ESAU, JACOB, ISRAEL

Genesis Volume Two

ESAU, JACOB, ISRAEL
FATHER, SON, SPIRIT

Rex Frost

Copyright © 2017 by Rex K. Frost.
All rights reserved. Fair use copyright law will be respected.
Genesis two-volume edition.

Published in the United States by Josiah ben David:

JOSIAH BEN DAVID
1111 JOHN ST
BROOKVILLE IN 47012-1041

http://www.josiahbendavid.com/

Editorial comments may be directed to admin@josiahbendavid.com. Theological questions may be directed to info@rexfrost.com.

Bible verses are taken from the King James Version standard English text printed by Holman Bible Publishers (originally published in 1611, with major editorial tuning completed by 1769). The King James Bible text is in the public domain.

Biblical word studies are derived from the *Brown-Driver-Briggs Hebrew and English Lexicon* (reprinted from the 1906 edition published by Houghton, Mifflin & Company), *Thayer's Greek-English Lexicon of the New Testament* (reprinted from the 1896 fourth edition published by T&T Clark), and *Strong's Exhaustive Concordance of the Bible . . . with . . . Brief Dictionaries of the Hebrew and Greek Words* (copyrighted 1890 by James Strong, thirty-eighth printing). These original source materials are also in the public domain.

Brief quotations from diverse commentaries and other source materials are footnoted, with annotations, for the purpose of critically analyzing the major hermeneutical traditions. All such materials are used in accordance with fair use copyright law and well within the widely accepted guidelines developed by the University of Chicago Press.

ISBN-13: 978-0-9834040-2-6
ISBN-10: 0-9834040-2-X

The title page illustration is a juxtaposition taken from the Bible moralisée Codex Vindobonensis 2554. The cover design and interior headers show details adapted from the 1611 King James Bible. The end page, connected with the author biographical sketch, shows a Fibonacci spiral. All employed images are in the public domain.

The **JbD** Publishing House medallion is taken from *Promptuarii iconum insigniorum* by Guillaume Rouille, also in the public domain.

All proceeds from the original purchase price of this book are donated to Christian charities and missions. Visit RexFrost.com for more information.

IN MEMORY OF Rebekah, who daringly obeyed the prophecy of the Lord concerning her two sons and put Jacob in the place of Esau. And truly the birthright and the blessing of the firstborn did rightfully belong to the younger, not the elder, for thus decreed the Lord God. Rebekah elevating the second born Jacob is a reflection of the Holy Spirit exalting the second man Jesus.

ΑΩ

PREFACE

This work is the second of two volumes covering the book of Genesis. The first volume focuses on the first half of the book of Genesis, while the present volume focuses on the second half. The first volume concludes with the death of Abraham in chapter twenty-five of Genesis, while the present volume begins with the births of Esau and Jacob, also in chapter twenty-five. The format and methodology of this volume is foremost a continuation of the first volume. The focus is not extra-Biblical materials, such as secular history and archaeology, but the Biblical text itself, expanded by concordance and lexicon studies. The Old and New Testaments are understood together to be a coherent and perfect whole that is breathed according to the one Holy Spirit, the person of God the Spirit. The reading of the Old Testament is Christological, guided by interpretation precedents established in the New Testament. The distinguishing characteristic marking this entire commentary series is an emphasis on elements, patterns, and motifs, not merely as literary structures, but as unique representations of the Trinity. This focus on elements and patterns could be termed a form of *structuralism* to distinguish it from *dispensationalism* and *covenantalism*, and so forth.

The hermeneutics employed in the present volume are identical with those of the previous volume, but the basic principles are further formalized and the prophetic implications are further detailed, which does distinguish the exact form of the exegesis. The first commentary volume, compared with this volume, focuses more on specific examples and less on the overall system, as is the normal pedagogy of first treating the basic rules of a thing before focusing on the abstract theory. The density of word studies, for example, is somewhat decreased in the present volume, partly to minimize the repetition of concepts from the first volume but also because of the shift of emphasis to the overall system. As in the previous volume, a sampling of Rabbinic, Orthodox, Roman Catholic, Protestant, and so forth, and also literary commentaries is presented in the footnotes in order to compare and contrast the present commentary with the ancillary context formed by the traditional teachings of our forefathers and our contemporaries. And maintaining such a context is absolutely essential to understanding the subtle but critical implications of diverging methodologies.

As with the first commentary volume, the intended audience is again the believer familiar with the New Testament ("New Covenant"). But now also assumed is a knowledge of the first commentary volume and a corresponding

PREFACE

understanding of the Old Testament ("Old Covenant"). The Old Testament, which is the focus of the present commentary series, is normally the purview of the more mature believer due to the abstract nature of the signs, types, and motifs that characterize the Old Testament. The new believer seeking a foundational understanding of the new covenant of Christianity is advised not to start with the present commentary, or actually any commentary, but rather to go directly to the books of the New Testament. It is the New Testament that offers the clearest call of the faithful to the life and testimony that is the life of Jesus Christ followed by the lives of his disciples. Since the essence of Christianity is the person of Jesus Christ and not any religious system, the child of God should feel a kinship with Christ when confronted with him, even if the nature of the kinship at first seems impossible (Matt 19:26). After reading the Gospels ("Good News") followed by the Acts of the Apostles, one should proceed through the Epistles ("Letters"), for it is the Epistles that represent the most explicit explanation of the meaning of the conception, death, and resurrection of Jesus Christ for the sake of us sinners. The faithful should guard against substituting any popular-culture beliefs or even church traditions for an honest and humble reading of the Bible. Christians are a people of the Book, and it is foremost by reading and obeying the written Word that we are led by the Holy Spirit into conformity with Jesus, who is the incarnate Word.

The New Testament is the correct focus of Christian study, but the New Testament is inextricably connected with the Old Testament. And therefore the Bible must ultimately be read from cover to cover. Jesus Christ is the fulfillment of the law (Matt 5:17). And thus to understand the meaning of the incarnation, the believer necessarily seeks a fluency in the Old Testament, namely, the Covenant of Law. Christ quoted the law each time he was tempted in the wilderness, whereby the faithful tempted in imitation of Christ should seek to understand the same law (Matt 4:1–11). One should be aware, however, that a palpable tension between law and grace does exist in the contrast between the Old and New Testaments. The carnal desire to dismiss the realities of law and justice must be resisted since the resolution of the tension between justice and mercy is the reality of God and likewise our redemption in God. Several readings of the Bible from cover to cover may be necessary to appreciate this fundamental paradox, but the child of God should feel impelled to continue in the Word (John 10:27). The Old Testament in its entirety is a prophecy, or promise, of Jesus Christ and likewise the Body of Christ. And therefore a knowledge of the implicit structure of the Old Testament promise is the essential foundation for understanding the explicit teaching of the New Testament that is the realization of the promise.

The author finally wishes to express his thankfulness for the selfless support and painstaking proofreading of his wife, Jennifer, and mother, Marlene, and also his sincere hope that the reader will abide in the truth.

Rex Frost
December 15, 2017

PROLOGUE

The first half of the book of Genesis spans the threefold progression from Adam to Noah to Abraham, while the second half of Genesis focuses on the personage of Jacob and, therein, the completion of the second threefold progression from Abraham to Isaac to Jacob. The progression from Adam to Noah to Abraham to Isaac to Jacob traces the Messianic bloodline. The nature of progressive revelation is to follow the Messianic bloodline, because redemption comes by the blood of the Messiah and only by the blood of the Messiah. In contrast to a simple proclaiming of factual information, revelation is a progressive unfolding with ever-increasing clarity, reflecting the opening and unfolding of space and time in the act of creation. This is the essential process of exercising freewill that necessarily occurs in space and time and throughout space and time. The implicit structure of the sacred text reflects and reinforces the explicit meaning because all levels of reality necessarily testify to the one God. The Bible is the revelation of the image of God and likewise the plan of God. And the plan of God is the Trinitarian sanctification of his children in conformity to his image and agreement with his image.[1]

The extreme symmetry that exists between the different levels of reality reflects the absolute perfection of God being a complete internal consistency of God and likewise an undeniable, or relentless, unity of all creation as formed in the image of God. The primal example of progressive revelation is the creation of Adam in the very image of God (Gen 1:26). This is not simply the formation of the one man Adam but also Eve proceeding from Adam followed by all humanity proceeding from Adam by Eve (Gen 1:27). God embodies a triune self-existence, existing outside time, inside time, and throughout all time. Father, Son, and Spirit. And therefore a simple static image alone in itself could never express the fullness of the character of God that is Trinity. But a sequence of

---

[1] "These decrees I pray that I may preserve, and keep to the end my faith and confession in one Father, one Son and one Holy Ghost. For the incarnation of the only begotten made no addition to the number of the Trinity. Even after the incarnation the Trinity is still a Trinity. This is the teaching I have received from the beginning; this has been my faith; in this was I baptized; this have I preached; in this have I baptized, this I continue to hold [Theodoret, *To the same*, i.e., *To Marcellus, Archimandrite of the Acoemetæ*]" (Schaff and Wace, *Nicene and Post-Nicene Fathers: Second Series* 3:309). The birth, death, and resurrection of the Son, necessary for the atonement of sin, is the eternal Sonship made visible, wherein the incarnation should be understood as changing not God but man.

PROLOGUE

progressive revelations of the different aspects of God being combined together does lead to an ever-increasing clarity of the image of God over time. And this process necessarily happens over time because we finite beings necessarily experience the infinite over time. The reality of God can only be experienced as the triunity of God, because the truth of God is the triunity of God. And the triunity of God is fundamentally progressive because the Spirit and the Son proceed from the Father.

Adam is the universal father of all mankind; Noah is the universal father of all postdiluvian mankind; and Abraham is the universal father of all the faithful. The threefold Adam, Noah, and Abraham reflect the triune God the Father, God the Son, and God the Holy Spirit and also the threefold progression of the formation of Adam in the image of God followed by the First and Second Advents of Christ. And the threefold Abraham, Isaac, and Jacob reflect the same Trinity and the same threefold creation. But the juxtaposition of the threefold Adam, Noah, and Abraham and the threefold Abraham, Isaac, and Jacob in the progressive revelation of the image of God represents more than a simple repetition or even the addition of information. God is not sometimes righteous and sometimes merciful but is always the perfect union of justice and mercy. And God is not sometimes one and sometimes three but always triune. The image of God has always displayed the perfect triunity of justice and grace from the very beginning, but the interplay between complement and contrast in the progressive revelation of creation provides depth and intensity to the image. The threefold Adam, Noah, and Abraham mark the death and resurrection of the world in the Flood, while the threefold Abraham, Isaac, and Jacob mark the establishment of the one tiny nation of Israel. And the connection between the destruction of the entire world and the formation of the one nation of Israel is the redemption of the entire world in the one man Jesus Christ.

The nation of Israel being formed after the recession of the floodwaters recalls the first man Adam being formed after the separation of the waters of the original creation (Gen 1:6–8). And the ark of Noah floating on the floodwaters recalls the Spirit of God, God the Spirit, hovering over the waters of the original creation (Gen 1:2). The body of living flesh, the expanse of the physical universe, and the spiritual domain of heaven are not separate but rather a unified whole just as the Son and the Father are one with the Spirit (John 17:21). The connection between the establishment of the nation of Israel and the creation of all mankind in Adam is the promised new Adam and new creation that will come through the Messiah of Israel.[2] The nation of Israel embodies the Messianic bloodline and, thereby, points to the promised new Adam. Creation and the Creator are not separate, but rather creation, in its entirety, is formed in the very image of God. And even though the creation has been corrupted by sin, the image of God is still unmistakable just as the love of God is undeniable—that is, relentless—despite the separation caused by sin (1

---

[2] Jesus Christ is the promised new Adam, not merely another Adam, for Adam was the created, or reflected, image of God while Christ is the actual, or perfect, image of God, being literally God in the flesh.

PROLOGUE

Cor 13:12). The centrality of the Lord God becoming flesh and thereby sanctifying flesh in himself is a testimony to the essentialness of the connection between Creator and creation. All levels of reality necessarily reflect the image of the one God, because God is the paradigm upon which all creation is based. And God is necessarily the one paradigm of all creation, because God is the only being that is self-existent.

1	2	3
GOD THE FATHER	GOD THE SON	GOD THE SPIRIT
ADAM	NOAH	ABRAHAM
(IMAGE OF GOD)	(RIGHTEOUS)	(FAITHFUL)
FORMATION OF ADAM	FIRST ADVENT OF CHRIST	SECOND ADVENT OF CHRIST
ABRAHAM	ISAAC	JACOB

The progressive revelation of God is ongoing even unto this day just as the divine act of creation is unfolding even unto this day. And that the original creation has not ceased is evident in the birth of every child. The progressive revelation of God continues not in the sense of adding to the reality of the Trinity but in the sense that the faithful continue to grow both in numbers and in understanding. And even the Bible continues to be progressively revealed in the sense that the prophecies of the Bible are still unfolding in history. The progressive revelation of the Creator and likewise the progressive revelation of creation will not be completed until the faithful become like Christ in the promised new creation (1 John 3:1–2). The progressive revelation of creation is the triunity of God and the corresponding participation of the faithful in the triunity of God. And this triune image of God is impressed upon all creation and all levels of creation. The oneness of God is revealed in the original creation by the two persons of the Spirit and the Son proceeding from the one person of the Father. The duality of the procession of the Spirit and the Son from the Father is affirmed by the incarnation of the Son, who is fully God and fully man. And the triunity of God is manifested in the new creation by the Spirit bringing the faithful in the Son unto to Father. The oneness and duality and triunity of the one God are the building blocks of the Scriptures and likewise the creation related by and embodied by the Scriptures. The essence of the oneness of God is freewill, which innately bifurcates into a twofold choice between the way of flesh and the way of the Spirit, that is, between the way of law and the way of grace. The two men Adam and Jesus Christ embody this fundamental dichotomy in creation. And the twofold natures of Christ, who is true man and true God, finally perfect this dichotomy in the one Body of Christ, which is established by the power of the Holy Spirit and according to the will of the Father.[3]

---

[3] "[L]et us believe that the Father, and the Son, and the Holy Spirit is one God . . . and that the Father is not the Son, nor the Holy Spirit either the Father or the Son, but a trinity of persons mutually interrelated, and a unity of an equal essence. And let us seek to understand this, praying for help from Himself, whom we wish to understand; . . . [Augustine, *On the Trinity*]" (Schaff, *Nicene and Post-Nicene Fathers: First Series* 3:125). The

PROLOGUE

The essential structuring of the progressive revelation of the triune image of God is evident in the fundamental elements of the sacred text constructing increasingly complex pattern types. The elemental pattern types *prime*, *twofold*, and *threefold* form the basis for the *serial*, *chiastic*, and *staircase* pattern types. The serial pattern type is formed by a simple repeating of elements, the chiastic pattern by a mirroring of elements, and the staircase pattern by a combined repeating and overlapping of elements. The temporal uniformity of the serial, chiastic, and staircase pattern types then points to an analogous nonuniformity represented by the *historical*, *individual*, and *generational* pattern types. The overarching image of God in creation, to which all other images are related, is the creation of Adam followed by the First and Second Advents of Christ. The first man Adam is followed by the second man Jesus Christ just as the First Advent of Christ is followed by the Second Advent of Christ, expressly the Second Advent of the Body of Christ. The repeating twofold pattern of first and second bodies thereby becomes the threefold creation of Adam followed by the First and Second Advents of Christ. The elemental pattern types prime, twofold, and threefold represent universal building blocks, inherently possessing a static, archetypal quality that evokes a sense of timelessness. And this quality of elements constructing a larger edifice, or reality, is the fundamental basis of all creation, including the promised new creation. And the basic patterns of revelation being demarcated by time reflects God existing simultaneously outside time, inside time, and throughout all time, which points, respectively, to God the Father, God the Son, and God the Spirit.

1	2	3
PRIME	TWOFOLD	THREEFOLD
SERIAL	CHIASTIC	STAIRCASE
HISTORICAL	INDIVIDUAL	GENERATIONAL

The three elemental pattern types prime, twofold, and threefold reflect the primacy of God the Father, the twofold natures of God the Son, and finally the threefold movement of God the Holy Spirit. The relatively abstract nature of such archetypal images reflects the universality of God. Trinitarian pattern types are manifested differently on different levels of reality and with different degrees of complexity, but all reality and all aspects of reality point to the one reality that is the one universal Trinity. The prime image in the account of Jacob is the person of Jacob himself in the progression of Jacob becoming the father of Israel. And the uniqueness of the nation of Israel reflects the oneness of God that is foremost the oneness of God the Father. Even Joseph is best understood as the son of Jacob, specifically the son of Jacob's old age (Gen 37:3). The multitude of the house of Jacob points to the multitude of the faithful being

---

Son has made known the Father, John 14:9, and the Father has sent the Holy Spirit, John 14:16, in accordance with which the faithful are not looking for some future revelation concerning the fundamental nature of God, John 15:15. God the Son and God the Spirit proceed eternally from God the Father, such that there was never a time nor ever will be a time when God is not triune.

gathered by God the Holy Spirit into the house of God the Father, wherein Jacob as the father of the twelve tribes of Israel reflects God the Father as revealed by God the Spirit (John 14:2).

The twofold image emphasized in the account of Jacob is his struggle with his older brother, Esau. The second born Jacob supplanting the firstborn Esau in both the birthright of the firstborn and the blessing of the firstborn reflects the second man Jesus taking possession of the lost dominion of the first man Adam (Gen 27:36). The twofold birthright and blessing of the firstborn reflect the twofold kingship and high priesthood of Christ and likewise the twofold natures of Christ, being fully man and fully God. The struggle between Jacob and Esau is paralleled by the struggle between Jacob and Laban, likewise the struggle between Laban's two daughters taken as wives by Jacob, and likewise the struggle between the offspring of Jacob by the two daughters of Laban (Gen 28:1–5). And the close identification of Jacob with his sons reflects the close identification of the Spirit with the faithful, who are indwelt by the Spirit. The parallel between the struggle in Padanaram in the east and the struggle in Canaan in the west reflects the parallel between the struggle in the heavenly domain and the struggle in the earthly domain. And the interplay between the struggle among men and the struggle among angels parallels the interplay between the struggle in the flesh and the struggle in the spirit.

The threefold image emphasized in the account of Jacob is the progression from Esau to Jacob to Israel, reflecting the threefold successive formation of Adam followed by the First and Second Advents of Christ. The second born Jacob supplanting the firstborn Esau prefigures Jacob becoming Israel just as the second man Jesus Christ supplanting the first man Adam prefigures the First Advent of Christ being completed in the Second Advent. The exaltation of Israel in becoming a nation under God prefigures the sanctification of the faithful in the Body of Christ, which is the kingdom of God proclaimed by Christ, in Christ, and through Christ (John 3:5, Rom 14:17). Jacob becoming Israel prefigures the resurrection of the faithful in the promised spiritual, or glorified, eternal bodies, necessarily supplanting the fallen natural body.[4] Esau is supplanted by Jacob just as Adam is supplanted by Christ, but Jacob becomes Israel just as the promise of Christ is fulfilled in the Body of Christ. Jesus Christ, in a sense, becomes the Body of Christ, uniting himself to the faithful. The threefold movement from Adam to Jesus Christ to the Body of Christ, which is reflected by the progression from Esau to Jacob to Israel, is the threefold movement of God the Holy Spirit.

---

[4] The distinction between the spiritual resurrection body and the present natural body is not based on corporeality, for both the spiritual and natural bodies are true physical bodies. Rather, the distinction is based on nature. The sinful nature of the natural body is governed by the law of flesh, whereas the glorified nature of the spiritual body is governed in the grace of the Holy Spirit.

PROLOGUE

1	2	3
PRIME	TWOFOLD	THREEFOLD
JACOB	ESAU & JACOB	ESAU, JACOB, ISRAEL
THE ONENESS OF GOD	TWOFOLD NATURES OF THE SON	THREEFOLD MOVEMENT OF THE SPIRIT
GOD THE FATHER	GOD THE SON	GOD THE SPIRIT

The three uniform pattern types serial, chiastic, and staircase reflect, respectively, God the Father as our creator, God the Son as our redeemer, and God the Holy Spirit as our sanctifier. The serial, chiastic, and staircase pattern types parallel the prime, twofold, and threefold pattern types, but the serial, chiastic, and staircase types show a unique emphasis on the flow of time. The threefold progression from creation to redemption to sanctification, which is unfolding in time, parallels the three uniform pattern types serial, chiastic, and staircase, which are rigidly uniform in time. And the specificity of the three titles, or attributes, of God—creator, redeemer, and sanctifier—also reflects the same rigidity characteristic of uniform pattern types. The threefold progression of sanctification represents the movement from creation to new creation. Patterns are manifested in different ways on different levels of reality, but all levels of reality point to the one reality that is the one Trinitarian movement from the original creation to the promised new creation according to the one will, or oneness, of the Godhead.[5]

The serial pattern is connected specifically with the original six days of creation in separation from the seventh day, which reflects the original creation and likewise the present fallen creation being separated from the promised new creation. And the creation proceeds from the Father just as the Spirit and the Son proceed from the Father. The present creation, particularly before the Fall of Man, is therefore most closely identified with the will and desire of the first person of the Trinity, which is for the well-being of his children, his faithful ones. The Son is commonly identified with the act of creation, but all things being made by or through the Son should be understood according to the full counsel of the Scriptures, namely, that all things are made according to the will of God the Father in and through God the Son by the power of God the Holy Spirit (John 1:3). And thus the primal font of all creation is the will of God the Father, which is identified with fatherhood, not in isolation, but in all creation.

The chiastic pattern emphasizes the pivotal fourth millennium, which is marked by the Davidic kingdom culminating in the conception of Christ as king of kings at the end of the fourth millennium. The Christ-child is conceived in the very midst of creation, space and time, humbly condescending in every sense to become part of creation and, thereby, redeeming all creation as the possessor of all creation. The Second Advent is traditionally but incorrectly

---

[5] "Let us then do the will of the Father, the will of the Son, the will of the Holy Ghost; because of this Trinity there is one will, one power, one majesty. Yet for that reason saith the Son, 'I came not to do mine own will, but the will of Him that sent me' [John 5:30]; . . . [Augustine, *Tractates on the Gospel of John*]" (Schaff, *Nicene and Post-Nicene Fathers: First Series* 7:150). The Trinity is one God.

identified with the kingship of Christ, and thus the church is now looking for an earthly military king as the time of the Second Advent approaches just as the Jews were looking for such a king at the time of the First Advent. The formal millennial kingdom will be established at the time of the Second Advent, but a faithful remnant has already received their conquering king in the victory of Christ over death. The faithful now await the Lord as a high priest, specifically our priest-king, who will anoint the Body of Christ in the spiritual, or glorified, resurrection body. It is ironically the faithless that will meet the Lord, not as their high priest, but in the form of a conquering and warring king, as embodied by the foretold coming destruction (Rev 19:11–16).[6]

The staircase pattern reflects the essence of the progressive revelation of God, which is the movement of the Holy Spirit leading the chosen faithful inexorably unto the sanctification of all things in the last days. The repeating and overlapping staircase structure reflects the progression of the generations of humanity. The ever-increasing clarity of progressive revelation parallels the ever-increasing body of faithful being called by the Spirit. The earthly parallels the heavenly. And the foretold convergence of heaven and earth will be the final revelation of the image of God in the Body of Christ (Rev 21:1–4). The eternal state of the faithful is traditionally but incorrectly connected with heaven, whereas the Bible itself speaks of a coming together of a new heaven and a new earth. The essential unity of earth and heaven in the promised new creation is the unity of the physical and the spiritual in the resurrection body, likewise the unity of true humanity and true divinity in the person of Christ, and likewise the unity of law and grace in the will of God.

1	2	3
PRIME	TWOFOLD	THREEFOLD
GOD THE FATHER	GOD THE SON	GOD THE SPIRIT
SERIAL	CHIASTIC	STAIRCASE
CREATOR	REDEEMER	SANCTIFIER

The chronological context of the account of Abraham, Isaac, and Jacob is the third millennium, which is marked by the call of Abraham and likewise the call of the children of Abraham. The patriarch Abraham represents the father of all the faithful (Gal 3:7). In relation to the serial pattern, the third millennium parallels the sixth millennium, with both the third and the sixth being marked by the sign of life. The life that marks the third millennium and connects the third millennium to the sixth millennium is the movement of the Holy Spirit establishing the chosen faithful. The chosen faithful are first established under the law in the third millennium and finally established in fulfillment of the law in the sixth millennium. Those born during the millennial kingdom will be born under law and grace, not under law of itself and the corresponding sinful nature, though necessarily still called to make a freewill decision for or against Christ.

---

[6] In Talmudic literature the essence of Rabbinic Judaism is expressed in the form of a social agenda aimed at building the kingdom of God here and now in the present life (Cohen, *Rabbinic Sages* xvii). The way of all the earth.

PROLOGUE

And the connection between the law and life is clear in the call to obey the law and live long in the land (Deut 4:40). The law points to life and grace.

The sixth millennium, like the sixth day, represents the completion of the original creation under the law, which is finally the fulfillment of the call to repentance under the law. The millennial kingdom is not the new creation, but it is the beginning of the new creation. The seventh millennium corresponding to the millennial kingdom is the Sabbath millennium. The present creation, likewise the original creation, is identified with the law of the flesh, while the promised new creation is identified with the grace of the Spirit. This is the mortal life that comes by law in contrast to the immortal life that comes by grace. The law precedes grace just as the natural body precedes the spiritual, or glorified, resurrection body. This is the essential nature of freewill since the power to choose life or death necessarily precedes eternal life. The Body of Christ will be increased during the millennial kingdom, but the call to repentance ends with the sixth millennium. Anyone who rejects Christ after his glorious reappearing will be lost forever, without any chance of repentance, because Christ cannot be crucified a second time (Heb 6:4–6). Likewise, the angels that reject the presence of God cannot be redeemed.[7]

The sign of life marking the third and sixth millennia in relation to the serial pattern is the blessing of the faithful that comes by the law, but a corresponding curse is simultaneously identified with the faithless. The law always represents a choice between a blessing and a curse (Deut 11:26). The blessing that Abraham received by faith reflects the grace of eternal life that the faithful receive in Christ (Rom 4:9). The promise of a multitude of offspring made to Abraham points to the multitude that will enter into kingdom of God, while the promise of the land made to Abraham points to the resurrection, or glorification, of corporeal man and the corresponding restoration, or re-creation, of physical creation (Gen 17:1–8). The call of Abraham in the third millennium heralds the Davidic kingdom of the fourth millennium just as the call of the faithful in the sixth millennium heralds the millennial kingdom of the seventh millennium. And the movement of the Spirit in the sixth millennium is even now denied by the people of the world just as the call of the one man Abraham in the third millennium went largely unnoticed by the people of the world. The separation of the Israelites from the nations in the third millennium foreshadows the separation of the faithful and the faithless in the sixth millennium. The schism of the earthly church is the visible, or physical, sign marking the sixth millennium, while the corresponding hidden, or spiritual, sign marking the sixth millennium is the separation of the faithful from the world that will culminate in the resurrection and rapture. The schism of the church signifies the coming judgment of the world according to the separate sins of each group and finally

---

[7] "The rabbis taught: . . . For six thousand years the world will continue, and in the seventh it will be destroyed. . . . As in the Sabbatic period, the seventh year is a release, so will it be with the whole world that one thousand years after six will be a release . . . ." (Rodkinson, *Talmud: Sanhedrin* 8[16]:302–3). The new creation will not be fully established until the end of the Sabbath millennium, Rev 21:1.

each individual. And the schism of the church is from God just as the schism of Israel and Judah was from God (1 Kgs 12:24).

In relation to the chiastic pattern, the third millennium is mirrored by the fifth millennium, with the fourth millennium forming the pivot. The central importance of the fourth millennium is the central importance of the kingdom of God, first announced by the Davidic kingdom at the beginning of the fourth millennium and fulfilled in the conception of Christ as king of kings at the end of the fourth millennium. The third and fifth millennia are both marked by the sign of life, again that life which comes expressly by the law. The third and sixth millennia are connected by the sign of life in relation to the serial pattern, while the third and fifth millennia are connected by the sign of life in relation to the chiastic pattern. A second-order relationship between the fifth and sixth millennia is therefore evident in the comparison between the serial and chiastic patterns. And the implied unity of the fifth and sixth millennia is the church age connecting the First and Second Advents of Christ. The life of the fifth millennium is the fulfillment of the law in the person of Christ, while the life of the sixth millennium is the fulfillment of grace by law in the Body of Christ, culminating in the resurrection and rapture. The serial pattern is most closely identified with God the Father, especially the Father as our creator, or spiritually procreator, while the chiastic pattern is most closely identified with God the Son, especially the Son as our redeemer through his own blood. And the agreement between the act of creation and the act of redemption points to the promised new creation that comes by the power of God the Holy Spirit in the act of indwelling sanctification.

The life of the third and fifth millennia points to the life of the fourth millennium, which represents the very font of true life being the eternal life in Christ. Our promised redemption is embodied by the conception of the Christ-child at the end of the fourth millennium. The Old Testament faithful looked forward to the promised incarnation, while the New Testament faithful now look backward to the incarnation. The separation of Israel from the nations beginning in the third millennium reflects the call of the faithful in Christ beginning in the fifth millennium. The blessing of the one nation of Israel reflects the anointing of the one man Christ and likewise the one Body of Christ. The life of the third millennium is the long life in the land that comes by simple obedience to the law (Deut 4:40). The emphasis on living long in the land represents an emphasis on the natural body, but the promise of the land further points to the restoration, or re-creation, of all things, including the resurrection of a physical body. The natural body itself is likewise a blurred reflection of the spiritual, or glorified, resurrection body. The life of the fifth millennium is then the eternal life that comes by the perfect fulfillment of the law on the cross by Jesus Christ. The resurrection of the fifth millennium is specifically the resurrection of Christ, but it is the resurrection of Christ that guarantees the resurrection of the faithful in Christ. This guarantee of life was made visible in the fifth millennium by a first movement of the Holy Spirit calling forth the faithful in Christ (John 16:7), but the call of the faithful in Christ will not be fulfilled until the time of the resurrection and rapture marking the conclusion of the sixth millennium (John 16:8). And it is exaltation of the faithful in Christ, heralding and marking the second coming, that will conclude the convicting work of the Holy Spirit.

In relation to the staircase pattern, the third millennium is part of a larger progression connecting Adam and the promised new Adam. The increasing clarity characteristic of progressive revelation is embodied by the progression from the first Adam to the new Adam. A clarity of understanding parallels a purity of material being. When understood properly, the spiritual and the natural are always in agreement. The third millennium parallels the fifth and seventh millennia in the staircase progression. And it is again the sign of life that connects the third, fifth, and seventh millennia in the staircase pattern, as it is the sign of life that connects the third and fifth millennia in the chiastic pattern, as it is the sign of life that connects the third and sixth millennia in the serial pattern. The comparison between the serial, chiastic, and staircase pattern types indicates a unity of the latter days corresponding to the fifth, sixth, and seventh millennia since all three are marked by the sign of life, specifically the fulfillment of the sign of life. The fifth, sixth, and seventh millennia are the three days of Christ connecting the cross and the foretold new creation to be established at the conclusion of the millennial kingdom (Rev 21:1). These are the last days, specifically the last three days, beginning at the time of the First Advent. The persecution of the early church in the fifth millennium is like the torment of Christ on the cross. The schism of the earthly church that marks the sixth millennium is like the scattering of the sheep when Christ lay in the earth (Zech 13:7, Matt 26:31). And the seventh millennium, corresponding to the millennial kingdom, is like the day of resurrection.

The three pattern types serial, chiastic, and staircase are identified, respectively, with the Father, Son, and Spirit, yet more specifically with creation, redemption, and sanctification. The identification of the sign of life (redemption) with the fifth millennium in relation to the chiastic pattern type points to the death and resurrection of Christ being the watershed event in history that changes everything. The identification of the sign of life (creation) with the sixth millennium in relation to the serial pattern type points to the culmination of creation in the resurrection and rapture of the faithful being our promised new creation in the glorified body. The identification of the sign of life (sanctification) with the seventh millennium in relation to the staircase pattern type points to the sanctification of the faithful being fully established in the Sabbath millennium. The interchange of the fifth and sixth millennia implied by the ordering of the signs of life marking the last three millennia (redemption, creation, and sanctification, in contrast to creation, redemption, and sanctification) foreshadows a reconstitution of the time of the First Advent, or a modern equivalent, as the time of the Second Advent approaches.[8] Further, the connection between the seventh and the fifth millennia in relation to the staircase pattern identifies the millennial kingdom of Christ with the kingdom of

---

[8] Likewise, the ordering of the blessings of Issachar and Zebulun, Leah's fifth and sixth sons, Gen 49:13–15, is reversed compared with the ordering of their births, 30:17–20.

PROLOGUE

God proclaimed by Christ at the time of the First Advent. The connection between the seventh and fifth millennia also reflects the unity of Christ and the Body of Christ in the kingdom of God.

Focusing on the staircase progression from the third millennium to the fifth millennium to the seventh millennium, it is the third millennium in the initial position, marked by father Abraham, that can be viewed as the font, or father, of the entire progression (Rom 4:16). The sign of life marking the third, fifth, and seventh millennia is ultimately the call of the faithful, which reflects Abraham being the father of all the faithful. The call of Abraham in the third millennium represents the promise, or prophecy, of the redemption of the children of Abraham, who, being identified with the faithfulness of their father, represent the very children of God (Gal 3:7). The death and resurrection of Christ in the fifth millennium embodies the guarantee of eternal life for all the faithful in the death and resurrection of all creation that is in reality the death and resurrection of Christ. The millennial kingdom, corresponding to the seventh, or Sabbath, millennium, represents the glorification of the faithful in the Body of Christ. The progression of revelation through the millennia represents the movement of the Holy Spirit throughout creation, leading the faithful unto the promised new creation that is the sanctification of the faithful in the Body of Christ. The account of Abraham, Isaac, and Jacob—echoed by the account of Esau, Jacob, and Israel—represents the establishment of the Messianic bloodline, likewise the chosen faithful to be redeemed through the Messianic bloodline, that is, to be redeemed by the blood of Christ.

1	2	3
SERIAL	CHIASTIC	STAIRCASE
THIRD/SIXTH MILLENNIA	THIRD/FIFTH	THIRD/FIFTH/SEVENTH
CREATOR	REDEEMER	SANCTIFIER
LIFE FROM THE FATHER	LIFE IN THE SON	LIFE OF THE SPIRIT

The account of Abraham, Isaac, and Jacob opens a larger period between Abraham and Christ that is marked by a dramatically increased density of narration focusing on the establishment of the one nation of Israel. This period begins with the call of Abraham as the first Hebrew (Gen 14:13) and culminates in the incarnation of Christ as the king of the Jews (Matt 2:2). The first half of the book of Genesis spans a period of more than 2,000 years. The last half of Genesis focuses on a period of less than 200 years, ending with the death of Joseph in Egypt. The first half of Genesis spans the 2,000 years between Adam and Abraham, while the whole of the remaining Old Testament focuses on the 2,000 years between Abraham and Christ.[9] The account of the establishment of Israel dominates the entire period between the Flood of Noah and the Passion of Christ, and this fact bears witness to the connection between the death and resurrection of the whole world and the death and resurrection of the one man

---

[9] Per Ussher's chronology, Adam was formed in 4004 BC (Ussher 17), Abraham, or Abram, was born in 1996 BC (Ibid. 22) and died in 1821 BC (Ibid. 28), Joseph died in 1635 BC (Ibid. 32), and Jesus Christ was born in 5 BC (Ibid. 779).

PROLOGUE

Christ (1 Pet 3:18–22). In this larger view, the foundation of the one nation of Israel begins with the Table of Nations, originally established through Noah (Gen 10:32) and divided at the tower of Babel (Gen 11:9).[10]

The period between the Flood of Noah and the Passion of Christ corresponds to the period of Biblical accounting in which the temporally nonuniform analogues of the serial, chiastic, and staircase pattern types are most clearly perceived. The three nonuniform analogues of the serial, chiastic, and staircase pattern types are, respectively, the historical, individual, and generational pattern types. First, a hierarchical parallel between man and the world characterizes the threefold construction of the historical pattern. And this hierarchical parallel recalls the sequential parallel between former and latter days that characterizes the threefold construction of the serial pattern. The serial and historical pattern types are also both connected to physical creation viewed as a whole. Second, the individual formed in the image of God reflects the singularity represented by the chiastic pivot and identified with the incarnation of Jesus Christ. And this relationship reflects the essential connection between the individual believer and the one man Jesus Christ. Third, the generational pattern type is the most obviously analogous to its uniform counterpart since it is characterized by an expansion (centrally) of the basic staircase pattern type.

The establishment of the nation of Israel defines the period between the baptism in the floodwaters and the baptism of the cross. The establishment of the one nation of Israel as the chosen people of God represents the Messianic bloodline proceeding from the new Adam as embodied by Noah. And the Messianic bloodline likewise proceeds from Christ in the establishment of the Body of Christ. The connection between the time of Noah and the time of Jesus Christ is the connection between the world as a whole and the one man Christ, likewise the connection between the Body of Christ and Jesus Christ as the Head of the Body. The intimate relationship between the one nation of Israel and the one man Jesus Christ is evident in the very life of Christ being a recapitulation of the history of the nation of Israel. The history of Israel is reflected in the life of Christ in minute detail, from the call out of Egypt (Matt 2:15) to the exaltation of Christ as king of the Jews (John 19:3). The relationship between the world of creation as a whole and the one man Jesus Christ is evident in the parallel between the baptism of the world in the floodwaters and the baptism of Christ on the cross (1 Pet 3:20–21). The death and resurrection of Christ is a recapitulation of the death and resurrection of the world at the time of Noah. The death and resurrection of Christ is the death and resurrection of creation.

---

[10] "Most successful stories are characterized by compression . . . . [N]othing is wasted . . . each word and detail are chosen for maximum effectiveness. . . . The writer achieves compression by exercising a rigid selectivity. He chooses the details and incidents that contribute most to the meaning he is after; he omits those whose usefulness is minimal. . . . [T]wo contributory resources . . . for gaining compression [are]: symbol and irony . . . [B]ut both demand awareness and maturity on the part of the reader" (Perrine 211). The reader should focus on what's written, minimize disconnected speculation about what has been left unwritten, and understand that there are always layers of meaning.

PROLOGUE

The meaning of recapitulation is sanctification just as the meaning of physical reality is spiritual reality. And the sanctification through recapitulation embodied by Christ is reinforced by the symmetry patterns that demarcate the progressive revelation of creation. All levels of reality reflect the one image of God, whether the exaltation of the one true image of God or the debasement and rejection of God in some corrupted image of God. And all levels necessarily reflect the same reality since all levels must be sanctified according to the one and only image of God. But it is the nonuniform pattern structures (historical, individual, and generational) that most clearly show the universality embodied by Jesus Christ, because it is the nonuniform pattern structures that are most obviously disconnected from a rigid uniformity in time. The nonuniform pattern types being disconnected from time expresses a sense of time and space as a whole (space-time). The reality of the recapitulation of all creation in the person of Christ is ultimately an image of the folding of all creation into the Body of Christ. This is not the end of physical existence but a vision of the Body of Christ being a restoration, or re-creation, of both ruddy man and the red earth together. The Body of Christ is the body of faithful, but the Body of Christ is material and spiritual just as Christ is true man and true God. The Body of Christ is all things just as Jesus Christ is over all.[11]

First, the historical pattern type reflects the universal parallel between creation as a whole and the individual person. The connection between physical creation and man is the essential connection between the body and the soul. And the restoration of creation parallels the resurrection of man. Our salvation resides in Christ alone and springs from Christ alone, but the Flood of Noah and the Passion of Christ still necessarily represent the same redemption because there is only one redemption. There is only one God, and therefore there is only one redemption in God. Second, the individual pattern type, which corresponds to the individuals of all the ages, points to the universal redemption of the faithful of all the ages and, thereby, testifies to the unity of the chosen people and the faithful as a whole, which is the unity of Jews and Gentiles. There is only one redemption for Old Testament saints, church age saints, and tribulation period saints because there is only one God. There is only one redemption for both Jew and Gentile because there is only one God. The decreased lifetimes proceeding from the days of Adam anticipates the ever-shortening time horizon preceding up to the judgment of the world and Adam-kind. And the world population increasing throughout the ages anticipates the multitude of faithful that will form the Body of Christ. Third, the generational pattern type points to the end times, which reflects the universal movement of the one Holy Spirit fulfilling all things in the redemption of all things. The

---

[11] Rabbis insist that God cannot in any way have a corporeal nature, and yet vivid anthropomorphic descriptions of God are numerous in Rabbinic literature, e.g., *Chagigah* and *Genesis Rabbah* (Cohen, *Rabbinic Sages* 7–8). It is impossible to speak of God caring about humanity without reference to the personal nature of God, existing in some way in space and time. And this reality should point us to the absolute necessity of the incarnation and, ultimately, to the eternal reality of the Son being begotten of the Father through the Spirit.

generational and staircase pattern types share this fundamental quality. But the multiplication of stairsteps between the Flood and Calvary in the generational pattern represents a unique emphasis on the universality of God, as reflected in the judgment of the world and the judgment of the cross being connected by the call of a chosen people under a universal law.

The historical type is identified with the re-creation of creation. The nonuniformity characterizing the historical type points to the restoration of the whole of creation, including the whole of physical creation and the faithful throughout all the ages. This is the transcendent, or overarching, will of God the Father. The correspondence between the Flood and Calvary implies a folding, or subsuming, of the intervening period, which represents the sanctification of the world concomitant with the sanctification of the chosen faithful. But this is not yet the fulfillment of all things. This is the baptism in water that precedes the baptism of fire just as the natural body precedes the spiritual, or glorified, resurrection body just as the law precedes grace. The individual type is then identified with the resurrection of the individual faithful. The nonuniformity characterizing the individual type points to the redemption of all the faithful throughout all the ages, Jew and Gentile, in the one person of God the Son, who is our personal savior. And the inclusion of all the believers throughout all the ages in the one Body of Christ evokes an image of the folding of all creation into the one Body of Christ. The generational type is lastly identified with the formation of the nation of Israel culminating in the establishment of the kingdom of God that is finally the Body of Christ. And the Body of Christ is understood to encompass the new earth and the new heaven just as the Son is true man and true God. It is the quality of being nonuniform in time that evokes a sense of encompassing all time and space (space-time). And it is exactly this nonuniformity characterizing the generational type that points to the eternal (infinite) nature of the Body of Christ, which, in the final analysis, should be recognized specifically as the universality of God the Holy Spirit indwelling all the faithful and likewise all creation.

1	2	3
HISTORICAL	INDIVIDUAL	GENERATIONAL
RE-CREATION OF CREATION	RESURRECTION OF THE INDIVIDUAL	ESTABLISHMENT OF THE BODY OF CHRIST
TRANSCENDENT FATHER	PERSONAL SON	UNIVERSAL SPIRIT
CREATION + MAN	JEW + GENTILE	NEW EARTH + NEW HEAVEN

TABLE OF CONTENTS

PREFACE vii

PROLOGUE ix

INTRODUCTION xxvi

PART I: ESAU

CHAPTER 1: JACOB AND ESAU 3
   ISAAC AND REBEKAH 25:19–23 4
   ESAU AND JACOB 25:24–28 10
   BIRTHRIGHT 25:29–34 17
   ABIMELECH 26:1–33 22
   BIRTHRIGHT AND BLESSING 26:34–27:40 39
   HATRED 27:41–46 67

CHAPTER 2: JACOB AND LABAN 79
   TO THE EAST 28:1–9 80
   BETHEL 28:10–22 87
   RACHEL AND LEAH 29:1–30 95
   ELEVEN SONS 29:31–30:24 104
   SHEEP AND GOATS 30:25–43 118
   FROM THE EAST 31:1–20 126
   GILEAD 31:21–55 132

PART II: JACOB

CHAPTER 3: JACOB AND GOD 159
   HOST OF GOD 32:1–21 160
   THE PRINCE WHO PREVAILS 32:22–32 167
   FACE OF GOD 33:1–17 171
   THE DEFILEMENT OF DINAH 33:18–34:31 176
   DEBORAH, RACHEL, ISAAC 35:1–29 183
   GENERATIONS OF ESAU 36:1–43 195

CHAPTER 4: JOSEPH BEN JACOB 208
- DREAMER OF DREAMS 37:1–11 209
- THE EVIL BEAST 37:12–36 213
- JUDAH AND TAMAR 38:1–30 220
- HOUSE OF POTIPHAR 39:1–23 230
- BAKER AND BUTLER 40:1–23 237
- INTERPRETER OF DREAMS 41:1–37 245
- HOUSE OF PHARAOH 41:38–57 254

PART III: ISRAEL

CHAPTER 5: TWELVE SONS 273
- THE FIRST JOURNEY 42:1–13 274
- SIMEON 42:14–24 279
- SILVER 42:25–35 284
- REUBEN AND JUDAH 42:36–43:14 287
- THE SECOND JOURNEY 43:15–28 292
- BENJAMIN 43:29–34 295
- THE SILVER CUP 44:1–13 297
- JUDAH 44:14–34 300
- PHARAOH, JOSEPH, JACOB 45:1–28 307

CHAPTER 6: TWELVE TRIBES 322
- THE THIRD JOURNEY 46:1–27 323
- GOSHEN 46:28–47:12 328
- TWO TITHES 47:13–31 333
- EPHRAIM AND MANASSEH 48:1–22 342
- TWELVE PROPHECIES 49:1–28 348
- THE DEATH OF JACOB 49:29–50:21 356
- THE DEATH OF JOSEPH 50:22–26 363

AFTERWORD 377

EPILOGUE 392

SELECTED BIBLIOGRAPHY 399

AUTHOR 407

INTRODUCTION

This commentary volume, focusing on the second half of the book of Genesis, follows the same organizational structure as volume one. Chapters are demarcated by Biblical personages or groups, reflecting the innate flow of progressive revelation. Biblical text and commentary text alternate in the minimum practical units that allow the development of complete thoughts. The King James Version standard English text is again used, with Strong's numbers connecting the Biblical text to word studies in the commentary text. Chapter introductions preview key chapter images, while chapter conclusions set the major chapter types and themes in the broader Biblical context of progressive revelation. Chapter introductions focus on the basic building blocks of the Biblical text, while chapter conclusions focus on the complex pattern types that characterize progressive revelation. Outlines of key chapter images and verse-by-verse interpretations follow each chapter conclusion. These summary tables highlight the universal parallel between the natural and the spiritual meanings of the Biblical text. Additionally, a sampling of Rabbinic, Orthodox, Roman Catholic, Protestant, and so forth, and also literary commentaries is surveyed in the footnotes. The interpretation precedents and anti-precedents detailed in the footnotes provide a critical comparison with the many and varied traditional and prevalent hermeneutical methodologies.

The lexicons used in the present volume, also the methods of their application, are the same as that in the previous volume. Biblical word studies are not restricted to *denotations* but also comprehend usage *connotations* and etymological *associations*.[1] The primary Old Testament Hebrew and Aramaic lexicon is *Brown-Driver-Briggs*, but a basic agreement is maintained with *Strong's Concise Dictionary of the Hebrew Bible*, published with the original *Strong's Exhaustive Concordance*. And the King James standard English text itself represents a distinct third witness testifying to the proper understanding of words and contexts. For

---

[1] "[M]eaning will never quite stay the same from context to context: the signified will be altered by the various chains of signifiers in which it is entangled" (Eagleton 112). It is a fundamental law of nature that all things are always altered by interactions with their environments; "Since the meaning of a sign is a matter of what the sign is *not*, its meaning is always in some sense absent from it too. Meaning, if you like, is scattered or dispersed along the whole chain of signifiers: . . ." (Eagleton 111). The subtlety or even nonexistence of certain relationships is also a tangible aspect of overall meaning.

INTRODUCTION

the small number of New Testament Greek word studies, *Thayer's* is used as the primary lexicon but likewise in conjunction with *Strong's Concise Dictionary of the Greek Testament*, also published with *Strong's Exhaustive Concordance*. Any significant deviations from *Brown-Driver-Briggs* or *Thayer's* in preference for *Strong's* are footnoted in this volume, as in volume one. Further, bottom-up and top-down views of Biblical texts are always compared. The analysis of words and literal imagery is the bottom-up view, while the analysis of overarching patterns is the top-down view. The bottom-up and top-down perspectives fit together to form a complete and unified reading just as the natural and spiritual levels of reality fit together to form a complete and unified reality. And the natural and the spiritual are both required for a full and correct exegesis to be completed. A fundamentally distorted hermeneutics will always yield a fundamentally distorted exegesis because interpretive frameworks inevitably produce the worldview or some aspect of the worldview that is assumed to exist in the first place. One could even say that exegesis is inevitably eisegesis.[2] And this is why a faithful hermeneutics must be fundamentally Trinitarian, likewise Christological, reflecting what is the true oneness of God.[3]

THEOLOGICAL SYSTEMS

An overview of several diverse modes of theological thought is useful to highlight the distinctive aspects of the hermeneutics developed in the present commentary series and, at the same time, to underscore the need for a new hermeneutics, or rather a purely Biblical hermeneutics. With these two basic goals in mind, the core concepts and logical implications of *dispensationalism*, *covenantalism*, and *scholasticism* are here reviewed. All such established theological systems do exist in multiple and varied forms, but it is the basic principles underlying each system that are of interest here, namely, the fundamental spirit, or worldview, of each system. All interpretive frameworks are formed by asserting the existence of some organizational principle or collection of principles, which inevitably reflects some particular worldview. A distinction can be made between hermeneutical methods and interpretive frameworks, but a functional hermeneutics necessarily establishes or defends some interpretive framework or set of frameworks. Further, an interpretive framework is necessarily formulated before or at the same time as the act of interpretation. And therefore the assumed worldview underlying any given interpretive

---

[2] "It [the book of Revelation] is a toxic book and . . . would appeal to people who, like the Joannine churches, felt alienated and resentful. . . . A thread of hatred runs through the [entire] New Testament" (Armstrong 76). A common saying is that any given interpretation of the Bible says more about the interpreter than about the Bible. And there is much truth in this, despite the fact that there is an absolute reality, for the heart of every individual will testify either according to the Spirit or to the flesh.

[3] In a process known as the hermeneutical circle, individual features are understood in terms of overall context while overall context is understood through individual features (Eagleton 64). This process assumes a unity of meaning, which, though not ever entirely true in the writings of men, is exactly true in the case of the Bible, the Word of God.

framework will largely predetermine the basic form of any interpretation, assuming, of course, that results are being logically derived from within the system of thought. Therefore required in the evaluation of the different aspects of theological systems is the normal process of forming some specific hypothesis, followed by testing and adjusting until a consistent explanation of the observables is formed or, in the case of Biblical hermeneutics, until a logical and moral understanding of the received revelation is realized. An iterative process of formulation and revision is used in all fields of inquiry, including theology, whether it is overt or admitted or known.

The reality of correspondence, which exists between interpreter and interpretation, is not surprising given the human frailties of ignorance and prejudice. It is also related to freewill. A correspondence exists between hermeneutics and exegesis, between interpretive frameworks and interpretation, between the belief system of the exegete and what the exegete will determine to be the meaning of, likewise the reality related by, the Biblical text. A more literal hermeneutics compared with a more historical-critical hermeneutics will produce predictably opposing interpretations of supernatural events, such as related to our original creation in Adam and our promised new creation in Christ. A more literal reading does reflect a recognition that the Bible is uniquely the written Word of God, likewise that Jesus Christ is uniquely the incarnate Word of God. And it is no coincidence that a more literal reading of the Word is a more humble reading of the Word. But ultimately it is only God the Holy Spirit who can guide the faithful through the myriad questions that arise both in the reading of the Bible and throughout life as a whole. For even supernatural revelations must be compared with the Bible, the God-breathed Word, in order to verify their authenticity, and therefore even supernatural revelations are ultimately connected to some fundamental interpretive framework used to understand the Bible (Gal 1:6–9). This does not mean that man judges God according to human understanding or methodologies; rather, this means that our very ability to receive revelation proceeds from God just as revelation itself proceeds from God.[4]

The common assertion that one or another way of reading, or form of hermeneutics, is purely literal should therefore be scrutinized. The claim to be simply presenting the plain meaning of the Bible, without any interpretation, could never be entirely true, because human judgment is necessarily part of the process of formulating any argument or explanation. If one truly wanted to relate a text without any interpretation, then one would simply read the text without any exposition. And in truth even the simple reading of some translation in isolation will still be marked by the interpretations and implications entangled with the specific wordings of the specific translation. Even in the original languages, our understanding is shaped by the specific formulations of our lexicons. And this is equally true for native speakers, who

---

[4] In the paradigm of structuralism, an ideal, or perfect, reader is assumed who has what is effectively an unlimited understanding of a given text (Eagleton 105). The perspective of God the Holy Spirit, indwelling and empowering the believer.

INTRODUCTION

are using the dictionaries of their minds.[5] Different organizational principles, actually patterns, are superimposed onto the Biblical text in the different theological systems, including the more literalistic systems. And thus one must always make a conscious or tacit judgment about whether the asserted principles and patterns actually exist in reality. If a Biblical pattern does exist, then it is divinely inspired and should be accepted just as the text it organizes is divinely inspired and should be accepted. Everything is language, including patterns, especially patterns. And language is ultimately literal, even when it's allegorical.[6] The Bible relates the totality of creation, and thus the lines are blurred between the spiritual and the literal, between overarching patterns and local meaning, between the Word of God and the world of God formed in the image of God. There are three witnesses: (1) natural creation as a whole, governed by natural law, (2) the human faculties, including reason and conscience, and (3) special revelation, which is first and foremost the Bible in the present age. The Word of God is our sure foundation, but the movement of the Holy Spirit in the world as a whole, likewise in the individual, cannot be denied.

With this general background, a development of the defining features and logical implications of the selected representative systems—dispensationalism, covenantalism, and scholasticism—can now begin. In this process, it is useful to recognize that a primary object of all major theological systems is explaining the obvious differences between the Old and New Testaments, that is, between the Covenants of Law and Grace. All the central theological issues, whether the perfection of God or the nature of man or the plan of salvation, are sooner or later related back to the paradox of law and grace, which is the dichotomy of the Old and New Testaments. It is also useful to recognize that everyone adheres to some theological system or systems, whether they realize it or not. And thus it is important to formalize our understanding of hermeneutics and, thereby, clarify the rules that we are either explicitly or implicitly using. Otherwise, one invites a fundamentally inconsistent understanding of God and salvation and, therein, a fundamentally incorrect understanding of God and salvation. And finally the organizing principles that characterize different theological systems and interpretive frameworks should be recognized as being nothing less than worldviews.

---

[5] "The idea that there is a single 'normal' language, a common currency shared equally by all members of society, is an illusion" (Eagleton 4). Yet the truth is still spoken forth.
[6] "All language . . . is ineradicably metaphorical, working by tropes and figures; it is a mistake to believe that any language is *literally* literal" (Eagleton 126). Rather, the figurative reading is the literal reading when dealing with what is obviously symbolic. And thus to reduce confusion on this point, Bible Christians will sometimes specify that they read the Bible not literally but seriously.

Dispensationalism

Classical dispensationalism[7] originated with John Nelson Darby (AD 1800–1882), though the basic concept of dividing history into dispensations is evident in the writings of the early church fathers, such as Irenaeus (ca. 130–ca. 200) and Augustine (354–430).[8] Dispensationalism was notably adopted by D. L. Moody (1837–1899) but was disseminated most broadly by C. I. Scofield (1843–1921), specifically via the Scofield Reference Bible.[9] The 1909 and 1917 editions of the Scofield Reference Bible relate a form of classical dispensationalism, whereas the 1967 New Scofield Reference Bible is a version more accurately identified with revised dispensationalism.[10] Dispensationalism in its various forms is among the most influential theological systems in modern Evangelical thought, with individuals holding various dispensational views being found in most Protestant denominations.[11] A strong distinction between the church and Israel, together with a strong rejection of replacement theology, is correctly identified with dispensationalism, but this specific area of belief is part of a larger worldview. The fundamental spirit of dispensationalism is characterized by an emphasis on the differences between the different eras of human history. And the different dispensations are viewed as purposeful discontinuities that exist according to the sovereign will of God. For example, the animal sacrifice required according to the Old Testament may be accepted as a type and foreshadowing of the sacrifice of Jesus Christ, but it is nonetheless considered most important to keep the different eras separate in order to avoid confusion and error. The supposition is that God in the past required animal, or blood, sacrifice, whereas in the present age God simply does not. The emphasis in dispensationalism is on the idea that the explicit requirements for serving God are different in the different dispensations, and this is the fundamental worldview from which the overall dispensational system is derived.

A dispensationalist will say that they believe God is unchanging, but the way in which God deals with or relates to humanity is changing.[12] And it is this incongruity that is the fundamental problem. A dispensationalist may state that the *grounds* of salvation throughout history remains the blood atonement of Jesus on the cross even though the *object* of saving faith changes according to the specific revelation that defines each different dispensation.[13] But adding this nuance does not alter the fundamental incongruity. The image of God is

---

[7] The actual label of *dispensationalism* was evidently not used until the 1920s (*Evangelical Dictionary of Theology*, s.v. "dispensation, dispensationalism").

[8] *Evangelical Dictionary of Theology*, s.vv. "Darby, John Nelson," "dispensation, dispensationalism."

[9] *Cambridge Dictionary of Christian Theology*, s.v. "dispensationalism."

[10] *Evangelical Dictionary of Theology*, s.v. "dispensation, dispensationalism."

[11] Blaising and Bock 9–13.

[12] *Evangelical Dictionary of Theology*, s.v. "dispensation, dispensationalism"; *Cambridge Dictionary of Christian Theology*, s.v. "dispensationalism."

[13] *Cambridge Dictionary of Christian Theology*, s.v. "dispensationalism."

INTRODUCTION

impressed upon all creation always (Rom 1:20). And thus physical reality is unchanging just as spiritual reality is unchanging. The rule of serving God and pleasing God has always been faith and will always be faith. This is affirmed in Abraham believing God, and it being accounted to him as righteousness (Gal 3:6). This is affirmed in the declaration that God desires mercy and not sacrifice (Hos 6:6).[14] This is affirmed in Jesus Christ not destroying the law but rather fulfilling the law and the prophets (Matt 5:17). Reality can never truly be compartmentalized. Reality is an organic whole just as God is one. And it is no coincidence that an emphasis on the separateness of dispensations tends to lead to bifurcating eschatologies and finally a belief in separate redemptions.

The paradox of an unchanging God repeatedly changing the requirements for being accepted by him can be addressed in dispensationalism by pointing to an unchanging sovereignty of God, which is viewed as unifying the different dispensations. God may sovereignly change the requirements for serving him, but the proposed constancy is that of bringing glory to his name.[15] The changing of the rules is viewed as necessary in this process in order to establish that man always fails regardless of the rules—and this is what then, at least by implication, proves the peerless perfection of God. But the idea that the failing of created man brings glory in any way to the Creator is untenable, as is the implication that God somehow needs to prove that man always fails. The separation between the different dispensations is fundamentally connected to the separation between man and God. And the parallel between the two kinds of separateness is no coincidence. God is sovereign, and God does have freewill. But just because God can do a thing, doesn't mean that God will choose to do the thing. God could violate our freewill and thereby sin against us, but God in his own perfect freewill chooses not to sin.[16] That the signs marking the different eras do change is incontrovertible. The blood of animals sacrificed on an altar does become the blood of Jesus Christ sacrificed on the cross. The first Adam is supplanted by the last Adam. But to emphasize the sovereign will of God implies that God is somehow arbitrary. To minimize the essential connectedness of the dispensations is to minimize the essential relationship between the two Adams; likewise, it is to minimize the essential unity of God and man formed in the very image of God.

Nothing, no system or any part of a system, exists in isolation, not the explicit suppositions of a system or the implicit worldview of a system. And the fundamental principles underlying any theological system are always going to have far-reaching implications, even unto salvation and eternity. The emphasis on the separateness of the different eras of world history is taken to its logical

---

[14] God prefers Torah study over blood sacrifice, *Shabbath* (Cohen, *Rabbinic Sages* 157). The goal is never the sacrifice itself, which corresponds to mere carnal reality, but rather the goal is understanding and accepting and finally internalizing the sacrifice—that is, the meaning, or sign, related by the sacrifice—and this is the same fundamental goal in all the many and varied dispensations.

[15] Ryrie 28–31.

[16] "An oft-quoted Rabbinic principle is, 'Everything is in the power of Heaven except the fear of Heaven' [*Berachoth*] . . . ." (Cohen, *Rabbinic Sages* 11). Freewill is sacrosanct.

eschatological and soteriological conclusions in classical dispensationalism in the assertion of completely separate earthly and heavenly programs of redemption.[17] And hyperdispensationalism shows this same tendency toward extreme separateness that is difficult to reconcile to the reality of there being one and only one salvation in the one person of Jesus Christ.[18] For example, hyperdispensationalism rejects the general (also known as catholic, or universal) Epistles, much of the book of Acts, and much of the four Gospels as not being directly relevant to the church age. Revised dispensationalism and progressive dispensationalism have softened the emphasis on separateness, but this is accomplished by imposing limits on the system of thought that are not derived organically from the basic principles that define dispensationalism. Revised dispensationalism dictates an artificial separation of anthropological significance and cosmological significance, while progressive dispensationalism dictates an artificial unity of covenantal and typological structures between the different dispensations.[19] But the simple reality is that hyperdispensationalism, not revised dispensationalism, is the logical conclusion of the fundamental principles of dispensational. And progressive dispensationalism is hardly recognizable as even a form of dispensationalism.

As a final specific example of the separateness that marks dispensational thought, Gentile races existing before the church age are generally viewed in the system as being excluded from the covenantal blessings of Israel.[20] And this assertion of dispensationalism should be recognized as inconsistent with the prophecy, or promise, that those who bless Israel will themselves be blessed (Gen 12:3). It is inconsistent with the proclamation that there is one law that applies equally to both Jew and Gentile (Exod 12:49). It is inconsistent with the commandment to accept the stranger dwelling in the land as one who is native-born (Lev 19:33–34). And it is inconsistent with the Moabitess Ruth claiming the God of Israel as her own God (Ruth 1:16–18) and ultimately taking her place in the genealogy of Jesus Christ (Matt 1:5). The organizing principle of separateness is assumed in dispensationalism, and therefore separateness is inevitably that which is concluded in dispensationalism. And any description of the different administrations in dispensationalism as being merely different aspects of one divine plan is simply not derivative of the fundamental worldview that is embodied by dispensationalism.

---

[17] *Evangelical Dictionary of Theology*, s.v. "dispensation, dispensationalism."
[18] "For the kingdom of the Father, of the Son, and of the Holy Ghost, is one, even as their substance is one and their dominion one. Whence also, with one and the same adoration, we worship the one Deity in three Persons, subsisting without beginning, uncreate, without end, and to which there is no successor [Methodius, *Palms*]" (Roberts et al., *Ante-Nicene Fathers* 6:396–97). One God, one dominion, one salvation.
[19] *Evangelical Dictionary of Theology*, s.v. "dispensation, dispensationalism."
[20] Ibid.

INTRODUCTION

Covenantalism

Covenant theology, which is closely related to federal theology and commonly connected with Reformed theology,[21] was first formally developed by Ulrich Zwingli (AD 1484–1531) and Heinrich Bullinger (AD 1504–1575) at the time of the Protestant Reformation, though the central importance of covenantal relationships is apparent in the Biblical text itself and also in the writings of patristic and medieval commentators.[22] Covenantal thought is also evident in the writings of John Calvin (1509–1564).[23] The fundamental spirit of covenantalism is characterized by an emphasis on unity in contrast to separateness, while the concept of a single overarching covenant forms the interpretive framework of covenantalism. The varied works of Zwingli are considered the first significant formulation of federal theology (1520s),[24] while an early influential work in covenant theology is Heinrich Bullinger's *One and Eternal Testament or Covenant* (1534).[25] The most influential work of Calvin is his *Institutes of the Christian Religion* (first edition 1536, fifth edition 1559).[26] Covenant theology was ultimately adopted in the Westminster Confession of Faith (1646) and, therefore, is identified with Anglican, as well as Reformed, traditions. The Westminster Confession has been largely adopted in British and American Presbyterian traditions and also many Congregational and Baptist assemblies.[27] John Gill (1697–1771) and Jonathan Edwards (1703–1758) are significant later advocates of federalism and Reformed theology.[28]

In covenant theology, two primary covenants are identified: a covenant of works and a covenant of grace. The covenant of works established Adam and mankind in Adam as the steward and ruler of creation under the sovereignty of God and in obedience to God.[29] The covenant of works promised eternal life, but only as a reward for an absolute perfect obedience. In covenant theology, the covenant of works is identified exclusively with the garden of Eden before the Fall of Man. And all subsequent covenants, including that represented by the law of Moses, are considered to be part of a singular overarching covenant of grace. The different individual covenants established since the Fall of Man are viewed as a progressive revelation of the one covenant of grace, and this progressive revelation is viewed as an organic whole, analogous to an acorn becoming an oak tree.[30] In the progressive revelation of the covenantal relationship between God and man, Adam is viewed as the federal head of the

---

[21] *Cambridge Dictionary of Christian Theology*, s.v. "federal theology."
[22] *Evangelical Dictionary of Theology*, s.v. "covenant theology."
[23] Ibid.
[24] *Cambridge Dictionary of Christian Theology*, s.v. "federal theology."
[25] *Evangelical Dictionary of Theology*, s.v. "covenant theology."
[26] Ibid., s.v. "Calvin, John."
[27] Ibid., s.v. "Westminster Confession of Faith."
[28] *Cambridge Dictionary of Christian Theology*, s.v. "federal theology."
[29] *Evangelical Dictionary of Theology*, s.v. "Calvinism."
[30] Ibid., s.v. "covenant theology."

human race under the covenant of works while Christ is viewed as the federal head of the faithful under the covenant of grace. Hence, the close relationship between covenant theology and federal theology.[31]

The resulting inclusion of the Mosaic covenant under a universal covenant of grace is an immediately surprising aspect of covenantalism since the Levitical rules are so clearly connected to the idea of blessing and long life being a reward for obedience and good works. And given that law is interpreted as grace or under grace, it is difficult not to conclude that obedience and good works are being added to faith as the rule for salvation in Christ. And if law is then viewed as merely a training mechanism to prepare humanity for the coming of Christ,[32] it is difficult not to conclude that obedience is being placed ahead of faith. Subsuming law under grace in such a way that minimizes the distinction between the two implies that law and grace are directly compatible. The reality is that the dichotomy of law and grace represents a fundamentally conflicted paradox and not a unified pair. The Old Testament does mandate a covenant of works as the basis for grace, but this should be understood exclusively as the works of Jesus Christ culminating in the work of the cross. And any blurring of this distinction means that the finite and imperfect works of the individual are being subsumed into the complete and perfect work of Christ in such a way that the finite works of the individual become themselves meritorious of the infinite blessing in Christ.[33] The risen Christ does send the Holy Spirit to empower the faithful to imitate him in life and death, but the fullness of the indwelling Holy Spirit does not precede the resurrection just as the faithful do not precede Christ. The works of sinful man are as filthy rags and should not in any way be equated with the work of Christ (Isa 64:6).

A distinct covenant of redemption, representing a third covenant existing exclusively within the Trinity, is sometimes also specified in covenantalism, wherein the Son promises to give his life for the redemption of the world. In this case, a purely spiritual covenant of redemption is normally viewed to be an essential complement to the covenant of grace in order to establish Jesus Christ as a mediator according to both the human and the divine natures.[34] And God establishing a covenantal relationship with humanity is then viewed as being founded upon or being a manifestation of the fundamental relationships existing within the Trinity.[35] And this organization scheme should be recognized as reflecting a belief in an intimate connection between the spiritual and natural domains of reality. The covenant of redemption is sometimes subsumed by the covenant of grace instead of being expressed as a distinct third covenant,[36] but in either case the close relationship between the covenants of redemption and grace is another aspect of the organic unity characterizing

---

[31] Ibid., s.v. "federal theology."
[32] Ibid., s.v. "covenant theology."
[33] *Cambridge Dictionary of Christian Theology*, s.v. "federal theology."
[34] Ibid.
[35] *Evangelical Dictionary of Theology*, s.v. "covenant theology."
[36] Ryrie 184, 187.

INTRODUCTION

covenant theology.[37] The relationship between grace and redemption in covenantalism correctly implies a universal parallel between the spiritual and natural, and it also correctly implies that all creation, including the unfolding of creation, is formed in the image of God. But the time-based language used to describe the relationships within the Trinity incorrectly implies that there was once a time when the Son had not agreed to die for the world.

In contrast to the emphasis on separateness and discontinuity that marks dispensationalism, the fundamental spirit of covenantalism is characterized by an emphasis on unity and continuity. The emphasis on unity in covenantalism is related to the attempt to describe the covenantal relationship between man and God, specifically between the elect and God, being established by God and God alone.[38] But the unity of man is not the unity of God. For example, in covenantalism the church is viewed as the fulfillment of Israel, the church being a new Israel. And therein the promises made to Israel are effectively transferred to the church.[39] And this is why covenant theology is sometimes labeled a form of supersessionism, or replacement theology. The problem with transferring to the church the promises made to Israel is that it inevitably requires allegorizing and, thereby, rejecting the literal and faithful promises of God. The promises made to Israel are simply too specific to be attributed to the church. To dismiss yet unfulfilled prophecies in this way or in any way flirts with the idea that God breaks covenants, and this is the incredible irony that marks covenant theology. The lack of distinction in covenantalism between the nation of Israel and the earthly church is a logical consequence of the emphasis on sameness, and therefore to reinstate the distinction between Israel and the church would require an interpretive framework that is fundamentally different from covenantalism. The organizing principle of unity and continuity is assumed in covenantalism, and therefore unity and continuity is inevitably that which is concluded in covenantalism.

The fundamental issue with allegorizing the promises of God is that it represents a denial of the true character of the Bible, likewise the true character of God related by the Bible. The Scriptures embody an innately simultaneous literal and spiritual significance, and thus to deny the literal is to deny the vital relationship between the literal and the spiritual. And to deny in any way the innate literal and spiritual meaning of the written Word equates to denying that Jesus Christ is simultaneously and eternally true man and true God. There is a parallel between the written Word and the incarnate Word. And this parallel is a purposeful reflection of the relationship between the humanity and divinity of Jesus Christ. It is the same inspired relationship between the human and divine perspectives that is embodied by the Bible. The two fundamental denials that mark allegorization are the denials that God means what he says and that God is who he is. And the parallel between these two denials also points to the essential relationship between the spiritual and the natural. The conclusion of

---

[37] *Evangelical Dictionary of Theology*, s.v. "covenant theology."
[38] Ibid.
[39] Ryrie 129–31.

allegorization is not simply error but an ever-increasing error caused by disregarding the fundamental relationship between the natural and the spiritual that is our compass in navigating the Scriptures and life as a whole.[40]

Another key characteristic of covenant theology is an emphasis on predestination in contrast to freewill, which is commonly folded into the concept of the elect. The covenant of grace is understood to establish the salvation of the faithful in eternal life by grace through faith in Jesus Christ, but the faithful that will be saved are very strictly viewed as a predetermined elect.[41] The emphasis on predestination to the negation of freewill is like the emphasis on unity and grace to the negation of law and is therefore a natural aspect of covenantalism. The emphasis on predestination is derived from an emphasis on the sovereignty of God Almighty.[42] But the problem with emphasizing either predestination or freewill is that it denies the essential paradox of predestination and freewill, which is the conflict between the sovereignty of God and the sacredness of the freewill of man. In order to correctly relate to God, one must comprehend the full counsel of God and, therefore, one must reconcile paradoxes and not simply ignore them. The sovereignty of God is the freewill of God, and thus the conflict between freewill and predestination is ultimately the universal conflict between the freewill of man and the freewill of God, between the way of flesh and the way of the Spirit.

The resolution of the paradox of freewill and predestination is commonly understood as the foreknowledge of God.[43] But foreknowledge still doesn't explain why God created some souls, knowing beforehand that they would be lost. Asserting that life is by nature an insoluble mystery or paradox is another common recourse.[44] But relegating the basic logic and morality of God, which is ultimately the life of God, as being beyond human comprehension, or separate from living reality, is incompatible with the very essence of Christianity being, not the way of ignorance and death separated from God, but the way of understanding and eternal life in accord with God. The Biblical resolution of the conflict between the freewill of man and the freewill of God is the person of Jesus Christ being fully man and fully God. And the corresponding resolution of law and grace is the cross. All creation is wrapped up in the humble condescension of God Almighty embodied by Jesus Christ, because all creation comes into being through the person of Jesus Christ (John 1:3). The condescension of the Lord God that is required for redemption and new creation is necessarily the same condescension required in the original act of creation, because the one man Christ is the one and only paradigm of all creation. The Lord allows our individual lives to be confounded by suffering,

---

[40] The spiritual sense of the Scriptures can be subdivided into allegorical, moral, and anagogical senses, but in a profound concordance all the spiritual senses are founded upon the literal sense (Rom. Catholic Church, *Catechism* 38–39). The literal and the spiritual, representing the natural and the spiritual, cannot be separated.
[41] *Evangelical Dictionary of Theology*, s.vv. "covenant theology," "elect, election."
[42] Ibid., s.vv. "predestination," "sovereignty of God."
[43] Ibid., s.v. "predestination."
[44] Ibid., s.v. "sovereignty of God."

INTRODUCTION

and the Lord likewise allows creation to be confounded by suffering. The Lord allows our individual human lives to be confounded by time and chance, and the Lord likewise allows the divine act of creation to be confounded by time and chance (Eccl 9:11). Any other situation would imply different parallel realities and, thereby, would imply more than one image of God. The observation that some souls are lost is proof not only of the sanctity of individual freewill but also of the oneness of God.

Scholasticism

Scholasticism is one of the systems of thought identified with the Roman Catholic Church and notably with Thomas Aquinas.[45] Aquinas was canonized in AD 1323 and decreed a doctor of the church in 1567. In 1879 Leo XIII formally advocated the methods of Aquinas as the proper model of Roman Catholic Theology, and Aquinas was pronounced the patron of Roman Catholic schools in 1880.[46] Prominent scholastic works of Thomas Aquinas are his *Summa theologica* ("Sum, or Total, of Theology") and *Quaestiones disputatae* ("Disputed Questions"). Scholasticism strives for rigorous definitions of terms and a precise systemization of logic. A basic form used in scholasticism is to pose two seemingly opposed views, and then synthesize them through a process of dialectic, or rational, dispute.[47] The foundation of scholasticism is human reason itself and the idea that the Bible and the world as a whole are essentially rational and, therefore, should yield to what are essentially secular modes of logical and analytical thought. The specific interpretive framework developed by Aquinas attempts to unite Christian theology with Greek philosophy, particularly the propositions of Aristotle. In his works Aquinas was influenced especially by the Islamic philosopher Averroes, who is closely identified with the view that philosophical reasoning should take precedence over the instruction of religious texts, whether that of the Bible or the Quran. Averroes (1126–1198) sought to reconcile Aristotelianism and Islam, while Aquinas (1225–1274) sought to reconcile Aristotelianism and Christianity.[48] Similarly, Maimonides, Rambam, (1135–1204) sought to reconcile Aristotelianism and Judaism.[49]

Anselm of Canterbury (AD 1033–1109), a forerunner of Thomas Aquinas, famously spoke of his worldview, quoting an Old Latin translation of Isaiah 7:9, as "faith seeking understanding."[50] But despite this assertion, the fundamental premise of scholasticism is that human knowledge and reason explain the Bible and God, and therefore the process should be described as "reason seeking

---

[45] *Cambridge Dictionary of Christian Theology*, s.vv. "Catholic theology," "Thomism."
[46] *Evangelical Dictionary of Theology*, s.vv. "Thomas Aquinas," "Thomism."
[47] *Evangelical Dictionary of Theology*, s.v. "scholasticism"; *Cambridge Dictionary of Christian Theology*, s.v. "Catholic theology."
[48] *Evangelical Dictionary of Theology*, s.vv. "Aristotle, Aristotelianism," "Averroes," "scholasticism."
[49] *Jewish Encyclopedia*, s.v. "Moses ben Maimon—RaMBaM, usually called Maimonides."
[50] *Evangelical Dictionary of Theology*, s.v. "Anselm of Canterbury"; *Cambridge Dictionary of Christian Theology*, s.v. "Anselm of Canterbury."

understanding or knowledge," or simply "knowledge seeking itself or its own way." The Latin *scholasticus*, Greek *scholastikós*, means "studious, learned," which of itself testifies that the fundamental spirit of scholasticism is human knowledge in contrast to divine revelation.[51] And Anselm is remembered for very consciously setting aside the Scriptures in order to freely speculate about the essential truths of the Christian faith.[52] And thus it is appropriate that a more complete understanding of Isaiah 7:9, in contrast to Anselm's position, is foremost to trust in God and not one's own power and reason. The correct starting point and ending point is faith, not human reason. Our sure foundation is the Word of God that speaks of Jesus Christ and the way of the Holy Spirit. Our sure foundation is not Greek philosophy, which speaks of Adam and the way of all the earth. The Spirit works through human reason and conscience, but the plain meaning of the Bible—not our flesh, or finite understanding—must be our counselor (Gal 1:8). Anselm reasoned that man is created in the image of God and, therefore, man is called to seek out the necessary reasons inherent in both creation and the Creator.[53] The flaw in this logic is that creation and likewise the human faculties were corrupted in the Fall of Man, and therefore human reason and conscience must be used primarily to respond to divine revelation, not anticipate it or prejudge it. Notable scholastic works of Anselm of Canterbury are *Proslogion* ("Colloquy"), originally titled *Faith Seeking Reason*, and also *Monologion* ("Soliloquy") *on the Rationale of the Faith*.[54]

Peter Abelard (1079–1142) is another pioneer of medieval scholasticism. In his influential work *Sic et Non* ("Yes and No"), Abelard elevates human reason, at least implicitly, to the same level as received tradition and divine revelation.[55] And this again is the root problem that has marked scholasticism from its foundation. Human reason is largely equivalent to human tradition and is therefore in perpetual conflict with divine revelation. The Bible is rational, and human beings are basically rational, and the individual can and actually must understand the revelations of God from a position of human reason. For though one could perhaps know a thing in separation from human reason—that is, without understanding it—one cannot, by definition, understand a thing separated human reason. Nonetheless, human beings habitually disagreeing with one another about basically everything should signal that human logic cannot be used by itself to determine absolute meaning and truth. Further, given that the dialectic tools of scholasticism are generally imparted by academic elites and that the intricacies of scholasticism are largely incomprehensible to the masses, it is difficult not to see a parallel between the esoteric nature of scholasticism and the esoteric nature of gnosticism. And given the elevation of self that is implied by the elevation of human reason, it is difficult not to remember the original sin of lucifer seeking to elevate himself to be like God (Isa 14:12–15).

---

[51] *Random House Unabridged Dictionary*, 2nd ed., s.v. "scholastic."
[52] *Evangelical Dictionary of Theology*, s.v. "Anselm of Canterbury."
[53] Ibid.
[54] Ibid.
[55] *Evangelical Dictionary of Theology*, s.v. "Abelard, Peter."

INTRODUCTION

And it is similarly difficult to dismiss the pagan roots of the Aristotelianism from which scholasticism springs up.[56]

The emergence of scholasticism has not been without controversy even within the Roman Catholic tradition.[57] Lanfranc, archbishop of Canterbury, refused to accept the methodology of Anselm, his eventual successor, to willfully set aside the Scriptures in the application of dialectic methods.[58] Over a century later in 1277, the archbishop of Canterbury, the bishop of Paris, and several doctors of Oxford condemned various propositions of Thomistic scholasticism, notably the principle of individuation being founded in some intrinsic way upon matter.[59] Also in 1277 the foundational works of Aristotle and Averroes were formally condemned by the Roman Catholic Church.[60] The problem has always been that the ethics underlying Thomistic scholasticism are not innately Christian but rather a form of Aristotelian eudaemonism.[61] The emphasis on the material and corporeal, not the spiritual, parallels the emphasis on human reason, in contrast to divine revelation. And the elevation of human reason should be recognized as a spirit of egocentricity and carnality. There is always a logical conclusion to every supposition, and simply denying or ignoring any such conclusion creates an incoherent reality. For example, the worldview of Aquinas regarding matter is substantially that of Aristotle. But where Aristotle derives the logical conclusion (within his system of thought) that matter is eternal, Aquinas places a (foreign) limit on the Aristotelian view of matter by asserting that matter is a created thing and therefore finite.[62] The latter is the Biblically correct view, but it is still foreign to the Aristotelian system. The Biblical accounting exists to measure all things, not to be mingled with pagan worldviews. And it seems that even Aquinas viewed scholasticism with some reservations, given the report that he ceased writing in 1273, despite urgings otherwise, because he had an insight that made everything he had ever written seem to be of little value.[63]

The first problem with scholasticism is that it elevates human reason to the primary position. The second problem with scholasticism is that it specifically

---

[56] "Christian thinkers, from the beginning, were confronted with the question: How are we to reconcile reason with revelation, science with faith, philosophy with theology? ... They [the first apologists] advanced the explanation that all the wisdom of Plato and the other Greeks was due to the inspiration of the Logos; that it was God's truth .... We find it [this hypothesis] in St. Basil, in Origen, and even in St. Augustine" (*Catholic Encyclopedia*, s.v. "scholasticism"). Yes, the origins of impious modern-day scholasticism can be traced to the beginning of and even before the church age, but a faithful remnant has always sought to use human reason, formed in the image of God, not to relegate divine revelation but to relate to and conform themselves to divine revelation.

[57] *Cambridge Dictionary of Christian Theology*, s.v. "Thomism."
[58] *Evangelical Dictionary of Theology*, s.v. "Anselm of Canterbury."
[59] *Catholic Encyclopedia*, s.vv. "Thomism," "matter."
[60] *Evangelical Dictionary of Theology*, s.v. "Aristotle, Aristotelianism."
[61] *Catholic Encyclopedia*, s.v. "scholasticism."
[62] Ibid., s.v. "matter."
[63] Ibid., s.v. "Thomas Aquinas."

elevates Greek modes of thought, which are rooted in humanism and paganism. For example, the form of Aristotelian scholasticism identified expressly with Aquinas, termed Thomism, is marked by the concept of the duality of the soul and the body.[64] In this school of thought the soul is viewed as the *substantial form* for man, separated from the *forma corporeitatis* ("physical body").[65] But this worldview is detached from the triune reality of body, soul, and spirit, which is the Biblical accounting (1 Thess 5:23). And it is appropriate, considering the fundamental carnality of Greek philosophy, that the difference between duality and triunity is the difference between animal and human life, between instinct and freewill. As another example, Thomism asserts that one cannot perceive or prove a priori the existence of God by some intuition—that is, from cause to effect, by deductive reasoning from a set of premises—but rather one proves the existence of God a posteriori—that is, from effect to cause, by inductive reasoning from that which is observed.[66] In contrast, the Biblical worldview is that God is evident both a priori and a posteriori. The Biblical worldview is that man has absolutely no excuse to deny the reality of God. Human beings intuitively, or morally, perceive the reality of God, that the perfect self-existence of God implies a perfecting existence, or creation, in his divine image. And all reality, or creation, confirms this innate knowledge, that the Creator can be inferred from the creation.[67] It is interesting to compare historical criticism with scholasticism since both are based on human rationalism and both are essentially atheistic or paganistic.[68] And given the philosophical parallels between scholasticism and historical criticism, it is not surprising that both theological systems permeate Roman Catholic theology.[69] Scholasticism and likewise historical criticism presuppose human rationalism and that is exactly

---

[64] Aquinas, *Summa theologica* 1:363–82.
[65] "[*Substantial form*:] The form or nature that according to the scholastics gives to an individual substance its specific or generic character" (*Webster's Third New International Dictionary of the English Language Unabridged*, s.v. "substantial form").
[66] *Catholic Encyclopedia*, s.v. "Thomism."
[67] "The choice is simple: one chooses either a self-existent God or a self-existent universe—and the universe is not behaving as if it is self-existent" (*Evangelical Dictionary of Theology*, s.v. "God, arguments for the existence of"). My sheep hear my voice (a posteriori), and I know them, and they follow me (a priori), John 10:27.
[68] "The achievements of the historical-critical method have been magnificent; it has given us unprecedented knowledge about the Bible but has not yet provided us with a spirituality" (Armstrong 226). It is often missed that the goal of the historical-critical method is as much to form a false religion as it is to destroy true religion.
[69] "In 1943 historical-critical exegesis was officially recognized as a legitimate form of biblical interpretation by Pope Pius XII . . . In 1964 the Pontifical Biblical Commission confirmed the validity of historical criticism . . . This more positive appreciation of historical criticism was confirmed by the Second Vatican Council (1962–1965). . . . This acceptance of historical criticism was reiterated on 23 April 1993, when the Pontifical Biblical Institute presented to Pope John Paul II a report entitled *The Interpretation of the Bible in the Church*" (Law 75). Historical criticism is a religion, and it has a priesthood.

INTRODUCTION

what is concluded, but the irony is that the final end of human rationalism is an animalistic irrationalism.[70]

STRUCTURALISM

The hermeneutics developed in this commentary series could be termed a form of structuralism because of the emphasis on types and patterns and how increasingly complex patterns are formed and organized. In comparison, the fundamental spirit of dispensationalism is marked by separateness and discontinuity. The concept of separateness is developed in dispensationalism by dividing the Biblical timeline of world history into distinct and completely separate, though potentially overlapping, eras or dispensations in which God deals differently with humanity at different times. Accordingly, the Old Testament, relating the law, and also much of the Gospels, fulfilling the law, are generally considered, in dispensational thought, not to be directly relevant to the church. The logical conclusion of dispensationalism is then the extension of the separateness of the present creation into eternity and, therein, the assertion of distinctly separate programs of redemption. In contrast, the testimony of the Bible is that there is only one salvation in the one man Jesus Christ.[71]

At the other extreme, the fundamental spirit of covenantalism is marked by an emphasis on unity and continuity. The concept of unity is developed in covenantalism by treating the entire Biblical timeline since the Fall of Man as being under a single covenant of grace. Accordingly, the Old and New Testaments are viewed as an organic whole, unified by a progressive revelation of the grace of God. The logical conclusion of covenantalism is, however, a blurring of the distinction between law and grace and likewise a blurring of the distinction between works and faith. The law that governs flesh simply being added to the grace of the Holy Spirit implies a salvation of faith plus works, in contrast to the one true salvation that comes by grace alone through faith alone in Christ alone.

A third discrete, nominally orthogonal point of comparison is scholasticism, the fundamental spirit of which is marked by an esoteric form of human rationalism. Scholasticism, which in the West is dominated by Thomism, blends Christian theology with Greek philosophy, primarily the philosophy of Aristotle. Consequently, the beginning and end of scholasticism is an elevating of human

---

[70] "Two charges, especially, are made against the Schoolmen [scholastic scholars]: First, that they confounded philosophy with theology; and second, that they made reason subservient to authority [dogmas]. As a matter of fact, the very essence of Scholasticism is, first, its clear delimitation of the respective domains of philosophy and theology, and, second, its advocacy of the use of reason" (*Catholic Encyclopedia*, s.v. "scholasticism"). The finite reasoning of mortal man fails to perceive that theology has no boundaries.

[71] "Structuralism, as the term suggests, is concerned with structures, and more particularly with examining the general laws by which they work" (Eagleton 82). The Biblical structuralism developed in the present work is distinct from traditional literary structuralism, most notably in that a perfect and complete text is assumed and also in that substantial meaning is not viewed as being negated by relational meaning.

philosophical predilections above the revelations of the Lord God. The innate problem with scholasticism is that the Scriptures, the Word of God—likewise the world as a whole, which is formed in the image of God—are viewed through a filter of Greek philosophy, which is fundamentally humanistic and paganistic, not Christological.

A first point about structuralism is that it is not a purely literary perspective. The Scriptures speak of life and the world, past and future, which means that the Scriptures are connected to the reality of creation as a whole. And therefore Biblical types and patterns must be understood as transcending the text and encompassing all reality. The patterns of the Scriptures are connected to space and time and to people. The progressive revelation of the Scriptures is the progressive revelation of the world, mankind as a whole, and individual man. For example, the seven millennia connecting the body of Adam and the Body of Christ represent the sevenfold creation of Adam. The sevenfold creation (seven days) of Adam is sanctified (subsumed) by the threefold creation (three days) of Jesus Christ. And the threefold creation is ultimately one creation just as the one God is triune. The exact form of one's hermeneutics is critical because the form of one's hermeneutics largely predetermines the form of one's exegesis. The basic construct of the dispensationalist is the separateness of the dispensations of God, and therein the dispensationalist assumes an absolute separation of law and grace that rends the vesture of Christ, not the veil of the temple (John 19:24, Matt 27:51). The basic construct of the covenantalist is the unity and sameness of the different covenants of God, which fails to make a crisp distinction between law and grace, and thereby the covenantalist implies a false equality between the works of the flesh and the faith in Christ that comes only by grace (Eph 2:8–10).

The transcendent form in structuralism is the relationship between the triune Father, Son, and Spirit and the threefold successive formation of Adam in the image of God followed by the First and Second Advents of Christ. And the formation of Adam followed by the First Advent followed by the Second Advent parallels the original creation followed by the destruction in the floodwaters followed by the promised new creation in the end times. All humanity proceeds from father Adam just as the Spirit and Son, likewise all creation, proceed from God the Father. And the First Advent of Christ, like the death and resurrection of the world at the time of Noah, is most closely identified with God the Son. Perhaps more subtly, the Second Advent is identified with God the Spirit. It is the power of the Holy Spirit that will raise the Body of Christ at the time of the Second Advent, and it is the promised resurrection, not the concomitant judgment of the world, that the faithful should recognize as the focus of God.

The immanent form in structuralism is the triunity of man—body, spirit, and soul—formed in the image of the triunity of God. And the triunity of man is ultimately manifested in the relationship between the triune Father, Son, and Spirit and the threefold successive formation of Adam, Eve, and their collective offspring, all of whom individually embody the image of the triunity of God. Eve and also Eve's offspring proceed from the side of Adam just as the Spirit and the Son proceed from the Father. The body of a person represents the creation that proceeds from God the Father. The spirit of a person corresponds to God the Spirit, while the living soul of a person is identified with the personal (living and breathing) nature of the Son. Further, since both the transcendent and the immanent forms are connected to the triunity of God, there exists a parallel between the two forms. And the parallel between the transcendent and the immanent, between the distant and the personal, represents a unity that spans and encompasses all reality, likewise a universality of the image of God in molding all levels of reality.

The general progression in structuralism is (1) identifying the fundamental elements and pattern types implicit to the Biblical text, (2) establishing how elements combine to construct increasingly complex patterns, especially the operation of Christological patterns in the construction of Trinitarian patterns, and (3) characterizing the relationship between implicit patterns and explicit meaning in the emergence, or convergence, of the fullness of the triune image of God. The identification of pattern types is therein understood to be the identification of the context of any given Biblical revelation or particular aspect of a Biblical revelation. And establishing the correct context is essential in understanding any narrative. For example, Adam followed by Noah followed by Abraham reflects the creation of Adam followed by the First and Second Advents of Christ, but Abraham followed by Isaac followed by Jacob also reflects the creation of Adam followed by the First and Second Advents of Christ. Abraham compared with Noah then reflects the Second Advent compared with the First Advent, but Abraham compared with Isaac reflects the first man Adam compared with the second man Christ. The account of Abraham, or different aspects of the account of Abraham, should therefore be simultaneously compared to the original formation of Adam and also the second coming of Christ. Such changing roles may seem confusing at first but is actually completely normal. It is like one man who is simultaneously a son to his father, a husband to his wife, and a father to his son.[72] The way of the Holy Bible is the way of all creation, and the way of all creation is the way of the Holy Spirit. It is something impossible that becomes inevitable, something strange that becomes familiar. And the way of a proper and holy Biblical hermeneutics is expected to be the exact same way.

There are three basic witnesses that should always agree: (1) the Bible, which is the explicit testimony of God, (2) the human faculties of conscience and reason, which are formed in the image of God, and (3) the nature of physical creation, which is governed by the natural laws of God. The Lord God is the one author and the one story of all three, and therefore all three should testify

---

[72] One man having different roles in life—for example, son, husband, and father—being further likened to the simultaneous oneness and triunity of God is often labeled modalism, which is a heresy, because only one person, not three, is involved. But I would point out that when people occupy such radically different roles, they normally report feeling and acting as if they truly were different people. A Biblical precedent for such an analogy—relating roles or aspects of an individual to separate personhoods—is the likening of individual believers to members of a single body, 1 Cor 12:12.

to the one and same God. Creation reflects the Creator. Likewise, all layers of reality reflect the one Creator. In this worldview, identifying the overarching pattern type, in which some aspect of a Biblical narrative is embedded, provides the correct context for developing word studies and understanding literal imagery. Pattern types represent a global top-down perspective, while word studies and literal imagery represent a local bottom-up perspective. And a fundamental agreement must exist between bottom-up and top-down perspectives, or something is wrong somewhere. All layers of reality are expected to tell the same story or contribute to the same story.

The fundamental agreement between global and local perspectives is one manifestation of the property of redundancy, which is in fact a universal property that always underlies the stability of functioning, or real, systems. The Bible represents a reliable guide for the faithful unto salvation, and thus the Bible, not surprisingly, also shows the essential property of redundancy. One consequence of Biblical redundancy is, however, that different word-study, key-image, and so forth, combinations can be used to derive what are effectively the same conclusions. In other words, any given exegesis, or analysis, can be correct but not necessarily unique. And though this may seem like a deviation from one-to-one correspondence and, as a result, an infringement of the concept of absolute truth, it is actually a natural result of our merely human faculties being finite, that is, our being fundamentally unable perceive every detail, much less every nuance of every detail. Similarly, one would never expect to exhaust the array of all possible commentaries on the Scriptures. For the Scriptures represent the Word of the infinite God.[73]

The Bible is often described as a history of salvation, but this is only true in so far as the will of God to redeem his faithful is a representation of the image of God. The Bible is the testimony of God, and the testimony of God is the visible image of God. There is a parallel between the written Word and the incarnate Word. The image of God envelopes the salvation of fallen man, Adam-kind, but the reality of God should be understood to be the Trinity. And the image of God made visible should be understood to be Jesus Christ, not Adam. Confusion naturally arises because fallen man is redeemed in the person of Christ, and there is a sense in which the faithful become one with Christ in the Body of Christ. But the distinction between Jesus Christ and Adam is critical because it is inextricably linked with a correct understanding of the Christological principle of Biblical interpretation. The Bible is, in its entirety, related to the person of Jesus Christ, and therefore to try to understand the Bible in separation from Christ inevitably leads to error and sin. To try to

---

[73] "It is an axiom of Rabbinic exegesis of the Bible that there is no tautology [needless repetition]; . . ." (Cohen, *Rabbinic Sages* 192 n. 1). When reading the Bible, the infinite Word of God, purposeful repetition should not be confused with needless repetition—repetition in the Word of God reflects the universality of God, the image of God, and in fact is always combining subtly different aspects or perspectives of God.

INTRODUCTION

understand the Word of God by focusing on fallen Adam inevitably yields a fallen, or corrupted, view of the Word.[74]

Jesus and the Bible that speaks of Jesus are the only two corporeal realities that are sinless and inerrant, and this parallel necessarily exists because the object of the Bible is the person of Jesus. Both the Holy Scriptures and Jesus Christ are conceived of the same Holy Spirit (Luke 1:35, 2 Tim 3:16). And it is also by the Holy Spirit that we relate to the Scriptures and also to the Son of God. Therefore, a complete hermeneutic, or interpretive framework, could only be based on the image of God itself. Any serious study of the Bible necessarily presupposes the inerrancy of the Biblical text and likewise the inerrancy of the fundamental organizing principles that characterize the Bible. The immanent principle is Christological, while the transcendent principle is Trinitarian. Jesus Christ, being the visible image of God, is properly understood only in the fullness of the context of the Trinity. And images are inherently the domain of types and patterns. This is the oneness of God, the twofold natures of Jesus Christ, and the triunity of the Godhead. The faithful truly understand God not through flawed analogies, such as the supposed three phases of water, but rather according to explicit Biblical proclamations undergirded by implicit Biblical types and patterns and principles.

A basis set of nine interlocking symmetry pattern types can be identified, specifically three sets of three pattern types. The three sets of three pattern types form a single, unique two-dimensional 3x3 matrix table. The first set of three is the set of *prime*, *twofold*, and *threefold* pattern types, representing a fundamental, or elemental, set, in that it builds the more complex patterns. This elemental set also shows internal construction, for example, as evident in the twofold type building the threefold type via a repeating, overlapping 1-2, 1-2 operation. The prime, twofold, and threefold set is the most basic and abstract, corresponding to an existence separate from time. The second set of three is the set of *serial*, *chiastic*, and *staircase* pattern types, which is characterized by a rigid uniformity in time. The third and final set of three is the set of *historical*, *individual*, and *generational* pattern types, representing nonuniform analogues of the second set. The three sets of three pattern types, though interrelated, are independent, representing a minimum set, because they are distinguishable according to the quality, or property, of time, itself an irreducible dimension. The three sets of pattern types are constructive in nature, as well as descriptive, in that both their structure and also their construction are significant. The image of fundamental patterns constructing more complex patterns reflects the Son and the Spirit, also all creation, proceeding from the Father. The emphasis on time reflects the primal requirement for freewill created in the image of God, namely, the body existing in time and space.

---

[74] "So thorough was the [early] Christian's *pesher* [deciphering] exegesis that there is scarcely a verse in the New Testament that did not refer to the older scriptures [Old Testament]" (Armstrong 68). Even unbelievers, innately opposed to the Word of God, unwittingly testify to the reality of the Word of God.

When interpreting the Word of God or the creation of God, seven basic principles, or properties, can be identified: (1) multiplicity, (2) parallelism, (3) apocalypsis, (4) Christosis, or the Christological principle, (5) duality, (6) structuralism, and (7) universality. The overall hermeneutics developed in the present work could be termed a form of structuralism, after the sixth principle, because of the dominant emphasis on types and patterns throughout all seven principles. But the emphasis on types and patterns should be understood to be an emphasis on the Trinity. Structuralism is Trinitarianism. The hermeneutics of structuralism is the Trinity. The exegesis of structuralism is the Body of Christ. The very nature of language is that of signifiers and signified, and thus to advocate an emphasis on types and patterns is simply to advocate an emphasis on the revelation of God itself, or what God is actually relating to us. And what God is relating to us is ultimately himself, our alpha and our omega, our first example and our final expectation.[75]

Multiplicity. The progression of creation is poetic, meaning that it has a multiplicity of horizons. And the fulfillment of prophecy is likewise poetic. The Lord declares the end from the beginning, and he will do all his pleasure (Isa 46:10). It is normal for prophecy and also physical creation to have simultaneously an immediate fulfillment, a progressive fulfillment, and a final and complete fulfillment. Physical creation embodies prophecy. It is normal for every utterance of the Lord, every creation of the Lord, to be prophetic and poetic, reflecting the infinite nature of God. The horizons of meaning are not arbitrary but intimately related, testifying to the extreme internal consistency of all creation and, thereby, to the absolute perfection of God. For example, the creation of life by the Lord is ultimately a promise of life in the Lord. For God does not bring life to the point of birth without bringing forth unto life (Isa 66:9). And the life that proceeds from God is surely the fullness of life. The progressive revelation of all creation is the one image of God and finally the promised new Adam formed in the one image of God, namely, the promised one Body of Christ. The revelation of creation is progressive—Adam followed by Christ followed by the Body of Christ—just as the nature of the Creator is progressive—the Father sending forth the Son and the Spirit.[76]

Parallelism. The nature of creation is fractal, meaning that the same forms and truths repeat on all scales and levels of reality, and thereby a parallelism exists between the different levels of reality. The voice of the Lord is like the sound of many waters (Ezek 43:2, Rev 1:15). It is normal for every aspect of the creation of the God of creation to be prophetic and fractal, reflecting the nature and presence of God being everywhere always. And it is normal for prophecy to simultaneously have a literal meaning and a spiritual meaning. The layers of creation are not arbitrary but intimately related, testifying to the wholeness and

---

[75] In one school of thought, structuralism is viewed as largely equivalent to semiotics, the systematic study of signs (Eagleton 87). Everything is language.
[76] Understanding social and historical context is foundational, but ultimately the sublime must be recognized in the banal (Eagleton 42). A historical-grammatical understanding is not the end but only the beginning.

INTRODUCTION

completeness and unity of God. For example, sin entering the one man Adam is also sin entering the whole world (Rom 5:12). And the condemnation of the one man Adam is also the condemnation of the whole world (Rom 5:14). Likewise, the death and resurrection of the one sinless man, Jesus Christ, is the death and resurrection of all creation and also the very process, or progression, of creation (Rom 5:19). The death and resurrection of Jesus Christ at the time of the First Advent parallels the death and resurrection of the world at the time of the Flood (1 Pet 3:18–22) and simultaneously points to the death and resurrection of all creation by fire that is identified with the Second Advent (2 Pet 3:5–9). The Lord is self-existent, the font of all life and all creation, and therefore the only practicable paradigm of everything that exists. All levels of reality naturally reflect the one image of God, and all aspects of reality combine to form the one image of God.[77]

Apocalypsis ("unveiling"). The Bible represents the special revelation of God, not simply from God. The Bible is the written Word of God and therefore inerrant, complete, and a unified whole. And it is specifically the Old and New Testaments that should be recognized as being a unified whole. The story, or image, related by the Bible is the very image of God, foremost the person of Jesus Christ, who is the eternal and perfect, or sinless, image of the invisible God (Col 1:15). The study of the Bible is the study of God. The Bible relates the history of mankind, but mankind, or Adam-kind, is formed in the image of God. The Bible relates the history of the redemption of fallen creation, but this is the will of God and therefore also relates the image of God. The correct focus of the believer is on God, not fallen creation, because a focus on the creation, which has been corrupted, will inevitably produce a corrupted image of God. Generally, the most common error in Bible study is to focus on the human authors and their supposed cultural settings and not on the Holy Spirit, who is the ultimate author of the Bible. The most basic truth of special revelation is that the Bible is the Word of God. Everything else is derivative of this one statement. Even the process of recognizing and interpreting revelation comes by the Holy Spirit and, therefore, is a matter not only of simple observation but is itself an expression of the image of God. And this is true of explicit revelation and also implicit revelation, including types and patterns.[78]

Christosis (Christological principle). The correct and complete interpretation of all creation—including the human condition, creation as a whole, and also the special revelation of the Scriptures—is necessarily Christological. Every detail of the Bible and likewise every detail of creation should be understood in relationship to Jesus Christ and only in relationship to Jesus Christ. Even sin is

---

[77] There can, by definition, be only one first, or unoriginated, principle, and the one unoriginated principle is rightly understood to be the oneness of God—Clement of Alexandria, *Stromata* (Roberts et al., *Ante-Nicene Fathers* 2:471). God the Father, from whom God the Spirit and God the Son eternally proceed, without beginning or end.

[78] The reader is an active participant in literature in that one's experience is in actuality expanded and refined in the act of reading (Perrine 556). The essential collusion between author and reader, which marks all literature and particularly the written Word of God, reflects the essential call of the faithful to unity in the Body of Christ.

understood with respect to Jesus Christ since it is Jesus Christ who became a curse on the cross for the sake of us sinners (Gal 3:13). The truth is that sin and evil are not something unto themselves but rather a corruption of something created by God. Even lucifer is a created being, who of himself cannot create anything. The evil one can only corrupt that which has already been created by the Lord God. Finally, Jesus Christ is the natural and correct focus of the believer, for Jesus Christ is our foremost example, being God in the flesh. But Jesus Christ, who is God the Son, is properly and fully understood only in the context of the Trinity. Jesus Christ is the visible image of God, but Jesus Christ is understood according to the Trinity and only according to the Trinity. Theology is Christology, and Christology is Trinitarianism.[79]

Duality. Our foremost experience of reality is twofold, material and spiritual, reflecting the duality of the Son, who is fully man and fully God. All things are made according to the Son and through the Son, and without him nothing is made (John 1:3). The distinction between the natural and the spiritual is reflected in the dichotomy of earth and heaven, likewise body and spirit, and likewise law and grace. The parallelism between the natural and the spiritual is fundamental because the natural and the spiritual together represent not some aspect of creation but rather the totality of all creation. Our twofold experience of reality connects us to the twofold natures of the Son, namely, the nearness of the Son and our personal relationship with the Son. Further, the natural and the spiritual are not separate but connected. The relationship between the natural and the spiritual, between the literal and the figurative, is not hidden or arbitrary just as the relationship between man and God is not distant and capricious.[80] The natural and the spiritual both testify to the same truth of God that is the image of God. For example, the written Word always has literal and spiritual dimensions just as the incarnate Word is simultaneously true man and true God. And the literal, bottom-up reality (earthly) always agrees with the spiritual, top-down reality (heavenly). Finally, our primal experience of creation is twofold, body and soul, or simply tangible versus intangible, but our final understanding

---

[79] "It [Christology] refers quite specifically to inquiry and reflection that are concerned with Jesus *in his messianic character*. . . . what is presupposed and implied by the fact that Jesus is the elect [only begotten] 'Son of God' . . . To understand or evaluate Jesus christologically means, on the one hand, to ask about his relation to God [the Father and the Holy Spirit] and, on the other, to seek a way of expressing his representative [propitiatory] character as a human being . . . the one in whom humanity's common destiny is both summed up and determined" (Norris 2). The relationship uniting the Father and the Son is the relationship uniting the Son and the faithful indwelt by the Holy Spirit, for the Trinity is the shape of our salvation.

[80] "The meaning of a literary symbol must be established and supported by the entire context of the story. The symbol has its meaning *in* the story, not *outside* it. . . . A symbol may have more than one meaning. It may suggest a cluster of meanings. At its most effective a symbol is like a many-faceted jewel: it flashes different colors when turned in the light. This is not to say that it can mean anything we want it to: the area of possible meanings is always controlled by the context" (Perrine 214–15). The Trinity is the paradigm of all creation and, therefore, the proper context for all interpretation.

of creation must be threefold, body, soul, and spirit. Our first creation in the natural body is governed by the flesh, but our promised new creation in the spiritual, or glorified, body must be governed by the Holy Spirit (1 Thess 5:23). The duality of Christ points us to the triunity of the Godhead just as the duality of Christ connects us to the triunity of the Godhead.[81]

Structuralism. Types and patterns are evident in the Biblical text, and therefore types and patterns, though implicit, are expected to reflect the image of God just as the explicit text reflects the image of God. And since there can only be one true image of God, the explicit and the implicit are expected to reinforce each other. The Bible relates a progressive revelation of creation and a corresponding progressive revelation of the Creator. The Bible relates the triunity of the Creator and a corresponding triunity of all creation formed in the image of God. Further, Biblical patterns are expected to be rational and systematic just as all creation is rational and systematic. Biblical patterns are expected to be governed by rules and laws just as natural creation is governed by rules and laws. And the rules that govern Biblical patterns are expected to be constructive, not merely descriptive, just as the laws that govern natural creation are predictive, not merely descriptive. Biblical patterns and the rules thereof actually must be constructive and creative in order to reflect the true, or complete, image of the Creator. The structures and rules of structuralism specifically reflect the reality of the progressive revelation of the triunity of God. Structuralism is not simply structure but construction. Structures are expected to not simply exist but, in some sense, to self-organize just as the Scriptures are understood to interpret themselves. Finally, the Bible proceeds from God, who clearly wishes his children to know him and to understand him. And therefore it should be practicable, with the guidance of the Holy Spirit, to identify and to interpret Biblical patterns. It should be practicable to comprehend their relationship to God and likewise their relationship to the whole of creation that is formed in the image of God. And it should be practicable to increasingly understand the relationship between the creation and the Creator.[82]

Universality. The triune reality of God is universal. The reality of all creation reflects the one Creator. The way we relate to creation reflects God, and the

---

[81] "Man is made in the image of God, and so he bears within him the unique likeness of God which is eternally and perfectly expressed in the divine Son of God . . . Thus, man is 'logical' . . . reflecting on the creaturely level the very nature of God . . . . Man also is 'spiritual' . . . . reflecting the divine nature because he is inspired [animated] by the Holy Spirit as is no other creature. . . . On the most basic level of creation, therefore, we see the Trinitarian dimensions of the being and action of God: the Word and the Spirit of God enter man and the world to allow them to be and to become that for which the Father has willed their existence" (Hopko, *Orthodox Faith* 1:143–44). Duality is the anatomy of Trinity.

[82] The justice of God, which is perfect justice, is based entirely upon equal substitution, *Sanhedrin* (Cohen, *Rabbinic Sages* 111). The propitiation, or substitution, of Jesus Christ on the cross in order to redeem all the faithful, along with physical creation, implies that creation as a whole is formed in the image of God, spiritually representing God and therein being symbolically, not literally but legally, interchangeable with God.

way we relate to God reflects God. And a triune understanding is necessary to relate to the triune God because a corrupted way of thinking will inevitably produce a corrupted image of God. There are three universal witnesses: (1) the Bible, which is the written Word of God, (2) the human condition, marked by freewill, comprising reason and conscience, and finally (3) the creation as a whole, which is governed by physical and also moral laws.[83] God is the one author and the one story of all three, and therefore all three should agree or something is wrong somewhere. The written Word of God is necessarily the primary and authoritative object of our study, at least in the present age, because the written Word represents special, or explicit, revelation—in contrast to the human condition and likewise creation as a whole, which both communicate general, or implicit, revelation. But the Word of God is not disconnected from reality as a whole, and therefore it is the totality of all three witnesses that reflects the fullness of the triunity of God. The Bible being our authoritative source reflects God the Father, wherein the explanation of all things proceeds from the Bible just as all creation proceeds from the Father like an offspring. The human condition reflects God the Son, who is the incarnation of God. And creation as a whole reflects God the Holy Spirit being everywhere always.

In summary, every aspect of Biblical hermeneutics is expected to reflect the nature of God. The multiplicity of revelation is the progressive revelation of the triune Father, Son, and Holy Spirit. The parallelism of revelation is the simultaneous separation and unity of the creation and the Creator. The apocalypsis of revelation is the special revelation of the written Word of God, which is not simply from God but of God, representing the very image of God. The Christosis of revelation is the realization that Jesus Christ, being the incarnate Word of God, is the correct interpretation, or absolute incarnation, of all things; Christosis is also the realization that Jesus Christ, being the image of God made visible, is correctly understood and related to only within the context of the Trinity. The duality of revelation is the dichotomy of flesh and spirit, embodying law and grace, that reflects the twofold natures of the Son, who is fully man and fully God; the duality of revelation characterizes all reality, which is formed through the Son. The structuralism of revelation is the innate triunity of the character and construction of the Scriptures, likewise that of reality as a whole. And the universality of revelation is the reality that nothing truly, or fully, exists in separation from God.

All things, including our understanding of all things, should finally be perceived to embody the innate structure and stream of creation as a whole. And therefore the seven principles of structuralism are themselves expected to reflect the progressive revelation that demarcates the seven millennia of creation. The multiplicity of reality is embodied by the one man Adam, from whom the multitude of humanity even now continues to proceed. The parallelism of reality is ultimately the parallel between heaven and earth,

---

[83] The Bible is a universal witness in that the Gospel must be and will be preached in all the world for a witness unto all peoples and nations, that is, unto all creation, ultimately throughout all time, Matt 24:14, 1 Pet 3:18–20.

INTRODUCTION

encompassing the whole of creation, and is therefore uniquely evident in the parallel judgments of the sons of God, or heaven, and the daughters of men, or the earth, spanning the whole of creation at the time of the Flood (Gen 6:1–7). The apocalypsis, or special revelation, of the written Word of God is heralded by Abraham, the first Hebrew, through whom the formal law of Moses would be received in Israel. The Christosis of reality is embodied foremost by the kingdom of David as fulfilled in the conception of Jesus Christ as king of kings. The duality of reality is ultimately the duality of Jesus Christ, who is fully man and fully God; the duality of reality is finally the death and resurrection of Christ, which is the fulfillment of law in grace. The structuralism of reality is most closely identified with the end times because the patterns of progressive revelation are clearly and completely discernible only in hindsight. And the universality of God will finally be made visible during the millennial reign over all the nations, when the Lord himself will personally rule over the whole of creation, earth and heaven.

THE HOLY BIBLE

There is no denomination, no corner of institutionalized Christianity, that has not become entangled, to one degree or another, with the systems of literary criticism, or analysis, commonly referred to as the historical-critical method, also known as historical criticism or higher criticism, sometimes as German rationalism or radical criticism.[84] The basic goal of historical criticism is to reconstruct an original meaning and context of the Biblical text.[85] The core presupposition of the method is that the Biblical text we have received is not the original text, and the implication is that the original text can never be known with complete certainty. This is essentially the view that the Bible doesn't exist. But the truth is that the Bible does exist, and we do possess the Bible today. The truth is that the Bible is the wholly and verbally inspired Word of God—that is, all aspects of the Bible, in whole and in part, down to the exact

---

[84] "The general acceptance of Semler's [Johann Salomo Semler, 1725–1791, sometimes called 'the father of German rationalism'] basic concept that the Bible must be treated like any other book has plunged theology into an endless chain of perplexities and inner contradictions.... In its development, what began as a *characteristicum protestanticum* (Protestant characteristic) culminated in a universal Christian sickness" (Maier 11); "The rationalistic premise [accepting human rationalism and rejecting Biblical authority] has led to radical criticism of the Scriptures.... This radical treatment of Scriptures reached its full tide in the nineteenth century ... [B]y the middle of the twentieth century most theological seminaries have accepted the basic theses of radical criticism, and many of its conclusions" (Ramm 63).

[85] "If he has ever inquired into the matter [of modern-day Bible revisions], the Bible-believing Christian has probably been told that the Greek text used by the [KJV] translators of 1611 is inferior to that used for more recent translations.... [T]he average believer probably has accepted such explanations from individuals he regards as qualified.... [B]ut [such believers] have never realized that what contemporary textual critics call inferior manuscripts actually make up a huge majority [80–90%] of all [extant] manuscripts [Z. C. Hodges]" (Fuller 25–27).

wordings, every jot and tittle, are God-breathed.⁸⁶ Historical-critical schools of thought also generally reject Biblical accounts of the miraculous as mere fables, possibly useful for instruction but not possibly true historically.⁸⁷ And this is essentially the view that God doesn't exist. But the truth is that God does exist, and God does supernaturally intervene in the affairs of men and in the stream of history as a whole. And the ever-expanding apostasy represented by the historical-critical method continuing to flourish among Bible scholars and nonprofessionals alike—despite an ever-growing preponderance of evidence supporting the inerrancy of the Bible—testifies to the supernatural character of the delusion.⁸⁸

Many devotees of the historical-critical method claim to believe that the Bible is the Word of God, but this assertion cannot be accepted as true in any real or meaningful sense. A common claim is that the supposed evolving text is somehow a greater testimony to the power of God than would be a received text, but this is just a complex form of humanism, celebrating the supposed human custodians of the text throughout human history.⁸⁹ Also, there are many

---

[86] "While the traditional view of verbal inspiration [the most essential constituents of which can be traced to the early church] sought to erect bulwarks against the new learning and partial inspiration made a major accommodation, plenary inspiration may be described as a minor accommodation" (*Evangelical Dictionary of Theology*, s.v. "plenary inspiration"); "In many quarters [in the late nineteenth century and into the twentieth century] the phrase 'plenary verbal inspiration' began to be used, but this was only a matter of wording, implying no change in the content of verbal inspiration" (*Evangelical Dictionary of Theology*, s.v. "verbal inspiration").

[87] "[T]he 'historical-critical method' . . . asserts that reality is uniform and universal and that one's present experience supplies an objective criterion for determining what could or could not have happened in the past. This anti-supernaturalist stance has led to a biblical criticism that seeks to explain the biblical books solely in terms of human processes unaided by divine revelation or inspiration . . . ." (*Evangelical Dictionary of Theology*, s.v. "higher criticism").

[88] "After the most careful scrutiny by scholars of the Old and New Testament texts, it is now evident that the Old and New Testaments are the best preserved texts from antiquity. The number of really important textual variations of the New Testament that cannot be settled with our present information is very small, and the new manuscripts available from the various caves around the Dead Sea show the remarkable purity of our present Old Testament text" (Ramm 8–9); "As much as is made over the proposed contradictions in Scripture, it is surprising how few examples of any possible merit can be supplied, and it is further surprising how difficult it is to make a successful case of these examples. . . . [I]n the conservative commentaries there are plausible explanations of every one of these alleged contradictions" (Ramm 205).

[89] "Historical-critical methodology cannot be claimed as a neutral discipline. It holds sway in 'scientific' theology pretty much as evolutionism rules the scientific disciplines. Theories multiply, often with total disdain for the facts, at times even though the facts contradict the conclusions. People finally believe what they want to believe. In the name of scholarship man sets himself up as lord . . . . [E. F. Klug]" (Maier 8). The profound parallel between evolution theory and the historical-critical method is no coincidence: they are two sides of the same coin, representing the same anti-supernatural, actually anti-God, worldview.

INTRODUCTION

who claim to simultaneously accept the incarnate Word of God and reject the written Word of God, but this simply means that the Jesus they have accepted is not the Biblical Jesus and, therefore, not the one true and faithful Jesus Christ.[90] The judgment of unbelievers is the domain of God and God alone, but there cannot be a middle ground between Christ and anti-christ. Further, it is commonly the case that apostate beliefs are prevalent despite not being immediately obvious in statements of faith or church constitutions or even sermons from the pulpits. To fully understand what is believed and what is being disseminated, one must carefully examine the exact wordings of church documents, the writings of church leaders, and also what is being taught at seminaries. Discerning the actual worldview that is being disseminated is also complicated by the fact that the most controversial ideas are usually taught not directly but by implication, with teachers maintaining some form of plausible deniability. The earthly church makes a purposeful distinction between clergy and laity, such that a church within a church normally exists, whereas in Biblical Christianity, clergy and laity alike are called to be kings and priests. Finally, the relative hiddenness of apostate views in our churches testifies that our church leaders know that their views are unacceptable. Yet the ever-increasing public assertions of such views indicate that they are nonetheless gaining a widespread respectability or, at least, a seeming irrelevance among the laity.[91]

A correct understanding of the nature of the Scriptures is essential because the special revelation of the Scriptures is our foremost schoolmaster, teaching us about the nature of Jesus Christ and likewise the Trinity. It is true that the Bible is not the only testimony of Jesus Christ in the world. Creation testifies to the Creator (Rom 1:20). And the human condition specifically—marked by freewill, reason, and conscience—testifies to the very nature of the Lord God (Rom 2:14–15). Nonetheless, the truths of creation are the domain of natural law and general revelation. The special revelation of the Bible is explicit, while the general revelation of creation is implicit. Special revelation is the clearest revelation, and this is why special revelation must stand above general revelation

---

[90] "The manner in which God's word is contained in Scripture must not be envisaged statically as a material content, but dynamically as a spiritual charge. The word and the Scripture are united in such a way that they constitute an organic unity; they are to each other as the soul to the body. . . . That relation is unique; its closest parallel is the relation of the divine and human natures in the person of Jesus Christ, who is the Word incarnate" (Metzger, *Canon* 288). Yes, there is a parallel between the written Word and the incarnate Word, wherein to say that the Bible changes is to say that the God of the Bible changes. Further, to have a wrong view of the inspired nature of the Bible is to have a wrong view of the God-man, Jesus Christ. And what is any wrong view of Christ, except anti-christ?

[91] "Religious liberals redefine inspiration. . . . [T]he inspiration of the Bible is its power to inspire religious experience. Revelation is redefined as human insight into religious truth, or human discovery of religious truths. . . . Whatever in the Bible is in accord with the 'spirit of Jesus' is normative, and whatever is below the ethical and moral level of the 'spirit of Jesus' is not binding. . . . [T]he doctrinal or theological content of Scripture is not binding. . . . [R]eligious experience is the heart of religion and theological forms are temporary" (Ramm 64–65). The tree of (experiential) knowledge of good and evil.

as our preeminent schoolmaster. And this situation will necessarily continue until the return of the Lord, because the faithful must await the resurrection in Christ to receive the fullness of God the Holy Spirit. In the resurrection body the fullness of the law will be written on our hearts and, therein, the distinction between special revelation and general revelation will cease to exist (Jer 31:33). Further, the emphasis on the Scriptures in no way disregards the work of the Holy Spirit in our hearts and in our daily lives, leading us unto Christ and convicting us of our sins, because the Scriptures represent the foremost visible sign of the movement of the Holy Spirit in the world (John 16:13–14). And this is the reason why Christians should consider themselves and themselves alone to be the people of the Book. And this is why Christians should be Bible Christians, not denominational Christians and certainly not followers of any specific person except the Lord himself.[92]

The reality of special revelation superseding general revelation is stranger than it may appear on the surface. One would more naturally expect that all the different revelations, or movements, of God the Holy Spirit would be equally clear just as God the Holy Spirit is in all ways and at all times perfect. The reason for the profound distinction between special and general revelation is that creation, which embodies general revelation, has been corrupted by sin and death. In contrast, the Bible is the inerrant and complete Word of God. Our ability to understand the Bible has been fundamentally corrupted in that the human condition, including human reason and conscience, has been corrupted as part of the overall corruption of creation. But the Word of God itself has not been corrupted, and this is literally all the difference in the world. There are actually only two corporeal realities that have not been corrupted and can never be corrupted: Christ and the Bible relating Christ. And the realization that there is a parallel between the written Word of God and the incarnate Word of God is the essential starting point for correctly understanding the fundamental nature and ultimate significance of the Bible and special revelation. The incarnate Word of God and the written Word of God are both perfect in the same sense, though on different levels of reality. To begin at some other point, even a statement of the inerrancy and completeness of the Scriptures, invites confusion and error, for our human understanding of even the basic nature of concepts such as inerrancy and completeness is bound up, not in the person of Jesus Christ, but in the corruption of the world.[93]

There are several statements of faith concerning the nature of the Bible that are commonly put forward by different Christian denominations. And these statements can seem very positive superficially, but they as a rule fail to affirm

---

[92] ". . . Jesus maintained that God's will could be found in the sacred texts . . . He read . . . studied . . . interpreted . . . adhered to . . . and taught these scriptures. His [Jesus's] followers were . . . unusual in the Roman Empire: like the Jews before them, but unlike nearly everyone else, they located sacred authority in sacred books. Christianity at its beginning was a religion of the book" (Ehrman 20). The written Word is inextricably connected with the incarnate Word.

[93] Ignorance of the Bible is ignorance of Jesus Christ, because the Bible is Christ (Rom. Catholic Church, *Catechism* 43). Do what they say, not what they do, Matt 23:3.

INTRODUCTION

the absolute authority of the Bible. One needs to understand the implications not only of what is being stated but also of what is not being stated. A common statement is that the Bible is inerrant in matters pertaining to faith and practice or salvation.[94] But one should not in any way limit, or make finite, the inerrancy of the Word of the infinite God. One cannot claim that some aspects of the Bible are perfectly true while some other aspects are not true at all. And one should neither assert that some aspects of the Word of God are irrelevant. There is a parallel between the written Word and the incarnate Word. To say that the Bible, which speaks of Christ, is sometimes true and sometimes false is like saying that the person of Christ is in some ways perfect but in other ways imperfect. To say that aspects of the Word of God are irrelevant is like saying that God is arbitrary. The fact is that the Scriptures we have received are impeccable according to any normal academic standard. And the Spirit testifies that all Scriptures are in fact God-breathed (2 Tim 3:16). The truth of the Bible is rejected by humanists simply because it is a demonstration of the reality of God that utterly condemns their unbelief.[95]

Another common statement is that the Scriptures are inerrant in the autographs, or original manuscripts. And it is a dark reality that the majority of modern scholarship is connected, not to elucidating the Scriptures, but to reconstructing the supposed autographs by deconstructing the actual Scriptures. The belief that the textual criticism of man restores the supposed original manuscripts of God could never be completely true even in principle, and it is no coincidence that this belief represents a subjection of the Word of God to the will of man.[96] Only copies, not the actual original manuscripts, still exist,

---

[94] *Evangelical Dictionary of Theology*, s.v. "Bible, inerrancy and infallibility of."
[95] "Anxious believers can be enormously reassured by the almost exact similarity between even the earliest of the biblical papyri from Egypt and the text as it has survived during its descent through countless scriptoria and printing shops of Europe. . . . No significant variations or deliberate falsifications have ever been found to shake public confidence in the Bible as a whole. No other text of comparable antiquity has come down to us with so few uncertainties about its transmission" (De Hamel 320). Academics emphasize the variations in extant manuscripts to the point that many, if not most, if not the vast majority of, laymen function as though the Bible doesn't exist in any well-defined or reliable form. The truth is actually the opposite. The Bible does exist. And the false impression to the contrary must be, in one way or another, intentional. No secular academic would have ever predicted the extreme uniformity across extant Biblical manuscripts. And through the emphasis on variations, academics and humanists effectively hide the truth about manuscript uniformity. But the faithful should recognize that the observed uniformity across extant manuscripts is a supernatural movement of the Holy Spirit. And the faithful should understand that the small variations that are observed are variations in individual manuscripts, not in the overall received tradition relating the Word of God.
[96] "[S]ince the original autographs no longer exist and since the doctrine [of inerrancy] applies only to them, inerrancy is meaningless. . . . [T]he doctrine of inerrant originals directs attention away from the authority of our present texts" (*Evangelical Dictionary of Theology*, s.v. "Bible, inerrancy and infallibility of"). The negation of the authority of the Bible is the elevation of the authority of man.

and neither did the originals ever exist together in one place. And thus a statement of belief in the originals is ironically a testimony not to the existence but to the nonexistence of the Bible. It is a belief in nothing that is finally to believe nothing, which would be perfectly normal apart from the reality of God. But the truth is that God does exist and so does the Word of God.[97] A related issue is that the dogmatic adherence to the original manuscripts is always connected with a dogmatic adherence to the original languages. And such a worldview is tantamount to believing that one cannot fully understand the Word of God outside the original languages. But the truth is that the Word of God was always intended to exist in all languages simultaneously (Acts 2:6). The truth is that it is not humanistic scholars but God the Holy Spirit who teaches us the Word of God.[98] There is a parallel between the written Word and the incarnate Word. The multitude of translated versions, or tongues, of the Bible were always intended to exist simultaneously just as the multitude of the faithful of God were always intended to exist as the one Body of Christ. The tongues of the Bible exist not in isolation of one another but together as a community of texts just as the multitude of the faithful exist not in conflict with one another but together in the one Body of Christ, bringing together the diversity of complementary gifts and perspectives of the Holy Spirit (1 Cor 12:1–14).[99]

The reality of the Bible existing as a community of texts, simultaneously in all tongues, is actually an essential distinctive of Biblical Christianity, testifying to the universal truth of Christianity. No particular Bible version or language, whether the King James Version English or the original languages, should ever be elevated to the point of worship. A tongue belongs to a man, whereas all tongues belong to God, whose voice is like a noise of many waters (Ezek 43:2).[100] The words of prophecy are not the object of worship but the revelation

---

[97] "The exegetes can no longer conceive of the New Testament [much less the Old and New Testaments together] as a unit.... For them it is an established fact that the formal canon cannot be equated with the Word of God.... [E]xegetes and systematicians have been searching for more than 200 years for the canon in the canon, i.e., for the binding Word of divine authority. This two-century undertaking has failed .... [E]ach theologian conceives of the canon in the canon differently ... uncontrolled subjectivity has the last word concerning what should have divine authority" (Maier 47). The authority of man, separated from God, is inevitably anarchy and finally nihilism.

[98] "Michael Fishbane's suggestion that we construct a 'canon within the canon' to moderate the religiously articulated hatred of our times is extremely apposite" (Armstrong 224–25). This is the normally hidden dimension of the search for a canon within the canon that is nothing less than a religion unto itself.

[99] "We cannot pass over the mystery of the *intermixing* [not mingling] of man's word with God's Word [represented by the Holy Scriptures]. The attempt to inquisitively unravel this intermixture and ultimately to divide it into quantitatively definable entities was the gross mistake of the higher-critical method. The comparison with the 'two natures' [true man and true God] in the Revelator, Jesus Christ, is closely related to what is divine and human in the revealed Word" (Maier 70). The denial of the written Word of God is the denial of the incarnate Word of God.

[100] The inspiration of the completed canon of the Scriptures, the written Word of God, originally occurring in the multiple and varied tongues of Hebrew, Aramaic, and Greek

INTRODUCTION

of the object of worship. And the absolute necessity of this reality is affirmed in the confounding of languages at Babel (Gen 11:9), the speaking in tongues at the first Pentecost after the crucifixion (Acts 2:4), and also the call to take the Gospel to all nations and therefore into all languages (Matt 28:18–20). To say the Bible is only inerrant and complete in the original languages is to imply that it would be better for the Bible to exist only in the original languages. And to say that the Bible should exist only in the original languages, when in fact it does not, is to deny either the sagacity or sovereignty of God. The way of man, which is false and carnal religion, is to assert an exclusivity based on language, which is ultimately a racist exclusivity based on ethnicity. In contrast, the way of the Spirit is to demand an exclusivity founded upon faith alone, calling all peoples of all languages and ethnicities unto the one true faith in the one man Jesus Christ. The parallel between ethnicity and language points to the parallel between the multitude of the faithful in Christ and the diversity of the gifts of the Spirit in the Body of Christ. The parallel between ethnicity and language testifies to the image of God being impressed upon all levels of reality.[101]

The primary justification for adhering in an exclusive way to the original languages of the Bible is based on misconceptions of the fundamental nature of language, the written Word of God, likewise misconceptions of the incarnate Word of God. The idea is that one can never completely translate words and sentence structures in all their subtlety of meanings and connotations and associations from one language to another. And this basic premise is correct, but it fails to comprehend that all the same fundamental ambiguities also exist in the original languages. Whether it is an original language or a translated language, an ancient language or a modern language, a foreign language or our native language, the meanings of words and passages can always be debated, in fact endlessly debated, because it is the fundamental nature of language to be ambiguous. There is no fundamental difference between picking up an English dictionary and picking up a Greek or Hebrew lexicon in order to clarify a Bible passage. And there is no fundamental difference between reading a judgment written in a lexicon and reading a judgment written in a Bible commentary. In fact the determination of the meanings of words represents the most basic and important commentary of all. The fundamental ambiguity of language, which

---

is itself a prophecy of the perfect, or complete, Word of God ultimately existing in all tongues and finally existing, or dwelling, in the individual hearts of all the faithful. And this reality embodies the essential testimony that the Word of God must come to us sinners individually by grace, in contrast to our working our own way to God.

[101] "They [the KJV translators] were quite explicit about their debt to the past. The king's own instructions had referred them to the sequence of sixteenth-century versions, and Miles Smith's [KJV] Preface is concerned to reiterate the point. . . . The idea, in fact, was not to make a new translation, Smith maintained, but to make 'out of many good ones, one principal good one.' And that was their triumph: a polished collation, a refinement of a century's translating, a book that became both clear and rich" (Nicolson 224). Academics claim that the King James Version is based on isolated and inferior original-language manuscripts, but the reality is far more inclusive and complicated. And perfect order arising from such complexity is the normal way of providence.

should ultimately be recognized as an essential ambiguity, is dramatically illustrated in Jesus's own disciples struggling to understand his teachings, even in their own native language and even in the exact context of Jesus's tone of voice, facial expressions, and so forth (John 13:7). Language is the medium of thoughts and feelings, the waters in which we swim, and therein language represents, or spiritually is, the mind and heart of man. The ambiguity of language reflects the time and chance of life, whereas the exactness of language reflects the certainty of God. And the movement from ambiguity to certainty reflects the essential process of freewill, choosing the good and rejecting the bad, ever growing in truth and love. We are the people of the Book.[102]

A closely related justification for adhering to the original languages is the idea that, whether or not the fundamental ambiguity remains the same, the process of translation still inevitably increases the magnitude of ambiguity. And this premise is also basically correct, at least when viewed in isolation, but it fails to comprehend the larger truth, which is that the process of translation actually increases our understanding of the Biblical text. For example, it's normal for Bible students to value each new translation that becomes available, because each new translation inevitably affords new perspectives of the Biblical narratives. It is true that some new perspectives are erroneous, but the majority is normally useful or at least not patently harmful. Careful discernment is required in this matter, but careful discernment is always required.[103] Further, the ubiquitous interplay between certainty and ambiguity that we experience when relating to the written Word of God, likewise the incarnate Word of God, is the inevitable consequence of finite creatures such as ourselves relating to the infinite God. We recognize Jesus Christ, but we are not yet like him (1 John 3:2). But this is not the complete story. The quality of ambiguity can be traced back to the original languages, testifying to the original, or underlying, intentions of God. The quality of ambiguity does not negate the certainty, or meaning, of the Biblical text but actually magnifies it, for it is through a purposeful ambiguity that the finite text becomes poetic and fractal and thereby infinite. And this quality of being infinite is also reflected in the Word of God existing in all languages. But neither is this the complete story. The reconciliation of the ubiquitous tension between ambiguity and certainty in the written Word of God

---

[102] "If the full meaning of the words of scripture can be grasped only by studying them in Greek (and Hebrew), doesn't this mean that most Christians, who don't read ancient languages, will never have complete access to what God wants them to know? And doesn't this make the doctrine of inspiration a doctrine only for the scholarly elite . . . What good does it do to say that the words are inspired by God if most people have absolutely no access to these words, but only to more or less clumsy renderings of these words into a language, such as English, that has nothing to do with the original words?" (Ehrman 7). Translation is theoretically impossible according to academics, despite the obvious reality to the contrary.

[103] All literary works are in a sense rewritten by each different reader because different aspects of any given work will always be understood to some degree differently by each individual reader (Eagleton 11). All the individual believers throughout all history are coming together to progressively form the one Body of Christ.

INTRODUCTION

reflects the reconciliation of the universal tension between flesh and spirit in the person of Jesus Christ, who is the incarnate Word of God.[104]

The Scriptures represent the wholly and verbally inspired Word of God. And the historical manuscripts are an irrefutable confirmation of the supernatural reality embodied by the Scriptures.[105] The vast majority of so-called errors in the extant manuscripts are obvious spelling, word-order, and so forth, variants, which are plainly insignificant to the literal meaning of the sacred text that has been firmly established by the totality of the corpus. And the small number of significant variations from the received text should be recognized as errors, not in the received text, but in the individual manuscripts themselves.[106] The minority Alexandrian texts, which have caused the most confusion in the modern day, should be rejected as a matter of course just as they have always

---

[104] "This [issue of transmission] became a problem for my view of inspiration, for I came to realize that it would have been no more difficult for God to preserve the words of scripture than it would have been for him to inspire them in the first place. If he wanted his people to have his words, surely he would have given them to them (and possibly even given the words in a language they could understand, rather than Greek and Hebrew)" (Ehrman 11). The original writing of the sacred text was inspired. The transmission continues to be inspired. And the reading of the text must also be inspired. It is the failure to perceive these things that is not inspired and ultimately reflective of an opposition to the Holy Spirit.

[105] "All too frequently the focus has been on variants found in particular manuscripts or editions . . . [I]t is all too easy to overlook the fact that the Byzantine Imperial text and the Alexandrian Egyptian text, to take two examples that in theory are diametrically opposed to each other, actually exhibit a remarkable degree of agreement, perhaps as much as 80 percent! Textual critics themselves, and New Testament specialists even more so, not to mention laypersons, tend to be fascinated by differences and to forget . . . how rarely significant variants occur—yielding to the common danger of failing to see the forest for the trees" (Aland 28). Any corruption at all of the received text would be incongruous, but the great uniformity between the majority Byzantine and minority Alexandrian texts explains how it is that people have in fact come to recognize the truth of God by reading modern translations.

[106] "To be sure, of all the hundreds of thousands of textual changes [variants] found among our manuscripts, most of them are completely insignificant, immaterial, of no real importance for anything other than showing that scribes [the individual scribes who produced the specific extant manuscripts in question] could not spell or keep focused any better than the rest of us" (Ehrman 207). Of course, to say that scribes can't spell any better than anyone else is like saying engineers can't build bridges better than anyone else; "[M]ore than 99 percent of the 400,000 differences [between extant New Testament Greek manuscripts] fall into this category of virtually unnoticeable variants [easily recognizable differences in spelling, word order, and so forth]! . . . Of the remaining 1 percent or so of variants, only a few have any significance for interpreting the biblical text. Most important, *none* of the differences affects any central element of the Christian faith" (Jones 44). I would disagree that any variant should be accepted as unimportant, but nonetheless the extreme uniformity across extant manuscripts does point to the perfection of the overall received text.

been rejected throughout all church history.[107] The Bible is inerrant and complete, and this reality is evidenced by all the facts. And yet the perfect written Word existing in an imperfect world is a paradox just as the incarnation of God in the flesh is a paradox. Both paradoxes are largely ignored under the banner of mystery. But the believer should recognize that Christianity is a religion of revealed mysteries, not a religion of hidden mysteries (Mark 13:23). The Scriptures do represent the wholly and verbally inspired Word of God, but the Scriptures further represent, simultaneously and without contradiction, a yet larger reality. There is a fundamental parallel between the written Word inspired by the Spirit and the incarnate Word conceived of the Spirit. The written Word and the incarnate Word embody the one and same paradox.

The medium of the written Word is language, and the fundamental paradox of language is ambiguity. It is the nature of language to be ambiguous, whether it is spoken or written, whether it is the original or a translation. And therefore ambiguity, including ranges of possible meaning and even uncertainty, cannot be mutually exclusive with inerrancy, if in fact inerrancy, which must mark the Word of God, is to have any meaning. The tension between uncertainty and inerrancy seems undesirable, and therefore it is not surprising that it is usually ignored. But the faithful should recognize that the juxtaposition of uncertainty and certainty is both fundamental and essential. The paradox of the written Word is best understood and ultimately only understood in relationship to the incarnation of the Son—stripping himself of the mantle of power, making himself in a sense finite, yet remaining infinitely perfect, or sinless, and therefore worthy of all praise and worship (Phil 2:6–11). The tension between ambiguity and certainty is the same tension between flesh and spirit. The flesh of man seems like a poor and lowly vessel for God just as the tongue of man seems like a poor and lowly vessel for the Word. Nonetheless, no true fault, or error, can be found with either the incarnate Word or the written Word. And though now we may not, actually cannot, understand every detail concerning the incarnate Word and likewise the written Word, we can still recognize the completeness and perfection of both, namely, the sinlessness of the incarnate Word and the inerrancy of the written Word (1 Cor 13:12).

The nature of the Scriptures being divinely inspired points uniquely to Jesus Christ being conceived of the Holy Spirit. The Holy Bible is twofold just as

---

[107] "Herein lies the greatest weakness of contemporary textual criticism. Denying to the Majority text any claim to represent the actual form of the original text, it is nevertheless unable to explain its rise, its comparative uniformity, and its dominance in any satisfactory manner. All these factors can be rationally accounted for, however, if the Majority text represents simply the continuous transmission of the original text from the very first. All minority text forms are, on this view, merely divergent offshoots of the broad stream of transmission whose source is the autographs themselves [Z. C. Hodges]" (Fuller 34); "Erasmus relied on manuscripts of the twelfth/thirteenth century which represented the Byzantine Imperial text, the Koine text, or the Majority text—however it may be known . . . This was the dominate form of the text in the fourteenth/fifteenth century manuscript tradition, and even where earlier uncial manuscripts were available they were not consulted" (Aland 4).

INTRODUCTION

Jesus Christ is twofold. The Lord is simultaneously and without contradiction fully man and fully God. Likewise, the Scriptures are simultaneously and without contradiction the finite words of the human writers and also the infinite Word of the one God. The Bible is the inspired Word of God, not the dictated Word of God. The one true God does not dictate just as the one true God is not a dictator. God does not violate freewill, because God is perfect and sinless. These are key distinctives of Christianity, authenticating that Christianity is the one true religion. And the key distinctives of Christianity are all closely related to one another, reflecting the oneness of God and likewise the universal truth of God. No other Word speaks forth inerrantly, in its very nature bridging the chasm between mankind and God. The reality of the inerrancy and the completeness of the Bible is irrefutable, such that no man can make an excuse for his unbelief. And thus the widespread denial of the obvious truth of the Bible is a testimony that our conviction comes not by the flesh but from the Holy Spirit. Our belief and the object of our belief must both necessarily be conceived of the same Holy Spirit in order for the Spirit to uniquely bear witness with our spirit (Rom 8:16). Our belief in Jesus Christ is ultimately united with the person of Christ in the Body of Christ, which is our promised inheritance in the twofold natures of Christ that is the final realization of the dichotomy of finite flesh and infinite Spirit. And the parallel between the written Word of God and the incarnate Word of God will persist in the eternal state, for the law must be written on the hearts of the faithful in the spiritual, or glorified, resurrection body that is a true body.[108]

A final point of controversy is the canon of Scripture itself, particularly the question of which texts form the Old Testament. Compared with the Old Testament books normally recognized by Jews and Protestants,[109] additional books and passages have been accepted by the Oriental Orthodox, Eastern Orthodox, and Roman Catholic traditions. The apocryphal texts added by the Roman Catholic Church are the books *Tobit*, *Judith*, *1 & 2 Maccabees*, *Wisdom*, *Sirach* (also known as *Ecclesiasticus*), and *Baruch* (incorporating the *Epistle of Jeremiah*), and also additions to the book of Daniel—including *Susanna*, and *Bel and the Dragon*, and the *Prayer of Azariah and Song of the Three Young Men*—and also six additions to the book of Esther.[110] The Greek and Russian Orthodox Churches, representing Eastern Orthodoxy, add the books *Tobit*, *Judith*, *1, 2 & 3 Maccabees*, *Wisdom*, *Sirach*, *Baruch*, and *Esdras* (grouped with Ezra or sometimes with Nehemiah, and called either *1* or *2 Esdras*), and also the *Epistle of Jeremiah*, and *Psalm 151*, and additions to the book of Daniel—including *Susanna*, and *Bel and the Dragon*, and the *Prayer of Azariah and Song of the Three Young Men*—and six additions to the book of Esther, and yet other books added as Biblical

---

[108] " 'It must be obvious . . . to any thoughtful reader of the Gospel records that Jesus regarded himself and his message as inseparable. . . .' [K. S. Latourette]" (McDowell, *Carpenter* 27). Christ and his message are inseparable, for Christ is the message.

[109] *New Unger's Bible Dictionary*, s.v. "canon of Scripture, the Old Testament."

[110] McDonald lists Nehemiah and Ezra as a single book, following the traditional Jewish canon organization of twenty-four books (McDonald 443–44).

appendices.[111] The Biblical canon of the Coptic Orthodox Church, representing Oriental Orthodoxy, has been in a state of flux at least into the twentieth century.[112] And the so-called *via media*, or "middle way," of the Anglican Communion generally views the Apocrypha as good for the instruction of manners and as an example of life but not for the establishment of doctrine.[113]

Viewing the apocryphal books as sometimes useful historical documents is completely reasonable. And personally reading the apocryphal texts is, of course, necessary to make a full evaluation of their veracity. In the end, however, the faithful should recognize that the apocryphal texts are not the divinely inspired Word of God. Further, this call to reject the bad and accept the good should be recognized as a microcosm of life as a whole (Gen 4:7). Encouraging a study of other religions is a fundamental characteristic of true Christianity, for the faithful are called to see firsthand that the one faith in the one man Jesus Christ is not only true but also unique. The faithful are called to know the difference between serving the kings of this world and serving the one true Lord (2 Chr 12:8). In stark contrast, it is a distinctive of false religions to oppose, often aggressively oppose, the study of other religions, especially Biblical Christianity, out of a cynical fear that people will be "fooled." And in the case of Biblical Christianity, this fear is ironically justified because the truth of Jesus Christ, likewise the truth of the Bible that speaks of Christ, is in fact indisputable. The culture of open dialogue in Christianity is a natural affirmation of our freedom and freewill in the Body of Christ that is the infinite importance of the individual and individuality to the one true God. And the faithful should finally recognize that adherence to the correct canon, the correct and complete Word of God, is a nonnegotiable priority, particularly when considering the parallel between the written Word of God and the incarnate Word of God.[114]

Several difficulties should be apparent when examining the apocryphal texts. First, Jewish tradition—the divinely ordained vehicle for the preservation and transmission of the Old Testament—has always rejected the Apocrypha.[115] And

---

[111] McDonald 443–44.

[112] Meinardus 40–41.

[113] "The official position of the Church of England regarding the books of the Apocrypha, like its position in certain other doctrinal disputes, was ambivalent" (Metzger, *Apocrypha* 190–91). A worldview never exists in isolation and inevitably affects all areas of thought.

[114] "The Word of God is the true holy thing above all holy things. Indeed, it is the only one we Christians acknowledge and have. . . . God's Word is the treasure that sanctifies all things" (Luther, *Large Catechism* 21). The Book of God is unique just as the God of the Book is peerless.

[115] "The Hebrew canon had been determined by long and approved usage of the books, and the Assembly at Jamnia [AD ca. 90] merely ratified what the most spiritually sensitive souls in Judaism had been accustomed to regard as holy Scripture. . . . In some undefined manner, certain books imposed themselves upon the Jewish community as the inspired oracles of God" (Metzger, *Apocrypha* 8–10). The recognition of the canon is inspired just as the assembly of the canon was inspired just as the original writings of the canon were inspired just as the reading of the canon must be inspired.

INTRODUCTION

neither were the apocryphal texts accepted by the early church.[116] This is not an absolute standard, but it should immediately raise concerns. Second, the so-called *deuterocanonicals*, or "second canon" (describing the Septuagint apocryphal texts), are distinguished from the *protocanonicals*, or "first canon" (describing what are the true canonical books), in that the deuterocanonical books were put forward as canonical not without controversy and not until a relatively late date.[117] This is not an absolute standard either, but it should again raise concerns. Third, the traditions that do embrace apocryphal texts tend to be, not coincidentally, aligned with the historical-critical worldview. And any such humanistic tradition is not expected to be aligned with the one true inspired canon, because the reality of inspiration transcends any merely carnal understanding of the world. Fourth, the Apocrypha contains historical and geographical errors.[118] And this is an absolute standard because the Word of God is expected to be inerrant in every way. Fifth, the apocryphal texts do not read as inspired literature. And though more nuanced, this is also an absolute standard. The Apocrypha depicts the world in a distinctly unrealistic manner, and it further lacks the normal prophetic character that marks the authentic Word of God.[119] The most basic characteristic of the Word of God is that every subtle detail is not merely inerrant but has meaning itself and meaning that reinforces the larger themes of progressive revelation.[120] Sixth, the validity of discounting the apocryphal texts is corroborated by them never being quoted or referenced in the canonical books.[121]

---

[116] "The small number of Fathers . . . who either had some personal knowledge of Hebrew (e.g., Origen and Jerome) or had made an effort to learn what the limits of the Jewish canon were (e.g., Melito of Sardis) were usually careful not to attribute canonicity to the Apocryphal books . . . . Jerome . . . spoke out decidedly for the Hebrew canon, declaring unreservedly that books which were outside that canon should be ranked as Apocryphal" (Metzger, *Apocrypha* 178–79).

[117] *Catholic Encyclopedia*, s.v. "canon of the Holy Scriptures."

[118] *New Unger's Bible Dictionary*, s.v. "Apocrypha."

[119] Ibid.

[120] Every aspect of the Biblical text unites to form an overwhelming concord, such that any discords must be understood as purposeful contrasts (Alter and Kermode, *Literary Guide* 44). Not only with regard to matters of theme and plot, but also with regard to every imaginable aspect, and with the understanding that only the one true Word of God can be held to such a standard.

[121] Metzger, *Apocrypha* 8–9, 171.

ESAU

יהוה

CHAPTER ONE

Jacob and Esau

The prime image marking the relationship between Esau and Jacob is the one blessing of Isaac being taken by Jacob while standing in the place of Esau (Gen 27:19). It is the taking of the blessing, more than any other event, that drives Jacob eastward to the house of Laban, and it is thereby the taking of the blessing that forms the context for Jacob establishing his own house. The second born son Jacob supplanting the firstborn son Esau reflects the second man Christ taking, or reclaiming, the dominion originally given to the first man Adam. Esau despising his birthright (Gen 25:34) recalls Adam rebelling against God and thereby despising God (Gen 1:27, 3:5). Jacob taking the blessing of Esau while presenting himself as Esau prefigures the incarnation of Christ, substituting himself for Adam, or mankind. Esau's hatred of his brother, with Esau seeking even to murder Jacob, portends the rejection of Christ by the world that is embodied by the crucifixion of Christ (Gen 27:41). The barrenness of Rebekah becoming a progressive separation of two nations prefigures the rejection of Christ becoming the progressive separation of the faithful and the faithless (Gen 25:23). The former separation is the opening of the womb of Rebekah through the prayer and supplication of Isaac, while the latter separation is the opening of the church age through the intercession of Jesus the Christ (Gen 25:21).

The twofold relationships emphasized in the account of the two sons of Isaac are the relationships between the first and second born and between father and mother. This is the relationship between the first man Adam and the second man Christ and likewise the relationship between the First Advent of Christ and the Second Advent. Jacob saving his brother from starvation through the act of purchasing his birthright with red soup (red pottage), or simply the "red," reflects Christ purchasing all mankind, or spiritually the life of Adam, with his blood (Rom 5:9). The second born son Jacob being urged by his mother to supplant her firstborn son, Esau, reflects the movement of the Holy Spirit (Gen 27:13). Jacob taking the blessing of Isaac by presenting himself as the firstborn represents the faithful being saved in the Body of Christ (Gen 27:15–16). The dichotomy of birthright and blessing is reinforced by the relationship between the land of Canaan and the land of Laban. Jacob faces the threat of certain death at the hands of Esau in Canaan, but the east country of Laban holds the promise of life as embodied by children (Gen 27:42–46). Isaac sending forth Jacob to form his household reflects the Son sending the Spirit. Rebekah lamenting her own life at the idea of Jacob taking a Hittite, or Canaanite, wife again connects the land of Canaan with the image of death (Gen 27:46). The birthright is connected with the natural body and likewise the death of the cross, while the blessing is connected with the spiritual, or glorified, resurrection body and likewise the resurrection unto life.

The threefold man, woman, and their offspring reflect the triune Father, Spirit, and Son. In the present account, this is Isaac, Rebekah, and their two sons. The birthright followed by the blessing proceeding from Isaac represents the original creation followed by the new creation proceeding from the Father. Rebekah putting Jacob ahead of Esau represents the movement of the Spirit anointing Christ in the place of Adam (Gen 27:8). The separation of Esau and Jacob because of the hatred of Esau represents the rejection of Jesus the Christ by the present world and the concurrent formation of the Body of Christ (Gen 27:44). The threefold man, woman, and their offspring always reflect the triune Father, Spirit, and Son. But Isaac sending forth Jacob to form his house, symbolically on behalf of Abraham, is simultaneously identified with the risen Christ sending the Spirit during the church age. And the sending of the Spirit is that which culminates in the resurrection and rapture and finally the Second Advent (John 16:7). The threefold Abraham, Isaac, and Jacob represent an overarching image of the Father, Son, and Spirit. But the ordering Father, Spirit, and Son always coexists with the ordering Father, Son, and Spirit. The former ordering emphasizes the connection between the original formation of Adam and the incarnation of Christ, while the latter ordering emphasizes the connection between the First and Second Advents of Christ. The former emphasizes creation, while the latter emphasizes new creation.

ISAAC AND REBEKAH

Genesis 25:19   And these [are] the generations [H8435] of Isaac, Abraham's son: Abraham begat [H3205] Isaac:

The word *generations* [H8435] (of Isaac) means "the account of a man and his descendants" in the Hebrew and is derived from the root word *begat* [H3205], which means "to bear, bring forth, beget." In the preceding account of the *generations* [H8435] of Ishmael, it is recorded that "Hagar the Egyptian, Sarah's handmaid, bare [Ishmael] unto Abraham," but the emphasis now is that "Abraham begat Isaac" (Gen 25:12). Abraham, Isaac, and Jacob reflect God the Father, God the Son, and God the Holy Spirit, whereby the emphasis on Isaac uniquely descending from Abraham affirms that the Son proceeds from the Father. The brothers Ishmael and Isaac reflect Adam and Christ. Hagar bearing and bringing Ishmael unto Abraham parallels Adam being first formed from the dust of the ground and only then being quickened by the breath of God (Gen

2:7). Man is formed at a specific point in time, a created being, as evident in our proceeding from the ground, but Christ is eternally begotten, like begetting like, as evident in the proceeding of Christ by the Holy Spirit, being conceived of the Spirit in the virgin (Matt 1:20).[1]

Genesis 25:20 And Isaac was forty years old when he took Rebekah to wife, the daughter of Bethuel the Syrian of Padan-aram, the sister to Laban the Syrian.

Isaac taking Rebekah as his wife when he is forty years old represents a very specific time of waiting and wanting, a period of forty, that reverberates down through progressive revelation. The twelve tribes would wander in the desert for forty years (Num 14:34), and Christ would ultimately be tempted in the desert for forty days (Mark 1:13). The number 40 in both the Old and New Testaments is connected with a period of purification through suffering and likewise with rebirth through death. The person of Isaac—especially in the context of Abraham, Isaac, and Jacob—is closely identified with Christ at the time of the First Advent. And when Isaac is identified with the First Advent, Rebekah can be identified with the movement of the Spirit in Israel at the First Advent or in the church age proceeding from the First Advent. The blood kinship of Isaac and Rebekah prefigures Christ being born a Jew and ministering only unto the Jews (Matt 15:24). But the emphasis on Rebekah being the sister of Laban, in contrast to Isaac's wife, portends a carnal apostasy, directly opposing the spirit of faith in Christ. This is the purification of the chosen faithful, separated from the rejected faithless, that points to the rebirth of all creation in Christ.[2]

In the global context, the number 40 connects the forty days of the Flood and the forty days of Christ in the desert (Gen 7:17, Mark 1:13). And this connection brackets the formation of national Israel as representing the call of the faithful unto repentance in Christ. And the call to repentance is the ultimate significance of waiting and wanting that is the waiting and wanting of God for the essential freewill turning away of his faithful ones from the world. Further, it is no coincidence that the Passion of Christ is identified so closely with the Flood of Noah (2 Pet 3:21). The intervening period is dominated by the call of Abraham's children, and this call is recapitulated in the very life of Christ (Matt 2:15, John 3:14). The different levels of reality reinforce one another to create a single image, which is characterized by an extreme internal consistency that

---

[1] "Repetition is used at practically every level of the hierarchy which the [Biblical] text constitutes, from sounds, words, and clauses to stories and groups of stories. . . . Thus a dialectic game of identity and difference is created which challenges us to compare parallelisms at various levels and to ask questions such as: What has remained unchanged, and why? What differences occur, and what do they mean?" (Alter and Kermode, *Literary Guide* 46). Every jot and tittle has meaning.

[2] The relationship between Rebekah and Laban points to Jacob's relationships with Esau and Laban being intertwined (Sarna 179; Gen 25:20). The flight from Esau to Laban and finally back to Esau is the formation of the house of Jacob.

reflects the absolute perfection of God. This is the image of God impressed upon all creation, or rather the image of God forming the fundamental paradigm of all creation. The repentance, or turning away, of God and the corresponding grief of God at the time of the Flood are connected to the repentance and suffering embodied by Christ on the cross (Gen 6:6). And the death and resurrection of Christ is the death and resurrection of the world and all creation, which will not be fully realized until the end times.[3]

Genesis 25:21   And Isaac intreated [H6279] the LORD for his wife, because she [was] barren: and the LORD was intreated [H6279] of him, and Rebekah his wife conceived.

The word *intreat* (entreat) [H6279] (Isaac intreated the Lord) means "to pray" and "to supplicate" in the Hebrew. Isaac makes supplication unto God for Rebekah just as the Son intercedes with the Father for the faithful (Rom 8:34).[4] Barrenness is an image of the unbeliever separated from the Lord God, likewise the perishable natural body under the law. Barrenness turned into fertility represents the exaltation of man in faith while yet in the mortal body and finally the resurrection of the immortal body by grace. The prophecy that the offspring of the barren woman is greater than she who has a husband (Isa 54:1) points to the Seed of woman being cut off from the living but yet and actually thereby establishing a multitude of offspring (Isa 53:8). The ubiquitous images of miraculous birth in the Scriptures ultimately point to the virginal conception in Mary (Luke 1:35) but finally prefigure our own miraculous rebirth in Christ through the barrenness of the cross (Rom 6:4). Rebekah came to Isaac freely in a testimony to faith being the fulfillment of freewill. But Rebekah cannot conceive until Isaac makes supplication unto the Lord just as the faithful are reborn only through Jesus the Christ and not of ourselves (Gen 24:58). We are not saved by faith of ourselves, or by simple belief, but rather by grace through faith in Christ (Eph 2:8).[5]

Isaac is a type of Christ, while his wife Rebekah is a type of the faithful called by the Spirit. And the identification with the faithful is likewise an identification with the movement of the Holy Spirit. The fulfillment of the union of man and woman is their offspring, representing an embodiment of the love between man

---

[3] Rebekah is a type of "God's church in the world" and the strife within her womb is a prophecy of "the great Apostasy itself in the womb of the historical Church" (Coffman 323–24; Gen 25:19–24). The human being is a microcosm of creation as a whole.

[4] "God is the thing to which he [the Christian] is praying—the goal he is trying to reach. God is also the thing inside him which is pushing him on—the motive power. God is also the road or bridge along which he is being pushed to that goal" (Lewis, *Mere Christianity* 143). True prayer is a Trinitarian event.

[5] "We all have needs enough, but the trouble is that we do not feel or see them. God therefore wishes you to lament and express your needs and wants, not because he is unaware of them, but in order that you may kindle your heart to stronger and greater desires and spread your cloak wide to receive many things" (Luther, *Large Catechism* 68). Our earthly domain is a mere shadow of the heavenly domain.

and woman. The persons of Isaac and Rebekah are most closely identified with the First Advent of Christ and also with the church age proceeding from the First Advent. The offspring of Isaac and Rebekah then represent the fulfillment of the union of Jesus Christ and the faithful that is our new creation in Christ, in the Body of Christ. But birth pangs precede actual birth just as the church age even now precedes the resurrection of the faithful. The breath of life animating our promised new creation is the same Holy Spirit animating our original formation from the dust of the ground, but our new creation will be animated by the fullness of the indwelling Holy Spirit (Gen 2:7, John 20:22). The born-again experience while yet in the natural body is likewise a foretaste of the resurrection in Christ that will be the fullness of rebirth. The threefold successive physical birth followed by the born-again experience in coming to faith followed by the resurrection echoes conception followed by the quickening in the womb followed by actual birth.[6]

Genesis 25:22 And the children struggled together within her; and she said, If [it be] so, why [am] I thus? And she went to inquire of the LORD.

The two nations struggling within Rebekah reflects good and evil struggling within every individual. The struggle within Rebekah proceeding from her in childbirth (as embodied by the continuing struggle between her sons) is a testimony to the struggle within the individual proceeding from man in the corruption of the whole of creation. Rebekah conceiving and giving birth to the struggle within her reflects the original corruption of all creation having proceeded from original, or personal, sin (1 Tim 2:14).[7] The struggle between evil and good is manifested on all levels of reality from the individual to the national to physical creation itself, even to the domain of angels. The two nations within Rebekah instinctively struggle against each other, reflecting the inherent and irreconcilable conflict between flesh and spirit. Flesh always contends against spirit (Gal 5:17). Rebekah giving birth to two nations finally represents a fundamental separation of the two outside the womb, or through birth. The separation in birth of Rebekah's first and second born sons prefigures the separation of evil and good in rebirth. There can be no fellowship

---

[6] From the beginning there has been only one promise, only one movement of the Spirit upon the face of the waters—namely, our promised inheritance of the indwelling Holy Spirit, the fullness of which cannot be simply a return to the garden of Eden where the promise was breathed but not realized.

[7] From the principle of like begetting like, original sin is necessarily passed down through the generations. For fallen humanity could no more conceive unfallen children than lower life-forms conceive higher forms. And according to the way of all flesh, the way of the present world, the sin of mankind necessarily defiles the rest of creation, because that which is unclean will always dirty that which is clean, never vice versa. The Lord, God Almighty, would have provided another way if another way existed, but the condemnation of the present fallen creation is irrevocable. For sin must be utterly destroyed in order to preserve the perfect righteousness of the Lord God, which is, after all, the font of our promised eternal life.

between the light and the darkness (2 Cor 6:14). Rebekah originally being surprised by the struggle within her womb is an image of the mystery of Christ, while the Lord ultimately answering Rebekah's inquiry concerning her struggle is an image of the revelation of the mystery of Christ (Eph 3:9). Christianity is not a religion, or way, of mystery and ignorance but rather the way of knowledge and understanding.

Isaac and Rebekah are identified with the First Advent and also with the church age proceeding from the First Advent. The sacrifice of Isaac in Moriah prefigures the sacrifice of Christ (Gen 22:2). The account of the union of Isaac and Rebekah closely follows the sacrifice of Isaac and, thereby, is closely connected with the sacrifice of Isaac (Gen 22:15, 22:23). The original, or beginning, barrenness of Rebekah represents the rejection of Christ by Israel, while the opening of Rebekah's womb represents the opening of the church age. And the end, or the beginning of the end, of the dispensation of Adam is marked by the account of the death of Sarah, which textually bridges the account of the sacrifice of Isaac to the account of the union of Isaac and Rebekah (Gen 23:1–2). The account of the death of Abraham immediately following the union of Isaac and Rebekah (Gen 25:7–11) then marks the formal end of the age of Adam, or fallen man—that is, the end of the age in which the faithful dead are interned unto the bosom of Abraham (Luke 16:22–23, 1 Pet 3:18–20).[8] The miraculous nature of the fertility of Rebekah, which comes through the intercession of Isaac, is an image of rebirth, specifically the rebirth experienced while yet in the natural body, since it is a rebirth characterized by physical struggle. And the rebirth in the natural body is like the establishment of the visible church since both are established according to the will of God and both are incomplete until the resurrection of the dead and the corresponding restoration of creation.[9]

Genesis 25:23 And the LORD said unto her, Two nations [are] in thy womb, and two manner of people shall be separated from thy bowels; and

---

[8] "Now as to Hades [sheol], wherein the souls of the righteous and unrighteous are detained . . . . In this region there is a certain place set apart as a *lake of unquenchable fire*; whereinto we suppose no one hath hitherto been cast; but it is prepared for a day aforedetermined by God . . . . [T]here is one descent into this region . . . but the just are guided to the *right hand* . . . unto a region of *light*, in which the just have dwelt from the beginning of the world; . . . This place we call the *bosom of Abraham*. . . . But as to the unjust, they are dragged by force to the *left hand* . . . allotted for punishment . . . . [F]or a *chaos* deep and large is fixed between them [the just and the unjust]; . . . This is . . . Hades, wherein the souls of all men are confined until a proper season . . . when he [God] will make a resurrection of all men [just and unjust] from the dead; . . . For all men, the just as well as the unjust, shall be brought before *God the Word*; for to him hath the *Father committed all judgment*; and he in order to *fulfill the will of his Father* shall come as judge, whom we call *Christ*" (Josephus 4:456–59).

[9] In death Jesus Christ descended into hell [unto the spirits in prison, 1 Pet 3:19] to deliver, not the damned, but those who had been received into the bosom of Abraham, Luke 16:22–26 (Rom. Catholic Church, *Catechism* 180). With the victory of the cross, the children of Abraham are exalted unto the presence of the Lord.

JACOB AND ESAU

[the one] people shall be stronger than [the other] people; and the elder [H7227] shall serve the younger [H6810].

The word *elder* [H7227] (elder brother) is synonymous with "greatness" in the Hebrew and is derived from the root "to become many, much" [H7231], while the word *younger* [H6810] (brother) has connotations of "littleness" and "insignificance." Accounts of older and younger brothers, or more generally former and latter things, are ubiquitous in the Scriptures, reflecting the relationship between Adam and Christ, likewise between law and grace, and likewise between the way of flesh and the way of the Spirit. The greatness of the firstborn in the eyes of the world is an image of the elevation of the way of flesh, while the firstborn becoming many is a vision of the multiplication of the way, or ways, of flesh that is the multiplication of sins (Rom 5:20). The elevation of the way of flesh is according to the flawed will of Adam-kind in conflict with the perfect will of God, while the multiplication of sins is a vain attempt to deny that the one way of all flesh, all the earth, is finally death. In contrast, the littleness and insignificance of the second born is an image of the humble condescension of God in the incarnation in the flesh of man. The way of the Spirit is the way of humbleness and patience and faith and love. The way of the firstborn is the broad way to death, while the way of the second born is the narrow way that leads to life (Matt 7:13–14).[10]

The parallel between the brothers and their future nations is an affirmation that all levels of reality reflect the same truth. The prophecy that the latter would be stronger than the former is an assertion that the will of God is undeniable despite original sin, that is, despite the sinful nature of man. The vision that the elder would serve the younger is a prophecy that the first man Adam would serve the second man Jesus Christ. The servitude of the believer to Christ is not, however, a form of annihilation, rather our promised redemption in Christ that comes by the power of the Holy Spirit. Freedom from God is slavery to sin, whereas slavery to God is the only true freedom (Rom 6:22). The servitude of the faithful unto God is the absolute necessity that God fill us with his love and faith and wisdom. No man knowingly chooses what is bad for himself, but rather men perish for a lack of knowledge (Isa 5:13). The faithful are given the discernment to choose the good, and we joyfully do so. But we do so of our own freewill—irrespective of the fact that the knowledge of right and wrong, as all knowledge and wisdom, ultimately comes from God. The evil remain in their ignorance because they desire in their souls to choose the good for themselves and the bad for others.[11]

---

[10] "[T]hat God chooses whom he will, according to his own good pleasure, he [the apostle Paul] adduces this testimony, 'the elder shall serve the younger' [Rom 9:7–8, 9:12]" (Calvin, *Commentaries* 2:46; Gen 25:23). The Epistles are not merely an adducing by men but rather a breathing of the Spirit. And the exaltation of the younger in the Spirit cannot be an arbitrary act, because the younger is always exalted above the elder.
[11] "It is only the Christians who have any idea of how human souls can be taken into the life of God and yet remain themselves—in fact, be very much more themselves than they were before" (Lewis, *Mere Christianity* 141). Salvation is a Trinitarian event, in which

ESAU, JACOB, ISRAEL

Esau and Jacob

Genesis 25:24 And when her days to be delivered [H3205] were fulfilled [H4390], behold, [there were] twins [H8380] in her womb [H990].

The word *delivered* [H3205] (days to be delivered) is elsewhere translated *travail* [H3205], which recalls Eve originally being cursed to bring forth children in suffering (Gen 3:16). A woman through sorrow giving birth to new life is a prophecy of the death and resurrection of the individual and also the concurrent destruction and re-creation of physical creation as a whole. The believer living in the current passing life, regardless of his age, is necessarily like a child, compared with the immeasurable eternal life that will be revealed in our rebirth in the resurrection. And this is one aspect of the teaching that a man must become like a child to enter the kingdom of God (Matt 18:3). The faithful are resurrected like children standing at the threshold of eternal life. But the faithless are resurrected like adults unto damnation—culpable as adults, being held responsible for their actions and being mature in the sense that they will never grow in the love of God (John 5:29). The word *womb* [H990] (twins in her womb) has a connotation of "body in contrast to the soul," representing an emphasis on the natural body and the present creation in contrast to the spiritual, or glorified, resurrection body and the promised new creation. And this again represents an emphasis on the present suffering in the natural body. The natural body must be sown like a seed to give rise to the promised spiritual body (1 Cor 15:44).

The word *fulfilled* [H4390] (days fulfilled) means "to be full, fill" and has a connotation "to consecrate." The appointed times and seasons in nature, the times of death and rebirth, reflect the preordained will of God and foreshadow the appointed time of the last days and finally the end times. The births of Esau and Jacob likewise point to the resurrection of all the dead to either condemnation or eternal life, that is, to the condemnation through Adam or the exaltation in Jesus Christ (John 5:28–29). The emphasis on Rebekah fulfilling the days of her pregnancy affirms the necessity that the days of the present age of suffering be completed in order to fulfill all righteousness (Matt 3:15). The Lord leaves no thing undone but rather completes all things to the fullest, because the Lord is perfect and whole himself. And there is no other template upon which to base the world other than the Lord because the Lord is all in all. The Lord does not bring to the birth and not cause to bring forth (Isa 66:9). All righteousness must be fulfilled, and this means the whole of the law must be fulfilled (Matt 5:17). First the Head, Christ himself, to be followed by the Body, the faithful in Christ.

The word *twins* [H8380] (in her womb) has an association "to be double" [H8382], elsewhere translated *coupled* [H8382], which reflects the fundamental

---

the faithful are called, in accordance with freewill, to be reconciled with the Father in the Son, the Body of Christ, by the power of the indwelling Holy Spirit.

union of the natural and the spiritual in the individual and also in the world as a whole. The twenty years separating the union of Isaac and Rebekah and the birth of Esau and Jacob represents a corresponding doubling, or coupling, of decades in waiting effectively ten years according to each son (Gen 25:20, 25:26). In the present context the number 10, epitomized by the Decalogue, or Ten Commandments, is connected specifically with law but generally with covenant. The first son and first ten is the natural, while the second son and second ten is the spiritual. Further, the twenty years that Isaac waited for his offspring in the promised land foreshadow the twenty years that Jacob would serve for his offspring in the east. But the twenty years of Jacob are divided into two seven-year periods and one six-year period, pointing to the fulfillment of the third and final seven in the promised land (Gen 31:38). The two decades of Isaac that point to the three sevens of Jacob are the two laws, or covenants— the Covenants of Law and Grace—that point to the triunity of all creation, specifically the new creation, or new seven, established in the three days of Christ. The twenty years of Isaac point to the twenty years of Jacob just as the First Advent points to the Second Advent just as the present creation points to the promised new creation.

Genesis 25:25–26 And the first came out red [H132], all over like an hairy [H8181] garment [H155]; and they called his name Esau. 26 And after that came his brother out, and his hand took hold on Esau's heel [H6119]; and his name was called Jacob: and Isaac [was] threescore years old when she bare them.

The word *hairy* [H8181] (describing Esau) is used in the Hebrew to denote both the "hair of animals" and the "hair of humans" and additionally has an association "to bristle, with horror" [H8175]. In contrast, the word *garment* [H155] (hairy garment) connotes "glory" and "magnificence." The undertones of horror and dread portend the cross, while the strange juxtaposition of horror and glory points to the victory of Jesus Christ over death. The first son Esau being hairy, even as one wearing a hairy garment, recalls the first son Adam wearing a coat of skins after the original fall (Gen 3:21). Esau figuratively wearing a garment of hair also evokes an image of a man being disguised as an animal. And this foreshadows the sacrifice of Christ being the fulfillment of the animal sacrifices required by the law of Moses. Esau can reflect both Adam and Jesus because the one man Adam prefigures the one man Jesus Christ (Rom 5:19). But the image of Esau being hairy will ultimately be supplanted by the image of Jacob disguising himself as hairy Esau just as Adam will be supplanted by Jesus Christ (Gen 27:16).

The word *red* [H132] (describing Esau) means "red, ruddy" and is related to the name *Adam* [H121] via the Hebrew "to be red" [H119]. Esau is specifically the first son of Abraham through Isaac just as Adam is the first son, or offspring, of God the Father through God the Son (John 1:3). Esau, the first son of Isaac, recalls Ishmael, the first son of Abraham. But the second born Isaac supplanting the firstborn Ishmael is most closely identified with the First

Advent while the second born Jacob supplanting the firstborn Esau is most closely identified with the church age that connects the First and Second Advents. The account of Esau and Jacob follows the account of Ishmael and Isaac just as the church age follows the First Advent. It is expressly the supplanting of Esau that is identified with the First Advent, or the beginning of the church age, while it is the exaltation of Jacob in the person of Israel that is identified with the coming Second Advent. The supplanting of Esau is the supplanting of Esau as the firstborn. This is Jacob purchasing the birthright of the firstborn (Gen 25:31). The exaltation of Jacob in the person of Israel is the blessing of Jacob. This is Jacob taking the blessing of the firstborn (Gen 27:36). The former is the birthright according to the flesh, while the latter is the blessing according to the Spirit. The natural precedes the spiritual just as the first man Adam precedes the second man Jesus Christ just as the First Advent of Jesus Christ precedes the Second Advent.

The word *heel* [H6119] (Esau's heel) is the same word used to describe the original curse that the serpent would bruise, or strike, the *Heel* [H6119] of the Seed of woman (Gen 3:15). And Jacob grasping the heel of Esau therefore recalls this prophecy. This identification of Jacob with the serpent is strange, but so is the identification of Christ with the serpent lifted up by Moses in the wilderness (Num 21:9, John 3:14). The original curse states that the head identified with the serpent would be struck first and that the Heel identified with the woman would be struck second. The former is the victory of Christ over death, while the latter is the aftermath of persecution that would follow the incarnation. The former is seen in the symbolic death and resurrection of Isaac in Moriah, while the latter is seen in Jacob grasping the heel of Esau (Gen 22:2). Isaac is again identified with the First Advent, while Jacob is identified with the Second Advent. The enmity between the woman and the serpent is closely connected with the pain of childbirth, and thus the twins struggling within Rebekah recalls the primordial struggle between good and evil (Gen 3:16). The struggle between the natural man Esau and the spiritual man Jacob reflects the primal struggle of the flesh against the Spirit, a struggle that always manifests itself in some form of suffering. And the struggle within the womb is only the beginning of a larger struggle that will culminate or, so to speak, come into maturity in the end times of the present creation.[12]

The word *heel* [H6119] (Esau's heel) has an association "to follow at the heel, figuratively assail insidiously, circumvent, overreach" [H6117]. The conflict between the natural man Esau and the spiritual man Jacob embodies the church age connecting the First and Second Advents. And Jacob grasping the heel of Esau points to Jacob supplanting Esau. The natural man Esau is most closely identified with the Jews under the law, while the spiritual man Jacob is most closely identified with the Gentiles under grace. Jacob grasping the heel of Esau represents Esau despising his birthright and consequently having his blessing

---

[12] Fundamental Rabbinic thought identifies the destruction of Jerusalem and the temple with the ceasing of honest men in the city, *Shabbath* (Cohen, *Rabbinic Sages* 227). The driving out of the early believers on the heels of the rejection of Jesus Christ.

seized (Gen 25:34). Jacob grasping his brother's heel is the observed physical reality, while Esau despising his birthright and likewise his blessing is the corresponding spiritual reality. Jacob grasping is Esau despising just as Adam choosing the tree of knowledge is Christ being crucified upon the tree of knowledge. Jacob grasping is Esau despising just as Christ blessing his faithful is Christ cursing the faithless. The serpent striking the Heel of the Seed of woman is foremost satan deceiving the Jews in the rejection of the risen Lord at the time of the First Advent. And it is this rejection that leads the Jews into being supplanted by the Gentiles. But Esau despising himself in this way is only the beginning of the rejection of the risen Lord as heralded by the one Jewish nation of Israel at the time of the First Advent. It will culminate with the rejection of the Lord in the end times by the nations of the whole world, nominally the Gentile nations. The one nation of Israel is thereby understood to be a microcosm of the world as a whole. And Jacob grasping the heel of Esau is finally understood as grace supplanting law.[13]

The word *heel* [H6119] also has a connotation of "hinder-part, rear (of a troop of men)," which again points to the last days and finally the end times (Isa 44:21–22). These are the latter generations of humanity finally connecting Adam to the promised new Adam. And it is humanity that is the object of salvation. Jacob grasping the heel of Esau is Jacob supplanting Esau and likewise Christ supplanting Adam, but Christ supplanting Adam is also Christ redeeming Adam (Hos 12:3). Jacob grasps his brother Esau just as the Spirit brings humanity unto the Father. The prophecy of the striking of the head identified with the serpent should ultimately be understood as the striking of the Head, the Head of the Body, Christ himself at the time of the First Advent. This identification of Christ with the serpent is that foretold through and by Moses in the lifting up of the serpent on a pole (Num 21:8), representing Christ becoming a curse on the cross (Gal 3:13). And the Lord effectively cursing himself in the cursing of the serpent in the garden is an affirmation of the absolute sovereignty of God—that God is always in complete control, even in death. No one would take the life of Christ, but rather he would lay it down freely (John 10:18). The prophecy of the striking of the Heel identified with the Seed should finally be understood as the striking of the Body of Christ, composed of both Jewish and Gentile believers throughout the church age, culminating in the Second Advent. The Covenant of Grace supplanting the Covenant of Law is, not simply Gentiles supplanting Jews, but the unity of Gentiles and Jews in Christ supplanting the disunity in Adam. The new encompasses the old just as grace fulfills law.

Genesis 25:27   And the boys grew [H1431]: and Esau was a cunning [H3045] hunter [H6718], a man [H376] of the field [H7704]; and Jacob [was] a plain [H8535] man [H376], dwelling [H3427] in tents [H168].

---

[13] Likewise, Paul ironically identifies Hagar and Ishmael with the Jewish people but Sarah and Isaac with the nominally Gentile church, Gal 4:22–31.

ESAU, JACOB, ISRAEL

The word *grew* [H1431] (Esau and Jacob grew) has connotations "to cause to grow" and "to bring up children" that reflects the Lord raising up the faithful, especially in the period between the First and Second Advents as identified with the persons of Esau and Jacob. The word *man* [H376] (of the field, of the tents) has a connotation "husband" that points to the intimate relationship between Esau and his domain of the field and likewise to the relationship between Jacob and his domain of the tents. Isaac's wife, Rebekah, is identified with Israel at the time of the First Advent and also with the church age proceeding from the First Advent. Isaac is identified with Christ throughout the corresponding periods. The offspring of Isaac and Rebekah represent the Jews and Gentiles populating the church age. Jews and Gentiles are called as one to Christ during the church age. But the Jews, as a matter of history, are most closely identified with those who reject Christ. And the Gentiles, when contrasted with the Jews, are most closely identified with those who accept Christ. The Jews represent those who remain under the law, while the Gentiles represent those who come into grace. And the Jews being closely identified both with the law and also with the rejection of Christ is no coincidence but points to the condemnation under the law apart from the grace in Christ.

The word *hunter* [H6718] (describing Esau) recalls Nimrod, the descendant of Ham, also being a *hunter* [H6718] before the Lord (Gen 10:9). Esau is the spiritual offspring of Ham just as Ham is the spiritual offspring of Cain just as Cain is the spiritual offspring of the serpent. The image of hunting represents the death of flesh, especially under the law, since a purposeful killing of any kind can be likened to execution. Eating the flesh of animals is also necessarily connected with killing animals. And so it is not surprising that the word *hunter* [H6718] (describing Esau) is elsewhere translated as *food* [H6718] (Job 38:41). And this connection between killing and eating is affirmed in the law by the priestly class being commanded to take meat to eat from the sacrificial altar (Lev 10:12). This is the death of Christ and the corresponding commandment to imitate Christ in death, which is represented by the commandment to eat the flesh of Christ (John 6:53). One should remember, however, that the crucifixion of Christ is not itself a positive thing. Christ willingly sacrificing himself is the ultimate manifestation of the love of God, but the unjust slaughter of Christ is itself indescribably appalling. It is the resurrection of Jesus Christ that is our great hope. Our eating the flesh of animals in our personal lives is likewise not a positive thing but rather a prophecy of death, specifically our own individual deaths under the law.

The word *cunning* [H3045] (describing Esau) has a connotation "to know by experience" and is the same word describing Adam and Eve *knowing* [H3045] good and evil and, thereby, becoming as God after eating from the tree of the knowledge of good and evil (Gen 3:22). The way of experiential knowledge is the way of flesh, specifically the way of flesh in conflict with the way of the Spirit. We must walk by faith, not by sight, because our true reality, the true reality, is foremost spiritual, not physical (2 Cor 5:7). The spiritual can be perceived in the physical (Rom 1:20), but the physical, or natural, because of sin, is only a blurred, or corrupted, image of the spiritual (1 Cor 13:12). And so the practice of walking by faith is primarily a matter of perceiving the true spiritual reality underlying the natural reality. This is ultimately the image of God impressed upon all creation. The faithful look forward to the promised new creation, the new earth and new heaven, and the corresponding passing away of the distinction between the natural and the spiritual and likewise the passing away of the distinction between the domains of earth and heaven. This is finally the image of God embodied by all creation.[14]

The word *plain* [H8535] (describing Jacob) has connotations of "complete, perfect" and also "morally innocent," reflecting the faithful being made complete and perfect in the Body of Christ, especially in the present church age. The perfection that appears plain and ordinary is that of Christ at the time of the First Advent (Isa 53:2). The faithful now also appear plain and ordinary in the natural body just as Christ appeared plain and ordinary as a true man in the incarnation. And this is one aspect of the call to imitate Christ. The word *tents* [H168] (Jacob dwelling in tents) has a connotation "tent of nomad" and is also the same word used to describe the tabernacle of the *tent* [H168] of the congregation, which was built by Moses (Exod 39:32). The faithful are nomads in the present world, awaiting the city that will be built by God (Heb 11:10). Tabernacles of tents are temporary and evanescent habitations just as the natural body is mortal and uncertain. The tabernacle (tent) is to the temple (house) as the natural body (perishable) is to the spiritual, or glorified, body (imperishable). And the Body of Christ is even now following Christ in death and resurrection. The world, or all creation, earth and heaven, will also follow Christ in the foretold destruction and renewal of all things (Rev 21:1). Christ as the Head precedes the Body of Christ just as the First Advent precedes the Second Advent just as the natural precedes the spiritual just as the Covenant of law precedes the Covenant of Grace.

The word *dwelling* [H3427] (dwelling in tents) has a connotation "to remain, stay, tarry," reflecting the present age of waiting and watching while yet in the natural body, the fleeting tent of the flesh. And even this is in imitation of the Lord who himself now tarries until the fulfillment of the appointed time. Jacob dwells in tents close to his father and mother just as the faithful live close to God, which is necessarily separated from the wilderness of the world. The word *field* [H7704] (Esau of the field) can refer to either a "pasture-land" or "home of beasts," but the latter is implied by the context of hunting game. The field of beasts is a place of death and dying representing the present world and finally the eternal death of the faithless in separation from Christ. The natural man Esau is a man of the field, a man of the world, while the spiritual man Jacob is a man of the tents, a man distinctly not of the world. The emphasis on the natural man being separated from the tents of his parents testifies to fallen man being opposed to the primordial image of the Trinity. The image of the tents that is

---

[14] In the Fall of Man, Adam and Eve conceived a distorted image of God (Rom. Catholic Church, *Catechism* 112). The distorted, or defiled, image of God that is birthed by sin is necessarily mortal life, or simply death, since the true and perfect image of God is life eternal, Rom 5:12.

ESAU, JACOB, ISRAEL

the image of the Trinity—Father, Spirit, Son—is the image of Adam and Eve and their promised Offspring, or generally man and woman and the collective offspring of the world, in a procession representing the faithful in Christ. The faithful are in the world but not of the world (John 17:15–16).

Genesis 25:28 And Isaac loved [H157] Esau, because he did eat [H6310] of [his] venison: but Rebekah loved [H157] Jacob.

The word *loved* [H157] recalls the same word used to describe the *love* [H157] of Abraham for Isaac at the time of the symbolic sacrifice of Isaac in Moriah (Gen 22:2). The overall context is the love of children within the covenant of marriage, both in the case of Abraham and his sons and also in the case of Isaac and his sons. The union of man and woman represents the union of justice and mercy, while the offspring of the union of man and woman represents the synthesis of justice and mercy that is the perfect love embodied by eternal, or childlike, life. Isaac is the embodiment of justice, and therefore he is identified with Esau since the firstborn Esau, the natural man, is the object of justice. This is the condemnation of the natural body under the law. Rebekah is the embodiment of mercy, and therefore she is identified with Jacob since the second born Jacob, the spiritual man, is the object of mercy. This is the exaltation of the spiritual, or glorified, resurrection body by grace. The love of Jacob being identified with the feminine connects the spiritual son Jacob with the foretold Seed of woman, the Christ, and likewise with the faithful in Christ (Gen 3:15). The love of Isaac and Rebekah for their sons proceeds from the love of Abraham for Isaac just as the Son proceeds from the Father. The love of Abraham proceeding to Jacob through Rebekah, not through Isaac, reflects the love of the Father proceeding through the death of the Son. The love of God that proceeds from Abraham to Jacob being closely identified with the sacrifice of Isaac in Moriah finally points to the death and resurrection of the Body of Christ in imitation of Jesus Christ. The connection between the marriage covenant and the death of the only begotten son points to the marriage supper of the Lamb, consummated in Christ, becoming a bridegroom of blood (Exod 4:25, Rev 19:9).[15]

The word *eat* [H6310] (Isaac did eat) means "mouth" and is elsewhere translated *commandment* [H6310] and, though not etymologically related, also recalls the word *covenant* [H1285], which is closely associated with the Hebrew "to eat (in the sense of cutting)" [H1262] (Gen 17:10). The love of Isaac for his firstborn being connected to eating the flesh of venison points to covenantal law being epitomized by blood sacrifice. But this is finally the commandment to eat the flesh of Christ that represents our own death to the flesh and likewise

---

[15] "Rebekah was mindful of the oracle of God, which had given the preference to Jacob ... And, if it be lawful for parents to make a difference between their children upon any account, doubtless Rebekah was in the right, that loved him whom God loved" (Henry 1:156; Gen 25:19–28). It is unlawful to bless what God has cursed, likewise to curse what God has blessed.

our own death in the flesh (John 6:53). The firstborn is always connected with the first covenant, the Covenant of Law. This is the first man Adam who is condemned under the law. This is the second man Christ who becomes the firstborn from the dead in fulfillment of the law. Isaac requiring that the firstborn prepare flesh for him points to the requirement of the cross for Christ himself and likewise for the Body of Christ in imitation of Christ (Mark 10:21). The love of Isaac for Esau being derived from his eating the venison of Esau points to the works of the law that are ultimately the work of Christ on the cross. The firstborn Esau killing the venison for Isaac is the first man Adam, or mankind in Adam, killing Christ. In contrast, no parallel reason is given for the unique love of Rebekah for Jacob and, thereby, the love of Rebekah for Jacob points to the unmerited gift of grace. The love of Isaac for the first son Esau reflects the desire of Christ to save the first man Adam, who is lost, or fallen, mankind. The love of Rebekah for the second son Jacob reflects an obedience to the prophecy of God, namely, that the elder Esau would serve and therefore must serve the younger Jacob (Gen 25:23). The servitude of the firstborn to the second born is the rebirth of the firstborn in the second born that is actually the only hope for the salvation of the firstborn. And so the love for the second born is the love for the firstborn.[16]

BIRTHRIGHT

Genesis 25:29–33 And Jacob sod [H2102] pottage [H5138]: and Esau [H6215] came from the field [H7704], and he [was] faint [H5889]: 30 And Esau [H6215] said to Jacob, Feed me, I pray thee, with that same [H122] red [H122] [pottage]; for I [am] faint [H5889]: therefore was his name called Edom [H123]. 31 And Jacob said, Sell me this day thy birthright [H1062]. 32 And Esau [H6215] said, Behold, I [am] at the point to die [H4191]: and what profit shall this birthright [H1062] do to me? 33 And Jacob said, Swear to me this day; and he sware unto him: and he sold his birthright [H1062] unto Jacob.

The word *sod* (cook) [H2102] (Jacob sod pottage) means "to boil, seethe, act proudly, rebelliously" in the Hebrew, while the word *pottage* (soup) [H5138] is derived from the word *sod* (cook) [H2102]. Esau eating red soup in exchange for his birthright is an image of Esau eating his birthright, recalling Adam being cursed to eat of the ground, or red earth, in sorrow (Gen 3:17).[17] The image of hot soup boiling represents the visceral anger and violence always connected with pride and rebellion. Esau eating his own birthright in the form of seething

---

[16] "*Esau* knew how to please him [Isaac] . . . treating him often with venison, which won upon him more than one would have thought. But *Rebekah* loved him [Jacob] whom God loved [script updated]" (Wesley 1:100; Gen 25:28). The effect of the venison seems disproportionate only when viewed in the purely natural, separated from the spiritual.
[17] "There was never any meat, except the forbidden fruit, so dearly bought as this broth of Jacob [Bishop Joseph Hall, AD 1574–1656]" (Jamieson et al. 1:190; Gen 25:33). Not a casual comparison, but an instinctive one.

soup represents Esau subsisting on his own degenerate desires, in contrast to seeking the desire of God that is the exaltation of his faithful. The Lord is not the one responsible for the suffering of mankind (Isa 5:4). Esau eats the red soup, or simply the red stuff; Adam eats of the ground, or of the red earth; and the serpent eats dust, or the red earth itself (Gen 3:14).[18] The mouth condemns the body, and thus the mouth is the condemnation of the body (Job 9:20). And the world is handed over to its own desires (2 Chr 12:8, Rom 1:22–24). But Esau selling the birthright is concomitant with Jacob buying the birthright. The curse of Adam and likewise the curse of all men under the law prefigure Christ on the cross for the sake of the whole world.[19]

The word *birthright* [H1062] literally means "right of the firstborn," which recalls the original dominion of the first son Adam created in the very image of God (Gen 1:28). Esau not understanding the value of his birthright reflects Adam not understanding the nature of his original birthright that is our creation in the image of God. Jacob buying Esau's birthright with red soup—or red food representing life—is an image of Jesus Christ purchasing Adam's birthright and dominion with his own blood—the red blood of Jesus relating true life (Deut 12:23). Jacob symbolically becomes the firstborn in the land (under the law) when he purchases the birthright from Esau just as Jesus would become Adam on the cross (under the law) in becoming a curse on the cross (Gal 3:13).[20] Esau swearing to Jacob represents the essential submission of Adam to Jesus Christ that is our salvation by grace through faith in Christ. The firstborn Esau is not saved from starvation until he sells his birthright to the second born Jacob just as the first man Adam representing mankind would have been eternally forsaken unless the birthright had passed to the second man Jesus. Esau can only be saved by Jacob just as Adam can only be saved by Jesus. Esau can only be saved if he sells his birthright of his own freewill just as every man must turn to Jesus Christ of his own freewill in order to be saved.[21]

The word *die* [H4191] (Esau) has connotations of "capital punishment" and "divine judgment," recalling the original judgment of death entering the world through Adam (Gen 2:17) and likewise the universal condemnation of the

---

[18] The Hebrew rendered *that same* [H122] *red* [H122] [*pottage*] means "red stuff, this red stuff!" (Waltke 363). Every detail of the sacred text has deep meaning.

[19] "It is well known that in biblical dialogue all the characters speak proper literary Hebrew, with no intimations of slang, dialect, or idiolect. The single striking exception is impatient Esau's first speech to Jacob . . . 'Let me gulp down [Feed me, I pray thee] some of this red red stuff.' Inarticulate with hunger, he cannot come up with the ordinary Hebrew term for 'stew' ['soup'], and so he makes do with . . . 'this red red' " (Alter, *Genesis* xxiv). The basic conformity of Biblical dialogue is a sign of the inspiration of the Spirit acting throughout all history, while the seeming deviation of Esau's speech at this seminal moment is a poignant testimony to the carnal degeneration of fallen man.

[20] "The birth-right was typical of spiritual privileges, those of the church of the firstborn . . . ." (Wesley 1:100; Gen 25:31). The church of the firstborn from the dead.

[21] "It was not out of pride or ambition that he [Jacob] coveted the birthright, but with an eye to spiritual blessings . . . ." (Henry 1:156; Gen 25:29–34). The Biblical text transcends the normal pride of life.

natural body under the law (Heb 9:27). And Esau being faint reinforces the image of death. Esau, as one who is *faint* [H5889], being linked with the *field* [H7704] recalls Adam being cursed through the ground and the concurrent degeneration of the natural order of all things after the original sin (Gen 3:17).[22] Esau being faint represents the weakness of the flesh and accordingly portends death, while the linking of Esau being faint with Esau being in the field of the earth is an identification of the flesh, or natural body, with the world, or with the present world order. But the revival of Esau through Jacob's red soup is a figurative death and resurrection of Esau through, or by, Jacob that reflects the death and resurrection of Adam in Jesus Christ that comes by the redeeming power of the blood of Christ shed for sins. The choice that Esau has between death and life may not seem like a real choice, but it is exactly the same choice that every Adam, or man, must make for himself. And the proof that freewill is not violated in this process is established by the fact that so many people choose death and not life.[23]

The name *Edom* [H123] is associated with the Hebrew "to be red" [H119], while the name *Esau* [H6215] is, according to the Biblical text itself, connected with "hairiness" and perhaps also "redness" (Gen 25:25).[24] The change from the name *Esau* [H6215] to the name *Edom* [H123] is again an image of death and resurrection. The name Esau is connected with flesh via the attribute of hairiness, while the name *Edom* is connected with blood and the life in the blood via the sign of red food, representing a life-giving sustenance. Esau would ultimately throw off the yoke of Jacob and thereby reject Jacob, which represents the unforgivable rejection of the Holy Spirit, but this does not negate in any way Jacob's original redemption of Esau from death (Gen 27:40). Christ likewise died for the sins of the whole world (1 John 2:2), even though his blood will finally serve as a ransom not for all but for many (Matt 20:28), according to as many who are willing to drink his blood (John 6:53). The name *Edom* [H123] and the word *red* [H122] (pottage eaten by Edom) and also the name *Adam* [H121] and the word *man* [H120] and the word *ground* [H127] are all closely related to the Hebrew "to be red" [H119]. This is an identification of the new man Edom with the old man Adam that also portends the final condemnation of Esau. Esau becoming Edom prefigures Jacob becoming Israel just as the fall through the one man Adam prefigures our exaltation through the

---

[22] "[H]e [Esau], being pinched with famine, resigned it [the birthright of the firstborn] up to him [Jacob], under an oath" (Josephus 1:136). The curse of the ground through the first man Adam points to a coming famine of the Word of God in the end times, the time of the last Adam, Amos 8:11.

[23] If man had not sinned, he would have remained immune from death (Rom. Catholic Church, *Catechism* 287). In Adam, death begets death, but in Jesus Christ, eternal life begets eternal life.

[24] The name *Esau* [H6215] is connected to the root "to do, make" [H6213] by *Strong's* and *Brown-Driver-Briggs*, but with *Strong's* alone adding that the relationship between [H6215] and [H6213] is evidently based on a sense of "handling; rough (sensibly felt)."

one man Jesus Christ (Rom 5:19). All men are resurrected, but only some to life, with others to condemnation (John 5:29).[25]

Genesis 25:34 Then Jacob gave Esau bread [H3899] and pottage [H5138] of lentiles; and he did eat [H398] and drink [H8354], and rose up [H6965], and went his way: thus Esau despised [H959] [his] birthright.

The word *bread* [H3899] (that Jacob gave Esau) recalls Adam cursed to eat *bread* [H3899] (that God gave man) in the sweat of his face until he would return unto the dust of the ground (Gen 3:19). The symbol of bread, or more specifically eating bread, is therefore connected with the curse of the natural body through the dust of the ground, which is according to the original curse of Adam. And the symbol of eating bread is now connected with Esau despising his birthright just as eating bread is connected with Adam despising his birthright. The linking of bread with the natural body and likewise with the present world is also evident in the image of the bread of affliction as established at the time of the Exodus (Deut 16:3). And Jesus Christ ultimately identifies his own body, or flesh, condemned under the law, with bread at the last supper (Matt 26:26). Esau *eating* [H398] and *drinking* [H8354] is connected, respectively, with *bread* [H3899] and *pottage* (soup) [H5138] since no other food or drink is recorded, whereby the solid bread and the (relatively) liquid red soup of Jacob are symbols, respectively, of the body and blood of Jesus Christ. Also note that the word ordering in the text of *bread* [H3899] followed by *pottage* (soup) [H5138] parallels the word ordering of *eating* [H398] followed by *drinking* [H8354]. Esau eating and drinking the bread and red soup of Jacob foreshadows the apostles, including Judas Iscariot, eating and drinking the bread and wine of Jesus Christ (Luke 22:19–23). And this is finally all mankind being called to eat the flesh and drink the blood of Christ in the subsequent church age connecting the First and Second Advents (John 6:53).[26]

The body and blood of Christ represent flesh and spirit, likewise justice and mercy, and likewise law and grace. The new covenant, the Covenant of Grace, does not simply replace the old covenant, the Covenant of Law, but rather the fullness of grace is the fulfillment of the law in the perfect union of justice and mercy. This is the unity of the body and blood that is the unity of flesh and spirit. The commandment to eat the body, or flesh, of Christ is the call to pick up our own crosses in this life and follow Christ in submission to the curse of Adam, which is the curse of the old covenant condemning the natural body unto death (Luke 9:23). The commandment to drink the blood of Christ, the

---

[25] The obscuration of the meanings of the names *Esau* (properly, "hairy") and *Jacob* (properly, "supplanter" or "heelcatcher") is a modern phenomenon that is based on unprovable and ultimately irrational scholarship (Coffman 325; Gen 25:25–26). The faithful should be wary of modern scholarship, that is, end-times scholarship.

[26] "Some varieties of lentils are reddish-brown, but when cooked they often lose the red hue. Hence, some suggest that Jacob added something to the stew [soup] that made it unusually red, maybe even what is called a 'blood soup' " (Waltke 364). Regardless of the exact details, Jacob's soup is clearly identified with the color red.

sign of the new covenant, is the call to salvation by grace alone through faith alone in Jesus Christ alone that is finally the resurrection of the eternal spiritual body in the Body of Christ (Matt 26:28). All men, good and evil, eat the flesh of Christ in that all men suffer and die, but good men glorify God whereas evil men suffer in vain (Ps 127:1). All men also drink the blood of Christ in that all men are resurrected, but the faithful are sanctified by drinking the blood of Christ whereas the faithless are condemned by the blood (John 5:29). The wicked drinking the blood of Christ is notably represented by the whore drunk on the blood of the martyrs (Rev 17:6). The martyrs are the children of God and, therefore, themselves embody the blood of Christ. The first son Esau symbolically eating and drinking the body and blood represents the first man Adam, or all mankind in the natural body, eating and drinking the body and the blood. This is the unity of the body and blood that is the brotherhood, or blood kinship, of Adam and Christ.

The word *pottage* (soup) [H5138] evokes an image of "boiling," which is an image of agitation and anger that is negative in tone. In contrast, the word *wine* [H3196] evokes a less violent, more uplifting image of "effervescence (frothiness)."[27] Soup and not wine being used to signify Esau drinking the blood of Christ thereby represents an emphasis on condemnation and wrath. A progression and also a parallel are evident in the comparison between "boiling" and "frothiness," reflecting the relationship between death and rebirth. The more negative image of drinking *pottage* (soup) [H5138] points to the more positive image of drinking *wine* [H3196] and, thereby, reflects our promised new creation being predicated on the destruction of the present creation. Note further that *pottage* (soup) [H5138] has qualities of both liquid and solid foods while *bread* [H3899], in comparison, represents a singularly solid food. Jacob presents bread followed by soup to Esau just as law is followed by grace, but soup incorporates the fundamental solidness of bread just as grace subsumes law in the perfect union of justice and mercy. Also, the tastiness of the soup, as well as the protein content, presumably exceeded that of the bread, or bread alone. And Esau eating *bread* [H3899], at least figuratively, before drinking *pottage* (soup) [H5138] is identified, in context, most specifically with the unfolding of the church age.[28] First the natural and visible church, second the spiritual church—the second, or latter, being the revelation of the true and complete Body of Christ in the end times.[29]

---

[27] The word *wine* [H3196] is derived from an unused root "to effervesce" per *Strong's*, not *Brown-Driver-Briggs*, but the relation to and relevance of an uplifting, or upward, effervescence is clear regardless of exact etymology.

[28] Esau very possibly raised the red soup to his mouth as if drinking from a cup, in contrast to using some utensil or sopping it up entirely with bread.

[29] "[T]he view that a new [everlasting] Law of God will be proclaimed by the Messiah is occasionally expressed [in Talmudic writings] . . . . [T]he Messiah will take upon himself the kingdom of the Law and make many zealous followers thereof. . . . The dietary and purity laws [all ceremonial laws] will no longer be in force . . . ." (*Jewish Encyclopedia*, s.v. "eschatology"). It has always been clear, or should have been, that the Mosaic laws point to some larger, future reality.

ESAU, JACOB, ISRAEL

The word *despise* [H959] (Esau despises) has a connotation "to regard with contempt," while the word *rose* [H6965] (Esau rose up) has connotations "to establish" and "to be fulfilled." Esau despising his birthright is closely connected with his rising up and symbolically separating himself from the very person of Jacob. The image of Esau *rising* [H6965] foreshadows the resurrection of Adam, or Adam-kind, representing all the dead, the righteous and the wicked. But the connection between Esau *despising* [H959] and Esau *rising* [H6965] represents an emphasis on the condemnation of the natural body that will finally be the resurrection of the faithless unto damnation. All mankind will be raised from the dead, but the faithful will be raised unto eternal life whereas the faithless will be raised unto eternal condemnation (John 5:28–29). The first son Esau is identified with the first people of God, those under the first covenant, the Covenant of Law, specifically those under the curse of the first covenant. This is not simply the Jewish nation but the totality of mankind in the natural body. And Esau as the brother of Jacob is further identified with the church age culminating in the end times and connecting the First and Second Advents. The rejection of Esau generally represents the condemnation of all men under the law, which is the condemnation of the natural body. This is the condemnation of all men that is the call to repentance of all men, the good and the evil. But Esau most specifically represents the condemnation of the faithless separated from grace, which is the condemnation in the eternal body. This is the utter rejection of the seed of the serpent. Finally, the complicated layering of imagery is itself a prophecy of the convergence of all things in the end times. The first man Adam embodying the first creation, the Covenant of Law marking a first covenant, the nation of Israel representing the first assembly of God, and the First Advent of Jesus Christ as our new Adam all point to the fulfillment of all things at the time of the Second Advent.[30]

ABIMELECH

Genesis 26:1 And there was a famine in the land, beside the first famine that was in the days of Abraham. And Isaac went unto Abimelech king of the Philistines unto Gerar.

The present account of Isaac and Abimelech is the third in a series of three accounts. The second is that of Abraham and Abimelech (Gen 20:1–17). The first is that of Abram and Pharaoh (Gen 12:10–20). The three accounts reflect the Fall of Man followed by the First and Second Advents of Christ. The key image connecting all three accounts and thereby demarcating the threefold set is a patriarch presenting his wife as his sister. The first and the third accounts are additionally connected by the sign of famine being in the land. Focusing on the

---

[30] "Why did Esau sell out [despise his birthright]? 'History shows that men prefer illusions to realities, choose time rather than eternity, and the pleasures of sin for a season rather than the joys of God forever. . . . Men still sell their birthright for a mess of pottage' [D. G. Barnhouse]" (Guzik 154; Gen 25:29–34). Adam-kind.

connection between the first and third accounts, the famine of the first account represents the curse of the ground through Adam—which is characterized by thorns and thistles, eating the herb of the field (like animals), eating bread in the sweat of our faces, and finally returning to the dust of the ground in death (Gen 3:17–21). The famine of the third account portends a famine of hearing the words of the Lord (Amos 8:11)—which will end in the sharp sword going forth from the mouth of the Lord to smite the nations (Rev 9:15). The first famine is distinctly natural, while the final famine is spiritual. The first famine represents the first death, while the final famine represents the second death (Rev 20:14). This is the first body of Adam supplanted by the final Body of Christ. The absence of famine in the second of the three accounts then points to there not being a famine of hearing the words of the Lord (or a literal famine) during the time of the First Advent. The children of the bridechamber do not mourn and fast while the bridegroom is still with them (Matt 9:15).

The first account, that of Abram and Pharaoh, represents the Fall of Man. This first of three accounts is positioned in the Biblical text immediately after the call of Abram from the east (Gen 12:1–9) and immediately before the separation of Abram and Lot (Gen 13:1–18). The call of Abram represents the original creation of Adam, while the separation from Lot represents the exile of man from the garden. The second account, that of Abraham and Abimelech, represents the First Advent. This second of three accounts immediately follows Lot being saved from the destruction of Sodom and Gomorrah (Gen 19:1–38) and immediately precedes the miraculous birth of Isaac and the corresponding rejection of Ishmael (Gen 21:1–21). The preservation of Lot represents the unmerited and preordained redemption of fallen man, while the birth of Isaac represents the virgin birth of Christ. The birth of Isaac and the corresponding rejection of Ishmael (Gen 21:1–21) is then bracketed by the account of the original conflict between Abraham and Abimelech (Gen 20:1–18) and the account of the resulting treaty between Abraham and Abimelech (Gen 21:22–34). The nesting of the account of the birth of Isaac within the overall account of Abraham and Abimelech further identifies the person of Isaac with the First Advent. The treaty between Abraham and Abimelech (Gen 21:22–34) is followed by the figurative sacrifice of Isaac in Moriah (Gen 22:1–19). And this connects the sacrifice of Isaac, representing the crucifixion of Christ (Gen 21:1–21), with the rescue of Lot, representing the promised salvation of fallen man (Gen 19:1–38). The third account, that of Isaac and Abimelech, represents the Second Advent. This third of three accounts immediately follows Jacob buying the birthright (Gen 25:27–34) and immediately precedes Jacob taking the blessing (Gen 27:1–40). The birthright reflects the kingship of Christ revealed in the First Advent, while the blessing reflects the priesthood of Christ that will be revealed in the Second Advent. The nesting of this third and final account between the birthright and the blessing then identifies Jacob, or rather Israel, with the culmination of the church age in the Second Advent.[31]

---

[31] The useful commentaries on this section of the Biblical text are almost nonexistent because of a fixation on imaginary sources and redactors, wherein the ongoing dispute

ESAU, JACOB, ISRAEL

Genesis 26:2–5 And the LORD appeared unto him, and said, Go not down [H3381] into Egypt; dwell [H7931] in the land which I shall tell thee of: 3 Sojourn [H1481] in this land, and I will be with thee, and will bless thee; for unto thee, and unto thy seed, I will give all these countries, and I will perform [H6965] the oath [H7621] which I sware [H7650] unto Abraham thy father; 4 And I will make thy seed to multiply as the stars of heaven, and will give unto thy seed all these countries; and in thy seed shall all the nations of the earth be blessed; 5 Because that Abraham obeyed my voice, and kept my charge, my commandments, my statutes, and my laws.

The word *go down* [H3381] (go not down into Egypt) means "to come or go down, descend" in the Hebrew and has a connotation "to be prostrated," representing the admonition that we must not go down to, or be conformed to, the ways of this world (2 Cor 6:17). The word *dwell* [H7931] (in the promised land) has a connotation "of the dead (dwelling in the dust)," while the word *sojourn* [H1481] (in the promised land) has associations "to stir up strife" [H1481] and also "to dread (to be afraid)" [H1481]. This is the death and dread portending the destruction that must precede the kingdom of God (1 Cor 15:36). The word *perform* [H6965] (the Lord will perform the oath) means "to arise, stand up," which points to the promised resurrection of the faithful unto eternal life, while the word *oath* [H7621] has a connotation "curse," which points to the faithless being raised unto condemnation (John 5:28–29). The word *sware* [H7650] (the oath which the Lord sware) literally means "to seven oneself, or bind oneself by seven things," reflecting the fulfillment of the original seven days of creation and likewise the seven millennia of creation.

The Fall of Adam followed by the First and Second Advents of Christ are reflected in the accounts of Abram and Pharaoh (Gen 12:10–20) followed by Abraham and Abimelech (Gen 20:1–18, 21:22–34) followed by Isaac and Abimelech (Gen 26:1–33). In the account of Abram and Pharaoh, God does not explicitly reveal himself to anyone. In the account of Abraham and Abimelech, God reveals himself to Abimelech. And in the account of Isaac and Abimelech, God reveals himself to Isaac. The silence that marks the first of the three accounts represents the condemnation of mankind in the Fall of Adam. God revealing himself in the second account unto the ruling power embodied by Abimelech represents the victory of Christ at the time of the First Advent. This is expressly the victory over the prince of this world, corresponding to Christ taking possession of the keys of hell and death (Rev 1:18). And God in the third account revealing himself to Isaac, the son of the promise, represents an emphasis on the fulfillment of all things in Christ, the Body of Christ, at the time of the Second Advent.

---

within modern scholarship over which imaginary sources are correct is reminiscent of the [representative, if not historical] dispute within medieval scholarship over how many angels can stand on the point of a needle (Coffman 330; Gen 26:1–5). Adding to the Word of God is the progenitor of subtracting from the Word.

JACOB AND ESAU

The kingdom of Abimelech, in contrast to the kingdom of Pharaoh, is within the geographical area of the promised land and is thereby identified with the promised land (Gen 15:18). The latter two accounts of Abraham and Abimelech followed by Isaac and Abimelech are both identified with sojourning in the promised land and, thereby, are distinguished from the first account of Abram and Pharaoh, which is identified with sojourning in separation from the land. The First and Second Advents of Christ are likewise identified with the physical presence of Christ in the earth, in contrast to the Fall of Adam, which is identified with the separation between man and God and likewise the separation between earth and heaven. But the name change from Abram to Abraham parallels the accounts of Abram and Pharaoh followed by Abraham and Abimelech, and thereby a connection between these two former accounts is also evident. This connection reflects the blood kinship between Adam and Jesus Christ. Abram becoming Abraham reflects the genealogical descent of Christ from the first man Adam. Abram and Abraham being in actuality the same person reflects Christ dying literally and legally in the place of Adam.

Abram originally sojourning under Pharaoh in Egypt represents an emphasis on our slavery to sin and thereby again the Fall of Adam, since the Israelites would ultimately live in bondage in Egypt (Exod 2:23). The latter two accounts of Abraham followed by Isaac sojourning under the Philistines in the promised land, not under the Egyptians in separation from the land, point to the freedom from sin we have in the Body of Christ. But since the nation of Israel would suffer continual warfare with the Philistines, the sojourning of Abraham and Isaac under Abimelech also points to the continual persecution of the faithful by the people of the world and that specifically during the period connecting the First and Second Advents (1 Sam 4:1–11).

Pharaoh and Abimelech are both kings of the world and, thereby, both reflect the universal dominion of God since the kings of the world necessarily receive their power from God (Prov 8:15–16). But the kingdom of Abimelech, being within the geographical area of the promised land, is expressly identified with the kingdom of God (Gen 15:18). Abraham followed by Isaac sojourning in the promised land under Abimelech foreshadows Christ proclaiming the kingdom of God uniquely unto Israel at the First Advent (Matt 15:24) followed by Christ returning uniquely to Israel at the Second Advent in order to establish the visible kingdom of God (Zech 14:4, Acts 1:6–11). In contrast, the kingdom of Pharaoh exists outside the promised land and, thereby, reflects a world system distinct from the kingdom of God, with this distinction culminating in the continued existence of the nations alongside the formal city, or kingdom, of God during the millennial kingdom (Rev 20:7–9). The dominion of God during the millennial kingdom will be universal, encompassing the whole of creation, even as the dominion of Pharaoh and Abimelech, which ultimately proceeded from God, represents a dominion over what signifies the whole of the world. But a distinction between the city of God and the cities of men will persist until the revelation of the new heaven and new earth at the end of the millennial kingdom of Christ (Rev 21:1).

Isaac had not yet been born at the time of the original sojourn of Abram under Pharaoh, and therefore Isaac was still in Abram at that time. And this hiddenness of Isaac, the son of promise, represents the hiddenness of the promise of God at the time of the Fall of Man. The birth of Isaac being closely linked with the account of Abraham and Abimelech then points to the revelation of the promise of God at the time of the First Advent. In contrast, Jacob is alive and presumably with Isaac at the time of Isaac's sojourn under Abimelech. And this nearness of Jacob represents the fullness of the reality of the kingdom of God being manifest in the resurrected Body of Christ at the time of the Second Advent. The blessing and multiplication of the seed of Isaac then points to the multitude of faithful forming the one Body of Christ. The emphasis on blessing and dominion being received through obedience to the law points to the perfection of the faithful in Christ. The blessing and dominion proceeding from God is our promised perfection in Christ. The promise of God is our inheritance of the fullness of the indwelling Holy Spirit.

Genesis 26:6–11 And Isaac dwelt in Gerar: 7 And the men of the place asked [him] of his wife; and he said, She [is] my sister: for he feared [H3372] to say, [She is] my wife; lest, [said he], the men of the place should kill me for Rebekah; because she [was] fair [H2896] to look upon. 8 And it came to pass, when he had been there a long time, that Abimelech king of the Philistines looked out at a window, and saw, and, behold, Isaac [was] sporting [H6711] with Rebekah his wife. 9 And Abimelech called Isaac, and said, Behold, of a surety she [is] thy wife: and how saidst thou, She [is] my sister? And Isaac said unto him, Because I said, Lest I die [H4191] for her. 10 And Abimelech said, What [is] this thou hast done unto us? one of the people might lightly have lien with thy wife, and thou shouldest have brought guiltiness upon us. 11 And Abimelech charged all [his] people, saying, He that toucheth [H5060] this man or his wife shall surely be put to death [H4191].

The word *fair* [H2896] (describing Rebekah) is the same word translated *good* [H2896] (very good) in describing the original creation (Gen 1:31). Our new perfect creation in the Body of Christ recalls our original very good creation in the body of Adam. The word *sporting* [H6711] (Isaac sporting with Rebekah) is previously translated *laugh* [H6711], recalling the laughter connected to the name *Isaac* [H3327]. The theme of laughing—originating with Abraham and Sarah but most closely connected with the person of Isaac and now finally extended to Rebekah—represents our joy and surprise in our redemption in Christ (Gen 17:17, Gen 18:12, Gen 21:9). The word *die* or *death* [H4191] (lest I die, shall be put to death) describing Isaac originally being afraid to *die* [H4191] and also the penalty of *death* [H4191] imposed by Abimelech is the same *death* [H4191] connected with eating from the tree of knowledge (Gen 2:17). The royal decree that anyone defiling the marriage of Isaac and Rebekah would die portends the judgment of the faithless under the law in the end times. The word *toucheth* [H5060] (toucheth . . . death) is the same word used by Eve to warn that anyone *touching* [H5060] the tree of knowledge would die (Gen 3:3). The final condemnation of mankind, or Adam-kind, in the end times will be the fulfillment of the original condemnation of Adam.[32]

The identity of Rebekah is hidden from Abimelech just as the identity of Sarah had been hidden from Abimelech (Gen 20:11–18) just as the identity of Sarai had been hidden from Pharaoh (Gen 12:10–20).[33] A wife is to her husband as the body of faithful is to Christ (Eph 5:32). The emphasis on wives always being hidden points to the mystery of salvation having been hidden from the foundation of the world. But the identities of wives in the end always being discovered points to the revelation of salvation in Jesus Christ in the last days (Col 1:26). Further, the revelation of hidden wives being connected with not only the Second Advent but also the Fall of Man and the First Advent represents the salvation in the one man Jesus Christ encompassing all the faithful throughout all the ages. Our redemption being a mystery represents the ignorance and hopelessness of natural man, while our redemption being made manifest represents the exaltation of spiritual man. The identity of Rebekah being hidden then points specifically to the ignorance of faithlessness persisting until the end times, since the account of Isaac and Rebekah in Gerar is identified with the Second Advent.

The emphasis on Isaac and Rebekah having been in the land for a long time before Abimelech discovered the true identity of Rebekah points to the revelation of the fullness of the Body of Christ being delayed until the end times. Rebekah is revealed as the wife of Isaac by the sporting of Isaac with her in public view just as the faithful will be identified with Christ by Christ himself before the whole world (Matt 24:30–31). Abimelech stating that someone might take Isaac's wife, Rebekah, portends the depravity of the world in the end times, particularly the wicked desiring to persecute, or defile, the faithful. Abimelech needing to ask Isaac why he had hidden the identity of Rebekah represents the ignorance of the faithless. And the ignorance of Abimelech recalls the primordial ignorance of Cain not knowing, or understanding, the spiritual nature of what had happened to Abel in death (Gen 4:9). The ignorance of sin is the mark of the spirit of disobedience, while the knowledge of Jesus Christ is the mark of the Holy Spirit. The natural man is ignorant even of his own self-condemnation (2 Sam 1:16).

In the account of Abram and Pharaoh, Abram gives no explanation for why he had hidden the identity of Sarai. Pharaoh asks Abram why he had hidden Sarai, but the Biblical text is silent regarding any response from Abram (Gen 12:18–20). The silence of Abram reflects Adam and likewise all mankind, though particularly antediluvian mankind, standing before God without excuse, or justification. In the account of Abraham and Abimelech, Abraham does

---

[32] "For Augustine Adam [the first man] was not merely the start of the human race, but the representative of humanity, so that 'we are all Adam' " (Augustine, *Confessions* 197 n. 20). Like begets like.

[33] *Abimelech* is a dynastic title that was used by early Philistine kings (Coffman 333; Gen 26:6–11). This is another subtle connection between Pharaoh and Abimelech, since both were named by titles of kingship.

explain himself and in doing so he equates his hiding of Sarah with there being no fear of God in the land (Gen 20:11–13). And Abraham further asserts that the mystery of Sarah is ironically the truth of Sarah in that his wife actually is his sister. Abraham explaining himself to Abimelech is dovetailed with Abraham praying for the healing of Abimelech. And thereby the truth of all Abraham's words is affirmed. And the revelation of the identity of Sarah is connected to the healing of the house, or body, of man. There being no fear of God in the land reflects the rejection of Christ at the time of the First Advent. The blood kinship between Abraham and Sarah is the blood kinship between God and humanity. The healing of Abimelech points to the healing of Adam. In the account of Isaac and Abimelech, Isaac also explains himself to Abimelech but, in that case, he equated his hiding of Rebekah very specifically with a fear of losing his life because of her (Gen 26:9). The figurative death of Isaac in Moriah is identified with the First Advent, while the much delayed literal, physical death of Isaac is identified with the end of the church age, or more generally with the end of the call to repentance, corresponding to the millennial kingdom. Isaac must not die prematurely just as the church age must not end prematurely.

The word *feared* [H3372] (Isaac feared) has a connotation in the Hebrew "to fear, reverence, honour," reflecting the reverential fear due to God and his sanctuary, that is, to God and his Son (Lev 26:2, Ps 89:7). In the account of Abram and Pharaoh, the presence of fear is not explicitly mentioned, which recalls the ignorance and arrogance of pride marking our original fall in Adam. In the account of Abraham and Abimelech, the entire court of Abimelech is seized by fear on account of Abraham, which reflects the crushing victory of Christ in the First Advent over the ruler of this world (John 12:31). In the account of Isaac and Abimelech, the emphasis is placed upon the fear that Isaac himself feels, which is startling since Isaac is identified with God. The life of Isaac following his figurative death in Moriah is identified with the church age, while the account of Isaac and Abimelech is identified specifically with the Second Advent. And thus the fear that characterizes Isaac can be identified with that which characterizes the world in the end times. Nonetheless, the image of God being afraid at the time of the final destruction (by fire) recalls the image of God repenting at the time of the first destruction (by water) (Gen 6:6). God repenting ultimately points to the nailing of Jesus Christ to the cross by which the repentance of man is accepted. Even our repentance comes from God just as our faith comes from God just as our very breath comes from God. And God being filled with reverential fear finally points to Christ moving swiftly and decisively to preserve the faithful from the fearful wrath to come. God is afraid for us, or in our place, even when we don't have the sense to be afraid for ourselves. Even our knowledge of the fear of God comes from God.[34]

---

[34] "[T]he essential vice, the utmost evil, is Pride [*sic*] . . . it was through Pride that the devil became the devil: Pride leads to every other vice: it is the complete anti-God state of mind" (Lewis, *Mere Christianity* 109). Pride is the original sin of man and devil alike— the mother of all other sins.

JACOB AND ESAU

Genesis 26:12–16   Then Isaac sowed in that land, and received in the same year an hundredfold: and the LORD blessed him. 13 And the man waxed great, and went forward, and grew until he became very great: 14 For he had possession of flocks, and possession of herds, and great store of servants: and the Philistines envied him. 15 For all the wells [H875] which his father's servants had digged [H2658] in the days of Abraham his father, the Philistines had stopped [H5640] them, and filled [H4390] them with earth [H6083]. 16 And Abimelech said unto Isaac, Go from us; for thou art much mightier than we.

In the account of Abram and Pharaoh, Abram is made wealthy when Sarai is taken, in contrast to when she is returned (Gen 12:10–20). This reflects the preservation of humanity after the Fall of Man, with an emphasis on the preservation of man being preordained. In the account of Abraham and Abimelech, Abraham is made wealthy when Sarah is returned (Gen 20:1–18) and the wealth that Abraham receives is marked by the sign of silver (Matt 27:9). This reflects the victory of the resurrection, or returning from death, at the First Advent. Abraham praying for Abimelech then represents the perpetual intercession of Jesus Christ for the faithful, the communion of Christ with the faithful, that proceeds from the victory of the cross (Heb 7:25). In the present account of Isaac and Abimelech, Rebekah is not taken at all (Gen 26:1–33). This reflects the faithful being secure in the Body of Christ. Isaac not being made wealthy by Abimelech but rather becoming wealthy by his own sowing in the land is a corresponding image of the exaltation of the faithful in Christ that is established expressly by the power of the Holy Spirit. This is the time of the Second Advent of Christ.[35]

The sign of harvesting that marks the account of Isaac and Abimelech points to the final harvest of the faithful in the end times (Matt 13:39). Isaac sowing and harvesting is Christ sowing and harvesting. Isaac sowing and harvesting solely in the promised land is an image of Christ establishing his chosen faithful ones and only his chosen faithful ones. Isaac both sows and reaps just as Jesus Christ is the author of our original creation and also the story, or ultimate meaning, of our new creation (John 1:3). Isaac becoming wealthy is identified with his reaping a hundredfold just as Jesus Christ is glorified by the multiplication of the faithful in the Body of Christ. The Philistines being envious of the visible wealth of Isaac portends the world hating Christ at the time of his glorious return (John 15:18). Abimelech acknowledges that Isaac is the mightier and greater one just as demons acknowledge the power and authority of Christ (Matt 8:29). Abimelech is the one that sends Isaac away just as it is the faithless that reject the grace of God. There is no fellowship between the darkness and the light (2 Cor 6:14).

---

[35] The Spirit of God, the Holy Spirit, is God, intrinsically and literally a person, not an abstract force or a personification of love. And thus the power of God the Spirit should be understood to be the relational movement unique to the person of the Holy Spirit.

The word *wells* [H875] (of Abraham) is derived from the root "to make distinct, plain (e.g., plainly written letters)" [H874]. The baptism in water marks the faithful and prefigures the water of life (Rev 22:17). And the envy of the Philistines is linked to their desire to keep the faithful from the water of life. The word *digged* [H2658] (Abraham's servants had digged the wells) connotes "to search for," while the word *stopped* [H5640] (Philistines stopped the wells) connotes "secret." The servants of God must necessarily repent (search out the water of life) before they can be redeemed (find the water of life). Seek and ye shall find (Matt 7:7). The Philistines stopping up the wells of Abraham represents the faithless secreting, or rejecting, the water of life that is the grace of God. The wells of father Abraham that are also the wells of his son Isaac point to our redemption in God the Son. The word *filled* [H4390] (filled the wells with earth) connotes "to be accomplished, ended," which portends the end times, while the word *earth* [H6083] (filled with earth) is the same *dust* [H6083] of the ground constituting Adam, which portends a corresponding end of the natural body (Gen 2:7). Earth is a symbol of death, particularly since man returns to the dust of the ground when he dies, whereby the act of stopping up the water of life with the dust of death represents a rejection of life in favor of death and likewise a rejection of the way of the Holy Spirit in favor of the way of the flesh (Gen 3:19).

Genesis 26:17–18 And Isaac departed thence, and pitched his tent in the valley of Gerar, and dwelt there. 18 And Isaac digged again the wells of water, which they had digged in the days of Abraham his father; for the Philistines had stopped them after the death of Abraham: and he called their names after the names by which his father had called them.

Isaac digs the same wells as his father and calls them by the same names as his father. Jesus Christ likewise does nothing of himself but only as the Father does (John 5:19). Isaac digging the same wells as his father and naming them the same names points to the person of Christ recapitulating first the history of Israel and finally creation as a whole. This is a process of sanctification through recapitulation in Christ. This is Christ embodying our sanctification. This is the Body of Christ. Just as the natural body proceeds from the one man Adam, so the spiritual, or glorified, resurrection body must proceed from the one man Christ (Gen 2:21–23, John 19:34).[36] Jesus is all in all because Jesus is God, and the ultimate meaning of all things is God and only God.[37] The wells of

---

[36] God created the one man Adam alone, not a community of first men, so that men would not [logically but erroneously] infer that there is more than one creator, *Sanhedrin* (Cohen, *Rabbinic Sages* 4). One God, one creation, and one salvation in the one Body of Christ are parallel realities that are necessarily consistent.

[37] "*Salvation* and *redemption* . . . as applied in the Messianic conception, are identical. As God is the *Moshia'* [savior], so He is also the *Go'el* [redeemer but also avenger] [Isa 44:23, 48:20, 52:9, 63:9, Ps 74:2]. This savior or redeemer is YHWH [Isa 44:24, 47:4, 48:17, 63:1] . . . ." (*Jewish Encyclopedia*, s.v. "salvation"). Law and grace, all things, are united in Jesus Christ, likewise the Body of Christ.

Abraham being the same wells of Isaac points to God being eternally unchanging. One and only one name has been given unto mankind for our salvation (Acts 4:12). But Isaac continues to dwell in tents after his figurative sacrifice in the land just as the faithful would continue in the natural body after the crucifixion of Christ just as sin would continue in the world even after the victory of Christ over death (Heb 11:19). And the new creation will continue to flow from the side of Christ until the Body of Christ is fully formed.

The period between the destruction of the world in the floodwaters and the crucifixion of Christ for the world is most closely identified with God the Son since this period is marked by the formation of national Israel and the concurrent formulation, or codification, of the law of Moses. The Jewish Messiah is national Israel. The First Advent is the Covenant of Law. Further, the antediluvian period is most closely identified with God the Father since this period is marked by the original creation that proceeds from God the Father, that is, from God as creator, or spiritually God as progenitor. Finally, the period following the crucifixion is most closely identified with God the Spirit since this period is marked by the call of the faithful by God the Spirit. The Body of Christ is animated by the power of the Spirit. The three distinct periods connecting the First Creation to the Flood to the Cross to the New Creation correspond to Adam followed by the First and Second Advents. And this threefold reality is also evidenced in the lives of the three patriarchs Abraham, Isaac, and Jacob.[38]

The Philistines stopping up the wells of Abraham is linked in the Biblical text with the death of Abraham. The patriarch Abraham is most closely identified with God the Father, or the God of Adam and creation, whereby the wells of Abraham are most closely identified with the original font of life established in the original creation of Adam. The death of Abraham then reflects the destruction by water, which marks the end of the antediluvian period. But the death of Abraham also reflects the death and resurrection of Christ, which marks the end of the dispensation of Adam, or the end of the bondage of death that proceeded from Adam (Rom 5:17). This seeming ambiguity results from the transcendent parallel between the Flood of Noah and the Passion of Christ, with both events representing the death and resurrection of all creation (1 Pet 3:20–21). The baptism in the floodwaters is the baptism of the cross. The stopping up of the wells of Abraham, signifying the water of life, reflects the death of God himself in the world, or rather the death of God in the hearts of the faithless, who embody the present world. This

---

[38] "[T]he verse 'A thousand years in thy sight are but as yesterday' [Ps 90:4] having suggested the idea that the present world of toil . . . is to be followed by a Sabbatical millennium . . . Of these the six millenniums were again divided . . . into three periods: the first 2,000 years devoid of the Law; the next 2,000 years under the rule of the Law; and the last 2,000 years preparing amid struggles and through catastrophes for the rule of the Messiah . . . ." (*Jewish Encyclopedia*, s.v. "eschatology"). The end of the Flood narrative is the call of Abraham, while the end of the dispensation of the law of Moses is the cross of Calvary.

is the rejection of God at the time of the Flood, and this is the rejection of God at the time of the First Advent.[39]

Genesis 26:19–22 And Isaac's servants digged in the valley [H5158], and found there a well of springing [H2416] water. 20 And the herdmen of Gerar did strive with Isaac's herdmen, saying, The water [is] our's: and he called the name of the well Esek [H6230]; because they strove with him. 21 And they digged another well, and strove for that also: and he called the name of it Sitnah [H7856]. 22 And he removed [H6275] from thence, and digged another well; and for that they strove not: and he called the name of it Rehoboth [H7344]; and he said, For now the LORD hath made room for us, and we shall be fruitful in the land.

The word *valley* [H5158] (dug wells in the valley) has an association in the Hebrew of "possession, property, inheritance" [H5159], reflecting the promised inheritance in the renewal of all things. A valley is a low place and, thereby, represents the earth in contrast to the high places of heaven, likewise the natural body in contrast to the spiritual resurrection body, and likewise the present world order in contrast to the promised future world order that is the new heaven and new earth (Rev 21:1). The word *springing* [H2416] (wells of springing water) means "alive, living" and, thereby, points to the promise of the resurrection of the dead in the end times. Isaac digging in the dust of the ground in expectation of finding the water of life represents the fulfillment of the prophecy that Adam, or all mankind in Adam, would work the ground until the time of death, that is, until the end times (Gen 3:19). And the emphasis on it being the person of Isaac digging in the dust points specifically to the incarnation of Christ in the flesh. And Isaac finding the water of life for his household represents the resurrection of the faithful in the Body of Christ. Isaac digging wells was previously connected with his obedience to his father (Gen 26:18). But now Isaac digging wells is connected with a strife that precedes peace. The will of the Father is the natural that precedes and points to the spiritual, that is, the law that precedes and points to grace. The will of God is opposed but will not be denied.

Isaac digging three successive wells reflects the threefold creation of Adam followed by the First and Second Advents and also the three millennia of Christ connecting the cross and the promised new creation. The name *Esek* [H6230] (first well dug by Isaac) means "contention" and has an association "to oppress, wrong, extort" [H6231] sometimes translated *deceived* [H6231], recalling the deception of Adam and portending the rejection of Christ and the oppression of his faithful. The name *Sitnah* [H7856] (second well) means "hostility" and is

---

[39] "Ye see, therefore, how great was the effect of the death of Christ, for no creature endured His fall with equal mind, nor did the elements His Passion . . . All things were in the Passion of Christ disturbed and convulsed [Alexander of Alexandria, *Arian Heresy*]" (Roberts et al., *Ante-Nicene Fathers* 6:301). The death and resurrection of Jesus Christ is the death and resurrection of the whole world.

derived from the word "adversary (satan)" [H7853], which points to the satanic disfiguring of the person of Christ at the First Advent and a corresponding disfiguring of the church, signifying the Body of Christ, in the end times. The name *Rehoboth* [H7344] (third well) is derived from the root "to be, or grow, wide, large" [H7337], which prefigures the millennial kingdom. The emphasis on Isaac becoming fruitful in the promised land after digging the third well reinforces the image of the glorification of the faithful on the earth in real bodies and in a literal millennial kingdom. The emphasis on the Lord making a separate place for Isaac and his household, distinct from the Philistines, points to the millennial kingdom being established in the midst of the kingdoms, or nations, of the world (Rev 20:7–9). The emphasis on the servants of Isaac doing the work of digging the wells testifies to the faithful in Christ even now striving while yet in the natural body.[40]

Genesis 26:23–25 And he went up [H5927] from thence to Beer-sheba [H884]. 24 And the LORD appeared unto him the same night, and said, I [am] the God of Abraham thy father: fear [H3372] not, for I [am] with thee, and will bless thee, and multiply thy seed for my servant Abraham's sake. 25 And he built [H1129] an altar [H4196] there, and called upon the name of the LORD, and pitched his tent there: and there Isaac's servants digged a well.

The word *up* [H5927] (went up to Beersheba) means "to go up, ascend, climb," while the word *removed* [H6275] (from Sitnah to Rehoboth) has a connotation "to become old" (Gen 26:22). The new place of Beersheba supplants the old place of Rehoboth. And the place of *Beersheba* [H884] is, at least figuratively, on high compared with all three of the previous locations, including *Rehoboth* [H7344]. The exalted state of Beersheba is further accentuated by the immediate appearance of the Lord and the corresponding blessing of the Lord. And Isaac testifies to the sanctity of Beersheba by building an altar. Nonetheless, *Beersheba* [H884] is still related to *Rehoboth* [H7344] since both locations are identified with dwelling in peace. Isaac digging Rehoboth in the valley, or low place, points to the new earth, while Isaac digging Beersheba in the high place points to the new heaven. The word *Beersheba* [H884] means "well of seven (as a place of swearing by seven)," which looks past the seven millennia of creation into eternity. The peaceful habitation that has been promised is not simply heaven, and neither is it only a new heaven and a new

---

[40] There is a striking parallel between the narratives that encompass the two wife-sister episodes of Sarah and Rebekah becoming imperiled, wherein the strife with Lot's men over the land, Gen 13:1–12, is identified with the strife with Abimelech's men over Abraham's wells, 26:14–22 (Waltke 366–67). The division over the land, or dust of the earth signifying flesh, that becomes a division over life-giving water, spiritually the water of life, is the separation of the faithful and the faithless in the two separate resurrections and resurrection bodies.

earth. It is the union of a new heaven and a new earth in the Body of Christ that is the nexus between God and man (Rev 21:1).[41]

The word *fear* [H3372] (fear not) has a connotation of "reverence, honour" and recalls Adam being *afraid* [H3372] after he ate from the tree of knowledge (Gen 3:10). Fear is the mark of the natural body, while love is the mark of the spiritual, or glorified, body. Accordingly, the call to not be afraid is the call from the nature of flesh to the nature of the Spirit. The nature of fear precedes the nature of love just as the natural body precedes the spiritual body just as law precedes grace. Fear is the beginning of wisdom (Ps 111:10), but love is the fulfillment of wisdom (1 John 4:16). The Lord telling Isaac to not be afraid is an affirmation of the victory of Christ over death, but the fullness of this victory over death will not be realized until the resurrection of the dead in the end times (Rom 5:12–21). The nature of fear continues to afflict the natural body even after the death and resurrection of Christ just as pain and suffering continue to afflict the physical world even after the death and resurrection of Christ. Psychological, or spiritual, fear and actual physical suffering are two aspects, or levels, of reality reflecting the same death and degradation of mankind because of sin. The admonition to not be afraid is an affirmation of the certainty of eternal life we have even now in Christ, but to truly cease from all fear and suffering necessarily awaits the resurrection of the dead and the corresponding re-creation of creation in the end times. The kingdom of Christ is not of this world; it is of the promised world to come (John 18:36).[42]

The word *builded* [H1129] (Isaac builded an altar) has a connotation "to establish" and is the same word used to describe God *making* [H1129] Eve from the rib (side) of Adam (Gen 2:22).[43] The original establishment of the union of man and woman in Adam and Eve (Gen 2:23) is an image of the covenantal union of Christ with the faithful and with creation as a whole (Eph 5:30–32), also the essential unity of the Father with the Son and with the Spirit (John 17:21). Jesus Christ is the bridegroom of blood establishing the covenantal relationship between deity and humanity (Exod 4:25). The word *altar* [H4196] is

---

[41] "This well they called *Rehoboth, enlargements* . . . in the two former wells [Esek and Sitnah] we may see what the earth is, *straitness* and *strife* . . . This well [Rehoboth] shows us what heaven is; it is *enlargement* and *peace*, room enough there, for there are many mansions" (Henry 1:161; Gen 26:12–25). The promise of life in God is not simply heaven but rather a new heaven together with a new earth.
[42] The unconditional blessing of Isaac, Gen 26:23–24, parallels the conditional blessing of Isaac, 26:2–5, in an alternating structure that spans 26:2–26:33 (Waltke 365). The original conditional blessing being tied to the promised land only to be realized as an unconditional blessing points to the natural body being supplanted by the promised spiritual, or glorified, resurrection body.
[43] "With Isaac God came first . . . [H]e built an altar and then waited there to call upon the Lord. Second came his home; he pitched his tent. Third came his business; his servants dug a well" (*Amplified Bible* 33 n. g; Gen 26:25). The covenantal altar, or act, of creation followed by the tabernacling of the First Advent of Christ followed by the final business of the Second Advent.

derived from the root "to slaughter for sacrifice" [H2076].[44] Isaac building an altar may imply blood sacrifice, but only his calling upon the name of the Lord is emphasized. The figurative sacrifice of Isaac in Moriah (Gen 22:2) does not need to be repeated just as Christ would die once and for all and never again (Heb 9:25–26). Jesus Christ is the only acceptable sacrifice, the only name given for our salvation (Acts 4:12). Beersheba was previously connected with the second flight of Hagar and Ishmael (Gen 21:14) and also with the second treaty of Abraham and Abimelech (Gen 21:32) and also with the aftermath of the sacrifice of Isaac in Moriah (Gen 22:19). The place of Beersheba—the place of the oath, or covenant—points to the second and final coming of Jesus Christ, likewise to the opening of eternity. Blessed are they which are called unto the marriage supper of the Lamb (Rev 19:9).[45]

Genesis 26:26–27 Then Abimelech [H40] went to him from Gerar, and Ahuzzath [H276] one of his friends, and Phichol [H6369] the chief captain [H8269] of his army [H6635]. 27 And Isaac said unto them, Wherefore come ye to me, seeing ye hate me, and have sent me away from you?

The words of Isaac are simple and true. Abimelech would not have sent him away if he did not hate him, and Abimelech's hatred, signified by his ongoing separation from Isaac, is in no way abrogated by his suing for peace. The hatred of Abimelech for Isaac and also the continuing separation between Abimelech and Isaac marks Abimelech and his party as representatives of the evil one and his children. The threefold Abimelech, Ahuzzath, and Phichol specifically represent an anti-trinity—respectively, the dragon, the beast, and the false prophet—counterfeiting the one true Trinity (Rev 16:13). In the account of Abram and Pharaoh, the emphasis is on the singular person of Pharaoh, representing the serpent and counterfeiting the oneness of God at the time of the Fall of Man. In the account of Abraham and Abimelech, the emphasis is on the twofold Abimelech and Phichol, counterfeiting the relationship between God the Father and God the Son at the First Advent. In the present account of Isaac and Abimelech, the emphasis is on the threefold Abimelech, Ahuzzath, and Phichol, counterfeiting the fullness of the revelation of the Trinity at the Second Advent. The third person of the Trinity and likewise the fullness of the revelation of the Trinity are identified with the Second Advent because it is the resurrection unto eternal life at the Second Advent that will be the realization of the fullness of the promised indwelling of God the Holy Spirit that is the fullness of the promised communion with God.

---

[44] H4196 is coded incorrectly as H4096 on page 258 of *Brown-Driver-Briggs*, per *Green's Interlinear* and also *Strong's*.

[45] "Abraham had reared an altar [grove] in Beer-sheba long before [Gen 21:33]; Isaac reared another [26:25], which, as has been remarked by Jewish writers, is the only one he [Isaac] is recorded to have raised" (Jamieson et al. 1:193; Gen 26:24–25). There is one redemption according to the one cross of Jesus Christ.

The name *Abimelech* [H40] evokes an image of "father" in the Hebrew, which points to the dragon, or serpent, as the father of lies (John 8:44). The name *Ahuzzath* [H276] means "possession (especially land by inheritance)," portending the possession of the land, above all the promised land, by the person of the anti-christ. This is also a possession by the dragon of the flesh (dust of the ground) of the beast, or anti-christ (Rev 13:2). The name *Phichol* [H6369] means "mouth of all," which portends the public ministry of the false prophet (Rev 13:13), while the office of *Phichol* [H6369] as the *chief captain* [H8269] of the *army* [H6635] portends a ministry of the false prophet that is characterized by intimidation and violent coercion (Rev 13:15–16). The treaty that the threefold Abimelech will seek foreshadows the false treaty of peace spoken of by and through the prophet Daniel (Dan 9:27). Abimelech had previously sworn that Abraham had dug Beersheba and, thereby, acknowledged the sovereignty of God and specifically the unassailable victory of the cross. But now Abimelech is silent on this point, relating a willful ignorance of the sovereignty of God, specifically the ignorance of the way of God that will characterize the end times. The interruption of the earlier account of Abraham and Abimelech by the birth of Isaac is an image of God delaying judgment for the sake of the faithful, while the absence of any such interruption in the present account of Isaac and Abimelech is an image of the haste of God fulfilling all things in Christ at the appointed time (Gen 21:1–21).[46]

Genesis 26:28–29 And they said, We saw certainly that the LORD was with thee: and we said, Let there be now an oath [H423] betwixt us, [even] betwixt us and thee, and let us make [H3772] a covenant [H1285] with thee; 29 That thou wilt do us no hurt [H7451], as we have not touched [H5060] thee, and as we have done unto thee nothing but good [H2896], and have sent thee away [H7971] in peace: thou [art] now the blessed of the LORD.

The phrase *make* [H3772] a *covenant* [H1285] evokes an image "to cut a covenant," recalling the covenant of the pieces (Gen 15:10) and also the covenant of circumcision (Gen 17:10), while all sacrifices ultimately evoke an image of being *cut off* [H3772] from the land of the living (Jer 11:19). The word *make* [H3772] (make a covenant) has a further connotation "to chew (between the teeth)" that foreshadows the commandment to eat the flesh of Christ (John 6:51). But Abimelech is a figure of satan, whereby his presumption to cut a treaty with Isaac represents a counterfeit of the true covenant of God that can only be cut by God himself. Abimelech seeking to establish an equality between himself and Isaac through a mutual treaty recalls Adam seeking to be like God

---

[46] "The Antichrist's deception already begins to take shape in the world every time the claim is made to realize within history that messianic hope which can only be realized beyond history through the eschatological judgment" (Rom. Catholic Church, *Catechism* 194). The Roman Catholic Church, for example, cannot be the promised fulfillment of the millennial reign of Christ.

(Gen 3:5) and likewise lucifer seeking to be like God (Isa 14:14). The word *oath* [H423] (let there be an oath) has a connotation "curse," reflecting the reality that Abimelech is calling down a curse upon himself, notably in that the Philistines would continue to oppose the chosen bloodline. Abimelech condemns himself with his own mouth just as man always condemns himself with his own mouth. The words *hurt* [H7451] (no hurt) and *good* [H2896] (nothing but good) used by Abimelech are the same words used to describe the *good* [H2896] and *evil* [H7451] connected with the tree of knowledge (Gen 2:9), whereby the words of Abimelech recall the original lies of the serpent (Gen 3:4). The one true God Almighty says "good and evil" as a matter of truth and fact, while the serpent says "no hurt," likewise "nothing but good," and likewise "ye shall not surely die."

The word *sent away* [H7971] (sent away in peace) recalls God *sending forth* [H7971] Adam-kind from the garden because of the rebellion of Adam—actually Adam sending away, or rejecting, God (Gen 3:23). And national Israel would likewise reject Christ at the time of the First Advent. The word *touched* [H5060] (touched not Isaac) is the same word Eve used to describe her not *touching* [H5060] the tree of knowledge. Abimelech figuratively touching Isaac in casting him out (though Abimelech denies it) is an image of the abuse of Christ caused by Adam effectively touching the forbidden tree and likewise the wooden cross (though it was actually Eve who touched the tree, or took from the tree) (Gen 3:3, 3:6). Isaac being blessed by the Lord is connected to his having been rejected, or literally not touched, by Abimelech and, thereby, points to the rejection of Christ by national Israel (from the time of the First Advent) becoming the acceptance of Christ by the whole world, including Israel (in the end times) (Rom 11:25–26). Abimelech not physically touching Isaac further points to the prophecy that the Holy Spirit must not be profaned, or blasphemed, by the world (Luke 12:10). The Son will be profaned, but not the Spirit. Isaac will be cast out, but not touched. The ambiguity about whether Abimelech should be considered to have touched Isaac in casting him out is itself a reflection of the Body of Christ called to be in the world but not of the world (John 17:15–16).[47]

Abimelech recognizing that the Lord is with Isaac foreshadows the revelation of the glorified Christ to the whole world in the end times (Matt 24:30). But acknowledging Christ is not the same as accepting Christ, or being anointed of the Holy Spirit. Abimelech claims to be seeking out Isaac because the Lord is with him, but if Abimelech had truly recognized Isaac, he would not have hated him in the first place and would not have maintained a physical separation from him. Abimelech cannot deny that the Lord is with Isaac just as the demons cannot deny the authority of Christ (Matt 8:29). But Abimelech seeks a blessing separated from God. In the earlier account of Abimelech and Abraham and also in the present account of Abimelech and Isaac, the Philistines were seeking a quid pro quo mutual nonaggression pact, representing

---

[47] A similar ambiguity exists in relation to the forbidden tree, for God says "do not eat," Gen 2:17, while Eve expands "do not touch," Gen 3:3.

a covenant of law. In the earlier account of Abimelech and Abraham, however, the Philistines, though seeking a covenant of law, ultimately find a covenant of grace by affirming Beersheba as the rightful possession of Abraham. This is the law that becomes grace at the time of the First Advent of Christ. In the present account of Abimelech and Isaac, the Philistines seek a covenant of law and that is exactly what they receive in the absence of affirming Beersheba as the rightful possession of Isaac. This is the condemnation of the faithless at the time of the Second Advent of Christ.

Genesis 26:30–33 And he made them a feast, and they did eat and drink. 31 And they rose up betimes in the morning, and sware one to another: and Isaac sent them away [H7971], and they departed from him in peace. 32 And it came to pass the same day, that Isaac's servants came, and told him concerning the well which they had digged, and said unto him, We have found water. 33 And he called it Shebah: therefore the name of the city [is] Beer-sheba unto this day.

Abimelech seeks to affirm with Isaac the earlier covenant of law established with Abraham just as the faithless affirm their rejection of the Son in their rejection of the Holy Spirit. Abraham followed by Isaac both willingly participating in a covenantal relationship with Abimelech foreshadows Christ surrendering himself to crucifixion in the incarnation followed by the Restrainer being removed in the end times (2 Thess 2:6–8). No specific treaty characterizes the relationship between Abram and Pharaoh, which recalls the original exile of Adam and Eve from the presence of God (Gen 12:10–20). Two distinct treaties characterize the relationship between Abraham and Abimelech, which reflects law and grace being embodied by the death and resurrection of Jesus Christ at the time of the First Advent (Gen 21:24, 21:27). And now only one treaty characterizes the relationship between Isaac and Abimelech, which portends the judgment of the world at the time of the Second Advent. The one treaty of the end times is law for the faithless but grace for the faithful, which is expressly grace subsuming law. Isaac finding the water of Beersheba after confirming the one treaty with Abimelech points to the water of life promised according to the sevenfold oath of God (Rev 21:6). And the account of Isaac finding water at Beersheba being interrupted by the final treaty with Abimelech is an affirmation of the great significance attached to Beersheba.

The making of a feast being connected exclusively with this latter-days treaty between Isaac and Abimelech, not with the earlier treaties with Pharaoh and with Abimelech, points to the wedding feast of the Lamb in the end times (Rev 19:7). Isaac preparing a feast for Abimelech is a vision of the call to eat the flesh and drink the blood of Christ (John 6:53). Nonetheless, Abimelech being sent away immediately after the oath is sworn portends many being called to the feast but few being accepted (Matt 22:14). Abimelech swearing the oath with Isaac represents the self-condemnation of the flesh (Job 9:20). Isaac swearing the oath with Abimelech represents the judgment through the Son (John 5:22). The emphasis on Isaac now *sending away* [H7971] Abimelech contrasts with

JACOB AND ESAU

Abimelech originally *sending away* [H7971] Isaac (Gen 26:27). The original sending away represents man rejecting God, while the final sending away represents God rejecting man. But Abimelech being sent away does not represent the rejection of all mankind but rather only the faithless. The person of Isaac represents both Christ and the faithful in Christ because the faithful are the Body of Christ. And Abraham having earlier planted a grove of trees after making the two treaties with Abimelech points to the long time delay between the First and Second Advents, as implied by the long time required to grow trees (Gen 21:33–34).

Birthright and Blessing

Genesis 26:34–35 And Esau was forty years old when he took to wife Judith the daughter of Beeri the Hittite [H2850], and Bashemath the daughter of Elon the Hittite [H2850]: 35 Which were a grief of mind unto Isaac and to Rebekah.

The firstborn Esau marries at forty in imitation of his father Isaac (Gen 25:20). But Esau marrying Canaanite women (unto condemnation) is a reverse image of Isaac marrying a near relative (unto exaltation) (Gen 24:3–4) just as our condemnation through Adam is the reverse image of our exaltation in Christ (Rom 5:19). The grief of Isaac and Rebekah over their firstborn son reflects the grief of God over the first man Adam. And Esau following after Canaanite women recalls Adam obeying Eve in disobedience (Gen 3:17, 1 Tim 2:14). The rejection of Esau further recalls the rejection of Ishmael, but Esau is most closely identified with the faithlessness in the church age culminating in the end times. In contrast, Ishmael is most closely identified with the faithlessness of Israel at the time of the First Advent. Likewise, Isaac is most closely identified with the First Advent of Christ while Jacob is most closely identified with the Second Advent.

Genesis 27:1–2 And it came to pass, that when Isaac was old, and his eyes were dim, so that he could not see, he called Esau his eldest son, and said unto him, My son: and he said unto him, Behold, [here am] I. 2 And he said, Behold now, I am old, I know [H3045] not the day [H3117] of my death [H4194]:

Isaac dying of old age recalls his symbolic dying in Moriah just as the completion and conclusion, or dying, of the Body of Christ in the end times will recall Christ himself dying at the time of the First Advent (Gen 22:2). But Isaac being sacrificed in Moriah is different in kind compared with his dying of old age. Also, Jesus Christ cannot be crucified twice (Heb 6:4–6). The sacrifice of Isaac reflects the First Advent, whereby Isaac growing old reflects the closing of the church age, which was originally opened by the rejection of Christ. And this connection between the conclusion of the First Advent of Christ and the conclusion of the church age is reflected in the one person of Isaac being identified with both the First Advent and also the church age opened by the First Advent. Isaac growing old is a graphic affirmation of the unity of Christ and his creation just as Isaac being sacrificed is a graphic affirmation of Christ becoming a curse for our sakes (Gal 3:13). The death of the Body being represented tangibly by the actual death of Isaac—in contrast to the death of the Head being represented figuratively in Moriah—is an escalation of intensity that itself represents an increasing suffering of the Lord because of an increasing suffering of his creation.

The word *death* [H4194] (Isaac's death) is derived from the root word *die* [H4191], which is connected with the tree of the knowledge of good and evil, while the word *day* [H3117] (day of death) is the *day* [H3117] of dying also connected with the tree of the knowledge of good and evil (Gen 2:17). The death of Isaac being linked to the death of Adam connects the final destruction in the end times with the original death of Adam. Death is the fruit of the tree of the knowledge of good and evil. Man's ignorance of the hour of his own death is an image of man's ignorance of death itself and likewise of man's ignorance of the law that governs flesh and death. Man does not know the hour of his own death just as man does not know to reject the bad (Gen 4:7). Adam truly died when he ate from the forbidden tree, whereby the hour of our death was the hour that Adam chose the fruit of the tree of the knowledge of good and evil (Gen 2:17). All humanity was in Adam when he incurred the curse of death, whereby the end of all flesh in the end times will be the final fulfillment of that curse. The death and resurrection of the faithful is the death of the body of Adam and the resurrection of the Body of Christ.

Isaac's eyes growing dim to the world while he yet lives in the world represents an increasing ignorance and apostasy of the visible church in the world, particularly in the period approaching the end times. Isaac, in his old age and figuratively on his deathbed, summoning Esau is an image of the final call to repentance of Adam-kind in the end times, that is, the final call of all nations in Adam to faith in Christ. But the ultimate rejection of Esau recalls the rejection of Ishmael just as the faithlessness of the end times even now recalls the faithlessness at the First Advent. The long delay between the figurative sacrifice of Isaac in Moriah and his actual death prefigures the long delay between the First and Second Advents, while the long delay between the dimming of Isaac's eyes and his actual death prefigures a protracted period of apostasy leading up to the final judgment (Gen 35:28–29). The dimming of Isaac's eyes recalls the opening of Adam's eyes just as the spiritual ignorance of the world in the last days recalls the original self-elevation of Adam in his own eyes (Gen 3:7). The wisdom of man is as foolishness to God (1 Cor 3:19).

The word *know* [H3045] (Isaac knows not) is the root word from which the word *knowledge* [H1847] is derived, describing the tree of the *knowledge* [H1847] of good and evil (Gen 2:9). Ignorance, or not knowing, is our inheritance in the original curse, as exemplified by Cain not knowing the spiritual fate of Abel (Gen 4:9). The ignorance of the flesh is especially the ignorance of the law that governs and likewise condemns the flesh. This curse of the flesh is the nature of the flesh, assumed even by Jesus Christ himself—standing in the place of man and, therefore, not knowing the day and hour of the coming judgment (Mark 13:32). This is one aspect of Christ becoming a curse for our sakes (Gal 3:13). This is Christ taking off the mantle of power and becoming the likeness of men (Phil 2:6–7). The life of Isaac reflects the First Advent opening the church age and culminating in the millennial kingdom, whereby Isaac does not know the hour of the death of his own flesh just as the Son would not know the appointed time of the end of all flesh.[48]

Genesis 27:3   Now therefore take [H5375], I pray thee, thy weapons [H3627], thy quiver [H8522] and thy bow [H7198], and go out to the field, and take me [some] venison;

Isaac in his old age sending Esau into the field to kill flesh portends the death of all flesh in the end times. The word *weapons* [H3627] (Esau's weapons) is derived from the root "to be complete, at an end, finished, accomplished, spent" [H3615], variously used to describe God *finishing* [H3615] the heavens and the earth (Gen 2:1) and *ending* [H3615] his work on the seventh day (Gen 2:2). The final judgment signified by the weapons of Esau points to the completion of the original creation. The emphasis on Esau points to man and not God as the true source of our condemnation. The word *bow* [H7198] (Esau's bow) is the same *bow* (rainbow) [H7198] of God, signifying the everlasting covenant between God and all flesh upon the earth (Gen 9:16). Water is a symbol of flesh, likewise the law that governs flesh, and likewise the repentance in the flesh. The promise that all flesh would never again be destroyed by water is an affirmation that we live only one transitory life in the natural body. Christ would likewise be crucified only once (Gen 9:15).

The word *take* [H5375] (take thy weapons) is the same word used to describe the ark of Noah *borne up* [H5375] by the floodwaters (Gen 7:17). The wooden ark being lifted up is connected to the wooden cross being lifted up. And the final judgment by fire will be the fulfillment of the first destruction that came by water. This layering of creation upon itself points to the oneness of God and likewise to the oneness of creation in God. The word *quiver* [H8522] (Esau's quiver) is derived from the root "to hang" [H8518], elsewhere used to describe being *hung* [H8518] upon a tree as being accursed (Deut 21:23). The hand of Esau holding the quiver reflects the hand of Adam nailing Christ to the tree of knowledge. Christ is the embodiment of all creation, whereby the final end of all flesh is connected to the death of Christ at the time of the First Advent. The death and resurrection of the Body of Christ is likewise connected to the death and resurrection of Christ as the Head. The faithful actually must participate in the death and resurrection of Christ (Rom 6:5).

---

[48] "Isaac's account has been gapped, and his life must be pieced together from other accounts. Considering that even the nonelect such as Ishmael and Esau are given separate, even if brief, accounts [25:12–18, 36:1–43], Isaac's gap seems deliberate. Why would Isaac, who had such miraculous beginnings, be gapped?" (Waltke 351). Another prophetic sign foreshadowing the brevity of the natural, or humbly condescending, life of Jesus Christ marking the First Advent.

ESAU, JACOB, ISRAEL

Genesis 27:4 And make [H6213] me savoury meat, such as I love [H157], and bring [H935] [it] to me, that I may eat [H398]; that my soul [H5315] may bless [H1288] thee before I die [H4191].

The word *love* [H157] (meat that I love) recalls the *love* [H157] of Abraham for Isaac (Gen 22:2) and also the *love* [H157] of Isaac for Rebekah (Gen 24:67). Isaac's love of savory meat, or symbolically flesh, is an image of the love of Christ for humanity and also for physical creation as a whole. Nonetheless, the body, or flesh, of humanity must be baptized with fire, or the Holy Spirit, just as the savory meat that Isaac loves must be prepared by fire (Luke 12:49). The aging Isaac embodies the church age, whereby his call for savory meat is the call to eat the flesh of Christ (John 6:51), which represents the death of the flesh, or natural body, in imitation of the death of Christ (Rom 6:23). The word *make* [H6213] (make savoury meat) recalls the same word used to describe God *making* [H6213] all things in the beginning (Gen 1:31), while the word *bring* [H935] (bring the meat) recalls the same word used to describe God *bringing* [H935] woman unto man in the beginning (Gen 2:22). The rebirth of the world in the end times will recall the original creation just as our new creation proceeding from the side of Jesus Christ (John 19:34) recalls humanity originally proceeding from the side of Adam (Gen 2:21). The word *eat* [H398] (that Isaac may eat) has a connotation "to consume by fire" that again points to the foretold destruction by fire and the concurrent purification of the body. The cooking of meat implies a purification, or refinement, by fire, whereby Isaac calls for savory meat just as the Lord God demands the absolute perfection of the flesh and creation as a whole(Gen 17:1).

The word *soul* [H5315] (Isaac's soul) has a connotation "that which breathes" and an additional association "to be refreshed" [H5314], elsewhere used to describe the *refreshment* [H5314] of the Sabbath rest that prefigures the foretold renewal in and through the millennial Sabbath (Exod 23:12). The soul, or breath, of Isaac seeking to bless his firstborn recalls the original breath of life being breathed into the first man (Gen 2:7). Our promised new creation in the first man redeemed from the grave, or ground, likewise recalls our original creation in the first man who was formed from the dust of the ground. But the word *die* [H4191] (Isaac to die) has a connotation "to die by capital punishment" that portends the condemnation of all flesh under the law. And the word *bless* [H1288] (Isaac's soul will bless) has a connotation "to kneel," which can be used to express either "blessing" or "cursing," foreshadowing the resurrection of all the dead to either condemnation or exaltation (John 5:28–29). The natural body must necessarily pass away in the rebirth of the spiritual, or glorified, body. The natural body is condemned under the law, but the spiritual body is resurrected by grace. Esau must bring savory meat, or blood sacrifice, unto Isaac before his death just as mortal, or natural, man must repent and rely upon the blood of Christ. Meat, or flesh, must be prepared for Isaac before a blessing can be received just as the birthright in the flesh must precede the blessing of the Spirit just as the natural body must precede the spiritual body just as repentance must precede redemption.[49]

Genesis 27:5–8 And Rebekah heard [H8085] when Isaac spake to Esau his son. And Esau went to the field to hunt [for] venison, [and] to bring [it]. 6 And Rebekah spake unto Jacob her son, saying, Behold, I heard [H8085] thy father speak unto Esau thy brother, saying, 7 Bring me venison, and make me savoury meat, that I may eat, and bless thee before the LORD before my death. 8 Now therefore, my son, obey [H8085] my voice [H6963] according to that which I command [H6680] thee.

The word *heard* [H8085] (Rebekah heard Isaac) is the same word translated *obey* [H8085] (Jacob obeys Rebekah), meaning "to hear (and obey)." Isaac commands that meat, or flesh, be brought unto him, and it is Rebekah that hears and obeys, and through her it is Jacob that hears and obeys. Isaac commanding his firstborn to arise, kill, and be blessed is an image of justification through the first covenant, the Covenant of Law. But it is the second man Jesus Christ that fulfills the law and not the first man Adam. Esau not perceiving the presence, or at least the intention, of his mother reflects the ignorance of the flesh inherited from the first man Adam. Esau hearing the promise of Isaac and trying to fulfill his commandments literally in his own flesh also reflects the ignorance of the flesh. In contrast, Rebekah hears the promise of Isaac and understands it correctly in relation to the prophecy that the firstborn son must serve the second born (Gen 25:23).

Man is the embodiment of flesh and likewise justice, while woman is the embodiment of spirit and likewise mercy. The natural man Esau is therefore identified with his father, Isaac, while the spiritual man Jacob is identified with his mother, Rebekah. Esau is the embodiment of natural man and therefore only perceives justice and not mercy, that is, Esau only perceives Isaac and not Rebekah. Jacob is the embodiment of spiritual man and therefore obeys his mother just as the Son is led by the Spirit of his Father (Luke 4:1, Rom 8:14). Isaac loves his firstborn Esau just as God longs to redeem the first man Adam and Adam-kind (necessarily under the law), while Rebekah substituting the second born Jacob for the firstborn Esau is an image of the second man Jesus Christ supplanting the first man Adam (necessarily by grace).

The word *heard* [H8085] (Jacob heard and obeyed) is the same word used to describe Adam and Eve *hearing* [H8085] the voice of the Lord God as the Lord walked in the garden of Eden, specifically after the Fall of Man (Gen 3:8). The words of Isaac represent the prophetic words of God concerning the condemnation and redemption of the world. The word *voice* [H6963] (voice of

---

[49] The birthright and blessing are innately inseparable, and since Jacob had previously purchased the birthright, it is technically the elder Esau, not the younger Jacob, that attempts to take illegitimate possession of the blessing (Coffman 344–45; Gen 27:1–4). Jesus Christ alone is both the king of kings and our high priest forever, eternally possessing both the birthright and the blessing.

Rebekah) is the same *voice* [H6963] heralding the presence of the Lord God in the garden and the same *voice* [H6963] from which Adam and Eve hid themselves among the trees of the garden (Gen 3:8). And the word *command* [H6680] (Rebekah commands Jacob) is the same word used to describe God *commanding* [H6680] Adam not to eat from the tree of the knowledge of good and evil (Gen 2:16–17). The voice of Rebekah, commanding her second born Jacob to receive the blessing of the firstborn, specifically represents the prophetic voice of God the Holy Spirit. Rebekah commanding her son Jacob to obey her voice represents the call of the Son and likewise the call of the faithful in the Son to perfect obedience unto the Father.

The command proceeding from Isaac to Jacob through Rebekah reflects the Father, Son, and Holy Spirit and likewise the formation of Adam followed by the First and Second Advents. The reality of man, woman, and child is always connected to the Godhead and likewise to the creation proceeding from the Godhead and in the image of the Godhead (Gen 1:27). The emphasis on the person of Rebekah in the present account of taking the blessing represents an emphasis on God the Holy Spirit, which connects the blessing of Isaac to the Second Advent. In contrast, Rebekah being absent from the previous account of Jacob purchasing the birthright represents an emphasis on God the Son in the First Advent (Gen 25:29–34). The birthright precedes the blessing just as law precedes grace just as the First Advent precedes the Second Advent just as the Son precedes the Spirit (John 16:7).[50]

The First Advent is the revelation of the kingship of Christ, which is the birthright of Christ, while the Second Advent is the revelation of the high priesthood of Christ, which is the blessing of the faithful in Christ. Jesus Christ is forever from eternity both king of kings and high priest, whereby both the First and Second Advents reflect both offices. Nonetheless, the emphasis in the First Advent is the kingship while the emphasis in the Second Advent is the high priesthood. The First Advent foreshadows the Second Advent, while the Second Advent subsumes the First Advent. The former foreshadows the latter, while the latter fulfills the former. The Jews would not accept the kingship of Christ in the First Advent because it was a kingship of servitude and suffering. And the visible church composed of Jews and Gentiles even now looks for the same kind of carnal kingship, as desired by the flesh, when the church should be expecting a divine high priesthood.

Genesis 27:9–10 Go now to the flock [H6629], and fetch me from thence two [H8147] good [H2896] kids [H1423] of the goats; and I will make them savoury meat for thy father, such as he loveth: 10 And thou shalt bring [it] to thy father, that he may eat, and that he may bless thee before his death.

---

[50] "... God left her [Rebekah] to herself to take this indirect course, that he might have the glory of bringing good out of evil" (Wesley 1:106; Gen 27:6). Because the present world is fallen, the way of providence necessarily involves good coming out of evil.

JACOB AND ESAU

The word *flock* [H6629] (goats from the flock) is the same word used to describe the *sheep* [H6629] kept by Abel (Gen 4:2) and also the firstlings of the *flock* [H6629] presented as an offering by Abel (Gen 4:4). Jacob fetching and necessarily killing the kids of the goats is an image of the death of the Son and likewise the death of the faithful in the Son. In the account of Cain and Abel, the offering of Abel is accepted but the offering of Cain is rejected (Gen 4:4–5). And this distinction is closely connected with Cain murdering Abel (Gen 4:6–8). In the present account of Esau and Jacob, the kids of the goats of Jacob are substituted for the venison of Esau. And this substitution is closely linked with Jacob taking the blessing of Esau. Cain murdering Abel parallels Esau being supplanted by Jacob. Likewise, Adam nailing Jesus Christ to the tree of knowledge parallels Adam being redeemed by Christ on the tree represented by the cross of Calvary.

Rebekah guiding events from behind the scenes and thereby elevating the second born in fulfillment of prophecy represents the movement of God the Holy Spirit. In the context of Isaac growing old, long after his sacrifice in Moriah, this is expressly the movement of the Spirit in the last days leading up to the Second Advent (Gen 22:2). Christ would not send the Spirit until after the time of the First Advent (John 14:26). The First Advent is most closely identified with the Son, while the Second Advent is most closely identified with the Spirit. Likewise, Jacob purchasing the birthright is most closely identified with the First Advent while Jacob taking the blessing is most closely identified with the Second Advent. The emphasis on Rebekah making the kids of the goats savory such that they will be loved by Isaac points to the glorification of the Son, likewise the faithful in the Son, by the power of the Holy Spirit. Distinguishing between the First and Second Advents is difficult, but this reflects the difficulty in distinguishing between the death and resurrection of the Head and that of the Body.

The number *two* [H8147] (two good kids of the goats) is emblematic of flesh and spirit, likewise of law and grace. The substitution of two kids of the flock for venison of the field reflects the twofold natures of Christ supplanting the singularly carnal nature of fallen man that exists in separation from God. This is the union of law and grace supplanting the mere condemnation under the law. This is the union of Jesus Christ and the faithful in Christ supplanting the utter isolation of fallen Adam-kind. The slaughter of two kids of the goats further points to the suffering of Christ in both the flesh and the spirit. Jesus Christ suffered in both the flesh and the spirit on the cross, but the suffering in the flesh is most closely identified with the First Advent while the suffering in the Spirit is most closely identified with the church age culminating in the Second Advent. Christ suffering in the spirit is Christ sending the Holy Spirit after the time of the First Advent (John 16:7). Christ suffering in the spirit is Christ suffering in sympathy for his faithful. There being two blood sacrifices finally points to the death and resurrection of the Body of Christ in imitation of the death and resurrection of Christ as the Head. And the slaughtering of *kids* [H1423] (of the goats) reflects the death of Christ before his natural time (being cut off) and also the end of the church age before its natural time (preternaturally). And these times of providence, not being natural, are not simply unnatural but supernatural.[51]

The word *good* [H2896] (kids of the goats) recalls the same word describing the original creation as very *good* [H2896] (Gen 1:31). The slaughtering of the kids of the goats represents the blood sacrifice required under law. This is the death and resurrection of Jesus Christ that is our new creation in the Body of Christ. The contrast between domesticated and wild animals recalls the contrast between Jacob dwelling in tents and Esau being a man of the field (Gen 25:27). The substitution of Jacob's offering for Esau's is the substitution of Jacob for Esau. We are saved by grace alone, but the natural reflects the spiritual. A domesticated animal from the flock is an image of the gentleness and humbleness of Jesus Christ, while a wild animal of the field is an image of the disobedience, or wildness, of Adam. The connection between rebirth (new creation) and substitution is the necessity of our being reborn in the Body of Christ. The connection between Esau and Jacob and their offerings reflects the universality of the one image of God that is impressed upon all creation. The image of God has been corrupted by sin throughout all creation, but the substitution of the promised new creation in the place of the present corrupted creation will finally bring the image of God and the reflected image of God into accord. This is the promised unity of flesh and spirit in the Body of Christ and likewise the promised unity of the new earth and new heaven in the new creation. And all these things are in accord with Jesus Christ, who is true man and true God.

Genesis 27:11–12 And Jacob said to Rebekah his mother, Behold, Esau my brother [is] a hairy [H8163] man, and I [am] a smooth [H2509] man: 12 My father peradventure will feel [H4959] me, and I shall seem [H5869] to him as a deceiver; and I shall bring a curse upon me, and not a blessing.

The word *smooth* [H2509] (describing Jacob) has a connotation of "flattery (smooth words)." The flattering word of the second born Jacob is the redemptive Word of the Spirit speaking in our behalf (Rom 8:26). The word *smooth* [H2509] (describing Jacob) also has an association "to divide, share (e.g., divide up plunder)" [H2505]. Jacob divides just as Christ judges (Rom 2:16). Jacob takes plunder just as Christ takes dominion (Matt 16:18). In contrast, the word *hairy* [H8163] (describing Esau) has an association "he-goat (for sin offering)" [H8163], connecting Esau with the goat of the flock used to represent him in the person of Jacob. And the word *hairy* [H8163] (describing Esau) has a further association "to bristle, with horror" [H8175], connecting

---

[51] God performing miracles is not questioned by the rabbis, *Sifré Deuteronomy*, but there is a strong preference for understanding the miraculous in accordance with the natural order of the universe, such that miracles throughout history are viewed as having been set in motion in the original act of creation, *Genesis Rabbah* (Cohen, *Rabbinic Sages* 11). Adding to the Word of God, as characterizes Talmudic literature, is the progenitor of subtracting from the Word of God, as marking modern-day historical criticism.

Esau with the nature of fear, in contrast to that of love. And the word *hairy* [H8163] (describing Esau) is also closely associated with the word "demon, satyr" [H8163], connecting Esau with the evil one (1 John 3:10). Jacob fearing that he would seem as a deceiver when he puts himself in the place of Esau ironically points to the person of Esau as the embodiment of the deceiver. Jacob fearing that a curse would fall upon him when he puts himself in the place of Esau is a prophecy of Christ becoming a curse on the cross in the place of Adam (Gal 3:13).

The word *seem* [H5869] (seem to Isaac as a deceiver) recalls the same word used to describe the *eyes* [H5869] of Adam and Eve being opened to their nakedness after being deceived by the serpent (Gen 3:7). Isaac, in his old age and afflicted with a dimness in his eyesight, represents the end of the church age, or the end of the call to repentance. And within this context, Esau represents the faithless while Jacob represents Christ and likewise the faithful in Christ. The dimness of the latter days began with the opening of the eyes of Adam and Eve and, thereby, affirms that the wisdom of man is as foolishness to God (Gen 3:5, 1 Cor 3:19). The knowledge of good and evil is the wisdom of man, or the flesh, which corresponds to an ignorance of the reality of the Spirit. The dimness of the church age began with the failure to recognize the Son and will culminate with the failure to recognize the Spirit. First the Son and finally the Spirit are dimly viewed as deceivers by the people of the world. This is Jacob incorrectly viewed as being wicked for purchasing the birthright and taking the blessing, even though he does so in complete accord with the prophecy of God (Gen 25:23). Jacob seems as a deceiver to Esau (Gen 27:36), but Jacob appears as the rightful heir to those that belong to him (Gen 31:16).

The word *feel* [H4959] (Isaac feels Jacob) has a connotation "to grope at noonday (in the darkness)" that portends a spiritual blindness, especially in the last days and necessarily despite the light of the Spirit. The darkness at noonday is foremost the darkening of the sun when Christ hung on the cross (Luke 23:44), but it is finally the darkening of the sun in the end times (Mark 13:24). This is again the rejection of the light of the Son that culminates in the rejection of the light of the Spirit. Nonetheless, the blindness of Isaac in his old age does not reflect only the apostasy culminating in the end times. The blindness of Isaac also represents the concurrent delay of the coming judgment embodied by the call to repentance. The apostasy of mankind and the call to repentance are two sides of the same coin, and therefore it is natural for both to be represented by the same dimness of the church age. And this same blindness of Isaac, as it represents God looking away from apostasy, foreshadows God not seeing or remembering the sins of the faithful, which is the Father accepting Jesus Christ in the place of the faithful (Ps 25:7). This is Isaac finally accepting Jacob in the place of Esau because of the dimness of his eyes and despite being able to distinguish between their voices and thereby between the two persons of the brothers (Gen 27:22–23). God does not, of course, literally forget anything.

Genesis 27:13 And his mother said unto him, Upon me [be] thy curse [H7045], my son: only obey my voice, and go fetch me [them].

The curse of Isaac being upon Rebekah represents the curse of the Son being upon the Spirit. This is the Son being raised from the dead by the power of the Spirit. This is the faithful, indwelt by the Holy Spirit, participating in the death and resurrection of the Son. Jacob's fear that his father will not accept him as Esau represents the reality of true justice, which is that each man must be judged according to his own sins (Deut 24:16). Nonetheless, Jacob's fear of being cursed becomes Jacob receiving the blessing, representing the death and resurrection of Christ and likewise that of the faithful in Christ. Jacob finally being accepted in the place of Esau is closely connected with his reliance upon Rebekah and, thereby, represents the power of the indwelling Holy Spirit, sanctifying the faithful in the Body of Christ.[52]

The word *curse* [H7045] (Jacob's curse upon Rebekah) is derived from the root "to be slight, swift, trifling" [H7043]. The slightness, or littleness, identified with the woman Rebekah represents the subtlety of the Holy Spirit that is mercurial in nature, as reflected in the floodwaters being *abated* [H7043] and returning whence they came, or figuratively returning unto God (Gen 8:11). The swiftness identified with Rebekah, or the Spirit, is the *swiftness* [H7043] of the whirlwind coming suddenly in judgment (Jer 4:13). The trifling identified with Rebekah is the movement of the Spirit from the *light thing* [H7043] of redeeming the faithful in the one tiny nation of Israel to finally redeeming all the faithful in Israel and all the Gentile nations (Isa 49:6).[53]

Genesis 27:14 And he went, and fetched, and brought [them] to his mother: and his mother made savoury meat, such as his father loved.

Isaac, Rebekah, and Jacob reflect the primordial image of God embodied by Adam, Eve, and the offspring of their union. Adam, Eve, Seed. Father, Spirit, Son. Jacob bringing the goats of the flock is a blood offering that represents the death and resurrection of Jesus Christ for the sins of the world. The savory meat being the object of Isaac's love points to the faithful being the object of the Father's love. Rebekah transforming the slaughtered animals into savory meat by fire represents the indwelling of the Holy Spirit redeeming and perfecting the faithful by the fire, or truth, of God. Isaac loving the offering brought by Jacob and prepared by Rebekah is the Father accepting the faithful in Christ by the power of the Holy Spirit. Also note that Isaac being sometimes identified with the Son and sometimes with the Father is itself a reflection of this fundamental acceptance of the Son by the Father that is ultimately the unity of the Father and the Son (John 14:9).

---

[52] "Augustine's defence of (e.g.) Samson's suicide or the sacrifice of Isaac or the fate of Jephthah's daughter (all favourite targets for Manichee attacks on Old Testament morality) is that seemingly unethical acts contain prophecy . . . ." (Augustine, *Confessions* 48 n. 39). The Old Testament is, in its entirety, prophetic.

[53] "The assurance of God's decree made her [Rebekah] bold [script updated]" (Whittingham et al., *Geneva Bible* 12R n. c [leaf 12, right-hand, note c]; Gen 27:13). The assurance of God the Holy Spirit, indwelling the faithful in Christ.

JACOB AND ESAU

Genesis 27:15 And Rebekah took goodly [H2532] raiment [H899] of her eldest [H1419] son Esau, which [were] with her in the house, and put them upon Jacob her younger [H6996] son:

The word *goodly* [H2532] (Esau's goodly raiment) is derived from the root "to desire, take pleasure in" [H2530], variously used to describe the tree of the knowledge of good and evil as a tree to be *desired* [H2530] (Gen 3:6) and in the warning to not *covet* [H2530] that which belongs to one's neighbor (Exod 20:17). The goodliness of Esau is as unrighteousness before the Lord. The word *raiment* [H899] (Esau's goodly raiment) is derived from the root "to act or deal treacherously" [H898], variously used to describe a master dealing *deceitfully* [H898] with his maidservant (Exod 21:8) and Israel dealing *treacherously* [H898] with the Lord (Jer 3:20). The raiment of Esau is as rags before the Lord. The *goodly* [H2532] *raiment* [H899], which Rebekah puts upon Jacob, rightly belongs to Esau and, thereby, represents the sins of Adam placed upon the back of Jesus. But the goodly raiment of Esau being found in the house of Rebekah represents an emphasis on the sins of the faithful, in contrast to those of the faithless. The seeming injustice of Rebekah, subverting the desire of Isaac to bless Esau, represents the seeming injustice of substituting Christ on the cross in the place of Adam. This is the seeming injustice of the condemnation of sinful man being assumed by the sinless Christ in his grace.

The word *eldest* [H1419] (describing Esau) has a connotation of "greatness," while the word *younger* [H6996] (describing Jacob) has a connotation of "insignificance." The greatness of the firstborn is a greatness in the eyes of Adam, or man. The insignificance of the second born is a corresponding insignificance of Jesus Christ, again in the eyes of man. The way of flesh always seeks to bless the firstborn over the second born. But there is also a greatness of the firstborn in the eyes of God. This is the desire of God to redeem Adam. This is the love of the Father for the Son, who is the firstborn from the dead. And there is also an insignificance of the second born in the eyes of God. This is the willing condescension of the infinite God in the person of Jesus Christ. This is the humility of Jesus Christ, even as a man and even unto death. The greatness of the firstborn is also the inviolable sanctity of freewill in the flesh. The insignificance of the second born is the intangible nature and seeming insignificance of the call to faith in Jesus Christ by which men are saved. The juxtaposition of greatness and insignificance is a paradox resolved in the person of Christ and only in the person of Christ, who is simultaneously and without contradiction fully God and fully man.[54]

Genesis 27:16 And she put the skins [H5785] of the kids of the goats upon his hands, and upon the smooth of his neck:

---

[54] Rabbinic teaching portrays God simultaneously and seemingly without contradiction as an approachable father and also an unapproachable infinite deity (Cohen, *Rabbinic Sages* 26). The necessity of the Trinity is inescapable.

ESAU, JACOB, ISRAEL

The word *skins* [H5785] (skins put upon Jacob) is the same word used to describe the coats of *skins* [H5785] that God placed upon Adam and Eve to cover their nakedness after the Fall of Man (Gen 3:21). The nakedness of Adam because of the tree of knowledge ultimately points to the nakedness of Christ on the tree of the cross for the sake of Adam and finally points to the nakedness, or death, of all the faithful in imitation of Christ. The word *skins* [H5785] (put upon Jacob) also has an association in the Hebrew "to be exposed, bare (into nakedness)" [H5783] that reinforces the image of nakedness. Our clothing testifies to our nakedness just as our experiential knowledge of good and evil testifies to our spiritual ignorance. Further, the figure of Jacob wearing animal skins evokes an image of animal sacrifice just as the crucifixion in fulfillment of the law recalls the animal sacrifices prescribed by the law. Jacob puts on the skins of animals in the place of Esau just as Jesus Christ puts on the sins of the world in the place of Adam.

Genesis 27:17 And she gave the savoury meat [H4303] and the bread [H3899], which she had prepared [H6213], into the hand of her son Jacob.

The word *prepared* [H6213] (Rebekah prepared the meat) recalls the same word used to describe God originally *making* [H6213] all things (Gen 1:31). But the thing prepared for Isaac by Rebekah is something unexpected, representing our promised new creation in the Body of Christ. The promised new creation is guaranteed by the cross but will not be fully manifested until the time of the Second Advent. The gifts of the Holy Spirit received during the church age are likewise a deposit on the promised inheritance of the fullness of the indwelling Spirit. The second born son takes the blessing not merely for himself but also for his whole house and his offspring. And this represents a preference for the offspring of the second born instead of the offspring of the firstborn. The offspring of the firstborn Adam is mortal life, which is death, while the offspring of the second born Christ is life eternal. The former is the birthright, while the latter is the blessing. The birthright is to the blessing as our original creation in Adam is to our promised new creation in Christ.

The word *bread* [H3899] (prepared by Rebekah) is derived from the root "to use as food, eat" [H3898] and has as an additional association in the Hebrew "to fight, do battle" [H3898], reflecting both the affliction of the flesh and also the victory of Christ over the flesh. This is Christ coming as a victorious king fighting and defeating sin and death at the time of the First Advent. This is the corresponding call to eat the flesh of Christ in imitation of Christ (John 6:55). The word *savoury meat* (savory meat) [H4303] (prepared by Rebekah) is derived from the root "to taste, perceive" [H2938] and has an additional association "taste, judgment" [H2940], which points to the essential exaltation of the faithful in understanding, or perception, and the concomitant judgment of the world. This is the judgment of the Second Advent that will be a blessing and a cursing administered in the office of the high priest. The life is in the blood, representing the indwelling Holy Spirit, whereby the faithful tasting, or perceiving, the blood is the faithful entering into eternal life by the power of God the Holy Spirit (Lev 17:11). This is the *tasting* [H2938] and seeing that the Lord God is good that is also the blessing of the faithful in the Lord (Ps 34:8). The birthright is to the blessing as the kingship of the First Advent is to the high priesthood of the Second Advent.[55]

Rebekah preparing savory meat and *bread* [H3899] in order to receive the blessing recalls Jacob preparing *bread* [H3899] and lentil soup (pottage of lentiles) in order to purchase the birthright (Gen 25:34). In the previous account of Jacob purchasing the birthright, it is bread and red soup that represent the body and blood of Christ (Gen 25:34). In the present account of Jacob taking the blessing, it is bread and meat that represent the body and blood of Christ whereby meat can be identified with blood because meat represents a blood sacrifice. The movement from purchasing the birthright to taking the blessing is a heightening of intensity, or reality, that is reinforced by the movement from the image of lentil soup (vegetable life, or lower form) to the image of savory meat (animal life, or higher form). The birthright is identified with flesh since it is received at the time of birth in the natural body, while the blessing is identified with spirit since the fullness of the blessing is received at the time of the rebirth in the spiritual, or glorified, resurrection body. The birthright is likewise identified with the death to sin while yet in the natural body, as represented by our repentance of sins in the natural body. The blessing is identified with the rebirth that comes by the power of the indwelling Holy Spirit that is our redemption in the spiritual, or glorified, resurrection body. The birthright (natural) is to the blessing (spiritual) as the natural body (lower form) is to the spiritual body (higher form).

Genesis 27:18 And he came unto his father, and said, My father: and he said, Here [am] I; who [art] thou, my son?

Only in God the Son—in the Body of Christ, glorified by God the Holy Spirit—may the faithful enter into the presence of God the Father. God the Holy Spirit, represented here by the person of Rebekah, is present with God the Son, represented prominently by Jacob standing in the place of Esau—wherein Rebekah, or at least Rebekah's purpose, is hidden, reflecting the essential subtlety of God the Spirit that is in accord with freewill.

Genesis 27:19 And Jacob said unto his father, I [am] Esau thy firstborn; I have done according as thou badest me: arise [H6965], I pray thee, sit [H3427] and eat [H398] of my venison, that thy soul [H5315] may bless [H1288] me.

---

[55] "Christ's militant reign is to cease with the accomplishment of His office as Judge ... but as King of the elect whom He has saved He will reign with them in glory for ever" (*Catholic Encyclopedia*, s.v. "eschatology"). The former office is that of king alone, while the latter office is that of king-priest and very specifically the kingship subsumed by the high priesthood.

Jacob presenting himself as Esau to Isaac is an image of the resurrection of the faithful in Christ. The faithful become Christ before the throne of God because we are the Body of Christ. The faithful before the throne of God must be one with Christ—that is, made perfect in Christ—because no sinfulness can enter into the fullness of the glory of God. And nothing truly exists, or lives, outside the fullness of the glory of God. The Lord commanding Abram to walk before him and be perfect is a prophecy of the perfection of the faithful in Christ (Gen 17:1), while the Lord warning Moses that no man can see the face of God and live is a prophecy of the judgment of the faithless (Exod 33:20). Isaac, who was previously sacrificed in Moriah, blessing Jacob in the place of Esau reflects the essential connection between the resurrection of Christ and that of the faithful in Christ. But the second son Jacob supplanting the first son Esau also reflects the second son Christ supplanting the first son Adam. The first man Adam is to the second man Christ as the First Advent of Christ is to the Second Advent of Christ. Rebekah substituting Jacob for Esau through the symbol of savory meat is our new creation in Christ through the sacrifice of Christ. Jacob presenting the required meat unto Isaac is an affirmation of the obedience of the Son unto the will of the Father that is finally the redemption of the faithful by the power of the Spirit. Our indignation at Jacob posing as Esau should be understood in light of the seeming injustice of substituting the sinless Christ in the place of sinful Adam.[56]

Jacob calling upon Isaac to *arise* [H6965], *sit* [H3427] and *eat* [H398], and finally to *bless* [H1288] reflects the First Advent pointing to the Second Advent. The word *arise* [H6965] (arise, I pray thee) has a connotation "to establish (a covenant)," reflecting the fulfillment of the Covenant of Law, the first covenant, in the First Advent. The resurrection, or arising, of Christ is the establishment of the faithful (Rom 6:5, 6:23). The word *sit* [H3427] (sit and eat) has connotations "to marry" and also "to tarry," reflecting the Son during the church age, sitting and waiting at the right hand of the Father until the appointed time of the marriage supper of the Lamb (Luke 22:69, Rev 19:7). The word *eat* [H398] (sit and eat) has a connotation "to devour, consume (by fire)," reflecting the commandment to eat the flesh of Christ (John 6:54) that will culminate in the destruction of all flesh by fire in the end times (2 Pet 3:7). The close relationship between *sitting* [H3427] (tarrying) and *eating* [H398] (consuming) also points to the destruction by fire as being the culmination of the suffering of the faithful that marks the church age. The word *bless* [H1288] (thy soul may bless) has a connotation "to kneel (down)," reflecting the righteous obedience of Christ and likewise the obedience of the faithful in

---

[56] "Jacob says to Isaac, 'I am Esau thy firstborn son,' and spiritually he spoke the truth, for he already partook of the rights of the first-born, which were perishing in his brother, and clothing himself with the goatskins he assumed the outward semblance of Esau, and was Esau all but the voice praising God, so that Esau might afterward find a place to receive a blessing. For if Jacob had not been blessed as Esau, neither would Esau perhaps have been able to receive a blessing of his own [Origen, *Commentary on John*]" (Roberts et al., *Ante-Nicene Fathers* 9:383). The blessing of the cross is deeply ironic, and therefore the prefiguring of the cross is also expected to be deeply ironic.

Christ. The word *soul* [H5315] (thy soul may bless) has a connotation "that which breathes" and is the same word used to describe the *life* [H5315] of the flesh that is the blood (Gen 9:4). The *soul* [H5315] of Isaac *blessing* [H1288] Jacob in the person of Esau points to the life that comes only through the blood of Christ and that is finally revealed in the resurrection of the faithful in Christ. The word *soul* [H5315] is also closely associated with the word *refreshed* [H5314] used to describe the Sabbath rest (Exod 31:17). This is finally the Sabbath millennium at the time of the Second Advent of Christ.

Genesis 27:20 And Isaac said unto his son, How [is it] that thou hast found [it] so quickly, my son? And he said, Because the LORD thy God brought [it] to me.

The emphasis on Jacob returning quickly to Isaac points to the haste with which Christ will return at the appointed time of the Second Advent. Jacob returning expressly unto his father Isaac reflects the Second Advent being the fulfillment of the First Advent. The image of the Lord himself bringing Jacob the meat offering points to Rebekah being a representation of God the Holy Spirit in the preparation of the meat offering.[57]

Genesis 27:21 And Isaac said unto Jacob, Come near, I pray thee, that I may feel thee, my son, whether thou [be] my very son Esau or not.

Isaac testing whether Jacob is Esau and confirming that Jacob is in fact Esau reflects the essential unity of Christ and the faithful in the Body of Christ. Adam must be Christ under the law because only Christ has fulfilled the law. Adam must be Christ in the eyes of the Father because no sin can exist in the presence of the perfect righteousness of God. Further, the Lord has freewill just as man has freewill, for man is created in the image of God. And thus God could choose to tolerate sin, but in so doing God would cease being perfect—God would cease being God. And all creation would necessarily unravel into some form of chaos because all creation is not only made in the image of God but is also sustained by the image of God. We know that all creation is made in the image of God because all things were created through Christ (John 1:3). We know that all creation is sustained by the image of God because Christ is the life that is the light of all creation (John 1:4). The Lord is all in all, and therefore nothing truly exists separated from the Lord. Not even that which is evil is something unto itself, but rather it is a corruption of the image of God.[58]

---

[57] "It is curious that Jacob referred to Jehovah in this episode as 'your God,' thus answering the question after the manner of the irreligious Esau . . . ." (Coffman 350: Gen 27:18–29). Jacob stands in the place of carnal Esau just as Christ stands in the place of fallen Adam, and it is only in so doing that the God of Isaac becomes the God of Esau, that is, fallen man is redeemed in Christ.

[58] "Goodness is, so to speak, itself: badness is only spoiled goodness. And there must be something good first before it can be spoiled" (Lewis, *Mere Christianity* 49). Only God can create, in contrast to the devil, who can only corrupt.

ESAU, JACOB, ISRAEL

Genesis 27:22 And Jacob went near unto Isaac his father; and he felt him, and said, The voice [H6963] [is] Jacob's voice [H6963], but the hands [H3027] [are] the hands [H3027] of Esau.

The word *voice* [H6963] (voice of Jacob) recalls the *voice* [H6963] of God—which was heard by Adam and Eve, mankind, as God walked in the garden of Eden (Gen 3:8)—while the word *hands* [H3027] (hands of Esau) recalls the *hand* [H3027] of Adam—which was forbidden to take, also, of the tree of life (Gen 3:22). The *voice* [H6963] of Jacob represents the spirit of man, while the *hands* [H3027] of Esau represent the flesh of man. The intangible *voice* [H6963] of a man represents his words, or what he believes, while the physical *hands* [H3027] of man represent the works of man. The former is the faith that comes by grace, while the latter is the works of the law in accordance with faith. Jacob speaking with his own voice but having the physical similitude of Esau is an image of the Holy Spirit indwelling the believer. Jacob speaking with his own voice (head) while having the physical similitude of Esau (body) is equally an image of Jesus Christ as the Head of the Body of the faithful in Christ.[59]

The inspiration of the indwelling Holy Spirit is not, however, a puppeteering of the believer. The Lord God, in all his perfection, choosing to not violate freewill is evident in the persistence of evil in the world. The indwelling Spirit is the revelation of truth, to which the faithful make a freewill choice to respond favorably. The faithful love the truth, while the faithless hate the truth. The eternal and inviolable sanctity of freewill necessitates the existence of an eternal physical body, likewise an eternal physical creation in which the individual is allowed to exercise freewill. The promised spiritual, or glorified, resurrection body is a true body—that is, the spiritual body, like the natural body, is a triune body, soul, and spirit (1 Thess 5:23). The triune image of the one God does not cease in eternity. The difference between the natural body and the spiritual body is that the former is governed by the way of carnal flesh whereas the latter is governed by the way of the Holy Spirit. The freewill response of the faithful is to love God and to desire the ways of God.

Genesis 27:23 And he discerned him not, because his hands were hairy [H8163], as his brother Esau's hands: so he blessed him.

The word *hairy* [H8163] (hairy hands) has an association "he-goat (for sin offering)" [H8163] that reflects the blood sacrifice required by the law and ultimately fulfilled in the flesh of Christ. Isaac accepting Jacob as Esau is signified by Isaac accepting the hands of Jacob and likewise the work of his hands, representing the work of the law. The work of the law that makes us

---

[59] "When pronouncing his blessing upon Jacob, Isaac said, 'The voice is Jacob's voice, but the hands are the hands of Esau.' Thus Isaac's blessings fixed upon each of his sons what should be his power. Jacob's power and function should be his voice=prayer, and Esau's might was to be in his hands [*Genesis Rabbah*]" (Rapaport, *Midrash* 82). God does answer all prayers, but the prayer, or desire of the heart, of carnal man is the way of all flesh, all the earth, which is ultimately death.

acceptable to the Father is the work of the Son on the cross. Isaac accepting and blessing Jacob in the place of Esau points to the redemption of the faithful being practicable only in Christ. The Bible is actually clear that the faithful are saved by works, but it is the perfect work of Christ, fulfilling the law, that the faithful participate in by grace and only by grace.[60]

Genesis 27:24–25 And he said, [Art] thou my very son Esau? And he said, I [am]. 25 And he said, Bring [it] near to me, and I will eat of my son's venison [H6718], that my soul may bless thee. And he brought [it] near to him, and he did eat: and he brought him wine [H3196], and he drank.

The repetition of the pronouncing of Jacob's blessing by Isaac recalls the repetition of the account of the creation of man and woman (Gen 1:27, 2:7). And this parallel is a sign of new creation. In the previous account of Isaac blessing Jacob, *bread* [H3899] and *savoury meat* (savory meat) [H4303] were emphasized, but now *venison* [H6718] and *wine* [H3196] are emphasized (Gen 27:17). The savory meat of Jacob has figuratively become the venison of Esau just as Jacob has figuratively become Esau. And the symbol of bread is replaced by the symbol of wine, which draws our attention from the First to the Second Advent. Bread, or broken bread, represents the affliction of the First Advent (Luke 22:19), while wine represents the lifeblood to be finally consumed at the Second Advent (Luke 22:20). Eating venison precedes drinking wine just as the animal sacrifices prescribed by the law precede the blood of Christ shed in fulfillment of the law. The death of the natural body under the law likewise precedes the resurrection of the spiritual, or glorified, body by grace. Jacob being required to present venison in order to be blessed points to the reality of blood sacrifice being required for our redemption. Jacob becoming Esau through the blood of goats points to the redemption of the faithful in Christ, in the Body Christ, through the blood of the cross.[61]

Genesis 27:26–27 And his father Isaac said unto him, Come near now, and kiss me, my son. 27 And he came near, and kissed him: and he smelled [H7306] the smell [H7381] of his raiment [H899], and blessed

---

[60] "This [statement that Jacob is Esau], if it be referred to those two twins, will seem a lie; but if to that for the signifying of which those deeds and words are written, He is here to be understood, in His body, which is His Church . . . . For so in a certain sort the younger brother did bear off the primacy of the elder brother, and transfer it to himself. Since then things so true, and so truthfully, be signified, what is there here that ought to be accounted to have been done or said lyingly? For when the things which are signified are not in truth things which are not, but which are, whether past or present or future, without doubt it is a true signification, and no lie [Augustine, *To Consentius: Against Lying*]" (Schaff, *Nicene and Post-Nicene Fathers: First Series* 3:492). Jesus Christ literally dies in our place, literally assuming our sins.

[61] Whether a thing or saying is understood symbolically [or spiritually] is normally determined by systemic markers, such as emphasis, repetition, and position (Perrine 214). The law is the pattern of life.

him, and said, See, the smell [H7381] of my son [is] as the smell [H7381] of a field which the LORD hath blessed:

The person of Isaac recalls the First Advent of Christ, while the person of Jacob points to the Second Advent of Christ. Isaac being kissed by Jacob then reflects the unity of the First and Second Advents of Christ. But Jacob kissing Isaac is also a strange prefiguring of Judas kissing Christ (Luke 22:48). And the ultimate suicide of Judas portends the condemnation of the natural body in general and the faithless in particular—which again connects the First and Second Advents, though in a distinctly negative way (Matt 27:5). The fate of Christ being sealed with a kiss of betrayal further reflects the connection between the crucifixion of Christ and the rebellion of Adam. The condemnation of all mankind in Adam is Jesus Christ nailed to the tree of knowledge. But the death of fallen man indeed must be joined to the death of Christ in order for the resurrection of forgiven man to be joined to the resurrection of Christ (Rom 6:5). And this is the connection between the Fall of Man and the First and Second Advents. And the necessity of this unity is again reflected in Jacob kissing Isaac before Jacob receives the blessing from Isaac. The enactment of the Judas kiss by Jacob is a further testimony that the fate of Christ was not sealed merely by the one man Judas but preordained from, actually cemented in, the foundation of the world (Rev 13:8). And Isaac actually calling upon Jacob to kiss him is an affirmation that Christ would not have his life taken from him but would lay it down of his own freewill (John 10:18).

The words *smelled* [H7306] (Isaac smelled) and *smell* [H7381] (the smell of his son) are the same words used to describe the Lord *smelling* [H7306] the sweet *savour* (savor) [H7381] of Noah's sacrifice after the Flood, a sweet *savour* (savor) [H7381] closely connected with the Lord promising to never curse the land with another Flood (Gen 8:21). The sweet savor of a sacrifice rising to heaven is an image of the prayers and hopes of the faithful rising unto God. This is likewise the faithful themselves rising unto God, especially in the resurrection of the dead. And Isaac accepting Jacob is connected with the smell of Esau's raiment just as the Lord accepting Noah is connected with the smell of his sacrifice. The word *raiment* [H899] (Esau's raiment) is derived from the root "to act or deal treacherously" [H898], whereby the raiment of Esau being placed upon Jacob represents the sins of Adam, or fallen man, placed upon Jesus Christ. The emphasis on Isaac's son smelling like and therefore being like a field the Lord has blessed recalls Adam having been formed from the dust of the ground (Gen 2:7). And this in turn points to the dominion of man in the world, especially in the resurrection of the body at the time of the restoration, or re-creation, of all creation (Isa 66:22). Isaac smelling and blessing Jacob but pronouncing that Jacob already smells as one blessed is an affirmation that the blessing of man, specifically the blessing of the Son of man, proceeds from heaven and that the blessing of man has been preordained from the foundation of the world.[62]

---

[62] "[A]s to the smell [of Esau's raiment], many interpreters consider this as a type and figure of the acceptance of believers with God, being clothed with . . . the righteousness

JACOB AND ESAU

Genesis 27:28–29 Therefore God give thee of the dew [H2919] of heaven [H8064], and the fatness [H4924] of the earth [H776], and plenty [H7230] of corn [H1715] and wine [H8492]: 29 Let people [H5971] serve [H5647] thee, and nations [H3816] bow down [H7812] to thee: be lord [H1376] over thy brethren [H251], and let thy mother's [H517] sons [H1121] bow down [H7812] to thee: cursed [H779] [be] every one that curseth [H779] thee, and blessed [H1288] [be] he that blesseth [H1288] thee.

Isaac blessing Jacob in the context of Jacob representing himself as the person of Esau points to the blessing of Christ encompassing Adam, or mankind in Adam. In having purchased the birthright and now taking the blessing, Jacob supplants Esau and becomes the firstborn just as the Body of Christ supplants the body of Adam. The blessing of Adam in Christ is the blessing of all the faithful of all the ages in Christ and, therefore, represents the summation and culmination of all creation in Christ. And this completion of all creation in the blessing of the one man Christ is evident in the progression of the blessing of Jacob, which marks the unfolding of the seven millennia of creation. Each millennium is marked by the dichotomy of flesh and spirit that is the foremost pattern of creation. But in the progression of the blessing, a convolution is additionally evident between the first and second millennia from Adam and also between the fifth and sixth millennia from Adam. The first closely related pair are the "dew of heaven" and the "fatness of the earth," reflecting the coupling of the first and second millennia. This is the connection between the original creation of Adam and the new creation, which is represented by the Flood following the death of Adam. The latter closely related pair are "be lord over thy brethren" and "thy mother's sons bow down to thee," reflecting the coupling of the fifth and sixth millennia. This is the church age connecting the First and Second Advents. The third and fourth millennia from Adam are then implicitly grouped together as a distinct period, marking the formation of the nation of Israel. The seventh and eighth millennia from Adam are likewise grouped together, representing the unity of the millennial reign and the opening of eternity.[63]

The two words *heaven* [H8064] and *earth* [H776] recall the same words used to describe the original creation heralding the first millennium (Gen 1:1). The words *earth* [H776] and *heaven* [H8064] evoke literal images of "land" and "sky." But land and sky parallel flesh and spirit, the union of which is the fundamental paradigm of all creation. The word *fatness* [H4924] (fatness of the earth) is derived from the root "to grow fat" [H8080], which has connotations "to

---

of Christ their elder brother . . . ." (Gill 1:149; Gen 27:27). Jesus Christ is simultaneously the second born and the firstborn.

[63] "Now, certainly more is comprised in this blessing [of Jacob] than appears at first; it must amount to an entail of the promise of the Messiah . . . First, That from him should come the *Messiah*, that should have a sovereign *dominion on earth*. . . . Secondly, That from him should come *the church* that should be particularly owned and favoured *by Heaven*" (Wesley 1:107; Gen 27:27). Christ the Head is followed by the faithful, the Body of Christ, just as the earthly, or natural, is followed by the heavenly, or spiritual.

become prosperous and arrogant" and also "to become dull and unreceptive." This is the apostasy of antediluvian man. The word *dew* [H2919] (dew of heaven) means "night-mist, dew," which reflects the connection between the destruction by the floodwaters and the darkness of the antediluvian period. The ironic comparison of the floodwaters to a mere mist points to a far greater destruction in the end times. The dew of heaven is further connected with the manna from heaven (Exod 16:14) and, thereby, reinforces the connection between the Flood and the First Advent since Christ himself would be the true manna from heaven (John 6:58). And the *fatness* [H4924] (of the earth) compared with the *dew* [H2919] (of heaven) again reflects the dichotomy of flesh and spirit. Also note that the symmetry marking the first and second millennia is ABA'B', that is, "dew" (A) "heaven" (B) paralleling "fatness" (A') "earth" (B'). This reflects the repetition of the act of creation represented by the time of the Flood. Also, the more common ordering of "flesh" followed by "spirit" is reversed in the text, with the "dew of heaven" being followed by the "fatness of the earth," which further implies a rotation of the original creation forward to the time of the destruction by water.[64]

The pair "corn" and "wine" mark the third millennium and again reflect flesh and spirit. The word *corn* (grain) [H1715] (plenty of corn) is derived from the root "to multiply, increase" [H1711], reflecting the call of Abraham in the third millennium to become a multitude literally in the flesh (Gen 17:5).[65] The symbol of corn, or grain, further evokes an image of bread that is also commonly used as a symbol of the body, or flesh, and thereby again of the multiplication of flesh (1 Cor 10:17). The word *plenty* [H7230] (plenty of corn) means "multitude, abundance, greatness" and, thereby, reinforces the image of the multiplication of flesh, specifically the multiplication of the faithful represented by the call of Abraham. The word *wine* [H8492] means "fresh or new wine," reflecting the newness of the new covenant in Christ that is signified by wine and blood. Additionally, the word *wine* [H8492] is derived from the root "to take possession of, inherit, dispossess" [H3423], which reflects spiritual man supplanting natural man in the new covenant. The images of *corn* (grain) [H1715] and *wine* (new wine) [H8492] being identified with the third millennium is further affirmed by Melchizedek offering bread and wine in the blessing of Abraham (Gen 14:18). Abraham being blessed with the bounty of the earth after the Flood marks the beginning of the establishment of the faithful in Christ. The corn and wine of Abraham point to the body and blood of Christ.

The pair "people serve" and "nations bow down" together mark the fourth millennium and again reflect the dichotomy of flesh and spirit. The fourth millennium begins with the proclamation of the Davidic kingdom and ends with the conception of Christ as king of kings. The contrast between *people* [H5971]

---

[64] The one God has created everything in pairs—for example, man and woman, earth and heaven, and this world and the next, *Deuteronomy Rabbah* (Cohen, *Rabbinic Sages* 4). All creation has been formed through the one person of Jesus Christ, God the Son, who is true man and true God.

[65] Etymology per *Strong's*, not *Brown-Driver-Briggs*, but regardless the image of corn, or grain, being as a multitude and thereby relating a multitude is self-evident.

and *nations* [H3816] and likewise the contrast between *serving* [H5647] and *bowing down* [H7812] represent a corresponding intensification rather than a distinction. The word *people* [H5971] (let people serve thee) has a connotation "kinsmen," reflecting the collective offspring of Jacob serving the single Messianic line through David. In contrast, the word *nations* [H3816] (let nations bow down to thee) points to the subjugation of the surrounding nations under the kingship of David. The emphasis on kinsmen is an emphasis on flesh, while the transition to nations represents something larger, or more significant. Spirit likewise transcends flesh. The word *bow down* [H7812] has a connotation "worship." The shift from *serving* [H5647] to *bowing down* [H7812] points to the culmination of the Davidic kingship in the birth of the Lord as king of kings. And this is ultimately natural man being supplanted by spiritual man. This is the way of flesh being supplanted by the way of the Spirit. This is the Covenant of Law being supplanted by the Covenant of Grace. The pair "people serve" and "nations bow down," focusing exclusively on the fourth millennium, point to the pivotal importance of the incarnation—which is the double portion belonging to the Lord himself, being true man and true God.

The closely related pair "be lord over thy brethren" and "thy mother's sons bow down" mark the fifth and sixth millennia and again exemplify flesh and spirit. The prophecy of becoming *lord* [H1376] represents the victory of Christ in the beginning of the fifth millennium. The prophecy of *bowing down* [H7812], which marks the sixth millennium, parallels the *bowing down* [H7812] that marks the fourth millennium—the one pointing to the birth of Christ at the First Advent, the other pointing to the rebirth in Christ at the Second Advent. The emphasis on *brethren* [H251] and *mother's* [H517] *sons* [H1121] points to the essential blood kinship between the faithful and Christ, while the shift from *brethren* [H251] to *mother's* [H517] *sons* [H1121] reflects the coming fullness of the Holy Spirit. The anointing of the Spirit is generally identified with the feminine and specifically with Jacob's mother, Rebekah, in the present context. The former "be lord over thy brethren" represents the victory over the flesh and likewise the submission and repentance in the flesh, while the latter "thy mother's sons bow down" represents the worship in the spirit and likewise the redemption by the Spirit. Also note that the pair "be lord over brethren" and "mother's sons bow down" show an AB|B'A' mirror symmetry, that is, "be lord over" (A) "brethren" (B) mirroring "mother's sons" (B') "bow down" (A'). The convolution of the fifth and sixth millennia reflects the unity of the church age connecting the First and Second Advents, while the mirror symmetry points to the reconstitution of the fundamental elements of the First Advent at the time of the Second Advent. A notable example of this mirroring is the reconstitution of the nation of Israel in the modern age.

The final pair "cursed be every one that curseth thee" and "blessed be he that blesseth thee" represent the resurrection of all the dead in the seventh millennium, either to condemnation or to eternal life (John 5:29). This final pair can also be compared to the seventh and eighth millennia, the former concluding the final judgment and the latter opening eternal life. The former curse is the condemnation of natural man, or figuratively flesh, while the latter blessing is the exaltation of spiritual man, or figuratively spirit. The *curse* [H779] of the faithless in the seventh millennium is the same *curse* [H779] of the serpent in the first millennium (Gen 3:14), while the *blessing* [H1288] of the seventh millennium is the same *blessing* [H1288] of the seventh day (Gen 2:3). Those who bless Jacob will be blessed, while those who curse Jacob will be cursed. For our salvation comes only through faith in the one man Jesus and only in the one man Jesus. The persistent pairing of images of flesh and spirit throughout the millennia testifies to the essential duality of flesh and spirit impressed upon all creation. This is Jesus Christ embodying the Covenants of Law and Grace. This is creation formed in the unity, or oneness, of the image of God, the twofold natures of Christ, and finally the fullness of the Trinity. The current world is truly like a blurred image of the world to come (1 Cor 13:12).[66]

Genesis 27:30 And it came to pass, as soon as Isaac had made an end [H3615] of blessing Jacob, and Jacob was yet scarce gone out from the presence [H6440] of Isaac his father, that Esau his brother came in from his hunting.

The word *presence* [H6440] (presence of Isaac) is the same word used to describe the *presence* [H6440] of the Lord God in the garden (Gen 3:8). The emphasis on Jacob and Esau both appearing before the presence, or face, of Isaac testifies to all peoples, both good and evil, being required to appear before God on the last day that is the last millennium (Rev 20:5). The rejection of Esau following the acceptance of Jacob reflects the resurrection unto damnation following the resurrection unto life (John 5:29). The faithful will be resurrected at the beginning of the last millennium, while the faithless will be resurrected at the end of the last millennium. But the rejection of Esau occurring on the very heels of the acceptance of Jacob simultaneously reflects the close relationship between the two resurrections, specifically the fundamental bifurcation of freewill. A choice must be made, and that choice is mutually exclusive. The Father recognizes and accepts the second born Christ in the place of the firstborn Adam, but the Father does not recognize, or accept, the firstborn Adam when he of himself enters in separation from the second born Christ. Esau following on the heels of Jacob further prefigures the tribulation that will immediately follow the resurrection and rapture of the faithful.[67]

---

[66] "More is certainly comprised in this blessing [of Jacob] than appears *prima facie* . . . It must amount to an entail of the promise of the Messiah, and of the church; . . . Jacob's dominion over Esau was to be only typical of this, [Gen 49:10], . . . [W]hen Isaac afterwards confirmed the blessing to Jacob, he called it *the blessing of Abraham*, [28:4]" (Henry 1:165–66; Gen 27:18–29). The blessing of father Abraham being given by his only legitimate son, Isaac, unto Jacob, the prolific offspring of Abraham and Isaac, is an image of the Trinity enveloping and thereby sanctifying the faithful.

[67] The formal tribulation period precedes the seventh, or Sabbath, millennium, but the final destruction by fire establishing the new creation follows the Sabbath millennium, such that there is a first and second destruction by fire, likewise a first and second casting into the lake of fire, and likewise a first and second death—testifying to the

JACOB AND ESAU

The word *end* [H3615] (end of the blessing) has a connotation "to perish, be destroyed" but is also the same word used to describe heaven and earth being *finished* [H3615] at the time of the original creation (Gen 2:1). The juxtaposition of death and life points to the renewal of all things in the end times. Isaac accepting Jacob in the place of Esau is an image of the resurrection unto eternal life of the faithful in Christ, while Isaac rejecting Esau is an image of the resurrection unto eternal condemnation of the faithless separated from Christ (John 5:28–29). The resurrection of the faithful precedes the resurrection of the faithless (Rev 20:4–6) because right judgment, which is necessarily righteous judgment, begins with the house of God (1 Pet 4:17). This is the case also because, not coincidentally, it is the faithful in Christ and only in Christ—or in accordance with Christ—that will finally participate in the judgment of the faithless (Heb 11:7, Matt 19:28, Rev 3:21). And in the renewal of all things—heaven and earth—the spiritual man necessarily preceding the natural man represents an essential reversal of the fallen world order, which recalls the second man Christ originally creating the first man Adam. The resurrection unto damnation following the resurrection unto life is also paralleled by the final tribulation period following the resurrection and rapture of the faithful. The first will be last, and the last will be first (Mark 9:35). The spiritual, or glorified, resurrection body will supplant the natural body.[68]

Genesis 27:31 And he also had made savoury meat, and brought it unto his father, and said unto his father, Let my father arise [H6965], and eat [H398] of his son's venison, that thy soul may bless [H1288] me.

Jacob and Esau both presenting blood sacrifices is an affirmation that all men must suffer and die in the flesh but that the wicked do suffer and die in vain (Gal 3:4). Jacob previously calling upon Isaac to *arise* [H6965], *sit* [H3427] and *eat* [H398], and finally to *bless* [H1288] reflects the First Advent pointing to the Second Advent. This is likewise the resurrection of the faithful at the beginning of the millennial kingdom (Rev 20:4–6) pointing to the renewal of all things at the end of the millennial kingdom (Rev 21:1). Esau now calling upon Isaac to *arise* [H6965], *eat* [H398], and finally to *bless* [H1288] parallels the previous account of Jacob and Isaac, but the call to *sit* [H3427] has been negated. The word *sit* [H3427] has connotations "to marry" and also "to tarry," reflecting the union of Christ and the faithful in Christ. This is the time of the church age preceding and awaiting the Second Advent. This is likewise the time

---

resurrection of life being separated from the resurrection of damnation, likewise the resurrection and rapture preceding the formal second coming of Christ, likewise the First and Second Advents of Christ, and likewise the first and second men Adam and Jesus Christ, Rev 19:20, 20:14–15.

[68] "The Jews, like Esau, hunted *after the law of righteousness* [Gen 27:31], yet missed of the blessing of righteousness, *because they sought it by the works of the law* [Gen 27:32]; while the Gentiles, who, like Jacob, sought it by faith in the oracle of God, obtained it by force, with that violence which the kingdom of heaven suffers [Matt 11:12]" (Henry 1:167; Gen 27:30–40). The law precedes grace, but grace finally subsumes the law.

of the millennial kingdom of Christ preceding and awaiting the renewal of all things. Esau negating the call to *sit* [H3427] therefore represents in his person a symbolic denial of the marriage of the Lamb. The word *bless* [H1288] has the same connotation "to kneel (down)" as it did in the account of Jacob. In the case of Esau, however, the blessing becomes a curse, referring not to the faithful worshipping the Lord God but to the faithless cowering before the incontestable power of God Almighty. Every knee shall bow, and every tongue shall confess (Phil 2:10–11). Even the demons believe that God exists, but they tremble at the knowledge (Jas 2:19). And Esau negating the call to *sit* (or tarry) [H3427] finally portends the devil knowing that his time is short (Rev 12:12).

Genesis 27:32   And Isaac his father said unto him, Who [art] thou? And he said, I [am] thy son, thy firstborn Esau.

The second man Jesus Christ (1 Cor 15:47) is the firstborn (Col 1:18) among many brothers (Rom 8:29). But Isaac not recognizing Esau portends the Lord not recognizing the faithless (Luke 13:27). No man knows the Son except the Father, and no man knows the Father except the Son and those to whom the Son reveals the Father (Matt 11:27).

Genesis 27:33   And Isaac trembled very exceedingly, and said, Who? where [is] he that hath taken venison, and brought [it] me, and I have eaten of all before thou camest, and have blessed him? yea, [and] he shall be blessed.

Isaac finally recognizing Esau is Isaac finally recognizing that Esau has been rejected. Isaac trembling at the rejection of Esau portends the sheer horror that will be the condemnation of the faithless. The initial questioning of who came before Esau represents the mystery of Christ, likewise the mystery of the Body of Christ, being only now revealed (Col 1:26). The strong statement that the one who came first would definitely be blessed is an affirmation of the undeniable nature of the will of God for the salvation of the faithful in Christ. But one should not think that God in any way violates freewill. The will of God is undeniable, or relentless, because it is the perfect union of justice and mercy, constituting the very fabric of creation.

Genesis 27:34   And when Esau heard [H8085] the words of his father, he cried [H6817] with a great and exceeding bitter [H4751] cry, and said unto his father, Bless me, [even] me also, O my father.

The word *heard* [H8085] (Esau heard the words) has a connotation "obey," reflecting the idea that Esau must submit himself to Isaac. And this is an affirmation of the power and authority of Jesus Christ over even the spirit of disobedience. Esau *crying* [H6817] recalls the same word used to describe the blood of Abel *crying* [H6817] from the ground (Gen 4:10). And the rejection of the firstborn Esau thereby recalls the rejection of the firstborn Cain (Gen 4:11).

JACOB AND ESAU

The emphasis on *bitter* [H4751] crying points to the *bitter* [H4751] water that brings a curse upon adultery (Num 5:18). And the adultery of man in the flesh represents a spiritual disobedience to God. Esau despised his birthright in accordance with his nature, and now his blessing is taken away in accordance with the providential will of God (Gen 25:23, 25:34, Heb 12:16–17).

Genesis 27:35 And he said, Thy brother came with subtilty [H4820], and hath taken [H3947] away thy blessing.

The word *subtilty* (subtlety) [H4820] (thy brother came with subtilty) means "deceit, treachery," reflecting not the wickedness of Jacob but rather the wickedness of Esau embodied by Jacob. Christ would likewise become a curse on the cross for the sake of us sinners (Gal 3:13). The Lord loves Jacob, but the Lord hates Esau (Rom 9:13). The word *taken* [H3947] (taken thy blessing) has a connotation "to be taken in marriage," which reflects the nature of the blessing of God as being like a marriage covenant. The blessing of the faithful in the marriage supper of the Lamb (Rev 19:9) is the result of the Lord taking the blessing for himself and those in him (Rev 17:14). And worthy is the Lamb that was slain to receive power and riches and wisdom and strength and honor and glory and blessing (Rev 5:12).

Genesis 27:36 And he said, Is not he rightly named Jacob? for he hath supplanted me these two times: he took away my birthright [H1062]; and, behold, now he hath taken away my blessing [H1293]. And he said, Hast thou not reserved a blessing for me?

The word *birthright* [H1062] means "right of the firstborn," representing the way of flesh. The word *blessing* [H1293] is derived from the root "to bless, kneel" [H1288] and, thereby, evokes an image of worship as the way of the Spirit. The birthright necessarily precedes the blessing just as the death in the flesh necessarily precedes the rebirth in the Spirit. All men die but this speaks of the death to sin that must precede the resurrection unto eternal life. And it is only the faithful, according to their own freewill, who embrace the death to sin. That the natural must precede the spiritual is therefore according to the inviolable sanctity of freewill. The birthright (right of the flesh) precedes the blessing (gift of the Spirit) just as the natural body (dominion of flesh) precedes the spiritual, or glorified, body (dominion of the Spirit) just as the First Advent (incarnation in the flesh of man) precedes the Second Advent (glorification by the Spirit) just as the kingship (authority, or victory, over flesh and death) precedes the high priesthood (administration of the Spirit).

The emphasis on Jacob having twice supplanted Esau points to the First and Second Advents of Christ and expressly to the dominions over flesh and spirit. Esau acknowledging that Jacob had been rightly named is a testimony that divine providence is undeniable even by fallen man in a fallen world. But Esau continuing to seek a blessing other than that of Jacob portends the faithless relentlessly following the desires of the flesh unto what is a complete destruction. The first is displaced by the second, and the first must be displaced by the second. Jesus Christ is the only begotten Son of the Father, conceived by the Holy Spirit (Matt 1:20). All things are delivered unto the Son (Matt 11:27). And it is Christ that is our hope. The second man Jesus Christ (1 Cor 15:47) is the firstborn (Col 1:18) among many brothers (Rom 8:29). The birthright and the blessing belong to the firstborn. Christ is king of kings and high priest (Heb 7:1) after the Order of Melchizedek (Heb 5:10).[69]

Genesis 27:37 And Isaac answered and said unto Esau, Behold, I have made him thy lord [H1376], and all his brethren have I given to him for servants [H5650]; and with corn [H1715] and wine [H8492] have I sustained him: and what shall I do now unto thee, my son?

The blessing of Jacob being described to Esau represents the blessing as viewed from the perspective of fallen man. This summary of the blessing of Jacob traces backward from the sixth millennium to the third millennium but excludes the first and second millennia. The Lord looks forward, while fallen man looks backward. And fallen man rejects the sovereignty of God that has been displayed in the original creation of the first millennium and also in the new creation through the floodwaters of the second millennium. The former word *serve* [H5647], identified with the blessing of Jacob, recalls the positive image of Adam being put into the garden of Eden to *dress* [H5647] it (Gen 2:15). In contrast, the latter word *servants* [H5650], now identified with Esau, recalls the negative image of Canaan being cursed to be a *servant* [H5650] of *servants* [H5650] unto his brethren (Gen 9:25). But the word *servants* [H5650] (brethren given for servants) is actually derived from the root "to work, serve" [H5647], which is a close relationship reflecting the fundamental unity of freewill, always presenting itself as a bifurcation or potential bifurcation into good and evil choices. Further, the same word *lord* [H1376] (made him thy lord), as previously used in the original blessing of Jacob, is here again used in the recounting of the blessing to Esau (Gen 27:29). And this reflects the fundamental dominion of Jesus Christ over both the living and the dead, over both Jacob and Esau, even though it is only the living, or the faithful, that belong to the Body of Christ.

The connection between the sixth and third millennia is the new creation, or new beginning, represented by the call of Abraham and that specifically following the Flood. The image of *corn* (grain) [H1715] and *wine* (new wine) [H8492], connected with the third millennium, represents the union of body and blood that is the union of flesh and spirit. This is the primordial union of the dust of the ground and the breath of God in Adam (Gen 2:7). And this is the promised union, or communion, of man and God in the Body of Christ

---

[69] "[H]e [Jacob] did not take it [the birthright] away from him either by force or fraud, Esau sold it to him for a mess of pottage; . . . he had bought of him the birthright, the blessing annexed to it went along with it, and of right belonged to Jacob . . . ." (Gill 1:150; Gen 27:36). The birthright and the blessing are one inheritance.

(Eph 5:32). This is our original creation and our new creation. The act of creation being identified with the call of Abraham points to the importance of the establishment of the chosen people after and only after the repentance signified by the Flood (Gen 6:6). The reordering of the blessing of Jacob—as described, or given, to Esau—reflects the significance of the life of Christ to fallen man. And this significance is foremost the recapitulation of the history of the call of Israel, representing the chosen faithful people of God (Gal 3:7). That the life of Christ is identified with the history of the Jews is evident, for example, in Christ retracing the steps of the Jews sojourning in Egypt (Hos 11:1, Matt 2:15). The importance of this new reality, expressly to fallen man, is that the recapitulation of the call of the chosen people in the life of Christ signifies the essential justification of fallen man in the Body of Christ.

Genesis 27:38 And Esau said unto his father, Hast thou but one blessing, my father? bless me, [even] me also, O my father. And Esau lifted up [H5375] his voice [H6963], and wept [H1058].

The firstborn Esau *lifting up* [H5375] his *voice* [H6963] and *weeping* [H1058] for his own sake recalls Hagar *lifting up* [H5375] her *voice* [H6963] and *weeping* [H1058] for her firstborn Ishmael (Gen 21:16). Jacob is most closely identified with the Second Advent, while Isaac is most closely identified with the First Advent. Esau is then most closely identified with the faithlessness of the whole world culminating in the final apostasy. And Ishmael is most closely identified with the faithlessness of Israel at the time of the First Advent. The supplanting of Esau recalls the supplanting of Ishmael just as the rejection of the faithless in the end times recalls the rejection of the faithless at the time of the crucifixion. Esau seeks a blessing separated from the blessing of Jacob just as the faithless seek a way of flesh separated from the way of the Holy Spirit. This is the way of the law that is the death required by the law. This is in contrast to the way of the Spirit that is the eternal life that comes by grace and only by grace. The identification of a false blessing with Esau portends the final apostasy in the end times being the culmination of all apostasy, spiritually the summation of all apostasy. Further, the supplanting of the firstborn Esau parallels not only the supplanting of the firstborn Ishmael but also the supplanting of the firstborn Cain, which testifies to the faithless throughout all time rejecting the second man Jesus Christ (Gen 4:25). The truth is that there is only one blessing in the one man Christ, namely, the blessing of the Holy Spirit.[70]

Genesis 27:39–40 And Isaac his father answered and said unto him, Behold, thy dwelling [H4186] shall be the fatness of the earth, and of the dew of heaven from above; 40 And by thy sword shalt thou live, and shalt

---

[70] "On the blessings pronounced on Jacob and Esau . . . . The truth is, it was their *posterity*, and not themselves, that were the objects of these blessings. Jacob, personally, gained no benefit; Esau, personally, sustained no loss" (Clarke 1:174; Gen 27:46). The nature of prophecy is fractal, encompassing but also transcending the individual.

serve thy brother; and it shall come to pass when thou shalt have the dominion, that thou shalt break his yoke from off thy neck.

Isaac had previously *given* [H5414] the "dew of heaven" and "fatness of the earth" to Jacob, but now Isaac pronounces that Esau would merely *dwell* [H4186] in the "fatness of the earth" and "dew of heaven," which rightfully belongs to Jacob (Gen 27:28). The blessing of Jacob, as previously described to Esau, traced backward from the sixth millennium to the third millennium but excluded the first and second millennia (Gen 27:37). In contrast, the blessing of Esau separated from Jacob now emphasizes the first and second millennia according to the "dew of heaven" and "fatness of the earth" and, thereby, identifies Esau with the Fall of Man and the closely related destruction by the Flood. Also, the ordering of the "fatness of the earth" and "dew of heaven" is here reversed for Esau, as compared with the original blessing of Jacob in the place of Esau (Gen 27:28). And this again connects the person of Esau to Adam, or fallen man, since the blessing of a person represents the nature of a person. The blessing of Esau is a reverse image of the blessing of Jacob just as the fall in Adam is a reverse of the exaltation in Christ (Rom 5:14). The person of Esau is most closely connected with the church age culminating in the end times, whereby Esau being connected with the original condemnation of Adamkind and the corresponding destruction by water points to the final apostasy in the end times and the corresponding final destruction by fire (2 Pet 3:6–8).[71]

The blessing of Esau is further marked by the sign of the sword, foreshadowing an unprecedented level of warfare in the end times. Man does war against man, and man will war against man, but man will finally war against God himself (Rev 17:14). And all wars prefigure this final war just as all wars represent war against God. Esau serving Jacob in the context of living by the sword represents the Lord working all things together for the good of the faithful (Rom 8:28). But the sword being viewed in the hand of Esau, in contrast to that of Jacob, is nonetheless an affirmation that man ultimately condemns himself, in contrast to being condemned by God. The prophecy that Esau would have the dominion and throw off the yoke of Jacob further portends the culmination of the final apostasy in the dominion of the dragon being cast down from heaven (Rev 12:9). Man warring against man parallels man warring against God just as the condemnation of man parallels the dragon being cast down. But in all these things, the sword of man ironically prefigures the sword of the Word of God just as the one man Adam prefigures the one man Jesus Christ (Rom 5:14). The sword of man is the sword of the flesh, while the sword of the Word of God is the sword of the Spirit (Eph 6:17). The sword

---

[71] "The rabbis taught: . . . Ben David [Messiah] will not come until the denouncers will increase. According to others [other rabbis], unless the disciples will decrease . . . And some others [other rabbis] also say unless they will renounce their hope to be redeemed" (Rodkinson, *Talmud: Sanhedrin* 8[16]:302). The nature of prophecy is poetic, always functioning on all levels of reality.

HATRED

Genesis 27:41 And Esau hated Jacob because of the blessing wherewith his father blessed him: and Esau said in his heart [H3820], The days of mourning for my father are at hand; then will I slay [H2026] my brother Jacob.

The word *heart* [H3820] (heart of Esau) recalls the Lord proclaiming that every imagination of the thoughts of the *heart* [H3820] of man is evil continually (Gen 6:5). The emphasis on Esau uttering his hatred in his heart speaks of the nature of his heart, that is, of his true innermost person being utterly evil (Matt 15:18).[73] The word *slay* [H2026] (I will slay my brother) recalls the same word used to describe Cain *slaying* [H2026] Abel and, thereby, reflects Esau's spiritual lineage from the serpent through Cain (Gen 4:8). Esau hates Jacob because Jacob's blood offering of the flock was accepted by their father (Gen 27:9) just as Cain hated Abel because Abel's blood offering of the flock was accepted by God (Gen 4:4–5). The text does not state that Esau hates Jacob because Jacob took the blessing, rather simply because of the blessing. The Lord had clearly decreed while the brothers were yet in the womb that the older would serve the younger, and neither father Isaac nor the firstborn Esau disputes this basic reality (Gen 25:23). The children of the devil hate the children of God without justification (1 John 3:10–15).[74]

The person of Isaac is most closely identified with the First Advent, while the person of Jacob is most closely identified with the Second Advent. The symbolic sacrifice of Isaac in Moriah represents the crucifixion at the time of the First Advent, while the old age of Isaac represents the end of the church age proceeding from the First Advent (Gen 22:2). Jacob being blessed by Isaac

---

[72] "We cannot be united with God [in eternal life] unless we freely choose to love him [in this life]. . . . This state of definitive self-exclusion from communion with God and the blessed is called 'hell' " (Rom. Catholic Church, *Catechism* 292). The reality of mortal life, or lesser life, is necessarily derived from and connected with immortal life, or true life, wherein the present life must have meaning and that meaning is necessarily freewill, the one thing that separates humanity, created in the image of God, from the rest of natural, mortal creation.

[73] In Talmudic literature—e.g., *Baba Bathra*—the heart is normally regarded as the seat of intelligence (Cohen, *Rabbinic Sages* 247). Contrary to the normal historical-grammatical method, which strives to relate to the original audience, the truth is that cultural vantage points are ancillary to the sacred text itself and also to natural law.

[74] "Cain despised his brother, and so, immediately after, he despised God. How despised Him? Mark his insolent answer to God; 'Am I my brother's keeper?' [Gen 4:9]. Again, Esau despised his brother, and he too despised God. Wherefore God said, 'Jacob have I loved, but Esau have I hated' [Rom 9:13, Mal 1:2–3] [Chrysostom, *Homilies on 2 Timothy*]" (Schaff, *Nicene and Post-Nicene Fathers: First Series* 13:501). To hate mankind is to hate the image of God.

specifically in Isaac's old age then represents the multitude of faithful being exalted specifically at the time of the Second Advent. And this is appropriate since it is Jacob, being the prolific son, who spiritually embodies the multitude of offspring promised to Abraham. The second son Jacob is raised up according to the will of his mother, Rebekah, to be presented as the firstborn to his father, Isaac. This represents the body of believers, or figuratively the first man Adam, being raised up from the dead by the power of the Holy Spirit in order to be presented in the Son unto the Father. Esau then devising in his heart to kill Jacob after the time of Isaac's death portends the final apostasy of the antichrist, seeking to fight even against God after the time of the resurrection and rapture (Rev 17:14). And Rebekah ultimately being told the words of Esau's heart foreshadows the revelation of the inner natures of all men in the final judgment of the living and the dead (1 Cor 4:5).[75]

Genesis 27:42   And these words of Esau her elder son were told to Rebekah: and she sent and called Jacob her younger son, and said unto him, Behold, thy brother Esau, as touching thee, doth comfort himself, [purposing] to kill thee.

The Holy Spirit leads the Son in the way of the flesh and in the way of the spirit, that is, in the way of death and resurrection (Luke 4:1).

Genesis 27:43   Now therefore, my son, obey [H8085] my voice [H6963]; and arise [H6965], flee [H1272] thou to Laban [H3837] my brother to Haran [H2771];

Rebekah calling upon Jacob to *obey* [H8085] (obey her voice), *arise* [H6965], and *flee* [H1272] reflects the threefold creation of Adam followed by the First and Second Advents. Jacob now being called to obedience recalls Adam originally being called to obedience (Gen 2:17). Jacob called to *obey* [H8085] the *voice* [H6963] of Rebekah specifically recalls Adam *hearkening* [H8085] unto the *voice* [H6963] of Eve and, thereby, emphasizes the original curse of mankind in Adam (Gen 3:17). The word *arise* [H6965] means "to arise, stand up" and has a connotation "to be established, confirmed," reflecting the resurrection of Jesus Christ and the corresponding establishment of the dominion of Christ over death. Jacob purchasing the birthright and taking the blessing also reflects the death and resurrection of Christ and likewise the First and Second Advents of Christ. The word *flee* [H1272] means "to go through, flee" and has a connotation "to hasten, come quickly," reflecting Christ hastening to establish the Body of Christ in the resurrection of the dead, specifically because of the suffering of the end times. The image of Jacob fleeing for his life represents the promised blessing of eternal life being preserved in Christ after his death and resurrection. Jacob leaving Canaan represents our continuing separation from

---

[75] "He [Esau] has good hope to recover his birthright by killing thee [Jacob]" (Whittingham et al., *Geneva Bible* 13L n. m; Gen 27:42). The vain hope of the devil.

the fullness of God even during the church age. The separation of mankind from God is because of sin and represents the visible sign of the call to repentance. Men still sin during the church age, and men are still called to repentance during the church age, and therefore men must remain separated from the fullness of the presence of God during the church age.

The original migration of Abram from Ur of the Chaldees to the land of Haran and finally to the land of Canaan represents the threefold promise, repentance, and redemption of God that is the threefold formation of Adam followed by the First and Second Advents. Jacob now fleeing to the land of *Haran* [H2771], in contrast to *Ur* [H218] of the *Chaldees* [H3778], therefore represents an emphasis on the First Advent, likewise the death represented by the baptism of repentance (Gen 11:31). This is the call of the faithful in the church age that proceeds from the First Advent. Jacob taking the blessing reflects the resurrection of Christ at the time of the First Advent and likewise the resurrection of the faithful in Christ at the time of the Second Advent. And thus the promise embodied by the resurrected Christ envelopes the entire church age, culminating finally in the resurrection of the faithful at the time of the Second Advent. The name *Laban* [H3837] (flee to Laban) is derived from the root "to be white" [H3835], which has a connotation "to be purified" and is connected with the image of burning bricks for the construction of the tower of Babel (Gen 11:3). The image of purification represents the perfecting and likewise the completing of the Body of Christ throughout the church age. The image of burning bricks, especially as related to the apostasy of the tower of Babel, portends the final destruction that will come by fire (2 Pet 3:7).

Genesis 27:44 And tarry [H3427] with him a few [H259] days, until thy brother's fury [H2534] turn away [H7725];

The word *tarry* [H3427] (tarry a few days) has a connotation "to marry," reflecting the union of Christ and the faithful in Christ, especially in death and resurrection (Rom 6:5) as marked by the sign of the third day (1 Cor 15:4). The word *few* [H259] (a few days until) has a connotation "once for all," which reflects the one death in the flesh (Heb 9:27–28) and, thereby, also points to the resurrection of Christ on the third day, likewise the resurrection of the Body of Christ in the third millennium from Christ (Matt 20:19). The word *few* [H259] is also connected with the word *eleven* [H6240, H259], foreshadowing the eleven sons born unto Jacob before his returning to Canaan (Gen 32:22). The word *fury* [H2534] (brother's fury) means "heat, rage" and has a connotation "burning anger," foreshadowing the raging of the nations (Acts 4:25–26) and likewise the raging of the dragon in the nations (Rev 12:12), culminating in the foretold destruction by fire (2 Pet 3:7). The word *turn away* [H7725] (brother's fury) means "to turn back, return," portending the final fury against the Body of Christ at the time of the Second Advent being an echoing of the first fury against Christ himself at the time of the First Advent.

ESAU, JACOB, ISRAEL

Genesis 27:45 Until thy brother's anger [H639] turn away [H7725] from thee, and he forget [H7911] [that] which thou hast done to him: then I will send, and fetch [H3947] thee from thence: why should I be deprived also of you both [H8147] in one [H259] day?

Rebekah actually sending for her son Jacob is nowhere recorded, which is a subtle testimony to the continuing depravity of Esau. But Jacob finally returning unto the promised land after twenty years is nevertheless connected to Rebekah now foretelling his return (Gen 31:38). And thus Rebekah never formally sending for Jacob finally represents the subtlety of the Holy Spirit, especially during the church age. The depravity of mankind and the subtleness, or separateness, of God are both identified with Rebekah never overtly sending for Jacob, which identifies the universal separation of man and God with the sinful nature of man. Rebekah lamenting that she should not be deprived of two sons in one day, Jacob followed by Esau, points to the corresponding separation between the First and Second Advents. The First Advent corresponds to the violence inflicted upon the second man, or son, Jesus Christ, while the Second Advent corresponds to the violence inflicted against the Body of Christ, or figuratively the first man, or son, Adam. The interim is the call to repentance.

The word *anger* [H639] (brother's anger) has a connotation "face," while the word *turn away* [H7725] (from Jacob) means "to turn back, return." The firstborn Esau being appointed to serve the second born Jacob represents the redemption of Adam in Christ. Esau turning away his face, or innate anger, back unto himself from Jacob ironically represents Adam rejecting his only redemption in Christ. And the expectation of Esau forgetting that Jacob had taken the blessing represents a prophecy of Esau rejecting his only possible blessing that is in Jacob. The word *fetch* [H3947] (Rebekah to fetch Jacob) has a connotation "to be taken in marriage," prefiguring the foretold marriage of the Lamb (Rev 19:9). Rebekah waiting to fetch Jacob until Esau turns away and forgets portends a corresponding time of judgment in the end times that will be a time of the fullness of evil (Gen 15:16). The prophecy that Esau would serve Jacob came directly from the Lord, whereby Esau hating Jacob on account of that reality represents Esau hating God himself (Gen 25:23).

Genesis 27:46 And Rebekah said to Isaac, I am weary [H6973] of my life [H2416] because of the daughters of Heth [H2845]: if Jacob take a wife of the daughters of Heth [H2845], such as these [which are] of the daughters of the land, what good shall my life [H2416] do me?

The word *life* [H2416] (life of Rebekah) is the same breath of *life* [H2416] proceeding from God in the formation of man as a *living* [H2416] soul (Gen 2:7). Rebekah represents the Holy Spirit—who is the wellspring of life, now and always—and thereby Rebekah also represents our present natural life. Rebekah being weary of her life represents a weariness of life itself, corresponding to the waning years of natural man, likewise natural creation. The word *weary* [H6973] (weary of my life) means "to feel a loathing, abhorrence, sickening dread," which reflects the foreknowing of God, awaiting the final apostasy of natural man that will be the final self-condemnation of natural man. The daughters of Heth being identified as the daughters of the land represents a further identification of the wickedness in the land with the original curse of the land, or natural creation, that came through Adam (Gen 3:17). The land, or dust of the ground, represents flesh, whereby the offspring of the land embodied by the daughters of the land represent a carnal nature separated from the Holy Spirit. Rebekah finally indicates her own death if Jacob were to accept Canaanite wives. And this is a testimony that the perfection of God would be corrupted—that God would figuratively die—if the faithless, the wicked, were allowed as members of the Body of Christ. But Jacob will not accept idolatrous Canaanite women just as Christ will not accept the faithless.

Ω Ω Ω

Abraham, Isaac, and Jacob embody the dominant pattern that overarches the last twenty-five chapters of the book of Genesis. But local context is global context. Abraham, Isaac, and Jacob reflect the Father, Son, and Spirit and likewise the formation of Adam followed by the First and Second Advents of Christ. And with respect to this global context, the three successive deaths of the three patriarchs Abraham, Isaac, and Jacob reflect the conclusions of three distinct periods, or dispensations, of progressive revelation that span the present creation. The first period was established in the first man Adam. The second period was established in the First Advent of Jesus Christ. And the third period will be established in the Second Advent of Christ. The book of Genesis is traditionally and correctly called a book of beginnings, but the book of Genesis is also a book of endings. And truly there is no one like God, declaring the end from the beginning (Isa 46:9–10).

1	2	3
FATHER	**SON**	**SPIRIT**
ADAM	**FIRST ADVENT**	**SECOND ADVENT**
ABRAHAM	**ISAAC**	**JACOB**

The three primary dispensations, which demarcate creation, are specifically the dispensations of Adam, the church age, and finally the millennial kingdom. And the successive deaths of Abraham, Isaac, and Jacob reflect the conclusions of these dispensations—namely, the end of the dispensation of Adam, the end of the church age, and finally the end of the present creation as a whole. The end of the dispensation of Adam began with the birth of Christ and was completed in the death and resurrection of Christ, for the life of Christ is that which liberates the children of God throughout all the generations, or all Adam-kind, allowing us to enter into the presence of God (Luke 23:43, 1 Pet 3:18–19). The dispensation of Adam was the dominion of the serpent, which related the enslavement of Adam-kind to sin and death, and thus the end of the dispensation of Adam could only come through the victory of Christ over death and the world. The end of the church age is then the end of the call to repentance that will begin with the resurrection and rapture but will not be completed until the formal Second Advent of Christ following the final tribulation period. And the end of the present creation will begin with the final tribulation period but will not be completed until the end of the millennial kingdom. Further, the account of Jacob and Esau follows closely after the account of the death of Abraham, coinciding with the end of the dispensation of Adam and the corresponding beginning of the church age. The account of the younger Jacob supplanting Esau reflects the second man Jesus supplanting Adam-kind, while the subsequent account of Jacob and Laban reflects the church age connecting the First and Second Advents.

1	2	3
ABRAHAM	ISAAC	JACOB
FALL OF ADAM	FIRST ADVENT	SECOND ADVENT
DEATH OF ABRAHAM	DEATH OF ISAAC	DEATH OF JACOB
THE END OF THE DISPENSATION OF ADAM	THE END OF THE CHURCH AGE	THE END OF THE PRESENT WORLD

The threefold Isaac, Rebekah, and Jacob—signifying man, woman, and child—are juxtaposed to the threefold Abraham, Isaac, and Jacob—signifying father, son, and their collective offspring. The threefold man, woman, and child reflect the ordering Father, Spirit, and Son, whereas the threefold father, son, and their offspring reflect the ordering Father, Son, and Spirit. The primal union of man and woman is obviously antecedent to the reality of their collective offspring, and yet the two fundamental Trinitarian sequences are always observed to coexist. Likewise, God the Son is eternally begotten. The (former) man, woman, and child emphasize the connection between the Fall of Man and the First Advent, while the (latter) man, son, and their offspring emphasize the connection between the First and Second Advents. The Spirit preceding the Son is epitomized by Eve preceding the offspring of Eve (Gen 3:20) and also the Spirit overshadowing Mary in the virgin conception of Christ (Luke 1:35). The Son preceding the Spirit is epitomized by Christ sending the Spirit only after his ascension unto the Father (John 16:7) and also the incarnation of Christ as the Head preceding the fullness of the indwelling Spirit in the Body of Christ (2 Cor 5:4–5). Therefore, the sequence Father, Spirit, Son can be further identified with the original, or present, creation. And the sequence Father, Son, Spirit can be identified with the promised new creation. The persistent coexistence of both threefold sequences reflects the reality that the Son and the Spirit both proceed from the Father. And this reality ultimately points to the coexistence of man and God, likewise law and grace, likewise the natural and the spiritual, persisting into eternity.[76]

---

[76] "When Christ is finally glorified, he can in turn send the Spirit from his place with the Father to those who believe in him: he communicates to them his glory, that is, the Holy Spirit who glorifies him" (Rom. Catholic Church, *Catechism* 199). The necessity of God the Son sending God the Spirit from the place of God the Father speaks of the Holy Spirit presenting the faithful in the Son, or Body of Christ, unto the Father.

JACOB AND ESAU

1	2
Isaac, Rebekah, Jacob	Abraham, Isaac, Jacob
Man, Woman, Child	Father, Son, Progeny
Father, Spirit, Son	Father, Son, Spirit
Fall of Man ↔ First Advent	First Advent ↔ Second Advent
Present Original Creation	Promised New Creation

The two brothers and nations Esau and Jacob reflect the relationship between the first and second men Adam and Jesus (Gen 25:23). The firstborn Esau is a natural man, a man of the field, whereas the second born Jacob is a spiritual man, a man of the tents, or tabernacles (Gen 25:27). Jacob purchasing the birthright of Esau with red soup (red pottage), or red stuff, points to Jesus Christ purchasing our lives, figuratively the life of Adam, with his blood at the time of the First Advent (Gen 25:30–31), while Jacob taking the blessing of Esau points to the kingdom of Christ being established by force for the sake of mankind, or figuratively Adam, at the time of the Second Advent (Gen 27:11–14). The first and second born Esau and Jacob also parallel the First and Second Advents just as the first and second men Adam and Jesus parallel the First and Second Advents. The rejection of the firstborn Esau, or spiritually Adam, reflects the rejection and crucifixion of Christ in the place of Adam, while the exaltation of the second born Jacob reflects the glorious return of Christ. The emphasis on Jacob being disguised as Esau when he takes the blessing of Isaac points to the faithful from Adam receiving the blessing of God in the Body of Christ and only in the Body of Christ (Gen 27:15–19). The birthright and blessing of the firstborn also reflect Adam and Christ and also the First and Second Advents. The birthright, which is guaranteed by birth, was originally established in the formation of Adam but ultimately in the conception of Christ at the First Advent, while the blessing of eternal life was established foremost in the resurrection of Christ at the First Advent and will be finally completed in the resurrection of the faithful in Christ at the Second Advent.

1	2
Esau	Jacob
Adam	Christ
Birthright of the Firstborn	Blessing of the Firstborn
First Advent	Second Advent

The account of Jacob purchasing Esau's birthright follows closely after the account of the birth of the two brothers, reinforcing the obvious but vital connection between birth and the birthright (Gen 25:24–26, 25:31). The close connection between physical birth and the purchasing of the birthright ultimately points to the close connection between the birth of Christ and his purchasing of the birthright, the right to be born again, on the cross. And this is also the close connection between the First Advent and the church age since the death and resurrection of Christ opens the church age. The subsequent separation of Jacob from Esau, which forms the context for Jacob establishing his own household, is closely connected to Jacob taking the blessing, for it is the dispute over the blessing that drives Jacob into the east country of his future near-kin wives (Gen 27:41–46). The connection between the blessing given by Isaac and the establishment of the house of Jacob points to the gifts of the Spirit proceeding from Christ at the time of the First Advent and culminating in the fullness of the indwelling Spirit at the time of the Second Advent. The birthright is to the blessing as the First Advent is to the Second Advent. And the establishment of the house of Jacob prefigures the Body of Christ forming throughout the church age and culminating in the Second Advent. The end of the dominion of the serpent over death is also connected to the birth of Esau and Jacob, but it cannot represent the end of death itself. For the condemnation of the natural body under the law is irrevocable. The end of death, likewise the end of suffering, also awaits the Second Advent of Christ and finally the end of the millennial kingdom (Rev 20:14).

JACOB AND ESAU

CHAPTER ONE OUTLINE

Key Images

Key images are organized in a twofold progression by order (prime, twofold, threefold) and by level (material, abstract, spiritual). The material level of reality—which is the literal, or immanent, level—is connected via an abstract, conceptual level to a spiritual level—which is the figurative, or transcendent, level. Prime, or singular, images reflect the oneness of God, foremost God the Father. Twofold images are identified with the duality of flesh and spirit, the two covenants of law and grace, and ultimately the twofold natures of God the Son, who is true man and true God. Threefold images relate the threefold movement of God the Holy Spirit in creation and new creation that is finally the revelation of the fullness of Trinitarian reality.

PRIME IMAGES		
Material	Abstract	Spiritual
The barrenness of Rebekah.	The natural body under the law.	Christ cut off out of the land of the living (Isa 53:8).
The hunger of Esau driving him to despise his birthright.	The famine of the present world.	A famine of the Word of God (Amos 8:11).
Jacob, disguised as Esau, receives the blessing of the firstborn.	The second born becomes the firstborn.	The second man Jesus is the firstborn of the dead (Col 1:18).
One blessing of the firstborn.	One bloodline.	One salvation in Christ.
The hatred and murderous intent of the firstborn Esau.	The way of all flesh, all the earth.	The apostasy of the last days, culminating in the end times.

TWOFOLD IMAGES		
Material	Abstract	Spiritual
Isaac and Rebekah.	Man identifies with the firstborn, woman with the second born. The firstborn by flesh, the second born by prophecy. Natural and spiritual. Law and grace. Flesh and spirit.	The bridegroom of blood, Jesus Christ, joined unto national Israel at the First Advent.
Esau and Jacob.	First and second born sons. Natural man and spiritual man. Flesh and spirit.	Adam and Jesus.
Birthright and blessing.	Material and spiritual. Flesh and spirit.	Kingship and high priesthood.
Land of Canaan, land of Laban.	Certain death, the hope of life. Flesh and spirit.	The First and Second Advents as connected by the church age.
Esau's wild game of the field supplanted by Jacob's kids of goats from the flock.	The offerings of Esau and Jacob. Wild versus domesticated. Violent versus gentle. Flesh and spirit.	The way of flesh supplanted by the way of the Spirit. The present fallen creation supplanted by the promised new creation.

THREEFOLD IMAGES		
Material	Abstract	Spiritual
Isaac; his wife, Rebekah; and their two sons, Esau and Jacob.	Father, wife, offspring. Man, woman, child.	{Adam, Eve}, all mankind. {Creation of Adam, conception of Christ}, Second Advent. {Father, Spirit}, Son.

Abraham, Isaac, Jacob.	Father, son, son's son. Father, son, collective offspring.	Adam, {Christ, Body of Christ}. Adam, {First Advent, New Creation of the Second Advent}. Father, {Son, Spirit}.
Abram and Pharaoh, Abraham and Abimelech, and Isaac and Abimelech.	Three successive covenants.	The formation of Adam, the First Advent of Christ, and the Second Advent.
The three wells of Abraham (Esek, Sitnah, Rehoboth).	Three fonts of life.	Father, Son, Spirit.

Synopsis

Parallel summaries of the material and spiritual levels of reality are arranged by Biblical chapters and verses and delimited by commentary chapter sections. The material level, or earthly perspective, corresponds to the explicit Biblical text, while the spiritual level corresponds to the implicit heavenly perspective. An intermediary abstract level is not developed, because it would be too intricate to be generally useful.

	ISAAC AND REBEKAH	
	Material	Spiritual
25:19–20	Abraham begets Isaac.	Jesus Christ, the only begotten Son.
	Isaac takes Rebekah as a near-kin wife.	Christ born a Jew and ministering to the Jews.
25:21	Rebekah is barren.	National Israel rejects Christ.
	Isaac intreats the Lord for Rebekah.	The Son intercedes with the Father.
	Rebekah conceives.	The opening of the church age.
25:22–23	Two nations struggle in the womb of Rebekah.	Flesh struggles against Spirit (Gal 5:17).
	The elder will serve the younger.	The first man Adam, representing all mankind, saved by the second man Christ.
	ESAU AND JACOB	
	Material	Spiritual
25:24	Rebekah fulfills her days to be delivered.	The last days.
25:25–26	The second born Jacob grasps the heel of the firstborn Esau.	Not coveting, but taking from the serpent that which belongs to the Seed.
25:27–28	Esau is a hunter, a man of the field. Jacob is plain, dwelling in tents.	Natural man. Spiritual man.
	Isaac loves Esau. Rebekah loves Jacob.	God longs to redeem Adam. Adam redeemed through the Seed of woman (Gen 3:15).
	BIRTHRIGHT	
	Material	Spiritual
25:29–34	Jacob purchases the birthright.	The faithful in Christ are bought with a price (1 Cor 6:19–20).
	Esau eats and drinks.	The body and blood of Christ (John 6:53).
	Esau leaves the presence of Jacob.	The condemnation of the natural body persists despite the death and resurrection of Christ.

JACOB AND ESAU

	ABIMELECH	
	Material	Spiritual
26:1–5	Famine in the land.	An image of death that recalls the original curse of the ground (Gen 3:17) and portends a famine of hearing the words of the Lord in the end times (Amos 8:11).
	Isaac must not leave Canaan.	Christ will return uniquely unto Israel at the Second Advent (Acts 1:6–11) just as Christ came uniquely unto Israel at the First Advent (Matt 15:24).
26:6–11	The identity of Rebekah is hidden.	The mystery of the Body of Christ (Eph 5:32).
	Abimelech recognizes the identity of Rebekah.	The Body of Christ acknowledged by the whole world in the end times.
26:12–16	Isaac sows in the land, and he receives an hundredfold.	The call of the faithful in the church age, which points to the harvest of mankind.
	The Philistines envy the greatness of Isaac.	Not the suffering Christ at the First Advent, but the glorified Christ at the Second Advent.
	The Philistines stop up the wells of Abraham.	The faithless reject the water of life.
	Abimelech sends Isaac away because of Isaac's greatness.	Jesus Christ is rejected, even the risen Christ (Luke 16:31).
26:17–18	Isaac digs again the wells of Abraham and gives them the same names as Abraham had.	The Son does nothing except what he sees the Father do (John 5:19).
26:19–22	Esek, Sitnah, Rehoboth.	The three millennia connecting the cross to the promised new creation.
26:23–25	Isaac goes up to Beersheba where he is blessed by the Lord.	The well of the sevenfold oath, representing the fulfillment of the present creation in the promised new creation.
26:26–27	Abimelech, Ahuzzath, and Phichol come to Isaac, the one whom they hate.	The dragon, the beast, and the false prophet (Rev 16:13).
26:28–33	Abimelech solicits a treaty with Isaac.	The law does not save, but rather condemns.
	BIRTHRIGHT AND BLESSING	
	Material	Spiritual
26:34–35	Esau takes Canaanite wives.	An image of faithlessness, particularly during the church age.
27:1–2	Isaac is old and near death.	The end of the church age draws near.
	Isaac's eyes grow dim in his old age.	Increasing apostasy in the end times.
	Isaac does not know the day of his death.	The Son does not know the appointed day and hour of judgment (Mark 13:32).
27:3–4	Isaac commands Esau to hunt and kill.	The coming judgment of the world.
	Isaac requires venison to be brought before he will give the blessing.	Blood sacrifice is required under the law before grace can be received.
27:5–10	Rebekah commands her second born son according to the blessing of the firstborn.	The Spirit calls the faithful unto Christ to receive the blessing of the Father.
	Rebekah seeks to substitute Jacob for Esau.	Jesus Christ must be substituted for Adam.
	A domesticated animal is substituted for a wild animal.	Obedience in contrast to disobedience.
27:11–14	A curse will be incurred if Isaac perceives that Jacob is not Esau.	Justice.
	Rebekah accepts the curse but reserves the blessing for Jacob.	Justice is fulfilled in mercy.

ESAU, JACOB, ISRAEL

27:15–25		Jacob comes quickly to Isaac.	The haste of the Second Advent.
		Jacob, disguised as Esau, presents himself before Isaac.	Christ assumes the faithful as his very Body.
		Isaac accepts Jacob as Esau.	The Father accepts the faithful in Christ.
27:26–29		They that curse Jacob will be cursed, and they that bless Jacob will be blessed.	Salvation comes only by grace through faith in Jesus Christ.
27:30–33		Esau presents himself to Isaac immediately after Jacob has departed.	The final tribulation period that will immediately follow the resurrection and rapture of the faithful. Also, the resurrection unto damnation that will follow the resurrection unto life.
		Isaac trembles exceedingly at the coming of his firstborn, Esau.	The horror that will mark the judgment of the faithless in the end times.
27:34–36		The birthright and blessing of the firstborn taken by the second born.	The kingship and high priesthood of Christ.
27:37–40		The blessing of Esau:	The curse of Adam:
		Your dwelling will be the fatness of the earth, and of the dew of heaven from above.	The preservation of the earth and heaven until the conclusion of the last days.
		You will live by the sword, and will serve your brother.	Death will proceed from the hand of man until the time of the Second Advent.
		And when you have the dominion, you will break your brother's yoke.	The great dragon is cast down into the earth (Rev 12:9).
	HATRED		
		Material	Spiritual
27:41–46		Esau plans to wait until the death of Isaac before killing Jacob.	The devil seeks the destruction of mankind in the end times.
		Rebekah instructs Jacob to flee to the east until the fury of Esau is turned away.	The fury of the devil is loosened in the end times (Rev 12:12).
		But Jacob will return to the promised land after the time of the wrath of Esau.	A prophecy of the millennial kingdom.

CHAPTER TWO

Jacob and Laban

The prime image in the account of Jacob's sojourn in the east is the blessing of Abraham resting upon Jacob and sanctifying all the work of his hands (Gen 30:27). Still, the corrupt dealings of Laban mark this time of Jacob specifically as a time of blessing during a time of suffering (Gen 31:6–9). The idols of Laban portend the image of the beast (Rev 13:14). Jacob taking the daughters and possessions of Laban reflects the movement of the Spirit establishing the Body of Christ. Jacob taking his inheritance from the hand of Laban, against Laban's will, represents Christ taking all dominion away from the devil (Gen 31:42). Leah selling her mandrakes to Rachel marks the end of the barrenness of both daughters and, thereby, connects the First and Second Advents by the progression of Jacob's latter sons, representing the latter days (Gen 30:16). The sojourn of Jacob in the east is bracketed by the pillar at Bethel (Gen 28:12, 28:18–19) and the pillar at Gilead (Gen 31:48, 31:52). The setting up of the former pillar represents the resurrection of Christ at the beginning of the church age, while the setting up of the latter pillar represents the resurrection and rapture of the faithful at the end of the church age. The prophetic tithe, or tenth, promised by Jacob at Bethel would be his eleventh son Joseph (Gen 28:20–22), while Jacob's prophetic curse of Rachel because of the idols of Laban portends the coming judgment of the world (Gen 31:32, 35:19).

The twofold relationships emphasized in the account of Jacob's sojourn in the east are those between Jacob and Laban, Leah and Rachel, and Isaac and Jacob. In Canaan, Jacob faces certain death at the hands of his brother Esau, but in the east, Jacob seizes his inheritance of life from the hands of his mother's brother Laban. Esau is identified with Laban just as the faithless are identified with the devil. That Jacob must take his inheritance and household from Laban represents the necessity that Jesus Christ must redeem his faithful from sin and death. The relationship between the daughters of Laban, Leah and Rachel, is paralleled by the relationship between Canaanite and near-kin wives and also the relationship between bondwoman and freewoman wives. The latter loved, the former not (Gen 29:30). The conflict between the firstborn Leah and the second born Rachel is resolved in their barrenness being supplanted by a miraculous fertility, representing the present world being supplanted by the promised new life and new creation (Gen 30:17, 30:22). The conflict between the first and second born is likewise law being supplanted by grace, that is, the natural being subsumed by the spiritual. And the blessing of Abraham passing from Isaac to Jacob represents a corresponding progression of the life of Christ to encompass all the faithful in Christ, specifically the progression from the First to the Second Advents of Christ (Gen 28:1–4).

The threefold progression of Esau taking Canaanite wives followed by Esau taking Ishmaelite wives followed by Jacob taking near-kin wives reflects the Fall of Man followed by the rejection and mocking of Christ at the time of the First Advent followed by the redemption in Christ at the time of the Second Advent (Gen 26:34, 28:8–9, 29:28). Adam followed by the First and Second Advents then reflects the Father, Son, and Spirit as creator, redeemer, and sanctifier. The threefold offspring of Jacob—demarcated by his firstborn of Leah followed by his firstborn of his bondwomen followed by his firstborn of Rachel—again represents the same progression from Adam to Christ to the Body of Christ (Gen 29:32, 30:6, 30:24). This is the offspring of the unloved followed by the offspring of bondage and suffering followed by the offspring of the beloved. The threefold journey of Jacob from Beersheba to Bethel to Padanaram—or rather from Beersheba to Bethel and then back to Bethel via Padanaram—represents the rejection of God by Adam, by Adam-kind, followed by the death and resurrection of Jesus Christ followed by the glorious return of Christ (Gen 28:10, 28:19, 35:1). This is the murderous intention of Esau followed by the tithe of Jacob unto God followed by the glorious return of Jacob unto the promised land (Gen 27:41, 28:20–22, 35:2–3). Further, the connection between the three days of the new creation and the seven days of the original creation is reflected by the three periods of seven years that Jacob works to gain the daughters of Laban together with Laban's possessions (Gen 31:41). The three days do not simply complete the four days; rather, the three days also subsume and amplify the seven days.

To the East

Genesis 28:1 And Isaac called Jacob, and blessed [H1288] him, and charged [H6680] him, and said unto him, Thou shalt not take a wife of the daughters of Canaan.

This is the third account of the one blessing of the second born Jacob in the place of the firstborn Esau. The three accounts reflect, respectively, Adam, the First Advent, and finally the Second Advent. The first account of the blessing of Jacob is repeated (Gen 27:23, 27:25), which recalls the original account of the formation of Adam being repeated (Gen 1:26–30, Gen 2:7–25). The first account is also connected with the six millennia of creation, though foremost with the original six days of creation culminating in the creation of the one man Adam. The second account of the blessing of Jacob is that which is recounted to Esau (Gen 27:37) and closely connected with the pseudoblessing, or rather the curse, of Esau separated from Jacob (Gen 27:39–40). The second account of the blessing of Jacob being identified with the rejection of Esau and the corresponding curse of Esau reflects Christ being in the place of Adam at the First Advent and, therein, becoming a curse on the cross (Gal 3:13). The second account of the blessing of Jacob emphasizes the millennia beginning with Abraham after the Flood and, thereby, emphasizes the new creation represented by the Flood—that is, the new creation beginning with the wooden cross of Christ, which is foreshadowed by the wooden ark of Noah.

The present third account of the blessing of Jacob is closely connected to the second account by the hatred of Esau for Jacob. Likewise, the First Advent is closely connected to the Second Advent by the hatred of the faithless for Christ. The word *charged* [H6680] (Isaac charged Jacob) is the same word used to describe God *commanding* [H6680] Adam to not eat from the tree of knowledge and, thereby, points to a symbolic fulfillment of the original creation in the obedience of Jacob to Isaac (Gen 2:16). Jacob now being charged to not accept Canaanite women as wives recalls the faithlessness of Adam, which was revealed in his obeying Eve and eating from the forbidden tree (Gen 3:17). But the fall of the first man Adam following Eve is now recast in the second man Christ preceding the faithful, the members of the Body of Christ (1 Tim 2:11–15). And this third account of Isaac blessing Jacob will be closely connected to God Almighty himself blessing Jacob (Gen 28:3) just as the blessing that marks the Second Advent is God himself being our promised inheritance of the indwelling of God the Holy Spirit (2 Cor 1:22).

Genesis 28:2 Arise [H6965], go [H3212] to Padan-aram [H6307], to the house of Bethuel thy mother's father; and take [H3947] thee a wife from thence of the daughters of Laban thy mother's brother.

Rebekah previously commanding Jacob to *obey* [H8085], *arise* [H6965], and *flee* [H1272] represents an overview of the seven millennia of creation that is the perspective of the Holy Spirit moving throughout all creation (Gen 27:43). Isaac now commanding Jacob to *arise* [H6965], *go* [H3212], and *take* [H3947] represents the death and resurrection of Christ pointing to the death and resurrection of the Body of Christ and, thereby, the three millennia connecting the First and Second Advents. The word *arise* [H6965] means "to arise, stand up" and has a connotation "to be established, confirmed," reflecting the resurrection of Jesus Christ and the corresponding establishment of the dominion of Christ. The word *go* [H3212] has a connotation "to depart, go away," reflecting the physical absence of Christ during the church age (John 14:30). The word *go* [H3212] also recalls the same word describing the serpent cursed to *go* [H3212] upon its belly eating dust, or figuratively flesh, and thereby portends the persecution of the faithful culminating in the final apostasy (Gen 3:14). And the word *take* [H3947] has a connotation "to be taken in marriage," prefiguring the foretold marriage of the Lamb that is the foundation of the millennial kingdom (Rev 19:9).[1]

Genesis 28:3 And God [H410] Almighty [H7706] bless thee, and make thee fruitful [H6509], and multiply [H7235] thee, that thou mayest be a multitude of people;

Isaac calling upon the name *God* [H410] *Almighty* [H7706] in the blessing of Jacob reflects the connection between the death of Christ at the time of the First Advent and the death of all flesh at the time of the Second Advent. The word *God* (El) [H410] is derived from the root "ram" [H352]—which recalls the ram substituted for Isaac in Moriah and, thereby, points to death being the final judgment of the law (Gen 22:13)—while the word *Almighty* (Shadday) [H7706] is derived from the root "to deal violently with, despoil, devastate, ruin" [H7703]—which foreshadows the utter condemnation of evil under the law in the end times (Rom 2:11–15).[2] The name *Almighty* [H7706] *God* [H410] is also the name connected with the covenant of circumcision and, thereby, further reinforces the image of flesh being cut off from the land of the living (Gen 17:1–10). And the blessing to be *fruitful* [H6509] and *multiply* [H7235] recalls the original blessing of Adam (Gen 1:28) and the subsequent blessing of Noah as the new Adam (Gen 9:1). The blessing of Jacob to be *fruitful* [H6509] and *multiply* [H7235] points to the Body of Christ and, thereby, represents the fulfillment of all the promises of creation in the Body of Christ.

Genesis 28:4 And give thee the blessing of Abraham, to thee, and to thy seed with thee; that thou mayest inherit [H3423] the land wherein thou art a stranger [H4033], which God gave unto Abraham.

Abraham, Isaac, and Jacob reflect the first man Adam followed by the First and Second Advents and likewise the Father, Son, and Holy Spirit. Isaac giving the blessing of Abraham to Jacob represents the Holy Spirit proceeding from the Father by virtue of the Son to be received by the faithful in the Son. The land represents the flesh, or the body, since flesh is derived from the dust of the ground (Gen 2:7), whereby the emphasis on our blessing being an inheritance in the land points to the spiritual, or glorified, body being a true, literal body (John 20:27). The land is the habitation of the body and therefore the natural extension of the body—which is one reason all creation must be restored, or itself resurrected, in parallel with our own personal rebirth in the spiritual body (Rev 21:1). The promised inheritance of the faithful is the resurrection and specifically the power of the resurrection that is the fullness of the indwelling

---

[1] "There have been several ingenious conjectures concerning the *retinue* which Jacob had, or might have had, for his journey; and by some he has been supposed to have been *well attended*. Of this nothing is mentioned here, and the reverse seems to be intimated elsewhere. . . . He had God alone with him" (Clarke 1:175; Gen 28:2). The suffering of the faithful in Christ.

[2] Etymologies per *Strong's*, not *Brown-Driver-Briggs*.

Holy Spirit and also the surrounding Holy Spirit. We now have a deposit of the Spirit, but we are awaiting the fullness of the Spirit (2 Cor 5:4–6). The faithful are currently not perfect, as should be obvious from our continuing sinfulness, but we absolutely must be made perfect in order to enter into the fullness of the presence of God (Exod 33:20).

The word *stranger* [H4033] (in the land) has a connotation "pilgrimage" and additional associations of "fear, terror" [H4032] and also "to dread" [H1481] (Gen 47:9). The faithful are merely pilgrims in the present world, making our way to the promised new creation (Heb 11:8–10). The fear of the pilgrim is his knowledge that he is an alien in a foreign land. And the pilgrim is easily recognized by the native inhabitants. The way of the natural body is fear, but the way of the spiritual body is love. The word *inherit* [H3423] (the land) means "to take possession of, inherit, dispossess" and has connotations "to take possession by force" and "to impoverish" and "to bring to ruin, destroy." The present king, or possessor, of the present world is the devil, but he will be chained and finally destroyed (Rev 20:1–10). The evil one possesses the present evil world just as evil individuals are themselves possessed by the evil one (Eph 6:12). The promise that Jacob will inherit the land is an affirmation that Christ will reclaim the lost dominion of Adam. And Christ necessarily takes the lost dominion of Adam by force because the dragon violently and relentlessly opposes Christ. Finally, Jacob does not earn the blessing of God, but God simply gives the blessing to Jacob. And the faithful are likewise exalted by an unmerited grace (Eph 2:8–9).[3]

Genesis 28:5 And Isaac sent away Jacob: and he went to Padan-aram [H6307] unto Laban, son of Bethuel the Syrian, the brother of Rebekah, Jacob's and Esau's mother.

---

[3] "His [Spanos'] cognitive-behavioral model of hypnosis is now the most influential perspective in the field [of psychopathology], largely replacing the earlier 'altered state' conception . . . Spanos [using the same line of reasoning] also made significant contributions to our understanding of a wide variety of related topics, including false memories, demonic possession, the Salem witchcraft trials, reports of alien abductions by UFOs, and multiple personality disorder" (Spanos vii). The natural must be weighed against the supernatural, likewise man must be weighed against the devil; "As the term implies, a victim of perfect Possession [*sic*] is absolutely controlled by evil and gives no outward indication, no hint whatsoever, of the demonic residing within. . . . Because there is no will left to call the victim's own—and because some part of the victim's will is necessary for any hope of successful Exorcism [*sic*]—remedy is unlikely to succeed even in the event the Possession should somehow be uncovered and verified as the problem" (Martin xxiii–xxiv). In the present order, the devil hides within mankind, such that the human and the demonic cannot always be distinguished; "To us [devils] a human is primarily food; our aim is the absorption of its will into ours . . . ." (Lewis, *Screwtape* 37). In the end, faithless men and godless demons alike will suffer the same fundamental annihilation of freewill, the only possible fate of those separated from the Lord God who is the font of freewill.

ESAU, JACOB, ISRAEL

The present journey of Jacob is the third in a series of three journeys connected with the native country of Abraham's relatives. The first journey is the original journey of Abram and Sarai from Ur of the Chaldees via the land of Haran, recalling the original formation of the first man Adam (Gen 11:31). The second journey is that of Abram's eldest servant in being sent on behalf of Isaac to call Rebekah to be Isaac's wife, which reflects the First Advent of Christ (Gen 24:2–4). And the third and present journey of Jacob to call Leah and Rachel and their handmaids points to the Second Advent. Further, Rebekah originally identifying the journey of Jacob with the land of *Haran* [H2771] connects the journey of Jacob with the original journey of Abram via *Haran* [H2771] and, thereby, connects the Second Advent with the First Creation (Gen 27:43). The land of *Haran* [H2771] is closely identified with the death of Terah and, thereby, represents an emphasis on the death of the natural body and likewise the baptism of repentance while yet in the natural body (Gen 11:32). The connection between the First Creation (journey of Abram) and the Second Advent (journey of Jacob) is the First Advent (Rebekah sending Jacob). The connection between the body of Adam and the Body of Christ is the Spirit, or breath of life. Finally, Isaac identifying the journey of Jacob with *Padanaram* [H6307] connects the journey of Jacob with the journey of Abram's eldest servant that was also to *Padanaram* [H6307] and, thereby, connects the First and Second Advents of Christ (Gen 25:20). The connection between the First Advent (journey of Abram's servant) and the Second Advent (journey of Jacob) is the person of Christ (Isaac sending Jacob). The emphasis on the journey of Jacob being to *Padanaram* [H6307]—representing the source, or font, of Rebekah—points to our promised new creation, which comes only by the indwelling Holy Spirit, the fullness of which is our promised inheritance.

Rebekah previously connected the journey of Jacob to the daughters of *Heth* [H2845], who is the ancestral father of the *Hittites* [H2850]. Rebekah thereby connects the journey of Jacob to the wives of Esau, which represents an emphasis on the contention between Jacob and Esau (Gen 27:46). The contention between Jacob and Esau is the contention between believers and unbelievers, especially in the church age and specifically because of the controversy surrounding the incarnation of Jesus Christ. Rebekah originally sending Jacob points to the First Advent, while Isaac finally sending Jacob points to the Second Advent. Rebekah first sending Jacob foreshadows the Holy Spirit revealing the Son, both in the conception of the Son and also in the call of the faithful in the Son throughout the church age (Luke 1:35). Isaac finally sending Jacob foreshadows the ascendant Son sending the Holy Spirit, both unto the faithful while yet in the world and also unto the faithful in the resurrection at the end of the age (John 16:7). And Isaac connects the journey of Jacob to the daughters of Canaan (Gen 28:1), which recalls the curse of Ham's son Canaan (Gen 9:25). The curse of Canaan is closely connected with the first destruction that came by water and, thereby, points to the foretold second destruction that will come by fire (2 Pet 3:12).

Isaac is the embodiment of the First Advent, while Jacob is the embodiment of the Second Advent. The Canaanites represent apostate humanity, affirming the curse of Ham's son Canaan (Gen 9:25). Jacob being forbidden from taking a Canaanite wife represents the glorified Christ accepting only the community of faithful as the bride of the Lamb, which is specifically by the one faith in the atoning blood of the one cross (Rev 21:9). The bridegroom represented by the Lamb is a bridegroom of blood (Exod 4:25). The emphasis on Jacob being required to take near kin, or blood kin, as wives is an affirmation that our blood kinship to Christ comes through the blood of the cross and only the blood of the cross (Matt 12:50). The union of male and female is a prophecy of the union of Christ and the faithful by blood, while the union of male and female producing righteous offspring is a prophecy of the rebirth of the faithful in the Body of Christ. The dichotomy of male and female represents justice and mercy, but the perfect union of justice and mercy is something new, even life itself, represented by the new life embodied by children.

Abraham previously insisted that his eldest servant bring a bride unto his son Isaac, but now Isaac insists that his son Jacob go himself to take a wife (Gen 24:3–4). Likewise, the First Advent of Christ would herald the call of the faithful unto Christ by the Holy Spirit but the Second Advent will be marked by Christ himself returning to take his faithful unto himself in the fullness of the Holy Spirit. Abraham's eldest servant purchased Rebekah for Isaac with a large dowry (Gen 24:53), which prefigures Christ purchasing the faithful with his own blood (Acts 20:28). And the blood of Jesus Christ represents life itself and likewise the font of life that is the person of the Holy Spirit (Lev 17:11). In contrast, Jacob is now sent for his bride empty handed. And Jacob having to work for his wives represents the work of the cross that is the sevenfold work of creation (Gen 29:20). Jacob needs no dowry of his own, because the price has already been paid in full (John 19:30). And Jacob finally taking his wives and his wealth from Laban, at least symbolically taking everything that had belonged to Laban, represents the glorified Jesus Christ taking the faithful and also creation itself as his rightful possession (Matt 24:30).

Rebekah originally hearing the command of her husband to bless the firstborn, followed by Rebekah directing her son Jacob to take that blessing, recalls the first revelation of the Trinity in creation—which is embodied by the formation of man, woman, and child (Gen 27:5–10). Adam being formed first by God followed second by Eve being taken from the side of Adam followed third by offspring proceeding from the womb of Eve represents the Father sending the Holy Spirit (the Spirit proceeding from the Father) to reveal the Son (Gen 2:21–24). This is the Holy Spirit of God—that is, God the Holy Spirit— moving upon the face of the waters in the original creation (Gen 1:2). And this is also the Holy Spirit of God overshadowing Mary in the virgin conception of Christ (Luke 1:35). The original creation of Adam, or man, is connected with the conception of Jesus Christ as the Son of man. And the first man Adam is to the second man Christ as the First Advent is to the Second Advent. The Son proceeding from the Spirit—denoted as Father, Spirit, and Son—is the First Advent and likewise the First Creation.

Isaac, son of Abraham, blessing and sending his own son Jacob represents the second revelation of the Trinity in creation—which is embodied by a father, his firstborn son, and their collective offspring through the firstborn son. This is the promised Messianic bloodline proceeding from the Father to the Son and finally to the faithful in the Son, who are themselves marked by the Holy Spirit and, thereby, identified with the Holy Spirit. This is the ascendant Son sending the Holy Spirit at the beginning of the church age (John 16:7). And this is also the Son bringing, or ushering in, the resurrection of the faithful at the time of the Second Advent, specifically by the power of the Holy Spirit (Rom 8:11). The resurrection of Christ at the time of the First Advent is connected with the resurrection of the faithful at the time of the Second Advent. And the first man Adam is to the second man Christ as the First Advent is to the Second Advent. The Spirit proceeding from the Son—denoted by Father, Son, and Spirit—is the coming Second Advent and likewise the present church age.[4]

Genesis 28:6–9 When Esau saw that Isaac had blessed Jacob, and sent him away to Padan-aram, to take him a wife from thence; and that as he blessed him he gave him a charge, saying, Thou shalt not take a wife of the daughters of Canaan; 7 And that Jacob obeyed his father and his mother, and was gone to Padan-aram; 8 And Esau seeing that the daughters of Canaan pleased not Isaac his father; 9 Then went Esau unto Ishmael, and took unto the wives which he had Mahalath the daughter of Ishmael Abraham's son, the sister of Nebajoth, to be his wife.

Though the natural man Esau cannot comprehend the true spiritual significance of the events, he does see the blessing of his brother, Jacob, and correctly connects it with Jacob taking wives from their near relatives. Christ does not come to be blessed himself but so that the faithful in him may be blessed. The emphasis on Jacob now being separated from the promised land points to the ascension of Christ after his death and resurrection (Acts 1:9). Jacob departing in order to form a family represents Christ departing in order to prepare many mansions for his faithful ones (John 14:2). Esau is already joined to the daughters of Canaan, represented by daughters of the Hittites, but he now seeks to join himself also to the daughters of Ishmael and, thereby, unite Canaan and Ishmael in one house (Gen 26:34). Neither Ishmael nor Canaan represents the son of the promise. But Ishmael does represent the offspring of Abraham—in contrast to Canaan, who represents apostate humanity, or the enemies of Abraham.[5]

---

[4] "The Church . . . is a reflection of the Trinity itself. For the Church, being many unique and distinct persons, is called to be one mind, one heart, one soul and one body in the one Truth and Love of God Himself" (Hopko, *Orthodox Faith* 1:145). All levels of reality, likewise all horizons of reality, are marked by a simultaneous unity and diversity.

[5] "These marriages by the patriarchs of wives closely akin to them were possible and permitted because, 'The race was young enough that the danger of accumulated mutational defects was minimized' [H. M. Morris]. Later, in the times of Moses, when genetic problems were more likely, the Law forbade the marriages of persons of near kinship" (Coffman 358; Gen 28:6–9). The Bible consistently testifies to the reality of entropy and, therein, denies the delusion of evolution.

JACOB AND LABAN

The daughters of Ishmael specifically represent a blood kinship in the promised land and, thereby, parallel the blood kinship in Padanaram. The parallel between Abraham's near kin in the promised land and Abraham's near kin in Padanaram represents the parallel between earth and heaven, especially during the church age culminating in the end of the age. And Padanaram being in the east reinforces this parallel (Gen 29:1) since it is the east that is connected with the return of Christ in the Second Advent (Matt 24:27). Esau attempting to imitate Jacob in the covenant of marriage then foreshadows the manipulations of the anti-christ. And the natural man Esau mingling the daughters of Ishmael and the daughters of Canaan specifically represents a corruption of the earth, or natural creation. Esau adding the daughters of Ishmael to the daughters of Canaan and not vice versa portends a willingness of humanity to be corrupted in the end times. And finally note that many, if not most, commentators see the natural man Esau, not the spiritual man Jacob, as having been unjustly cheated in the matter of the inheritance of the firstborn, which itself portends a universal acceptance of the coming anti-christ.[6]

Bethel

Genesis 28:10 And Jacob went out from Beer-sheba [H884], and went toward Haran [H2771].

The account of Jacob being blessed and his being sent to take wives in the east is framed by the place, or rather the signification, of *Beersheba* [H884]. And Jacob being blessed and his taking of wives are therefore again closely connected. The previous arrival of Isaac at *Beersheba* [H884] is connected with Esau taking Canaanite wives (Gen 26:32–35). But Jacob now departs from *Beersheba* [H884] to take wives from among his mother's close relatives. The dwelling place at *Beersheba* [H884], which means "well of seven (as a place of swearing by seven)," is identified with the Second Advent—which corresponds to the seventh, or Sabbath, millennium, likewise the conclusion of the totality of the seven millennia of creation. And the close connection between the blessing of Jacob and his taking of wives also points to the Second Advent.

Rebekah previously identified Jacob's destination as *Haran* [H2771] (Gen 27:43), while Isaac identified Jacob's destination as *Padanaram* [H6307] (Gen 28:2). The name *Haran* [H2771] is most closely identified with the First Advent, while the name *Padanaram* [H6307] is most closely identified with the Second Advent. But the two names are intertwined. The journey of Jacob to the east and back again to the promised land represents the movement of the Holy

---

[6] "Although Jacob was assured of this blessing by faith: yet he did evil to seek it by lies and the more because he abuses God's Name thereunto" (Whittingham et al., *Geneva Bible* 12R n. d; Gen 27:19); "It [the account of Jacob taking the blessing] is certainly written, not for our imitation, but for our admonition" (Henry 1:165; Gen 27:18–29); "[H]e [Jacob] can by no means be excused; . . ." (Gill 1:148; Gen 27:19); "[I]t is painful to think of the deliberate falsehoods, as well as daring profanity, he [Jacob] resorted to" (Jamieson et al. 1:195–96; Gen 27:18–27).

Spirit during the church age. The emphasis on *Haran* [H2771] testifies to the call of the faithful to repentance and likewise to our death and resurrection in imitation of the death and resurrection of Christ. The baptism in water becomes the baptism of the Holy Spirit.

Genesis 28:11 And he lighted [H6293] upon a certain place [H4725], and tarried there all night, because the sun was set; and he took [H3947] of the stones [H68] of that place [H4725], and put [them for] his pillows, and lay down in that place [H4725] to sleep.

The word *lighted* [H6293] (upon a certain place) is the same word used by the prophet Isaiah to foretell the *intercession* [H6293] of Christ (Isa 53:12). The word *place* [H4725] (lighted upon, stones of, lay down in) is derived from the root "to arise, stand up, stand" [H6965], which has a connotation "to be established, confirmed" and, thereby, reflects the resurrection of Jesus Christ and the corresponding establishment of the dominion of Christ. The word *place* [H4725] being used three times in this single passage points to the threefold resurrection that is the resurrection of Christ followed by the faithful followed by the faithless. The nighttime then reflects the absence of Jesus Christ during his entombment after the crucifixion and also the absence of Christ during the church age after his ascension. But the coming dawn foreshadows the resurrection of Christ followed by the foretold resurrection at the end of the age. The three millennia following the rejection of Christ are like the three days following the crucifixion of Christ. Arise, Arise, Arise.

The word *stone* [H68] (of that place) is the same word used to describe the unhewn *stone* [H68] required to build the Lord's altar (Exod 20:25) and also the tables (tablets) of *stone* [H68] required to teach the law of Moses to the people of Israel (Exod 24:12). The image of Jacob sleeping upon stones represents Christ offered upon the altar required by the law. And the sacrificial altar of Christ being represented by the stone tables of the law is a testimony that the work of the cross fulfills the law. The word *took* [H3947] (of the stones) has connotations "to buy" and also "to be taken in marriage," reflecting the wages of sin being paid in full on the cross (Rom 6:23) and the corresponding union of Christ and the faithful, inherent in Christ purchasing the faithful for himself (1 Cor 6:20). In life Christ had no place to lay his head, but in his death and resurrection, we all find rest (Matt 8:20). Christ is the stone the builders have rejected and yet has become the cornerstone (Mark 12:10).

Genesis 28:12 And he dreamed, and behold a ladder [H5551] set up on the earth, and the top [H7218] of it reached [H5060] to heaven: and behold the angels [H4397] of God ascending and descending on it.

The vision of angels ascending and descending between earth and heaven prefigures the union of earth and heaven that is the promised new creation (Rev 3:12). This is the foretold union of flesh and spirit and likewise the union of law and grace.[7] The union of the faithful and Christ does not and can not happen in isolation. The image of angels ascending and descending is repeated in the book of John and is specifically related to the Son of man. Hereafter ye shall see heaven open, and the angels of God ascending and descending upon the Son of man (John 1:51). Further, the specific ordering, ascending being followed by descending, reflects the ascension of the Son being followed by his glorious return in the end times (Acts 1:11). Christ is the man from heaven, and so he necessarily first descended (John 3:13). But the emphasis here is new creation and, therefore, the timeline following his death and resurrection. Jesus Christ is likewise the second man as compared with Adam (1 Cor 15:47), even though Adam was created through Christ (John 1:3). In the life of Jacob, this ascending and descending will be embodied by his leaving the promised land and going to the east but then finally returning from the east with his wives and children as well as great wealth. The life of Jacob is most closely identified with the movement of the Holy Spirit, but it is the movement of the Holy Spirit that connects the First and Second Advents of Christ.[8]

The word *ladder* [H5551] (reaching heaven) is derived from the root "to lift up, cast up" [H5549], which has a connotation "to exalt oneself," recalling the peoples of Babel seeking to exalt themselves (Gen 11:6). And the word *top* [H7218] (of the ladder) is the same word used to describe the *top* [H7218] of the tower of Babel that was intended to reach to heaven (Gen 11:4). The word *reach* [H5060] (to heaven) recalls the same word used to describe the *touching* [H5060] of the tree of knowledge that leads to death, which reflects the parallel between the tree of knowledge and the tower of Babel (Gen 3:3). Further, it is not clear in Jacob's dream who sets up the ladder. And one would presume that angels don't need a ladder to ascend and descend between earth and heaven. Also, there is no ladder in the account of the angels ascending and descending in the book of John (John 1:51). A ladder is inherently something men set up to elevate themselves, whereby the ladder to heaven portends a tower of Babel in the end times. The positive image of the ministering angels of God being superimposed upon the negative image of the ladder foreshadows the Second Advent being heralded by a final apostasy. This is the death that necessarily precedes rebirth. The ascending and descending of the angels of God reflects the ascension and return of Christ, but the ladder extending from the earth to heaven represents the concurrent rejection of God. This is the crucifixion that precedes the church age and likewise the final apostasy that precedes the millennial kingdom.[9]

---

[7] "[H]e [Christ] may be fitly represented hereby [Jacob's ladder] as the Mediator, who has reconciled things in heaven and things on earth, and has as it were joined and united heaven and earth together...." (Gill 1:154; Gen 28:12). Jesus Christ is fully man and fully God, simultaneously the Son of man and the Son of God.

[8] "Jesus refers to the ascending and descending angels on the stairway as [a] picture of himself as the true axis between heaven and earth [John 1:51]. He is the only mediator between God and human beings [1 Tim 2:5]" (Waltke 398). The ladder is the cross.

[9] "This [dream of the ladder] might represent 1. The *providence of God*, by which there is a *constant correspondence kept up* between heaven and earth.... 2. The *mediation of Christ*. He

ESAU, JACOB, ISRAEL

The journey of Jacob from the promised land and then back to the promised land prefigures the ascension and glorious return of Christ that demarcates the church age. Jacob will return with his wives and children just as Christ will return with the faithful of all the ages. And this ascending and descending of Jacob thereby points to the promised union of earth and heaven, likewise flesh and spirit, and likewise law and grace. But the emphasis is on the progression from earth to heaven and, thereby, reflects the progression from law to grace and likewise from the natural body to the spiritual, or glorified, body. This is the death that is required by the law pointing to the eternal life that comes only by the Spirit. The law leads us unto the grace that is eternal life. And the law is thereby recognized as the visible sign of the invisible Holy Spirit, who is the very breath of life, that is, the embodiment of life itself. And the death of the natural body that precedes the eternal life in the spiritual body parallels the final apostasy that will precede the glorious return of Jesus Christ.

The vision of the angels of God ascending and descending between earth and heaven is connected to the time of Jacob departing from the promised land. And this connection reflects the Son sending the Holy Spirit as our comforter at the beginning of the church age (John 16:7). The Son ascending by the power of the Holy Spirit (Rom 8:11) parallels the Holy Spirit descending from the Son (John 14:26). The Holy Spirit is the breath of life that animates the perfect union of flesh and spirit, likewise law and grace, in the Body of Christ. The Holy Spirit is God and no mere angel, but angels are identified with protecting and edifying the Body and, thereby, are identified with the Spirit. The word *angel* [H4397], meaning "messenger, representative," therefore reflects the Holy Spirit, who is the messenger, or giver of the Word, in contrast to the Word made flesh (John 1:14). The Spirit following the Son represents the specific ordering Father, Son, and Spirit that is connected to the promised new creation. The Head must come before the Body in the act of new creation because it is the Head that redeems the Body in the act of new creation. This is the faithful resurrected in the Body of Christ by the power of the Holy Spirit.

Genesis 28:13 And, behold, the LORD [H3068] stood above it, and said, I [am] the LORD [H3068] God [H430] of Abraham thy father, and the God [H430] of Isaac: the land whereon thou liest, to thee will I give it, and to thy seed;

The Biblical text draws our eyes up the ladder to see a vision of the Lord God standing above the ladder and there opposing all who would pass into heaven by their own power. The complex name *Lord* [H3068] *God* [H430] represents the union of mercy and justice, but the emphasis is on justice in contrast to mercy since the name *Lord* [H3068] by itself represents the fullness

---

is this ladder: the foot on earth in his human nature, the top in heaven in his divine nature; or the former is his humiliation, the latter is his exaltation" (Wesley 1:111; Gen 28:12). The two realities are not mutually exclusive, and actually the two reflect the one and same reality.

of life. The Lord restates his promises to Abraham's children, promises originally made to Abraham, which affirms that the promises of God are undeniable and inviolable. And the many promises of God are ultimately one promise, namely, the inherent promise of all creation that is the one image of God. The Lord as signified by the God of father Abraham represents God the Father, while the Lord as signified by the God of Abraham's son Isaac represents God the Son. The seed, or offspring, embodied by Jacob then represents the Body of Christ and, thereby, God the Holy Spirit who animates and indwells the Body of the faithful in Christ. The emphasis on giving the land to the chosen people points to the rebirth of creation that will parallel the resurrection of the individual faithful. The emphasis on the land is equally a testimony that the promised spiritual, or glorified, body is, without qualification, a true tangible body.

Genesis 28:14 And thy seed shall be as the dust of the earth, and thou shalt spread abroad to the west, and to the east, and to the north, and to the south: and in thee and in thy seed shall all the families of the earth be blessed.

Jacob and his offspring represent Christ and the faithful in Christ. Counting the seed of Jacob as the dust of the earth, in contrast to the stars of heaven, represents an emphasis on the natural body, as preceding the spiritual, or glorified, resurrection body. And this is likewise the church age that precedes the millennial kingdom. The promise that the families of the earth will be blessed in Jacob and his seed is an affirmation of the promise that Japheth will be blessed in the tents of Shem (Gen 9:27). The blessing of the faithful in the church age is not merely the promised gifts of the Holy Spirit but also and most importantly the call of the chosen by the Holy Spirit to faith in the Son. And the blessing of the faithful in the church age prefigures the fullness of the blessing of the faithful at the time of the Second Advent. And the seed of Jacob spreading in all directions is a prophecy of the universal dominion of Christ.[10]

Genesis 28:15 And, behold, I [am] with thee, and will keep thee in all [places] whither thou goest, and will bring thee again into this land; for I will not leave thee, until I have done [that] which I have spoken to thee of.

The Lord promising to be with Jacob and to bring him again into the promised land prefigures the Son sending the Holy Spirit to abide with the faithful forever (John 14:16). And this is the same promise of the Lord to always be with the faithful even unto the end of the world (Matt 28:20).

---

[10] "Christ is the great blessing of the world . . . none of any family are excluded from blessedness in him, but those that exclude themselves" (Wesley 1:111; Gen 28:14). The concurrent inclusivity and exclusivity of the cross reflects the dichotomy of grace and law, the way of the Spirit in contrast to the way of all the earth.

Nevertheless, there is an ominous implication that the Lord will leave Jacob after he has fulfilled what he has spoken, which portends the Restrainer, God the Holy Spirit, being removed in the end times (2 Thess 2:7).

Genesis 28:16–17 And Jacob awaked out of his sleep, and he said, Surely the LORD is in this place; and I knew [it] not. 17 And he was afraid [H3372], and said, How dreadful [H3772] [is] this place! this [is] none other but the house of God, and this [is] the gate of heaven.

Jacob is most closely identified with the Second Advent of Christ, but his journey out of the promised land and then back again represents the church age that connects the First and Second Advents. The journey of Jacob specifically represents the movement of the Spirit beginning with the resurrection of Christ and culminating in the resurrection of the faithful in Christ. Jacob awaking from sleep at the very gate of heaven before leaving the promised land prefigures the resurrection of Christ himself. The dreadful fear that Jacob feels is the sympathetic fear that Christ feels for the world, particularly looking forward to the coming judgment in the end times. The word *afraid* [H3372] (Jacob was afraid) is the same word used to describe Adam being *afraid* [H3372] of the voice of the Lord and, thereby, connects the universal fear in the end times to the primordial fear of the universal man Adam (Gen 3:10). And the word *dreadful* [H3372] (dreadful place) is the same word used to describe the coming of the great and *dreadful* [H3372] Day of the Lord (Mal 4:5). Woe unto you that desire the Day of the Lord . . . the Day of the Lord is darkness, and not light (Amos 5:18). The emphasis on Jacob being surprised by the appearance of the gateway to heaven is an affirmation that times and seasons are appointed by the Father and not by the Son or the Spirit (Mark 13:32, Acts 1:7).

Genesis 28:18 And Jacob rose up early in the morning, and took the stone that he had put [for] his pillows, and set it up [for] a pillar [H4676], and poured oil upon the top of it.

Jacob sleeping upon stones represents Christ sacrificed upon the altar of the law. The pillows of stone being set up in the form of a pillar points to the resurrection of Christ that in turn prefigures the resurrection of the faithful in Christ. The resurrection of Jesus Christ represents the firstfruits, while the redemption of the faithful in Christ represents the harvest (1 Cor 15:23, Lev 23:10–12). Anointing the pillar with oil represents the anointing, or power, of the Holy Spirit in the resurrection of Christ (Rom 8:11) and also Christ sending the Holy Spirit after his death, resurrection, and ascension (John 16:7). Jacob forming the pillar using the stone that he had used for a pillow represents an emphasis on Christ as the Head of the Body. And this is appropriate since it is the resurrection of Christ that enables the resurrection of the faithful in Christ. But ultimately the resurrection of the Head is directly connected to the resurrection of the Body, so much so that the two events can be considered one resurrection of one Body, that is, the Head and Body together.[11]

Genesis 28:19 And he called the name of that place [H4725] Beth-el [H1008]: but the name of that city [H5892] [was called] Luz [H3870] at the first.

The name *Luz* [H3870] has an association "almond tree, almond wood" [H3869], which is the same *hazel* [H3869] Jacob will use to conceive strong animals for his flock (Gen 30:37). In contrast, the name *Bethel* [H1008] has the dramatic meaning "house of God." The former name *Luz* [H3870] reflects the wooden cross by which the faithful are conceived (Rom 6:4), while the latter name *Bethel* [H1008] points to the promised familial relationship between the faithful and Christ (Matt 12:50). Further, the word *city* [H5892] (city of Luz) has an association "excitement (of terror)" [H5892], while the word *place* [H4725] (place of Bethel) means "standing-place, place" and has connotations "place of human abode (home)" and also "place of the Lord (heaven)." The former reflects the city of man, while the latter points to the place of God that is the Body of Christ. And truly the city of God is not like the cities of men, for it is the house of Jacob alone that will be the house of God (Heb 11:9–10).

Genesis 28:20–22 And Jacob vowed a vow, saying, If God will be with me, and will keep me in this way that I go, and will give me bread [H3899] to eat, and raiment [H899] to put on, 21 So that I come again to my father's house in peace [H7965]; then shall the LORD be my God: 22 And this stone, which I have set [for] a pillar [H4676], shall be God's house: and of all that thou shalt give me I will surely give the tenth [H6237] unto thee.

Jacob is not negotiating with God. Jacob vowing is Jacob prophesying. Jacob can only come back again to his father's house if God blesses him and leads him. The *bread* [H3899] that God gives Jacob is the *bread* [H3899] from heaven (Exod 16:4), which is the *bread* [H3899] of affliction representing the fulfillment of the law (Deut 16:3). The *raiment* [H899] that God gives Jacob represents the very *garments* [H899] of salvation and even a *robe* [H4598] of righteousness, signifying the exaltation of Christ and likewise the exaltation of the faithful in Christ in the resurrection of the dead (Isa 61:10). The word *peace* [H7965] (to my father's house in peace) means "completeness, soundness, welfare, peace" and is derived from the root "to be complete, sound" [H7999]. The completeness of the house of the Father is our promised union with the Son that is the embodiment of the perfect union of law and grace, likewise of flesh and spirit.

---

[11] Interwoven throughout Gen 28:10–28:22 is God's revelation being directly paralleled by Jacob's response, wherein the memorial pillar raised by Jacob is identified with the ladder connecting earth and heaven (Waltke 387–88). The promised resurrection of all the faithful, the Old and New Testament saints together, in the one Body of Christ.

The stones being set up as a pillar foreshadows the resurrection of Christ and finally the faithful in Christ, whereby the pillar becoming the very house of God points to the promised fullness of the indwelling of the Holy Spirit. The body of believers is literally the temple of God (1 Cor 6:19).[12]

The *tenth* [H6237] promised by Jacob points to the tithe that Levi while yet in Abram gave to Melchizedek and also the tithe that Levi himself would receive from all Israel (Heb 7:4–10). The tithe, or tenth, points to the Decalogue, which is the heart of the law, while the law as a whole is a prophecy of the redemption that comes by the cross of Christ (Matt 5:17). The tithe that Jacob personally pays will be his firstborn son Joseph. And the firstborn Joseph is specifically Jacob's second firstborn, of a freewoman, following Reuben just as Christ is the second firstborn, by the power of the Spirit, following Adam. Jesus Christ is counted as second because he is born after Adam (1 Cor 15:47), and Jesus Christ is simultaneously counted as first because he is the firstborn from the dead (Col 1:18). The tithe and the firstborn are closely related since both represent that which is set apart for the Lord. And the tithe is further connected with the firstborn in that the Levites are sustained by the tithe (Num 18:24) in their substitution for the firstborn of all Israel (Num 3:12). This is the law that governs the firstborn Adam, the same law that is fulfilled in the firstborn Jesus Christ.[13]

Joseph is literally the eleventh son of all the sons of Jacob, but he can be counted as the tenth, or tithed, son in that Levi belongs to the Lord and not to Jacob. That Levi should be subtracted from his brothers is also evident in Levi not receiving an inheritance in the land among his brothers (Deut 18:1). Further, Joseph is also the seventh son of Jacob's freewomen, Leah and Rachel, when viewed separately from the sons of Jacob's bondwomen, Zilpah and Bilhah. And the tithe embodied by Joseph, which is set apart for God, represents the inheritance of God that is finally the faithful in Christ themselves, to be first established in the millennial kingdom corresponding to the seventh, or Sabbath, millennium. The tithe is simultaneously that which is given to God and that which was originally received from God, whereby the tithe given to God finally points to our faith in God since the faith required by God must itself have originally come from God. Counting Joseph as the tenth, or tithed, son of all Jacob's sons is according to the inheritance, which represents the law, while counting Joseph as the seventh son of Jacob's sons by freewomen is according to honor and prestige, which represents grace. But who is the second firstborn son Joseph that is the seventh son fulfilling the role of the tenth son?

---

[12] "He [Jacob] binds not God under this condition but acknowledges his infirmity, and promises to be thankful" (Whittingham et al., *Geneva Bible* 13R n. h; Gen 28:20). God Almighty freely binds himself unto his children in his covenantal promises.

[13] "Jacob seems to make this vow rather for his *posterity* than for *himself*... for he particularly refers to the promises which God had made to him, which concerned the *multiplication of his offspring*, and *their establishment in that land*" (Clarke 1:178; Gen 28:20). Prophecy is innately fractal, simultaneously focusing on the individual and looking beyond the individual.

JACOB AND LABAN

This speaks of a second creation that comes by grace, beginning with the seventh millennium and fulfilling the whole of the tenfold law.[14]

Rachel and Leah

Genesis 29:1 Then Jacob went on his journey, and came into the land of the people of the east [H6924].

The necessity of Jacob leaving the promised land and journeying to the east recalls the necessity of Adam being driven from the way of the garden of Eden, also in the east (Gen 3:22–24). The exile of Adam represents the irrevocable condemnation of all mankind in Adam, but the concurrent preservation of Adam represents the call to repentance of all mankind in Christ, the new Adam. Jacob being sent away represents the corresponding condemnation of Christ that would open the church age, but Jacob seeking to establish his house represents the redemption of the faithful in Christ. Jesus Christ is the second Adam. The east is the place of the rising sun, representing the font of life, whereby Jacob, representing the Lord, will one day return from the east. This is the glorious return of Christ that will be like lightning coming from the east and shining even unto the west (Matt 24:27).

Genesis 29:2 And he looked, and behold a well in the field, and, lo, there [were] three flocks of sheep lying by it; for out of that well they watered the flocks: and a great stone [was] upon the well's mouth.

Jesus Christ is the font of living water (John 4:10). The three flocks of sheep reflect the three millennia connecting the First and Second Advents and culminating in the millennial kingdom.

Genesis 29:3 And thither were all the flocks gathered: and they rolled the stone [H68] from the well's mouth, and watered the sheep, and put the stone [H68] again upon the well's mouth in his place.

The word *stone* [H68] (upon the well's mouth) is the same word used to describe the *stone* [H68] that Jacob used at Bethel for his pillows (Gen 28:11) and ultimately set up as a pillar (Gen 28:18). Jacob lying upon a stone represents the sacrificial altar required by the law and fulfilled by Jesus Christ. Jacob setting up a pillar with this same altar stone prefigures the resurrection and directly

---

[14] "*Tithes* in their origin appear to have been a sort of *eucharistic offering* made unto God, and probably were something similar to the *minchah* [offering], which we learn from [Gen 4] was in use almost [almost?] from the foundation of the world" (Clarke 1:179; Gen 28:22). The offerings (minchah) of Cain and Abel, respectively, of the dust of the ground (fruit of the ground) and of blood (firstlings of his flock) represent bread and wine, the body and the blood—and finally the condemnation of the present natural body in Adam followed by the promised resurrection unto eternal life that comes by the blood of the new covenant in Christ.

connects the promise of resurrection to the sacrifice of Christ. The stone rolled away from the well's mouth to water the sheep is the stone rolled away from the opening of Jesus's sepulcher (Matt 28:2).

Genesis 29:4 And Jacob said unto them, My brethren, whence [be] ye? And they said, Of Haran [H2771] [are] we.

Jacob meeting his brethren of the land of *Haran* [H2771] is Jacob retracing the original steps of Abram to the land of Canaan through *Haran* [H2771] from Ur of the Chaldees (Gen 11:31). But the land of *Haran* [H2771] is specifically identified with death, as established by the death of Abram's father, Terah, at *Haran* [H2771] (Gen 11:32). And the death identified with the place of *Haran* [H2771], poised between Ur of the Chaldees and the promised land, is the death experienced in the baptism of repentance that is signified by water. This is the sign of the well's mouth identified with this place of meeting.

Genesis 29:5 And he said unto them, Know [H3045] ye Laban the son of Nahor? And they said, We know [H3045] [him].

The word *know* [H3045] (know ye Laban?) is the same "experiential knowledge" connected with the tree of the knowledge of good and evil (Gen 3:5). And the place of Haran is closely identified with death (Gen 11:32). The emphasis on the men of Haran *knowing* [H3045] Laban then points to a connection between the person of Laban and the death under the curse of the tree that is required by the law. This is the death to sin first marked by the baptism in water but not finally fulfilled until the baptism of fire. This is the call to repentance that connects the First and Second Advents of Christ.[15]

Genesis 29:6 And he said unto them, [Is] he well [H7965]? And they said, [He is] well [H7965]: and, behold, Rachel his daughter cometh with the sheep.

The word *well* [H7965] (is Laban well?) is elsewhere translated *prosperity* [H7965] (Job 15:21) and is the same *peace* [H7965] that Jacob is seeking from God in his journey to the east (Gen 28:21). Jacob inquiring after the wellness of Laban is Jacob seeking the peace of God. But the connection between the prosperity of Laban and the peace of God will prove to be bitterly ironic. The first sign of the prosperity, or wellness, of Laban is Rachel, who will be closely

---

[15] "Poetry takes all life as its province. Its primary concern is not with beauty, not with philosophical truth, not with persuasion, but with experience.... [B]eautiful or ugly, strange or common, noble or ignoble, actual or imaginary" (Perrine 559). The whole of the Scriptures is poetically experiential, uncomfortably candid, in the same sense that our relationship with Jesus is personal and transcendent, being innately unmerited, wherein the written Word points to the incarnate Word just as the tree of (experiential) knowledge points to the tree of life.

identified with the idolatry of Laban and will finally be cursed by Jacob because of that idolatry (Gen 31:32).

Genesis 29:7–8 And he said, Lo, [it is] yet high day, neither [is it] time that the cattle should be gathered together: water ye the sheep, and go [and] feed [them]. 8 And they said, We cannot, until all the flocks be gathered together, and [till] they roll the stone from the well's mouth; then we water the sheep.

The necessity that all the flocks be gathered together reflects the reality that there is only one redemption in the one Body of Christ. But the redemption of the faithful in Christ cannot be revealed until the appointed time of the glorious return of Christ (2 Pet 3:8). The rolling away of the stone to reveal the water of life is the resurrection of the dead and also the exaltation of the living. The long delay between the First and Second Advents is the visible expression of the long-suffering of God in the call of the faithful to repentance (2 Pet 3:9). And the emphasis on it being yet high day points to this long delay. Jacob seeking to water the flocks before the appointed time represents the longing of Christ to redeem his faithful ones. And the faithful in Christ have always felt this imminency of Christ (2 Pet 3:10).

Genesis 29:9 And while he yet spake with them, Rachel came with her father's sheep: for she kept them.

It is Rachel that keeps her father's sheep, and thereby it is Rachel, not Leah, that is most closely identified with their father, Laban.

Genesis 29:10 And it came to pass, when Jacob saw Rachel the daughter of Laban his mother's brother, and the sheep of Laban his mother's brother, that Jacob went near, and rolled the stone from the well's mouth, and watered the flock of Laban his mother's brother.

The flock of Rachel represents the last flock to be gathered. Rachel will ultimately suffer premature death, but she nevertheless represents one group, or aspect, of saved humanity. Jacob now removes the stone from the well's mouth in great haste just as Jesus Christ will return in great haste at the appointed time. And the only time that is acceptable to the Lord is the time when all believers have been assembled.[16]

---

[16] "... Jacob ... hastening to seek a bride, met Rachel unexpectedly at the well. And a great stone lay upon the well ... But Jacob alone rolls away the stone, and waters the flocks of his spouse [to be]. The thing is, I think, a dark saying, a shadow of what should come. For what is the stone that is laid but Christ Himself? ... [Gregory of Nyssa, *On the Baptism of Christ*]" (Schaff and Wace, *Nicene and Post-Nicene Fathers: Second Series* 5:521). The marriage supper of the Lamb must await the end times, Rev 19:9.

ESAU, JACOB, ISRAEL

Genesis 29:11 And Jacob kissed [H5401] Rachel, and lifted up [H5375] his voice, and wept [H1058].

Jacob *kissing* [H5401] Rachel recalls the Lord originally breathing the breath of life into humanity, while Jacob *lifting up* [H5375] his voice reflects the exaltation of the Word in the flesh. And Jacob finally *weeping* [H1058] portends the final judgment of the world in the end times. This is the formation of Adam followed by the First Advent followed by the Second Advent. Jacob weeping when he first meets Rachel further anticipates her death and also what can be considered a corresponding loss of her son Joseph (Gen 37:35). This is the lamenting of the Lord in the last days.

Genesis 29:12 And Jacob told Rachel that he [was] her father's brother, and that he [was] Rebekah's son: and she ran and told her father.

Jacob reveals himself first to Rachel, and only then does Laban come to know the identity of Jacob. The Lord likewise reveals himself directly to the faithful, and only afterward does the ruling power of the current world recognize the coming of the Lord in great power and glory (Mark 13:26). Laban will first see Jacob coming as one who is lowly and meek, but Laban will finally recognize that it is Jacob alone who possesses the singular birthright and blessing that proceeds from the one Lord Almighty (2 Cor 6:18).

Genesis 29:13 And it came to pass, when Laban heard the tidings of Jacob his sister's son, that he ran to meet him, and embraced him, and kissed him, and brought him to his house. And he told Laban all these things.

Jacob identifies himself as a near kin, but he does not have any tangible proof. Rather, Jacob has only his own testimony, and that by itself is recognized as accurate and true. Jesus likewise identifies himself by the Holy Scriptures, which testify to him, or are his testimony, and that alone is sufficient for the faithful, who recognize it as the truth. The supernatural sign of the Holy Spirit that marks the faithful is faith itself in Jesus Christ. Other supernatural signs do arise, but it is the sign of faith and faith alone that seals the faithful.

Genesis 29:14 And Laban said to him, Surely thou [art] my bone [H6106] and my flesh [H1320]. And he abode with him the space of a month [H2320].

Laban asserting that Jacob is his *bone* [H6106] and *flesh* [H1320] recalls Adam testifying that Eve is *bone* [H6106] of his *bones* [H6106] and *flesh* [H1320] of his *flesh* [H1320] (Gen 2:23). But there is, however, a subtle progression in phraseology. And that progression does not affirm the unity of flesh but rather testifies to the corruption of all flesh. The unity with Laban is that of the tares and the wheat growing together in one field, or one body. The two will be separated in the end times, and the tares will be consigned unto the fire (Matt 13:30). This is the fate of all flesh that belongs to Laban. Further, the word *month* [H2320] (abode a month) evokes an image in the Hebrew of a "new moon" (Amos 8:5). And the relationship of Jacob and Laban being identified foremost with the moon represents an emphasis on the nighttime, or a relative darkness, a spiritual darkness (Amos 8:9). This points to the physical absence of Jesus Christ during the church age, a famine of hearing the words of the Lord, which is also a kind of relative darkness and is even now culminating in the end times (Amos 8:11).

Genesis 29:15 And Laban said unto Jacob, Because thou [art] my brother, shouldest thou therefore serve me for nought? tell me, what [shall] thy wages [be]?

Jacob sets his own wages. In contrast, Laban does not and can not set Jacob's wages. The devil is merely a created being and in no way has the power to dictate conditions to the Lord.[17]

Genesis 29:16–17 And Laban had two daughters: the name of the elder [was] Leah, and the name of the younger [was] Rachel. 17 Leah [was] tender eyed; but Rachel was beautiful and well favoured.

The wives of Jacob, together with their respective offspring, represent the different groups of faithful that will enter into the one Body of Christ. The elder Leah and the younger Rachel represent, respectively, Jews and Gentiles embodying law and grace. And Jacob will finally receive Leah and Rachel together just as the Jews and Gentiles will finally enter together into the one Body of Christ. Leah then precedes Rachel just as the Covenant of Law precedes the Covenant of Grace. And the Lord will similarly speak of the southern kingdom of Judah and the northern kingdom of Israel as two sisters being his two wives (Jer 3:8). Rachel is chosen before Leah just as the Lord always intended from the very beginning to call all nations, including Israel, into the Body of Christ. Rachel will not replace Leah just as grace does not replace the law. Rather, grace is added to the law, or one could say that grace fulfills the law (Matt 5:17–18). The two sisters Leah and Rachel likewise represent the former days and the latter days, whereby the emphasis on Leah and Rachel being the daughters of Laban is finally a dark testimony that the devil would represent the de facto prince of this world throughout all the ages, even after

---

[17] "There is no uncreated [self-existent] being except God. God has no opposite [since an exact opposite would imply a form of equality] . . . [F]or when you have taken away [from the devil] every kind of good thing (intelligence, will, memory, energy, and existence itself) there would be none of him left" (Lewis, *Screwtape* vii). Nonetheless, the final annihilation of freedom, likewise freewill, in the lake of fire should not be equated with the annihilation of existence or the annihilation, or ending, of consciousness, for the condemnation of the corruption of creation is not the simple opposite of the exhortation implicit to the original act of creation.

the time of the cross. And this reality is now indubitable given the increasing corruption of the visible church, continuing even unto the modern era.[18]

Genesis 29:18–19 And Jacob loved Rachel; and said, I will serve thee seven years for Rachel thy younger daughter. 19 And Laban said, [It is] better that I give her to thee, than that I should give her to another man: abide with me.

Jacob does not ask to be paid with material wealth but rather with a wife and the implied offspring of a wife. Christ neither seeks the kingdoms of the world but rather the redemption of the faithful (Matt 4:8–10). One must first seek the kingdom of God, and to that will be added material wealth—that is, the spiritual, or glorified, body established as a true body (Matt 6:33). Any sign of wealth in this life merely points to our promised inheritance in the spiritual body. Jacob working for and actually against Laban in order to establish his offspring points to Jesus Christ working against the evil one in order to take possession of his faithful ones, particularly during the church age. Laban acknowledging that Jacob should receive his younger daughter reflects even the devil acknowledging that Christ is the rightful bridegroom of blood, specifically as coming in the last days (Rev 19:7).

Genesis 29:20 And Jacob served seven years [H8141] for Rachel; and they seemed unto him [but] a few days [H3117], for the love he had to her.

The seven years that Jacob will serve for his beloved Rachel reflect the original seven days of creation. This is likewise the seven millennia of creation in which the Son seeks his beloved faithful ones. Jacob's experience of *years* [H8141] (seven years) seeming as only *days* [H3117] (a few days) reflects a thousand years being as a day with the Lord (2 Pet 3:8). This is the seven original days of creation heralding the seven millennia of creation. This is the three days that the Head would be in the earth heralding the three millennia the Body would be in the earth (Matt 12:40, Matt 16:4). Rachel is identified with death in childbirth (Gen 35:16–19), whereby Jacob's love for Rachel points to the desire, or lamenting, of Christ for those who are perishing despite the call to be reborn (Matt 18:14). And Leah ultimately being placed ahead of Rachel reflects the necessity that the law precedes grace, likewise that the natural body precedes the spiritual body, and likewise that repentance precedes redemption (Gen 29:25). Jacob receiving both Leah and Rachel together at the end of the first seven years reflects the redemption of the faithful of all the ages together in the one Body of Christ at the end of the present creation (Gen 29:27–30).[19]

---

[18] "Leah who was tender-eyed and Rachel whom Jacob loved signify the synagogue and the church [Jerome, *To Ageruchia*]" (Schaff and Wace, *Nicene and Post-Nicene Fathers: Second Series* 6:235). The people of the law compared with the people of grace.

[19] ". . . Jacob here respects not so much the time as the toil and labour of service he endured in it; he thought that seven years' service was a trifle . . . ." (Gill 1:157; Gen

JACOB AND LABAN

Genesis 29:21 And Jacob said unto Laban, Give [me] my wife, for my days [H3117] are fulfilled, that I may go in unto her.

The emphasis on Jacob serving *days* [H3117], in contrast to *years* [H8141], points to the original seven *days* [H3117] of creation. Jacob has fulfilled all righteousness in the formation of his household just as the Lord has fulfilled all righteousness in the creation and formation of the world (Gen 1:31).

Genesis 29:22 And Laban gathered together all the men of the place, and made a feast.

This is not yet the marriage supper of the Lamb (Rev 19:9). Just as in the days preceding the original destruction that came by water, this is mankind eating, drinking, and marrying in the days preceding the final destruction that will come by fire (Luke 17:27, 2 Pet 3:10).

Genesis 29:23 And it came to pass in the evening, that he took Leah his daughter, and brought her to him; and he went in unto her.

Leah precedes Rachel in the order of natural birth just as humanity is governed first by the law and second by grace in the timeline of world history. The foremost desire of Jacob is for Rachel just as the foremost desire of the Lord is the redemption of humanity that comes only by grace. Nonetheless, Jacob receives Leah as his wife before he receives Rachel just as the law must precede grace and just as the natural must precede the spiritual. And all these things are in accordance with the inviolable sanctity of freewill. The Lord has freewill himself just as man formed in his image has freewill. And thus the Lord could sin and violate our freewill if he so desired, but in any such event, the Lord would cease being the Lord. And what is the hope of the devil in tempting the one true God to sin, except the vain hope that God will somehow cease being God (Matt 4:1)?

Genesis 29:24 And Laban gave unto his daughter Leah Zilpah his maid [for] an handmaid.

Leah is a freewoman, while Zilpah is her bondwoman. The elder Leah, in contrast to the younger Rachel, is most closely identified with the primordial dispensation of law, in contrast to the promised dispensation of grace. And Zilpah is therefore also identified with the law since she belongs to Leah. The dispensation, or administration, of the law is not simply the time of the formal law given by Moses, but rather it is the whole of the present creation that exists under the law, including the incarnation of Christ under the law and in fulfillment of the law. The rule of law is death, specifically the death of the

---

29:20). The sufferings of this present time, of the whole of the present creation, are not worthy to be compared with the glory that will be revealed in us, Rom 8:18.

natural body. And thus one knows that the time of the law encompasses the whole of the present creation, for the natural body has been subjected to death throughout the whole of the present creation. The movement of Leah and Zilpah from the house of Laban to the house of Jacob then represents the struggling of the Lord God to redeem humanity, especially with respect to the requirements of the law. And the struggling of God under the law is specifically the suffering of the Son, especially on the cross. Yet death and hell will not be cast into the lake of fire until the conclusion of the millennial kingdom, being the final conclusion of the dispensation of law and death (Rev 20:14).

Genesis 29:25 And it came to pass, that in the morning, behold, it [was] Leah: and he said to Laban, What [is] this thou hast done unto me? did not I serve with thee for Rachel? wherefore then hast thou beguiled [H7411] me?

Laban is the beguiler, and it is Jacob that identifies him as such. The word *beguiled* [H7411] (why hast thou beguiled me) means "to beguile, deal treacherously with" and has a connotation "to deceive." That the deceiver, who is the devil, would be the instrument of providence is at first shocking, but this should finally be recognized as the fundamental way, or nature, of the present world. The evil one would likewise be allowed to nail Jesus to the cross in order for the grace of God to be revealed. And providence likewise moves in all our lives despite the reality that we are ourselves all sinners.

Genesis 29:26 And Laban said, It must not be so done in our country, to give the younger before the firstborn.

The natural body must precede the spiritual, or glorified, body just as law must precede grace just as repentance must precede redemption.[20]

Genesis 29:27 Fulfil her week, and we will give thee this also for the service which thou shalt serve with me yet seven other years.

In total, Jacob will serve Laban three sevens (Gen 31:41). The first period of seven years for Leah. The second seven years for Rachel. And the third and final seven years for Laban's flocks—the final year of which to be completed, at

---

[20] "Dr. [John] Lightfoot [AD 1602–1675] makes Leah and Rachel [respectively] to be figures of the two churches, the Jews under the law and the Gentiles under the gospel [of grace in Christ]: [Rachel] the younger, the more beautiful, and more in *the thoughts of Christ* . . . but the other, like Leah, first embraced: yet in this the allegory does not hold, that the Gentiles, the younger, were more fruitful, [Gal 4:27]" (Henry 1:177; Gen 29:15–30). Henry's argument against the parallel between the two daughters of Laban and the two covenants of God, law and grace, must be faulty, for the same argument could be used against the inspired identification of Ishmael and Isaac also with, respectively, law and grace, Gal 4:25–28, in that Ishmael, in the purely natural, has always been more prolific than Isaac, Gen 25:16.

least symbolically, in Jacob's return unto the promised land. The three sevens served by Jacob finally point to the three sevens of the book of Revelation—namely, the seven seals, the seven trumpets, and the seven vials. Jacob receiving, at the end of the first seven, Leah and Rachel with their handmaids and, thereby, spiritually his twelve offspring points to the sealing of the 144,000, as predicating the end of the first seven of Revelation (Rev 7:4–8). And Jacob finally returning to the promised land, suddenly and secretly, at the end of the third and final seven points to Jesus returning like a thief, suddenly and unexpectedly, which predicates the end of the third and final seven of Revelation (Gen 31:20, Rev 16:15).[21]

Genesis 29:28 And Jacob did so, and fulfilled her week: and he gave him Rachel his daughter to wife also.

To receive his wives and offspring, Jacob fulfills all righteousness under Laban, even though the dealings of Laban are unjust. Jesus likewise fulfills all righteousness under the law in order to receive his faithful, even though the law, which is the law of death, has no power over him (Matt 3:14–16).

Genesis 29:29 And Laban gave to Rachel his daughter Bilhah his handmaid to be her maid.

Rachel is a freewoman, while Bilhah is her bondwoman. The younger Rachel, in contrast to the elder Leah, is most closely identified with the latter dispensation of grace, in contrast to the former dispensation of law. And Bilhah is therefore also identified with grace since she belongs to Rachel. The dispensation, or administration, of grace is not only the church age beginning with the cross but rather the totality of the grace of God throughout the whole of creation. Christ is the lamb slain from the foundation of the world (Rev 13:8). The grace of God began with the original act of creation—as affirmed in the preservation of all mankind despite sin—and will be fulfilled radically and finally in the unmerited exaltation of the faithful in the spiritual, or glorified, body at the conclusion of the present creation.[22]

The blood of Jesus Christ spilled on the cross is the suffering of God in the act of our redemption made visible at a specific point in time, but the blood of Christ covers the whole of creation just as it is the whole of creation that must be redeemed. The movement of Rachel and Bilhah from the house of Laban to the house of Jacob then represents the struggling of God to redeem humanity, especially with respect to the final revelation of grace in the last days. And the struggling of God in the revelation of grace in the end times is specifically the

---

[21] "It is evident that the marriage of both sisters took place nearly about the same time, and that such a connection was then allowed, though afterwards prohibited [Lev 18:18]" (Jamieson et al. 1:203; Gen 29:23). The sealing of the 144,000 out of the twelve tribes.
[22] "The [Rabbinic] belief was general that the sending of the Messiah was part of the Creator's plan at the inception of the Universe [e.g., *Pesachim* and *Pesikta Rabbah*]" (Cohen, *Rabbinic Sages* 347). God is in control, even in the face of suffering and death.

suffering of the Body of Christ in imitation of Christ. The suffering and struggling of the Body of Christ in imitation of Christ is most closely identified with God the Spirit, not God the Son, since it is the Spirit who indwells and empowers and inspires the Body. This struggling and suffering of the Body of Christ is the groaning of the Holy Spirit in the childbirth that brings forth the faithful unto eternal life.

Genesis 29:30 And he went in also unto Rachel, and he loved also Rachel more than Leah, and served with him yet seven other years.

The elder Leah is most closely identified with law, while the younger Rachel is most closely identified with grace. Jacob desires Rachel more than Leah just as Jesus desires the exaltation of the spiritual, or glorified, resurrection body by grace more than the condemnation of the natural body under the law. The pain we feel seeing Leah not loved is the pain that always accompanies the law, that is, the law of death that necessarily exists apart from the life in grace.

Eleven Sons

Genesis 29:31 And when the LORD saw that Leah [was] hated [H8130], he opened her womb: but Rachel [was] barren.

The firstborn Leah being *hated* [H8130] parallels the firstborn Esau being *hated* [H8130] (Mal 1:3). The ironic hatred and rejection of the firstborn, who holds the birthright and the blessing, represents the condemnation of the natural body, which must precede the exaltation of the spiritual, or glorified, body. The firstborn Leah being hated represents the condemnation and exile of fallen mankind, while her fertility represents the concurrent preservation of mankind for the purpose of redemption. The original barrenness of Rachel represents the faithful waiting until the appointed time of the revelation of the fullness of grace in the end times. The second born Jacob being united with the firstborn Leah represents the second man Jesus fulfilling the first covenant, or marriage contract, the Covenant of Law. The second born Jacob being united with the second born Rachel represents the second man Jesus fulfilling the second covenant, or marriage contract, the Covenant of Grace.[23]

Genesis 29:32 And Leah conceived, and bare a son, and she called his name Reuben [H7205]: for she said, Surely the LORD hath looked [H7200] upon my affliction [H6040]; now therefore my husband will love [H157] me.

---

[23] "This statement [that God saw Leah was hated] is of great importance in the progressive development of the covenant. It is not to be considered . . . merely in the style of Scripture, which ascribes all ordinary events to the agency of God; but purposely to show that . . . the Israelitish nation originated not from nature but from grace" (Jamieson et al. 1:204; Gen 29:31). Individual events always have meaning, and they also always fit into an overall flow of progressive revelation.

JACOB AND LABAN

The elder Leah, the firstborn, is most closely identified with the first covenant, the Covenant of law, and likewise with the present creation, the first creation, that is governed by the first covenant. The six sons of Leah thereby reflect the six millennia of the present creation, beginning with Adam in the first millennium. The close succession of the births of Leah's first four sons in the Biblical account reflects the unity of the first four millennia leading up to the watershed that is the birth of Christ. The *affliction* [H6040] of Leah identified with the conception and birth of the firstborn Reuben reflects the original condemnation of all mankind in the person of Adam (Gen 3:17), while the sign of new life represented by the birth of Reuben reflects the concurrent preservation of mankind in the world despite sin (Gen 3:20). And the expectation that Jacob will finally *love* [H157] Leah being expressly because of the birth of Reuben points to the Messianic bloodline by which the faithful will realize the redemptive love of Jesus Christ (Gen 22:2). That the firstborn Reuben is not himself a member of the Messianic bloodline foreshadows the delay of the redemption that is the call to repentance in the flesh (Matt 1:1–17).

The name *Reuben* [H7205] (given by Leah) means "behold a son," which again points to the promised Seed of woman, who is God the Son (Gen 3:15). And therefore the firstborn Reuben being a type of the Messiah, even though he is not a member of the Messianic bloodline, represents an emphasis on Jesus being the true firstborn. And Jesus is not only the firstborn from the dead, even though the Lord would be born, or revealed, after the original formation of Adam (Col 1:18). All things have, after all, come into existence through God the Son, who is the Christ, and therefore the Lord originally preceded Adam (John 1:3). Further, the name *Reuben* [H7205] (she called his name) and the word *looked* [H7200] (the Lord hath looked) are closely related in the Hebrew. And Leah connects the image of the Lord *looking* [H7200] upon her affliction with the name of her firstborn *Reuben* [H7205], again "behold or look a son." And thereby Leah identifies the promised Seed of woman with the sign of affliction. This is not the death of the cross in isolation but also the affliction and death of the whole world throughout the whole of time and space, both before and after the cross, as embodied by the Messiah on the cross.

Genesis 29:33 And she conceived again, and bare a son; and said, Because the LORD hath heard [H8085] that I [was] hated [H8130], he hath therefore given me this [son] also: and she called his name Simeon [H8095].

The name *Simeon* [H8095] (given by Leah) means "heard" and is closely related to the word *heard* [H8085], which has a connotation "to obey".[24] The image of Leah being *hated* [H8130] (because I was hated), identified with her second born son, recalls the apostasy and hatred and violence that filled the earth in the second millennium (Gen 6:5, 6:11). The image of the Lord hearing and obeying Leah, or rather acting in response to the hatred toward Leah,

---

[24] *Simeon* [H8095] literal meaning and etymology per *Strong's*, not *Brown-Driver-Briggs*.

recalls the Lord acting in response to the corruption and wickedness of all flesh at the time of the Flood (Gen 6:13). But the new life represented by the birth of Simeon recalls the concurrent preservation of Noah and his family despite the condemnation of all flesh (Gen 6:18).[25]

Genesis 29:34 And she conceived again, and bare a son; and said, Now this time will my husband be joined [H3867] unto me, because I have born him three sons: therefore was his name called Levi [H3878].

The name *Levi* [H3878] (given by Leah) means "joined" and is closely related to the word *joined* [H3867] (as husband and wife). Levi is the third son, and this fact is connected with the desirable and also prophetic union of man and woman. This connection points to the call of the faithful embodied by the call of Abraham in the third millennium in what is fundamentally a marriage covenant. And the person of Levi is again identified with the third millennium by the formal Levitical priesthood that would also be established in the third millennium (Num 3:6–7). The first three millennia embodied by Adam, Noah, and Abraham reflect the unity of the Trinity and also the call of the faithful to unity with God, in God, and through God. This is the call of the faithful to be joined unto the Father in the one Body of Christ through the power of the indwelling Holy Spirit (Rom 12:5). And the union of man and woman is the revelation of just this union of Christ and the faithful (Eph 5:30–32).

Genesis 29:35 And she conceived again, and bare a son: and she said, Now will I praise [H3034] the LORD: therefore she called his name Judah [H3063]; and left bearing.

The name *Judah* [H3063] (given by Leah) means "praised," while the word *praise* [H3034] (praise the Lord) connotes "to confess the name of God" and also "to confess sins." This points to the one and only name that has been given unto mankind for our salvation (Acts 4:12). The birth of Jacob's fourth son Judah prefigures the fourth millennium, beginning with the kingship of David and culminating in the birth of Jesus as the king of kings. The person of Judah is directly connected to the fourth millennium in that David and Christ would descend from the line of Judah (Gen 49:10). The image of Leah *praising* [H3034] the Lord, which is identified with the birth of Judah, reflects Jesus being the very incarnation of God in the flesh. But the sign of barrenness being attached to Leah immediately following the birth of Judah portends the Messiah being cut off from the land of the living (Isa 53:8). And the barrenness of Leah following her fourth son foreshadows a second and final barrenness following her sixth son just as the time of the First Advent foreshadows the time of the

---

[25] The word *heard* [the Lord hath heard] is etymologically linked in the text with the name *Simeon* [she called his name] (*Tanakh* 45 n. f; Gen 29:33) as is the word *joined* [my husband unto me] with the name *Levi* [was his name called] (Ibid. 45 n. g; Gen 29:34).

Second Advent. The two periods of barrenness correspond to the rejection of Christ followed by the rejection of the Body of Christ.

The first period of barrenness experienced by Leah is identified with the births of sons unto Jacob by his bondwomen, Bilhah and Zilpah. And the naming of the sons of the bondwomen, corresponding to the birthrights of the sons, is thereby identified with the First Advent of Jesus Christ. But when Jacob finally blesses all his sons at the end of his life, the position of the sons of his bondwomen, Bilhah and Zilpah, will be shifted to follow Leah's sixth and final son. This again identifies the sons of the bondwomen with the barrenness of Leah, but this time it is the second and final period of barrenness experienced by Leah. And the blessings of the sons of the bondwomen are thereby identified with the Second Advent of Christ (Gen 49:16–21). The naming, or the birthrighting, of Jacob's sons in the order of their natural births in the flesh is most closely identified with the incarnation of Christ in the flesh. The blessing of Jacob's sons in a spiritual reordering, or new ordering, is most closely identified with the glorious reappearing of Christ and the concomitant judgment of the world. The First Advent is to the birthright as the Second Advent is to the blessing.

Genesis 30:1 And when Rachel saw that she bare Jacob no children, Rachel envied [H7065] her sister; and said unto Jacob, Give me children, or else I die [H4191].

The sons of the bondwomen Bilhah and Zilpah do not reflect the millennia of creation as do the sons of the freewomen Leah and Rachel, but rather the sons of the bondwomen collectively reflect the revelation of Jesus Christ. The bondwomen are subordinate to the freewomen in the natural chronology of creation just as the bondwomen themselves are subordinate to the freewomen in the societal order of the present creation. In the context of the first period of barrenness experienced by Leah, the sons of Jacob's bondwomen specifically reflect the First Advent of Christ. And the emphasis in the First Advent is Christ as the Son of man in contrast to the Son of God. And the emphasis is likewise the birthright in contrast to the blessing. The interjection of bondwomen intervenes unnaturally in the normal progression of the offspring of the freewomen just as the Holy Spirit overshadowing Mary in the conception of Christ intercedes supernaturally in the normal progression of the generations of man (Luke 1:35). The interjection of bondwomen to bear children is unnatural in the sense that it represents an intervention in the normal incidence and progression of barrenness in the world. The intercession of Christ is likewise a supernatural intervention in the natural progression of the spiritual barrenness of the world. The First Advent of Christ being most closely connected with bondwomen, in contrast to freewomen, points to the earthly ministry of Christ as the servant of all humanity (Mark 10:44–45). And the account of the births of the sons of the bondwomen Bilhah and Zilpah being succinct and uninterrupted reflects the brevity of the First Advent.

The younger Rachel is most closely identified with grace, while the elder Leah is most closely identified with law. Rachel becoming *envious* [H7065] because of the offspring of Leah reflects the Lord being provoked to *jealousy* [H7065] because of the sins, or figurative offspring, of Judah (1 Kgs 14:22). The elder Leah is fertile and gives birth to natural offspring, while the younger Rachel is barren and therefore seeks supernatural offspring. The natural offspring of Leah are identified with the current natural creation, as represented by the first six millennia of creation, while the supernatural offspring of Rachel are identified with the promised new creation, as represented by the seventh and eighth millennia. The sons of Rachel follow the sons of Leah just as the spiritual follows the natural. The sons of Rachel will be a minority compared with the sons of Leah just as the faithful are a minority. The sons of Rachel, led by Joseph, will be preeminent compared with the sons of Leah just as the Body of Christ will transcend the body of Adam. Rachel proclaiming that she will *die* [H4191] if she does not receive children recalls the original *dying* [H4191] connected with the tree of knowledge (Gen 2:17). And the fertility that Rachel seeks will follow the fertility of Leah just as grace completes the law in the resurrection of the dead unto eternal life. And the first sign of fertility given to the freewoman Rachel will be the fertility of her bondwoman, Bilhah, representing, together with Zilpah, the First Advent of Jesus Christ.[26]

Genesis 30:2 And Jacob's anger [H639] was kindled [H2734] against Rachel: and he said, [Am] I in God's stead, who hath withheld from thee the fruit of the womb?

The word *kindled* [H2734] (Jacob's anger kindled) means "to burn, be kindled, of anger." In contrast, the word *anger* [H639] (Jacob's anger) is the same word *nostrils* [H639], closely identified with the original breath of life that proceeds from God (Gen 2:7). Jacob will act to give Rachel offspring through Bilhah, and thereby Jacob will act in the place of God, as a type, or representation, of God. The image of Jacob flaring his nostrils at Rachel recalls the original spark of life that is our hope. But the dominant image of a burning anger is negative and portends the coming destruction by fire that will precede the renewal of all things. The ubiquitous juxtaposition of hatred and hope, representing law and grace, points to the death that must precede eternal life. This is the death and resurrection embodied by Jesus Christ and likewise the faithful in Jesus Christ.

Genesis 30:3–4 And she said, Behold my maid Bilhah, go in unto her; and she shall bear upon my knees [H1290], that I may also have children

---

[26] "... 'The world will endure six thousand years—two thousand years in chaos, two thousand with Torah, and two thousand years will be the days of the Messiah' [*Sanhedrin*]" (Cohen, *Rabbinic Sages* 356). In this schema, the days of the Messiah can be interpreted as the parenthetical church age connecting the First and Second Advents.

by her. 4 And she gave him Bilhah her handmaid to wife: and Jacob went in unto her.

The word *knees* [H1290] (bear upon my knees) is derived from the root "to kneel, bless" [H1288]. The person of Rachel, the second born, or latter offspring, is identified with the dispensation of grace, in contrast to that of law. And Rachel's bondwoman, Bilhah, expressly in the act of bearing offspring, is identified with the revelation of Jesus Christ at the time of the First Advent. The bondwoman Bilhah travailing in childbirth on the knees of Rachel reflects the blessing that the faithful receive by grace through the submission and suffering of Christ in the incarnation. But the relationship between Rachel and Bilhah specifically points to the relationship between God the Spirit and the virgin Mary and, thereby, again connects God the Holy Spirit to the feminine, in contrast to the masculine. Rachel giving Bilhah to Jacob reflects God the Spirit overshadowing Mary in the conception of God the Son according to the will of God the Father (Luke 1:35). Jacob, in isolation, is normally identified with God the Holy Spirit, but in this case Rachel assumes the active role of giving while Jacob assumes the more passive role of receiving. This is the conception of the Son that is by the power of the Holy Spirit. Further, the relationship between Mary and the Holy Spirit should be viewed as the parallel between flesh and spirit in conceiving the unity of flesh and spirit, likewise the unity of law and grace. Mary conceiving Christ is also the Holy Spirit conceiving Christ. The virgin conception should absolutely not be viewed as a masculine God the Holy Spirit inseminating Mary.[27]

Genesis 30:5–6 And Bilhah conceived, and bare Jacob a son. 6 And Rachel said, God hath judged [H1777] me, and hath also heard [H8085] my voice, and hath given me a son: therefore called she his name Dan [H1835].

The name *Dan* [H1835] (given by Rachel) means "judge" and is derived from the root "to judge" [H1777] (God hath judged), which has connotations not only "to execute judgment" but also "to plead a cause." And this contrast reflects the connection between the death and resurrection of Jesus Christ in the place of the faithful and the perpetual intercession of Christ for the faithful, the communion of Christ with the faithful, that is our personal justification, or new creation, in Christ. Further, the image of the Lord *hearing* [H8085] is connected with the birth of Dan and also the earlier birth of Simeon (Gen 29:33). And this parallel reflects the connection between the First Advent of Christ and the Flood of Noah. The Lord hearing is connected with humanity being delivered and, thereby, points to the necessity of man repenting and calling upon the name of the one true Lord in order to be saved (Acts 2:21).

---

[27] "These are all the children of Jacob . . . eight were legitimate, viz. six of Lea [Leah], and two of Rachel, and four were of the handmaids, two of each; . . ." (Josephus 1:135). The illegitimacy of the second man is the legitimacy of the first man.

Genesis 30:7-8 And Bilhah Rachel's maid conceived again, and bare Jacob a second son. 8 And Rachel said, With great wrestlings [H5319] have I wrestled [H6617] with my sister, and I have prevailed: and she called his name Naphtali [H5321].

The name *Naphtali* [H5321] (given by Rachel) means "wrestling" and is closely related in the Hebrew to the words *wrestlings* [H5319] and *wrestled* [H6617]. The younger Rachel is most closely identified with grace, while the elder Leah is most closely identified with law. Rachel *wrestling* [H6617] with Leah and prevailing over Leah then represents grace superseding law. In the present context, which is the birthright in contrast to the blessing, the prevailing of Rachel over Leah signifies the victory of the cross that would be the fulfillment of the law. And this is specifically the law of death in contrast to the life that comes by grace. The firstborn *Dan* [H1835], the first son of Rachel's bondwoman, Bilhah, focuses our attention on judgment, while the second born *Naphtali* [H5321], the second son of Rachel's bondwoman, focuses our attention on victory. This is the death and resurrection of Jesus Christ in the First Advent by which the children of God receive grace through faith in Christ. Rachel's claim of victory over her sister, Leah, being somewhat hollow, in that Rachel has not yet herself given birth, foreshadows the long delay between the resurrection of Jesus Christ at the First Advent and the resurrection of the faithful in Christ at the Second Advent.

Genesis 30:9 When Leah saw that she had left bearing, she took Zilpah her maid, and gave her Jacob to wife.

This specific juncture, marked by the two bondwomen Bilhah and Zilpah, represents a time of barrenness for both Rachel and Leah, who are identified, respectively, with grace and law. The failure of Leah and also Rachel to themselves produce offspring at this juncture portends the time of the First Advent, which is marked by the rejection of the offspring of the Messiah that is the promised new life in Christ. The fertility of Leah becoming barrenness represents the failure of the law to yield salvation, or offspring. The original and continuing barrenness of Rachel represents the promise of grace being unfulfilled even at the time of the First Advent. The grace of God cannot be considered complete, even after the death and resurrection of Christ, because the faithful in Christ continue to suffer in the natural body. The six sons of Leah reflect the six millennia of creation between the formation of Adam and the establishment of the Second Advent of Christ. And Rachel will be barren during this entire period. The barrenness of Leah and Rachel, representing the failure of the law and the concurrent rejection of grace, points to the barrenness of Christ at the time of the First Advent, being cut off from the land of the living without offspring, that is, without completing the promised rebirth of the faithful (Isa 53:8). The spiritual, or glorified, body is the offspring of Christ just as the natural body is the offspring of Adam.

JACOB AND LABAN

The sons of bondwomen being interjected unnaturally into the natural progression of the sons of freewomen represents the conception of Christ being interposed supernaturally into the natural progression of the generations of man. The present context is the natural birth order of the sons of Jacob—reflecting the birthright and the corresponding kingship of Jesus Christ and, therefore, the First Advent of Christ. But within this context, the sons of Jacob's bondwomen do represent different aspects of the First Advent. Leah is identified with the law, and therefore her bondwoman, Zilpah, is also identified with the law. Rachel is identified with grace, and therefore her bondwoman, Bilhah, is also identified with grace. Bilhah's offspring are identified specifically with Jesus Christ as the Head of the Body and the corresponding grace in eternal life that is received by virtue of the Head. Zilpah's offspring are identified with the Body of Christ and the corresponding law of righteousness that must be fulfilled in the Body. The Head is identified with the intangible, such as speaking words, and accordingly reflects grace, which is also intangible, or spiritual. The Body is identified with the tangible, such as doing works, and accordingly reflects the works required by the law, which are also tangible, or physical. The Head is also over the Body just as the Covenant of Grace is greater than the Covenant of Law. And Bilhah's offspring precede Zilpah's offspring just as the Head precedes the Body in death and resurrection.

Genesis 30:10–11 And Zilpah Leah's maid bare Jacob a son. 11 And Leah said, A troop [H1409] cometh: and she called his name Gad [H1410].

The name *Gad* [H1410] (given by Leah) is closely related to the word *troop* [H1409], meaning "troop" or perhaps denoting "good fortune." The birth of *Gad* [H1410] points to the blessing of the multitude of the faithful in the Body of Christ, which comes only by the shed blood of Christ.[28]

Genesis 30:12–13 And Zilpah Leah's maid bare Jacob a second son. 13 And Leah said, Happy [H837] am I, for the daughters [H1323] will call me blessed [H833]: and she called his name Asher [H836].

The name *Asher* [H836] (given by Leah) means "happy" and is closely related to the words *happy* [H837] and *blessed* [H833]. The name *Asher* [H836] is derived from the root "to go straight, go on, advance" [H833], which has a connotation "to go straight in the way of understanding." The birth of *Asher* [H836] (to Leah), like the birth of *Gad* [H1410] (also to Leah), points to the blessing and exaltation in the Body of Christ. But the image of *daughters* [H1323] calling Leah *blessed* [H833] represents an emphasis on the feminine that points specifically to the anointing of the indwelling Holy Spirit, who animates and edifies and empowers the faithful in the Body of Christ. This sign, or intimation, of the presence, or nature, of the Spirit is subtle, but it is, after all, the very nature of

---

[28] The word *troop* [H1409] denotes "fortune" per *Strong's*, "fortune, good fortune" per *Brown-Driver-Briggs*.

the Spirit to be subtle. And it is uniquely the feminine that is marked by the sign of subtlety, or silence (1 Cor 14:34).

Genesis 30:14 And Reuben went in the days of wheat harvest, and found mandrakes in the field, and brought them unto his mother Leah. Then Rachel said to Leah, Give me, I pray thee, of thy son's mandrakes.

The firstfruits of the wheat harvest mark the Feast of Weeks, which is also called Pentecost (Exod 34:22).[29] The account of the firstborn Reuben finding mandrakes in the days of wheat harvest immediately follows the account of the offspring of Bilhah and Zilpah just as the coming of the Holy Spirit on Pentecost immediately follows the First Advent of Christ (Acts 2:1–4). The giving of mandrakes in this context then represents the freewill offering connected with the Feast of Weeks, or Pentecost (Deut 16:10). Leah is identified with law, while Rachel is identified with grace. Leah's firstborn Reuben is identified with Adam, or all men born in the natural body under the law. Reuben giving an offering of mandrakes to Leah represents the repentance of the faithful that is required under the law, while Rachel commanding Leah to give her Reuben's mandrakes represents the redemption of man that comes only by grace. The identification of the mandrakes with a freewill offering points to the necessity that man must himself choose to turn to God of his own freewill. And the connection with Pentecost, in contrast to Passover or Tabernacles, points to the repentance that heralds the Holy Spirit (Acts 2:38).[30]

The Feast of Unleavened Bread, the Feast of Weeks (Pentecost), and finally the Feast of Tabernacles (Ingathering) are the three times that all males must appear before the Lord (Exod 34:18–23, Deut 16:16). The Feast of Unleavened Bread, beginning with Passover and affirmed by Firstfruits, signifies the promise embodied by the death and resurrection of Jesus Christ as the new Adam (Lev 23:10–12). The faithful are not yet exalted in the spiritual, or glorified, resurrection body, but the promise of our redemption is absolutely guaranteed by the death and resurrection of Jesus Christ as the Head of the Body of the faithful. Pentecost then signifies the call to repentance that marks the quickening of the indwelling Holy Spirit in our lives while we are yet in the natural body. The conviction that comes by the Spirit is the revelation of the truth of Christ (John 16:8–11). We repent from our sins, but our sins are exactly what nailed Christ to the cross (Acts 2:36–38). We are spiritually repenting from the crucifixion of Christ. And thus the Son must come before the Spirit in the act of new creation (John 16:7). And the Feast of Ingathering finally signifies the completion of the harvest of mankind that is finally the fulfillment of our promised redemption in the resurrection of the Body of Christ.

---

[29] *Pentecost* [G4005] means "fiftieth," referring to the completion of seven Sabbaths of days as counted from Passover, Lev 23:15–16, Deut 16:9.

[30] "Whatever strange agencies God may allow to be used (such as mandrakes), the real factor is His sovereign will . . . ." (Guzik 175; Gen 30:14–18). The providence of God, working through a fallen creation, is necessarily always using "strange" agencies.

JACOB AND LABAN

Genesis 30:15 And she said unto her, [Is it] a small matter that thou hast taken my husband? and wouldest thou take away my son's mandrakes also? And Rachel said, Therefore he shall lie with thee to night for thy son's mandrakes.

The present juncture—following the births of the first four sons of Leah, also following the births of the four sons of Bilhah and Zilpah—represents the beginning of the church age opened by the First Advent. The emphasis at this juncture on the second born Rachel having taken Jacob from the firstborn Leah reflects the ascension of Christ concluding the First Advent (Acts 1:6–9). Leah is to Rachel as law is to grace as earth is to heaven. Rachel now seeking to take away the mandrakes of Leah's son Reuben, after taking Leah's husband Jacob, points to the faithful in Christ being accepted and also taken in the exaltation by the grace of the Holy Spirit just as Christ was accepted and taken in the resurrection and ascension by the power of the Spirit. In this role the firstborn Reuben reflects the faithful as taken expressly out of the first man Adam. And the mandrakes again represent the freewill offering connected with the Feast of Weeks, or Pentecost. The close connection in the narrative between Rachel taking Leah's husband and Rachel taking the mandrakes of Leah's son reflects the unity of Jesus Christ and the faithful in the Body of Christ. Note also that the acceptance of Christ is a "small matter" in the sense that Christ is sinless. In contrast, the acceptance of the faithful in Christ is a "big matter" in that all men, including the faithful, are undeserving sinners.

The emphasis changing from Rachel having taken Jacob away from Leah to Rachel now giving Jacob back to Leah represents the quickening of the Spirit in the faithful that comes only by grace and only after the ascension of Christ. Since Leah is identified with law and likewise the flesh governed by law, Rachel giving Jacob to Leah principally represents the quickening of the Spirit in the individual while yet in the natural body. The emphasis on Leah receiving Jacob in exchange for Rachel receiving the freewill offering of her firstborn, Reuben, points to the faithful receiving Christ—the anointing of the Holy Spirit—only upon repenting and turning unto Christ of their own freewill. And the firstborn Reuben again reflects the faithful being called out of the first man Adam as specifically connected with the first Pentecost following the death and resurrection of Christ. This is the essential repentance identified with the crucifixion of Christ, in accordance with it being Adam and likewise mankind in Adam that nailed Christ to the cross. And the union of Jacob and Leah at this point in time represents the union of the ascendant Christ and the faithful while the faithful are yet in the natural body. It is exactly this union, or betrothal, that defines the church age. And the subsequent two sons of Leah will accordingly reflect the fifth and sixth millennia constituting the church age.[31]

---

[31] "In still another correspondence with the story of Jacob and Esau, one sibling barters a privilege for a plant product [mandrakes compared with lentiles], though here the one who sells off the privilege is the younger, not the elder" (Alter, *Genesis* 160; Gen 30:15). The younger man Jacob buying his birthright is Christ assuming the dominion of Adam,

Genesis 30:16 And Jacob came out of the field in the evening, and Leah went out to meet him, and said, Thou must come in unto me; for surely I have hired thee with my son's mandrakes. And he lay with her that night.

The final two offspring of Leah and Jacob that will proceed from this point forward reflect the fifth and sixth millennia following the time of the First Advent. Leah hiring Jacob with Reuben's mandrakes represents the repentance of the firstborn, or first man, Adam. And this connects the church age with the call to repentance of all mankind in Adam and from Adam, which corresponds to the formation of the body of faithful in Christ, the new Adam. The idea that Jacob is actually required to lay with Leah because she has hired him points to the righteousness of God in delaying the final judgment so that the faithful have time to repent and turn unto God (2 Pet 3:9). The freewill offering of the firstborn being used to purchase additional offspring represents the blood of the firstborn from the dead, Jesus Christ, being offered as a ransom for many (Matt 20:28). This again connects the firstborn Adam and the firstborn Christ. And the offering of the firstborn ultimately being repentance itself points to the firstborn from the dead repenting in the place of all the faithful on the cross. The baptism of repentance is the baptism of death and resurrection on the cross. And the repentance of the faithful in Christ actually must be the same repentance of Christ on the cross. Adam formed in the image of God embodies the promise of God that is the image of God, while the First Advent of Christ embodies the repentance of all the faithful in Christ. And the Second Advent of Christ will finally embody the redemption of all the faithful in Christ.

Genesis 30:17 And God hearkened [H8085] unto Leah, and she conceived, and bare Jacob the fifth son.

The word *hearkened* [H8085] (God hearkened unto Leah) has a connotation "to obey." Leah is most closely identified with the law, so God *hearkening* [H8085] unto Leah especially reflects the perfect righteousness of God that is in accord with the law. But the image of God *hearkening* [H8085] is connected not only with the fifth son Issachar but also with the sequence of Simeon (Gen 29:33), Dan (Gen 30:6), Issachar (Gen 30:17), and Joseph (Gen 30:22). The connection between Jacob's sons Simeon, Dan, Issachar, and Joseph is the connection between the Flood, the First Advent, the opening of the church age, and the Second Advent. This is the God of Abraham, Isaac, and Jacob hearkening first unto Leah and second unto Rachel and, thereby, affirming the fulfillment of law in grace.

Genesis 30:18 And Leah said, God hath given me my hire, because I have given my maiden to my husband: and she called his name Issachar [H3485].

---

whereas the elder woman Leah buying her offspring—representing the Bride, or Body, of Christ—is Adam-kind accepting the gift of grace in Christ.

JACOB AND LABAN

Leah connects the birth of Issachar with her having given Zilpah to Jacob. The offspring of Leah's bondwoman, Zilpah, are identified with the call of the faithful at the time of the First Advent, while Leah's fifth son Issachar is identified with the corresponding call of the faithful that opens the church age in the fifth millennium. The name *Issachar* [H3485] means "recompense," which represents the blessing of the faithful by the Holy Spirit, specifically in the church age and expressly because of the fulfillment of the law by Christ.[32] The primary blessing, or gift, of the Spirit that we receive while yet in the natural body is not wealth and power but rather the one true faith. And the primary sign of the Spirit is not the works of the visible church or even supernatural miracles but rather the Bible that is the very Word of God. The only sign that a wicked and adulterous generation will receive is the sign of Jonah. And the sign of Jonah is not only the three days but also the preaching unto Nineveh that follows the three days and represents the Gospel going unto the Gentiles (Matt 16:4). This is the Great Commission that is foremost the call to faith and salvation, which is expressly that faith and salvation that exists in the Trinity and only in the Trinity (Matthew 28:18–20).[33]

Genesis 30:19 And Leah conceived again, and bare Jacob the sixth son.

The sixth son of the firstborn Leah prefigures the sixth millennium of the present creation. And the sixth millennium, as the fifth millennium, continues to be governed by the Covenant of Law, the first covenant, as from the time of the first man Adam. That the present creation continues to be governed by law, even after the time of the cross, should be obvious from the fact that suffering and death continue to reign over the present creation, including the faithful yet in the world. The kingdom of God is not of this world (John 18:36).

Genesis 30:20 And Leah said, God hath endued me [with] a good dowry; now will my husband dwell [H2082] with me, because I have born him six sons: and she called his name Zebulun [H2074].

The name *Zebulun* [H2074] (given by Leah) means "habitation" and is derived from the root "to reside (dwell)" [H2082].[34] The birth of Leah's sixth and final son prefigures the coming fullness of the indwelling Holy Spirit that

---

[32] "Two sons *Leah* was now blessed with . . . reckoning herself well repaid for her *mandrakes* . . . which is a strange construction of the providence . . . rewarded for *giving her maid to her husband*" (Wesley 1:119; Gen 30:17). The movement of a sinless God in a sinful world is necessarily always strange and foreign.
[33] "The book of Jonah is most likely a prophetic allegory intended to foretell the Lord's salvation of the gentiles in the time of His final messianic presence in the world. . . . It is read in its entirety in the Church at the Easter vigil of Great Saturday as it was directly referred to by Christ Himself as the sign of His messianic mission in the world [Matt 12:38, Luke 11:29]" (Hopko, *Orthodox Faith* 3:25). The Scriptures, in their entirety, are simultaneously literal and prophetic, with all realities converging in the end times.
[34] *Zebulun* [H2074] literal meaning and etymology per *Strong's*, not *Brown-Driver-Briggs*.

will be the conclusion of the sixth millennium and the culmination of the church age in the resurrection and exaltation of the faithful. The births of Leah's fifth and sixth sons are closely connected with each other in the Biblical account and are also markedly separated from the births of Leah's first four sons. The church age following the incarnation of Christ is likewise distinct and separate from the first four millennia of creation following the formation of Adam. Leah is identified with the law and likewise the natural body governed by the law, whereby Leah's six sons represent the completion of the six millennia of natural creation that precedes the supernatural seventh millennium. And it is the seventh, or Sabbath, millennium that is finally the millennial kingdom of Christ (Rev 20:6). Leah connecting the totality of her six sons with Jacob finally dwelling with her as a husband points to the fulfillment of the six millennia of creation in the seventh millennium. This is the marriage of the Lamb (Rev 19:7). And the good wedding dowry that Leah receives represents the exaltation of the faithful throughout the millennia of Adam in the one Body of Christ.

Genesis 30:21 And afterwards she bare a daughter, and called her name Dinah [H1783].

The name *Dinah* [H1783] (given by Leah) means "judgment," whereby the birth of Dinah following her six brothers portends the final judgment that will conclude the six millennia of creation. And the person of Dinah is specifically identified with the destruction of Shalem (a city of Shechem), executed by Simeon and Levi on the third day following the sign of circumcision (Gen 33:18, 34:25).[35] There is a parallel between the circumcision required by the Old Testament and the baptism required by the New Testament. The third day following the circumcision of all flesh points to the third millennium following the baptism of Christ on the cross. The third day from Christ corresponds to the seventh day from Adam, subsuming the seven days of Adam. This is the new creation supplanting the original creation.

Genesis 30:22 And God remembered [H2142] Rachel, and God hearkened [H8085] to her, and opened her womb.

The word *hearkened* [H8085] (God hearkened unto Rachel) has a connotation "to obey." Rachel is most closely identified with the grace of God, and thus God *hearkening* [H8085] unto Rachel reflects the promised redemption of the faithful coming only by the grace of God. But the image of God *hearkening* [H8085] is linked all together with the births of Simeon (Gen 29:33), Dan (Gen 30:6), Issachar (Gen 30:17), and Joseph (Gen 30:22). The connection between

---

[35] The *Shalem* [H8004] ultimately destroyed by Simeon and Levi, Gen 33:18, can be identified with the *Salem* [H8004] originally ruled by Melchizedek, Gen 14:18, which is a testimony to the kingdom and dominion of Christ being founded upon grace but established through law and, therefore, not being merely of the present world, Heb 7:17. Law preceded grace, but grace subsumes law. Adam preceded Jesus Christ, and yet simultaneously Adam proceeds from Christ.

Simeon, Dan, Issachar, and Joseph is the hearkening of God first unto Leah and second unto Rachel, representing the fulfillment of law in grace. This is the progression marked by the Flood, the First Advent, the opening of the church age, and finally the Second Advent. God *remembering* [H2142] Rachel in the barrenness of her womb recalls God *remembering* [H2142] Noah and his family forlorn in the ark (Gen 8:1). Noah's ark is then the womb from which humanity would be born though the birth pains of the Flood. And the destruction by water is to the First Advent as the coming destruction by fire is to the Second Advent (2 Pet 3:1–12).[36]

Genesis 30:23–24 And she conceived, and bare a son [H1121]; and said, God hath taken away my reproach [H2781]: 24 And she called his name Joseph [H3130]; and said, The LORD shall add [H3254] to me another son [H1121].

Leah's son Reuben is Jacob's first firstborn, in contrast to Rachel's son Joseph who is Jacob's second firstborn. Reuben is identified with Adam and likewise with the death that came through Adam, while Joseph is identified with Jesus Christ and likewise with the life that is only in Christ. The first firstborn Reuben is to the second firstborn Joseph as the original formation of mankind in Adam is to the promised rebirth of the faithful in Christ at the time of the Second Advent. But the Second Advent of Christ is simultaneously both an ending and a beginning. The first son of Rachel, together with the six sons of Leah, forms a distinct group since these first seven sons were all born in the land of Laban, in contrast to the land promised to Abraham. The promised land is to the land of Laban as the promised new creation is to the present creation. And the person of Joseph points specifically to the seventh, or Sabbath, millennium. The unity of Rachel's firstborn and Leah's six sons, demarcated by the land of Laban and representing the fallen world, points to the present heaven and earth not being supplanted by the new heaven and earth until the end of the millennial kingdom (Rev 21:1). And this corresponds to the end of the seventh, or Sabbath, millennium.

The name *Joseph* [H3130] (given by Rachel) means "he adds, increases" and is closely related to the word *add* [H3254] (add another son). This connects the birth of Joseph in the east and the yet future birth of Benjamin to be added to the birth of Joseph in the promised land (Gen 35:18). And the connection between Benjamin and Joseph is the connection between the eighth and seventh millennia, which is the opening of eternity at the time of the millennial reign. The word *reproach* [H2781] (God hath taken away) has a connotation "condition of shame, disgrace" and is derived from the root word *reproach*

---

[36] The exaltation of Jacob through having offspring in the east forms the pivot in an overarching chiastic structure framed by his fleeing and his returning to Esau, while also evident is an alternating structure in which establishing equality with Aram (Laban) parallels establishing equality with Edom (Esau) (Waltke 385–86). Jacob struggling to establish his house, against Esau on one side and against Laban on the other, represents the parallel struggle in the natural and spiritual domains.

[H2778], which is variously translated *blasphemed* [H2778] (Isa 65:7) and *betrothed* [H2778] (Lev 19:20). The younger Rachel is identified with grace, while her firstborn Joseph is identified with the Sabbath millennium. And the emphasis on Rachel's reproach being taken away by Joseph's birth points to the redemption of the faithful at the time of the Sabbath millennium.[37]

Joseph being the seventh son of Jacob by a freewoman points to the fulfillment of the promised redemption in the seventh millennium. Joseph being the second firstborn son of Jacob by a freewoman points to the exaltation of the faithful in the Body of Christ that is the new, or second, Adam. The unfolding of the plan of God in history being signified by the offspring of freewomen represents an emphasis on the sanctity of freewill. The supernatural conception of Christ being signified by the unnatural interjection of the children of bondwomen represents an emphasis on the humble condescension of Christ as a suffering servant. A set of seven millennia will be completed before the opening of the eighth millennium, representing eternity, just as a set of seven days was completed before the opening of the present creation (Gen 2:2). And the seven in each case is specifically six plus one. And the eighth day, or millennium, finally represents a new beginning, or new week, following the completion of the present creation that is signified by a completed week of days, or week of millennia. And this promised new beginning will be marked by the birth of the eighth son Benjamin in the promised land.[38]

Sheep and Goats

Genesis 30:25–26 And it came to pass, when Rachel had born Joseph, that Jacob said unto Laban, Send me away, that I may go unto mine own place, and to my country. 26 Give [me] my wives and my children, for whom I have served thee, and let me go: for thou knowest my service which I have done thee.

The birth of Joseph is here directly connected to the completion of Jacob's servitude for his wives and children. The birth of Joseph prefigures the advent

---

[37] The promised new and eternal life in Christ should be understood as endless but not timeless, whereby the newness of eternity is naturally compared to the long and literal period of a millennium, specifically the eighth millennium corresponding to a new week and signifying a new creation. A creation of timeless existence, as distinct from the self-existence of the Creator, is untenable because freewill implies a tangible body with which to exercise freewill, likewise a tangible environment, or creation, in which to exercise freewill. Further, the assertion of a future state of timeless existence ultimately represents a denial of God the Son who, by his very nature, eternally embodies the fullness of God in the humble condescension of God in space and time.

[38] The birth of Joseph, Gen 30:22–24, marks the turning point from Laban back to the promised land, as reinforced by being the pivot of a chiastic structure spanning 29:1–31:55 (Waltke 353). Jacob's one son Joseph uniquely embodies the return of the Lord at the time of the millennial kingdom, reflecting the oneness of Jesus Christ and likewise the oneness of the Body of Christ.

of the seventh millennium, whereby the end of Jacob's required servitude in establishing his household prefigures a corresponding gathering of the faithful. And this is not only the gathering of the faithful throughout the church age but also throughout the totality of the six millennia of creation as signified by Leah's six sons. The unrighteous dominion of Laban over the house of Jacob reflects the dominion of the serpent, the authority governing the present creation. And the devil is clearly the god of this world, even following the cross, because this world continues to be marked by suffering and death (2 Cor 4:4). But Jacob asking for the approval of Laban does not represent any equality between the Lord God and satan. Rather, this is God fulfilling an unassailable righteousness that is perfect by an absolute standard. The evil one governing creation is the tempter, the slanderer, and the adversary, but the time is coming when every knee shall bow to Christ and every tongue shall confess that Christ is God (Rom 14:11). And Jacob seeking to return to the promised land is finally an image of the Son longing for the redemption of his faithful at the time of the Second Advent. But Jacob continuing to serve his father-in-law is an affirmation that the Son obediently awaits the time appointed by the Father.

Genesis 30:27 And Laban said unto him, I pray thee, if I have found favour [H2580] in thine eyes, [tarry: for] I have learned by experience [H5172] that the LORD hath blessed [H1288] me for thy sake [H1558].

The person of Jacob, compared with Isaac and Abraham, is most closely identified with the time of the Second Advent. And the three sevens of Jacob foreshadow the three sevens of the revelation of Jesus Christ recorded in the book of Revelation—namely, the seven seals, the seven trumpets, and the seven vials. Jacob now receives Joseph at the end of the second seven years of servitude to Laban, marking the conclusion of his offspring to be received in the east and, thereby, representing the totality of Jacob's offspring in the east. In a sense, Joseph represents the totality of all Jacob's offspring, east or west, even though Benjamin would not be received until the end of the third and final period of servitude (Gen 35:16). And this is reinforced by the person of Joseph being closely identified with adding Benjamin as another son (Gen 30:24). Also, Jacob received both Leah and Rachel at the end of the first seven years of servitude to Laban, even though Jacob would serve the second seven years for Rachel (Gen 29:26–30). Jacob will finally receive herds of livestock at the end of six more years of servitude to Laban, but the final six years of Jacob represents a third and final period of seven years to be completed specifically in the promised land (Gen 31:41).

The end of the first seven of Jacob is marked by Jacob receiving his wives and the corresponding promise, or assurance, or seal, of the offspring they would conceive. The end of the first seven of Jacob points to the sealing of the 144,000 of the offspring of Jacob, likewise connected with the end of the first seven of the book of Revelation, namely, the seven seals (Rev 7:4–8). The end of the second seven of Jacob is marked by the birth of Joseph, representing the conclusion, or totality, of the offspring that Jacob would receive in the land of

Laban. The end of the second seven of Jacob points to the fulfillment, or completion, of creation in the seventh, or Sabbath, millennium. And this corresponds to the establishment of the promised kingdom of God, which is closely identified with the end of the second seven of Revelation, namely, the seven trumpets (Rev 11:15). The third and final seven of Jacob being fulfilled in the promised land points to the glorious return of Jesus Christ, also to be fulfilled in the promised land (Zech 14:4), as connected with the end of the third seven of Revelation, namely, the seven vials (Rev 16:15).

The word *favour* (favor) [H2580] (tarry if I have found favour) means "favour, grace" in the Hebrew and is the same word used to describe the *grace* [H2580] that Noah found in the eyes of the Lord at the time of the first destruction that came by water (Gen 6:8). Jacob will tarry with Laban but not for the sake of Laban. Jacob will tarry in order to fulfill all righteousness and, thereby, to establish his own house in all righteousness. And yet the first destruction (by water) foreshadows the second and final destruction (by fire). Further, the word *learned by experience* [H5172] (Laban learned by experience) has connotations "to observe signs or omens" and also "divination" and is the same word used to describe the *divining* [H5172] connected with the reign of Joseph in Egypt (Gen 44:5). The sign of signs that marks the last days is the grace of God manifest in the call to repentance, but the men of the world will not repent, even unto the time of the end (Rev 9:20, 9:21, 16:9, 16:11). Laban recognizes by observation, or experience, the blessing that comes by Jacob just as the devil knows very well that Christ is God, but Laban seeks to steal that blessing just as the devil seeks to steal the glory of God.

The word *blessed* [H1288] (Laban blessed for Jacob's sake) is variously translated as *blessing* [H1288] (Gen 22:17) and *curse* [H1288] (Job 2:5). The simultaneous curse and blessing that proceeds from the Lord is the call to reject the bad and choose the good, which is finally the death of the natural body and the corresponding rebirth in the spiritual, or glorified, resurrection body. The word *sake* [H1558] (for Jacob's sake) is the same word used to describe the house of the Egyptian Potiphar being blessed for the *sake* [H1558] of Joseph (Gen 39:5). This is again the delay of judgment for the sake of the faithful, particularly the final delay in the end times. And the word *sake* [H1558] is also closely related to the word *roll* [H1556], describing the stone that Jacob *rolled* [H1556] from the well's mouth upon first arriving in the east country (Gen 29:3). And the well of water covered by a stone is nothing less than the tomb of Christ that is the font of eternal life. The blessing that is received for the sake of Jacob represents the blessing that comes only by the cross.[39]

Genesis 30:28 And he said, Appoint [H5344] me thy wages [H7939], and I will give [it].

---

[39] Even the wicked are blessed in this life by the presence of the righteous in the world (Jamieson et al. 1:206; Gen 30:27). The fallen world is currently being preserved for a season in order to call the faithful unto repentance in Christ.

JACOB AND LABAN

The word *appoint* [H5344] (appoint thy wages) has a connotation "to pierce" and is variously translated *curse* [H5344] (Num 23:8) and *blaspheme* [H5344] (Lev 24:16). Jacob appointing his own wages prefigures Jesus Christ willingly accepting the death of the cross (John 10:18). That Jacob must receive his wages from Laban portends the death of the cross being demanded (not commanded) by the slanderer who is the devil. The wages of sin is death, but Christ takes payment for us all (Rom 6:23). However, the primary context here is the church age leading up to the Second Advent, in contrast to the First Advent opening the church age. Accordingly, the wages appointed unto Laban most specifically represent the faithful in Christ picking up their own crosses in imitation of Christ (Mark 8:34). Jacob being blessed by God, simultaneously fulfilling all the requirements of Laban, in the establishment his own household and wealth and position is finally a vision of Christ sitting at the right hand of God the Father until his enemies are made his footstool (Ps 110:11, 1 Cor 15:25–26). Laban, representing the devil, does not have the power to appoint the wages of Jacob; it is Jacob, representing Christ, that is sovereign and has complete control over all things, even death.[40]

Genesis 30:29 And he said unto him, Thou knowest how I have served thee, and how thy cattle was with me.

The devil knows very well that even he is a created being and that all things were originally created through the Son (John 1:3).

Genesis 30:30 For [it was] little which thou hadst before I [came], and it is [now] increased unto a multitude; and the LORD **hath blessed thee since my coming: and now when shall I provide for mine own house also?**

The blessing of God—who is the self-existent one—is life, or existence, itself. And in this sense, even the devil is blessed by God. But the fleeting existence that we now experience is only a foretaste, a lowest common denominator, prefiguring the fullness of eternal life. This is the breath of life (Gen 2:7) that precedes the fullness of the indwelling Spirit of God (2 Cor 5:5). The former things are received by all, but the latter things are received only by the faithful. The multitude of Laban represents the present world, whereas the multitude of the Lord will be established in the world to come. The blessing of the Lord is now experienced by all men, including the faithless. But the time is coming when the blessing of the faithless will be taken away and added to the blessing of the faithful. And the blessing of the faithful will become boundless

---

[40] "Death was held [in Rabbinic thought] to be the consequence of sin, and a sinless person would necessarily be immortal. 'There is no death without sin' [*Shabbath*]" (Cohen, *Rabbinic Sages* 73). The garden of Eden was not the kingdom of God. The garden of Eden was not a destination. The garden was a path, or way, that would have, if Adam-kind had followed it, led to the kingdom of God, namely, the fullness of the presence of God.

(Luke 19:22–27). And when the blessing of the Lord is finally withdrawn from the present creation, the only thing that will remain will be the lake of fire. This is the second death, representing nothing less than a never-ending torment, which is the sole reality in separation from the love of God (Rev 20:10, 20:14).[41]

Genesis 30:31 And he said, What shall I give thee? And Jacob said, Thou shalt not give me any thing: if thou wilt do this thing for me, I will again feed [H7462] [and] keep [H8104] thy flock [H6629].

The word *feed* [H7462] (Jacob feeds the flock) has connotations of "friendship" and "companionship," reflecting our fellowship with the Lord that is practicable only because of the humble condescension of the Lord. And this is actually a very surprising fellowship that is absolutely unique to the one true faith. The word *keep* [H8104] (Jacob keeps the flock) means "to keep, watch, preserve" and is the same word used to describe Adam originally placed in the garden of Eden to dress it and to *keep* [H8104] it (Gen 2:15). Jacob keeping and preserving the flock of Laban is an image of the preservation of the present world that is necessary during the call to repentance. One could also say the preservation of the world is the visible manifestation of the call to repentance. The word *flock* [H6629] (of Laban) is derived from an unused root "to migrate," reflecting the restlessness of the faithful in this world and likewise the movement, or migration, of the faithful unto the next world.[42]

Laban seeking, or rather presuming, to give Jacob his wages as if a gift is an image of the dragon, that old serpent, called the devil and also satan, seeking an indebtedness, or enslavement, of Jesus Christ (Matt 4:9). This is the evil one seeking a dominion over Christ or, at a minimum, a dominion over the faithful in Christ. The tempter, the serpent, desires power that he cannot have. Jacob then asserting that he wants nothing from Laban is an affirmation that Christ himself has paid the full price for our redemption in full accordance with the law and without any indebtedness to anyone else (John 19:30). The slanderer, the devil, pretends to have power that he does not have. The emphasis on Jacob feeding and keeping the flocks of Laban throughout this time is a testimony that the present world endures only for a time and only by the grace of God. And in the end, the adversary, satan, will think he has power that he does not have.

---

[41] "To-day's festival [Pentecost], dearly-beloved, which is held in reverence by the whole world, has been hallowed by that advent of the Holy Ghost, which on the fiftieth day after the Lord's Resurrection, descended on the Apostles and the multitude of believers, even as it was hoped. And there was this hope, because the Lord Jesus had promised that He should come, not then first to be the Indweller of the saints [by sending the Holy Spirit], but to kindle to a greater heat, and to fill with larger abundance the hearts that were dedicated to Him, increasing, not commencing His gifts, not fresh in operation because richer in bounty [Leo the Great, *On Whitsuntide*]" (Schaff and Wace, *Nicene and Post-Nicene Fathers: Second Series* 12.1:191). The breath of life that becomes the fullness of eternal life.

[42] Root per *Strong's*, not *Brown-Driver-Briggs*, but the link between flocks and migration is inherent regardless of exact etymology.

JACOB AND LABAN

Genesis 30:32 I will pass through all thy flock to day, removing from thence all the speckled and spotted cattle, and all the brown cattle among the sheep, and the spotted and speckled among the goats: and [of such] shall be my hire.

Jacob passing through the flock of Laban represents Christ sending the Holy Spirit during the church age, particularly during the end times (John 7:37–40). The ensuing struggle between Jacob and Laban over the flock of Laban represents Christ seeking to save the faithful from the evil one. The emphasis on the cattle being speckled, spotted, and brown points to the sins that mark all mankind, especially the universal apostasy that will mark the end times (2 Thess 2:3). Jacob delaying his return unto the promised land, as required to take possession of the cattle of Laban, represents the delay of the judgment of the world for the sake of the faithful, again particularly during the end times (Rev 6:11). Laban accepting, without hesitation or negotiation, the wages appointed by Jacob points to the undeniable, or relentless, will of God, which is the salvation of all his children (Matt 18:12–14).

Genesis 30:33 So shall my righteousness answer for me in time to come, when it shall come for my hire before thy face: every one that [is] not speckled and spotted among the goats, and brown among the sheep, that shall be counted stolen with me.

The righteousness of Jacob will be self-evident and will also form the very foundation of the business relationship between himself and Laban. The righteousness of God is likewise self-evident and also forms the foundation of all creation. If the accuser could find any real fault with God—any sin at all, no matter how small—then God would cease to be God. And actually God would have already ceased being God—for no sin can be truly hidden, not even in God—and chaos would have already overrun cosmos and pervaded all creation. But it is also true that God is fundamentally unchanging and that the discovery of any sin—that is, incompleteness—in God would imply that sin had always existed in God and, thus, had always defined God. Therefore, not only the continuance of creation but also the very existence of creation testifies that the perfection of God is not only undeniable but also eternal. The first man Adam points to the second man Jesus Christ.

Genesis 30:34 And Laban [H3837] said, Behold, I would it might be according to thy word.

The devil is playing a game that he cannot win.

Genesis 30:35 And he removed that day the he goats that were ringstraked and spotted, and all the she goats that were speckled and spotted, [and] every one that had [some] white [H3836] in it, and all the brown among the sheep, and gave [them] into the hand of his sons.

The word *white* [H3836] (every goat that had some white) is derived from the root "to be white" [H3835], which has connotations "to become morally pure" (Isa 1:18) and also "to be purified (by fire)" (Gen 11:3). These images point to the foretold judgment by fire that will purify the whole world (2 Pet 3:7). And the separation of the flocks of Laban and Jacob foreshadows the corresponding separation of the sheep and the goats in the end times (Matt 25:31–33). The word *white* [H3836] is also closely related to the name *Laban* [H3837], but this connection points to that which is destroyed by fire, not that which is saved through the fire. All men are sinners, but the person of Laban, marked by an opposition to the blessing of Jacob, is consistently identified with the evil one. And such identifications are normally subtle because the distinctions between Christ and anti-christ are normally subtle. This is because the devil, seeking to substitute himself for Christ, presents himself as Christ. And one actually has no hope of distinguishing between Christ and anti-christ, in separation from the wisdom of God the Holy Spirit, who is the Spirit of truth, prophecy, and life.

Genesis 30:36 And he set three days' journey betwixt himself and Jacob: and Jacob fed the rest of Laban's [H3837] flocks.

The three days' journey between Jacob's own flocks and Laban's flocks tended by Jacob represents a separation of Jacob—a separation between Jacob and Jacob—that points to the three millennia separating the First and Second Advents of Christ. The imposition of the three days' journey reflects the imperative to believe in the three days of Christ that is the death and resurrection of Christ. The separation between the flocks of Jacob and Laban likewise represents the separation of the faithful and the faithless that is based expressly upon the belief or denial of the three days of Christ. The sign of Jonah is not only the three days in the heart of the earth but also the call of Gentiles as represented by Nineveh, and thereby the sign of Jonah also points to the three millennia separating the First and Second Advents of Christ (Luke 11:29–36).[43]

---

[43] "It is extremely difficult to find out, from [Gen 30:32 and 30:35], in *what* the bargain of Jacob with his father-in-law properly consisted. It appears from [30:32], that Jacob was to have for his wages all the *speckled, spotted,* and *brown* among the sheep and the goats; and of course that all those which were not party-coloured [parti-colored] should be considered as the property of Laban. But in [30:35] it appears that Laban separated all the *party-coloured* cattle, delivered them into the hands of *his own sons*; which seems as if he had taken these for his own property, and left the others to Jacob. . . . [T]he true meaning appears to be this: Jacob had agreed to take all the party-coloured for his wages. As he was now only *beginning* to act upon this agreement, consequently none of the cattle as yet belonged to him; therefore Laban separated from the flock, [30:35], all such cattle as Jacob might afterwards claim in consequence of his bargain, (for as yet he had no right;) therefore Jacob commenced his service to Laban with a flock that did not contain a single animal of the description of those to which he might be entitled; and the others were sent away under the care of Laban's sons, three days' journey from those of which Jacob had the care" (Clarke 1:188; Gen 30:35). In this reading, the flock that is separated can still be viewed as symbolically representing the future possession of Jacob since the separated flock is otherwise indistinguishable from Jacob's rightful

JACOB AND LABAN

Genesis 30:37–39 And Jacob took him rods of green poplar, and of the hazel and chesnut tree; and pilled white [H3836] strakes in them, and made the white [H3836] appear which [was] in the rods. 38 And he set the rods which he had pilled before the flocks in the gutters in the watering troughs when the flocks came to drink, that they should conceive when they came to drink. 39 And the flocks conceived before the rods, and brought forth cattle ringstraked, speckled, and spotted.

The rods with white strakes made by Jacob compared with the ringstraked, speckled, and spotted cattle desired by Jacob represents the parallel between the physical and the spiritual and likewise the parallel between law and grace. The connection between the cattle drinking water and the cattle conceiving the desired offspring points to the well of living water springing up inside the believer and corresponding to our promised new birth (John 4:14). The image of Jacob, by his own hand, increasing his flocks at the expense of Laban reflects Jesus Christ, by force and expressly by the power of the Holy Spirit, taking his rightful dominion over creation at the expense of, or negation of, the prince of this world who is the devil (John 14:22–31). The beginning of the kingdom of God is the individual, but the end of the kingdom of God is all creation.[44]

Genesis 30:40 And Jacob did separate the lambs, and set the faces of the flocks toward the ringstraked, and all the brown in the flock of Laban; and he put his own flocks by themselves, and put them not unto Laban's cattle.

There can be no communion between light and darkness (2 Cor 6:14).

Genesis 30:41–42 And it came to pass, whensoever the stronger cattle did conceive, that Jacob laid the rods before the eyes of the cattle in the gutters, that they might conceive among the rods. 42 But when the cattle were feeble, he put [them] not in: so the feebler were Laban's, and the stronger Jacob's.

The faithful are conceived of the Holy Spirit, and thereby the faithful express the strength and power of the Spirit.

Genesis 30:43 And the man increased exceedingly, and had much cattle, and maidservants, and menservants, and camels, and asses.

---

possession. And it should be recognized that such an abstraction is encouraged, within this supposition, by what must be a purposeful ambiguity of the account.

[44] "Jacob herein used no deceit: for it was God's commandment as he declares in [Gen 31:9 and 31:11]" (Whittingham et al., *Geneva Bible* 14R n. l; Gen 30:37). Jacob is the righteous one, the chosen of God, not Laban and not Esau.

ESAU, JACOB, ISRAEL

The multitude of Jacob represents the rebirth of the faithful in the Body of Christ, while the material wealth of Jacob represents the corresponding renewal of all creation, both earth and heaven.

From the East

Genesis 31:1 And he heard the words of Laban's sons, saying, Jacob hath taken away all that [was] our father's; and of [that] which [was] our father's hath he gotten all this glory.

The glory of Laban represents the dominion of the devil over the present world. The glory of Laban becoming the glory of Jacob points to the kingdoms of this world becoming the kingdoms of Christ (Rev 11:15).

Genesis 31:2 And Jacob beheld the countenance of Laban, and, behold, it [was] not toward him as before.

The darkening countenance of Laban toward Jacob portends the dragon becoming consumed by fury because he knows his time is short (Rev 12:12).

Genesis 31:3 And the LORD said unto Jacob, Return unto the land of thy fathers, and to thy kindred; and I will be with thee.

The glorious reappearing of Christ will be like lightning coming from the east and shining even unto the west (Matt 24:27). The Lord now commanding Jacob to return from the east unto the promised land points to exactly that time which has been appointed by God the Father for the Second Advent of God the Son (Mark 13:32). The flocks of Laban becoming the flocks of Jacob affirms the Second Advent as a time of the harvest of mankind (Matt 13:39) and points to the promise that in the end not a single sheep will be lost (Matt 18:14). And the emphasis on Jacob returning unto his blood relatives in Canaan points to the essential blood relationship between Jesus Christ and the faithful in Christ, which is according to God the Holy Spirit (Matt 12:50).

Genesis 31:4 And Jacob sent and called Rachel and Leah to the field unto his flock,

The elder Leah is most closely identified with law and the corresponding six millennia of creation governed by law. In contrast, the younger Rachel is most closely identified with grace and the corresponding seventh, or Sabbath, millennium, which will be the first manifestation of the government of grace. Jacob calling his wives in the order of the younger Rachel followed by the elder Leah represents a looking backward from the time of the Second Advent. And Jacob now setting the stage to recount his past dealings with Laban reinforces this sense of looking backward (Gen 31:5–13). The emphasis on being called unto the flock points to the gathering of the faithful throughout all the ages.

JACOB AND LABAN

And the emphasis on being called unto the field points to the wilderness of the present world in which the faithful have dwelt throughout the ages.

Genesis 31:5 And said unto them, I see your father's countenance, that it [is] not toward me as before; but the God of my father hath been with me.

Laban represents the devil, whose countenance is ever against humanity, particularly the faithful. But the God of Jacob's father, representing God the Father, is with Jacob, who embodies the faithful empowered by God the Holy Spirit. And the opposition of Laban and the devil to Jacob will therefore be in vain. The desire of God to save his children is undeniable—that is, relentless—and the faithful do testify that all things work together providentially in the plan of God, who knows and foreknows all things (Gen 50:20).

Genesis 31:6 And ye know that with all my power [H3851] I have served [H5647] your father.

The power of Jacob represents that of the Holy Spirit. Righteous Jacob serving wicked Laban reflects Jesus Christ fulfilling all righteousness even though he is the font of righteousness. And the emphasis on Rachel and Leah recognizing the extreme service of Jacob points to the righteousness of God being self-evident throughout all creation and throughout all the ages. Note also that evil Cain *tilled* [H5647] in vain for the *strength* [H3581] of the earth, or creation, specifically the present creation (Gen 4:12). In contrast, the *power* [H3581] of righteous Jacob proceeds from within him according to the Holy Spirit, and thereby Jacob's *service* [H5647] becomes the fruitfulness of new life and new creation.

Genesis 31:7 And your father hath deceived [H2048] me, and changed my wages ten [H6235] times; but God suffered [H5414] him not to hurt me.

The emphasis on the number *ten* [H6235] (wages changed ten times) points to the law of flesh. This is the administration of the law by wicked Laban and the corresponding fulfillment of the law by righteous Jacob. The elder Leah and the younger Rachel are identified with the successive ages of creation, whereby their father Laban represents the god of this world who is the devil (2 Cor 4:4). And it should be no surprise that the present fallen world is governed by the fallen one. The present world governed by the law of flesh is fundamentally unjust (Eccl 12:8). The father of Leah and Rachel is the *deceiver* [H2048], the father of lies and a murderer from the beginning (John 8:44). But God not *suffering* [H5414] Laban to hurt Jacob points to the promised redemption of the faithful in the Body of Christ.

Genesis 31:8 If he said thus, The speckled shall be thy wages; then all the cattle bare speckled: and if he said thus, The ringstraked shall be thy hire; then bare all the cattle ringstraked.

The devil thinks that he can use the law of God against God, but the devil plainly does not understand the true meaning of the law of God. All things work together providentially in the plan of God, who knows and foreknows all things (Gen 50:20). The greatest evil of all would be the condemnation of Jesus Christ under the law, but even the death of Christ would become the victory of Christ and actually that by which the faithful receive grace. And it is no coincidence that the greatest evil of all would become the greatest good of all, since the greatest evil is exactly that which necessitates the greatest good. The law entered that the offence might abound, but where sin abounded, grace did much more abound (Rom 5:20). If the evil one understood the truth of the law that is fulfilled in grace, then he would never have sought the life of Christ, nor would he even now seek the life of the Body of Christ.

Genesis 31:9 Thus God hath taken away the cattle of your father, and given [them] to me.

The kingdoms of this world are become the kingdoms of our Lord, and of his Christ, and he shall reign for ever and ever (Rev 11:15).

Genesis 31:10 And it came to pass at the time that the cattle conceived, that I lifted up mine eyes, and saw in a dream, and, behold, the rams which leaped upon the cattle [were] ringstraked, speckled, and grisled.

Jacob is previously described setting pilled (peeled) rods before the flocks so that they would conceive ringstraked, speckled, and spotted offspring (Gen 30:37–39). But now Jacob is described as seeing a vision of the conception of ringstraked, speckled, and spotted cattle in a dream. The natural precedes the spiritual just as the law precedes grace. But the account of the dream follows the account of the reality, when in actuality the dream certainly preceded the reality. Likewise, the birth of Jesus follows the formation of Adam, when in actuality Jesus certainly preceded Adam. And this is finally the first and second men, Adam followed by Christ, paralleling the First and Second Advents, Christ followed by the Body of Christ.[45]

Genesis 31:11 And the angel [H4397] of God [H430] spake unto me in a dream, [saying], Jacob: and I said, Here [am] I.

The designation *angel* (Angel) [H4397] means "messenger," but angels also have names just as men have names. And names are important to God just as

---

[45] The focus should be the actual narrative, not speculation about whether pilled rods could have affected the siring of cattle in the purely natural order of things.

individuals are important to God. The importance of individuals and thus their names to God is evidenced by the numerous earthly genealogies recorded in the Scriptures (Luke 3:23–38) and also by the heavenly names given to the angels (Luke 1:19). Designating the angel of God without a name therefore represents an emphasis on God himself. Accordingly, such relationships as the *angel* (Angel) [H4397] of *God* [H430] and elsewhere the *word* (Word) [H1697] of *God* [H430] represent, or symbolize, the actual manifestation of God (Gen 21:17, 1 Kgs 12:22). The relative ambiguity of such descriptions, compared with the primordial view of the Lord himself literally walking in the garden of Eden, reflects the distance, or separation, between man and God that has arisen because of sin and as required by the law (Gen 3:8). But the *Word* (Logos) [G3056] of God ultimately becomes flesh, full of grace and truth, so that the faithful in Christ can receive the grace that is the truth of the law (John 1:14–17). And the spiritual man Jacob here responding affirmatively to the angel of God represents just that coming of the faithful unto the Lord.

Genesis 31:12 And he said, Lift up now thine eyes, and see, all the rams which leap upon the cattle [are] ringstraked, speckled, and grisled: for I have seen all that Laban doeth unto thee.

Jacob is called upon to lift up his eyes and see the reality of what is happening. And the true reality is the spiritual reality of the Lord intervening in what is a hopelessly fallen creation. The flocks of Laban being given to Jacob is directly connected to the evil dealings of Laban. And the authority to take back the possession of creation is based on the perfect righteousness of Christ, as testified to by the righteous dealings of Jacob.

Genesis 31:13 I [am] the God of Beth-el, where thou anointedst the pillar [H4676], [and] where thou vowedst a vow unto me: now arise, get thee out from this land, and return unto the land of thy kindred.

The return of Jacob unto the promised land is here connected to the original departure of Jacob from the promised land. Jacob setting up and anointing the pillar of Bethel at the time of his departure from the promised land represents the resurrection of Christ at the time of the First Advent. And the vow of Jacob at this time prefigures Christ promising that he would indeed return in the end times to establish his faithful ones (John 14:3). And the emphasis on Jacob returning to a land that is the land of his blood kindred testifies to the essential blood kinship that must exist between Christ and the faithful in Christ.

Genesis 31:14–16 And Rachel and Leah answered and said unto him, [Is there] yet any portion or inheritance for us in our father's house? 15 Are we not counted of him strangers? for he hath sold us, and hath quite devoured also our money. 16 For all the riches which God hath taken from our father, that [is] ours, and our children's: now then, whatsoever God hath said unto thee, do.

Jacob's two wives, Leah and Rachel, speaking in one voice is an affirmation of the unity of law and grace and likewise the unity of the faithful throughout all the ages in Christ. Rachel and Leah asserting that they have no inheritance at all in Laban's house is a testimony that the condemnation of the natural body in the present world is utterly irrevocable. Rachel and Leah proclaiming that the riches God had taken from Laban belong exclusively to the house of Jacob is an affirmation that the faithful receive their inheritance in the Body of Christ and only in the Body of Christ.[46]

Genesis 31:17 Then Jacob rose up, and set his sons and his wives upon camels;

Abraham previously sent his eldest servant on camels and with precious gifts to bring Rebekah back to be the wife of Isaac (Gen 24:10). But now Jacob himself returns on camels not only with his own wives but also with a great many offspring and also with a great wealth. And the wealth that Jacob takes from Laban is, at least figuratively, the same wealth previously given to the house of Laban by Abraham's eldest servant on behalf of Isaac (Gen 24:53). The gifts that father Abraham gave on behalf of his only son, Isaac, represent the gifts of the Holy Spirit that would proceed from the Father after the ascension of the Son (John 16:7). And the great wealth that Jacob now brings back to the promised land represents the fullness of the Holy Spirit. This is the church age that connects the First and Second Advents. And this is finally the anointing of the faithful and the concomitant rejection of the faithless.

Genesis 31:18 And he carried away all his cattle, and all his goods which he had gotten, the cattle of his getting, which he had gotten in Padan-aram [H6307], for to go to Isaac his father in the land of Canaan.

The person of Isaac is most closely identified with the First Advent of Christ, while the person of Jacob is most closely identified with the Second Advent. And the emphasis on Jacob returning unto Isaac in the promised land points to the unity of the First and Second Advents of Christ. Jacob emphasizing the name *Padanaram* [H6307] recalls Isaac emphasizing the same name *Padanaram* [H6307] and, thereby, reinforces the connection between the First and Second Advents (Gen 28:2). And the place of Padanaram is further identified with the font, or source, of Rebekah, representing the faithful and likewise the Holy Spirit, who calls the faithful. This is again the coming of the Holy Spirit that demarcates the church age and connects the First and Second Advents. The Spirit, who is the giver of life, precedes the Son just as Adam

---

[46] "The marriages of Jacob were types of that which Christ was about to accomplish.... Leah is your people and synagogue; but Rachel is our Church. And for these, and for the servants in both, Christ even now serves [Justin Martyr, *Dialogue with Trypho*]" (Roberts et al., *Ante-Nicene Fathers* 1:267). The Jews preceded the Gentiles just as law preceded grace, but the law is subsumed by grace, not simply supplanted, just as Jews and Gentiles alike are called to form the one Body of Christ.

precedes Christ in the original creation. And the Spirit, who indwells the faithful, also follows the Son just as the Body of Christ follows Christ in our promised new creation. The former is the original creation proceeding from God (Father, Spirit, and Son), while the latter is our new creation returning unto, or in communion with, God (Father, Son, and Spirit).

Genesis 31:19 And Laban went to shear [H1494] his sheep: and Rachel had stolen [H1589] the images [H8655] that [were] her father's.

The person of Rachel is most closely identified with the seventh millennium, specifically the time beginning with the seventh millennium. And the seventh millennium begins, in some sense at least, with the rebellion of the dragon (Rev 20:1–3) and ends with the judgment of the dragon (Rev 20:7–10). And Rachel stealing the idols, or images, of Laban represents the event that will define the beginning of the end that she embodies. The beloved Rachel stealing the idols of Laban portends the rejection of even the glorified Christ at the time of the Second Advent. Our surprise and distress at Rachel stealing the idols of her father and what such an act represents points to just this unbelievable but foretold and therefore certain apostasy in the end times (Rev 9:20).

Nevertheless, Rachel is simultaneously and without contradiction the wife of Jacob and also the daughter of Laban. And it is also true that Laban does lose his idols because of the action of Rachel. The word *images* (idols) [H8655] (Rachel had stolen) is derived from the root "to heal" [H7495].[47] The idols of Laban being stolen thereby foreshadows a failure of the covenant with death in which the faithless falsely believe they have an agreement with hell (Isa 28:15). And Laban losing his idols is further connected with his shearing his sheep. The word *shear* [H1494] (his sheep) has a connotation "to be cut off (destroyed)" that points to the devil tormenting his children, the faithless, in the end times. The children of the devil are the children of destruction. And the sheep that belong to Laban represent the children of the devil.

Genesis 31:20 And Jacob stole away [H1589] unawares to Laban the Syrian [H761], in that he told him not that he fled.

The word *stole away* [H1589] (Jacob stole away) is the same word used to describe Rachel *stealing* [H1589] the idols of her father, Laban (Gen 31:19). And this reinforces the connection between these two events, which is already evidenced by their close proximity in the Biblical text. Laban does not perceive the time of Jacob's returning unto the promised land just as the devil does not know the time of the promised glorious reappearing of Jesus Christ (Matt 24:36). And Laban having his idols stolen at this same time is a concurrent testimony to the impotence of satan in all these things. The idols, or images, of Laban represent the supernatural power of the evil one. And thereby the idols

---

[47] Root per *Strong's*, not *Brown-Driver-Briggs*, but the identification of household idols with the seeking of blessing and healing is clear regardless of exact etymology.

of Laban being stolen portends the dragon being cast down to the earth, which is closely connected with the end times and also with the Second Advent (Rev 12:9). And the emphasis on Laban being *Syrian* [H761] finally points to the significance of Damascus in the end times (Isa 17:1), Damascus being the head of *Syria* [H758] (Isa 7:8).

Gilead

Genesis 31:21 So he fled with all that he had; and he rose up, and passed over the river, and set his face [toward] the mount Gilead [H1568].

The emphasis on Jacob passing over the river in order to return unto the promised land testifies to the necessity that the faithful in Christ experience the baptism of repentance in order to enter into the Body of Christ.[48] This is not only the baptism in water that signifies death and resurrection but also our literal death and resurrection in the flesh. And this is likewise the born-again experience that begins with the repentance in the natural body and finally culminates in the resurrection of the spiritual, or glorified, body. In contrast, Jacob not being described as passing over the river when he originally left the promised land reflects the sinlessness of Christ, especially the sinlessness of the ascendant Christ sending the Holy Spirit at the time of the First Advent. Further, the mount *Gilead* [H1568] is identified with Reuben, the firstborn of Leah, together with Gad, the firstborn of Leah's handmaid, Zilpah (Num 32:29). The emphasis on Jacob pointing his face toward the mount *Gilead* [H1568], the place of the firstborn, points to Jesus Christ taking his rightful possession of the birthright and blessing of the firstborn, especially in the Body of Christ that is animated by the power of the Spirit.

Genesis 31:22 And it was told Laban on the third day that Jacob was fled.

The connection between the third day and Jacob returning to Canaan points to the resurrection of Jesus Christ on the third day—as counted from the crucifixion—and likewise to the resurrection of the faithful in Christ in the third millennium—also counted from the crucifixion. Jacob being discovered missing on the third day prefigures the tomb of Jesus Christ being discovered empty on the third day and finally the faithful in Christ being discovered missing in the third millennium. The former is the resurrection of Christ as the Head, while the latter is the promised resurrection and rapture of the Body of Christ. And the two are necessarily one. Laban not being told until after the fact that Jacob

---

[48] "The river here is the Euphrates, which in the Bible is called, 'by preeminence, *the river* [1 Kgs 4:21, Ezra 4:10, 4:16]'" (Coffman 387; Gen 31:17–21). The preeminence of the Euphrates River is derived not from size, location, and so forth, but from the person of Abraham, our father, the first *Hebrew* [H5680], or "one from beyond [the Euphrates River]," wherein the Euphrates is recognized as the baptismal waters of repentance, or turning from the world.

was returning to the promised land reflects the devil not knowing the time that has been appointed for the glorious return of Christ (Matt 24:36).

Genesis 31:23 And he took his brethren with him, and pursued [H7291] after him seven days' journey; and they overtook [H1692] him in the mount Gilead [H1568].

The word *pursued* [H7291] (Laban pursued Jacob) means "to pursue, chase, persecute," reflecting the unjust persecution of the children of God. Laban pursuing, or persecuting, Jacob for seven days represents the devil opposing the Lord throughout the totality of the seven millennia of creation. Additionally, Laban was not told, until the third day, that Jacob had fled (Gen 31:22). And Laban pursuing Jacob for seven days following the third day then represents a total of ten days, which reflects the Covenant of Law being closely connected with the number 10 (Deut 4:13). Also, the mount *Gilead* [H1568] (Jacob overtook in Gilead) is identified with Reuben, Leah's firstborn, and also with Gad, Zilpah's firstborn (Num 32:29). The emphasis on Laban overtaking Jacob in Gilead, which is the place of the firstborn, again points to the Covenant of Law, which is the first, or old, covenant. Further, the word *overtook* [H1692] (Laban overtook Jacob) means "to cling, cleave, keep close" and has a connotation "man to wife (as in marriage)," reflecting the distinctly covenantal relationship between humanity and the Lord.

The seven days of Laban compared to the three days of Jacob represents the sevenfold creation in Adam compared to the coming threefold creation in Jesus Christ to be established at the end of seven millennia (Rev 21:1). But the three being followed by the seven represents a looking backward from the time of the Second Advent. This looking backward is the restoration of the first man Adam in the last man Christ. And the three plus seven that becomes ten points to the new creation being founded upon the fulfillment of the law in the person of Jesus Christ. But the ten that must finally come is also a concurrent judgment of the natural body under the law that is the law of death. And this is the final seven years of tribulation that follows the three days of Christ (Dan 9:27). This is the final seven years that will reflect the totality of the seven millennia that is the sevenfold creation. The book of Revelation is likewise a book of sevens that reflects the sevenfold creation.

Genesis 31:24 And God came to Laban the Syrian in a dream by night, and said unto him, Take heed that thou speak [H1696] not to Jacob either good [H2896] or bad [H7451].

The words *good* [H2896] and *bad* [H7451] are the same words used to describe the tree of the knowledge of *good* [H2896] and *evil* [H7451] by which the serpent deceived humanity (Gen 2:9). Laban represents the evil one, while Jacob represents the faithful in Christ, or the new Adam. Laban not being allowed to speak either good or evil unto Jacob then stands in stark contrast to the serpent originally being allowed to speak and lie as he wished unto Adam and Eve in the garden of Eden (Gen 3:1). In the fullness and unity of the Body of Christ, the devil is finally silenced and likewise the sin nature inherited from the first Adam is finally destroyed. This is the promised new Adam. Further, the word *speak* [H1696] (Laban will not) is variously translated *promise* [H1696] (Exod 12:25) and *commune* [H1696] (Exod 25:22) and *command* [H1696] (Num 27:23). The vain promises and commandments of the evil one are utterly rejected by Christ and likewise in Christ.[49]

Genesis 31:25 Then Laban overtook Jacob. Now Jacob had pitched his tent in the mount: and Laban with his brethren pitched in the mount of Gilead.

The Biblical text emphasizes a plurality of Laban as embodied collectively by Laban together with his brethren, and this plurality of Laban is contrasted against the one man Jacob. The former represents the devil together with his host of fallen angels, while the latter represents the one man Jesus Christ and likewise the one Body of Christ empowered by the one Holy Spirit (Rev 12:9). The former is disunity, the latter is unity. The former is chaos, the latter is cosmos. The plurality of the devil corresponds to the broad gate that leads to destruction, while the oneness of Jesus Christ corresponds to the narrow gate that leads to eternal life (Matt 7:13–14). It is the blood of Christ and that alone which overcomes the dragon and his angels (Rev 12:11). The different levels of reality reflect different aspects, or perspectives, of the one and same reality that is the one truth of the one God.

Genesis 31:26 And Laban said to Jacob, What hast thou done, that thou hast stolen away unawares to me, and carried away my daughters, as captives [taken] with the sword?

The sword of Jacob represents the sword that proceeds from the mouth of Christ (Rev 19:15), namely, the sword of the Spirit (Eph 6:17). Laban accuses Jacob of having carried away his daughters as captives with the sword. And it is true that the body of faithful are the captives, or bondservants, of the Lord, being in accord with the grace of the indwelling Holy Spirit (Rom 1:1, 1 Cor 6:19–20). Also, Jacob stealing away points to Christ returning like a thief in the night (1 Thess 5:2). And Jacob stealing away unto the land of his closest, or true, blood kindred points to our redemption coming by the blood of Christ and only by the blood of Christ (Heb 9:22). Jacob stealing away with the

---

[49] "... Thou hast come to earth, and hast sought for the members of Thy fashioning, undertake for man who is Thine own, receive that which is committed to Thee, recover Thine image, Thine Adam. . . . to offer before His Father, not gold or silver, or precious stones, but the man whom He had formed after His own image and similitude; . . . [Alexander of Alexandria, *Arian Heresy*]" (Roberts et al., *Ante-Nicene Fathers* 6:301–2). In undertaking for Adam-kind what we sinners could never do for ourselves, our Lord cannot simply be another Adam as before the Fall of Man. Neither can the promised kingdom of God be merely a return to the garden of Eden.

daughters of Laban reflects the faithful being redeemed from the hand of the adversary (Ps 107:2). Jacob stealing away unawares to Laban is a testimony that the devil does not know the appointed time of the glorious return of Christ (Isa 46:9–10). And all these things prefigure the promised resurrection and rapture, or catching up, of the faithful away from the evil one (1 Thess 4:17).

Genesis 31:27–28 Wherefore didst thou flee away secretly [H2244], and steal away [H1589] from me; and didst not tell me, that I might have sent thee away [H7971] with mirth, and with songs, with tabret, and with harp? 28 And hast not suffered me to kiss my sons and my daughters? thou hast now done foolishly in [so] doing.

The word *secretly* [H2244] (Jacob fled secretly) recalls the same word used to describe Adam and Eve *hiding* [H2244] from the presence of the Lord in the garden of Eden (Gen 3:8). The serpent figuratively, or spiritually, hid Adam and Eve, or humanity, from the Lord, but now it is the Lord who hides the faithful from that same dragon. The former represents the old humanity governed by the flesh that becomes sin and death, while the latter represents the new humanity governed absolutely and finally by the indwelling Holy Spirit. The former is our separation from the Lord, while the latter is our promised communion with the Lord. Further, the word *sent away* [H7971] (with tabret and harp), describing Laban's desire to have sent Jacob away, recalls Adam being *sent forth* [H7971] from the garden of Eden by the Lord God himself (Gen 3:23). However, the faithful will not be *sent forth* [H7971] into the land from the east but rather *stolen away* [H1589] out of the land, or world, from the east, representing an exaltation in the land, or body. The new Adam will not be *hidden* [H2244] in the land from the presence of the Lord. But Laban identifying himself with mirth and songs and the tabret and harp again points to the evil one, who is also closely identified with musical instruments and music (Ezek 28:13). This is the eating and drinking and marrying and giving in marriage that always precedes destruction (Matt 24:38).

Genesis 31:29 It is in the power [H410] of my hand to do you hurt [H7451]: but the God [H430] of your father spake unto me yesternight, saying, Take thou heed that thou speak not to Jacob either good or bad.

The word *power* (el) [H410] (of Laban's hand) is elsewhere used as a title of the one true *God* (El) [H410] (Gen 14:18) and is closely related to the title *God* (Elohim) [H430] identified with the present passage. The disquieting connection between Laban and the Lord reflects the parallel between Laban's vain boasting over Jacob and the devil seeking to elevate himself to the very throne of God (Isa 14:12–14). Laban boasts about his *power* (el) [H410] to hurt Jacob but at the same time admits his impotence in that Jacob is being protected by *God* (Elohim) [H430]. The former is the boast of the devil to Adam, or mankind, while the latter is the utter impotence of the devil before God Almighty. Further, the word *hurt* [H7451] (power to hurt) means "evil." This is the power of the hand of Laban that is only to do evil and not good, likewise only to corrupt and not to create. But this should not be confused with Laban being unable to speak either good or bad unto Jacob, which represents the complete powerlessness of the devil to either bless or curse the faithful in Christ. It is the true power of God, specifically God the Holy Spirit, who blesses and curses and who restrains the false and lying power of the devil until the appointed time of the end, the time of judgment (2 Thess 2:7).[50]

Genesis 31:30 And now, [though] thou wouldest needs be gone, because thou sore longedst after thy father's house, [yet] wherefore hast thou stolen my gods?

Laban can see a connection between Jacob leaving and his gods being stolen, but Laban cannot understand it or the reality it represents. The gods of Laban reflect the supernatural power and dominion of the devil that is permitted by God for a time and only for a time (Rom 13:1–3). From the perspective of the earth, Rachel taking and, at least figuratively, acknowledging and accepting the gods of her father, Laban, represents the apostasy and idolatry that will mark the end times. From the perspective of heaven, Laban having his gods taken from him and, at least figuratively, destroyed by his younger daughter, Rachel, represents the devil being cast down in the end times (Gen 35:4). Therefore rejoice ye heavens and ye that dwell in them but woe to the inhabiters of the earth and of the sea because the devil is come down unto you (Rev 12:12).

Genesis 31:31 And Jacob answered and said to Laban, Because I was afraid: for I said, Peradventure thou wouldest take by force thy daughters from me.

Laban has to ask Jacob to explain the meaning of all these things, and thereby Laban personifies the ignorance of the way of God that marks the devil and likewise his children. Also, Jacob is not afraid for himself but rather for the daughters of Laban. Jacob secrets away his wives just as the Holy Spirit seals the faithful. And the daughters of Laban being finally affirmed to be the wives of Jacob represents the redemption of the faithful in the one Body of Christ.

Genesis 31:32 With whomsoever thou findest thy gods, let him not live: before our brethren discern thou what [is] thine with me, and take [it] to thee. For Jacob knew not that Rachel had stolen them.

Jacob unknowingly, or rather prophetically, curses Rachel. And thereby the younger, or last, wife Rachel embodies the last generation of humanity. This is the generation that will enter into the final tribulation period after the time of

---

[50] "He [Laban] was an idolater, and therefore would not acknowledge the God of Jacob for his God" (Whittingham et al., *Geneva Bible* 15L n. g; Gen 31:29). The children of the devil are the earthly, or carnal, representatives of the devil.

the resurrection and rapture of believers. And the corresponding apostasy will not be characterized by just any form of idolatry but specifically that of the idols, or images, taken from the dragon himself, represented here by the idols taken from Laban. The image of the devil that proceeds from the devil is the beast and the image of the beast (Rev 13:2, 13:14–15). And anyone found with the image, or mark, of the beast will be condemned (Rev 14:9–11).

Genesis 31:33 And Laban went into Jacob's tent, and into Leah's tent, and into the two maidservants' tents; but he found [them] not. Then went he out of Leah's tent, and entered into Rachel's tent.

Laban, who represents the devil, is seeking the possessor of his personal idols, or images, and therefore he is figuratively seeking out his own devotee. The one adhering to the images of Laban, representing the religion advocated by Laban, can and should be viewed as adhering to Laban himself. And the one found with the images of Laban will be put to death by Jacob (Gen 31:32) just as those who worship the beast and his image will be condemned by God (Rev 14:9–11). Laban is simultaneously seeking out his devotee and the one who stole his images, because his devotee is the one who stole his images. And the devotee of Laban is actually his own child, so to speak, born in his own image. The devil is simultaneously seeking out his own children and those who lie, steal, and murder, because his children are those who lie, steal, and murder. But with the final apostasy also comes the final condemnation. This is Rachel taking the idols of Laban that is simultaneously Laban losing his idols.

Leah's tent is here mentioned twice, which implies that Laban is most closely focused on the tent of his firstborn. And the firstborn Leah is identified with the six millennia of creation and correspondingly natural man. The devil is seeking to condemn not only the last generation but all creation throughout all time. Leah is identified with the first six millennia, while Rachel is identified with the seventh millennium, or the time beginning with the seventh millennium. The emphasis on Laban moving from the tent, or place, of Leah to that of Rachel then points to the key movement from the sixth to the seventh millennium. And Laban searching the tent of Jacob followed by the tents of his wives also reflects the devil first tempting, or testing, Christ followed second by the Body of Christ. But Laban not being able to find his images in the tent of Rachel finally represents the devil not being able to condemn the faithful in Christ, despite the reality of sin having originally marked us all.

Genesis 31:34 Now Rachel had taken the images, and put them in the camel's furniture, and sat upon them. And Laban searched all the tent, but found [them] not.

The younger Rachel is identified with the seventh and eighth millennia, corresponding to the millennial reign and the opening of eternity, which together represent the totality of the Second Advent. Rachel taking the idols of her father, Laban, then portends the idolatry connected with the final apostasy that precedes the Second Advent. We see here a woman figuratively sitting upon a beast that itself embodies the idolatry hidden within it. And the woman that sits upon the beast is the whore of Babylon (Rev 17:3). The woman does not so much ride the beast as sits, or dwells, upon the beast. Rachel being the daughter of Laban prefigures a blood kinship between the harlot and the dragon that is the blood of the saints (Rev 17:6). Laban seeking to accuse his daughter Rachel, yet not being able to accuse her, foreshadows the period before the ten horns upon the beast turn on and consume the woman (Rev 17:16).

Genesis 31:35 And she said to her father, Let it not displease my lord that I cannot rise up before thee; for the custom of women [is] upon me. And he searched, but found not the images.

Rachel is, at least figuratively, sitting upon her menstrual blood and, thereby, represents the whore sitting upon many waters (Rev 17:1). The many waters, or bloods, are peoples and multitudes and nations and tongues (Rev 17:15), specifically the inhabitants of the earth whose names are not written in the Book of Life (Rev 17:8). The flow of menstrual blood represents a judgment against life in contrast to conception. And the flow of blood also makes a woman unclean and likewise anyone who touches her unclean (Lev 15:19). Rachel not being able to rise up represents the condemnation of the children of the devil. This is Rachel not being able to rise up, figuratively not being exalted in the resurrection, because of the idols she rests upon. And this is Rachel not being able to rise up before Laban, spiritually because of Laban.

Genesis 31:36 And Jacob was wroth [H2734], and chode with Laban: and Jacob answered and said to Laban, What [is] my trespass [H6588]? what [is] my sin [H2403], that thou hast so hotly pursued after me?

The word *trespass* [H6588] (what is my trespass?) is derived from the root "to rebel, transgress" [H6586], while the word *sin* [H2403] (what is my sin?) is the same *sin* [H2403] that desired and consumed evil Cain at the time of Adam (Gen 4:7). And the connection in the Biblical text between *sin* [H2403] and *trespass* [H6588] thereby points to the primeval rebellion that is the root of all sin. The image here is that of Christ condemning the devil, the accuser, specifically condemning the devil with the devil's own accusations against the Body of Christ, which are ultimately accusations against Christ the Head. The faithful in Christ become guiltless in the Body of Christ just as Jesus Christ himself is guiltless. Further, the word *wroth* [H2734] (Jacob wroth at Laban) means "to burn, be kindled, of anger," whereby the burning anger of Jacob portends the coming judgment of the world by fire, likewise the judgment of the god of this world also by fire (2 Cor 4:4, 2 Pet 3:7).

Genesis 31:37 Whereas thou hast searched all my stuff, what hast thou found of all thy household stuff? set [it] here before my brethren and thy brethren, that they may judge betwixt us both.

JACOB AND LABAN

Laban cannot find any of the things of his house mingled with the things of the house of Jacob. For there is truly no fellowship between the light and the darkness (2 Cor 6:14). Neither the brethren of Jacob nor the brethren of Laban can make a judgment against Jacob. Neither the children of God nor the children of the devil can find any fault, or sin, in the way of the Holy Spirit. The images of Laban, representing the sins of Laban, are actually present in the household of Jacob, but they are hidden so that no one can find them. Likewise, the faithful while yet in the natural body are all sinners but our original sins will be remembered no more, or hidden from sight, in the promised spiritual, or glorified, resurrection body (Jer 31:34).

Genesis 31:38 This twenty years [have] I [been] with thee; thy ewes and thy she goats have not cast their young, and the rams of thy flock have I not eaten.

The twenty years of Jacob's servitude reflects the totality of the seven millennia of creation. The faithful servitude of Jacob represents the movement of the Holy Spirit throughout all the past and future ages. The person of Laban is identified with the prince, or authority, of the present world that is the devil (John 14:30). The she-goats of Laban not casting—that is, losing—their young represents the multitude of humanity being brought forth and preserved throughout all the ages. Jacob not eating the rams of Laban, not killing them and roasting them in fire, reflects the delay of the judgment by fire that has been decreed from the time of the first man Adam (Gen 3:19). This is the first man Adam that embodied all humanity, likewise the curse of all humanity, just as the second man Jesus Christ would ultimately embody all humanity and likewise the curse of all humanity.

Genesis 31:39 That which was torn [of beasts] I brought not unto thee; I bare the loss of it; of my hand didst thou require it, [whether] stolen by day, or stolen by night.

Laban requiring that Jacob bear all his loses throughout their long history points to the condemnation of Jesus Christ for all the sins of the world throughout all the ages of creation. And this strict expectation placed upon Jacob is specifically the condemnation of Christ under the law and in fulfillment of the law. The beasts that steal and tear apart are the offspring of the devil, but it is Jesus Christ, not the devil, who has borne the consequent suffering and hopelessness and death, even that of the entire world throughout all time. And it is the Spirit moving throughout all the ages that testifies to all these things.

Genesis 31:40 [Thus] I was; in the day the drought consumed me, and the frost by night; and my sleep departed from mine eyes.

The cross of Christ is the suffering and rejection of God made visible, but God has suffered and been rejected throughout all the ages, both before and after the time of the cross. That the cross transcends time is evident in the redemptive power of the cross reaching backward and forward in time.

Genesis 31:41 Thus have I been twenty years in thy house; I served thee fourteen years for thy two daughters, and six years for thy cattle: and thou hast changed my wages ten times.

The two women for whom Jacob serves signify the faithful who come out of the dispensations of law and grace, represented by Jews and Gentiles. The elder Leah is identified with the old covenant, the Covenant of Law, while the younger Rachel is identified with the new covenant, the Covenant of Grace. The six millennia from Adam, including the two millennia from the time of the incarnation of Christ, are most closely identified with the Covenant of Law. This is because all creation remains in the natural body under the death sentence of the law during this entire time, including the period following the cross. In contrast, the seventh, or Sabbath, millennium, which corresponds to the millennial kingdom, is most closely identified with the Covenant of Grace. And this is because the millennial kingdom begins the rule, or governance, of the spiritual, or glorified, resurrection body, which is the law of eternal life and not death. The cattle and possessions for which Jacob serves represent the physical creation that will be and must be renewed in conjunction with the rebirth of humanity. This renewal, or rebirth, of all things begins in the establishment of the millennial kingdom (Rev 20:6) and will be finally completed in the foretold new heaven and new earth of eternity (Rev 21:21).[51]

The number 7 is identified with completion, whereby Jacob returning to the promised land without completing a third seven-year period points to this third and final seven-year period of Jacob being fulfilled in the promised land itself. The final seven of Jacob is served for cattle, representing material wealth and possessions. And the connection between the final seven and the promised land is an affirmation that the land, or earth, is the material possession that has been promised to the children of Abraham (Gen 12:7, Gal 3:7). This is the physical creation, or true body, that has been promised to the faithful. Further, the number 10 is identified with the law, whereby the wages of Jacob's servitude being changed ten times reflects the connection between the servitude of Christ and the fulfillment of the law. The emphasis on Laban changing the wages, or laws, governing his relationship with Jacob points specifically to the evil one who will seek to change the times and laws (Dan 7:25). And the final seven of sevens will be a gathering together unto the promised land in a place called in the Hebrew tongue, Armageddon (Rev 16:16).

---

[51] In Talmudic literature, the time of the Messiah is sometimes viewed as the promised world to come and sometimes as a transitory period connecting this world and the next (Cohen, *Rabbinic Sages* 364). The confusion in Rabbinic thought over the distinction between the seventh and eighth millennia is like the confusion over the distinction between the First and Second Advents.

JACOB AND LABAN

Genesis 31:42 Except the God of my father, the God of Abraham, and the fear of Isaac, had been with me, surely thou hadst sent me away now empty. God hath seen mine affliction and the labour of my hands, and rebuked [thee] yesternight.

The First Advent is by virtue of the crucifixion most closely identified with God the Son. And this reality is reflected by the person of Isaac being sacrificed in Moriah (Gen 22:2). The Second Advent is most closely identified with God the Holy Spirit and likewise the Body of Christ animated by the Spirit. And this reality is reflected by the person of Jacob being the progenitor of the tribes of Israel, representing the multitude that is the kingdom of God (Rev 11:15). Jacob returning with great wealth and possessions is then connected to the fear of Isaac just as the glorious return of Christ at the Second Advent will be founded upon the kingship established at the First Advent. The power to overcome the dragon is the blood of the Lamb (Rev 7:14, 12:11). And the life that is in the blood, or represented by the blood, is the Holy Spirit.

The present emphasis on the God of Jacob's father being the God of Abraham, in contrast to the God of Isaac, points to the connection between father Abraham and God the Father. The concurrent emphasis on the fear of Isaac being with Jacob—which is connected with the God of Abraham, the God of Jacob's father—points to the unity of the Father, Son, and Holy Spirit. The connection between the affliction of Jacob and the labor of his hands hearkens back to the work of the cross. The tribulation of the Body likewise recalls the tribulation of the Head. But Laban, because of Isaac, has no power over Jacob just as the devil, because of Jesus Christ, has no power over the Body of Christ. The power to overcome the dragon is the blood of the Lamb (Rev 7:14, 12:11). And the life that is in the blood, or represented by the blood, is the Holy Spirit.

Genesis 31:43 And Laban answered and said unto Jacob, [These] daughters [are] my daughters, and [these] children [are] my children, and [these] cattle [are] my cattle, and all that thou seest [is] mine: and what can I do this day unto these my daughters, or unto their children which they have born?

The devil truly is the prince of this world (John 14:30).

Genesis 31:44 Now therefore come thou, let us make a covenant, I and thou; and let it be for a witness between me and thee.

Laban now demanding a covenant with Jacob and likewise with the house of Jacob portends the final covenant that will be confirmed with many for one week. And the covenant bearing witness to itself portends the ceasing of the sacrifice and oblation in the midst of the week (Dan 9:27).

ESAU, JACOB, ISRAEL

Genesis 31:45   And Jacob took a stone [H68], and set it up [for] a pillar [H4676].

The *stone* [H68] *pillar* [H4676] now set up at Gilead (Gen 31:25) is a repetition of the *stone* [H68] *pillar* [H4676] that Jacob had previously set up at Bethel (Gen 28:18). The two pillars demarcate Jacob's sojourn in the east and, thereby, prophetically demarcate the church age. Jacob setting up the first pillar at Bethel represents the resurrection of Jesus Christ as and with the firstfruits of the dead (1 Cor 15:20, Matt 27:52–53), while Jacob setting up the second pillar at Gilead represents the foretold resurrection and rapture of all the faithful, which is the beginning of the final harvest of humanity (Matt 13:39). The mount *Gilead* [H1568] is identified with the firstborn sons of Leah, representing natural creation, and thereby connects the resurrection of all the faithful with the firstborn Adam (Num 32:29). The first man Adam prefigures the new Adam, but not all those in Adam will become the new Adam—rather only those born again, or born anew. The faithless of the world are not the children of God, formed in the very image of God, but the children of the serpent of the garden, embodying the defacement of the image of God. Finally, the subsequent return of Jacob to Bethel will mark the formal return of Christ following the tribulation period, which, though closely related, is distinct from what is normally considered the end of the church age (Gen 28:21, 35:1).

Genesis 31:46   And Jacob said unto his brethren, Gather stones; and they took stones, and made an heap: and they did eat there upon the heap.

The marriage supper of the Lamb (Rev 19:7).

Genesis 31:47   And Laban called it Jegar-sahadutha [H3026]: but Jacob called it Galeed [H1567].

The one pillar is here called by two different names.[52] There are likewise two gatherings, or resurrections, the faithful unto life and the evil unto damnation (John 5:29). Both resurrections bear witness to the one Lord as the one and same pillar of life. But the setting up of the current pillar at Gilead is most closely identified with the first resurrection of the faithful unto life that will signal the coming of the millennial kingdom (Rev 20:6). And Jacob taking the last word, effectively renaming the pillar, represents Jacob correcting Laban with regard to the immediate significance of the current pillar. A treaty is identified with the current pillar of resurrection, but there will be no treaty, only

---

[52] "Moses, in using the name of Galeed, does it proleptically; . . ." (Calvin, *Commentaries* 2:180; Gen 31:47). The correct and righteous question is never founded upon historical criticism, rather why the Holy Spirit would inspire any certain construction or usage.

judgment, at the second resurrection, occurring at the end of the millennial kingdom (Rev 20:5, 20:12). The delay of judgment cannot stand forever.[53]

Genesis 31:48–49 And Laban said, This heap [is] a witness between me and thee this day. Therefore was the name of it called Galeed [H1567]; 49 And Mizpah [H4709]; for he said, The LORD watch between me and thee, when we are absent one from another.

The one pillar is here again called by two different names, reinforcing the idea that two different events are signified. There are two judgments, or acts of witnessing, the good unto a blessing and the evil unto a curse (2 Cor 5:10). That the two resurrections reflected by this one pillar, or treaty, are separated in time is reinforced by the reality that the established treaty will inevitably be violated. The treaties made with the faithless are always violated by the faithless because the faithless are faithless. The present peace will be followed by war just as the resurrection unto life will be followed by the resurrection unto damnation (John 5:29). And the separation of the two resurrections in time represents this same fundamental and essential separation of light and darkness that must typify every aspect of the promised new creation.[54]

Genesis 31:50 If thou shalt afflict my daughters, or if thou shalt take [other] wives beside my daughters, no man [is] with us; see, God [is] witness betwixt me and thee.

The emphasis throughout this account is on Laban being the one who initiates and enunciates the covenant between himself and Jacob. But this represents the devil and likewise the children of the devil condemning themselves before God with their own mouths. Laban poses as one seeking the welfare of his offspring, but Jacob and also Laban's own daughters testify unequivocally against Laban (Gen 31:14–15, 31:42). The house of Jacob represents the house of God, while the house of Laban represents the house of the devil. And thus it is the testimony of Jacob, not that of Laban, which is accepted as faithful and true. Further, the wives of Jacob embody the totality of the present creation. Therefore, Laban, in proclaiming the end of Jacob taking wives, ironically foretells the end of the present fallen creation that is the devil's dominion. Laban proclaiming that Jacob would not afflict his wives foretells of the promised redemption of the faithful in Christ from death and judgment.

---

[53] The belief in resurrection, partly because of its connection to the belief in reward and punishment, is of central importance in the Rabbinic concept of the hereafter, *Sanhedrin* (Cohen, *Rabbinic Sages* 357). The present temporal world is a prophecy, or promise, of the eternal world to come.

[54] "[T]o take God's name in vain ... [I]t is either simply to lie and assert under his name something that is not so, or to curse, swear, conjure, and, in short, to practice wickedness of any sort.... We are not to swear in support of evil ... but in support of the good ...." (Luther, *Large Catechism* 17). The truth of God is an oath under God that is simultaneously a blessing unto the faithful and a curse unto the faithless.

And Jacob himself setting up the first, or foundational, stone for the pillar of the covenant and then directing the gathering of more stones reflects the providential movement of the Holy Spirit from the foundation of creation and throughout all the ages (Gen 31:45–46). God the Spirit is the giver of the breath of life that marks the faithful and sets up the pillar of resurrection.[55]

Genesis 31:51 And Laban said to Jacob, Behold this heap, and behold [this] pillar [H4676], which I have cast betwixt me and thee;

Laban again asserts that it is he who sets up the covenantal pillar between himself and Jacob. But it was Jacob who set up the foundational stone for the pillar, and it was Jacob who then directed the gathering of the subsequent stones for the pillar (Gen 31:45–46). It is the Lord who has all power and authority, and yet it is simultaneously true that the devil and his children actually condemn themselves with their own mouths. The providential nature of the judgments of God is a seeming paradox, but the strange concurrence of the will of God and the way of creation follows the fundamental paradigm of all creation, which is the union of spirit and flesh in imitation of God the Son. And this is the objective reality, or judgment, of all creation that cannot be denied.

Genesis 31:52 This heap [be] witness, and [this] pillar [H4676] [be] witness, that I will not pass over [H5674] this heap to thee, and that thou shalt not pass over [H5674] this heap and this pillar [H4676] unto me, for harm [H7451].

The word *harm* [H7451] (not pass over for harm) is the same word used to describe the *evil* [H7451] connected with the tree of knowledge of *good* [H2896] and *evil* [H7451] (Gen 2:9) and is also the same word used to describe God warning Laban to not speak either *good* [H2896] or *bad* (evil) [H7451] to Jacob (Gen 31:24). But Laban does now speak thus to Jacob despite the warning of God. And by proclaiming that no one will pass over the pillar, he is ironically foretelling of just such a day and hour. The resurrection represented by the pillar will itself bear witness to *good* [H2896] and *evil* [H7451] in accordance with the judgment that every knee shall bow and every tongue shall confess (Rom 14:11). The pillar will bear witness, and the pillar will be passed over. And just as Laban demands, it will be for good and not for evil—that is, the good work of Jesus Christ, which is the destruction of all evil.

But the covenant presumed here by Laban also portends the final covenant to be established by the anti-christ, a covenant that will mark the final seven foretold through and by Daniel (Dan 9:27). And the cross-purposes of Jacob and Laban in establishing the pillar points to the connection between the

---

[55] "... Jacob is obligated to treat Laban's daughters [his wives] rightly and not to take other wives [Gen 31:50] ... The words of Laban suggest that the agreement is really a nonaggression pact [31:51–52] ...." (Murphy, *New Jerome* 33; Gen 31:48–52). The two aspects are clearly connected, and the connection should not be dismissed.

resurrection of the dead and the final seven, specifically the beginning of the resurrection of all the dead at the beginning of the final seven. The covenant between Laban and Jacob seems like a covenant with death, annulling death, but it is in truth a covenant of death, even calling down death. The overflowing scourge will *pass through* (pass over) [H5674] in accordance with the judgment of God (Isa 28:18–21). The eternal life that is only in God must come through death, or mortal life, just as the spiritual, or glorified, resurrection body in Christ must supplant the natural body of Adam. And likewise a perfected grace must complete, or fulfill, all law and righteousness.

Genesis 31:53 The God of Abraham, and the God of Nahor, the God of their father, judge betwixt us. And Jacob sware by the fear of his father Isaac.

Laban with his own mouth calls down the judgment of God upon himself as is always the case with the faithless following the way of all flesh, the way of all the earth (Prov 13:3). And Laban, not coincidentally, confuses the identity of the God of Abraham (Josh 24:2). The one true God calls himself the God of Abraham, Isaac, and Jacob—not Abraham, Nahor, and Terah (Exod 3:6). This skewing of reality from the God of Abraham to the god of Abraham (Abram) and Nahor's father, Terah, represents a looking away from the one true God of the new Adam to the god of the old Adam, which is the dragon, that old serpent. The three sons Nahor, Haran, and Abram parallel the three sons Cain, Abel, and Seth and likewise the three sons Ham, Shem, and Japheth. These are the three persons Father, Son, and Holy Spirit and likewise the three persons Adam, Jesus Christ, and the Body of Christ. And in what represents a purposeful contrast to Laban, Jacob swears singularly by the fear of his father Isaac and Isaac alone—thereby affirming the power and authority that comes by the cross and only by the cross. Jacob, unlike Laban, does not call down the judgment of God. Jacob, himself asking nothing of Laban, says neither good nor evil unto Laban, which portends the annihilation of freewill in the body of anti-christ, as represented by Laban. And wicked Laban, standing before righteous Jacob, publically condemns himself.

Genesis 31:54 Then Jacob offered sacrifice upon the mount, and called his brethren to eat bread: and they did eat bread, and tarried all night in the mount.

The covenant between Jacob and Laban is sealed with bread alone and not with wine, and their eating bread together is directly connected to Jacob offering sacrifice. The breaking of bread represents the death of the natural body, while the drinking of wine represents the promised rebirth of the resurrection, or glorified, spiritual body. The eating of bread without wine then represents an emphasis on death and judgment. And surely the covenant with death will be disannulled (Isa 28:18).

ESAU, JACOB, ISRAEL

Genesis 31:55 And early in the morning Laban rose up, and kissed his sons and his daughters, and blessed them: and Laban departed, and returned unto his place.

The covenant with Laban, marked by the God (god) of Terah, is closely connected with the curse of Rachel, which is marked by the idols, or gods, of Laban (Gen 31:32, 31:53). All gods and idols represent the one devil, whether or not their devotees know it. The person of Rachel is identified with the seventh millennium, or the era beginning with the seventh millennium. Rachel taking the idols of her father, Laban, unto herself portends the apostasy marking the end of the millennial kingdom and also that marking the beginning of the millennial kingdom. The beginning of the end is the final seven foretold through and by Daniel (Dan 9:27), while the end itself is the final rebellion of the dragon foretold through and by John (Rev 20:7–9). The beginning is the curse of Rachel that seals her fate, while the end is the actual physical death of Rachel. Laban heatedly pursuing Jacob and his family, but not being allowed to harm them, reflects the dragon seeking in vain to destroy the promised child and also the mother of the child (Rev 12:4–5, 12:13–14). And the absence of Laban from this point forward in the Biblical text foreshadows the second death of the lake of fire, which marks the beginning of the millennial kingdom of Christ (Rev 20:14). The second death will not be complete until the end of the thousand years, but it is sealed at the beginning of the thousand years (Rev 19:20, 20:10). Lord God have mercy.

Ω Ω Ω

The second born Jacob purchases the birthright and takes the blessing, but it is expressly the taking of the blessing that necessitates Jacob leave Canaan and sojourn in the east country (Gen 27:41). And Laban testifying in the east to the blessing that rests upon Jacob reinforces the connection between the blessing of Jacob and his sojourn (Gen 30:27). The birthright is most closely connected with Canaan, particularly before Jacob's sojourn in separation from the land, while the blessing is most closely connected with the sojourn itself and finally the long anticipated return back unto the promised land. The birthright is to the blessing as law is to grace. The freewill tithe pledged by Jacob at Bethel before his sojourn in the east identifies the land of Canaan with the Covenant of Law (Gen 28:20–22), while the perpetual separation of the righteous house of Jacob out of the wicked house of Laban, guaranteed at Gilead, identifies the return of Jacob from the east with the Covenant of Grace (Gen 31:52). The birthright is to the blessing as the kingship is to the high priesthood. The birthright points to the birth of Christ (in the land) as a rightful king at the time of the First Advent, while the blessing points to the glorious return of Christ (unto the land) as a ministering high priest at the time of the Second Advent. The sojourn of Jacob in the east foreshadows the church age connecting the conception of Christ at the First Advent (fulfilling the law as our king) and the sanctification of the faithful at the Second Advent (subsuming law in grace as our high priest).

JACOB AND LABAN

1	2
The Land of Canaan	The Promised Land
Birthright	Blessing
The Pillar of Bethel	The Pillar of Gilead
Covenant of Law	Covenant of Grace
The First Advent	The Second Advent
Kingship	High Priesthood

Jacob faced certain death in Canaan at the hands of his older brother, and thereby the second born Jacob did figuratively die (Gen 27:41–45). But in Padanaram, in the east, Jacob finds not only his own life but life eternal represented by his offspring. The symbolic death of the second born Jacob at the hands of the firstborn Esau reflects the death of the second man Christ being literally because of, but spiritually for the sake of, the first man Adam. And Jacob not only preserving his own life but also establishing his offspring reflects the connection between the resurrection of Christ and the resurrection of the Body of Christ. The one man Jacob becoming the nation of Israel points to the one man Christ establishing the multitude of his faithful in himself, in the Body of Christ. And Jacob formally becomes Israel specifically at the time of his leaving Padanaram and returning unto the promised land (Gen 32:28). And it is also at this time of returning that Jacob's house is completed in the birth of his twelfth and final son, Benjamin (Gen 35:18). The sojourn of Jacob in the east country represents the church age connecting the First and Second Advents of Christ. And the connection between the First and Second Advents is the relationship between Christ as the Head and the faithful as the Body of Christ.

1	2
Land of Canaan	Sojourn in the East
Certain Death	Hope of Life
The Firstborn Esau	The Second Born Jacob
The First Man Adam	The Second Man Christ
Jacob Departs	Israel Returns
Christ as Head	Body of Christ

The necessity of Jacob establishing his offspring by separating himself from his older brother is the barrenness of his mother becoming a struggle between two nations (Gen 25:21–24). And the symbolic death of Jacob at the hands of Esau is another kind of barrenness, in that Jacob is effectively cut off from the land of the living as represented by the promised land (Isa 53:8). But the younger Jacob establishing his household in his exile, or out of his exile, reflects a barrenness becoming fertility, which is finally recognized as a death and resurrection. The two future nations embodied by Jacob and Esau represent the faithful and the faithless. And their struggle is the struggle between the light and the darkness (2 Cor 6:14). Jacob being forced to separate himself from his brother reflects the rejection of Jesus Christ by his kinsmen at the time of the First Advent. Jacob building his household while being physically separated from the promised land represents the church age. And Jacob finally returning from the east country unto the promised land prefigures the glorious return of Christ at the time of the Second Advent.

The theme of barrenness becoming fertility is reinforced by the barrenness of Rachel and also the barrenness of Leah becoming fertility (Gen 30:1, 30:9). The barrenness of Leah is an intervening barrenness between her fourth and fifth sons, which points to the opening of the parenthetical church age following the fourth millennium (Gen 29:35). The barrenness of Rachel becoming fertility is identified with Jacob's old age, which points to the establishment of the Body of Christ in the last days, beginning with the First Advent but culminating in the Second Advent (Gen 37:3). The theme of barrenness becoming fertility is also evident in the account of the flocks of Laban and Jacob. The relative barrenness of Laban's flocks becomes fertility through the blessing of Abraham that rests upon Jacob, which represents a preservation and blessing while yet in the natural body (Gen 31:16). The flocks of Laban ultimately becoming the flocks of Jacob represents a death and resurrection, specifically that of the present creation being fulfilled in the promised new creation, which is the true significance of barrenness becoming fertility. And the blessing of the flocks of Jacob, which is finally a blessing not only in the east country but also in the promised land, points to the restoration of creation occurring together with the redemption of mankind. The promised new creation is flesh and spirit, earth and man, a new earth and a new heaven.

1	2
THE FIRSTBORN ESAU	THE SECOND BORN JACOB
DARKNESS OF DEATH	LIGHT OF RESURRECTION
THE DAUGHTERS OF LABAN	THE WIVES OF JACOB
BARRENNESS	FERTILITY
THE FLOCKS OF LABAN	THE FLOCKS OF JACOB
PRESENT FALLEN CREATION	PROMISED NEW CREATION

The three persons Abraham, Isaac, and Jacob reflect the three persons of the Father, Son, and Spirit and likewise the three revelations represented by the formation of Adam followed by the First and Second Advents of Christ. Jacob is sent forth by Isaac to sojourn in the land of Laban, not merely to flee from the face of his brother Esau, but expressly to raise up a family and finally a nation (Gen 28:1–2). Jacob building up his household in the east represents the Holy Spirit calling the faithful during the church age. And the connection between the second born Jacob being sent forth and the firstborn Esau losing the blessing is the connection between the call of the faithful to repentance and the original curse of Adam (Gen 27:41–46). The necessity that Jacob must take a near-kin wife points to the essential blood relationship between Christ and the faithful in Christ that is the blood of Christ (Gen 27:46). And the formation of Adam followed by the First and Second Advents can be viewed as the three persons represented by the first man Adam followed by the second man Jesus Christ followed by the one Body of Christ, corresponding to the last Adam.

Jacob being sent forth after the time of the sacrifice of Isaac in Moriah, but before the literal death of Isaac in old age, again points to the church age connecting the First and Second Advents (Gen 22:2, 35:28–29). The unrelenting

JACOB AND LABAN

struggle between Jacob and Laban represents the Holy Spirit striving to save the faithful in Christ from the power of hell and death, which is the dominion of the great dragon, that old serpent, called the devil and also satan (Rev 12:9). The trickery of Laban is the serpent. The deceitfulness of Laban is the devil. And the grasping nature and desire to do harm marking Laban, likewise his sons, is satan. Jacob finally taking his wives and children and possessions from the hand of Laban represents the necessity that the faithful in Christ be redeemed from the present fallen world governed by the evil one (2 Cor 4:4, John 18:36). And Jacob not only returning unto the promised land but returning in what is a surprising peace with his brother, Esau, prefigures the supernatural peace that will only come with the millennial kingdom of Christ (Gen 33:10).

1	2	3
ABRAHAM	ISAAC	JACOB
FORMATION OF ADAM	FIRST ADVENT OF CHRIST	SECOND ADVENT OF CHRIST
ESAU LOSES THE BLESSING	JACOB SENT FORTH BY ISAAC	JACOB RETURNS
(ESAU REJECTED)	(STRUGGLE WITH LABAN)	(PEACE WITH ESAU)
ADAM, TOGETHER WITH ALL CREATION, CURSED	THE FIRST ADVENT OPENING THE CHURCH AGE	THE MILLENNIAL KINGDOM OF THE SECOND ADVENT

The children of Jacob reflect the recapitulation in Christ of the totality of the millennia connecting Adam, or the body of Adam, and the promised new Adam, which is finally the Body of Christ. The firstborn Leah is identified with the first covenant, the Covenant of Law, while the second born Rachel is identified with the second covenant, the Covenant of Grace. Likewise, the present First Creation, which is fallen, is identified with the law and also the condemnation under the law, while the promised New Creation, or Second Creation, is identified with grace and also with the exaltation that comes only by grace. The six sons of the firstborn Leah embody the six millennia of the present creation, which connect the original formation of Adam and the redemption of the faithful from Adam-kind at the Second Advent. The two sons of the second born Rachel are then identified with the seventh and eighth millennia of creation, representing the millennial kingdom and the subsequent opening of eternity.

The children of Jacob by bondwomen are identified with bondage and therefore with suffering just as Jesus Christ himself would be identified with bondage and servitude and also with suffering and death. The interjection of Jacob's offspring by bondwomen, following Leah's fourth son, points foremost to the suffering, or tribulation, of Christ in fulfillment of the law, specifically as following the fourth millennium. And the supernatural conception of Christ is the interjection, or intercession, of the incarnation of Christ. The significance of recapitulation, which is ultimately embodied by Christ, is that the promised new creation must necessarily comprehend the totality of the original creation. This is the spiritual, or glorified, resurrection body—which is a true body and must be a true body, physical and spiritual. Jacob establishing his house represents the establishment of humanity and ultimately the church, but the true significance of the present age is the constitution of the promised new body, the Body of

Christ, formally beginning in the last days with the incarnation of Jesus Christ as the Head of the Body.[56]

1	2	3
THE FIRSTBORN LEAH (FIRST WIFE)	THE INTERJECTION OF BILHAH & ZILPAH	THE SECOND BORN RACHEL (SECOND WIFE)
THE COVENANT OF LAW (FIRST LAW)	THE FULFILLMENT OF THE COVENANT OF LAW	THE COVENANT OF GRACE (SECOND LAW)
THE FIRST MAN ADAM	THE SECOND MAN CHRIST	THE BODY OF CHRIST
THE FALLEN CREATION	THE INTERCESSION OF CHRIST	THE NEW CREATION

The struggle between Jacob and Laban, which marks the establishment of the house of Jacob, reflects the struggle between the Spirit and anti-spirit, marking the establishment of the church of God. The offspring of the house of Jacob being taken out of the house of Laban represents the faithful being called out of the present fallen world (Gen 31:14–17). The pillar that Jacob sets up at Bethel when he departs from Canaan points to the death and resurrection of Jesus Christ at the time of the First Advent (Gen 28:18–19). The angels of God that Jacob sees ascending and descending on the ladder between earth and heaven represent the ministering of God the Holy Spirit during the church age, connecting the First and Second Advents (Gen 28:12). And the Lord God standing above the ladder represents the ascendant Christ, likewise during the church age (Gen 28:13). Jacob pledges a tithe of all he has at Bethel in exchange for the safety of his household, and Jacob's tithe would be fulfilled in the sacrifice and suffering of his beloved second firstborn son, Joseph (Gen 28:20–22). The tithe symbolizes the law. And the judgment of the law is the death of Adam, the death of Christ in the place of Adam, and also the death of the faithful in imitation of Christ.

The children of Jacob represent the totality of creation. The six sons of Leah are identified with the six millennia connecting Adam and the promised new Adam. The interjection of Jacob's sons by bondwomen represents the intercession of Jesus Christ at the time of the First Advent. And the two sons of Rachel are identified with the millennial reign and eternity. Jacob finally taking possession of the great material wealth of Laban points to the restoration of all creation that will be concomitant with the resurrection of the physical body (Gen 31:17–18). The 7+7+6 years that Jacob struggles with Laban portends the 7+7+7 seals, trumpets, and vials foretold in the book of Revelation (Gen

---

[56] "There is a deep mystery in this number of twelve: . . . Our Lord spoke of twelve thrones . . . . The expression is typical of a sort of universality, as the Church was destined to prevail throughout the whole world: whence this edifice is styled a building together into Christ: and because judges come from all quarters, the twelve thrones are spoken of, just as the twelve gates, from the entering in from all sides into that city. . . . There are four quarters of the globe: East, West, North, and South: and they are constantly alluded to in the Scriptures. . . . And how called? On every side it is called in the Trinity: no otherwise is it called than by Baptism in the name of the Father, the Son, and the Holy Ghost: four then being thrice taken, twelve are found [Augustine, *Expositions on the Psalms*]" (Schaff, *Nicene and Post-Nicene Fathers: First Series* 8:421). The three fathers Abraham, Isaac, and Jacob fathered the twelve tribes.

JACOB AND LABAN

31:38–42). And the third and final 7 of Jacob's 7+7+6 trouble will be completed in the promised land just as the final tribulation period will be completed in the promised land (Jer 30:7–9). The pillar that Jacob sets up at Gilead when he finally and forever separates himself from the house of Laban points to the resurrection and rapture of the faithful at the time of the Second Advent (Gen 31:44–54). But the cursing of Rachel because of the idols of Laban portends a universal apostasy in the end times (Gen 31:32).

ESAU, JACOB, ISRAEL

CHAPTER TWO OUTLINE

Key Images

PRIME IMAGES		
Material	Abstract	Spiritual
Jacob builds his household in the east, at a distance far removed from the land of Canaan.	The place of the rising sun, or new day, representing new life.	The ascendant Christ, through the ministry of the Holy Spirit, builds the house of the Father during the church age (John 14:2, 14:16).
The person of Laban.	The deceitful and greedy lord who rules over the house of Jacob.	The god of this world, who is the devil (2 Cor 4:4).
The idols of Laban.	All false gods represent the devil and his demons.	The last-days apostasy of mankind culminating in the end times.
The mandrakes of Leah purchased by Rachel.	A sign marking the end of the barrenness of Rachel and Leah, but most specifically the end of the latter-days barrenness of Leah.	Jacob's latter sons by the elder Leah reflect the latter days connecting the First and Second Advents of Christ.
Against Laban's will, Jacob takes as his rightful inheritance Laban's daughters and possessions.	A people and dominion taken by force but in accordance with the sovereign will of God.	Christ takes his rightful dominion over creation away from satan, the adversary.
Rachel is prophetically cursed to die because of the idols of Laban.	A death in childbirth identified with Jacob's last born son.	The death and resurrection of the whole world, all creation, in the end times of apostasy.
The tithe, or tenth, promised by Jacob unto God.	The tithe paid by Jacob would be the eleventh son Joseph.	The Father gives the Son in order to save the world (John 3:16).
TWOFOLD IMAGES		
Material	Abstract	Spiritual
Laban and Jacob.	Evil lord versus righteous usurper. Cursed and blessed. Flesh and spirit.	The god of the current world, the devil, versus the one true God, the Lord over the world to come.
Leah and Rachel.	First and second born. Not loved versus loved. Flesh and spirit.	The present creation followed by the promised new creation.
Canaanite wives versus near-kin wives.	Pagans and believers. Faithless and faithful offspring. Flesh and spirit.	The children of the devil versus the children of God.
Bond versus free wives.	Slavery and freedom. Law and grace. Flesh and spirit.	The suffering Messiah in contrast to the glorified Messiah.
Barrenness supplanted by fertility.	Lifelessness versus life. Flesh and spirit.	Mortality supplanted by immortality.
Isaac and Jacob.	Dying versus prolific. Death and life. Flesh and spirit.	The First and Second Advents of Christ.
The pillars of Jacob that are set up at Bethel and Gilead, bracketing his sojourn in the east.	Two being built, or raised up. Life and new life. Natural and resurrection bodies. Flesh and spirit.	The resurrection of Christ at the time of the First Advent followed by that of the faithful in Christ at the Second Advent.
THREEFOLD IMAGES		
Material	Abstract	Spiritual
Abraham, Isaac, Jacob.	Covenantal father, only son, twelve offspring representing a great nation.	Adam formed in the image of God followed by the First and Second Advents of Christ.

JACOB AND LABAN

Esau taking Canaanite wives followed by Esau taking Ishmaelite wives followed by Jacob taking kinswoman wives.	The offspring of pagans followed by the offspring of Ishmael, who mocked Isaac, followed by the offspring of blood relationship representing faithfulness.	The Fall of Man followed by the rejection of Christ at the time of the First Advent followed by the sanctification in Christ at the time of the Second Advent.
Jacob's firstborn offspring of Leah followed by that of his bondwomen followed by that of his beloved Rachel.	The offspring of the unloved woman followed by the offspring of bondage followed by the offspring of the loved woman.	The original curse of Adam, the bondage of Christ at the First Advent, and finally the blessing in Christ at the Second Advent.
Jacob's journey from Beersheba to Bethel and finally to Padanaram, or rather back to the promised land via Padanaram.	The place of the murderous intention of the firstborn followed by the place of the tithe of the second born followed by the place of the return of the second born.	The rejection of God by the first man Adam; the tithe, or offering, of Christ at the First Advent; and finally the glorious return at the Second Advent.
Jacob's seven years of service for Leah followed by another seven for Rachel followed by six for the possessions of Laban.	The offspring of the firstborn followed by the offspring of the second born followed by the material inheritance.	The formation of Adam followed by the First and Second Advents of Christ. (The three subsume and amplify the sevenfold creation.)

Synopsis

To the East

	Material	Spiritual
28:1–5	Isaac commands Jacob to arise, go, and take a wife from among his relatives in the east.	The establishment of the Body of Christ during the church age that connects the First and Second Advents.
	Isaac proclaims that God Almighty will make Jacob into a multitude of people.	The Body of Christ.
	Jacob will inherit the land that God gave unto Abraham.	The restoration, or re-creation, of all creation that follows the resurrection of the faithful.
28:6–9	Esau seeks to imitate the sign of marriage that marks the person of Jacob.	The anti-christ seeks to imitate Christ.
	Esau adds daughters of Ishmael to the daughters of Canaan as his wives.	Humanity is willingly corrupted in the end times of apostasy.

Bethel

	Material	Spiritual
28:10	Jacob goes out from Beersheba toward Haran.	The sevenfold oath represented by creation will be fulfilled in the house of Jacob.
28:11–17	Jacob sleeps upon pillows of stones.	Jesus sacrificed upon the altar of the law.
	Jacob dreams of a ladder reaching from the earth unto heaven.	The promised redemption of all creation will be the union of earth and heaven.
	And Jacob awaked out of his sleep.	The resurrection of Jesus Christ.
28:18	Jacob sets up a pillar with the stone he had used as pillows and then pours oil upon it.	The death and resurrection of the Son is the fulfillment of the law that brings the Spirit.
28:19	Jacob names the place Bethel.	The house of Jacob will be the house of God.
28:20–22	Jacob vows a tithe unto God and connects that tithe to the blessing of God.	The tithe, or law, of the First Advent that points to the grace of the Second Advent.

Rachel and Leah

	Material	Spiritual
29:1–6	Then Jacob came into the land of the east.	The east, the place of the rising sun, from which Christ will return (Matt 24:27).

ESAU, JACOB, ISRAEL

	And behold, a well, and three flocks, and a great stone upon the well's mouth.	Three flocks representing the three millennia that connect the First and Second Advents.
	Jacob meets his brethren of the land of Haran.	The land of Haran is identified with the death of the baptism of repentance, which must precede the life of the baptism of redemption.
29:7–10	And Jacob rolled away the stone and watered the flock that was kept by Rachel.	Christ possesses the living water by virtue of his death and resurrection.
29:11–14	Jacob reveals his identity first unto Rachel and then unto the entire household of Laban.	The resurrection and rapture followed by what is the formal Second Advent.
29:15–21	Jacob submits to serving Laban, but it is Jacob that sets his own wages.	The righteous One fulfills all righteousness.
29:22–30	Leah must precede Rachel.	The Covenant of Law must precede the Covenant of Grace.
	Jacob loved Rachel more than Leah.	Christ desires grace over law.

ELEVEN SONS

	Material	Spiritual
29:31	Leah is hated.	The fallen state of humanity.
	The Lord opens Leah's womb.	The preservation of humanity for redemption.
29:32–35	Leah bears her first four sons, but then she ceases to bear children.	The four millennia connecting the formation of Adam and the First Advent of Christ.
30:1–13	Rachel's bondwoman, Bilhah, gives birth to Dan and Naphtali followed by Leah's bondwoman, Zilpah, giving birth to Gad and Asher.	The unnatural interjection of the offspring of bondwomen points to the supernatural conception of Christ as a suffering servant at the time of the First Advent.
30:14–16	At the time of the wheat harvest, Leah hires Jacob from Rachel with the mandrakes of her firstborn, Reuben.	The first Pentecost, or Feast of Weeks, following the First Advent and marking the coming of the Holy Spirit.
30:17–20	Leah bears her fifth and sixth sons, Issachar and Zebulun.	The fifth and sixth millennia corresponding to the church age and connecting the First and Second Advents of Christ.
30:21	Leah bears her daughter, Dinah, between her sixth and seventh sons, Zebulun and Joseph.	The name *Dinah* means "judgment," which portends the judgment connecting the sixth and seventh millennia.
30:22–24	And God remembers Rachel and opens her womb, and she bears Joseph.	Jacob's seventh son by a freewoman, relating the seventh, or Sabbath, millennium.

SHEEP AND GOATS

	Material	Spiritual
30:25–26	Jacob seeks to return unto Isaac at the time of Joseph's birth.	The end of the church age connecting the First and Second Advents.
30:27	Laban urges Jacob to stay longer in the land of the east.	The final delay before the judgment of the world in the end times.
30:28–32	Jacob to appoint his own wages.	God alone has the dominion.
	Laban will give nothing unto Jacob.	Christ alone has paid the price of redemption.
30:33–34	The flock of Jacob will be the proof of the righteousness of Jacob.	The redemption of the faithful in Christ is the proof of the righteousness of Christ.
30:35	The flocks of Jacob and Laban are separated.	The separation of the faithful and the faithless.
30:36	A three-day journey is set between the flocks of Laban tended by Jacob and the flocks belonging to Jacob himself.	The sign of three days connecting the death and resurrection of Christ, and also the three millennia connecting the First and Second Advents of Christ.
30:37–42	The weak animals bear offspring unto Laban, while the strong animals bear offspring unto Jacob.	The faithful are conceived of the Spirit, and thereby the faithful express the strength and power of the Spirit.
30:43	Jacob increases exceedingly.	The exaltation of the faithful in the Body of Christ, and the corresponding new creation of heaven and earth.

JACOB AND LABAN

From the East

	Material	Spiritual
31:1–3	Laban's sons proclaim that Jacob has gotten all the glory of their father.	Christ takes formal possession of all creation away from the devil in the end times.
	The countenance of Laban changes.	The dragon cast down in fury (Rev 12:12).
	The Lord commands Jacob to return unto the land of his blood kindred.	The time appointed for the glorious return of the Son.
31:4–12	Jacob proclaims his righteousness unto his wives, Leah and Rachel.	The righteousness of Christ is proclaimed unto all peoples throughout all the ages.
	Jacob proclaims that Laban is a deceiver.	The father of lies is rebuked (John 8:44).
31:13	The Lord remembers the pillar and the vow that Jacob established at Bethel.	The promised resurrection of the faithful that is connected with the resurrection of Christ.
31:14–16	Leah and Rachel affirm the wickedness of their father and also that their husband is being directed by the Lord.	The faithful in Christ throughout all the ages are redeemed in the one Body of Christ.
31:17–20	Rachel steals the idols of Laban.	The final apostasy.
	Laban does not perceive the return of Jacob unto the promised land.	The evil one, satan, does not know the time appointed by the Father (Mark 13:32).

Gilead

	Material	Spiritual
31:21–23	Jacob flees toward Gilead.	The place of the firstborn signifying the birthright and blessing of the firstborn.
	Laban pursues.	The evil one persecuting the faithful.
31:24	God warns Laban in a dream by night not to speak to Jacob either good or bad.	The evil one not being able to bless or curse represents the silencing of the sin nature.
31:25–28	Laban questions Jacob in Gilead.	The devil is ignorant of the way of the Spirit.
31:29	Laban claims the power to harm Jacob.	The devil is the father of lies (John 8:44).
31:30	Laban accuses Jacob of stealing his idols.	The apostasy that is the dragon cast down.
31:31	Jacob proclaims that he feared Laban would take Leah and Rachel by force.	The faithful throughout the ages are protected from the evil one.
31:32	Jacob proclaims a judgment of death for the one that has Laban's idols.	The final tribulation period after the time of the resurrection and rapture of the faithful.
31:33–35	Rachel sits upon the idols of Laban as one having a flow of blood.	The mother of harlots (idolatresses) sitting upon the scarlet beast (Rev 17:3–6).
31:36–37	Jacob is wroth and chides Laban.	The coming judgment of the world that will come by fire (2 Pet 3:7).
31:38–42	Jacob recounts his twenty years of suffering in the service of the wicked Laban.	The works and judgments of the Lord God are righteous, fulfilling all righteousness.
31:43–54	Laban calls upon Jacob to make a covenant.	A covenant with death that will be broken (Isa 28:18, Dan 9:27).
31:55	Laban departs and returns unto his place.	The proper place of the dragon is the lake of fire (Rev 19:20, 20:10).

JACOB

יהוה

CHAPTER THREE

Jacob and God

The prime images in the account of Jacob's return to the promised land are the angels of God meeting him at Mahanaim (Gen 32:2), Jacob wrestling with God at Peniel (Gen 32:30), Dinah being defiled at Shechem (Gen 34:2), and Jacob's entire sojourn in the east being bookended by Bethel (Gen 28:19, 35:1). The meeting of the camps of Jacob and God at Mahanaim reflects the parallel movement of the natural and the spiritual in the progressive revelation of God. Jacob wrestling God at Peniel represents the conflict between flesh and spirit that is resolved in the blessing of God. The destruction of Shechem because of the defilement of Dinah portends the tribulation that will herald the glorious return of Christ. The parallel between the defilement of Dinah by Shechem and the defilement of Bilhah by Reuben represents the parallel between the apostasy of faithless Gentiles and the apostasy of faithless Jews (Gen 34:5, 35:22). The place of Bethel, signifying the house of God, relates the presence of God on earth, specifically in the person of Christ at the times of the First and Second Advents. The return of Jacob from the east is preceded by Esau rushing to meet Jacob just as the Second Advent of Christ will be preceded by the resurrection and rapture of the faithful in Christ (Gen 33:4).

The twofold relationships emphasized in the return of Jacob to Canaan are those between Jacob and Esau, Jacob and God, and Jacob and the new Jacob that is Israel. Isaac is most closely identified with the First Advent, while the struggle between Isaac's two sons, Esau and Jacob, reflects the church age culminating in the Second Advent. The sending away of Jacob to the east reflects the rejection of Christ at the time of the First Advent (Gen 27:41). Jacob becoming Israel represents the movement of God the Spirit throughout the church age culminating in the millennial kingdom (Gen 32:28). The wealth accumulated by Esau during Jacob's sojourn represents the gifts of the Spirit given during the church age, while the gifts given to Esau by Jacob upon his return point to the fullness of the indwelling Spirit that will be received in the end times (Gen 32:20, 33:9). But the final separation of the nation of Israel from the nation of Edom portends the eternal separation of the faithful from the faithless (Gen 36:6–8). Further, the destroying of Shechem by the second and third sons Simeon and Levi reflects the connection between the first destruction administered in the second millennium and the first covenant administered in the third millennium (Gen 34:24–29). The two names *Benoni* and *Benjamin*, given sequentially by Rachel followed by Jacob, reflect the curse of the present natural body necessarily preceding the blessing in the spiritual, or glorified, resurrection body (Gen 35:18–19).

Jacob splitting his household into three waves as he enters into the promised land reflects the Fall of Adam followed by the First and Second Advents (Gen 33:1–2). The bondwomen with their children being placed first recalls the bondage that came through Adam. The firstborn Leah with her firstborn children of Jacob being placed second points to the fulfillment of the law, the first covenant, at the time of the First Advent. The second born Rachel with her second firstborn son of Jacob, Joseph, being placed in the final position prefigures the exaltation of the faithful by grace at the time of the Second Advent. And the three closely connected deaths of Deborah followed by Rachel followed by Isaac again reflect the threefold reality of creation that is the promised new creation in Christ. The death of Rebekah's nurse, Deborah, representing the death of a mother figure, recalls the death that entered the world through the first woman Eve, the mother of all the living (Gen 35:8). The death of Rachel giving birth to Benoni, who would become Benjamin, reflects the First Advent pointing to the Second Advent (Gen 35:18–19). The death of Isaac in his old age points to the end of the church age corresponding to the Second Advent (Gen 35:28–29). Adam followed by the First and Second Advents then reflects the Father, Son, and Spirit. And the overarching threefold reality of creation is also reflected by the three days, or millennia, connecting the First and Second Advents of Christ.

HOST OF GOD

Genesis 32:1 And Jacob went on his way, and the angels [H4397] of God [H430] met [H6293] him.

The word *God* (Elohim) [H430] (angels of God) has connotations of "rulers" and "judges" in the Hebrew, which represents an emphasis on authority and power and righteousness, in contrast to condescension and obedience and faithfulness. The title *angel* [H4397] (angels of God) means "messenger," which reflects the Word of God proceeding from God. And the Word of *God* (Elohim) [H430]—relating a word of "ruling" and "judging," or simply "justice"—can only be the condemnation and destruction of the wickedness of mankind. Nonetheless, the title *God* (Elohim) [H430] is also identified with the original creation and, thereby, points to the promised new creation that will be born out of, or through, the foretold destruction (Gen 1:1). The word *met*

[H6293] is elsewhere translated *intercession* [H6293] (he bare the sin of many and made intercession) and, thereby, also points from justice to mercy (Isa 53:12).[1]

Genesis 32:2 And when Jacob saw them, he said, This [is] God's host [H4264]: and he called the name of that place Mahanaim [H4266].

The name *Mahanaim* [H4266] means "two camps" and is closely related to the word *host* [H4264], meaning "encampment, camp." The meeting of the camp of Jacob and the camp of God reflects the dichotomy of flesh and spirit, or more specifically the exaltation of the flesh by the Spirit. The camp of angels and the camp of Jacob forming two camps together also prefigures the host of angels coming with the Son of man to exalt the faithful and to restore creation (Matt 16:27). Further, the image of the two camps meeting together represents the internalization of the image of God in the individual believer. And the implication that the two camps are moving together into the promised land represents the externalization, or projection, of the image of God on to creation as a whole in the promised renewal of all things. The former internalization is a microcosm, while the latter externalization is a macrocosm. But both levels of reality, representing all levels of reality, always work together.[2]

Genesis 32:3 And Jacob sent messengers [H4397] before him to Esau his brother unto the land of Seir, the country of Edom [H123].

The word *messengers* [H4397] (sent by Jacob) is the same word previously translated *angels* [H4397] (sent by God) (Gen 32:1). Jacob sending *messengers* [H4397] unto his brother, Esau, prefigures Christ sending the Spirit of truth unto mankind, or figuratively unto his brother Adam, particularly in the end times (John 16:8–11). The connection between the *messengers* [H4397] of Jacob and the *angels* [H4397] of God is indicated, not only by the use of the same word in each account, but also by the close proximity in the text of the two accounts and also by the otherwise extraneous nature of the account of meeting the *angels* [H4397] of God. Further, the name *Edom* [H123] is closely related to the name *Adam* [H121] (Gen 2:21). The first son *Edom* [H123] and the first man *Adam* [H121] both represent the natural man and likewise the present world.

---

[1] In an alternating structure, Gen 32:1–33:17, the two-camps encounter of Jacob with angels at Mahanaim, 32:1–2, parallels Jacob wrestling with God at Peniel, 32:22–32, while simultaneously in a separate alternating structure, 32:3–32, Jacob dividing his household into two camps, 32:7–8, parallels Jacob dividing himself from his household before wresting with God, 32:22–23 (Waltke 437–38). The universal dichotomy of flesh and spirit testifies to the simultaneous humanity and deity of Jesus Christ being the one paradigm of all creation.
[2] "[T]he church is [elsewhere] called *Mahanaim, two armies*, [Song 6:13]. Here were Jacob's family, which made one army, representing the church militant and itinerant on earth; and the angels, another army, representing the church triumphant and at rest in heaven" (Henry 1:191; Gen 32:1–2). Earth and heaven, flesh and spirit, law and grace—relating the one Body of Christ.

Jacob sends *messengers* [H4397] not unto the land of Canaan, the promised land, representing the promised world to come, but rather Jacob sends *messengers* [H4397] unto the country of *Edom* [H123], representing the present world order. And the name *Edom* [H123] is directly connected to Jacob buying the birthright (Gen 25:30), in contrast to Jacob taking the blessing (Gen 27:37). The birthright is to the blessing as the natural man is to the spiritual man as the present world is to the promised world to come. Jacob sending word of his coming to Edom represents the call to repentance, particularly in the end times.

Genesis 32:4–5 And he commanded them, saying, Thus shall ye speak unto my lord Esau; Thy servant Jacob saith thus, I have sojourned with Laban, and stayed there until now: 5 And I have oxen, and asses, flocks, and menservants, and womenservants: and I have sent to tell my lord, that I may find grace in thy sight.

The emphasis on Jacob being the servant of Esau points to Christ being the suffering servant of all mankind (Mark 10:42–45). The image of Jacob being poised between Laban on the one side and Esau on the other side represents the parallel between the spiritual and the physical. Laban represents the devil, who is the ruler of the present world, while Esau represents the peoples of the present world. We wrestle not against flesh and blood, but against principalities, against powers, against the rulers of the darkness of this world, against spiritual wickedness in high places (Eph 6:12). The emphasis on the great wealth and possessions of Jacob testifies to the power and authority of Christ, even in his servitude to mankind and actually because of his servitude to mankind. Worthy is the Lamb that was slain to receive power and riches and wisdom and strength and honor and glory and blessing (Rev 5:12). Jacob seeking grace in the sight of Esau represents Christ seeking to be accepted by the world and thereby seeking to save the world.

Genesis 32:6 And the messengers [H4397] returned to Jacob, saying, We came to thy brother Esau, and also he cometh to meet thee, and four hundred men with him.

The return of Jacob unto the promised land represents the promised return of Jesus Christ unto the earth. And Esau represents the peoples of the earth, whereby Esau coming to meet Jacob with a numbered contingent represents the faithful among the peoples of the world being numbered, or known unto God. Esau coming to meet Jacob en route before Jacob has formally arrived in the promised land represents the resurrection and rapture of the faithful to meet Christ in the air (1 Thess 4:17). And the catching up of the faithful is here seen as the first in a series of events that will culminate in the visible return of Christ in the Second Advent. The formal departure of Jacob from the promised land was marked by the pillar at Bethel, and it is therefore the return to Bethel that will mark the formal return of Jacob to the promised land (Gen 28:10, Gen 35:1). And it is this formal return that represents the visible return of Christ in the Second Advent. This same Jesus shall return from heaven in the same manner as he departed to heaven (Acts 1:11).

The image of Jacob being poised between Laban on the one side and Esau on the other side represents the parallel between the spiritual and the physical and likewise the parallel between heaven and earth. Jacob setting up the pillar with Laban compared with Jacob meeting with Esau reflects the spiritual and physical aspects of the one and same resurrection. And the symbolic covenant with Laban compared with the giving of physical possessions to Esau reflects the spiritual and physical aspects of the one and same covenant. Laban represents the invisible ruler, or authority, of the present world, while Esau represents the visible ruler, or authority, of the present world. Jacob standing between Laban and Esau represents Christ, who is true God and true man, moving between heaven and earth and uniting the two under his singular dominion. The Lord is opposed by both devil and man, but the Lord God is undeniable, or relentless. And the covenant that God will make in the end times points to the covenant that God will allow in the end times (Dan 9:27).

Genesis 32:7 Then Jacob was greatly afraid and distressed: and he divided the people that [was] with him, and the flocks, and herds, and the camels, into two bands [H4264];

Jacob is not afraid for himself but for his family, representing the faithful in Christ. Jacob dividing his house into two *bands* [H4264] recalls the camps of Jacob and God forming two respective *camps* (hosts) [H4264] at *Mahanaim* [H4266] (Gen 32:2). The camp of Jacob compared with the camp of God represents the dichotomy of flesh and spirit, of earth and heaven. And the two camps composing Jacob's house likewise represent flesh and spirit, also law and grace. The two respective camps of Jacob and God represent the macrocosm, while the two unified camps of Jacob's house represent the microcosm. But both levels of reality embody the one and same reality. And the two camps of Jacob's house ultimately are the two respective camps of Jacob and God, as established in the Body of Christ according to the God-man Jesus Christ—namely, the two camps, or two natures, of flesh and spirit and finally the two camps, or two covenants, of the Jews and Gentiles (1 Cor 12:13).[3]

Genesis 32:8 And said, If Esau come to the one company [H4264], and smite it, then the other company [H4264] which is left shall escape.

The person of Esau represents the totality of the peoples of the earth. Esau coming with great haste to meet Jacob represents the resurrection and rapture of the faithful. But the fear that Esau will smite one of the camps of Jacob represents the faithless rejecting the Lord, either because of law or because of

---

[3] "Among us also in his Christ God has made a heaven and an earth, meaning the spiritual and carnal members of his Church" (Augustine, *Confessions* 280). Jesus Christ embodies all creation.

grace. The rule of law is the condemnation of the natural body, while the gift of grace is the exaltation of the spiritual, or glorified, resurrection body. The rejection of law represents an exaltation of the natural body, while the rejection of grace represents the rejection of the spiritual body. The rejection of law is the physical aspect, while the rejection of grace is the spiritual aspect. The rejection of law is some version of humanism, while the rejection of grace is some version of satanism. But both rejections represent the same rejection of the one truth of the one true God.

Nonetheless, the assurance of one camp escaping destruction is a positive image, even though the possibility (not the certainty) of one of the camps being destroyed is a negative image. In this light, the camp of grace being viewed as surviving represents the law passing away for those under grace (Rom 6:14, Heb 7:18–19) while the camp of law being (simultaneously) viewed as surviving represents those who are a law unto themselves because they have never heard the law (Rom 2:14–16). The overlapping of images of attacking Christ and also being redeemed by Christ reflects the reality that all men are sinners, including the faithful but not for Christ. And this is also the universal juxtaposition of law and grace, likewise flesh and spirit, that can only be reconciled in Christ, in the Body of Christ. This is the fundamental unity of death and resurrection that is the essential unity of justice and mercy.

Genesis 32:9 And Jacob said, O God of my father Abraham, and God of my father Isaac, the LORD which saidst unto me, Return unto thy country, and to thy kindred, and I will deal well with thee:

The one true God is the God of Abraham, Isaac, and Jacob reflecting the triune Father, Son, and Spirit. And the one true God calls his children home to their one true family (Rom 11:17–18).

Genesis 32:10 I am not worthy of the least of all the mercies [H2617], and of all the truth [H571], which thou hast shewed unto thy servant; for with my staff I passed over this Jordan; and now I am become two bands.

When Jacob speaks of his own unworthiness, he is not speaking of Christ as the Head but rather of the Body of Christ. The faithful are saved by grace alone through faith alone and not by any works (Eph 2:8). The truth and mercy of God is law and grace. The emphasis on Jacob becoming two bands, or camps, points to the dichotomy of the law and grace of God. And Jacob connecting the *mercy* [H2617] and *truth* [H571] of God to the establishment of his own family recalls Abraham's eldest servant connecting the *mercy* [H2617] and *truth* [H571] of God to the establishment of Isaac's family (Gen 24:27). The respective families of Isaac and Jacob themselves relate the Body of faithful in Christ, as represented by Jews and Gentiles, and thereby themselves parallel the dichotomy of law and grace.[4]

Jacob passing over the Jordan when he originally departed Canaan is the first baptism—namely, the baptism of repentance by water, or in the flesh. The first baptism represents the death to sin that is the death of the natural man. Jacob now passing over the Jordan a second time in his return to Canaan is the second baptism—namely, the baptism of redemption by fire, or in the Spirit. The second baptism represents the resurrection and exaltation of the spiritual man. The former (first) passing out of, or leaving, the land is most closely identified with death, while the latter (second) passing into, or entering, the land is most closely identified with life. Thereby, the former passing and the latter passing represent yet another parallel between law and grace. The baptism by water marks the natural body governed by flesh, while the baptism by fire marks the resurrection body governed by the Spirit.

Genesis 32:11 Deliver me, I pray thee, from the hand of my brother, from the hand of Esau: for I fear him, lest he will come and smite me, [and] the mother with the children.

The prayer of the second born for a deliverance from the hand of the firstborn is the prayer of the righteous man for deliverance from the sinful man that is finally the deliverance from the sinful nature itself. This is the promised resurrection and exaltation of the spiritual man and the corresponding condemnation of the natural man. This is the promised new birth of creation and the corresponding destruction of the present fallen creation.[5]

Genesis 32:12 And thou saidst, I will surely do thee good, and make thy seed as the sand of the sea, which cannot be numbered for multitude.

The multitude of offspring proceeding from Jacob represents the multitude of faithful composing the Body of Christ.

Genesis 32:13 And he lodged there that same night; and took of that which came to his hand a present for Esau his brother;

The gifts prepared for the natural man Esau proceed from God through the spiritual man Jacob just as the gifts of the Holy Spirit that we receive now in the natural body proceed from the Father through the Son.[6]

---

[4] "A man who sees himself in the light of God will ever feel that he has no good but what he has received, and that he deserves nothing of all that he has" (Clarke 1:201; Gen 32:10). The promised resurrection body will proceed from the second man Christ just as the fallen natural body proceeded from the first man Adam.
[5] "The best we can say to God in prayer is what he [God] hath said to us" (Wesley 1:129; Gen 32:12). God is triune: the object, the medium, and the power of worship.
[6] "Jacob, having piously made God his friend by a prayer, is here prudently endeavouring to make Esau his friend by a present. . . . When we have prayed to God

Genesis 32:14–15 Two hundred she goats, and twenty he goats, two hundred ewes, and twenty rams, 15 Thirty milch camels with their colts, forty kine, and ten bulls, twenty she asses, and ten foals.

The emphasis on owning and gifting livestock affirms the reality that all the gifts of the Holy Spirit all point to the one gift of life itself, whether mortal life in the natural body or eternal life in the spiritual, or glorified, body.

Genesis 32:16 And he delivered [them] into the hand of his servants, every drove by themselves; and said unto his servants, Pass over before me, and put a space betwixt drove and drove.

The emphasis on the droves being separated by spaces evokes a sense of the passing of time. This is the time of the Spirit, marked by the gifts of the Spirit, that must precede both the glorious return of the Son and the corresponding revelation of the fullness of the Spirit, the Holy Spirit. The call to repentance must likewise precede the promised redemption.

Genesis 32:17–18 And he commanded the foremost, saying, When Esau my brother meeteth thee, and asketh thee, saying, Whose [art] thou? and whither goest thou? and whose [are] these before thee? 18 Then thou shalt say, [They be] thy servant Jacob's; it [is] a present sent unto my lord Esau: and, behold, also he [is] behind us.

The firstborn natural man does not recognize, or understand, the coming of the second born spiritual man. The person of the firstborn represents the first birth, while the person of the second born represents the second birth.

Genesis 32:19 And so commanded he the second, and the third, and all that followed the droves, saying, On this manner shall ye speak unto Esau, when ye find him.

The three droves of Jacob reflect the three millennia following the First Advent of Jesus Christ. The messengers of Jacob speaking unto Esau in the exact same manner with regard to each passing drove represents the exact same message of Christ being proclaimed with each passing millennium. The one message of the Holy Spirit is the call into the Body of Christ by grace alone through faith alone in Christ alone. And the repeating of the same message over and over again reflects the relentlessness of God in the calling of the faithful to repentance throughout the millennia of creation.

---

for any mercy, we must second our prayers with our endeavours; else, instead of trusting God, we tempt him; we must so depend upon God's providence as to make use of our own prudence" (Henry 1:194; Gen 32:13–23). The natural and the spiritual always work together and always on all levels of reality.

JACOB AND GOD

Genesis 32:20–21 And say ye moreover, Behold, thy servant Jacob [is] behind us. For he said, I will appease [H3722] him with the present that goeth before me, and afterward I will see his face; peradventure he will accept of me. 21 So went the present over before him: and himself lodged that night in the company.

The word *appease* [H3722] (Jacob will appease Esau) means "to cover over, pacify, make propitiation," which reflects Jesus Christ being the propitiation for the sins of the whole world (1 John 2:2). Esau does not seek to appease Jacob, but rather it is Jacob that seeks to appease Esau. The natural man cannot appease the spiritual man. And the affirmation that the spiritual man must appease the natural man reflects the necessity of death and resurrection. Jacob seeks to be accepted by Esau for the sake of his household just as Jesus Christ seeks to be accepted by the world for the sake of the world. If Esau had chosen to attack Jacob, then the Lord would surely have struck down Esau in order to preserve the promises given to Jacob. And the natural man likewise perishes in his own sins unless he accepts the propitiation that comes only through faith in the blood of Christ (Rom 3:25).

THE PRINCE WHO PREVAILS

Genesis 32:22–24 And he rose up that night, and took his two wives, and his two womenservants, and his eleven [H6240, H259] sons, and passed over the ford Jabbok. 23 And he took them, and sent them over the brook, and sent over that he had. 24 And Jacob was left alone; and there wrestled [H79] a man [H376] with him until the breaking [H5927] of the day.

The word *wrestle* [H79] (Jacob wrestled a man) has a connotation "to become dusty," which recalls the original formation of man from the dust of the ground (Gen 2:7). The struggle of Jacob is the struggle in the dust of the flesh that is the struggle to redeem the whole man—body, spirit, and soul. The word *man* [H376] (Jacob wrestled a man) has a connotation "husband" and is the same word describing *woman* [H802] being taken out of *man* [H376] (Gen 2:23). The man with whom Jacob wrestles is the man from whom all creation proceeds. The man is God the Son. In this struggle to redeem the world, the Son is struggling against Jacob and not against the devil, actually not even against Jacob since Jacob prefigures the glorious return of Christ. The person of Jacob represents God the Son, while the man against which he wrestles is also God the Son. And the emphasis on Jacob staying alone and wrestling alone, separated from his camp, reinforces the image of a solitary struggle.

The image of the Son struggling against himself does not represent an internal struggle of God but affirms that all power and authority are embodied by the Son. And the Son struggling against himself likewise affirms that the presumed power of the evil one has no power at all over the unfolding redemption of the world. Further, this struggle to redeem flesh reflects the suffering of the Son in the flesh. The struggle of Jacob against the man can then be viewed as the struggle of the Son of man against the Son of God—that is, the suffering of the Son in the flesh according to the will and urging of the Holy Spirit, which is perfectly embodied by the Son. And the emphasis on Jacob wrestling through the night at this critical moment of his triumphal return unto the promised land points to the darkness of the anti-christ that will herald the dawn of the millennial kingdom of Christ.[7]

Genesis 32:25 And when he saw that he prevailed not against him, he touched [H5060] the hollow of his thigh [H3409]; and the hollow of Jacob's thigh [H3409] was out of joint, as he wrestled [H79] with him.

The word *touched* [H5060] (touched his thigh) means "to touch, reach, strike" and is elsewhere translated *plagued* [H5060] (Gen 12:17). The man plagues the thigh of Jacob because he is not prevailing against Jacob. There would be no prevailing, or overcoming, unless the flesh of Christ had been plagued. This is the victory of the cross. And the victory of the cross is also the victory of the end times because it is by the blood of the Lamb and only by the blood of the Lamb that we overcome the evil one (Rev 12:11). The man touching, or plaguing, Jacob's *thigh* [H3409] further recalls Abraham's eldest servant swearing by his *thigh* [H3409] to take a kinswoman wife unto Isaac (Gen 24:2). The thigh of Abraham signifies the marriage covenant of Isaac that is the Covenant of Law fulfilled in the First Advent of Christ, while the thigh of Jacob now signifies the covenant of prevailing that is the Covenant of Grace to be fulfilled in the Second Advent.

Abraham, Isaac, and Jacob reflect the Father, Son, and Spirit and likewise the formation of Adam in the image of God followed by the First and Second Advents of Christ. The fulfillment of the law is the original commandment of the Father and is identified with the original obedience of father Abraham (Luke 22:42). The fulfillment of the law is then reflected by the sacrifice of Isaac by Abraham in Moriah (Gen 22:2). The gift of grace is the Holy Spirit animating the Body of Christ and is identified with the multitude of offspring proceeding from the person of Jacob (John 16:7). The image of Jacob's thigh being wrenched out of joint represents the Covenant of Law being superseded by the Covenant of Grace. And Jacob continues to wrestle seemingly unaffected by his thigh being wrenched just as the glorious return of Christ in the Second Advent proceeds despite and even as a direct result of the suffering that marked the time of the First Advent.

Genesis 32:26 And he said, Let me go, for the day breaketh [H5927]. And he said, I will not let thee go, except thou bless me.

---

[7] "The mode by which this wrestling was maintained and conducted to an ultimate victory was by 'strong crying and tears' . . . in which Jacob was a type of Christ . . . . It is [further] evident that Jacob was aware of the character of Him with whom he wrestled; . . ." (Jamieson et al. 1:215; Gen 32:24–26). Two simultaneous images representing the reality that God the Son is true man and true God.

JACOB AND GOD

The word *breaketh* [H5927] (the day breaketh) means "to go up, ascend, climb." The man proclaims that he must be let go at the time of the ascending of daylight. Jacob proclaims that the man must then bless him in order to be let go at the time of the ascending of light. And the blessing of Jacob is thereby connected to the same time of ascending. The blessing of the injured Jacob is the blessing of the Son of man in being injured for the sake of his faithful ones. And the letting go of the man represents the glorious return of the Son of God. The letting go of the man by the injured Jacob is a testimony that the authority of the Second Advent is based on the First Advent. And the ascending that marks the end of this struggle is the resurrection of the faithful in the Son.

Genesis 32:27–28 And he said unto him, What [is] thy name? And he said, Jacob [H3290]. 28 And he said, Thy name shall be called no more Jacob [H3290], but Israel [H3478]: for as a prince hast thou power with God and with men, and hast prevailed.

The name *Jacob* [H3290] being changed to *Israel* [H3478] speaks of new creation. The name *Jacob* [H3290] means "supplanter" and is connected to the second born Jacob originally grasping the heel of the firstborn Esau and ultimately supplanting the firstborn Esau (Gen 25:26, 27:36). The name *Israel* [H3478] means "he will rule as God" and is now connected to Jacob finally prevailing in his struggling with man and with God (Gen 32:24–32).[8] Jacob supplanting Esau reflects the Son of man supplanting Adam in the First Advent, while Israel finally ruling as God reflects the promised visible dominion of the Son of God in the Second Advent. Jesus Christ is simultaneously the Son of man and the Son of God, but his humanity is emphasized in the First Advent while his divinity is emphasized in the Second Advent. And Jacob having struggled and prevailed with both man and God reflects the Son having dominion over both flesh and spirit. And the name *Jacob* [H3290] being changed to *Israel* [H3478] now at the time of returning unto the promised land points to the fullness of the revelation of Jesus Christ not occurring until the time of the Second Advent.[9]

Genesis 32:29 And Jacob asked [him], and said, Tell [me], I pray thee, thy name. And he said, Wherefore [is] it [that] thou dost ask after my name? And he blessed him there.

---

[8] Literal meaning of the name *Israel* [H3478] per *Strong's*, not *Brown-Driver-Briggs*.
[9] "If any one, again, will look into Jacob's actions, he shall find them not destitute of meaning, but full of import with regard to the dispensations. Thus, in the first place, at his birth, since he laid hold on his brother's heel, he was called Jacob, that is, the *supplanter*... striving and conquering... For to this end was the Lord born, the type of whose birth he set forth beforehand.... [Irenaeus, *Against Heresies*]" (Roberts et al., *Ante-Nicene Fathers* 1:493). Not only be willing to look, but be willing to look with a spirit of humility, in accordance with the Holy Spirit.

In the naming of Israel, the Lord has, in one sense, implicitly revealed that his own name is *the God of Israel*. In another sense, the man with whom Jacob wrestles does not explicitly answer Jacob and, thereby, the man indicates that his true name is yet hidden. The true name of the Lord must still be hidden at this point in time because the true name of the Lord represents the fullness of the understanding of the nature of the Lord. And the fullness of the understanding of God will be realizable only at the appointed time of the fullness of the new creation of all things. The first and immediate revelation of the name of God as *the God of Israel* or *the God of the chosen people* reflects the resurrection and rapture of the faithful at the beginning of the final tribulation period, while the implied but yet future second revelation of a hidden name of God reflects the glorious return of the Lord at the ending of the final tribulation period. And the hidden name of the Lord will at that time be established, or revealed, in relation to *the God of all nations* or *the God over all nations*.[10]

The imminent catching up of the faithful points to the glorious return just as the one nation of Israel points to all nations collectively. In the same sense, the redemption of mankind points to the redemption of the whole of creation. The identification of the resurrection and rapture with Israel is an identification with law in contrast to grace. The Jew is to the Gentile as law is to grace. And the catching up of the faithful in Christ compared with the glorious return of Christ parallels the First Advent compared with the Second Advent. The resurrection and rapture of all believers at the time of the end is the exaltation of the Body of Christ, while the resurrection of Christ at the time of the First Advent, in the midst of time, is the resurrection of the Head. And the resurrection of the Head and the Body should be considered spiritually one event in accordance with the law fulfilled perfectly in Christ (Col 2:12). And the salvation of a sinful world on the brink of destruction at the ending of the final tribulation period will then be the final revelation of the grace of God in the formal return of Christ at the time of the Second Advent (Mark 13:20).

Genesis 32:30 And Jacob called the name of the place Peniel: for I have seen God [H430] face to face, and my life is preserved.

The person with whom Jacob wrestles was first described as a *man* [H376] but now as *God* [H430] himself (Gen 32:24). Jesus would likewise reveal himself first as the Son of man and second as the Son of God. The first emphasizes humanity, while the second emphasizes divinity. And Jacob finally realizing that the man is God reflects the realization that the Son of man is the Son of God (Matt 16:15–17). The name *Son of man* is to the name *Son of God* as the First Advent is to the Second Advent, whereby the realization that the man is God

---

[10] "The name [of anyone] . . . was always significant . . . descriptive of the nature and rank of the bearer. But His name [the name of God] was ineffable, because His nature was wonderful, mysterious, and incomprehensible . . . ." (Jamieson et al. 1:216; Gen 32:29). Everything, every jot and tittle, has meaning, and amazingly even that which is absent has meaning.

should be most closely identified with the end times. The fundamental duality of Christ being the Son of man and the Son of God parallels the dichotomy represented by Jacob and Jacob's contender and, thereby, reflects the image of God being impressed upon the nature and character of all creation. And the progression from Jacob's initial experience of the man to his final realization that the man is God reflects the image of God being impressed upon the very movement of history, manifested in time itself. Jacob finally proclaiming the preservation of his own life is not simply a realization that God could have destroyed him but ultimately that seeing the face of God is the preservation of one's life and finally the only way to preserve one's life.

Genesis 32:31 And as he passed over Penuel the sun rose upon him, and he halted upon his thigh.

And they, Jews and also Gentiles, shall look upon him whom they have pierced, not only at the time of the First Advent (John 19:37), but also at the time of the Second Advent (Zech 12:10).

Genesis 32:32 Therefore the children of Israel eat not [of] the sinew which shrank, which [is] upon the hollow of the thigh, unto this day: because he touched the hollow of Jacob's thigh in the sinew that shrank.

Israel continuing unto this day in not eating the sinew, or flesh, touched by God represents a false piety portending a false religion of the end times that will be the final rejection of God in the flesh. Except ye eat the flesh of the Son of man, and drink his blood, ye have no life in you (John 6:53).

FACE OF GOD

Genesis 33:1–3 And Jacob lifted up his eyes, and looked, and, behold, Esau came, and with him four hundred men. And he divided the children unto Leah, and unto Rachel, and unto the two handmaids. 2 And he put the handmaids and their children foremost, and Leah and her children after, and Rachel and Joseph hindermost. 3 And he passed over before them, and bowed himself to the ground seven times, until he came near to his brother.

Jacob proceeds first at the head of his family just as Christ is the Head of the Body. Jacob, the spiritual man, bowing seven times as he comes near to his brother, the natural man Esau, reflects the seven millennia of creation that separates the natural man from the spiritual man, or rather separates the natural man from becoming the spiritual man. Jacob's family also reflects the seven millennia of creation, whereby Jacob dividing them into three groups represents the three millennia of Christ supplanting the seven millennia of Adam. And Jacob previously sending ahead the three droves of flocks can be compared with Jacob now dividing his family into three groups (Gen 32:13–19). This is the revelation of prophecy compared with the fulfillment of prophecy. The Covenant of Law likewise precedes the Covenant of Grace. And the three complete and subsume the seven just as the promised new Adam will perfect and supplant the old Adam.

The dividing of Jacob into three groups can further be related to the three millennia connecting the First and Second Advents. In this view, Joseph can be identified with the millennial reign of Christ that marks the seventh, or Sabbath, millennium while the offspring of the bondwomen can be identified with the servitude of Christ that marks the fifth millennium. And the offspring of Leah, particularly Reuben and Judah, are then identified with the rejection of Joseph, signifying the rejection of the glorified Christ, that marks the sixth millennium (Gen 37:22, 37:26–27). The three groups of Jacob can also be related to the time of Adam followed by the First and Second Advents. Joseph being the child of Jacob's old age points to the Second Advent at the end of the age, while the offspring of Jacob's bondwomen reflect the original enslavement, or servitude, of Adam to sin. The offspring of Leah, particularly Judah, then embodies the Messianic bloodline and, thereby, the First Advent.

Genesis 33:4 And Esau ran to meet him, and embraced him, and fell on his neck, and kissed him: and they wept.

The firstborn Esau reflects Adam—the totality of humanity, the faithful and the faithless—culminating in the end times. The coming of Esau represents the call of the faithful, while the subsequent departing of Esau represents the rejection of the faithless. Esau running to meet Jacob prefigures the catching up of the faithful into the air to meet Christ at the time of the first resurrection (1 Thess 4:17). And Esau embracing and falling upon and kissing Jacob speaks of the unity of the faithful with Christ and also the dependence of the faithful upon Christ. And the firstborn Esau and the second born Jacob weeping together finally reflects the long-suffering of the second man Jesus, together with the first man Adam.

Genesis 33:5 And he lifted up his eyes, and saw the women and the children; and said, Who [are] those with thee? And he said, The children which God hath graciously given thy servant.

The firstborn Esau must ask the second born Jacob to explain the identity, or meaning, of his wives and children. The natural man does not recognize, or understand, the offspring that come by the grace of God. Nonetheless, the fullness of the grace of God will be revealed in the end times.

Genesis 33:6–7 Then the handmaidens came near, they and their children, and they bowed themselves. 7 And Leah also with her children came near, and bowed themselves: and after came Joseph near and Rachel, and they bowed themselves.

JACOB AND GOD

The family of Jacob being divided into three groups represents the totality of the seven millennia of Adam being organized, or understood, as the three millennia of Jesus Christ. The three groups of Jacob, each in its turn, bowing unto Esau represents God the Spirit calling the whole world, every generation in its turn, unto repentance and grace.[11]

Genesis 33:8 And he said, What [meanest] thou by all this drove which I met? And he said, [These are] to find grace in the sight of my lord.

The three droves of flocks previously sent ahead by Jacob, compared with his family now divided into three groups, represents the revelation of prophecy compared with the fulfillment of prophecy (Gen 32:13–19). The prophecy of God is the proof of God that is given unto the world so that the world can believe God and receive the grace of God. This is the call to repentance that must precede redemption in accordance with the inviolability of freewill. This is the grace in the Spirit that can only be received by the faith of the Spirit.

Genesis 33:9 And Esau said, I have enough [H7227], my brother; keep that thou hast unto thyself.

The natural man does not comprehend, much less believe, that he must receive the gift of grace from the hand of God in order to be saved.[12]

Genesis 33:10 And Jacob said, Nay, I pray thee, if now I have found grace in thy sight, then receive my present at my hand: for therefore I have seen thy face, as though I had seen the face of God, and thou wast pleased with me.

The imperative that the firstborn Esau must receive this gift from the hand of the second born Jacob is directly connected to his finding grace and finally to his having the very likeness of God. To receive the gift of grace from the hand of Christ is to receive the very face, or image, of God unto oneself. And the believer, or first man, in so doing, becomes like the second man Jesus Christ (1 John 3:1–2), who is our great God and our Savior (Titus 2:13). Not of ourselves, but only in Christ.[13]

---

[11] "Jacob and his family are the image of the Church under the yoke of tyrants, who for fear are brought to subjection" (Whittingham et al., *Geneva Bible* 16L n. c; Gen 33:6). God handing us over to the world is God calling us unto repentance.

[12] Esau has *enough* (rab) [H7227], meaning "much," Gen 33:9, whereas Jacob has *enough* (kol) [H3605], meaning "everything [the whole]," 33:11 (Coffman 407; Gen 33:8–11). The wholeness that Jacob possesses is the Holy Spirit.

[13] A concentric pattern, framed by Esau and Jacob making confessions of material blessings, spans Gen 33:9–11 and centers around Jacob seeing the face of Esau as the very face of God, 33:10b (Waltke 452). The promised blessing of the Lord is nothing less than God himself, namely, the indwelling Holy Spirit.

ESAU, JACOB, ISRAEL

Genesis 33:11 Take, I pray thee, my blessing [H1293] that is brought to thee; because God hath dealt graciously with me, and because I have enough [H3605]. And he urged him, and he took [it].

Jacob urging Esau to take his blessing represents the Holy Spirit urging all mankind to accept the Son. And note that the blessing proceeds from God through Jacob unto Esau according to the grace of God that is the will of God. Jacob previously taking the *blessing* [H1293] of the firstborn from Esau and then departing to the east is an image of Christ taking up the lost dominion of Adam at the time of the First Advent. And Jacob now *blessing* [H1293] Esau upon his returning unto the promised land is an image of the blessing of the faithful in Christ at the time of the Second Advent (Gen 27:27–29). Esau may appear, according to the way of man, to be the powerful party in this meeting, but it is Jacob, according to the way of God, that blesses Esau. And surely it is the lesser person that is blessed by the greater (Heb 7:7).

The second born Jacob purchased the birthright of the firstborn (Gen 25:31), and he took the blessing of the firstborn (Gen 27:35). But Jacob having to flee to the east was a direct result of his taking the blessing and not because of his purchasing the birthright (Gen 27:41). And thus Jacob's sojourn in the east and his corresponding return from the east are most closely connected with the blessing and not with the birthright. Esau now being blessed by Jacob and thereby partaking of the blessing of Jacob reinforces this connection between the blessing of the firstborn and the glorious return of the second born. The First Advent is to the Second Advent as the birthright is to the blessing as the flesh is to the spirit as the kingship is to the priesthood as law is to grace. And surely the latter things are greater than the former things, since the latter things complete the former things (Rom 5:20).

Genesis 33:12 And he said, Let us take our journey, and let us go, and I will go before thee.

The first man Adam is not the Head of the Body and cannot be accepted as such. It is the second man Jesus who is the Head of the Body of Christ.

Genesis 33:13 And he said unto him, My lord knoweth that the children [are] tender, and the flocks and herds with young [are] with me: and if men should overdrive [H1849] them one day, all the flock will die.

The way of the natural man Esau, which represents the way of Adam, leads to death and only to death. And the spiritual man Jacob, who represents the Lord, knows very well how to avoid the way of flesh and death. Nonetheless, the herds not now being overdriven even one day is connected to the present time of tender youth and, thereby, points to a yet future time of maturity when they will be overdriven one day. The word *overdrive* [H1849] (the flocks) means "to beat, knock (violently)." The one day of being overdriven portends the Day of the Lord in the end times (Mal 4:5, 2 Pet 3:10).

JACOB AND GOD

Genesis 33:14 Let my lord, I pray thee, pass over before his servant: and I will lead on softly, according as the cattle that goeth before me and the children be able to endure, until I come unto my lord unto Seir.

The relatively slow movement of the spiritual man Jacob as compared with the natural man Esau reflects the perception of mankind that the Lord is slow moving to fulfill his promises. But Jacob directly connects his slow movement to the well-being of his flocks. The Lord is not slack concerning his promise, as the carnal man reckons, but is long-suffering, not willing that any should perish, desiring that all should come to repentance (2 Pet 3:9).

Genesis 33:15–16 And Esau said, Let me now leave with thee [some] of the folk that [are] with me. And he said, What needeth it? let me find grace in the sight of my lord. 16 So Esau returned that day on his way unto Seir.

The firstborn Esau represents Adam, or the totality of humanity, particularly in the end times. The coming of Esau represents the call of the faithful, while the going of Esau represents the rejection of the faithless. The person of Esau reflects different aspects of the faithless and the faithful. This is the evil and good in all of us while we yet remain in the natural body. Esau seeking to help Jacob in his journey represents the works of the flesh, but Jacob does not need help just as the Lord does not need help and actually cannot, in his perfection, accept the tainted help, or works, of sinful man. And Jacob directly connects his not needing help with his desire to find grace in the sight of his brother. The faithful are saved by the grace of the Spirit, not by the works of the flesh.

Genesis 33:17 And Jacob journeyed to Succoth [H5523], and built him an house [H1004], and made booths [H5521] for his cattle: therefore the name of the place is called Succoth [H5523].

The sacrifice of the Passover lamb prefigures the propitiatory sacrifice of Christ (Exod 12:21–23). The Feast of Weeks, also called the Feast of Harvest and also Pentecost, is identified with the firstfruits of labor and, thereby, prefigures the coming of the Holy Spirit, which would be the first sign, or deposit, of our promised redemption (Exod 23:16, Num 28:26). But Jacob building booths specifically points to the Feast of Ingathering, also called the Feast of Booths and also Tabernacles. The Feast of Ingathering at the end of the year marks the end of the harvest cycle and, thereby, prefigures the glorious return of Christ and the corresponding harvest of the world (Exod 23:16). Jacob building himself a house represents the establishment of the house of God that is the exaltation of the faithful. Jacob building his house along with booths for his flock represents the Lord literally dwelling among us. And the current pause of Jacob at Succoth, before his journey to Shalem (a city of Shechem) and finally to Bethel, prefigures the resurrection and rapture that will precede the formal return of Christ (Gen 33:18, 35:1). A booth, or tabernacle, being a

THE DEFILEMENT OF DINAH

Genesis 33:18–20 And Jacob came to Shalem [H8004], a city of Shechem, which [is] in the land of Canaan, when he came from Padan-aram; and pitched [H2583] his tent before the city. 19 And he bought a parcel of a field, where he had spread his tent, at the hand of the children of Hamor, Shechem's father, for an hundred pieces of money. 20 And he erected there an altar, and called it El-elohe-Israel.'

The return of Jacob from Padanaram to the land of Canaan is here formally announced, prefiguring the visible return of Christ at the time of his second coming. Jacob built a house at Succoth, but now he pitches a tent at Shalem, a city of Shechem. The children of Hamor represent all the people of the land, and in the act of accepting Jacob's money, they acknowledge Jacob's right to pitch his tent in the land. But the people do not understand that the coming of Jacob is the coming of their destruction. The word *pitched* [H2583] (pitched his tent) connotes "to encamp against (lay siege)." Jacob buying a parcel of a field prefigures Christ taking formal and legal possession of all creation at the time of his second coming.[15]

Genesis 34:1–2 And Dinah [H1783] the daughter of Leah, which she bare unto Jacob, went out to see the daughters of the land. 2 And when Shechem the son of Hamor the Hivite, prince of the country, saw her, he took her, and lay with her, and defiled her.

---

[14] The firstling sheaf (of barley) is presented at the time of the Feast of Unleavened Bread before the grain harvest begins, Lev 23:10–11, while the firstling loaves (made of wheat) are presented at the time of the Feast of Weeks after the completion of the grain harvest, Lev 23:17 (*New Unger's Bible Dictionary*, s.v. "first fruit"). The offering of the firstling sheaf, not the firstling loaves, is commonly called the Feast of Firstfruits, but the firstling sheaf and firstling loaves are connected just as Passover and Pentecost are connected; Per Exod 23:16, Deut 16:13, and Lev 23:39, the Feast of Ingathering is held after the completion of the annual harvest cycle and, therefore, corresponds to the harvest of fruits and specifically grapes, being the final harvest in the annual cycle (*New Unger's Bible Dictionary*, s.v. "festivals"). The Feast of Ingathering is the time of the treading of the winepress, corresponding to the end times.

[15] The account of Dinah and Shechem, Gen 33:18–34:31, mirrors the earlier account of Rebekah and Abimelech, 26:1–33, in a chiastic structuring that spans 25:19–35:29 and pivots around the account of the births of Jacob's first eleven sons, 29:31–30:24 (Waltke 352). The account of Shechem being destroyed and also the account of Isaac fearing Abimelech both point to the end times, wherein Reuben, Simeon, Levi, and so forth—specifically the sons preceding the twelfth and last son, Benjamin—represent the seven millennia of the present creation and, thereby, the culmination of the present creation in the seventh millennium.

The devil is the prince of this world, that is, the defiler of this world (John 14:30). And the emphasis on Dinah being the daughter of Leah points to the defilement of Dinah being the defilement of Leah. The firstborn Leah is identified with the six millennia of natural creation proceeding from the first man Adam, and thereby Leah is identified with the conclusion of the same six millennia of creation in the end times. And the birth of Dinah after her six brothers also points to the conclusion of the six millennia of creation (Gen 30:21). The name *Dinah* [H1783] is derived from the root "to judge" [H1777], which foreshadows the judgment of the world in the end times. This is not simply the judgment of the extant world at the time of the end but rather the judgment of the whole of the six millennia of creation.[16]

Genesis 34:3 And his soul [H5315] clave [H1692] unto Dinah the daughter of Jacob, and he loved [H157] the damsel, and spake kindly unto the damsel.

The word *clave* [H1692] (Shechem clave unto Dinah) is the same word used to prophesy that man would *cleave* [H1692] unto his wife and be one flesh, but Shechem defiling Dinah is a desecration of the image of becoming one flesh (Gen 2:24). The word *loved* [H157] (Shechem loved Dinah) is the same word used to describe Isaac *loving* [H157] Rebekah, but Shechem defiling Dinah is a desecration of the image of man loving woman (Gen 24:67). And all these things ultimately represent the desecration of the image of Christ, the very image of God, and finally the desecration of the Body of Christ. The word *soul* [H5315] (soul clave unto Dinah) means "living being, life." The desire of the dragon is to defile the image of God, because his life depends upon defiling the image of God and thereby defiling God himself. For if the perfection of God could be corrupted, then no judge would exist to condemn the dragon. Shechem, the prince of this world, speaking kindly unto Dinah represents the speaking of smooth things in contrast to right things (Isa 30:10).

Genesis 34:4 And Shechem spake unto his father Hamor, saying, Get me this damsel to wife.

The relationship between Hamor and his son, Shechem, reflects the relationship between the dragon and the beast who receives the power and throne of the dragon (Rev 13:2). Shechem asking his father to get him Dinah represents the beast relying upon the power of the dragon. And the power of the evil one is primarily that of a seducing spirit (1 Tim 4:1).

---

[16] "For her violator (i.e., Dinah's) [Shechem] is called the prince of the country [Gen 34:2], by whom the devil is plainly denoted . . . And he [Shechem] also seeks her for his wife, because the evil spirit hastens to possess lawfully the soul which he has first corrupted by hidden seduction [Gregory the Great, *To Domitian, Metropolitan*]" (Schaff and Wace, *Nicene and Post-Nicene Fathers: Second Series* 12.2:142). The lost dominion of Adam and Eve, of Adam-kind.

Genesis 34:5 And Jacob heard that he had defiled Dinah his daughter: now his sons were with his cattle in the field: and Jacob held his peace until they were come.

Jacob hearing that Dinah had been defiled is an affirmation that nothing is hidden from the Lord. But Jacob now holding his peace represents the delay of the foretold glorious return of Christ, particularly the delay represented by the final tribulation period. Jacob's sons are identified with the unfolding of the millennia of creation connecting Adam and the promised new Adam, whereby the emphasis on his sons remaining yet in the field, or wilderness of the present world, further testifies that the end has not yet come.

Genesis 34:6 And Hamor the father of Shechem went out unto Jacob to commune with him.

The evil one thinks that he can negotiate with the Lord, because he does not understand the Lord. The evil one mistakes the humble suffering of God as mere weakness. The evil one mistakes the humble condescension of God as something less than infinity. But the will of the Lord God Almighty for the redemption of his faithful ones cannot be withstood. And the judgment of God necessarily precedes the justification in God.

Genesis 34:7 And the sons of Jacob came out of the field when they heard [it]: and the men were grieved, and they were very wroth, because he had wrought folly in Israel in lying with Jacob's daughter; which thing ought not to be done.

The time of Jacob's trouble (Jer 30:7).

Genesis 34:8–9 And Hamor communed with them, saying, The soul of my son Shechem longeth for your daughter: I pray you give her him to wife. 9 And make ye marriages with us, [and] give your daughters unto us, and take our daughters unto you.

The person of Dinah is here connected to all the daughters of Jacob, whereby the defilement of Dinah is connected to the defilement of all Israel, particularly in the end times since all of Israel will not have been revealed until the end of the present creation.

Genesis 34:10 And ye shall dwell with us: and the land shall be before you; dwell and trade ye therein, and get you possessions therein.

The proposal of intermarriage between Israel and the world foreshadows the ecumenism, or religious union, that will be attempted in the end times, while the emphasis on trade and possessions points to the corresponding economic union that will also be attempted in the end times.

JACOB AND GOD

Genesis 34:11–12 And Shechem said unto her father and unto her brethren, Let me find [H4672] grace [H2580] in your eyes [H5869], and what ye shall say unto me I will give. 12 Ask me never so much dowry and gift, and I will give according as ye shall say unto me: but give me the damsel to wife.

Shechem now seeking to *find* [H4672] *grace* [H2580] in the *eyes* [H5869] of Israel recalls Israel seeking to *find* [H4672] *grace* [H2580] in the *sight* [H5869] of Esau and, thereby, reaffirms the connection between the two accounts already evidenced by their close proximity in the text (Gen 33:15). The former account of Esau represents the call of the faithful, while the latter account of Shechem represents the concomitant rejection of the faithless. Jacob sought to bless Esau, but now Shechem seeks to bless himself. The promises of Shechem represent the false promises of the evil one. Those who join themselves unto the beast are promised all things in the flesh; and the death that governs all things in the flesh is exactly that which is received. It is Jacob representing the Body of Christ that alone finds the grace that is only in God.

Genesis 34:13 And the sons of Jacob answered Shechem and Hamor his father deceitfully [H4820], and said, because he had defiled Dinah their sister:

The sons of Jacob answering Shechem *deceitfully* [H4820] recalls the *subtilty* (subtlety) [H4820] of Jacob in taking the blessing of Esau (Gen 27:35). And Shechem does not discern the intention of Jacob's sons just as Esau did not discern the intention of Jacob. The natural man does not understand, much less foresee, the coming of the spiritual man. And the sons of Jacob answering Shechem *deceitfully* [H4820] is directly connected to Shechem having defiled Dinah. The mystery of God is hidden from the children of the devil. The mystery of God is our promised new creation in Christ that comes by grace through faith in Christ.

Genesis 34:14–15 And they said unto them, We cannot do this thing, to give our sister to one that is uncircumcised; for that [were] a reproach unto us: 15 But in this will we consent unto you: If ye will be as we [be], that every male of you be circumcised;

The practice of circumcision is a mark of blood in the flesh (Exod 4:26) and the primary symbol representing the law (Gen 17:11). And the natural connection between circumcision and procreation points to Christ being cut off without offspring in accordance with the law (Isa 53:8). That only a man can be circumcised under the law points to the reality of the incarnation of God as a man. The masculine is identified with justice, while the feminine is identified with mercy. And the judgment of the law is death and destruction, whereby the call to circumcision is finally the condemnation of the fallen natural body and likewise the condemnation of the present fallen natural creation. And the demand that the defiler of woman must be circumcised and thereby condemned points to the judgment of the original defiler of woman that is the serpent who beguiled Eve in the garden (2 Cor 11:3). And the obvious but uncomfortable identification of Christ with the serpent is explained by the fiery serpent that Moses raised upon a pole in the desert (Num 21:8).

Genesis 34:16–17 Then will we give our daughters unto you, and we will take your daughters to us, and we will dwell with you, and we will become one people. 17 But if ye will not hearken unto us, to be circumcised; then will we take our daughter, and we will be gone.

That the camp of Israel will depart with their daughters unless the men of the place are circumcised is a testimony that there is no judgment apart from the law that is marked by circumcision. That the men will indeed be circumcised is a testimony that there is a law under which all men are judged, in separation from the grace received through faith in the one man Jesus Christ.[17]

Genesis 34:18 And their words pleased Hamor, and Shechem Hamor's son.

The words of Israel pleasing Hamor ironically foreshadows the time when even the wicked will acknowledge the righteousness of Christ and accordingly his authority to judge all creation (Rom 14:10–12).

Genesis 34:19 And the young man deferred not to do the thing, because he had delight in Jacob's daughter: and he [was] more honourable [H3513] than all the house of his father.

The emphasis on Shechem being the most honorable in the house of his father recalls lucifer being perfect in beauty and full of wisdom in the mountain of God (Ezek 28:12–16). The Lord of hosts has purposed to bring into contempt the *honourable* (honorable) [H3513] of the earth (Isa 23:9). And woe unto those that desire the Day of the Lord (Amos 5:18). The wicked man Shechem does not delay his wrongful claim to his bride, but the righteous man Christ does delay his rightful claim to his bride. The evil one seeks to complete the defilement of his bride, but the Lord desires that none of his faithful should perish (2 Pet 3:9). The person of Dinah reflects different aspects of the faithless and also the faithful just as the person of Esau reflects different aspects of the faithless and the faithful. And the difficulty in distinguishing the different aspects is the same difficulty in distinguishing Christ and anti-christ.

---

[17] Coffman submits that Jacob's sons never expected the Shechemites to accept their offer, that they never intended to destroy Shechem, rather the sons were trapped into action by an attempt at guile (Coffman 417; Gen 34:13–17). The focus should be on prophetic types and patterns relating the image of God, not judging degrees of personal guilt. And this truth is affirmed by the observation that it simply isn't possible for us to know personal perceptions, motivations, and so forth, with any certainty.

JACOB AND GOD

Genesis 34:20 And Hamor and Shechem his son came unto the gate of their city, and communed with the men of their city, saying,

The city of Shechem represents the cities of fallen mankind, especially in opposition to the one city of God. The men of the earth speak with one voice, calling for the defilement of woman and likewise the defilement of her offspring (Rev 12:13–13:1).

Genesis 34:21 These men [are] peaceable with us; therefore let them dwell in the land, and trade therein; for the land, behold, [it is] large enough for them; let us take their daughters to us for wives, and let us give them our daughters.

The men of the city prophesy a false peace and a false prosperity, to be established in a false marriage covenant (Dan 11:21–24).

Genesis 34:22–23 Only herein will the men consent unto us for to dwell with us, to be one people, if every male among us be circumcised, as they [are] circumcised. 23 [Shall] not their cattle and their substance and every beast of theirs [be] ours? only let us consent unto them, and they will dwell with us.

The false marriage covenant with the house of Jacob is here identified with the wicked receiving all the wealth of the house of Jacob, representing the glory of the house of God. And the sign of circumcision, which represents the law and likewise the judgment of death, is also identified with this same marriage covenant. This is the covenant with death that will fail (Isa 28:15). And this is the devil seeking in vain to ascend unto the throne of God (Isa 14:12–15).

Genesis 34:24 And unto Hamor and unto Shechem his son hearkened all that went out of the gate of his city; and every male was circumcised, all that went out of the gate of his city.

The gates of hell will not prevail against the assembly of the faithful in Jesus Christ, not against the Body of Christ (Matt 16:18).

Genesis 34:25 And it came to pass on the third day, when they were sore, that two of the sons of Jacob, Simeon and Levi, Dinah's brethren, took each man his sword, and came upon the city boldly, and slew all the males.

The men of the city being judged on the third day portends the judgment of the world in the third millennium following the First Advent. The men of the city suffer throughout this three-day period because of the circumcision required by the law. And all creation likewise groans in pain, particularly since the time of the crucifixion of Jesus under the law (Rom 8:21–23). The three millennia of the law connecting the First and Second Advents are a testimony to the three days of the law connecting the death and resurrection of Jesus Christ. Further, the persons of Simeon and Levi also connect the destruction of the city of Shechem with the judgment that is required by the law. The second and third sons Simeon and Levi are identified with the second and third millennia from the first man Adam. Simeon connects the first destruction (by water) in the second millennium to the foretold second destruction (by fire), as connected with the closing of the sixth millennium. And Levi connects the formal law given in the third millennium to the fulfillment of all things, or the law as a whole, which is connected with the seventh millennium.[18]

Genesis 34:26 And they slew Hamor and Shechem his son with the edge of the sword, and took Dinah out of Shechem's house, and went out.

The sword of the Spirit is the Word of God (Eph 6:17).

Genesis 34:27 The sons of Jacob came upon the slain, and spoiled the city, because they had defiled their sister.

The wicked city is destroyed because of the defilement of woman.[19]

Genesis 34:28–29 They took their sheep, and their oxen, and their asses, and that which [was] in the city, and that which [was] in the field, 29 And all their wealth, and all their little ones, and their wives took they captive, and spoiled even all that [was] in the house.

The women and children being taken out of the destruction of the city represents the redemption of a final remnant of faithful during the time of the final tribulation period. Jesus Christ will take his rightful possession of all creation in the end times. And not a single one of his faithful will be lost.

Genesis 34:30 And Jacob said to Simeon and Levi, Ye have troubled me to make me to stink among the inhabitants of the land, among the Canaanites and the Perizzites: and I [being] few in number, they shall

---

[18] ". . . He [Christ] is spiritually interpreted to be Jacob against Simeon and Levi, which means against [respectively] the scribes and the Pharisees . . . Like Simeon and Levi, they [the scribes and Pharisees] consummated their wickedness by their heresy, with which they persecuted Christ [Tertullian, *Against Marcion*]" (Roberts et al., *Ante-Nicene Fathers* 3:336). Per *Strong's*, the name *Simeon* [H8095] means "heard" and is closely related to the word *heard* [H8085], having a connotation "to obey," consistent with the scribes' work, or words of the law, being heard and obeyed.

[19] In an alternating structure spanning Gen 34:1–31, the rape of Dinah parallels the spoiling of the city of Shechem (Waltke 458). The serpent, the tempter, knows very well that the defilement of woman, the womb, is nothing less than the defilement of the whole of creation.

JACOB AND GOD

gather themselves together against me, and slay me; and I shall be destroyed, I and my house.

The Canaanites and the Perizzites represent the wicked of the earth, particularly during the end times. And Jacob becoming a stink among them portends Christ becoming a stink among the wicked, particularly in the end times. Jacob being made a stink among the wicked, specifically by Simeon and Levi, foreshadows the rejection of Christ, specifically because of the law. The perfect fulfillment of the law forms the basis of the authority of Christ over the whole of creation. But Jacob being only a small group, few in number, foreshadows only a remnant, or relative few, being saved through the foretold devastation of the tribulation period. The image of a great many wicked assailing a few righteous is ubiquitous in the Scriptures and reflects the broad road unto destruction that is ever juxtaposed to the narrow road unto life (Matt 7:13–14). But Jacob here foreseeing the people of the land uniting against him specifically portends a diversity of wicked in the world waging war against the one man Christ in the end times. That the people of the land will not actually be able to attack Jacob foreshadows the utter impotence of the wicked in seeking to attack Christ, who is our mighty God (Gen 35:5).[20]

Genesis 34:31 And they said, Should he deal with our sister as with an harlot?

Dinah being treated as a harlot portends the great whore that sits upon many waters (Rev 17:1), while the destruction of the city of Shechem portends the destruction of the city of Babylon (Rev 18:10). Dinah going out to commune with the women of the land of Canaan (Gen 34:1) prefigures the inhabitants of the earth being made drunk with the wine of the whore (Rev 17:2). And Dinah being defiled by the Canaanites (Gen 34:2) portends the whore being made desolate and naked (Rev 17:16). The suddenness of the destruction of Shechem portends the suddenness of the destruction of Babylon (Rev 18:8). And the surrounding peoples not attacking Jacob because of the terror of God being upon them (Gen 35:5) prefigures the kings of the earth standing afar off in terror at the judgment of Babylon (Rev 18:10).[21]

Deborah, Rachel, Isaac

Genesis 35:1 And God said unto Jacob, Arise [H6965], go up [H5927] to Beth-el, and dwell [H3427] there: and make [H6213] there an altar unto

---

[20] The phenomenal objectivity of the Bible, never hiding the sins of the people of God, is itself a proof of the inspired nature of the text (Coffman 420; Gen 34:30–31). The truth, to be true, must be complete.

[21] "[W]ith the unprejudiced reader the ample and detailed relation which we have here of this barbarous transaction will appear an additional proof of the veracity and impartiality of the sacred historian" (Clarke 1:210; Gen 34:31). The naked candor of the written Word reflects the naked, or humble, condescension of the incarnate Word.

God, that appeared unto thee when thou fleddest from the face of Esau thy brother.

Bethel is the place from which Jacob originally fled from the promised land, and therefore the return to Bethel marks the formal return of Jacob to the promised land. The covenantal pillar established against wicked Laban at Gilead marks the beginning of the final delay before the final judgment of the world (Gen 31:52). Esau coming in haste to meet Jacob en route prefigures the catching up of the faithful to meet Christ in the air (Gen 32:6). The destruction of Shechem immediately following the reconciliation with Esau portends the coming final tribulation period (Gen 34:25). Jacob now returning to Bethel just as he had originally departed from Bethel prefigures the glorious and visible return of Christ to the earth at the Second Advent just as he had originally ascended to heaven at the First Advent (Acts 1:11). Jacob being called to return to Bethel specifically from the destruction of Shechem prefigures the coming of Christ in glory expressly to end the time of the tribulation (Matt 24:22).[22]

Genesis 35:2 Then Jacob said unto his household, and to all that [were] with him, Put away the strange gods that [are] among you, and be clean, and change your garments:

Jacob returning unto Bethel prefigures Christ establishing his millennial kingdom at the ending of the tribulation period (Rev 20:4). Jacob returning with all his household represents Christ returning with all his saints (1 Thess 3:13). The emphasis on the household of Jacob changing their garments points to the faithful washing their robes and making them white in the blood of the Lamb (Rev 7:14). And the call to put away strange gods is here closely connected to the destruction of Shechem. The destruction of Shechem represents the physical dimension of the tribulation period, while the putting away of strange gods represents the spiritual dimension.[23]

Genesis 35:3 And let us arise [H6965], and go up [H5927] to Beth-el [H1008]; and I will make [H6213] there an altar unto God, who answered me in the day of my distress, and was with me in the way which I went.

---

[22] "Also in the LXth [Ps 60], 'I will rejoice, I will divide Shechem:' here [Ps 108] 'I will be exalted, and will divide Shechem.' Where is shown what is signified in the division of Shechem, which it was prophesied should happen after the Lord's exaltation, and that this joy doth refer to that exaltation; so that He rejoiceth, because He is exalted [Augustine, *On the Psalms*]" (Schaff, *Nicene and Post-Nicene Fathers: First Series* 8:536). The exaltation of Jesus Christ is one resurrection together with his faithful ones, Head and Body, and necessarily precedes the tribulation-period judgment of the faithless world by the Head and Body, 1 Cor 6:2.

[23] "Why did they [the camp of Jacob] have to *change . . . garments*? 'Throughout the Bible, garments symbolize character. The inward life of the unregenerate is compared to a polluted garment' [D. G. Barnhouse]" (Guzik 202; Gen 35:2–4). The outward and the inward are linked just as the natural and the spiritual are linked.

JACOB AND GOD

Jacob was first told by God to *arise* [H6965] and *go up* [H5927] to Bethel, and now Jacob likewise tells his household to *arise* [H6965] and *go up* [H5927] to Bethel (Gen 35:1). The Father calls his only Son, and then the Son calls his faithful ones. The Son represents the firstfruits, while the faithful represent the harvest (Lev 23:10–12). Jacob was specifically told to *dwell* [H3427] in Bethel and *make* [H6213] an altar, but now Jacob firmly resolves that he will immediately *make* [H6213] an altar. The former emphasis on *dwelling* [H3427] in the house of God represents the delay between the First and Second Advents, while the latter emphasis on immediately *making* [H6213] the altar represents the haste with which Christ will return at the appointed time of the Second Advent.

The word *arise* [H6965] has a connotation "to establish." The word *go up* [H5927] has a connotation "to exalt." And the word *make* [H6213] has a connotation "to accomplish." The commandments *arise* [H6965] and *go up* [H5927] and *make* [H6213] reflect our original creation through Christ (establish), our resurrection with Christ (exalt), and finally our new creation in Christ (accomplish). The formation of Adam is followed by the First and Second Advents of Christ. The Father, Son, and Spirit are creator, redeemer, and sanctifier. The word *dwell* [H3427] means "to sit, remain, dwell," reflecting the Son sitting at the right hand of the Father during the church age, as identified with the sending forth of the indwelling Holy Spirit (Ps 110:1, Matt 22:44). The three persons Father, Son, and Spirit are one God.[24]

Genesis 35:4 And they gave unto Jacob all the strange gods which [were] in their hand, and [all their] earrings which [were] in their ears; and Jacob hid them under the oak [H424] which [was] by Shechem.

The purification of the household of Jacob is here again directly connected to the city of Shechem and finally to the destruction of Shechem. The act of hiding articles of idolatry beneath a tree reflects our sins being nailed to the cross, or tree, of Christ (Col 2:13–14). The judgment of Shechem under the law points most directly to the Second Advent, but the dominion of the Second Advent is the blood of the First Advent. The affliction of the fifth millennium is followed by the division of the sixth millennium is followed by the exaltation of the seventh millennium. The three days of Christ.[25]

---

[24] ". . . '[There is] one God and Father from whom all things are, and one Lord Jesus Christ through whom all things are, and one Holy Spirit in whom all things are' [Council of Constantinople II, AD 553]" (Rom. Catholic Church, *Catechism* 77). The act of creation is uniquely identified with the will of God the Father but is simultaneously a Trinitarian event. And this is true whether considering the original creation or the promised new creation or the two creations as one.

[25] "[C]onsider what we used to do in our blindness . . . . every person selected his own saint and worshiped and invoked him in time of need. . . . All these fix their heart and trust elsewhere than in the true God" (Luther, *Large Catechism* 10). The myriad schisms that mark the sixth millennium are a portent of the separation of the faithful from the faithless in the seventh millennium.

Genesis 35:5 And they journeyed: and the terror of God was upon the cities that [were] round about them, and they did not pursue after the sons of Jacob.

The surrounding Canaanites do not pursue Jacob, for the terror of God is upon them. Likewise, the kings of the earth will stand afar off in terror because of the judgment of Babylon (Rev 18:10). The way of the flesh is fear and terror, but the way of the Spirit is love and truth.

Genesis 35:6 So Jacob came to Luz, which [is] in the land of Canaan, that [is], Beth-el [H1008], he and all the people that [were] with him.

The name *Bethel* [H1008] means "house of God." The house of Jacob coming to the house of God represents the house of Jacob becoming the house of God. This is the faithful in Christ, the Body of Christ, that will be visibly revealed in the establishment of the millennial kingdom at the time of the Second Advent of Christ.

Genesis 35:7 And he built there an altar, and called the place El-beth-el [H416]: because there God appeared unto him, when he fled from the face of his brother.

Bethel is here again identified as the place from which Jacob fled from his brother Esau, whereby it is the return to Bethel that now marks the formal return of Jacob unto the promised land. The firstborn Esau is the embodiment of flesh and likewise the law that governs flesh, whereby Jacob fleeing Esau recalls the death of Christ under the law. And Jacob returning to Esau foreshadows Christ returning to judge the world, likewise under the law. Jacob originally fleeing his brother represents the rejection of Christ at the time of the First Advent. And Jacob now returning unto the promised land with great wealth and a multitude of offspring represents the glorious return of Christ with his faithful at the time of the Second Advent.

The name *Bethel* [H1008] means "house of God," while the name *Elbethel* [H416] means "God of the house of God." The shift in emphasis from the house of God to the God of the house reflects the shift from the call of the faithful by God to the exaltation of the faithful in God. The former is the visible church, while the latter is the true Body of Christ. The house of God points to the God of the house of God just as the First Advent points to the Second Advent. This is the Son of man revealing himself as the Son of God. The creation likewise points to the Creator. The first man Adam points to the second man Christ. The Covenant of Law points to the Covenant of Grace. This is the natural that always points to the spiritual.[26]

---

[26] "The name for God in this passage is plural, just as in earlier chapters. . . . It is only another example of 'singular-plural polarity in Israel's idea of God' [C. T. Francisco]. We join many others in finding here intimations of the triune godhead . . . ." (Coffman

JACOB AND GOD

Genesis 35:8 But Deborah Rebekah's nurse [H3243] died, and she was buried beneath Beth-el under an oak [H437]: and the name of it was called Allon-bachuth [H439].

The word *nurse* [H3243] (Rebekah's nurse died) evokes an image of "suckling a baby." And Rebekah's nurse, Deborah, can be identified with the infancy of Jacob because Deborah has remained with Jacob. And the death of Deborah then reflects the end of the infancy, or the end of the beginning, of Jacob. The person of Jacob is most closely identified with the Second Advent. And the end of the beginning of the Second Advent is the ending of the tribulation period, which follows the resurrection and rapture but precedes the establishment of the visible millennial kingdom. The name *Allonbachuth* [H439] means "oak of weeping." And the burial of Deborah beneath an *oak* [H437] at Bethel recalls the house of Jacob hiding their idols, or images, beneath an *oak* [H424]—which is a further connection to Bethel, specifically the going up unto Bethel (Gen 35:4). The death of Deborah, which foreshadows the ending of the tribulation period, is thereby connected to the putting away of false gods and finally to the beginning of the millennial reign and the casting of the beast and the false prophet, likewise the image of the beast, into the lake of fire (Rev 19:20).[27]

Genesis 35:9 And God [H430] appeared unto Jacob again, when he came out of Padan-aram, and blessed him.

At the time of Jacob's fleeing from Esau, the *Lord* [H3068] *God* [H430] promised that in Jacob all the families of the earth would be blessed (Gen 28:13–14). But now at the time of Jacob's returning unto the promised land *God* [H430] blesses Jacob himself. The former blessing is the promised blessing of the faithful, which would be guaranteed by the blood of Christ at the time of the First Advent and affirmed by the sign of faith throughout the church age. The latter blessing is the blessing of Jesus Christ himself, which represents the realization of the blessing of the faithful in the Body of Christ, the fullness of which will not be revealed until the time of the Second Advent. The focus in the present context of returning unto the promised land is on the name *God* [H430] in contrast to the name *Lord* [H3068]—representing an emphasis on justice and righteousness, specifically that which will be manifested in the coming judgment of the world.

427; Gen 35:1–7). The Father and Son relationship implies the person of the Spirit and, therein, represents not a fundamental duality but an essential triunity.

[27] Coffman asserts that the timing of Deborah's death with respect to other events can be viewed as occurring either chronologically or not and that both views are equally acceptable since the timing is not stated explicitly in the Biblical text (Coffman 428; Gen 35:8). The correct perspective, or worldview, is not the timing of things according to the flesh, or way of man, but when and where and in what context the Holy Spirit chooses to emphasize any particular event.

ESAU, JACOB, ISRAEL

Genesis 35:10 And God said unto him, Thy name [is] Jacob [H3290]: thy name shall not be called any more Jacob [H3290], but Israel [H3478] shall be thy name: and he called his name Israel [H3478].

The three patriarchs Abraham, Isaac, and Jacob reflect the triune Father, Son, and Spirit and likewise the threefold progressive revelation of the Trinity represented by Adam followed by the First and Second Advents of Christ. This is why the Lord refers to himself in such a distinct manner as the God of Abraham, Isaac, and Jacob, in contrast to what is a multitude of other seemingly appropriate but nonetheless happenstance combinations of Biblical names.[28] God changing the name of father *Abram* [H87] to *Abraham* [H85] should then be recognized as the promise embodied by the first man Adam becoming a multitude, or Adam-kind (Gen 17:5). God naming *Isaac* [H3327] even before he was born and then never changing his name points to the sinlessness of Christ, who himself would have no need of a transformative redemption (Gen 17:19). And God finally changing the name of *Jacob* [H3290] to *Israel* [H3478] is a prophecy of the redemption, or rebirth, of the faithful in the Body of Christ that is the promised new Adam and the corresponding new creation.

Focusing on the last days that connect the First and Second Advents, it is Isaac who sends Jacob unto the east but it is Israel whom God calls back into the promised land. And thus the name *Israel* [H3478] is most closely identified with the return unto the promised land while the name *Jacob* [H3290] is most closely identified with the original fleeing from Esau (Gen 28:5). The name *Jacob* [H3290] is then identified with the solitary Jacob fleeing his brother Esau, which prefigures the rejection of the one man Christ at the time of the First Advent, likewise the continuing absence of the (visible) person of Christ throughout the church age. In contrast, the name *Israel* [H3478] is used to denote the individual person *Jacob* [H3290] and simultaneously his collective offspring as embodied by national *Israel* [H3478], whereby the name *Israel* [H3478] reflects the unity of the faithful in the Body of Christ (Exod 14:5, 14:30). National Israel composed of the chosen people prefigures the millennial kingdom of Christ composed of the faithful in Christ. But the (visible) Body of Christ will not be established until the time of the Second Advent of Christ.

Genesis 35:11 And God said unto him, I [am] God Almighty: be fruitful and multiply; a nation and a company of nations shall be of thee, and kings shall come out of thy loins;

Jacob is the patriarch that is most closely identified with the promise to be fruitful and multiply, because Jacob is the patriarch that founded the twelve

---

[28] Other Trinitarian titles are "the God of Shadrach, Meshach, and Abednego," Dan 3:29, and "the God of Abraham, and the God of Nahor, the God of their father [Terah]," Gen 31:53. But these titles of deity are not emphasized beyond their local context and, not coincidentally, neither are they applied by God to himself, rather by the people of the world to God, Exod 3:6.

tribes. The multiplication of the chosen people prefigures the multiplication of the faithful. That Jacob will become a company of nations is a prophecy of the kingdoms of the world becoming the kingdoms of God (Rev 11:15). That Jacob will become both a nation and a company of nations prefigures the city of God being surrounded by the nations during the reign of the millennial kingdom (Rev 20:7–9). And the emphasis on a plurality of kings proceeding from Jacob is finally a prophetic testimony to the faithful becoming kings themselves in the kingdom of God (Rev 5:10).

Genesis 35:12 And the land which I gave Abraham and Isaac, to thee I will give it, and to thy seed after thee will I give the land.

The promises of God are uniquely identified with Abraham, Isaac, and Jacob just as the Lord is uniquely called the God of Abraham, Isaac, and Jacob.[29] The body of man is formed from the dust of the ground, spiritually from the land that has been promised (Gen 2:7). The original dominion given to man was correspondingly the earth as a whole (Gen 1:28). And the promise to inherit the land, or earth, is finally a prophecy of the resurrection of a true body and likewise a literal dominion of man over the earth, or creation. The spiritual, or glorified, resurrection body is a true body just as the millennial kingdom is a true kingdom. The image of God is reflected not only in the creation but also in the progression of creation. The image of God is reflected not only in individual man but also in mankind as a whole.

Genesis 35:13–15 And God went up from him in the place where he talked with him. 14 And Jacob set up a pillar [H4676] in the place where he talked with him, [even] a pillar [H4678] of stone: and he poured a drink offering thereon, and he poured oil thereon. 15 And Jacob called the name of the place where God spake with him, Beth-el.

This pillar is the third in a series of four pillars set up by Jacob. The first pillar set up by Jacob at Bethel when he fled from Esau represents the resurrection of Christ himself at the time of the First Advent (Gen 28:22). The second pillar set up at Gilead, against Laban, represents the resurrection and rapture of the faithful in Christ (Gen 31:51). The third pillar now set up in Bethel, following the destruction of Shechem and also the death of Deborah, represents the subsequent exaltation in Christ of the new believers, or newly believing, who will suffer throughout the final tribulation period. And the fourth pillar that will be set upon the grave of the accursed Rachel represents the resurrection unto damnation (Gen 35:20). Jacob poured oil on the first pillar (Gen 28:18). Jacob and Laban ate bread on the second pillar (Gen 31:46, 31:54).

---

[29] The totality of those who accept Jesus Christ, Jews and Gentiles, together form the one Body of Christ, but the law embodied by the Jews, the physical offspring of father Abraham, necessarily precedes the grace embodied by the Gentiles, the spiritual offspring of Abraham.

Jacob pours a drink offering and oil on this third pillar (Gen 35:14). But Jacob will offer nothing over the fourth pillar (Gen 35:20).

Further, the first and third pillars are connected by Bethel, both pillars having been set up in Bethel. And the connection between the first and third pillars is the connection between the personal tribulation endured by Jesus Christ at the time of the First Advent and the final tribulation period that will be endured by the new believers, or newly believing, in Christ at the time of the Second Advent. Jacob pouring oil on the first pillar at Bethel represents the anointing of Jesus Christ and likewise the sending of the Holy Spirit during the church age. Jacob now pouring oil on the third pillar, again at Bethel, represents a double portion, or fullness, of the Holy Spirit to be received in the fullness of the Body of Christ. Jacob adding a drink offering, representing the blood of the new covenant (Matt 26:28), to the third pillar prefigures the faithful being washed clean with the blood of Christ, that is, all the faithful of all the ages being exalted by grace in the millennial reign of Christ over creation (Rev 7:14). The second pillar being connected with eating bread, or figuratively flesh, represents an emphasis on the condemnation of the natural body and likewise the condemnation of the present fallen creation in the end times.[30]

Genesis 35:16 And they journeyed from Beth-el [H1008]; and there was but a little way to come to Ephrath: and Rachel travailed, and she had hard labour.

The six sons of Leah are identified with the six millennia of creation. Rachel's firstborn, Joseph, is identified with the seventh, or Sabbath, millennium, while Rachel's second born, Benjamin, is identified with the eighth millennium, representing eternity. The place of *Bethel* [H1008], meaning "house of God," marks the beginning and end of Jacob's sojourn in the east, representing the church age, and thereby *Bethel* [H1008] connects the First and Second Advents. The First and Second Advents can be viewed as one uninterrupted whole, separated from the parenthetical church age, just as the resurrection of the Head and the resurrection of the Body should be viewed as one resurrection. This is the one Body of Christ. And the camp of Jacob now departing from *Bethel* [H1008], the "house of God," finally marks the end of the Sabbath millennium, or one could say the end of the First and Second Advent periods as viewed collectively. Rachel travailing in hard labor prefigures satan going out to deceive the nations at the end of the millennial kingdom period (Rev 20:7–9). But the birth of Benjamin will mark the beginning of the eighth millennium that is the opening of eternity.[31]

---

[30] "The first mention [in the Scriptures] of the drink-offering. . . . It was always 'poured out,' never drunk, and may be considered a type of Christ in the sense of [Ps 22:14] and [Isa 53:12]" (Scofield 51 n. 2; Gen 35:14).

[31] Ephrath, called Bethlehem Ephratah in Mic 5:2, is the same Bethlehem where Jesus Christ would be born (Coffman 430; Gen 35:16–20). The house of bread (Bethlehem) proceeds from the house of God (Bethel).

JACOB AND GOD

Genesis 35:17 And it came to pass, when she was in hard labour, that the midwife said unto her, Fear [H3372] not; thou shalt have this son also.

The word *fear* [H3372] (fear not) recalls Adam originally being *afraid* [H3372] in the garden because of his nakedness (Gen 3:10). But Rachel's midwife now telling her to not be afraid represents the call from fear to love, likewise the call from the natural body to the spiritual, or glorified, body, and likewise the call from the present fallen creation to the promised new creation. This is the call from law unto grace, or more specifically the fulfillment of law in grace. The command to not be afraid is here directly connected to the birth of the second son Benjamin, corresponding to the eighth millennium and representing the promised new creation to be revealed in the opening of the eighth millennium from the first man Adam (Rev 21:1).

Genesis 35:18 And it came to pass, as her soul was in departing, (for she died) that she called his name Ben-oni [H1126]: but his father called him Benjamin [H1144].

Rachel, at least symbolically, dies under the curse of Jacob because of Laban's idols that she had taken, whereby her death reflects the necessary end of idolatry that is concomitant with our promised new creation (Gen 31:32). The second creation embodied by the birth of the second son Benjamin is a fulfillment of the prophecy that another son would be added to the firstborn Joseph and, thereby, represents the continuation of the millennial reign into eternity (Gen 30:24). The millennial kingdom corresponding to the seventh, or Sabbath, millennium is, not the final revelation of the promises of God, but rather it is the eighth millennium, or the first day of the new week, representing the promised new day, or new creation (Rev 21:1). Only when death and hell, likewise the children of hell, are cast into the lake of fire (Rev 20:14–15) will the first heaven and the first earth pass away and the new heaven and new earth be established, or revealed (Rev 21:1). Eye hath not seen, nor ear heard, neither have entered into the heart of man, the things which God hath prepared for them that love him (1 Cor 2:9).

The name *Benoni* [H1126] means "son of my sorrow," while the name *Benjamin* [H1144] means "son of (the) right hand." The former name represents death and destruction, while the latter name represents resurrection and exaltation. This is the end of the current world and the corresponding revelation of the promised world to come. The six sons of Leah are identified with the six millennia of creation, while the preeminent son Joseph is identified with the seventh millennium. And the seventh, or Sabbath, millennium compared with the original six millennia represents our rest, or grace, in Christ compared with our works under the law of Adam. In turn, the singular Joseph followed by the twofold Benoni and Benjamin represents Adam followed by the First and Second Advents of Christ. Our promised fullness of communion with God in eternity as represented by the eighth millennium is the culmination and also unification of the First and Second Advents. This is the union of the Covenant of Law and the Covenant of Grace and specifically the fulfillment of the Covenant of Law in the Covenant of Grace.

Genesis 35:19 And Rachel died, and was buried in the way to Ephrath, which [is] Beth-lehem [H1035].

The name *Bethlehem* [H1035] means "house of bread," reflecting the house of flesh, or man, in contrast to the house of God, likewise the title *Son of man* in contrast to the title *Son of God*, and likewise the kingship in contrast to the priesthood. The emphasis on the symbol of bread represents an emphasis on the Adamic natural body and likewise the condemnation of the natural under the law (Matt 26:26). This is the condemnation borne perfectly by Christ on the cross and the same condemnation borne imperfectly by the faithful in imitation of Christ. Bethlehem would become the birth place of Christ and, thereby, points to the First Advent and the suffering and death of Christ in the flesh at the First Advent (Matt 2:1–6, Mic 5:2). And Rachel dying at the birth place of Christ while giving birth to Jacob's eighth son of a freewoman, Benjamin, connects the end of the millennial kingdom with the death of Christ as king of kings. And the parallel between the death and resurrection of creation and the death and resurrection of the Creator finally points to the whole of creation following Christ in death and resurrection. And the whole of creation surely groans and travails in pain together even until now (Rom 8:22).

Genesis 35:20 And Jacob set a pillar [H4676] upon her grave: that [is] the pillar [H4678] of Rachel's grave unto this day.

This pillar is the fourth in a series of four pillars set up by Jacob. And the emphasis on this fourth and final pillar not being removed from its place throughout time points to the end of the time of the present creation. Jacob not pouring oil or a drink offering on this fourth pillar portends a curse and not a blessing. And this reinforces the image of Rachel dying under the curse of Jacob because of the idols of the accuser (Gen 31:32). This fourth pillar represents not the resurrection unto eternal life at the beginning of the millennial kingdom but the resurrection unto damnation at the end of the millennial kingdom (John 5:29, Rev 20:11–15). It is no coincidence that Rachel herself had connected her life and death with the bringing forth of children (Gen 30:1).[32]

Genesis 35:21 And Israel journeyed, and spread his tent beyond the tower [H4026] of Edar [H4029].

---

[32] "Rachel's death was in tragic fulfillment of the curse Jacob himself had pronounced on the one who stole the idols of Laban . . . . Rachel pleaded with Jacob, 'Give me children, or else I die!' . . . both became true. She had children, and died as a result" (Guzik 205; Gen 35:19–20). Truly, all prayers are answered.

JACOB AND GOD

Thou, O tower of the flock, the stronghold of the daughter of Zion, unto thee shall it come, even the first dominion; the kingdom shall come to the daughter of Jerusalem. . . . Be in pain, and labour to bring forth, O daughter of Zion, like a woman in travail: . . . the Lord shall redeem thee from the hand of thine enemies (Mic 4:8–10).[33]

Genesis 35:22a And it came to pass, when Israel dwelt in that land, that Reuben went and lay with Bilhah his father's concubine: and Israel heard [H8085] [it].

The first son Reuben reflects the first man Adam, whereby the depravity of Reuben reflects the universal apostasy of natural man, which is the corruption of the whole of creation embodied by Adam. And the defilement of Rachel's handmaid, Bilhah, by Reuben is closely connected to the immediately preceding account of the death of Bilhah's mistress, Rachel (Gen 35:19). The pillar set upon Rachel's grave represents the resurrection unto damnation (John 5:29). And the emphasis on Israel hearing that Reuben had defiled his concubine points to the books being opened at the white throne judgment (Rev 20:11–15). Further, the word *heard* [H8085] (Israel heard) has a connotation "to obey." The image of Israel, representing God, hearing and obeying the sin of Reuben reflects the perfect righteousness of God in allowing the freewill choice of the wicked to reject him. And finally, the parallel between the defilement of Bilhah by Reuben and the defilement of Dinah by Shechem points to the parallel apostasies of faithless Jews and Gentiles (Gen 34:5, 35:22). The defilement of Bilhah corresponds to the time of the First Advent, while the defilement of Dinah corresponds to the time of the Second Advent.

Genesis 35:22b-26 Now the sons of Jacob were twelve: 23 The sons of Leah; Reuben, Jacob's firstborn, and Simeon, and Levi, and Judah, and Issachar, and Zebulun: 24 The sons of Rachel; Joseph, and Benjamin: 25 And the sons of Bilhah, Rachel's handmaid; Dan, and Naphtali: 26 And the sons of Zilpah, Leah's handmaid; Gad, and Asher: these [are] the sons of Jacob, which were born to him in Padan-aram.

The sons of Jacob are identified with the progression of creation down through the millennia. The recounting of the sons of Jacob thereby represents a retelling of the plan of God from the original creation to the fulfillment of all things in the end times. And the recounting of all creation ultimately represents a review of the perfect righteousness and perfect faithfulness of the Lord himself throughout all the ages. And the retelling of all creation is finally the revelation of the promised new heaven and new earth that is the fulfillment of the present creation and likewise the fulfillment of the perfect righteousness of God (Rev 21:1). The promised new creation in Christ being the fulfillment of the present creation through Adam then points to the life of Christ being the

---

[33] The name *Edar* [H4029] means "tower [H4026] of the flock [H5739]."

recapitulation of all creation. The recapitulation of all creation in the life of Christ corresponds to the redemption of all creation being in the Body of Christ and only in the Body of Christ.[34]

Genesis 35:27–29 And Jacob came unto Isaac his father unto Mamre, unto the city of Arbah, which [is] Hebron, where Abraham and Isaac sojourned. 28 And the days of Isaac were an hundred and fourscore years. 29 And Isaac gave up the ghost, and died, and was gathered unto his people, [being] old and full of days: and his sons Esau and Jacob buried him.

The person of Isaac is most closely identified with the First Advent, while the person of Jacob is most closely identified with the Second Advent. The symbolic sacrifice of Isaac in Moriah prefigures the death and resurrection of Jesus Christ at the First Advent (Gen 22:2), while the old age and blindness of Isaac prefigures the end of the church age proceeding from the First Advent (Gen 27:1). And the old age of Isaac being connected with the time of Jacob's blessing is a testimony to the promised blessing in Christ that will be received in the Second Advent of Christ at the end of the church age and finally at the end of the present creation as a whole. The old age of Isaac is the end, or old age, of the present age, corresponding to the last days. The dimness of the eyes of Isaac is the spiritual blindness and universal apostasy that even now marks the end of the church age. And Jacob being sent away by Isaac represents the rejection of Christ beginning at the time of the First Advent and being completed in the final apostasy that will herald the Second Advent (Gen 28:1–5).[35]

Jacob finally returning unto the promised land with great wealth and a multitude of offspring represents the glorious return of Christ at the Second Advent (Gen 31:16–18). And the great wealth that marks the house of Jacob at this time prefigures the promised fullness of the blessing in Christ that will be the fullness of the indwelling Holy Spirit. The literal, physical death of Isaac when he is old and full of days then most specifically represents the end of the

---

[34] "The reason for inserting the names of Jacob's sons in this part of the history is to show, on his return to his father, that Isaac's prayer for him, pronounced at his departure to Padan-aram [Gen 28:3], had been graciously answered" (Jamieson et al. 1:225; Gen 35:22–26). The prayer and blessing of Isaac represents the prayer and blessing of Jesus Christ.

[35] "Isaac conveys a figure of God the Father; Rebecca [Rebekah] of the Holy Spirit; Esau of the first people and the devil; Jacob of the Church, or of Christ. That Isaac was old, points to the end of the world; that his eyes were dim, denotes that faith had perished from the world, and that the light of religion was neglected before him; . . . [Hippolytus, *On Genesis*]" (Roberts et al., *Ante-Nicene Fathers* 5:168). The distinction between God the Father and God the Son is often difficult to perceive, likewise the distinction between God the Holy Spirit and the faithful indwelt by the Holy Spirit, likewise the distinction between the Body of Christ—that is, the true church—and Christ as the Head, and likewise the distinction between fallen mankind and the serpent as the lord of fallen mankind.

JACOB AND GOD

First and Second Advent periods, viewed as an uninterrupted whole. This is foremost the end of the church age corresponding to the beginning of the Second Advent, but it is finally the end of the millennial kingdom of Christ corresponding to the end of the Second Advent. Isaac being old and full of days represents the conclusion of the foretold last days in which the Christ would come (Heb 1:1–2). The last days are the three days and the three millennia connecting the First and Second Advents. This is again the First and Second Advents viewed as an uninterrupted whole. And the last days will conclude the seventh, or Sabbath, millennium and herald the eighth millennium, representing eternity. The emphasis on the natural man Esau and the spiritual man Jacob together burying Isaac is a testimony that both the faithless and the faithful will acknowledge that Jesus Christ is God (Isa 45:23).[36]

GENERATIONS OF ESAU

Genesis 36:1 Now these [are] the generations of Esau, who [is] Edom.

The emphasis on Esau being Edom represents an emphasis on the circumstances under which Esau became Edom, namely, Esau despising his birthright and selling it to Jacob (Gen 25:29–34).

Genesis 36:2–5 Esau took his wives of the daughters of Canaan; Adah the daughter of Elon the Hittite, and Aholibamah the daughter of Anah the daughter of Zibeon the Hivite; 3 And Bashemath Ishmael's daughter, sister of Nebajoth. 4 And Adah bare to Esau Eliphaz; and Bashemath bare Reuel; 5 And Aholibamah bare Jeush, and Jaalam, and Korah: these [are] the sons of Esau, which were born unto him in the land of Canaan.

The emphasis on all Esau's children having been born in Canaan stands in sharp distinction to the emphasis on all Jacob's children having been born in Padanaram, in the east (Gen 35:23–26). All of Esau's offspring are considered to be the offspring of the land of Canaan even though the Ishmaelites are blood relatives. And this is a testimony that his offspring are innately unacceptable to God. The land of Canaan compared with the east represents the earth compared with heaven. And the difference between the east and the west is the difference between the rising sun and the setting sun. And Jacob, in direct contrast to Esau, is credited with all his children having been born in the east even though Benjamin was born near Bethlehem in Canaan (Gen 35:16–19).[37] Esau took an Ishmaelite wife because Isaac and Rebekah were displeased with

---

[36] "Abraham is the most perfect character under the Old Testament, and even under the *New* he has no parallel but St. Paul. Isaac, though falling far short of his father's excellences, will ever remain a pattern of piety and filial obedience" (Clarke 1:214; Gen 35:29). The humble condescension of the Son in the procession from the Father.
[37] Jacob's last son, Benjamin, was very possibly conceived in the east country.

his Canaanite wives (Gen 28:6–9). But the offspring of Esau are still distinct and separate from the offspring of Jacob.

Esau's Canaanite wives trace their lineage from Ham through Canaan, while Esau's Ishmaelite wife traces her lineage from Ham through Mizraim (Egypt) via the Egyptian Hagar (Gen 10:6, 16:1–2, 16:11). Esau is thereby doubly identified with the sin of Ham against his father Noah (Gen 9:22). And Esau's double identification with Ham is a sign of the certainty of his condemnation (Gen 41:32). The defilement of Noah by Ham prefigures the defilement of Christ, whereby Esau's identification with Ham represents an identification of Esau with the defilement of Christ. And the violent rejection of Christ will finally and inevitably become the violent rejection of the Body of Christ. Esau originally coming in haste to meet Jacob en route to Canaan represents the catching up of the faithful unto the Lord (Gen 32:6), while Esau's subsequent separation from Jacob represents those faithless that will not be caught up unto the Lord (Gen 33:16–17). Nevertheless, the emphasis in the present context is on the latter rejection of the faithless, specifically those who will continue to reject the Lord throughout the tribulation period.

Genesis 36:6 And Esau took his wives, and his sons, and his daughters, and all the persons of his house, and his cattle, and all his beasts, and all his substance, which he had got in the land of Canaan; and went into the country from the face of his brother Jacob.

The land represents the body of man that is formed from the dust of the ground (Gen 2:7). And the emphasis on the firstborn Esau gaining great wealth in the land of Canaan points to the blessing of the first man Adam, or mankind in Adam, in the first body that is the natural body. Nonetheless, Esau separating himself from the promised land, likewise from the face of his brother, Jacob, represents a rejection of the promise of the spiritual, or glorified, resurrection body, which will be in the likeness of our risen Lord (1 John 3:2). It is Esau that separates himself from Jacob and not vice versa. It is likewise natural man, loving his own sin, that separates himself from God.[38]

Genesis 36:7–8 For their riches were more than that they might dwell together; and the land wherein they were strangers could not bear them because of their cattle. 8 Thus dwelt Esau in mount Seir: Esau [is] Edom.

The possessions of Esau and Jacob cannot dwell together. There can be no communion between the light and the darkness (2 Cor 6:14). The possessions of Esau and Jacob represent their respective desires. Where a man's treasure is, there also is his heart (Matt 6:21). The desires of Esau are the things of man,

---

[38] The Lord blessed the firstborn Esau in the flesh in accordance with the desire and nature of the firstborn (Guzik 207; Gen 36:6–8). God does answer our prayers, but sadly the majority would fare better, infinitely so in eternity, if God didn't give them, or hand them over to, the desire of their hearts.

JACOB AND GOD

while the desires of Jacob are the things of God. The disparate desires of Esau and Jacob cannot coexist in the one body represented by the promised land, prefiguring the one Body of Christ and the exclusivity thereof.[39]

Genesis 36:9–30 And these [are] the generations of Esau the father of the Edomites in mount Seir: 10 These [are] the names of Esau's sons; Eliphaz the son of Adah the wife of Esau, Reuel the son of Bashemath the wife of Esau. 11 And the sons of Eliphaz were Teman, Omar, Zepho, and Gatam, and Kenaz. 12 And Timna was concubine to Eliphaz Esau's son; and she bare to Eliphaz Amalek: these [were] the sons of Adah Esau's wife. 13 And these [are] the sons of Reuel; Nahath, and Zerah, Shammah, and Mizzah: these were the sons of Bashemath Esau's wife. 14 And these were the sons of Aholibamah, the daughter of Anah the daughter of Zibeon, Esau's wife: and she bare to Esau Jeush, and Jaalam, and Korah. 15 These [were] dukes of the sons of Esau: the sons of Eliphaz the firstborn [son] of Esau; duke Teman, duke Omar, duke Zepho, duke Kenaz, 16 Duke Korah, duke Gatam, [and] duke Amalek: these [are] the dukes [that came] of Eliphaz in the land of Edom; these [were] the sons of Adah. 17 And these [are] the sons of Reuel Esau's son; duke Nahath, duke Zerah, duke Shammah, duke Mizzah: these [are] the dukes [that came] of Reuel in the land of Edom; these [are] the sons of Bashemath Esau's wife. 18 And these [are] the sons of Aholibamah Esau's wife; duke Jeush, duke Jaalam, duke Korah: these [were] the dukes [that came] of Aholibamah the daughter of Anah, Esau's wife. 19 These [are] the sons of Esau, who [is] Edom, and these [are] their dukes. 20 These [are] the sons of Seir the Horite, who inhabited the land; Lotan, and Shobal, and Zibeon, and Anah, 21 And Dishon, and Ezer, and Dishan: these [are] the dukes of the Horites, the children of Seir in the land of Edom. 22 And the children of Lotan were Hori and Hemam; and Lotan's sister [was] Timna. 23 And the children of Shobal [were] these; Alvan, and Manahath, and Ebal, Shepho, and Onam. 24 And these [are] the children of Zibeon; both Ajah, and Anah: this [was that] Anah that found the mules in the wilderness, as he fed the asses of Zibeon his father. 25 And the children of Anah [were] these; Dishon, and Aholibamah the daughter of Anah. 26 And these [are] the children of Dishon; Hemdan, and Eshban, and Ithran, and Cheran. 27 The children of Ezer [are] these; Bilhan, and Zaavan, and Akan. 28 The children of Dishan [are] these; Uz, and Aran. 29 These [are] the dukes [that came] of the Horites; duke Lotan, duke Shobal, duke Zibeon, duke Anah, duke Dishon, duke Ezer, duke Dishan: these [are] the dukes [that came] of Hori, among their dukes in the land of Seir.

---

[39] The division of Esau and Jacob, which is founded upon limited natural resources, recalls the division of Lot and Abraham, Gen 13:7–8 (Sarna 249; Gen 36:7). Esau is to Lot as Jacob is to Abraham.

ESAU, JACOB, ISRAEL

The detailed genealogies recorded in the Scriptures are a testimony to the omniscience of God. Every name and every deed and every thought are known unto God. And God knows an immeasurable amount about each individual just as every individual has immeasurable value to God. But the offspring of Esau recorded here, specifically at the time of their separation from Jacob, prefigure the names and deeds recorded in the books that will be opened at the time of the white throne judgment of the faithless (Rev 20:11–15).[40]

Genesis 36:31–43 And these [are] the kings that reigned in the land of Edom, before there reigned any king over the children of Israel. 32 And Bela the son of Beor reigned in Edom: and the name of his city [was] Dinhabah. 33 And Bela died, and Jobab the son of Zerah of Bozrah reigned in his stead. 34 And Jobab died, and Husham of the land of Temani reigned in his stead. 35 And Husham died, and Hadad the son of Bedad, who smote Midian in the field of Moab, reigned in his stead: and the name of his city [was] Avith. 36 And Hadad died, and Samlah of Masrekah reigned in his stead. 37 And Samlah died, and Saul of Rehoboth [by] the river reigned in his stead. 38 And Saul died, and Baal-hanan the son of Achbor reigned in his stead. 39 And Baal-hanan the son of Achbor died, and Hadar reigned in his stead: and the name of his city [was] Pau; and his wife's name [was] Mehetabel, the daughter of Matred, the daughter of Mezahab. 40 And these [are] the names of the dukes [that came] of Esau, according to their families, after their places, by their names; duke Timnah, duke Alvah, duke Jetheth, 41 Duke Aholibamah, duke Elah, duke Pinon, 42 Duke Kenaz, duke Teman, duke Mibzar, 43 Duke Magdiel, duke Iram: these [be] the dukes of Edom, according to their habitations in the land of their possession: he [is] Esau the father of the Edomites.

The kings of the world will stand before the King of kings at the time of the final judgment. The kings of Edom precede the kings of Israel just as the dominion of Adam precedes the dominion of Christ just as the Covenant of Law precedes the Covenant of Grace. The father of the Edomites is the one man Esau representing the one man Adam, or fallen mankind in Adam—standing alone and separated from God. In contrast, the father, or progenitor, of the Israelites is not only Jacob representing the Holy Spirit but also Isaac representing the Son and also Abraham representing the Father.[41]

---

[40] "The truth is, the Messiah must spring from *some one family*, and God chose *Abraham's* through *Isaac, Jacob*, etc., rather than the same through *Ishmael, Esau*, and the others in that line; but from this choice it does not follow that the first were all *necessarily saved*, and the others *necessarily lost*" (Clarke 1:219; Gen 36:43). God is no respecter of persons, Acts 10:34.

[41] "To some the *genealogical lists* in this chapter will doubtless appear uninteresting, especially those which concern *Esau* . . . but it was as necessary to register the generations of *Esau* as to register those of *Jacob* . . . . These registers were religiously preserved among the Jews till the destruction of Jerusalem [AD 70], after which they

JACOB AND GOD

Ω Ω Ω

The first and second born sons of Isaac, Esau followed by Jacob, reflect the first and second men of God, Adam followed by Christ, and likewise the First and Second Advents of Christ, namely, Christ the Head followed by the Body of Christ. The conflict between Esau and Jacob represents the conflict between mankind, or Adam-kind, and Jesus Christ. This is the primordial conflict between natural man and spiritual man that is the conflict between the faithless and the faithful. Esau seeking to kill his younger brother when Jacob takes possession of the birthright and blessing represents Adamic mankind rejecting Christ at the time of the First Advent (Gen 27:36, 27:41). Isaac sending Jacob forth to establish his offspring prefigures the Son sending the Holy Spirit during the church age (Gen 28:1–2). And Jacob finally returning unto Canaan with a great house and great wealth points to the Second Advent (Gen 31:16). The first and second men Adam and Christ parallel the First and Second Advents of Christ, Christ and the Body of Christ. The rejection and condemnation of the first man Adam prefigures the rejection and crucifixion of Jesus Christ in the place of Adam. And the resurrection of the second man Christ prefigures the resurrection of the faithful in Christ.

1	2
FIRSTBORN ESAU	SECOND BORN JACOB
THE FIRST MAN ADAM	THE SECOND MAN CHRIST
ESAU REJECTED	JACOB ACCEPTED
THE REJECTION OF CHRIST	THE REDEMPTION IN CHRIST
BY ALL MANKIND	OF ALL THE FAITHFUL

Esau reflects Adam, or all mankind in Adam, but not simply fallen mankind in Adam, for the whole of mankind, the faithful and the faithless, are the offspring of Adam in the natural body. Esau represents the whole of mankind at the time of Jacob's departing from Canaan and also at the time of Jacob's returning. Esau represents all mankind at the time of Jacob's departing in the sense that all mankind is culpable for the death of Jesus Christ. And Esau represents all mankind at the time of Jacob's returning in the sense that all mankind is called to repent and receive the glorified Christ. The gifts of the three droves of livestock that Jacob, upon his return from the east, gives unto Esau represent the gifts of the Spirit culminating in the fullness of the promised indwelling of the Holy Spirit (Gen 32:17–19). The three droves precede the

---

were all destroyed . . . consequently, all expectation of a Messiah *to come* is . . . *nugatory* and *absurd*, as nothing remains to legitimate his birth. . . . When St. Matthew and St. Luke wrote, all these registers were still in existence; . . ." (Clarke 1:219; Gen 36:43); "It is characteristic of Scripture that the kings of Edom should be enumerated before the kings of Israel. The *principle* is stated in [1 Cor 15:46]. First things are 'natural,' man's best, and always fail; second things are 'spiritual,' God's things, and succeed. Adam—Christ; Cain—Abel; Cain's posterity—Seth's posterity; Saul—David; Israel—the true Church, etc." (Scofield 53 n. 1; Gen 36:31).

camp of Jacob just as the gifts of the Spirit precede the fullness of the Spirit (Gen 32:21). The whole of mankind, represented by Esau, benefits either directly or indirectly from the gifts of the Spirit. But only the faithful will receive the fullness of the indwelling Holy Spirit, which is the singular inheritance of the children of God. The focus on there being three droves, or at least the emphasis on the first three droves, points to the three millennia connecting the First and Second Advents of Christ, likewise connecting the coming of the Spirit and the promised fullness of the indwelling Spirit (John 16:7).

1	2
THE FIRSTBORN ESAU	THE SECOND BORN JACOB
ALL MANKIND FROM ADAM	THE FAITHFUL IN CHRIST
THE DROVES PRECEDING JACOB	THE CAMP OF JACOB
THE GIFTS OF THE SPIRIT	THE INDWELLING HOLY SPIRIT

Esau meeting Jacob en route to the promised land prefigures the resurrection and rapture of the faithful caught up into the clouds to meet Christ in the air (Gen 32:6, 1 Thess 4:15–17). In contrast, the subsequent formal return of Jacob, especially unto Bethel from which he originally departed, points to the glorious return of Christ at the time of the establishment of the millennial kingdom (Gen 28:19–22, 35:1). The personage of Esau represents all mankind in Adam—that is, all mankind in the natural body, which includes the faithless and the faithful. Esau meeting Jacob and embracing him represents the faithful of mankind embracing Jesus Christ as Lord and Savior (Gen 33:4, Rom 10:9). But Esau and Jacob finally being separated into the two nations of Edom and Israel represents the fundamental separation of the faithless and the faithful, corresponding to the rejection of the faithless of mankind (Gen 36:6–8). Esau embracing Jacob prefigures the promised Body of Christ animated by the fullness of the Holy Spirit, whereas Esau separating himself from Jacob prefigures the body of Adam, or fallen man, which in separation from grace constitutes the body of the serpent.

1	2
THE FIRSTBORN ESAU	THE SECOND BORN JACOB
FAITHLESS & FAITHFUL	FAITHFUL IN CHRIST
ESAU MEETS JACOB EN ROUTE	JACOB RETURNS UNTO BETHEL
RESURRECTION & RAPTURE	FORMAL SECOND ADVENT OF CHRIST

The rape of Dinah and the corresponding destruction of Shechem mark the return of Jacob unto Bethel, representing the return unto the promised land (Gen 34:25–31, 35:5–6). The rape of Dinah and the resulting destruction of Shechem specifically portend the tribulation period, which will precede the glorious return of Christ to establish the millennial kingdom. The destruction of Shechem follows the meeting with Esau but precedes the return unto Bethel. Likewise, the tribulation period follows the resurrection and rapture of the faithful but precedes the return of Jesus Christ in glory. The removal of all idols from the camp of Jacob during this time of great fear prefigures the purification of a remnant to be saved during the final tribulation period (Gen 35:2). The deaths of Isaac and Rachel and Rebekah's nurse, Deborah, are closely identified with this same period and, thereby, reinforce the images of tribulation and judgment that mark the end of the age (Gen 35:8, 35:19, 35:28–29). The defilement of Rachel's bondwoman, Bilhah, by Jacob's firstborn, Reuben—which is also connected to this time of fear and death—portends a universal apostasy of Adamic mankind, or figuratively the first man Adam (Gen 35:22). The threefold resurrection and rapture followed by the tribulation period followed by the glorious return of Christ echoes the threefold preservation of Adam followed by the tribulation of Christ at the time of the First Advent followed by the revelation of the promised new Adam, which is finally the Body of Christ, at the time of the Second Advent of Christ.

1	2	3
ESAU MEETS JACOB EN ROUTE	DESTRUCTION OF SHECHEM	RETURN UNTO BETHEL
RESURRECTION & RAPTURE	TRIBULATION	RETURN OF CHRIST IN GLORY
CREATION OF ADAM	FIRST ADVENT OF CHRIST	SECOND ADVENT OF CHRIST
PRESERVATION OF ADAM	DEATH OF CHRIST IN THE PLACE OF ADAM	REVELATION OF THE NEW ADAM

The emphasis on Simeon and Levi, the second and third born sons, being the ones who destroy Shechem points to the second and third millennia from Adam and also the second and third millennia from Jesus Christ. (The second and third millennia from Christ being the sixth and seventh millennia from Adam.) The parallel between the second millennium from Adam and the sixth millennium from Adam is the parallel between the first destruction, which came by water, and the second destruction, which will come by fire. The parallel between the third millennium from Adam and the seventh millennium from Adam is the parallel between the Covenant of Law and the Covenant of Grace, specifically the law formally established by Moses in the nation of Israel and the grace that will be visibly established in Christ during the millennial kingdom. The emphasis on the men of Shechem being circumcised according to the requirement of Simeon and Levi, figuratively by Simeon and Levi, finally points to the judgment of natural man being a judgment under the law that comes by both water and fire (Gen 34:14). These are the two deaths (Rev 21:8), the twofold *destroying* [G622], or "putting out of the way entirely," of the body and the soul (Matt 10:28).[42]

1	2
THE SECOND BORN SIMEON	THE THIRD BORN LEVI
SECOND MILLENNIUM	THIRD MILLENNIUM
THE FIRST DESTRUCTION (WATER)	THE FIRST COVENANT (LAW)
SIXTH MILLENNIUM	SEVENTH MILLENNIUM
THE SECOND DESTRUCTION (FIRE)	THE SECOND COVENANT (GRACE)

---

[42] G622 connotation "put out of the way entirely" per *Brown-Driver-Briggs*, but is also evident in *Strong's* etymology connecting G622 and G575.

ESAU, JACOB, ISRAEL

The threefold Esau followed by Jacob and Israel reflect the threefold Adam followed by the First and Second Advents of Christ. The rejection of the firstborn Esau recalls the rejection of the first man Adam (Gen 25:23). Esau seeking to kill Jacob reflects the rejection and execution of Christ at the time of the First Advent (Gen 27:41). The glorious return of Jacob as Israel prefigures the Second Advent, while Jacob becoming Israel embodies the essential unity of the First and Second Advents of Christ (Gen 32:28). Jacob separating his household into three groups, or waves, as he prepares to meet Esau reflects again the threefold successive Adam followed by the First and Second Advents (Gen 33:2). The first group formed by Jacob's bondwomen and their offspring recalls the bondage to sin and death that came by the first man Adam (Rom 5:12). The second group formed by Jacob's wife Leah and her offspring reflects the Messianic bloodline embodied foremost by her son Judah and ultimately revealed at the First Advent (Matt 1:2–3, Luke 3:33–34). The third group formed by Jacob's wife Rachel and her offspring prefigures the promised kingdom embodied by her princely son, Joseph, and finally established in the millennial kingdom at the Second Advent (Gen 41:41–43).

The threefold deaths of Deborah followed by Rachel and Isaac again reflect the threefold progression of Adam followed by the First and Second Advents. The death of Rebekah's nurse, Deborah, represents the death of a mother figure and, thereby, recalls the original condemnation of Eve, the mother of all the living (Gen 3:20, 35:8). The death of Rachel giving birth to Benoni reflects the death of Christ that marks the First Advent, while Benoni, "son of my sorrow," being renamed Benjamin, "son of (the) right hand," reflects the essential unity of the First and Second Advents (Gen 35:18). And the literal death of Isaac in his old age finally prefigures the end of the present age that is foremost the end of the church age and finally the end of the millennial kingdom (Gen 35:28–29). The convergence of multiple threefold images pointing to the end times reflects the fulfillment of all things in the Body of Christ. The primary local framework for the account of Jacob returning to the promised land is the threefold sequence of Esau meeting Jacob followed by the destruction of Shechem followed by the return to Bethel, which ultimately also reflects the threefold successive Adam followed by the First and Second Advents of Christ.

1	2	3
Esau	Jacob	Israel
Adam	First Advent	Second Advent
Bondwomen	Leah	Rachel
(First Group)	(Second Group)	(Third Group)
Bondage in Adam	Messianic Bloodline	Millennial Kingdom
Death of Deborah	Death of Rachel	Death of Isaac
Fall of Man	Cross of Christ	End of the World

The account of the pillar of Jacob and Laban immediately precedes the account of Jacob preparing to meet Esau (Gen 31:44–54). The continual struggle between Jacob and Laban in the establishment of Jacob's household represents the struggle against the rulers of darkness and spiritual wickedness during the church age (Eph 6:12). The pillar of Jacob and Laban, which is set up between Jacob and Laban, represents the resurrection and rapture of the faithful in the end times and the concomitant rejection of the faithless. And the account of Esau coming to meet Jacob en route to the promised land, which is closely connected to the account of the pillar of Jacob and Laban, reinforces the image of the resurrection and rapture and the faithful (1 Thess 4:17). The gifts of the three droves of livestock, which Jacob sends ahead of him unto Esau, reflect the gifts of the indwelling Holy Spirit, which mark the three millennia connecting the First and Second Advents and opening eternity (Gen 32:19). And Jacob being renamed Israel because he has overcome both God and man reflects the essential nexus between God and man that is the promised new creation in the Body of Christ (Gen 32:28).

Jacob separating his household into three camps, or waves, demarcated by his bondwomen followed by Leah and finally by Rachel, represents the threefold progression of Adam followed by the First Advent of Jesus Christ and finally by the Second Advent of Christ (Gen 33:1–3). The threefold camp of Jacob is a testimony to the person of Christ and finally the Body of Christ being a recapitulation and finally a sanctification of the totality of creation formed in the image of the Trinity. The person of Esau represents the whole of mankind. Esau running to meet Jacob and embracing him and kissing him represents the resurrection and rapture of the faithful (Gen 33:4), but Esau finally separating himself from Jacob represents the rejection of the faithless (Gen 36:6–8). The destruction of Shechem—following the meeting with Esau but preceding the formal return unto Bethel—portends the final tribulation period (Gen 34:25–26). The threefold deaths of Deborah, Rachel, and Isaac during this period of great fear portend the coming judgment of the whole world and the corresponding end of the age (Gen 35:8, 35:19, 35:29).

ESAU, JACOB, ISRAEL

CHAPTER THREE OUTLINE

Key Images

	PRIME IMAGES	
Material	Abstract	Spiritual
The return to the promised land.	The fulfillment of the tithe.	The Second Advent of Christ.
Mahanaim.	The meeting of the camp of God and the camp of Jacob en route to the promised land.	The parallel between the natural and the spiritual in progressive revelation.
Peniel.	Jacob wrestles God.	The conflict between flesh and spirit resolved in Christ, who is true man and true God.
Shechem.	A destruction marked by the law of circumcision.	The condemnation of the world under the law.
The meeting with Esau when Jacob returns from the east.	The firstborn rushes to meet the second born en route.	The resurrection and rapture of the faithful to meet the Lord in the air (1 Thess 4:16–17).
Bethel.	The house of God.	The Body of Christ.
	TWOFOLD IMAGES	
Material	Abstract	Spiritual
Esau and Jacob.	The second born supplanting the firstborn is followed by the second born being accepted by the firstborn. Way of flesh, way of the Spirit. Flesh and spirit.	The church age connecting the First and Second Advents.
Jacob and God.	Jacob wrestles with God before Jacob is blessed by God. Flesh and spirit.	The curse of man supplanted by the blessing of God.
Jacob and Israel.	The name according to the flesh supplanted by the name according to the Spirit. Flesh and spirit.	The movement of the Holy Spirit during the church age culminating in the Body of Christ.
Edom and Israel.	Cursed nation, blessed nation. Flesh and spirit.	The kingdom of man, the kingdom of God.
Simeon and Levi.	Second and third sons. Second and third millennia. The Flood followed by the formation of national Israel. Death versus life (in the land). Flesh and spirit.	The death and resurrection of the world.
Benoni and Benjamin.	Son of my sorrow, son of the right hand. Way of flesh, way of the Spirit. Flesh and spirit.	The exaltation of the faithful from the natural body to the spiritual, or glorified, resurrection body.
	THREEFOLD IMAGES	
Material	Abstract	Spiritual
The spiritual man Jacob separates his camp into three groups of waves in preparation to meet the natural man Esau en route to the promised land.	The camp of bondwomen; the camp of Leah, who is not loved; the camp of Rachel, who is loved. The bondage of sin, the curse of the law, the love that is grace.	Adam followed by the First and Second Advents of Christ.

JACOB AND GOD

The deaths of Rachel's nurse, Deborah, followed by Rachel herself and finally Isaac.	The death of a mother figure, the death of a mother in childbirth, and finally the death of the child of promise.	The curse through Eve, the rejection of the Seed of woman, and finally the end of the age.
The two brothers Simeon and Levi destroy Shechem on the third day after the circumcision required by the one covenant.	A death of all flesh following a sign in the flesh given to all flesh.	The destruction on the third day, or millennium, from the First Advent that is the foretold final tribulation.

Synopsis

	HOST OF GOD	
	Material	Spiritual
32:1–2	The host, or camp, of God meets the camp of Jacob at Mahanaim.	The parallel between the spiritual and the natural, and finally the exaltation of the natural by the spiritual in the end times.
32:3–6	Jacob sends messengers unto his brother, Esau, in order to find grace, or acceptance.	The call of the Holy Spirit to faith in Christ and a corresponding repentance of sins.
	Esau and a great company come to meet Jacob while he is still en route to Canaan.	The resurrection and rapture of the faithful to meet the Lord in the air (1 Thess 4:17).
32:7–12	Jacob fears that Esau will kill him and his entire household.	The Lord fearing for the world, expressly because the Lord cannot die a second time for the world (Heb 6:4–6).
	Jacob divides into two camps.	The Lord comes by water and blood, by law and grace (1 John 5:6).
32:13–21	Jacob sends three droves of gifts ahead of him unto Esau.	The three millennia connecting the First and Second Advents.
	The messengers of Jacob speak in the same manner unto Esau with each passing drove.	The singular call into the one Body of Christ that comes by grace alone through faith alone.
	THE PRINCE WHO PREVAILS	
	Material	Spiritual
32:22–24	Jacob is left alone and wrestles a man until the breaking of the day.	The struggle between flesh and spirit that is the striving to redeem flesh.
32:25	The man puts Jacob's thigh out of joint because he was not prevailing.	There is no prevailing in separation from the plaguing of the flesh of Christ.
32:26	The man proclaims that he must be let go.	The glorious return of Christ.
	Jacob proclaims that the man must bless him.	The blessing of the faithful in Christ.
32:27–28	Jacob is renamed Israel by the man, for as a prince he has power with God and man and has prevailed.	The establishment of the millennial kingdom.
32:29	Jacob asks what the man's name is, and the man blesses him.	Who can the man be, except Jesus Christ?
32:30	Jacob names the place Peniel, for he saw God face to face and his life was preserved.	The man revealed to be God is Jesus Christ, who is true man and true God.
32:31–32	The children of Israel unto this day do not eat the sinew that shrank.	Except ye eat the flesh of Christ, and drink his blood, ye have no life in you (John 6:53).
	FACE OF GOD	
	Material	Spiritual
33:1–3	Jacob bows seven times as he approaches his older brother Esau.	The seven millennia of creation connecting the old man and the promised new man.
	The bondwomen and their offspring proceed first, followed by Leah and her offspring, and finally by Rachel and her only son, Joseph.	The Creation followed by the First and Second Advents, likewise the three millennia connecting the First and Second Advents.

ESAU, JACOB, ISRAEL

33:4	The firstborn Esau runs to meet the second born Jacob. Esau embraces and kisses Jacob, and the two brothers weep together.		Esau meeting Jacob is the acceptance in Christ of the faithful at the time of the resurrection and rapture, but their subsequent separation will be the concomitant rejection of the faithless separated from Christ (1 Thess 4:17).
33:5	Esau asks Jacob to explain the identity of his wives and children.		The natural man cannot recognize the offspring of the spiritual man, but still God's grace will be revealed in the end times.
33:6–7	The three groups of Jacob's offspring, each in their appointed order, bow unto Esau.		The one and same call of the Holy Spirit, throughout all the ages of creation.
33:8	Esau asks the meaning of the three droves of animals that went ahead of Jacob.		The revelation of prophecy that precedes the reality, or fulfillment, of prophecy.
33:9–11	Esau asserts that he doesn't need to receive the gifts of the droves.		The condemnation of the natural man under the law.
	But Jacob insists that Esau must receive the gifts of the droves.		The redemption and exaltation of the spiritual man by grace.
33:12–16	Esau seeks to lead Jacob into the promised land.		Adam is not the Head of the Body.
	For the sake of his flocks, Jacob proceeds slowly without Esau.		The grace of God that cannot come by the works of man.
33:17	Jacob builds a house and booths at Succoth.		The resurrection and rapture of the faithful followed by the glorious return of Christ will be the fulfillment of the Feast of Tabernacles.
	THE DEFILEMENT OF DINAH		
	Material		Spiritual
33:18–20	Jacob buys a parcel of a field just outside the city of Shechem, pitches his tent upon the parcel, and erects an altar upon the parcel.		A token of land signifying Christ taking formal and legal possession of the whole of the earth at the time of the second coming.
34:1–2	Dinah goes out to commune with the daughters of the land of Canaan.		Dinah, born between Jacob's sixth and seventh sons by freewomen, prefigures the end times, specifically the end of the call to freewill repentance (Gen 30:21).
	And Shechem, the prince of the land, takes Dinah and defiles her.		The devil is the prince of the present world and the defiler thereof (John 14:30).
34:3	The soul of Shechem cleaves unto Dinah.		The desire of the devil is to defile creation so that he may possess creation.
34:4	Shechem asks his father Hamor to get him Dinah as his wife.		The beast receives from the dragon his power and authority (Rev 13:2).
34:5	Jacob hears that Dinah is defiled, but he holds his peace until his sons come.		The final delay before the judgment of the world in the end times.
34:6–23	A false covenant marked by circumcision is established between the house of Hamor and the house of Jacob.		A false blood covenant prefiguring the false peace treaty foretold through and by Daniel the prophet (Dan 11:21–24).
34:24–29	On the third day, Simeon and Levi slay the men of Shechem with the sword.		Prefigures the final tribulation period that will connect the sixth and seventh millennia.
34:30	Jacob tells Simeon and Levi that they have made him a stink among the Canaanites.		The rejection of the Lord specifically because of the Covenant of Law.
34:31	Simeon and Levi ask if their sister should be dealt with as a harlot.		Babylon will be destroyed (Rev 18:8).
	DEBORAH, RACHEL, ISAAC		
	Material		Spiritual
35:1	God commands Jacob to go up unto Bethel and dwell there, the same place from which he had fled Esau.		The glorious return of Jesus Christ.
35:2–4	Jacob commands his household to put away strange gods, be clean, and change garments.		The sanctification of faithful in Christ.

JACOB AND GOD

	Jacob is given all the strange gods, and he hides them beneath a tree.	The sins of the faithful are nailed to the tree that is the cross of Christ.
35:5	The terror of God falls upon the Canaanites, and they do not attack the camp of Jacob.	The children of the devil are helpless to stop the establishment of the house of God.
35:6–7	Jacob with his entire household arrives at Bethel, and he calls the place Elbethel.	The "house of God" becomes the "God of the house of God," representing the fullness of the indwelling Holy Spirit.
35:8	Rebekah's nurse, Deborah, dies and is buried under a tree in Bethel.	The end of the beginning, of the infancy, that is the ending of the final tribulation period.
35:9–12	God blesses Jacob and affirms his new name, Israel.	The promised resurrection body.
	A nation and a company of nations will be of Jacob, and kings will come out of his loins.	The kingdoms of the world have become the kingdoms of God (Rev 11:15).
	And Jacob and his seed will inherit the land of Abraham and Isaac.	A literal millennial kingdom.
35:13–15	Jacob sets up a pillar and pours a drink offering and also oil onto it.	The third of four pillars, representing the exaltation of the tribulation saints.
35:16–26	Rachel dies in childbirth delivering Benjamin as Jacob's eighth son by a freewoman.	The death and resurrection of heaven and earth, marking the opening of the eighth millennium that is the opening of eternity.
	Jacob sets a pillar upon the grave of Rachel.	The fourth of four pillars, representing the resurrection unto damnation concomitant with the opening of eternity.
	The firstborn Reuben defiles Rachel's handmaid, Bilhah, and Jacob hears of it.	The apostasy of the first man, Adam-kind, will not escape judgment.
35:27–29	And Isaac, being old and full of days, dies and is gathered unto his people.	The end of the millennial kingdom and the corresponding conclusion of the last days opened by the First Advent of Christ.
	And Isaac is buried by his two sons, Esau and Jacob.	Both the natural man and the spiritual man will affirm the righteousness of God.

GENERATIONS OF ESAU

	Material	Spiritual
36:1	The generations of Esau, who is called Edom.	The red man who despises his birthright because of the red soup, representing the rejection of the blood of Christ (Gen 25:30).
36:2–5	Esau took wives of the daughters of Canaan and Ishmael.	Esau's offspring are the offspring of the land, in contrast to Jacob's offspring being the offspring of blood relationship (Gen 27:46).
36:6–8	Esau took his household and possessions and departed from the face of Jacob.	The faithless of their own freewill separate themselves from the presence of God.
	Esau is established outside Canaan.	The nations are preserved until the end of the millennial kingdom (Rev 20:7–8).
36:9–30	The descendants of Esau are listed by name.	The books will be opened at the time of the white throne judgment (Rev 20:11–15).
36:31–43	The kings of Edom are listed, who began reigning in the nation of Edom before any king reigned in Israel.	The kings of Edom preceded the kings of Israel just as the dominion of Adam precedes the dominion of Jesus Christ.

CHAPTER FOUR

Joseph ben Jacob

The prime image in the establishment of the dominion of Joseph is his ascendancy through a period of great suffering. Joseph being raised up through a period of intense suffering to rule Egypt, effectively to rule the whole world, prefigures the dominion of Jesus Christ during the millennial reign being founded upon his sacrifice at the time of the First Advent. Joseph being stripped and sold into slavery by his brothers foreshadows the rejection of Jesus Christ by the Jews at the time of the First Advent (Gen 37:23, 37:28). But Joseph rising above all adversity points to the glorified Christ at the time of the Second Advent. The relentless blessing resting upon Joseph reflects the undeniable will of God to redeem his faithful ones. Further, Joseph being very specifically the second firstborn son of Jacob by a freewoman prefigures the second man Christ becoming the firstborn from the dead (Col 1:18). The person of Jacob is most closely identified with God the Spirit, whereby the unique love of Jacob for Joseph reflects the testimony of the Spirit concerning the Son. The coat of many colors fashioned by Jacob as a covering for Joseph represents the multitude forming the Body of Christ, which is a covering of glory for the Son (Gen 37:3). And Joseph is not only the dreamer of dreams but also the interpreter of dreams just as Jesus Christ is the origin of all creation and also the paradigm of our creation (Gen 37:5, 41:12).

The twofold image, or sequence, framing the account of the ascendancy of Joseph is his being cast into a pit by his brothers (Gen 37:20) followed by his being cast into prison because of Potiphar's wife (Gen 39:20). The former reflects the death and resurrection of Christ at the time of the First Advent, while the latter reflects the death and resurrection of the Body of Christ at the time of the Second Advent. The firstborn Reuben casting Joseph into a pit reflects the death of Christ in the place of the first man Adam (Gen 37:21–22), while the fourth born Judah selling Joseph into slavery reflects the connection between the formation of Adam in the first millennium and the conception of Christ in the fourth millennium (Gen 37:26–27). The connection between Adam and Christ, likewise between Christ and the Body of Christ, is the bloodline of Christ, or simply the blood of Christ. Further, the account of

JOSEPH BEN JACOB

Pharez and Zerah, the twin sons of Judah by Tamar, progressively reinforces the ongoing theme of the first and second men, with the presumptive firstborn Zerah being supplanted by Pharez even while yet in the womb (Gen 38:28–30). The account of Manasseh and Ephraim, the two sons of Joseph in Egypt, also reinforces the theme of the first and second men, with the hand of Jacob, representing providence, supplanting the firstborn with the second born Ephraim (Gen 48:17–19). And the baker and the cupbearer of Pharaoh testify unto the body and blood of Christ, likewise the First and Second Advents of Christ (Gen 40:20–22).

The threefold Abraham, Isaac, and Jacob embody the overarching image of the Father, Son, and Spirit in the account of the lives of Jacob and Joseph. But in the local context, not contradicting but reinforcing the overarching context, the threefold Pharaoh, Joseph, and Jacob also reflect the Father, Son, and Spirit. And the threefold Pharaoh, Joseph, and Jacob can equally be expressed Pharaoh, Joseph, and Joseph ben Jacob to emphasize the dominion of Joseph being established for the benefit of Jacob, or all Israel, and also to distinguish the suffering Joseph from the exalted Joseph. The triunity of God related by the formation of Adam followed by the First and Second Advents of Christ is echoed in the account of the three sons of Judah being betrothed unto Tamar (Gen 38:6–11). The first son is evil and dies; the second son spills his seed, which represents rejecting the Seed; and the third son lives, literally and also spiritually, through the offspring of Judah by Tamar. And the threefold progression of the person of Tamar herself also reflects the Fall of Adam followed by the First and Second Advents of Christ. The progression of Tamar from widow to shrine prostitute to mother of the Messiah, or Messianic line, represents death followed by conceiving in shame, or humble condescension, followed by the appearance of newborn life (Gen 38:11, 38:15, 38:24). Further, the baker and the cupbearer being lifted up on the third day reflects the three days of Christ, likewise the three millennia connecting the First and Second Advents of Christ (Gen 40:20). And Joseph being brought out of prison in Egypt in the third year (after two full years) also reflects the three days and three millennia of Christ (Gen 41:1).

Dreamer of Dreams

Genesis 37:1 And Jacob dwelt in the land wherein his father was a stranger, in the land of Canaan.

Jacob formally dwelling in the land that was promised is directly connected to his father having been a stranger in that same land and, thereby, represents a fulfillment of the original promise of the land to his father. The persistent connection between Abraham, Isaac, and Jacob reflects the universality of the triunity of the Father, Son, and Spirit. And the second born Jacob dwelling in Canaan stands in direct contrast to the firstborn Esau dwelling in Seir, which is an affirmation that it is the second man Jesus and not the first man Adam that possesses the birthright and blessing of the firstborn (Gen 36:6–8). But the text now turns to the seventh son born of a freewoman and likewise to the seventh, or Sabbath, millennium that represents the tangible manifestation of our promised peace and freedom in the land, the Body of Christ.

Genesis 37:2 These [are] the generations of Jacob. Joseph, [being] seventeen years old, was feeding the flock with his brethren; and the lad [was] with the sons of Bilhah, and with the sons of Zilpah, his father's wives: and Joseph brought unto his father their evil report.

The sons of Bilhah and Zilpah are the sons of bondwomen and, thereby, reflect the bondage and suffering of Jesus Christ and likewise that of the Body of Christ in imitation of Christ. The person of Joseph is most closely identified with the seventh millennium, whereby his evil report against Jacob's sons of bondwomen points to the rejection of Christ and likewise the rejection of the Body of Christ, which marks the beginning and the end of the millennial kingdom. But the emphasis on the young age of Joseph represents an emphasis on the beginning of the seventh millennial period and thereby an emphasis on the final tribulation period. Jacob compared with Abraham and Isaac reflects the Second Advent compared with the formation of Adam and the First Advent of Christ. And Jacob compared with Abraham and Isaac likewise reflects the Spirit compared with the Father and the Son. The relationship between Jacob and Joseph reflects the relationship between the Spirit and the Son—which is embodied by the faithful in the Son, or in the Body of Christ—but specifically at the time of the establishment of the Body of Christ in the millennial kingdom. And Joseph bringing an evil report to his father, Jacob, concerning Jacob's sons of bondwomen therefore represents the rejection of Christ at the time of the Body of Christ.[1]

Genesis 37:3 Now Israel loved Joseph more than all his children, because he [was] the son of his old age: and he made him a coat of [many] colours.

The sons of Jacob reflect the seven millennia of creation proceeding from the body of Adam unto the fullness of the Body of Christ. Joseph embodies the new creation beginning in the seventh millennium, in contrast to his brothers who embody the original six millennia of fallen creation. The emphasis on Joseph being the son of Jacob's old age implies the exclusion of Benjamin from this comparison of Jacob's children, given that Benjamin was born after Joseph (Gen 35:18). The love of Jacob for Joseph being unique represents the Spirit of God resting fully upon the one person of Christ. And the unique love identified

---

[1] Coffman notes that some commentators idolize figures such as Joseph to the point of rejecting what the Bible actually says about them—such as Joseph bringing an evil report (Coffman 448; Gen 37:2). The fact that Joseph brought an evil report concerning his brothers should not be denied and neither should the event be judged beyond its significance to the coming of the Messiah.

with Joseph is signified by Jacob making Joseph a coat of many colors. The coat of many colors represents a covering unto Joseph just as the multitude of the Body of Christ represents a covering of glory unto Christ. And the Body of Christ signifies the unique love of God since it is the Body of Christ that is the visible manifestation of the love of God in his giving the life of his only begotten Son (John 3:16). The identification of Jacob's love of Joseph with Jacob's old age finally points to the last days of creation being the time of the manifestation of the Holy Spirit in the establishment of the Body of Christ.[2]

Genesis 37:4 And when his brethren saw that their father loved him more than all his brethren, they hated him, and could not speak peaceably unto him.

Joseph is hated by his brothers, who represent the totality of the six millennia of creation. And Jesus Christ would likewise be hated by the world, that is, by the whole of fallen creation (John 15:18–19). The brothers hating Joseph is based on Jacob loving Joseph, and thereby the hating of Joseph reflects the rejecting of the love of the Son, likewise the rejecting of the redemption that exists only in the Son. The emphasis on Joseph's brothers seeing and rightly understanding that their father, Jacob, indeed does uniquely love Joseph represents an emphasis on their condemnation being justified. For the brothers see and understand the love resting upon Joseph but even so reject it. And this hating of Joseph that does not allow his brothers to speak peaceably unto him reflects the faithless not being able under any circumstances to enter into the peace of the Son.

Genesis 37:5 And Joseph dreamed a dream, and he told [it] his brethren: and they hated him yet the more.

The second firstborn son Joseph is identified with the Sabbath millennium, while his brothers are identified with the preceding six millennia. Joseph dreaming a dream and telling his brothers represents the prophetic revelation of the Son throughout all the ages. And Joseph's brothers hating the revelation of Joseph's dream represents the rejection of the clear and undeniable truth of the Son. The telling of the dream points to a universal revelation in the last millennium, while the hating of the dream points to a corresponding universal apostasy in the last millennium.

Genesis 37:6 And he said unto them, Hear [H8085], I pray you, this dream which I have dreamed:

---

[2] "Why had Joseph, representing Christ, a coat of many colours? Why does the Apostle say to the Romans: '. . . For even as we have many members in one body, and all the members have not the same office: so we, who are many, are one body in Christ, and severally members one of another. And having gifts differing according to the grace that was given to us . . . .' [Jerome, *Against Jovinianus*]" (Schaff and Wace, *Nicene and Post-Nicene Fathers: Second Series* 6:404–5). The unity of all races and peoples in Christ.

The word *hear* [H8085] (hear the dream) has a connotation "to obey."

Genesis 37:7 For, behold, we [were] binding sheaves in the field, and, lo, my sheaf arose, and also stood upright; and, behold, your sheaves stood round about, and made obeisance [H7812] to my sheaf.

The word *obeisance* [H7812] has a connotation "to worship God," which is a testimony that the person of Joseph represents nothing less than God in the flesh. The single sheaf of Joseph stands up as a monarch, while the sheaves of his brothers bow down in obeisance. Joseph and his brothers all work together in the field, but the work of Joseph stands up while the works of his brothers are laid low. The work of Joseph represents the work of the cross that is ultimately realized in the resurrection of Christ. In contrast, the works of Joseph's brothers are the works of men, the works of the flesh, which are always in vain and always lead down to death.

Genesis 37:8 And his brethren said to him, Shalt thou indeed reign over us? or shalt thou indeed have dominion over us? And they hated him yet the more for his dreams, and for his words.

Joseph's brothers understand very well the meaning of Joseph's dreams. The faithless are without excuse. Joseph's words are true and faithful, but Joseph's brothers hate that which is true and faithful. The faithless condemn themselves with their own mouths. Joseph's brothers hate him for who he is, but they hate him most of all for who he says he is. The faithless likewise hate God, but most of all they hate the appearing of God.[3]

Genesis 37:9–11 And he dreamed yet another dream, and told it his brethren, and said, Behold, I have dreamed a dream more; and, behold, the sun and the moon and the eleven stars made obeisance to me. 10 And he told [it] to his father, and to his brethren: and his father rebuked him, and said unto him, What [is] this dream that thou hast dreamed? Shall I and thy mother and thy brethren indeed come to bow down ourselves to thee to the earth? 11 And his brethren envied him; but his father observed the saying.

The brothers of Joseph are most closely identified with the dream of the earthly sheaves, while the parents of Joseph are most closely identified with the dream of the heavenly bodies. The brothers envying Joseph represents the flesh contending with the Holy Spirit, while Jacob observing the saying of Joseph

---

[3] "Thou that art the youngest, over us that are elder? The reign of Jesus Christ, our *Joseph*, is despised, and striven against by an unbelieving world, who cannot endure to think that *this man* should *reign over them*" (Wesley 1:146; Gen 37:8). The present reign of man is that of the elder, or firstborn, Adam-kind. The promised new reign of man will be of the younger, or second firstborn, Christ-kind.

represents the Spirit affirming the Son. The dream of the earthly sheaves is to the dream of the heavenly bodies as the earthly is to the heavenly. The former testifies to the dominion of the Son over the earth, while the latter testifies to the dominion of the Son over heaven. The Father gives all things over into the hands of the Son (John 3:35). The Son is true man and true God and, thereby, embodies the nexus of earth and heaven, that is, the natural and the spiritual. Jacob originally rebuking Joseph before observing the saying of Joseph represents the suffering of the Son at the First Advent that precedes the exaltation of the Son at the Second Advent. The original dream of the earthly sheaves compared with the second dream of the heavenly bodies also reflects the First Advent compared with the Second Advent. The former represents the dominion of the Son over the earth, while the latter represents the dominion of the Son over heaven, or rather over the union of earth and heaven in the promised new creation.[4]

The Evil Beast

Genesis 37:12–14 And his brethren went to feed their father's flock in Shechem [H7927]. 13 And Israel said unto Joseph, Do not thy brethren feed [the flock] in Shechem [H7927]? come, and I will send thee unto them. And he said to him, Here [am I]. 14 And he said to him, Go, I pray thee, see whether it be well with thy brethren, and well with the flocks; and bring me word again. So he sent him out of the vale of Hebron, and he came to Shechem [H7927].

Jacob sending his beloved Joseph unto his brothers reflects the Son proceeding according to the Spirit, particularly at the time of the First Advent (Luke 1:35). The person of Joseph is most closely identified with the millennial kingdom at the time of the Second Advent, but the First and Second Advents are inextricably linked. The First Advent of Christ is identified most closely with the kingship of Christ (Matt 2:2, 27:37), while the Second Advent is most closely identified with the high priesthood of Christ (Heb 9:11, 9:28). But the Second Advent is finally understood to be the union of the kingship and the high priesthood (Heb 7:1, 6:20, Rev 5:10). The Covenant of Grace likewise replaces the Covenant of Law but also subsumes the Covenant of Law.[5]

Genesis 37:15–17 And a certain man found him, and, behold, [he was] wandering in the field: and the man asked him, saying, What seekest thou? 16 And he said, I seek my brethren: tell me, I pray thee, where they

---

[4] The dreams of Israelites are understandable, whereas the dreams of Egyptians require an interpreter, Gen 40:8, 41:8 (Sarna 256; Gen 37:8). The dualistic nature of parables is to be simultaneously clear and confounded, Luke 8:10.

[5] Joseph's body would later [hundreds of years later] be interred in Shechem, Josh 24:32 (Sarna 258; Gen 37:12). Joseph ultimately being buried in Shechem reinforces the image of his symbolic, or spiritual, death being at the hands of his brothers at the time of his fateful journey unto them at Shechem.

feed [their flocks]. 17 And the man said, They are departed hence; for I heard them say, Let us go to Dothan. And Joseph went after his brethren, and found them in Dothan.

The earlier destruction of Shechem portends the coming judgment of the law, the judgment of the end times (Gen 34:24–26). And Jacob now sending Joseph to Shechem to look for his brothers identifies his brothers with the same final judgment of the law (Gen 37:12). The millennia of creation proceeding from Adam are as a whole under the judgment of the law. But Shechem is already desolate as signified by an empty field, which points beyond the six millennia of creation and beyond the final tribulation period to the promised millennial kingdom. And Joseph not finding his brothers at Shechem points to the promised redemption of the faithful in Christ. An unidentified man directing Joseph to his brothers prefigures the angels serving Christ in his journey unto his brothers at the time of the First Advent (Matt 4:11) and also at the time of the Second Advent (Matt 16:27). The life of Joseph reflects the essential unity of the First and Second Advents, but the emphasis in the account of Joseph is on the Second Advent and the corresponding millennial kingdom.

Genesis 37:18 And when they saw him afar off, even before he came near unto them, they conspired against him to slay him.

The whole of the world has truly rejected Christ from the time of Adam, as evidenced by the wickedness of man throughout the millennia of creation. The wickedness of man is great in the earth, and every imagination of the thoughts of his heart is only evil continually (Gen 6:5). The reality of the incarnation transcends the time of the incarnation just as the redemption of the cross encompasses all the generations of Adam-kind throughout all time.[6]

Genesis 37:19 And they said one to another, Behold, this dreamer cometh.

The coming of Joseph as the despised dreamer of dreams represents the first coming of Christ. In contrast, the future coming of Joseph when he is exalted as the interpreter of dreams represents the second coming of Christ (Gen 41:39–40). Joseph now comes lowly and weak, but in the future Joseph will come exalted and with great power (Gen 45:3). Joseph now comes unto his brothers, but in the future his brothers will be called unto him (Gen 45:19–20). The testimony of Jesus is the spirit of prophecy (Rev 19:10).

---

[6] "The holy Ghost covers not men's faults, as do vain writers who make vice virtue" (Whittingham et al., *Geneva Bible* 18L n. g; Gen 37:18). The truthfulness of the Holy Scriptures with regard to visible things is a testimony to the truthfulness of the Holy Scriptures with regard to invisible things.

JOSEPH BEN JACOB

Genesis 37:20 Come now therefore, and let us slay him, and cast him into some pit [H953], and we will say, Some evil beast hath devoured him: and we shall see what will become of his dreams.

The evil beast being fictitious reflects the spiritual, or symbolic, nature of the beast being the evil that is committed under its name, or image. And the evil beast that devours is finally understood to be the devil. The spiritual nature of the beast prefigures the fundamentally incorporeal manifestation of the devil at the time of the First Advent (John 13:2). Joseph being cast into a pit by his brothers (the pit of his brothers) prefigures the death of Christ going down into the pit of the flesh that is the grave (Ps 30:3). Joseph's brothers mocking him in the pit by looking to see what would become of him and his dreams prefigures the faithless mocking Jesus Christ by looking to see if he would come down from the cross (Mark 15:32). But the mockers will, despite themselves, prove to be prophets. And the evil beast will prove to be real at the time of the Second Advent of Christ.[7]

Genesis 37:21–22 And Reuben heard [it], and he delivered him out of their hands; and said, Let us not kill him. 22 And Reuben said unto them, Shed no blood, [but] cast him into this pit that [is] in the wilderness, and lay no hand upon him; that he might rid him out of their hands, to deliver him to his father again.

The first firstborn son Reuben is identified with casting the second firstborn son Joseph into a pit, representing the grave. It is likewise the first man Adam that is identified with nailing the second man Christ to the cross, since it was by Adam that sin entered the world, and death by sin (Rom 5:12). And Reuben denying that they had laid their hands upon Joseph reflects the unrepentant nature of carnal man. Nonetheless, the firstborn Reuben ultimately having had good intentions in casting Joseph into the pit reflects the first man Adam having sinned in ignorance. Adam sinned in ignorance, in stark contrast to the serpent who sinned knowingly. This difference is why a fallen man can be redeemed, but a fallen angel cannot be redeemed (Jude 1:6). And Reuben's supposition that Joseph must be cast into the pit in order to deliver him again unto his father points to the reality that the death of Christ must necessarily precede the resurrection and ascension of Christ and likewise the faithful in Christ.

Genesis 37:23 And it came to pass, when Joseph was come unto his brethren, that they stript Joseph out of his coat, [his] coat of [many] colours that [was] on him;

---

[7] "How they [Joseph's brothers] agreed to keep one another's counsel, and to cover the murder with a lie: *We will say, Some evil beast hath devoured him*; whereas in thus consulting to devour him they proved themselves worse than the most evil beasts; . . ." (Henry 1:214; Gen 37:12–22). The relationship between the ten brothers and the evil beast is manifest, intrinsic to the inspired narrative.

The nakedness of Christ on the cross (Matt 27:35).

Genesis 37:24 And they took him, and cast him into a pit: and the pit [was] empty, [there was] no water in it.

The thirst of Christ on the cross (John 19:28).[8]

Genesis 37:25 And they sat down to eat bread: and they lifted up their eyes and looked, and, behold, a company of Ishmeelites came from Gilead with their camels bearing spicery and balm and myrrh, going to carry [it] down to Egypt.

The eating of bread by the brothers points to the breaking of bread at the last supper and, thereby, portends the death of the natural body under the law (Matt 26:26). The caravan that bears Joseph to Egypt also carrying balm and myrrh foreshadows the body of Jesus Christ being prepared for burial with a mixture of myrrh and aloes (John 19:39–40) and also the intended anointing of Christ with sweet spices (Mark 16:1).

Genesis 37:26 And Judah said unto his brethren, What profit [is it] if we slay our brother, and conceal his blood?

The first son Reuben, reflecting the first man Adam, is most closely identified with Joseph being cast into a pit, representing the death of Christ in contrast to the resurrection of Christ (Gen 37:22). Reuben casting Joseph into the pit reflects Adam nailing Jesus to the cross that is spiritually the tree of the knowledge of good and evil. And the death of Jesus Christ in the place of Adam is thereby seen as the condemnation, or death, of the old man Adam. The fourth son Judah, embodying the Messianic bloodline, is most closely identified with the selling of Joseph and the corresponding raising up of Joseph out of the pit (Gen 49:10). The Messianic bloodline that marks Judah connects Jesus Christ to the figurative resurrection of Joseph. And the death and resurrection of Jesus is thereby seen as the death of the old man Adam, or Christ in the place of Adam, followed by the rebirth of the new man Christ and likewise the faithful in Christ. Finally, the image of the brothers shedding and then concealing the blood of Joseph, which they effectively do even though they deny it, prefigures the rejection of the risen Lord. But the connection between Joseph being sold and his being raised out of the pit is the same connection

---

[8] Sarna puts forward Gen 42:21 as proof that Joseph protested his fate in a loud manner (Sarna 259; Gen 37:24). While Gen 42:21 does tell us that Joseph pleaded for his life, the local narrative, 37:23–28, does not record this fact and, thereby, implies a relative silence, perhaps shock, compared with what might be expected. The incongruity, or seeming incongruity, should be recognized as a prophecy of Jesus Christ being as silent as a lamb to the slaughter, Acts 8:32, but also opening his mouth to his accusers, Matt 26:62–65. The speaking that follows silence is the resurrection and exaltation that follows the condemnation and crucifixion.

between Judas Iscariot selling the life of Christ (Acts 1:16–18) and the life of Christ purchasing many (Matt 20:28).[9]

Genesis 37:27 Come, and let us sell him to the Ishmeelites, and let not our hand be upon him; for he [is] our brother [and] our flesh. And his brethren were content.

Joseph's brothers vainly try to avoid having blood on their hands by selling Joseph into Egypt. Likewise, Jesus's brothers, or fellow Jews, would vainly try to avoid having blood on their hands by handing Jesus over to the Roman authorities (Matt 27:1–6).[10]

Genesis 37:28 Then there passed by Midianites merchantmen; and they drew and lifted up Joseph out of the pit, and sold Joseph to the Ishmeelites for twenty [pieces] of silver: and they brought Joseph into Egypt.

The life of Joseph being valued in pieces of silver prefigures the life of Jesus being valued in pieces of silver (Matt 27:9). Isaac is identified with the First Advent, whereby Isaac's brother Ishmael is also identified with the First Advent (Gen 22:2). And Ishmael mocking Isaac (Gen 21:9) prefigures Israel rejecting Christ (Matt 27:41). Caiaphas would connect the rejection of Christ to the welfare and prosperity of Israel at the time of the First Advent (John 11:49–50). But the emphasis on merchants conducting Joseph to Egypt also looks past the First Advent to the time of the Second Advent and the merchants that will be closely identified with Babylon (Rev 18:11–19).

Genesis 37:29 And Reuben returned unto the pit; and, behold, Joseph [was] not in the pit; and he rent his clothes.

---

[9] "And as *Joseph* was sold by the contrivance of *Judah* for twenty pieces of silver, so was our Lord Jesus for thirty, and by one of the same name too, *Judas*" (Wesley 1:148; Gen 37:26). The Greek name *Judas* corresponds to the Hebrew name *Judah*, whereby Judas Iscariot betraying Christ reflects all of the nation of Judah, or Israel, rejecting Christ.
[10] "He was sold with Joseph, and He guided Abraham; was bound along with Isaac, and wandered with Jacob; with Moses He was Leader, and, respecting the people, Legislator. He preached in the prophets; was incarnate of a virgin; born in Bethlehem; received by John, and baptized in Jordan; was tempted in the desert, and proved to be the Lord [Irenaeus, *Fragments*]" (Roberts et al., *Ante-Nicene Fathers* 1:577). Creation is a capitulation to the life of Christ, our Lord being the only begotten Son of God, while the life of Christ, our Lord also being the Son of man, is a recapitulation of creation. Therein, the Trinity—by which we understand Christ and in which we relate to Christ—is necessarily the paradigm of creation, the shape of our salvation, and the mode of our prayer. And as such, the Trinity must be our one true hermeneutics, our way to read and understand the Bible, likewise our way to interpret the human condition and creation as a whole.

Reuben is the son of Jacob most closely identified with the suffering, or passion, of Joseph. The first son Reuben reflects the first man Adam, or fallen man, for whom Christ would die in order to redeem. And Reuben rending his clothes in this context represents an identification with the nakedness of Joseph being stripped of his coat of many colors (Gen 37:23). The faithful are raised with Christ because the faithful are buried with Christ (Rom 6:5).

Genesis 37:30 And he returned unto his brethren, and said, The child [is] not; and I, whither shall I go?

Reuben is correct to say that he has nowhere to go, no way to escape his guilt, no work that he can do of himself to save himself.[11]

Genesis 37:31 And they took Joseph's coat, and killed a kid of the goats, and dipped the coat in the blood;

The symbolic death of Joseph being connected with the slaughter of a goat points to the animal sacrifices required by the law for the atonement of sin. And the sacrificial system of the law is a prophecy of the death of Jesus Christ for the sins of the world (Matt 5:17). The shedding of blood is therefore a symbol of the love of God (Heb 9:22). And the reality of the love of God is the life represented by the blood that is the redemption of the faithful by the blood (Lev 17:11). The coat of Joseph being dipped in blood then connects his coat to the life that is in the blood. And the coat, or covering, of Joseph is a symbol of the unique love of Jacob for Joseph, which represents the love of God for the Son and for the faithful in the Son (Gen 37:3). The Father loves the Son because the Son lays down his life for the faithful (John 10:17). The covering of Christ that embodies the love of God is the Body of Christ. And the robes of the faithful are washed in the blood and made white (Rev 7:14).

Genesis 37:32 And they sent the coat of [many] colours, and they brought [it] to their father; and said, This have we found: know now whether it [be] thy son's coat or no.

The blood of Christ represents the life in Christ. And Joseph being identified by the sign of his coat, or covering, being covered with blood represents Jesus Christ being identified by the sign of love marking the faithful (John 13:35). Jacob testifies to the identity of Joseph just as the Holy Spirit indwelling the faithful testifies to the identity of the Son (John 15:26).

---

[11] "As the firstborn, he [Reuben] realized what a terrible crime had been injected into the heart of the chosen nation. Long centuries of slavery for all of them would result [from the crime against Joseph]" (Coffman 455; Gen 37:29–30). The slavery to sin and death in the present life that proceeds from the rejection of the Lord God by Adam, likewise by all Adam-kind.

Genesis 37:33 And he knew it, and said, [It is] my son's coat; an evil beast hath devoured him; Joseph is without doubt [H2963] rent in pieces [H2963].

The evil beast is the dragon, that old serpent, called the devil and also satan (Rev 12:9). Joseph being *without doubt* [H2963] *rent in pieces* [H2963] represents a doubling of the verb "to tear, rend, pluck" [H2963] in the Hebrew, which points to the death of the Body of Christ in imitation of the death of Christ the Head. From the perspective of God, the death and resurrection Christ, together with the death and resurrection of the faithful in Christ, forms one event (Col 2:12). And the perspective of God is the one true perspective.[12]

Genesis 37:34 And Jacob rent his clothes, and put sackcloth upon his loins, and mourned for his son many days.

God the Son, not God the Father, is the person of the Trinity that was nailed to the cross. Nonetheless, Christ becoming a curse on the cross (Gal 3:13) represents a separation between the Son and the Father because of sin (Matt 27:46). And the Father surely suffers when the Son suffers just as any good father would suffer at the idea of his son suffering. And the Spirit likewise also broods over the suffering of the Son. The suffering of the cross represents a state of separation, or forsakenness, and therefore necessarily reverberates throughout the Trinity and even throughout the whole of creation formed in the image of God, which is the reality of the Trinity. Reuben followed by Jacob rending their clothes represents their identifying with the nakedness of Joseph, specifically his being stripped of his coat of many colors (Gen 37:23). But Reuben previously rending his clothes in fear reflects the call of fallen man to the repentance that is an identification with the Son (Gen 37:29). And Jacob now rending his clothes in empathetic love reflects the unity, or mutual identification, of the Spirit and Son proceeding from the Father.[13]

Genesis 37:35 And all his sons and all his daughters rose up to comfort him; but he refused to be comforted; and he said, For I will go down into the grave unto my son mourning. Thus his father wept for him.

The Comforter cannot come until the Son ascends back unto the Father at which time the Comforter, who is the Spirit of truth, will testify of the Son (John 15:26). And when the Spirit is come, the Spirit will reprove the world of sin, and of righteousness, and of judgment (John 16:7–11). The progression

---

[12] "Above all, the movement [experienced by Joseph] from exaltation to humiliation to exaltation foreshadows the career of the Son of God. Believers have an exemplar by which to interpret their experiences" (Waltke 523). Jesus Christ the Head followed by the faithful in the Body of Christ.

[13] The Lord could exclaim from the cross that he had been forsaken, because he had so fully assumed the sins of mankind, Mark 15:34 (Rom. Catholic Church, *Catechism* 171). The literal and spiritual levels of reality necessarily always fit together.

Father, Son, and Spirit reflects the promised new creation that finally comes by the power of the indwelling Holy Spirit. Jacob will mourn until Joseph is returned unto him at which time Joseph's brothers, who represent the world, will stand convicted of their sin against Joseph. The Holy Spirit would come unto the church at the time of Pentecost in the form of a deposit (Acts 2:1–4), but the fullness of the indwelling Holy Spirit cannot be realized until the resurrection unto eternal life at the time of Tabernacles (2 Cor 5:5). The partial cessation of the mourning of Jacob implied by his many but finite days of mourning represents the deposit of the Holy Spirit (Gen 37:34), while the indescribable jubilation of Jacob when Joseph is finally returned unto him represents the fullness of the Spirit (Gen 46:30).[14]

Genesis 37:36 And the Midianites sold him into Egypt unto Potiphar, an officer of Pharaoh's, [and] captain of the guard.

We are not our own, for we are bought with a price (1 Cor 6:19–20).[15]

Judah and Tamar

Genesis 38:1 And it came to pass at that time, that Judah went down from his brethren, and turned in to a certain Adullamite, whose name [was] Hirah.

Judah going down from his brothers represents Judah being considered alone in isolation from his brothers. The person of Judah is identified with the Messianic bloodline, likewise with the Messianic kingship, which corresponds to the birthright, or bloodright, in contrast to the blessing (Gen 49:10). The blessing necessarily comprehends the birthright, but the emphasis is on the birthright. Delimiting the account of Judah and Tamar are the account of Joseph being thrown into a pit by his brothers, which represents the death and resurrection of Christ (Gen 37:20), and the account of Joseph being thrown into prison in Egypt, which represents the death and resurrection of the Body of Christ (Gen 39:20). The spiritual context of the account of Judah and Tamar is therefore the church age connecting the First and Second Advents.[16]

---

[14] "There is no concept of 'heaven' and 'hell' in the Hebrew Bible. The underworld [the grave, or sheol] received all men—good and bad, great and small . . . ." (Sarna 262; Gen 37:35). The bosom of Abraham, Luke 16:22, would not become the presence of the Lord, 2 Cor 5:8, until the time of the death and resurrection of Christ, 1 Pet 3:18–22.
[15] ". . . Joseph being reckoned as dead by his father, and yet alive, may be herein an emblem of Christ's death, and his resurrection from the dead" (Gill 1:196; Gen 37:36). This is without doubt the case.
[16] Accounts such as that of Judah and Tamar appear superficially to be intrusions into a larger narrative but, if understood properly, are actually thematically integrated into the whole (Alter and Kermode, *Literary Guide* 39–40). A superficial reading of the Bible will inevitably correspond to some carnal level of reality, in which can never be found the true, or complete, image of God, who is simultaneously immanent and transcendent.

Genesis 38:2 And Judah saw there a daughter of a certain Canaanite, whose name [was] Shuah; and he took her, and went in unto her.

The Canaanites represent fallen humanity and particularly the unrepentant fallen, whereby Judah taking a Canaanite wife portends a wicked generation and finally the judgment of that generation (Gen 24:3).[17]

Genesis 38:3–5 And she conceived, and bare a son; and he called his name Er. 4 And she conceived again, and bare a son; and she called his name Onan. 5 And she yet again conceived, and bare a son; and called his name Shelah: and he was at Chezib [H3580], when she bare him.

The name *Chezib* [H3580] (the place of bearing offspring) is derived from the root "to lie, be a liar" [H3576], which reflects a spiritual lineage from the father of lies who is the devil (John 8:44). The three sequential sons of Judah's Canaanite wife reflect the three millennia connecting the First and Second Advents and culminating in the apostasy that demarcates the beginning and the end of the Sabbath millennium (Rev 19:19, 20:7–8).

Genesis 38:6 And Judah took a wife for Er his firstborn, whose name [was] Tamar.

The genealogy of Tamar is nowhere specified, and thereby Tamar is symbolically disconnected from any blood relationship to Adam and from the corresponding fallen nature inherited from Adam. As a point of comparison, the person of Melchizedek is likewise disconnected from any genealogy (Heb 7:3). Tamar being named as an individual without her ethnicity stands in stark contrast to Judah's nameless Canaanite wife being named only by her ethnicity.

Genesis 38:7 And Er, Judah's firstborn, was wicked in the sight of the LORD; and the LORD slew him.

The wickedness of Judah's first son, Er, represents the wickedness of the first millennium following the rejection of the Messianic bloodline at the time of the First Advent. (The first millennium from Christ being the fifth millennium from Adam.) The wickedness of the first millennium of the First Advent is the rejection of Christ followed by the persecution of Christians followed by the corruption of the institutionalized church. And the emphasis on Er being wicked in the sight of the Lord points to a literal physical presence of God at the time of the incarnation. Er being judged wicked without any specific reason

---

[17] "[A]t first sight, the dignity of Christ seems to be somewhat tarnished by such dishonour [incurred by Judah]: . . . it rather redounds to his glory . . . [W]e wrong Christ, unless we deem him alone sufficient to blot out any ignominy . . . . [L]et us remember that Christ derives no glory from his ancestors; . . ." (Calvin, *Commentaries* 2:278; Gen 38:1). To think otherwise is tantamount to believing that God is not peerless.

being recorded portends the condemnation and rejection of Christ and likewise the rejection of the Gospel of Christ without reason or cause (John 15:25). And the slaying of Er represents the first millennium of Christ ending without the promised return of Christ.

Genesis 38:8 And Judah said unto Onan, Go in unto thy brother's wife, and marry her, and raise up seed to thy brother.

Judah seeking to raise up an heir for his firstborn is a prophecy of the man-child who would embody the promise of new life that is eternal, or continuing, life. The second son Onan represents the second millennium from Christ that is also the sixth millennium from Adam. The call of Onan to raise up seed for the firstborn represents the call to raise up the Body of Christ that precedes the judgment of the world. Christ the Head is first, the Body of Christ is second. Judah represents the Messianic bloodline, whereby Judah seeking to raise up offspring for his firstborn, Er, represents Judah affirming the Messianic bloodline. And the bloodline continues spiritually through Jesus Christ unto his offspring by the grace that establishes the faithful in the Body of Christ (John 15:5). The death of the firstborn represents the condemnation of Adam. And the call to raise up seed for the firstborn represents the desire to redeem the firstborn, not of himself but rather only by the second born who represents the second man Christ.[18]

Genesis 38:9 And Onan knew that the seed should not be his; and it came to pass, when he went in unto his brother's wife, that he spilled [it] on the ground, lest that he should give seed to his brother.

The second son Onan refusing to raise up seed for the firstborn is a prophecy of increasing apostasy in the final millennium preceding the Second Advent. Onan knows that the seed will not be his, and he is ironically correct because he spills it upon the ground and, thereby, rejects the one true Seed. The faithless condemn themselves. The seed that is spilled upon the ground, or goes upon the ground, recalls the seed of the serpent cursed to go on its belly and eat dust (Gen 3:14–15).

Genesis 38:10 And the thing which he did displeased the LORD: wherefore he slew him also.

The slaying of the second born Onan portends the ending of the second millennium from Christ that is the sixth millennium from Adam. This last millennium preceding the Second Advent is the millennium of apostasy.

---

[18] A man taking his brother's wife is forbidden in Lev 18:16 and 20:21, but it is required in Deut 25:5 in the case of the brother having died without a son (Sarna 266; Gen 38:8). Every nuance of the law speaks of death and resurrection.

Genesis 38:11 Then said Judah to Tamar his daughter in law, Remain a widow at thy father's house, till Shelah my son be grown: for he said, Lest peradventure he die also, as his brethren [did]. And Tamar went and dwelt in her father's house.

The third son Shelah represents the third millennium from Christ that is also the seventh, or Sabbath, millennium from Adam. Shelah will not die but will be supplanted in the Messianic bloodline by the offspring of Tamar. The supplanting of the third born Shelah with the offspring of Tamar represents the death and resurrection of the Body of Christ that embodies the millennial kingdom. And the fear of Judah for the life of Shelah portends the final tribulation period that will precede the millennial kingdom. The necessity of the supplanting of Shelah waiting until the time of his maturity prefigures the necessity of the harvest of mankind waiting until the time of the maturity of the call to repentance that is also the time of the maturity of sin. Tamar being marked by the sign of widowhood distinguishes her from the whore of Babylon who says that she will never be a widow (Rev 18:7). Tamar the widow waiting to give birth to the Messianic bloodline represents the other woman of the book of Revelation, the woman clothed with the sun, the moon under her feet, and a crown of twelve stars upon her head (Rev 12:1). And this vision of the sun and the moon and twelve stars is the exact context of the present account of Judah and Tamar, which is Joseph's dream of the sun and the moon and the twelve stars (Gen 37:9).

Genesis 38:12 And in process of time the daughter of Shuah Judah's wife died; and Judah was comforted [H5162], and went up unto his sheepshearers to Timnath, he and his friend Hirah the Adullamite.

The word *comforted* [H5162] (Judah comforted) is the same word used to prophesy that Noah would be a *comfort* [H5162] from the work and toil of our hands (Gen 5:29) and also at the time of Noah to describe it *repenting* [H5162] the Lord that he had made man on the earth (Gen 6:6). The connection between the first destruction that came by water and the second destruction that will come by fire (2 Pet 3:5–7) is ubiquitous, for the second destruction will be the final fulfillment of the destruction of all flesh, together with the earth, prophesied by the first destruction (Gen 6:13). The strange relationship between repenting and being comforted is the same relationship between death and rebirth and likewise between destruction and renewal. The three sons of Judah's Canaanite wife represent the three millennia connecting the First and Second Advents, whereby her death and the concomitant end of her childbearing represents the end of this period that is ostensibly the church age. The death of Judah's Canaanite wife following the deaths of her first and second sons but preceding the death of her third son points very specifically to the juncture connecting the second and third millennia from the First Advent. This is the end of the church age that is the foretold tribulation heralding the millennial kingdom of Jesus Christ.

Genesis 38:13 And it was told Tamar, saying, Behold thy father in law goeth up to Timnath to shear his sheep.

The time of shearing the sheep is like the time of harvesting the fields that prefigures the harvesting of the world.

Genesis 38:14 And she put her widow's garments off from her, and covered her with a vail, and wrapped herself, and sat in an open place, which [is] by the way to Timnath; for she saw that Shelah was grown, and she was not given unto him to wife.

The contrast between Tamar the widow and Tamar the whore reflects the two women of the book of Revelation. The third son Shelah prefigures the third millennium from Christ that is the Sabbath millennium from Adam, whereby Shelah becoming a very young adult points to the beginning of the millennial kingdom and likewise the end of the church age. Tamar the widow waiting to give birth in the Messianic bloodline represents the woman clothed with the sun, the moon under her feet, and upon her head a crown of twelve stars (Rev 12:1). Tamar sitting as a harlot in an open place represents the whore of Babylon who says in her heart that she sits as a queen and is not a widow and will never see sorrow (Rev 18:7). The woman clothed with heavenly bodies and the whore of Babylon being represented by the same woman Tamar portends a time of great deception when people will not be able to distinguish Christ from anti-christ. The stark comparison of Tamar the prostitute to the degradation of Christ also reflects this same subtlety. And this is finally the subtlety of the serpent (Gen 3:1). The subtlety between Tamar the whore and Tamar the mother is the same subtlety between the rider on the white horse going forth conquering and to conquer (Rev 6:2) and the rider on a white horse righteously judging and making war (Rev 19:11).

Genesis 38:15 When Judah saw her, he thought her [to be] an harlot; because she had covered her face.

Tamar is a widow who becomes a harlot who will become a mother and specifically the mother of the Messianic bloodline. Tamar the widow reflects the fall through Adam, with an emphasis on death having entered into the world at that time. Tamar the harlot reflects the rejection of Christ, with an emphasis on the harlotry, or idolatry, inherently connected with the rejection of the one true God. But Tamar the mother of the Messianic bloodline reflects the rebirth of the faithful in the promised Body of Christ. The death of Christ precedes the resurrection of Christ just as the harlot precedes the mother. And the death of the natural body likewise precedes the rebirth of the spiritual, or glorified, resurrection body. The offensive nature of the faithful being conceived through an act of harlotry reflects the offensive nature of the death of the sinless Christ on the cross in the place of us unworthy sinners (1 Pet 3:18).

The personage of Judah is most closely identified with the fourth millennium from Adam, marked by the conception of Christ as the king of kings at the end of the fourth millennium. But the overarching context of the local (nested) account of Judah and Tamar is Joseph being sold into Egypt, with the personage of Joseph being most closely identified with the seventh, or Sabbath, millennium. The connection between Judah and Joseph reflects the connection between the fourth and seventh millennia, namely, the birth of Christ viewed as one event with the rebirth of the faithful in the Body of Christ. This is the essential perspective of God in the redemption of the faithful. The faithful in Christ are truly buried with Christ and are truly raised with Christ (Rom 6:4). Judah going into the harlot and her conceiving the Messianic bloodline testifies to the conception of the Body of Christ being not of ourselves, or by our own virtue, but only by Christ in accord with the grace of the Spirit.[19]

Genesis 38:16 And he turned unto her by the way, and said, Go to, I pray thee, let me come in unto thee; (for he knew not that she [was] his daughter in law.) And she said, What wilt thou give me, that thou mayest come in unto me?

Judah not recognizing Tamar prefigures the end times being a time of deception and confusion. The people of the world will not be able to distinguish between the widow and the whore. The emphasis on giving something in payment to the harlot points to the kings of the earth fornicating with Babylon the great, which itself parallels the merchants of the earth waxing rich through the abundance of Babylon's delicacies (Rev 18:3).

Genesis 38:17–18 And he said, I will send [thee] a kid from the flock. And she said, Wilt thou give [me] a pledge, till thou send [it]? 18 And he said, What pledge shall I give thee? And she said, Thy signet [H2368], and thy bracelets [H6616], and thy staff [H4294] that [is] in thine hand. And he gave [it] her, and came in unto her, and she conceived by him.

The payment required for the coming forth of the promised man-child is a kid from the flock, representing the blood sacrifice required by the law. But the death here required by the law and represented by the kid from the flock points

---

[19] "Tamar went forth, and in the darkness stole the Light, and in uncleanness stole the Holy One, and by uncovering her nakedness she went in and stole Thee, O glorious One, that bringest the pure out of the impure. . . . For holy was the adultery of Tamar, for Thy sake. Thee it was she thirsted after, O pure Fountain. . . . She was a widow for Thy sake. Thee did she long for, she hasted and was also an harlot for Thy sake. Thee did she vehemently desire, and was sanctified in that it was Thee she loved. . . . May Tamar rejoice that her Lord hath come and hath made her name known for the son of her adultery! [Ephraim the Syrian, *Hymns on the Nativity*]" (Schaff and Wace, *Nicene and Post-Nicene Fathers: Second Series* 13:240). If the Lord only worked through righteous things, he would not work at all, for there is nothing in the present fallen world that is not tainted in comparison with the perfect righteousness of the Lord.

most specifically to the death and resurrection of the Body of Christ in imitation of Christ, or with Christ. The pledge of Judah is the seal of Judah representing the Messianic kingship. The pledge of the Messianic kingship that precedes the death and resurrection of the Body of Christ is the Holy Spirit (John 16:7). The incarnation in the flesh points to the promise of the Spirit just as the kingship points to the high priesthood just as the birthright points to the blessing just as the law points to grace.

The one pledge of Judah being threefold—consisting of a signet, bracelets, and staff—represents the triunity of the one true God. The *signet* [H2368] represents the authority of the Father. The *bracelets* (cord, twisted thread) [H6616] represent the Son and likewise the faithful bound unto the Son. The *staff* [H4294] of Judah is the staff of the Son that is the person of the Holy Spirit indwelling the tribe of the faithful. God the Father, God the Son, and God the Spirit are three distinct persons, but nonetheless the totality of the Trinity is the testimony of the one person of God the Holy Spirit, here represented by the pledge of Judah. And the sequence Father, Son, Spirit, implicit in Judah's pledge, should be identified with redemption and with the promised new creation, in contrast to the original creation or the present fallen creation.[20]

Genesis 38:19 And she arose, and went away, and laid by her vail from her, and put on the garments of her widowhood.

Tamar is a widow who becomes a harlot who becomes a mother and specifically the mother of the Messianic bloodline. The birth of a son unto Tamar, which was first promised by Judah and is now conceived by Judah, prefigures the resurrection and rebirth of the faithful in Christ. The emphasis on Tamar being a widow as she awaits the birth of the promised man-child points to the separation from Christ that marks the church age and also the mourning that will mark the final tribulation period.

Genesis 38:20 And Judah sent the kid by the hand of his friend the Adullamite, to receive [his] pledge from the woman's hand: but he found her not.

Judah's Adullamite friend, Hirah, is connected to the account of Judah and Tamar in three places, corresponding to the threefold Fall of Adam followed by the First and Second Advents of Christ. First, Judah taking a Canaanite wife is connected to Judah departing from his brothers and lodging with Hirah (Gen 38:1). Second, Judah going into Tamar after his Canaanite wife dies is connected to Judah going up to his sheepshearers with Hirah (Gen 38:12). And Third,

---

[20] "Hear, then, how this Man, of whom the Scriptures declare that He will come again in glory after His crucifixion, was symbolized both by the tree of life . . . and by those events which should happen to all the just. . . . [For example:] it was a rod [wooden staff] that pointed out Judah to be the father of Tamar's sons by a great mystery [Justin Martyr, *Dialogue with Trypho*]" (Roberts et al., *Ante-Nicene Fathers* 1:242). The Holy Spirit comes by virtue of the wooden cross.

Judah sends Hirah with the promised kid of the flock to Tamar (Gen 38:20). Judah originally taking a Canaanite wife and fathering wicked offspring reflects the Fall of Adam. Judah fathering the Messianic bloodline by Tamar in an act of adultery reflects the redemption of humanity at the Second Advent proceeding from the rejection of Christ at the First Advent (Gen 38:26).

The death of Judah's Canaanite wife at this specific juncture connects the death of Christ and the death of the Body of Christ, which together define the totality of the church age. Judah not being able to recompense Tamar with a kid from the flock as a sign of the law points to a salvation by grace and by grace alone at the time of the Second Advent. The pledge of Judah representing the Spirit and the grace that comes by the Spirit is irrevocable. That Tamar will in the end send the pledge back unto Judah does not represent a surrender of the pledge but rather an authentication of her possession of the pledge, or seal, of Judah (Gen 38:25). The account of Judah and Tamar points primarily to the time of the Second Advent, but the Second Advent and also the First Advent both individually embody the triune image of the one God. Likewise, the Spirit and the Son both individually personify the fullness of divinity.

Genesis 38:21–22 Then he asked the men of that place, saying, Where [is] the harlot, that [was] openly by the way side? And they said, There was no harlot in this [place]. 22 And he returned to Judah, and said, I cannot find her; and also the men of the place said, [that] there was no harlot in this [place].

The harlot that sits openly is Babylon the great, the mother of harlots and abominations of the earth (Rev 17:5). The harlot not being found where she was expected is the sudden judgment of Babylon coming in one hour (Rev 18:10). The implication that there never had been a harlot represents the utter destruction of Babylon, to be found no more at all (Rev 18:21).

Genesis 38:23 And Judah said, Let her take [it] to her, lest we be shamed: behold, I sent this kid, and thou hast not found her.

The kid from the flock represents the blood sacrifice required by the law. And the seal of Judah given as a pledge represents the Holy Spirit. The shame of Judah is connected to his payment, or offering, of the kid not being accepted, representing the condemnation under the law. The pledge of Judah's seal being given in the place of the kid points to the death and resurrection of Christ being the ultimate fulfillment of the law. It now being found impossible to exchange the kid from the flock in return for the seal of Judah represents grace forever supplanting the law. The law cannot produce eternal life in separation from Christ and the Spirit who comes by Christ (Rom 8:1–4).

Genesis 38:24 And it came to pass about three months after, that it was told Judah, saying, Tamar thy daughter in law hath played the harlot; and

also, behold, she [is] with child by whoredom. And Judah said, Bring her forth, and let her be burnt.

The discovery of the whoredom of Tamar being connected with the third month of her pregnancy points to the whoredom that will characterize the earth at the time of the Second Advent, corresponding to the third millennium from the First Advent. The judgment that Tamar should be burned for her harlotry points generally to the universal destruction by fire (2 Pet 3:7) and specifically to the destruction of Babylon by fire (Rev 18:8). And Tamar the harlot is figuratively burned just as Isaac was figuratively offered as a burnt offering in Moriah (Gen 22:2). And Judah showing no mercy portends the final judgment under the law being utterly separated from grace. Tamar being condemned together with her only child still in her womb portends the destruction of all flesh and the corresponding end of the natural body. The body of Adam is finally supplanted by the Body of Christ.[21]

Genesis 38:25 When she [was] brought forth, she sent to her father in law, saying, By the man, whose these [are, am] I with child: and she said, Discern, I pray thee, whose [are] these, the signet, and bracelets, and staff.

Tamar is a widow who becomes a harlot who finally becomes a mother and specifically the mother of the Messianic bloodline. Tamar the harlot being supplanted by Tamar the mother with child represents the whore of Babylon being supplanted by a mother with child. And the latter woman is clothed with the sun, the moon under her feet, and upon her head a crown of twelve stars (Rev 12:1–2). The immediate meaning of the sun and moon and stars is as a representation of a father, mother, and offspring according to the dream of Joseph (Gen 37:9–10), but the ultimate meaning of the sun and moon and stars is the Father, Son, or Seed of woman, and Spirit according to the revelation of Jesus Christ (Rev 1:1, 12:1). The raiment of the woman with child is the triunity of God. The raiment of Tamar is likewise the threefold signet, bracelets, and staff of Judah. Tamar producing the pledge of Judah represents her authenticating her possession of the seal of Judah, which signifies the Holy Spirit and likewise the offspring of the Spirit.

Genesis 38:26 And Judah acknowledged [them], and said, She hath been more righteous than I; because that I gave her not to Shelah my son. And he knew her again no more.

---

[21] Stoning is the more common penalty for sexual crimes, Deut 22:21, 22:24, Ezek 16:40, but in two instances burning is also prescribed, Lev 20:14, 21:9 (Sarna 269; Gen 38:24). Stoning a person, or body, compared with the symbolic annihilation of burning, Ezek 16:40–41, is like the first death compared with the second death, Rev 21:8.

The quality of righteousness is directly connected to bringing forth the Messianic bloodline. Tamar alone bringing forth the Messianic bloodline without the consent or knowledge of Judah, figuratively without Judah at all, points to the Messiah being the promised Seed of woman (Gen 3:15). Christ is physically the Seed of woman by the virgin Mary, and simultaneously Christ is spiritually the Seed of the Holy Spirit (Matt 1:20). The conception of Jesus Christ thereby reflects the parallel between the Spirit being the help meet of mankind and woman being the help meet of man (Gen 2:18). The nature of man is justice, while the nature of woman is mercy. The Messiah coming by woman is a testimony that Christ comes by mercy and grace and not by the law that condemns all flesh. And Judah not fathering any more children by Tamar points to the singular nature of the one man Jesus Christ and likewise the one Body of Christ.[22]

Genesis 38:27 And it came to pass in the time of her travail, that, behold, twins [were] in her womb.

The travail of Tamar portends the tribulation period in the end times. The struggle between brothers that is ubiquitous in the Bible reflects the relationship between Adam and Christ, the relationship between the First and Second Advents of Christ, and the relationship between Christ the Head and the Body of Christ. And this is finally the struggle between anti-christ and Christ. The one man Christ is God the Son—the only begotten of the Father by, or through, the Spirit—and thus the relationship between Christ and created beings should not be understood as an equality. The relationship, or brotherhood, between the Creator and creation exists in the person of Christ, who is true God and true man, in accord with the will of the Father and by the power of the Spirit. And to deny the brotherhood of Jesus Christ and humanity is actually to deny the humanity of Christ, likewise to deny the salvation that exists by virtue of the humanity of Christ. The dominion of the first man Adam precedes the dominion of the second man Christ just as the rule of the anti-christ precedes the rule of the one true Christ. The natural body likewise precedes the spiritual, or glorified, resurrection body. And the law likewise precedes grace.

Genesis 38:28 And it came to pass, when she travailed, that [the one] put out [his] hand: and the midwife took and bound upon his hand a scarlet thread [H8144], saying, This came out first.

The *scarlet* (scarlet thread) [H8144] that marks the firstborn represents the sins of the firstborn, or more specifically the sinful nature of the firstborn (Isa

---

[22] " 'More righteous than I . . .' A better word would have been, 'She [Tamar] is less sinful than I [Judah]'; . . ." (Coffman 466; Gen 38:26). Coffman consistently defends the Bible against historical criticism, which seeks to subtract from the text, but he then falls into the error of trying to moralize, or purify, the text by the standards of man, which represents an adding to the Bible.

1:18). The firstborn representing the first man is specifically Adam but generally natural man, or sinful man, and finally the man of sin who will come in the end times (2 Thess 2:3).[23]

Genesis 38:29–30 And it came to pass, as he drew back his hand, that, behold, his brother came out: and she said, How hast thou broken forth? [this] breach [be] upon thee: therefore his name was called Pharez. 30 And afterward came out his brother, that had the scarlet thread upon his hand: and his name was called Zarah.

Pharez was the second after Zerah (Zarah) but became the first just as Jesus would be born second after Adam but would become the firstborn from the dead (Col 1:18). The faithful in Christ likewise follow Christ but are exalted in Christ and made like Christ (1 John 3:2). The surprise of the midwife at the second son becoming the first represents the surprise and joy of the faithful at the incarnation of God and the corresponding death and resurrection of God for our sakes. And our surprise at the death and resurrection of Christ is like our surprise at the promised death and resurrection of the faithful in Christ. Nonetheless, the midwife originally failing to correctly identify the firstborn portends humanity not being able to distinguish Christ from anti-christ, particularly in the end times.[24]

House of Potiphar

Genesis 39:1 And Joseph was brought down to Egypt; and Potiphar, an officer of Pharaoh, captain [H8269] of the guard [H2876], an Egyptian, bought him of the hands of the Ishmeelites, which had brought him down thither.

The account of Judah and Tamar is inserted after the account of Joseph being raised from the pit by his brothers (Gen 37:28) and directly into the account of Joseph being sold to Potiphar (Gen 37:36, 39:1). The emphasis in

---

[23] "The *Jews*, as *Zarah* [Zerah], bid fair for the birth-right . . . but the *Gentiles*, like *Pharez*, . . . got the start of them, by that *violence* which the *kingdom of heaven* suffers . . . ." (Wesley 1:151; Gen 38:28). The birthpangs of new creation.

[24] ". . . Zara [Zerah or Zarah], upon whom was the scarlet line, [was born] the second: the Scripture clearly pointing out that people which possessed the scarlet sign, that is, faith in a state of circumcision, which was shown beforehand, indeed, in the patriarchs first; but after that withdrawn, that his brother [Pharez] might be born; and also, in like manner, him who was the elder [Zerah], as being born in the second place, [him] who was distinguished by the scarlet token, which was [fastened] on him, that is, the passion of the Just One, which was prefigured from the beginning in Abel, and described by the prophets, but perfected in the last times [or last days, beginning with the First Advent] in the Son of God [Irenaeus, *Against Heresies*]" (Roberts et al., *Ante-Nicene Fathers* 1:496). The sign of circumcision points to the blood of the cross just as the law points to grace just as the dead man Adam points to the living man Jesus Christ.

the account of Judah and Tamar is the struggle of Tamar to give birth, which reflects the church age leading up to the Second Advent. The abrupt, even awkward, insertion of the account of Judah and Tamar reflects the unexpected and parenthetical nature of the church age. The juxtaposed account of the ascension of Joseph in Egypt also prefigures the church age leading up to the Second Advent, but the account of Joseph represents the perspective of Christ while the account of Tamar represents the perspective of the church. Joseph originally being cast into a pit by his brothers prefigures the death of Christ at the time of the First Advent (Gen 37:23–24), while Joseph's rise to prominence in the house of Potiphar prefigures the ascension of Christ marking the church age (Gen 39:2). Joseph finally being cast into prison by Potiphar foreshadows the end of the church age marked by the final tribulation period and corresponding to the death and resurrection of the Body of Christ in imitation of the death and resurrection of Christ himself.

Genesis 39:2 And the LORD was with Joseph, and he was a prosperous man; and he was in the house of his master the Egyptian.

The paradox of Joseph being a prosperous slave reflects the Son of God being a suffering servant (Isa 53:11). And the ascendant Christ after the time of the crucifixion remains identified as a suffering servant because the faithful in Christ are still suffering in the world. The Head and the Body are one. The Lord being with Joseph reflects the Spirit and actually the fullness of the Spirit indwelling the Son. And the ascendant Christ remains anointed by the fullness of the Spirit even though he sends the Spirit unto the faithful (John 16:7). Christ in no way diminishes his own baptism of the Spirit even though he baptizes the faithful with the Spirit (John 1:33). This is the prime subtlety of the Holy Spirit being everywhere always, in contrast to the personal character of the Son being first and foremost in one place at one time.[25]

Genesis 39:3 And his master saw that the LORD [was] with him, and that the LORD made all that he did to prosper in his hand.

The person of Joseph reflects God the Son, while Joseph's master, Potiphar, reflects God the Father. And the presence of the Lord being with Joseph reflects God the Spirit. Joseph's master, Potiphar, acknowledging that the Lord is with Joseph reflects the Father testifying that the Son possesses the font of life that is the Holy Spirit (Luke 3:22). And it is only the ascendant Christ—glorified (bodily, as well as spiritually) by the Father with the fullness of the Spirit—that can in turn give the fullness of the Spirit to his faithful of the church (John 16:7). The image of God impressed upon all creation and forming

---

[25] To denote the incorporeal presence of God simultaneously on earth and in heaven, a term *Shechinah*, literally "dwelling," was coined in Rabbinic teaching—e.g., *Sanhedrin* (Cohen, *Rabbinic Sages* 42). An obscure view of the person of God the Holy Spirit, who indwells the faithful.

all creation is the progression Father, Son, Spirit that is ultimately embodied by the drawing forth of the faithful unto the Godhead.

Genesis 39:4 And Joseph found grace in his sight, and he served him: and he made him overseer over his house, and all [that] he had he put into his hand.

Joseph finding grace in the sight of his master, Potiphar, is connected to Joseph serving Potiphar. Likewise, the grace (of the Holy Spirit) that proceeds from the Father is connected to the Son sacrificing himself according to the will of the Father (Luke 22:42). The service that is acceptable flows from grace and not vice versa. Joseph managing the house of Potiphar reflects the ascendant Christ preparing the house of his Father (John 14:2). Potiphar putting all that he has into the hand of Joseph reflects the Father giving all things into the hand of the Son (John 3:35).

Genesis 39:5 And it came to pass from the time [that] he had made him overseer in his house, and over all that he had, that the LORD blessed the Egyptian's house for Joseph's sake; and the blessing of the LORD was upon all that he had in the house, and in the field.

The blessing of the house of the Father for the sake of the Son is the blessing of the faithful in the Son. The blessing of the faithful in the Son is our promised inheritance that is the indwelling Holy Spirit. The blessing of the house and the field together is the rebirth of both man and earth together that is the rebirth of the totality of spiritual and natural creation.

Genesis 39:6 And he left all that he had in Joseph's hand; and he knew not ought he had, save the bread which he did eat. And Joseph was [a] goodly [person], and well favoured.

The significance of bread is the body, while the significance of eating bread is the death of the body. And the authority of Joseph is connected with the image of eating bread. Likewise, the authority of Jesus Christ is connected with his sacrificing his physical body on the cross. And Joseph being a goodly person and well favored reflects the essential sinlessness of Jesus that well pleases the Father (Matt 3:17).

Genesis 39:7 And it came to pass after these things, that his master's wife cast her eyes upon Joseph; and she said, Lie with me.

Potiphar represents God the Father, Joseph represents God the Son, and the blessing of Joseph represents God the Spirit. And the Father, Son, and Spirit are most closely identified as creator, redeemer, and sanctifier. The wife of the Father, who is the creator, is humanity as a whole, or all those who have been created. In contrast, the wife of the Son, who is the redeemer, is specifically the body of believers, or those who are redeemed. Potiphar's wife then represents the whole of humanity and specifically the culmination of humanity leading up to the end times. And the Son cannot accept the whole of humanity but rather only the faithful. The relationship that Potiphar's wife seeks is adulterous, which emphasizes the sacrilegious nature of the faithless seeking to become one body with Christ, that is, members of the Body of Christ. Potiphar's wife seeking to become one body with Joseph prefigures a false church, or anti-church, in the end times. Potiphar's adulterous wife prefigures the whore of Babylon.

Genesis 39:8 But he refused, and said unto his master's wife, Behold, my master wotteth not what [is] with me in the house, and he hath committed all that he hath to my hand;

Joseph refuses to take his master's wife expressly because he had received all things from his master. The Son likewise receives all things from the Father because the Son does all things according to the will of the Father. That which the Son receives from the Father is the will, or nature, of the Father that is the fullness of the Holy Spirit (John 3:34–35, 5:19–20).

Genesis 39:9 [There is] none greater in this house than I; neither hath he kept back any thing from me but thee, because thou [art] his wife: how then can I do this great wickedness, and sin against God?

The continuing emphasis on Joseph being the greatest person in the house of Potiphar points to the relationship between God the Son and God the Father. It is a strange situation for one man to be the greatest in another man's house, but that is exactly the relationship between the Son and the Father. Joseph identifies sinning against his master, Potiphar, as sinning against God himself and, thereby, reinforces the connection between Potiphar and God the Father. Joseph lying with his master's wife is finally identified with a great wickedness and, thereby, connects the person of Potiphar's wife with great wickedness. The great wickedness of Potiphar's wife prefigures the final adultery, or idolatry, opposing God himself in the end times.[26]

Genesis 39:10 And it came to pass, as she spake to Joseph day by day, that he hearkened not unto her, to lie by her, [or] to be with her.

Joseph remaining faithful day by day reflects Jesus remaining faithful millennium by millennium. These are generally the days from the time of Adam and specifically the days from the time of the First Advent.

---

[26] Joseph uses the term *God* (Elohim), not *Lord* (YHWH), because Potiphar's wife is not of the people of Israel (Sarna 273; Gen 39:8–9). The strict otherness of Potiphar's wife reflects the faithless being utterly separated from the faithful.

Genesis 39:11 And it came to pass about this time, that [Joseph] went into the house to do his business [H4399]; and [there was] none of the men of the house there within.

The word *business* [H4399] (Joseph's business) is the same word used to describe the *work* [H4399] of God in the original act of creation (Gen 2:2–3). The work of Joseph is the work of his master just as the work of the Son is the work, or will, of the Father. Joseph being alone while he completes his work reflects God being alone, or peerless, in the creation of all things.

Genesis 39:12 And she caught him by his garment, saying, Lie with me: and he left his garment in her hand, and fled, and got him out.

Joseph is here stripped of his bodily garment for a second time. The first time was when he was stripped by his brothers and cast into a pit (Gen 37:23–24). Now he is stripped by Potiphar's wife before he is to be cast into prison (Gen 39:16–20). The former nakedness points to the death and resurrection of Jesus Christ at the time of the First Advent, while the latter nakedness points to the death and resurrection of the Body of Christ at the time of the Second Advent. The garment that is stripped is the natural body and likewise the law that governs the natural body. The ultimate covering of a man is his body. Joseph stripped is Jesus striped (Isa 53:5). And the covering of Jesus Christ is likewise the Body of Christ.

Genesis 39:13–15 And it came to pass, when she saw that he had left his garment in her hand, and was fled forth, 14 That she called unto the men of her house, and spake unto them, saying, See, he hath brought in an Hebrew [H376, H5680] unto us to mock us; he came in unto me to lie with me, and I cried with a loud voice: 15 And it came to pass, when he heard that I lifted up my voice and cried, that he left his garment with me, and fled, and got him out.

The word *Hebrew* (Hebrew man) [H376, H5680] identifies Joseph with the first *Hebrew* [H5680], Abraham (Gen 14:13). And the implication is that Joseph can be identified by his garment as a Hebrew and specifically as a child of Abraham. The faithful can likewise be identified by their covering that is made white with the blood of the Lamb (Rev 7:14). Joseph's garment was dipped in blood the first time he was stripped (Gen 37:31). But Joseph's garment is not dipped in blood this second time, which represents just this quality of being made white, a quality reinforced by Joseph's innocence. The emphasis in the First Advent is the shedding of the blood of Christ, while the emphasis in the Second Advent is the glorification of the Body of Christ. The blood of Christ was spilled once and for all and never again at the time of the First Advent. And the shedding of the blood of the Body connected with the Second Advent is only meaningful with regard to the glorification of the Body in so far as it is connected with the blood of Christ.

JOSEPH BEN JACOB

Genesis 39:16–18 And she laid up his garment by her, until his lord came home. 17 And she spake unto him according to these words, saying, The Hebrew servant, which thou hast brought unto us, came in unto me to mock me: 18 And it came to pass, as I lifted up my voice and cried, that he left his garment with me, and fled out.

Joseph being falsely accused by Potiphar's wicked wife prefigures the whore of Babylon and all she represents, falsely accusing the faithful in Christ in the end times. The cup of the whore is full of abominations and filthiness of her fornication (Rev 17:4), and she is drunk with the blood of the saints (Rev 17:6). The abomination of the whore, the blood of the saints, is the abomination of desolation (Mark 13:14).

Genesis 39:19 And it came to pass, when his master heard the words of his wife, which she spake unto him, saying, After this manner did thy servant to me; that his wrath was kindled.

The wrath of Potiphar portends the wrath of God being poured out in the end times. It is, however, the words of his wicked wife, not the deeds of righteous Joseph, that kindles Potiphar's anger, for after all Joseph is innocent. The wicked words of Potiphar's wife portend the blasphemies of the whore of Babylon. The person of Joseph is the formal object of the wrath of his master, which points to those who will be redeemed during the tribulation period, following the resurrection and rapture. But those who will be saved and exalted in Christ during the final tribulation period are not of themselves the object of the wrath of God just as Christ was not of himself the object of the wrath of God on the cross. Jesus Christ suffered in the place of us sinners, but he himself was sinless.

The new believers, or newly believing, who will suffer during the tribulation will not be sinless but will be in a state of forgiveness. The faithful believers who will be saved and exalted in Christ during the tribulation period, after the time of the resurrection and rapture, represent a final (earthly) remnant of the Body of Christ. And the Body of Christ will suffer up until the time of the Second Advent of Christ just as Christ himself suffered at the time of the First Advent. The death and resurrection of the Body follows the death and resurrection of the Head. The Second Advent will comprise a series of events—beginning with the resurrection and rapture of the faithful and culminating in the millennial kingdom of Christ—just as the First Advent comprised a series of events—beginning with the conception and birth of Jesus Christ and culminating in the ascension of Christ.

Genesis 39:20 And Joseph's master took him, and put him into the prison, a place where the king's prisoners [were] bound: and he was there in the prison.

Joseph was first thrown into a pit because of the unjust hatred of his wicked brothers, and he is now thrown into a prison because of the unjust hatred of Potiphar's adulterous wife. The former represents the death and resurrection of Christ at the time of the First Advent, while the latter represents the death and resurrection of the Body of Christ at the time of the Second Advent. Joseph being thrown into a pit alone because of his brethren prefigures the death of Christ alone for the sins of the world. Joseph now being thrown into a prison, not alone but surrounded by other prisoners, prefigures the multitude called into the Body of Christ. The emphasis on the prisoners being the king's prisoners points to humanity being under the judgment of God because of our transgressions against God.[27]

Genesis 39:21 But the LORD was with Joseph, and shewed him mercy, and gave him favour in the sight of the keeper of the prison.

The irony of Joseph being in prison but also being blessed prefigures Christ being dead in the flesh but nonetheless preaching in accord with the Spirit to those imprisoned by death (1 Pet 3:18–20). Christ calls forth the faithful out of the prison of sin and death, and Christ does this by virtue of his own death and finally by the authority of his resurrection (John 5:29).[28]

Genesis 39:22 And the keeper of the prison committed to Joseph's hand all the prisoners that [were] in the prison; and whatsoever they did there, he was the doer [of it].

The keeper of the king's prison is a proxy for the king himself, who represents God the Father. The prison keeper putting all the prisoners into Joseph's hand reflects God the Son judging all the peoples of the world according to the will of God the Father (John 5:30). The king represents God the Father, while Joseph represents God the Son. The keeper of the prison is the one who gives the power of the king unto Joseph, and thereby the keeper represents God the Spirit.

Genesis 39:23 The keeper of the prison looked not to any thing [that was] under his hand; because the LORD was with him, and [that] which he did, the LORD made [it] to prosper.

---

[27] "Such are God's ways of ordering: the very things by which we are hurt, by these same are we benefited [Chrysostom, *Homilies on the Acts*]" (Schaff, *Nicene and Post-Nicene Fathers: First Series* 11:295). Death must precede resurrection just as repentance must precede redemption just as law must precede grace.

[28] "Irony is a term with a range of meanings, all of them involving some sort of discrepancy or incongruity. . . . Like symbolism, irony makes it possible to suggest meanings without stating them. . . . The ironic contrast generates meaning" (Perrine 215–18). Irony and paradox are the coins of the realm in the kingdom of God.

Potiphar previously putting all things into the hand of Joseph is connected with the symbol of eating bread (Gen 39:6). But now the keeper of the prison putting all things into the hand of Joseph is connected with the symbols of bread and also wine as embodied by the king's baker and butler (Gen 40:20–22). The former emphasis on the symbol of bread alone represents an emphasis on the death of Christ at the time of the First Advent. The latter emphasis on bread and wine together represents an emphasis on the resurrection of the Body of Christ at the time of the Second Advent.

Baker and Butler

Genesis 40:1 And it came to pass after these things, [that] the butler [H8248] of the king of Egypt and [his] baker [H644] had offended their lord the king of Egypt.

The butler and the baker of the king of Egypt represent the blood and the body of the King of kings. The wine of the butler is the blood, while the bread of the baker is the body.[29] The body is to the blood as the First Advent is to the Second Advent. Christ died in the body at the time of the First Advent, but Christ will not exalt the faithful by the power of his blood until the time of the Second Advent. The overarching context of Joseph being cast into prison by Potiphar is the Second Advent, while the context of Joseph originally being cast into a pit by his brothers is the First Advent (Gen 37:23–24). And consistent with the context of the Second Advent, the butler is persistently listed before the baker, which represents the perspective of the Second Advent looking back to the First Advent. The body and blood being identified with the Second Advent points to the First Advent being the foundation of the Second Advent, likewise the Second Advent being the culmination of the First Advent. The Second Advent subsumes the First Advent just as the Covenant of Grace subsumes the Covenant of Law.

Genesis 40:2 And Pharaoh was wroth against two [of] his officers, against the chief of the butlers, and against the chief of the bakers.

The offenses of the baker and butler against their master represent the sins of the body and blood against God, which are the sins of the flesh and spirit. And Pharaoh being wroth against his butler and baker represents the judgment of all sins, whether seen or unseen, whether visible or invisible. The offense, or sin, of the baker points to Christ the Head dying in the flesh (body) at the time of the First Advent. The offense, or sin, of the butler points to the dying of the Body of Christ to the sinful nature (body and spirit) as culminating in the time of the Second Advent. The one man Christ fulfilled the law in his life and death and resurrection, but the death penalty of the law nevertheless remains, as

---

[29] The title *butler* [H8248] is connected with wine in Gen 40:11; the title *baker* [H644] is connected with bread in Gen 19:3.

evident by the faithful continuing to die even after the resurrection of Christ. And in this sense the Body of Christ must fulfill the law in imitation of Christ. The natural body, or carnal flesh, must die because the purely natural cannot enter into the fullness of the presence of God, but the promised inheritance of the faithful received by virtue of the blood, or Spirit, of Christ is the spiritual, or glorified, resurrection body.

Genesis 40:3 And he put them in ward in the house of the captain of the guard, into the prison, the place where Joseph [was] bound.

Joseph reflects God the Son, while the butler and the baker reflect the twofold natures of the Son, who is fully God and fully man. The emphasis on Joseph being bound in the same place as the baker and the butler affirms just this unity, or binding together, of the totality of the one person of the Son.

Genesis 40:4 And the captain [H8269] of the guard [H2876] charged Joseph with them, and he served them: and they continued a season in ward.

Joseph reflects God the Son, while the butler and the baker reflect the twofold natures of the Son, who is true God and true man. The emphasis on Joseph serving the butler and the baker testifies to the Son being God and man in action, as well as nature, and also revealing himself as such.[30]

Genesis 40:5 And they dreamed a dream both of them, each man his dream in one night, each man according to the interpretation [H6623] of his dream, the butler and the baker of the king of Egypt, which [were] bound in the prison.

The butler and baker dreaming their dreams in one night reflects the unity of the butler and baker that is the unity of the one man Christ, who is fully God and fully man. The word *interpretation* [H6623] means "interpretation (of a dream)" and is derived from the root "to interpret (a dream)" [H6622]. The implication that the dreams proceed from their interpretations and not vice versa is generally a statement of the sovereignty of God but specifically points to the butler and baker as representing something uniquely of God. The sovereignty of God over all things, heaven and earth, is embodied by the Son, who is all things, true God and true man. The whole of creation proceeds from God and the whole of creation reflects God, whereby true God not only can be true man but true God must be true man.

---

[30] Guzik identifies the *captain* [H8269] of the *guard* [H2876] in Gen 40:4 as the same as Joseph's original Egyptian master, Potiphar, because one of Potiphar's titles in Gen 39:1 is *captain* [H8269] of the *guard* [H2876] (Guzik 225; Gen 40:1–4). Whether or not this is true, the key point is that the death and resurrection of Joseph in the house of Potiphar is purposefully linked to the death and resurrection of Joseph in prison.

JOSEPH BEN JACOB

Genesis 40:6–7 And Joseph came in unto them in the morning, and looked upon them, and, behold, they [were] sad [H2196]. 7 And he asked Pharaoh's officers that [were] with him in the ward of his lord's house, saying, Wherefore look ye [so] sadly [H7451] to day?

The butler and baker are here again viewed collectively. The word *sad* [H2196] means "to be out of humour, vexed, enraged," while the word *sadly* [H7451] means "bad, evil." The evil vexation of the baker and butler, the body and blood, represents the rejection of the Body of Christ culminating in the Second Advent, but viewed as the rejection of the Head and Body together. The rejection of the Body of Christ at the time of the Second Advent comprehends the rejection of Christ at the time of the First Advent.

Genesis 40:8 And they said unto him, We have dreamed a dream, and [there is] no interpreter of it. And Joseph said unto them, [Do] not interpretations [belong] to God? tell me [them], I pray you.

Joseph affirms that the interpretation of dreams belongs to God and only to God, but then Joseph proceeds to interpret the dreams himself. Joseph thereby simultaneously distinguishes himself from God and also identifies himself with the Lord God, in testimony to the oneness of the Trinity. The one given the interpretation of dreams is Joseph representing God the Son, who is fully man and fully God. The actual dreaming of dreams according to their interpretations represents the movement of God the Holy Spirit. And Pharaoh's servants, representing Pharaoh, originally dreaming the dreams represents God the Father, from whom the Spirit and Son proceed.

Genesis 40:9–10 And the chief butler told his dream to Joseph, and said to him, In my dream, behold, a vine [was] before me; 10 And in the vine [were] three branches: and it [was] as though it budded, [and] her blossoms shot forth; and the clusters thereof brought forth ripe grapes:

The one vine with three branches represents three days, likewise three millennia, and ultimately the triunity of God. The three days connecting the death and resurrection of Christ are like the three millennia connecting the First and Second Advents of Christ. The emphasis in the First Advent is the death of Christ, while the emphasis in the Second Advent is the resurrection of the Body of Christ. The vine budding and blossoming represents the emergence of new life and, thereby, reflects the culmination of the call to faith in Christ that is the resurrection of the faithful in Christ. The symbol of grapes represents the blood of the new covenant that is the Covenant of Grace (Matt 26:27–29). The emphasis on the grapes being ripe and therefore ready for harvest points specifically to the end times. The Covenant of Law is identified most closely with the death of Christ at the time of the First Advent, while the Covenant of Grace is identified most closely with the resurrection of the Body of Christ at the time of the Second Advent. The Covenant of Law precedes the Covenant of

Grace just as the First Advent precedes the Second Advent just as the Head precedes the Body.

Genesis 40:11 And Pharaoh's cup [was] in my hand: and I took the grapes, and pressed them into Pharaoh's cup, and I gave the cup into Pharaoh's hand.

Pharaoh's butler pressing grapes into Pharaoh's cup represents the winepress of the wrath of God (Rev 14:19) filling the cup of his indignation (Rev 14:10). Pharaoh is not depicted as drinking from the cup but rather as holding the cup. Pharaoh's butler pressing the grapes and putting the cup into Pharaoh's hand points to the Son acting as the hand of God in the judgment proceeding from the Father. The cup of God represents the cup of the new covenant of the grace of God and also the cup of the fierceness of the wrath of God just as the blood of Christ shed on the cross represents both the grace of God and also the judgment, or law, of God (Luke 22:20).

Genesis 40:12–13 And Joseph said unto him, This [is] the interpretation of it: The three branches [are] three days: 13 Yet within three days shall Pharaoh lift up thine head, and restore thee unto thy place: and thou shalt deliver Pharaoh's cup into his hand, after the former manner when thou wast his butler.

Joseph is not God and therefore does not interpret dreams by his own power, but nonetheless Joseph does represent God and specifically God the Son (Gen 40:8). Joseph reflects God the Son, while the butler and the baker reflect the twofold natures of the Son, who is fully God and true man. Joseph giving the interpretation of the dream without specifically attributing the interpretation to God, the Father, points to the deity of the Son. The butler being restored to a former estate, or life, reflects not only the death and resurrection of Christ at the time of the First Advent but also the death and resurrection of the First and Second Advents viewed collectively.

Genesis 40:14 But think on me when it shall be well with thee, and shew kindness, I pray thee, unto me, and make mention of me unto Pharaoh, and bring me out of this house:

The imprisonment of Joseph foreshadows the death and resurrection that will be embodied by the tribulation period ending with the glorious return of Jesus Christ. Joseph asks the butler to bring him out of prison at the time when all is well with the butler and, thereby, prophesies that he will be brought out of prison at just such a time when all is well. The persons of the baker and butler reflect flesh and spirit, likewise law and grace, and finally the twofold natures of the Son, who is fully man and fully God. The time when all will be well is the time of grace, that is, the time of the resurrection of the faithful in the Son. The emphasis in the First Advent is the Son of man, while the emphasis in the Second Advent is the Son of God.

Genesis 40:15 For indeed I was stolen away out of the land of the Hebrews: and here also have I done nothing that they should put me into the dungeon.

Joseph having been stolen out of the land represents the lost dominion of Adam, likewise mankind, while the innocence of Joseph represents the sinlessness of Christ and likewise the redeemed in Christ. The land of the Hebrews, or the land that has been promised, signifies the whole of physical creation, including the physical body and our corresponding dominion over physical creation. And such a material, or literal, dominion is a prerequisite for freewill, or one could say it is an attribute of freewill. The image of being out of the land represents the death of the flesh. And the connection between the physical body and physical creation is affirmed in the promised renewal of physical creation, which is part and parcel of the resurrection, or rebirth, of the physical body (Rev 21:1). Physical creation is the inherent extension of the physical body, while the whole of physicality represents the realm, or dominion, of freewill. One cannot be said to have freewill unless one has both the freedom and the ability to exercise freewill. The natural body precedes the spiritual body, but both the natural body and the spiritual bodies are true physical bodies. The difference between the natural body and the spiritual, or glorified, body is that the natural body is governed by the law of the flesh, which is death, while the spiritual body is governed by the Spirit of grace, which is eternal life.

Genesis 40:16 When the chief baker saw that the interpretation was good, he said unto Joseph, I also [was] in my dream, and, behold, [I had] three white baskets on my head:

The fate of the baker is bad, while the fate of the butler is good. The two persons of the baker and butler embody flesh and spirit and likewise law and grace. The bad fate is the death of the mortal natural body, while the good fate is the resurrection of the immortal spiritual, or glorified, body. The baker and butler exist side by side just as the bad and good fates exist side by side, in accordance with freewill. The baker seeks the good interpretation of Joseph and, thereby, symbolically submits to the person of Joseph because of the good fate of the butler. Jesus Christ would likewise endure the cross in the flesh because of the joy that was set before him (Heb 12:2).

Genesis 40:17 And in the uppermost [H5945] basket [there was] of all manner [H3978] of bakemeats for Pharaoh; and the birds [H5775] did eat them out of the basket upon my head.

The word *uppermost* [H5945] (uppermost basket) is elsewhere used to describe the *most high* [H5945] (the most high God), which points to the coming of the person of Jesus Christ (Gen 14:18). The uppermost basket is the third basket furthest from the condemned head of the baker and, thereby, points to the third millennium from the condemnation of the Head at the time of the First Advent. The third millennium from the First Advent is the uppermost, or most high, millennium, signifying the presence of the most high in the millennial kingdom. The person of the baker is identified with the body, or flesh, in contrast to the butler who is identified with the blood, or the life in the blood, representing the Spirit. The image of *birds* [H5775] eating all *manner* [H3978] of bakemeats from off the third basket of the baker portends the coming judgment of all flesh. And this imagery is echoed in the warning of Jeremiah that the flesh of the faithless will be *meat* (or food) [H3978] for the *fowls* [H5775] of heaven (Jer 16:4, 19:7, 34:20). And it is foretold that in the end times the fowls that fly in the midst of heaven will be called together unto the supper of the great God, unto the supper of the flesh of the enemies of God (Rev 19:17–18). Nonetheless, the condemnation of the world is intimately related to the condemnation of Christ for the sake of the world.

The condemnation of the baker prefigures the condemnation of Christ, likewise the condemnation of the Body of Christ in imitation of Christ and in communion with Christ. And the condemnation of Christ for the whole world can also be compared to the condemnation of the whole world. Christ embodies the whole of creation because the whole of creation has been made according to him and through him, whereby the whole of creation is of him (John 1:3). The parallel between the death and resurrection of the world and the death and resurrection of Christ for the world is seen in the parallel between the wooden ark of Noah and the wooden cross of Christ (1 Pet 3:17–22). The baptism of Christ on the cross for the world is the baptism of the world, or it would not be efficacious. It is correct to say that God speaks and creates something out of nothing. But it is more correct to say that God speaks and his Word is creation, whereby creation belongs to God because creation is from God and of God. The Word of God is the world, and therefore the world is intimately connected with the Word. Christ calling the faithful to be his brother and sister and mother is shocking, but he does not exaggerate and his call in and of him is not vain (Matt 12:50). Christ is all things to all people at all times, whereby the death of his body portends the death of all creation (1 Cor 9:22).

Genesis 40:18–19 And Joseph answered and said, This [is] the interpretation thereof: The three baskets [are] three days: 19 Yet within three days shall Pharaoh lift up thy head from off thee, and shall hang thee on a tree; and the birds shall eat thy flesh from off thee.

The tree to which Christ and likewise the Body of Christ are nailed is the tree of the knowledge of good and evil (Gen 2:16–17). The three days of the baker and the three days of the butler are the same three days, as evident in their meeting their fates on the same day. The three days of the baker and butler point to the third millennium from the time of the crucifixion of Christ. The two fates of the baker and the butler are connected and shared but also different and separate. The shared but separate fates of the baker and butler represent death and resurrection, specifically as embodied by the tribulation period in the end times.[31]

Genesis 40:20 And it came to pass the third day, [which was] Pharaoh's birthday, that he made a feast unto all his servants [H5650]: and he lifted up the head of the chief butler and of the chief baker among his servants [H5650].

The word *servant* [H5650] (Pharaoh's servants) means "slave, servant." The idea that Pharaoh on his own birthday would make a feast for his slaves, or servants, is strange even though the servants may be high ranking officials. One would rather expect the feast to be held strictly in honor of Pharaoh himself and without any reference to his servants. But Pharaoh represents the one true God, and therefore the birthday of Pharaoh represents the birthday not only of God but also of those who are one with God. And the birthday of God can be considered the day of the appearing, or revealing, of God. The emphasis on Pharaoh's birthday being on the third day points to the third millennium from the First Advent, corresponding to the Second Advent. And it is the Second Advent that is the day of the birth, or rebirth and resurrection, of the Body of Christ. The feast that Pharaoh makes for his servants on the third day is the wedding supper of the Lamb in the third millennium from the First Advent (Rev 19:9). The heads of the baker and butler, representing law and grace, being lifted up together reflects the essential unity of the First and Second Advents. The unity of the First and Second Advents is the unity of death and resurrection. This is the wedding supper of the Lamb, in contrast to the wedding supper of the Lion (Rev 5:5). The faithful are united with Jesus Christ at the time of the Second Advent by virtue of the First Advent and only by virtue of the First Advent.[32]

The person of Pharaoh represents God the Father, in contrast to the person of Joseph, who represents God the Son, while the blessing that rests upon Joseph represents God the Holy Spirit. The birthday of God the Father, the day of revealing God, is the time of the formation of Adam in the image of God. The original image of God before the Fall of Man is most closely identified with the Father, not the Son, because the original creation embodies birth, in contrast to rebirth and redemption. Adam, or created man, is created in the image of the Father, who is the creator, or spiritually procreator. The day of revealing God the Son is the First Advent, while the day of revealing God the Holy Spirit is the Second Advent. The First Advent is the time of the birth of

---

[31] In contrast to the butler's dream, the baker's dream does not show him, the baker, actually in the presence of Pharaoh or personally preparing his delicacies and, also, his bakemeats never even reach the hand of Pharaoh (Sarna 279; Gen 40:18–19). The condemnation of the natural body is irrevocable.

[32] "Joseph's fellow-sufferers were like the two thieves that were crucified with Christ—the one saved, the other condemned" (Henry 1:227; Gen 40:20–23). Law compared with grace is death compared with life.

Christ, while the Second Advent is the time of the birth, or rebirth, of the Body of Christ, which comes by the power of the Spirit. But the progressive days of revealing the triunity of God finally forms one image of the one God. The lifting up of the baker and butler on Pharaoh's birthday marks the validation of Joseph's interpretations and, thereby, marks the beginning of the liberation of Joseph from prison as if a birthday. And this is also the day of revealing the blessing that rests upon Joseph, which is God the Spirit. The resurrection of Christ and the resurrection of the Body of Christ should be viewed as one event, according to the one promise (of the indwelling Holy Spirit) related by the original formation of Adam in the very image of God.

Genesis 40:21–22 And he restored the chief butler unto his butlership again; and he gave the cup into Pharaoh's hand: 22 But he hanged the chief baker: as Joseph had interpreted to them.

The dream is followed by the interpretation of the dream, which is finally followed by the manifestation of the reality of the dream. The original dream represents a prophecy and a promise that can be likened to the promise of life inherent in the original creation of Adam. The interpretation of the dream represents an explicit explanation of the promise, which can be likened to the incarnation of Christ at the time of the First Advent in fulfillment of the law and prophets. The manifestation of the reality of the dream represents the fulfillment of the promise, which can be likened to the fulfillment of all things in the Body of Christ at the time of the Second Advent. The threefold creation of Adam followed by the First and Second Advents of Christ reflects the triune Father, Son, and Spirit that is the fabric of creation and likewise the pattern, or meaning and significance, of creation. To have a dream, or promise, that is connected to reality without an interpretation, or without the correct interpretation, is to be separated from this basic fabric of creation, likewise to be separated from the triunity of God. To have a dream, or promise, that is connected to reality without the person of Jesus Christ is to be separate from the Body of Christ.

Genesis 40:23 Yet did not the chief butler remember Joseph, but forgat him.

The butler forgetting Joseph in prison represents the delay between the First and Second Advents, especially the final delay during the final tribulation period. The person of the butler is identified with Jesus Christ and particularly with the divinity of Christ, whereby the forgetfulness of the butler represents nothing less than a divine forgetfulness. The forgetfulness identified with the tribulation at the time of the Second Advent recalls the forsakenness identified with the tribulation of the cross at the time of the First Advent, whereby the two tribulations embodied by the First and Second Advents are viewed together as one (Mark 15:34). The forsakenness identified with the tribulation of the First Advent is also connected to the forgetfulness identified with the tribulation of the Flood (Gen 8:1). The first destruction (by water) is fulfilled in the second destruction (by fire) just as the death and resurrection of Christ is fulfilled in the death and resurrection of the Body of Christ. The delay of judgment, or the figurative forgetting of judgment, is the call to repentance established from the foundation of the world.

The Lord God is omniscient, and thus God forgetting cannot be a purely literal, or human, reality. The image of God forgetting represents a putting away of a thing from the mind, or presence, of God. And a thing being put away from the mind, or presence, of God is like the thing not existing at all. The thing that God puts outside the fullness of his presence is sin and likewise sinful man, or Adam-kind (Exod 33:20). The Lord God remembering our sins no more is the new covenant (Jer 31:31–34). But how is this possible? When we become the new creation in Christ, in the Body of Christ, the old creation in Adam is destroyed and therefore no longer exists, whereby the new creation can be considered to have no connection to the old creation. To say the new creation is guilty because of the old creation would be like saying that one man is responsible for the sins of another man (Deut 24:16). If one says that God creates things out of nothing, then conversely when God destroys a thing, it is truly nothing. If one says that the words, or thoughts, of God are creation, or reality, then conversely when God destroys a thing, it is in a very real sense no longer in the presence, or mind, of God.[33]

Interpreter of Dreams

Genesis 41:1 And it came to pass at the end of two full years, that Pharaoh dreamed: and, behold, he stood by the river.

Joseph originally being cast into a pit by his brothers prefigures the death of Christ at the time of the First Advent (Gen 37:23–24), while Joseph being cast into prison prefigures the death of the Body of Christ at the time of the Second Advent (Gen 39:20). The baker and the butler reflect the twofold natures of Christ, being true man and true God. The baker and butler having their heads lifted up on the third day reflects the resurrection of Christ on the third day and the corresponding resurrection of the Body of Christ in the third millennium (Gen 40:20). The dream of Pharaoh now coming after two full years is connected to Joseph finally being brought out of prison and, thereby, points to the promised millennial kingdom following two full millennia from the time of the First Advent (Gen 41:14). An obvious parallel exists between days and years because both represent the completion of a cycle, but the parallel between days and millennia is more subtle, being established by special revelation.

---

[33] "How prone are men to forget and neglect in prosperity . . . But, although reflecting no credit on the butler, it was wisely ordered, in the providence of God, that he [the butler] should forget Joseph. The Divine purposes required that the son of Israel should obtain his deliverance in another way, and by other means" (Jamieson et al. 1:241; Gen 40:23). The nature of man is the providence of God.

A day is the completion of the cycle of darkness and light, while a year is the completion of the cycle of the seasons of cold and hot. The parallel between days and millennia is not obvious but is formally defined by special revelation in the Scriptures (2 Pet 3:8). The parallel between days and millennia can also be perceived in the parallel between the original seven days of creation and the seven millennia of the Biblical, or historical, timeline. And the cycle of revelation established by the millennia can be perceived in the progression from Adam, Noah, and Abraham, and so forth, in relation to the millennia. The baker and butler being lifted up before Joseph is lifted up is like prophecy preceding the fulfillment of prophecy, likewise law preceding grace, and likewise days preceding years and millennia. The progression from days to years to millennia is like the progressive revelation of the Trinity. The days of the original creation reflect God the Father, who is our creator. The years of creation reflect the years of the earthly ministry of God the Son, who is our redeemer. And the millennia of creation, representing the most subtle of cycles, reflect the movement throughout all creation of God the Holy Spirit, who is our sanctifier and not coincidentally the most subtle person of the Trinity.[34]

Genesis 41:2–7 And, behold, there came up out of the river seven well favoured kine [H6510] and fatfleshed; and they fed in a meadow. 3 And, behold, seven other kine [H6510] came up after them out of the river, ill favoured and leanfleshed; and stood by the [other] kine [H6510] upon the brink of the river. 4 And the ill favoured and leanfleshed kine [H6510] did eat up the seven well favoured and fat kine [H6510]. So Pharaoh awoke. 5 And he slept and dreamed the second time: and, behold, seven ears of corn [H7641] came up upon one stalk, rank and good. 6 And, behold, seven thin ears [H7641] and blasted with the east wind sprung up after them. 7 And the seven thin ears [H7641] devoured the seven rank and full ears [H7641]. And Pharaoh awoke, and, behold, [it was] a dream.

The *kine* (cows) [H6510] being followed by *ears* (ears of corn, or grain) [H7641] suggests a looking backward in time because *kine* [H6510] represent a higher life-form compared with *ears* [H7641]. The nature of progressive revelation is to expand in scope and not to contract. And cows eat grain and not vice versa. The exaltation of the second firstborn Joseph began with two dreams and now ends with two dreams. The original two dreams of Joseph were the dream of the sheaves followed by the dream of the sun and the moon and the stars (Gen 37:7, 37:9). The original two dreams dreamed by Joseph were forward looking, while the present two dreams interpreted by Joseph are backward looking. The imagery of the sun and the moon and the stars

---

[34] "If we do not believe that God's love is almighty, how can we believe that the Father could create us, the Son redeem us, and the Holy Spirit sanctify us?" (Rom. Catholic Church, *Catechism* 81). The will of God Almighty, which is mercy and grace for his children, is itself almighty, or unflagging, pressing inexorably unto the fulfillment of all things in the end times.

compared with the imagery of sheaves represents the heavenly compared with the earthly, likewise the spiritual compared with the natural, and likewise grace compared with law. The two pairs of dreams connect the First and Second Advents of Christ. The first pair of dreams is connected with Joseph being cast into a pit in Canaan and corresponds to the death of Jesus Christ (Gen 37:20). The final pair of dreams is connected with Joseph being brought out of prison in Egypt and corresponds to the resurrection of the Body of Christ in communion with Jesus Christ (Gen 41:14).[35]

Genesis 41:8 And it came to pass in the morning that his spirit was troubled; and he sent and called for all the magicians of Egypt, and all the wise men thereof: and Pharaoh told them his dream; but [there was] none that could interpret them unto Pharaoh.

Pharaoh represents God Almighty, while the magicians and wise men of Egypt represent the people of the world. The magicians and wise men of Pharaoh further represent the people of the earthly church, particularly the apostate church in the end times, not relying upon the Lord but striving to use human power and wisdom. The dream of Pharaoh represents the will of God, whereby Pharaoh calling upon the magicians and wise men of Egypt to interpret his dream represents the call to understanding and repentance. Therefore, the magicians and wise men not being able to interpret Pharaoh's dream reflects the apostate not perceiving the warning signs that increasingly announce the coming judgment of the world. Such spiritual blindness and apostasy has marked all history, but will increasingly mark the end times and especially the church of the end times.

Genesis 41:9–13 Then spake the chief butler unto Pharaoh, saying, I do remember my faults [H2399] this day: 10 Pharaoh was wroth with his servants, and put me in ward in the captain of the guard's house, [both] me and the chief baker: 11 And we dreamed a dream in one night, I and he; we dreamed each man according to the interpretation of his dream. 12 And [there was] there with us a young man, an Hebrew, servant to the captain of the guard; and we told him, and he interpreted to us our dreams; to each man according to his dream he did interpret. 13 And it came to pass, as he interpreted to us, so it was; me he restored unto mine office, and him he hanged.

The word *fault* [H2399] (my faults) means "sin." The butler remembering his faults, or sins, is connected with the baker being hanged and also to the butler being restored to his prior estate. The fates of the baker and butler are distinct but coupled. The baker and butler are identified with flesh and spirit, likewise

---

[35] Pharaoh being a mere observer within his dreams, not an actual participant, indicates a national significance, not a personal one (Sarna 282; Gen 41:8). The Body of Christ, in contrast to Christ the Head.

law and grace, likewise the twofold natures of the Son, and likewise the First and Second Advents. The faults, or sins, that are remembered at the time of the Second Advent are the sins that were nailed to the cross at the time of the First Advent. This is not the remembrance of the sins themselves but the reality that they were nailed to the cross. For the butler does not recount, or name, his sins but simply states that he had escaped the judgment of the baker. Thus figuratively the baker died in the place of the Butler. There is actually no account anywhere in the Bible of what specific sins the butler or baker committed, which testifies that our sins, or sinful nature, are truly taken away in Christ and that in Christ there is not any sin anymore (1 John 3:5).

Genesis 41:14 Then Pharaoh sent and called Joseph, and they brought him hastily out of the dungeon: and he shaved [himself], and changed [H2498] his raiment, and came in unto Pharaoh.

Joseph being stripped was emphasized when his brothers cast him into a pit (Gen 37:23–24) and again when Potiphar cast him into prison (Gen 39:12–20). But Joseph changing his raiment is emphasized now at the time of his being brought up out of prison. And the new raiment of Joseph represents a first sign of his new stature that will be finally established when Pharaoh arrays him in vestures of fine linen (Gen 41:42). The new stature of Joseph prefigures the glorification of the Body of Christ at the time of the millennial kingdom. Joseph now *changes* [H2498] his raiment before he warns Pharaoh of the coming seven evil years. But immediately after Joseph warns Pharaoh of the evil seven years, Pharaoh will *array* [H3847] him in fine vestures. The *changing* [H2498] of raiment that precedes the being *arrayed* [H3847] in fine vestures prefigures the resurrection and rapture of the faithful that will precede the millennial kingdom. The warning of the evil seven years that separates the *changing* [H2498] and the being *arrayed* [H3847] portends the final tribulation period.[36]

Genesis 41:15–16 And Pharaoh said unto Joseph, I have dreamed a dream, and [there is] none that can interpret it: and I have heard say of thee, [that] thou canst understand a dream to interpret it. 16 And Joseph answered Pharaoh, saying, [It is] not in me: God shall give Pharaoh an answer of peace.

Pharaoh as the dreamer represents the originator of the dream that is God the Father. Joseph as the interpreter, or speaker of the meaning, of the dream represents the Word made flesh that is God the Son. And the movement of God the Spirit is perceived indirectly by the manifestation of the dream itself. Joseph distinguishes himself from God just as the Son distinguishes himself from the Father (Matt 26:39). But in foretelling an answer of peace without

---

[36] When at long last the proper time appointed by God had arrived, the suddenness of Joseph's liberation and exaltation was breathtaking (Guzik 229; Gen 41:8–14). And so it will be in the end times, when everything changes in the twinkling of an eye.

even hearing the dream, Joseph also identifies himself with God just as the Son identifies himself as God (John 14:9).[37]

Genesis 41:17–24 And Pharaoh said unto Joseph, In my dream, behold, I stood upon the bank of the river: 18 And, behold, there came up out of the river seven kine, fatfleshed and well favoured; and they fed in a meadow: 19 And, behold, seven other kine came up after them, poor and very ill favoured and leanfleshed, such as I never saw in all the land of Egypt for badness: 20 And the lean and the ill favoured kine did eat up the first seven fat kine: 21 And when they had eaten them up, it could not be known that they had eaten them; but they [were] still ill favoured, as at the beginning. So I awoke. 22 And I saw in my dream, and, behold, seven ears came up in one stalk, full and good: 23 And, behold, seven ears, withered, thin, [and] blasted with the east wind, sprung up after them: 24 And the thin ears devoured the seven good ears: and I told [this] unto the magicians; but [there was] none that could declare [it] to me.

The extreme nature of the coming seven evil years is further emphasized in this second telling of the dream of Pharaoh (Gen 41:1–8). Pharaoh having never seen such kine (cows) in the land of Egypt is emphasized (Gen 41:19) and also emphasized is the seven ill favored kine remaining ill favored even after eating the seven fat kine (Gen 41:21). And the coming reality of the seven evil years will be yet more traumatic as compared with the mere foretelling of the seven evil years (Gen 47:13). The escalating anxiety evident in the progression from the telling, or foretelling, of Pharaoh's dream to the reality of Pharaoh's dream is itself a harbinger of the escalating apostasy and concomitant suffering that will culminate in the end times. There being none other than Joseph who can declare the dream unto Pharaoh is a testimony to the exclusivity of the one salvation in Jesus Christ and likewise to the oneness of the God of the Bible.

The first and second foretelling of the seven evil years followed by the reality of the seven evil years reflects the Fall of Man followed by the rejection of Christ at the First Advent followed by the rejection of the Body of Christ culminating in the Second Advent. The Fall of Man is the original rejection of the promise of life (Gen 2:8–9). The rejection of the First Advent is the rejection of the call to repentance (Mark 1:15). And the rejection of the Second Advent is the final rejection that is the rejection of the gift of redemption itself (Luke 21:28). The rejection of the original promise of life corresponding to the Fall of Man represents a rejection of the plan of God, which is the temporal natural body (Gen 3:19). The rejection of the First Advent represents a rejection of God the Son and also the Father, which can at least in principle be forgiven,

---

[37] "It was obviously to Joseph's advantage that the chief butler . . . had not mentioned Joseph's name to Pharaoh until all the astrologers had failed . . . Otherwise, if Joseph had been called before them, it might have been thought that they [the astrologers] were able to interpret the dream [*Genesis Rabbah*]" (Rapaport, *Midrash* 85–86). The natural must precede the spiritual just as the law must precede grace.

or tolerated, for a time (Luke 23:34). But the rejection of the Second Advent represents a rejection of God the Holy Spirit along with the Son and the Father, which can in no way ever be forgiven (Luke 12:10).

Genesis 41:25 And Joseph said unto Pharaoh, The dream of Pharaoh [is] one: God hath shewed Pharaoh what he [is] about to do.

Proclaiming that the two dreams of Pharaoh are in fact one dream represents an emphasis on the comparison between cows and corn, in contrast to the comparison between bad and good cows or between bad and good corn. The ears of corn compared with the cows reflects the dichotomy of flesh and spirit and likewise law and grace. Cows are a higher form of life than corn, or grain, just as grace transcends law just as spirit animates flesh. The two dreams of Pharaoh being one dream further reflects the unity of law and grace, likewise the unity of the First and Second Advents, and likewise the one person of the Son being true man and true God. The unity of Pharaoh's two dreams is connected to God showing Pharaoh what he is about to do and, thereby, reflects the character of God the Son. One aspect of the incarnation is God showing us what he is about to do, that is, God showing what we shall be like in the resurrection (1 John 3:2). And this is the unity of the First and Second Advents. This is the death and resurrection of Christ the Head and the Body of Christ viewed as one single event.

The two dreams of Pharaoh are the third pair in a series of three pairs of dreams. The first pair is the dream of the sheaves followed by the dream of the sun and the moon and the stars (Gen 37:7, 37:9). The second pair is the dream of the baker followed by the dream of the butler (Gen 40:4–5). These three pairs of dreams form a group demarcating the journey of Joseph from the house of Jacob to the house of Potiphar to the house of Pharaoh. The persistent pairing of dreams reflects the universal dichotomy of flesh and spirit and likewise law and grace. And the pairs of dreams forming a distinct threefold series reflects the formation of Adam followed by the First and Second Advents of Christ. The first pair is dreamed by Joseph himself, reflecting the original act of creation. The second and third pairs are interpreted by Joseph, reflecting the unity of the First and Second Advents of Christ and likewise the unity of Jesus Christ and the Body of Christ. And the pairwise construction of this threefold revelation points to God the Son being the one who reveals, or makes visible, the reality of the Trinity.[38]

Genesis 41:26 The seven good kine [are] seven years; and the seven good ears [are] seven years: the dream [is] one.

---

[38] "The name *God*, not *Jehovah*, is used in speaking to foreigners and heathens [who are distinguished from the chosen people]" (Jamieson et al. 1:243; Gen 41:25). The name *God* (Elohim) is to the name *Lord* (YHWH) as the law is to grace, as the flesh is to spirit, as the earth is to heaven, as man is to the God-man Christ.

Pharaoh at first tells his dream in vain to his magicians and wise men and, thereby, shows a reliance upon flesh and not the Spirit, which reflects the Fall of Adam (Gen 41:8). Pharaoh then telling his dream to Joseph, who recounts his dream with its interpretation, reflects the First Advent of Jesus Christ. And the dream of Pharaoh in the end being understood throughout Egypt, spiritually the whole world, represents yet a third telling, which reflects the manifestation of the power of the Holy Spirit throughout all creation at the time of the Second Advent. Joseph recounting the dream to Pharaoh is not a separate telling but rather a response to Pharaoh's second telling, whereby Pharaoh telling his dream to Joseph being juxtaposed to Joseph retelling the dream to Pharaoh reflects the twofold natures of the Son. This is the dichotomy of flesh and spirit and likewise law and grace. The simple telling of the dream reflects the explicit reality of the flesh, while the interpreting of the dream reflects the implicit reality of the Spirit.

Further, the telling and interpreting and proclaiming of Pharaoh's dreams are simultaneously a threefold pattern reflecting the Trinity. And the dreams of Joseph followed by the dreams of the baker and butler followed by the dreams of Pharaoh also reflect the Trinity (Gen 37:7–9, 40:5, 41:1–7). An alignment, or convergence, marked by the dreams of Pharaoh is therefore evident, particularly as represented by the final universal telling of Pharaoh's dreams, and thereby the fullness of the Trinity, or the fullness of revelation, can be connected to the millennial kingdom of Christ to be set up in the end times, which is so clearly and dramatically signified by Joseph ruling under Pharaoh.

The seven years of famine represent seven evil years, specifically seven years of a famine of the Word of God (Amos 8:11). The seven evil years of Pharaoh portend the tribulation period of seven years at the time of the Second Advent (Dan 9:27). The correct context being the Second Advent is established and affirmed by the existence and layering of threefold, or Trinitarian, series within the text. The dreams of Pharaoh are the third and final pair demarcating the overall journey of Joseph (Gen 37:19–20, 40:14, 41:14). Also, the rise of Joseph to authority over his brothers follows his being rejected by his brothers (Gen 37:23–24), which follows Joseph being the son uniquely identified with his father, figuratively his creator (Gen 37:3). And the person of Joseph represents the crowned head not merely of Egypt under Pharaoh but also of the kingdom established by Jacob in fulfillment of the threefold progression from Abraham to Isaac to Jacob (Gen 49:26). But what then are the seven years of plenty that precede the seven evil years?

The years of famine represent a famine of the Word of God, while the years of plenty represent an outpouring of the Word. And the time of the greatest outpouring of the Word before the seven years of tribulation is the period encompassing the public ministry of Christ and the subsequent outpouring of the Holy Spirit. The seven years of plenty are then separated from the seven years of famine by the church age, though ultimately the First and Second Advents are still viewed as one event. And since Christ embodies all things, the death and resurrection of Christ is further connected to the death and resurrection of the entire world. Tribulation marks both the beginning and end of the millennial kingdom, whereby the seven of plenty that precede the seven of famine can finally be compared to the totality of the seven millennia of natural creation that are concluded and destroyed by the final tribulation, which bookends the Sabbath millennium of Christ.

Genesis 41:27 And the seven thin and ill favoured kine that came up after them [are] seven years; and the seven empty ears blasted with the east wind shall be seven years of famine.

The seven years of famine being marked by the blasting by the east wind prefigures the coming of Christ at the ending of the tribulation period, as lightning out of the east that shines as far as the west (Matt 24:27).

Genesis 41:28 This [is] the thing which I have spoken unto Pharaoh: What God [is] about to do he sheweth unto Pharaoh.

What God is about to do is not simply one thing but everything, because God is all things. The dreams of Pharaoh apply to his time and also to our time. The overarching nature of God is infinite even when he acts in the finite, whereby the specific manifestations of God in the natural always reflect a larger spiritual reality.

Genesis 41:29–31 Behold, there come seven years of great plenty throughout all the land of Egypt: 30 And there shall arise after them seven years of famine; and all the plenty shall be forgotten in the land of Egypt; and the famine shall consume the land; 31 And the plenty shall not be known in the land by reason of that famine following; for it [shall be] very grievous.

The years of plenty being forgotten during the years of famine portends a universal apostasy of people during the tribulation period, forgetting God and likewise the goodness of God. The emphasis on the famine consuming the land portends a terrible desolation of the world in the end times.

Genesis 41:32 And for that the dream was doubled unto Pharaoh twice; [it is] because the thing [is] established by God, and God will shortly bring it to pass.

The doubling of Pharaoh's dream represents the certainty and imminence of God. The thing being already established by God represents the certainty of God, while God shortly bringing the thing to pass represents the imminence of God. The two qualities of certainty and imminence are like the birthright and the blessing that belong to the firstborn (Gen 27:36).[39] The firstborn represents all mankind in the first man Adam. And that which is shortly to come to pass is the promised redemption of the firstborn in Jesus, who is himself the firstborn from the dead (Exod 13:11–15, Col 1:18). The birthright is the natural body and likewise the law that governs the natural body, while the blessing is the spiritual, or glorified, resurrection body and likewise the grace that governs the spiritual body. The natural is the certainty of God, while the spiritual is the imminence of God. The birthright precedes the blessing just as law precedes grace just as the natural body precedes the spiritual body just as the First Advent precedes the Second Advent. And the certainty of redemption is established in the First Advent, while the imminence of redemption will be fulfilled in the Second Advent. The significance of doubling is finally the unity of law and grace, likewise the unity of flesh and spirit, in the one Body of Christ, sanctified by the Holy Spirit in accordance with the will of the Father.

Genesis 41:33 Now therefore let Pharaoh look out a man discreet and wise, and set him over the land of Egypt.

Pharaoh represents God the Father, while Joseph represents God the Son. Pharaoh sets Joseph over all the land just as the Father sets the Son over all things (John 3:35). The Son is the man who is discreet and wise.

Genesis 41:34 Let Pharaoh do [this], and let him appoint officers over the land, and take up the fifth part of the land of Egypt in the seven plenteous years.

Pharaoh represents God the Father, while the officers of Pharaoh represent the angels of God. The emphasis on taking up a fifth part of the land points to the time of the First Advent. The fifth part taken up during the whole of the first seven points to the fifth of the seven millennia from Adam.[40]

Genesis 41:35 And let them gather all the food of those good years that come, and lay up corn under the hand of Pharaoh, and let them keep food in the cities.

The corn, or grain, taken up by Pharaoh represents the Bread of Life (John 6:48). And the cities of Pharaoh represent the city of God (Heb 11:10). The first good seven reflects the First Advent, while the second evil seven reflects the tribulation period that will herald the Second Advent. The number 7 represents

---

[39] The inheritance of a material double portion also belongs to the firstborn, but the material double portion, representing the beginning of strength, itself ultimately points to the spiritual significance of the dual birthright and blessing, Deut 21:17.

[40] Joseph uses the same verb stem ["to do" = H6213] to describe the urgently needed actions of Pharaoh and also the soon-coming actions of God as foretold by the dreams of Pharaoh, and thereby Joseph likens Pharaoh unto God, Gen 41:25, 41:28, 41:32 (Sarna 285; Gen 41:34). Every level of reality tells the same story.

completeness and wholeness, particularly the completeness and wholeness of creation. The good seven is the new creation promised by Christ and guaranteed by Christ at the First Advent. The evil seven is the utter destruction and desolation in separation from Christ that will precede the reality of the promised new creation in Christ at the Second Advent. The First and Second Advents are viewed together as the one Body of Christ.

Genesis 41:36 And that food shall be for store to the land against the seven years of famine, which shall be in the land of Egypt; that the land perish not through the famine.

The food that saves is the flesh of Christ that is the bread of life (John 6:51).

Genesis 41:37 And the thing was good in the eyes of Pharaoh, and in the eyes of all his servants.

The Father is well pleased with the Son (2 Pet 1:17).[41]

House of Pharaoh

Genesis 41:38 And Pharaoh said unto his servants, Can we find [such a one] as this [is], a man in whom the Spirit of God [is]?

And the spirit of the Lord shall rest upon him, the spirit of wisdom and understanding, the spirit of counsel and might, the spirit of knowledge and of the fear of the Lord (Isa 11:2). God the Son and God the Holy Spirit are distinct persons; nonetheless, the Spirit indwells the Son just as the Spirit indwells the faithful in the Son. The Head and the Body are one Body. The difference between the Son and the faithful is that the absolute fullness of the Holy Spirit indwells the Son. And it is only in the Son, in the Body of Christ, that the faithful can participate in the fullness of the Spirit, which is the promised communion with the Father.

Genesis 41:39 And Pharaoh said unto Joseph, Forasmuch as God hath shewed thee all this, [there is] none so discreet and wise as thou [art]:

God showing Joseph all things, or all necessary things, reflects the Father showing the Son absolutely all things (John 5:20). And there being no other man so discreet and wise as Joseph is directly connected to the things of God. Likewise, there is no other man like the Son, growing strong in the spirit, filled with wisdom, and with the grace of God upon him (Luke 2:40).

---

[41] Joseph doesn't merely predict affliction, but immediately offers a remedy (Sarna 285; Gen 41:37). The law is subsumed by grace.

Genesis 41:40 Thou shalt be over my house, and according unto thy word shall all my people be ruled: only in the throne will I be greater than thou.

The house of Pharaoh represents the house of God that is the Body of faithful. Joseph rules over the house of Pharaoh just as Jesus Christ is the Head of the Body. The word of Joseph by which all Pharaoh's people are ruled represents the word of Christ by which all the faithful are edified and guided. The word of Christ is truth, namely, law and grace. Pharaoh being greater than Joseph only in the throne reflects the relationship between God the Father and God the Son. The Father is greater than the Son because the Son proceeds from the Father, but yet the Father and Son have the same, or equal, nature, or essence, exactly because the Son proceeds from the Father.

Genesis 41:41 And Pharaoh said unto Joseph, See, I have set thee over all the land of Egypt.

The Son is given all power in heaven and in earth (Matt 28:18).

Genesis 41:42 And Pharaoh took off his ring from his hand, and put it upon Joseph's hand, and arrayed him in vestures of fine linen [H8336], and put a gold chain about his neck;

Joseph having the ring of Pharaoh put upon his hand, also his being arrayed with vestures of fine linen and having a gold chain put around his neck, prefigures the glorification of Christ, likewise the Body of Christ. The ring of Pharaoh represents the authority of the Father given unto the Son. The vestures of fine linen are robes of righteousness, representing the faithful redeemed by the righteousness of Christ. The gold chain around the neck of Joseph represents the glory of Christ specifically as the Head of the Body. The threefold ring of Pharaoh, vestures of fine linen, and gold chain reflect, respectively, the authority of the Father, the animation and sanctification of the Body by the Holy Spirit, and the headship of the Son over the Body. The Father, Son, and Spirit are three distinct persons, but the totality of the Trinity is nonetheless evident in the one person of the Son. The sequence of the ring followed by the vestures of fine linen followed by the gold chain point from Adam to the cross to the promised new creation in Christ.

Focusing on the garments of Joseph, a garment is understood to be a covering for the body and, thereby, signifies the body. Joseph being stripped by his brothers when they cast him into a pit represents the physical death of Christ at the First Advent (Gen 37:23–24). Joseph again being stripped when Potiphar cast him into prison represents the death of the Body of Christ culminating in the Second Advent (Gen 39:12, 39:20). And Joseph finally being arrayed in fine vestures by Pharaoh represents the resurrection and rapture of the Body of Christ. Joseph being clothed in new garments was implied but not emphasized at the time he was brought up out of the pit and sold into Egypt, because the emphasis in the First Advent is the death of Christ. And Joseph's garment was dipped in blood by his brothers, representing the blood of Christ spilled at the time of the First Advent (Gen 37:31). In contrast, Joseph's garment was not dipped in blood by Potiphar, affirming that the blood of Christ would be spilled once and for all and never again at the time of the First Advent (Heb 9:25–28). The emphasis in the First Advent is the shedding of the blood of Christ, while the emphasis in the Second Advent is the glorification of the Body of Christ. The shedding of the blood of the Body connected with the Second Advent is meaningful with regard to the glorification of the Body only in so far as it is connected with the blood of Christ.[42]

Genesis 41:43 And he made him to ride in the second chariot which he had; and they cried before him, Bow the knee: and he made him [ruler] over all the land of Egypt.

Pharaoh riding in the first chariot represents God the Father, the first person of the Trinity. Joseph riding in the second chariot represents God the Son, the second person of the Trinity. And the heralds proclaiming Joseph represent God the Holy Spirit, the third person of the Trinity. The heralds calling upon every knee to bow before Joseph is a prophecy of the time when every knee will bow and every tongue will confess to God (Rom 14:11).

Genesis 41:44 And Pharaoh said unto Joseph, I [am] Pharaoh, and without thee shall no man lift up his hand or foot in all the land of Egypt.

There is no conflict between Pharaoh being sovereign over all Egypt and Joseph governing all Egypt. Joseph exercises the power and authority of Pharaoh, while the power and authority itself originates uniquely with Pharaoh. It is likewise the Father who commits all judgment unto the Son (John 5:22). The Biblical accounts taken collectively, not any analogies conceived by men, is that which relates the correct Trinitarian image of the one God of the Bible.

Genesis 41:45 And Pharaoh called Joseph's name Zaphnath-paaneah; and he gave him to wife Asenath the daughter of Poti-pherah [H6319] priest of On. And Joseph went out over [all] the land of Egypt.

To be given a new name signifying a newfound prestige is emblematic of rebirth and glorification. The overarching context is the time of the Second Advent, and so this is specifically the exaltation of the faithful in Christ. And the implicit connection between Joseph being given a name and his being given a wife points to this very union of the faithful and Christ. Joseph's wife being the daughter of an Egyptian priest reflects the connection between the Second

---

[42] The *fine linen* [H8336] in which Joseph is arrayed is the same basic type of fabric used for the tabernacle and also for the priestly garments [Exod 26:31, 28:6] (Sarna 286; Gen 41:42). The temple of God is the Body of Christ.

Advent of Christ and the priesthood of Christ.[43] The First Advent is to the Second Advent as the kingship is to the high priesthood as the birthright is to the blessing as the law is to grace. And Joseph's wife being Egyptian prefigures the predominantly Gentile nature of the church.[44]

Genesis 41:46 And Joseph [was] thirty years old when he stood before Pharaoh king of Egypt. And Joseph went out from the presence of Pharaoh, and went throughout all the land of Egypt.

Jesus would likewise be around thirty years old when he begins his public ministry at the time of the First Advent (Luke 3:23). But the emphasis here is the priesthood of the Second Advent, in contrast to the kingship of the First Advent. And the age of thirty is not coincidentally the minimum age required by the law to begin priestly service in the tabernacle of the congregation (Num 4:3). The high priesthood of Jesus Christ is his ministry of eternal intercession that proceeds from his death and resurrection as king of kings (Heb 7:25). The ministry of grace as high priest (over Jews and Gentiles alike) is connected to the crucifixion as king under the law (as the king of the Jews) just as redemption is connected to repentance just as the Body is connected to the Head just as the Second Advent is connected to the First Advent (Matt 2:2, 27:37).

Genesis 41:47–49 And in the seven plenteous years the earth brought forth by handfuls. 48 And he gathered up all the food of the seven years, which were in the land of Egypt, and laid up the food in the cities: the food of the field, which [was] round about every city, laid he up in the same. 49 And Joseph gathered corn as the sand of the sea, very much, until he left numbering; for [it was] without number.

The seven plenteous years that precede the seven years of dearth represent the First Advent of Christ that precedes the Second Advent, specifically the victory of Christ over death that precedes the wrath to be poured out during the tribulation period. The plenteous seven also represents the totality of the seven millennia of creation just as the death and resurrection of Christ represents the death and resurrection of the whole world. And the gathering of corn, which occurs throughout the seven good years, represents the redemption of the faithful throughout the whole of creation by the one man Jesus Christ, who embodies the whole of creation. The cities to which the corn is gathered point

---

[43] The name *Potipherah* [H6319] is nearly identical with *Potiphar* [H6318] (Sarna 263; Gen 37:36). The exaltation of Joseph in the house of Potiphar is closely connected with the exaltation of Joseph in the house of Pharaoh.

[44] "Asenath, the Gentile bride espoused by Joseph the rejected one [John 19:15], type of the Church, called out from the Gentiles to be the bride of Christ during the time of His rejection by His brethren, Israel [Acts 15:14, Eph 5:31–32]" (Scofield 59 n. 1; Gen 41:45). Not simply Gentile, but Jew and Gentile together, just as the children of Joseph would be a mixed ethnicity, Israelite and Egyptian.

to the city of God. And the corn being without number prefigures the multitude forming the Body of Christ.

Genesis 41:50 And unto Joseph were born two sons before the years of famine came, which Asenath the daughter of Poti-pherah priest of On bare unto him.

The seven plenteous years reflect the totality of the seven millennia of creation, especially that embodied by Christ at the time of the First Advent. The two sons of Joseph, who are born during the seven plenteous years before the famine, also reflect the totality of creation. The firstborn Manasseh is to the second born Ephraim as the first man Adam is to the second man Christ. And the first man Adam is to the second man Christ as the First Advent of Christ is to the Second Advent of Christ. This is creation and new creation, representing the whole of creation. The original creation of Adam followed by the First and Second Advents of Christ reflect the Father, Son, and Spirit. And the Trinity is the fullness of the image of God in which Adam, likewise the whole of creation proceeding from Adam, is formed.[45]

Genesis 41:51 And Joseph called the name of the firstborn Manasseh: For God, [said he], hath made me forget all my toil, and all my father's house.

The toil of Joseph being connected with the birth of his firstborn Manasseh recalls the first man Adam being cursed to eat bread in the sweat of his face (Gen 3:19). But Joseph forgetting his toil prefigures Jesus Christ, by virtue of the work of the cross, sending the Comforter (John 15:26). The firstborn Manasseh reflects the first man Adam and likewise reflects Jesus Christ nailed to the tree of the cross in the place of Adam. Joseph figuratively, or spiritually, forgetting his father's house is primarily a reference to his brothers—themselves representing creation, the generations of Adam-kind, particularly the first six millennia of natural creation. Joseph forgetting his brothers is Joseph forgetting, or rather forgiving, their sins against him.[46]

Genesis 41:52 And the name of the second called he Ephraim: For God hath caused me to be fruitful in the land of my affliction.

The fruitfulness of Joseph is connected with the birth of his second born, Ephraim. The one who becomes fruitful in the land of his affliction is the second man Jesus Christ who takes possession of all creation by virtue of the cross. This is the death and resurrection of Christ as the Head and

---

[45] "*Ephraim* signifies *fruitfulness*, and *Manasseh forgetfulness*" (Wesley 1:161; Gen 41:50). The way of the flesh is forgetfulness and death, whereas the way of the Spirit is fruitfulness and the resurrection unto eternal life.

[46] "The name which Joseph here used for God was *Elohim*, the great Creator-God, and not *Jehovah* [YHWH], the God of the covenant . . . ." (Coffman 495; Gen 41:46–53). The God of the new covenant, the Covenant of Grace.

simultaneously the death and resurrection of the faithful in Christ as the Body. The second born Ephraim will displace the firstborn Manasseh just as the second man Christ will displace the first man Adam just as the spiritual, or glorified, body will displace the natural body (Gen 48:13–20).[47]

Genesis 41:53 And the seven years of plenteousness, that was in the land of Egypt, were ended.

Time moves so slowly that the present order of things can seem to have no end, and this is especially true while we are yet young and, so to speak, very small compared with creation as a whole. But this is merely our finite experience and limited understanding of the patience and long-suffering of God calling us sinners to repentance (2 Pet 3:9). There is an appointed time of the end, and there always has been, though it may seem remote and distant (Mark 13:32).

Genesis 41:54 And the seven years of dearth began to come, according as Joseph had said: and the dearth was in all lands; but in all the land of Egypt there was bread.

Even during the final tribulation period, there will be a place to find the bread of life. This is the call to repentance that will be extended even during the final tribulation period. And the emphasis on Joseph having foretold the coming seven years of dearth points to our present modern world being forewarned of the coming judgment of God.

Genesis 41:55 And when all the land of Egypt was famished, the people cried to Pharaoh for bread: and Pharaoh said unto all the Egyptians, Go unto Joseph; what he saith to you, do.

The people throughout the land must come unto Joseph and not unto Pharaoh for their bread. It is the Son who is uniquely the manna from heaven, the bread of life, because it is the Son who died for the sins of the world (John 6:58). The people crying out for the bread of life when they are famished, presumably only when they are famished and dying, portends the remnant that will finally repent of their apostasy during the final tribulation period.

Genesis 41:56 And the famine was over all the face of the earth: And Joseph opened all the storehouses, and sold unto the Egyptians; and the famine waxed sore in the land of Egypt.

---

[47] "Now, as Isaac's two sons, Esau and Jacob, furnished a type [respectively] of the two peoples, the Jews and the Christians . . . so the same thing happened in Joseph's two sons . . . . [T]he one [elder] according to the flesh, the other [younger] according to faith" (Augustine, *City of God* 565). The Jew is to the Christian as the law is to grace as the present mortal life is to the promised eternal life.

The famine raging over the whole land portends the final destruction of the whole earth that will come by fire. Famines are normally connected with heat and dryness in addition to hunger. The first destruction was by water, the second destruction will be by fire (2 Pet 3:3–7). The baptism in water, which is the baptism of repentance, likewise precedes the baptism of the Spirit, which is the baptism of redemption, just as law precedes grace just as the natural body precedes the spiritual, or glorified, resurrection body. The storehouses are opened, but the famine still waxes sore in the land, even in the promised land. The remnant to be saved and exalted in Christ during the final tribulation period, after the time of the resurrection and rapture, will be saved through tribulation and not out of tribulation.

Genesis 41:57 And all countries came into Egypt to Joseph for to buy [corn]; because that the famine was [so] sore in all lands.

The famine being sore in all countries portends a final tribulation period affecting the whole of the earth. All countries coming unto the one man Joseph prefigures all peoples acknowledging that Jesus Christ alone is Lord and Savior. Lord God have mercy.[48]

Ω Ω Ω

Rachel's son Joseph is Jacob's second firstborn son (by a freewoman), while Leah's son Reuben is Jacob's first firstborn son. Adam and Jesus Christ are likewise the first and second firstborn sons of God in the sense that Adam is the first man formed in the image of God (1 Cor 15:47) and Christ is the firstborn from the dead (1 Cor 15:20). The second firstborn Joseph prefigures the second man Jesus Christ in both the first coming and the second coming. The condemnation of Christ in the place of mankind, or Adam-kind, at the First Advent parallels the original condemnation of the first man Adam (Gen 2:16–17), while the resurrection of the faithful in Christ, the Body of Christ, at the Second Advent parallels the original resurrection of Christ at the First Advent (Rev 1:18). The providential image of first and second sons, specifically the second son supplanting the first, is reinforced by the account of Judah's sons by Tamar, Zerah and Pharez, and also by the account of Joseph's sons, Manasseh and Ephraim, though different aspects of the fundamental twofold relationship are, as always, stressed in the different accounts.

Judah's offspring form the Messianic bloodline from which the Lord would proceed, and thereby Judah's offspring are identified with the birthright of Jesus Christ, who would ultimately become the firstborn from the dead, guaranteeing the rebirth of the faithful in the Body of Christ (Matt 1:3). And Zerah being

---

[48] "[A]s Joseph had all the stores of corn under his care, and the needy were bid to go to him for it, so Christ has all the treasures of grace in his hand, and all that are sensible of their need of it are directed to go to him for it; . . ." (Gill 1:212; Gen 41:57). Jesus Christ is the bread of life, the manna from heaven.

supplanted by Pharez while yet in the womb testifies to the undeniable, or inherent, nature of the promised rebirth of the faithful in the Body of Christ (Gen 38:27–30). Joseph's offspring are identified with Jacob and the blessing that they receive from Jacob and, thereby, the promised blessing of the indwelling Holy Spirit that Jacob embodies, the fullness of which can only be received in the resurrection body (Gen 48:5, 48:19). The names of Manasseh and Ephraim are identified, respectively, with images of forgetfulness and fruitfulness, wherein forgetfulness is symbolically supplanted by fruitfulness, representing death and resurrection (Gen 41:50–52).

1	2
ADAM	CHRIST
REUBEN	JOSEPH
ZERAH	PHAREZ
MANASSEH	EPHRAIM

Joseph is the dreamer of dreams who becomes the interpreter of dreams just as Jesus Christ is both the author of our redemption and the story, or meaning, of our redemption (Gen 37:5, 37:9, 41:16). The dream, or prophecy, precedes the fulfillment just as Adam precedes the promised new Adam, who is Christ the Head and finally the Body of Christ. Joseph being cast into a pit by his brothers prefigures the death and resurrection of Christ at the First Advent (Gen 37:20), while Joseph subsequently being cast into prison because of Potiphar's wife prefigures the death and resurrection of the Body of Christ at the Second Advent (Gen 39:20). Joseph's brothers figuratively killing him because of his dreams concerning himself (Gen 37:20) prefigures Jesus Christ being formally executed because of his prophecies concerning himself (Matt 26:64), while Potiphar's wife figuratively killing Joseph because she cannot defile his body prefigures the rejection of the Body of Christ that will culminate in the resurrection and rapture of the faithful (Gen 39:6–7). Pharaoh's baker and cupbearer—identified with the person of Joseph, specifically in prison—signify bread and wine, likewise body and blood, and likewise flesh and spirit (Gen 40:4). And the fundamental dichotomy of flesh and spirit ultimately points to the twofold natures of Jesus Christ, being fully man and fully God. The Lord embodies the perfect union of flesh and spirit just as he embodies the perfect union of law and grace.

1	2
DREAMER OF DREAMS	INTERPRETER OF DREAMS
CREATION THROUGH CHRIST	NEW CREATION IN CHRIST
THE PIT IN CANAAN	THE PRISON IN EGYPT
(BROTHERS=JEWS)	(EGYPTIANS=GENTILES)
THE REJECTION OF CHRIST	THE REJECTION OF THE BODY OF CHRIST
BAKER OF PHARAOH	CUPBEARER OF PHARAOH
COVENANT OF LAW	COVENANT OF GRACE

Pharaoh's dream of seven good followed by seven bad represents, in the immediate context, seven good years followed by seven bad years (Gen 41:1–7). But the seven good followed by the seven bad, in the broader context, represents the totality of natural creation being concluded in the sevenfold judgment that bookends the seventh millennium. (The tribulation following the millennial kingdom is connected to the tribulation preceding the millennial kingdom just as the Second Advent is connected to the First Advent just as the last Adam is connected to the first Adam.) The seven fat being devoured by the seven gaunt represents the totality of the seven millennia of creation destroyed by the seven years of the final tribulation. The contrast between the good and bad cows, likewise the contrast between the good and bad corn, represents a contrast between distinct and separate time frames, while the distinguishing modifiers "fatness" and "gauntness" represent a difference in the magnitudes of the time frames. Big cows or corn represent long periods, while small cows or corn represent short periods. And the big compared with the small specifically represents millennia compared with years.

The image of cows eating cows and also the image of corn eating corn are both preternatural, but the image of corn eating is further beyond the normal order than the image of cows eating. The image of cows eating cows is actually distinctly more realistic than the image of ears of corn eating ears of corn. The more realistic image of cows eating cows reflects the seven millennia of natural creation, whereas the more fantastic image of corn eating corn prefigures the supernatural nature of the coming final seven years of tribulation. The strange but conceivable death of the cows followed by the quite inconceivable death of the ears of corn represents the two deaths, that is, the natural death of the natural body followed by the supernatural death in the lake of fire (Rev 20:14). The emphasis on the gaunt cows not being sated by the fat cows portends a complete destruction, but no similar declaration being made concerning the seven gaunt ears of corn hints at a temporary reprieve. The new earth and new heaven are not to be established until the opening of eternity at the end of the millennial kingdom (Rev 21:1).

1	2
COWS EATING COWS	CORN EATING CORN
MORE REALISTIC, OR NATURAL	MORE FANTASTIC, OR SUPERNATURAL
SEVEN FAT, OR BIG, YEARS	SEVEN GAUNT, OR SMALL, YEARS
SEVEN MILLENNIA OF CREATION	SEVEN YEARS OF TRIBULATION

The threefold Abraham, Isaac, and Jacob—reflecting the triune Father, Son, and Spirit—relate the overarching image of the Trinity in the account of Joseph and Jacob. But Pharaoh, Joseph, and Jacob relate the Father, Son, and Spirit in the local context. Isaac originally sent Jacob into the east with the blessing of Abraham in order to establish his personal household, but now Joseph proceeds from Jacob into the west in order to make the house of Jacob a great nation and a kingdom. The former reflects God the Son sending forth God the Spirit at the time of the First Advent (John 14:16–17), while the latter reflects God the Spirit establishing God the Son, specifically the Body of Christ, at the time of the Second Advent (John 15:26). Jacob taking his house from the hand of Laban represents God the Holy Spirit calling the faithful out of the world during the church age. Joseph ultimately reigning with the authority of Pharaoh reflects

JOSEPH BEN JACOB

God the Son reigning with the authority of God the Father (Gen 41:40). And Jacob bringing his house unto Joseph in Egypt in order to live and not die represents God the Holy Spirit directing the faithful unto God the Son and unto the life that is only in God the Son (Gen 42:1–2).

The threefold Pharaoh, Joseph, and Jacob can also be expressed Pharaoh, Joseph, and Joseph ben Jacob, which emphasizes the Body of Christ animated by the fullness of the Holy Spirit. Joseph ben Jacob comprehends the entire house of Jacob, representing the Body of Christ, in that all of Jacob is nourished under the auspices of Joseph. But the position of Judah in Joseph ben Jacob is unique since Judah embodies the Messianic bloodline, which ultimately leads to Christ and finally the Body of Christ. (And it is completely normal for more than one personage to contribute to the image of God in any given narrative.) Focusing on the literal, or explicit, Messianic bloodline, the fates of the three sons of Judah betrothed to Tamar (Gen 38:6–11) parallel Tamar herself becoming a widow and ultimately a prostitute and finally a mother in the bloodline of Christ (Gen 38:11, 38:15, 38:27). The death of Judah's firstborn son, which corresponds to the widowhood of Tamar, reflects the death of Adam and likewise all mankind in Adam. The death of Judah's second born, which is connected with his failure to sire offspring, portends Jesus Christ being cut off without offspring (Isa 53:8). But the righteous prostitute Tamar giving birth to the sacred bloodline reflects the death and resurrection of Jesus Christ, who is exalted in his being defiled (Matt 1:3). And the life of Judah's third born son being spared points to the promised inheritance of eternal life just as the motherhood of Tamar points to the resurrection, or rebirth, of the faithful in Christ in the end times.

1	2	3
FATHER	SON	SPIRIT
PHARAOH	JOSEPH	JOSEPH BEN JACOB
ADAM	FIRST ADVENT	SECOND ADVENT
TAMAR THE FORLORN WIDOW	TAMAR THE RIGHTEOUS PROSTITUTE	TAMAR THE MOTHER OF CHRIST

Joseph being stripped and cast into a pit by his brothers prefigures the death and resurrection of Jesus Christ (Gen 37:23–24). The firstborn Reuben being identified with casting Joseph into the pit recalls the first man Adam nailing Christ to the tree of knowledge (Gen 37:21). Judah embodies the Messianic bloodline, and therefore Judah being identified with saving Joseph, or figuratively resurrecting him, points to the power of the blood of Christ, representing the Holy Spirit and connecting the First and Second Advents (Gen 37:26–28). And the bloodline, or blood, of Christ is thereby understood to be the essential connection between the death and resurrection of Christ and the death and resurrection of the Body of Christ. The sojourn of Joseph as a foreigner in Egypt then prefigures the church age, while the interjection of the account of Judah and Tamar, testifying to the bloodline of Christ, underscores the parenthetical nature of the church age. The three sons of Judah connected with Tamar are the three days connecting the death and resurrection of Christ, likewise the three millennia connecting the First Advent (revealing Christ) and the Second Advent (fulfilling the Body of Christ).

The account of Potiphar's wife portends the persecution in the end times that is identified with the whore of Babylon. And the second death and resurrection of Joseph, which is represented by his being cast into prison because of Potiphar's wife, prefigures the resurrection and rapture of the faithful—that is, the formal, or visible, death and resurrection of the Body of Christ (Second Advent) that must be joined to the death and resurrection of Christ (First Advent). The identification of the person of Joseph with the baker and cupbearer of Pharaoh, who embody bread and wine, points to the unity of body and blood, flesh and spirit, and law and grace, which characterizes the natural body but is perfected in the resurrection body. And the identification of Joseph with the baker and cupbearer in the context of being physically imprisoned reinforces the essential unity of the physical body and affirms the physical reality of the resurrection body. The seven years of famine in the land during the time of Joseph foreshadow the final seven years of desolation in the end times (Gen 45:11, Dan 9:27). But Joseph taking possession of all the land and all the people of the land for Pharaoh prefigures the establishment of the Body of Christ during the millennial kingdom of Christ.

JOSEPH BEN JACOB

CHAPTER FOUR OUTLINE

Key Images

	PRIME IMAGES	
Material	Abstract	Spiritual
Joseph.	The second firstborn son of his father by a freewoman.	The second man Jesus, who is the firstborn from the dead.
The unique love of Jacob for his one son Joseph.	To have many brothers, but yet to be peerless.	Jesus is the only begotten Son of the Father.
Joseph's coat of many colors.	A covering of the body relating the love of a father.	The Body of Christ.
Betrayed by his brothers and sold for pieces of silver.	One who becomes a curse.	The First Advent.
The ascendancy of Joseph.	One who is exalted.	The Second Advent.
	TWOFOLD IMAGES	
Material	Abstract	Spiritual
Dreamer of dreams, interpreter of dreams.	To proclaim a thing, to explain a thing. Flesh and spirit.	The author of creation; the story, or meaning, of creation. Son of man, Son of God.
Joseph being cast into a pit by his brothers followed by his being cast into prison on account of Potiphar's wife.	A pit and a prison. A grave versus a judgment. A judgment of the body versus a judgment of the being, or soul. Flesh and spirit.	The death and resurrection of the Head followed by the death and resurrection of the Body. The First and Second Advents.
Pharez and Zerah.	Firstborn and second born. Firstborn supplanted by the second while yet in the womb. Flesh and spirit.	The undeniable will of God to redeem his faithful ones.
Baker and cupbearer.	Bread and wine. Body and blood. Flesh and spirit.	The body and blood of Christ. The First and Second Advents.
Manasseh and Ephraim.	Firstborn and second born. By the hand of Jacob the firstborn is supplanted by the second born. Flesh and spirit.	The hand of Jacob represents the providential movement of God the Holy Spirit.
	THREEFOLD IMAGES	
Material	Abstract	Spiritual
Er, Onan, Shelah.	The first son, who is evil; the second, who rejects the Seed; and the third, who lives.	The Fall of Adam, the First Advent of Jesus Christ, and the Second Advent of Christ.
Tamar the widow, Tamar the prostitute, Tamar the mother of the Messianic bloodline.	Death followed by shame followed by glory.	Adam, First Advent, and Second Advent.
The signet, bracelets, and staff of Judah.	The threefold pledge of Judah guaranteeing the lamb of Judah.	The triunity of God proclaimed and also embodied by Christ.
The baker and cupbearer lifted up on the third day.	The judgment of the bread and the wine, representing natural man (body of Adam) and spiritual man (blood of Christ).	The judgment of the faithless and the exaltation of the faithful on the third day, or millennium, from the First Advent.
Joseph brought out of prison after two full years.	A prison sentence originally determined by an adulteress, or figuratively an idolatress, but now finally ended.	The death and resurrection of the Body of Christ on the third day, or millennium, from the rejection of Jesus Christ.

ESAU, JACOB, ISRAEL

Synopsis

Dreamer of Dreams

	Material	Spiritual
37:1	Jacob dwells in the land wherein his father was a stranger.	The children of God are promised a true land and a true body.
37:2	Joseph brings an evil report to his father concerning his offspring of bondwomen.	The rejection of the Son at the time of the establishment of the millennial kingdom.
37:3	Jacob loves Joseph more than all his children because he is the son of his old age.	The love that marks the Son, especially in the old age, or last days, of creation.
	Jacob makes Joseph a coat of many colors.	The Body of Christ.
37:4	Joseph is hated by his brothers because their father loves him more than them.	The children of the devil reject the unique love that rests upon the Son.
	Joseph's brothers cannot speak peaceably unto him.	The faithless cannot enter into the peace of God that is the Body of Christ.
37:5	Joseph dreams a dream, and he is hated yet the more.	The wicked hate the Lord, and they hate the coming of the Lord even more.
37:6–10	In Joseph's first dream, his sheaf stands upright while the sheaves of his brethren bow down in obeisance unto it.	The dominion of the Son over the earth.
	In Joseph's second dream, the sun, the moon, and the stars make obeisance unto him.	The dominion of the Son over heaven.
37:11	Joseph's brothers envy him.	Flesh contends with the Spirit.
	Jacob rebukes Joseph, but he nonetheless observes the saying of Joseph.	The suffering of the Son must precede the exaltation of the Son.

The Evil Beast

	Material	Spiritual
37:12–14	Jacob sends Joseph unto his brothers in Shechem.	The Son proceeds according to the Spirit at the time of the First Advent.
37:15–17	Joseph does not find his brothers in Shechem.	The First Advent points to the Second.
37:18	Joseph's brothers conspire against him.	All mankind in Adam has rejected Christ.
37:19	Behold, the dreamer cometh.	The dreamer of dreams compared with the interpreter of dreams reflects the first coming compared with the second coming.
37:20	Let us kill Joseph and blame some evil beast.	The evil beast that devours is the devil.
37:21–22	The firstborn Reuben delivers Joseph by casting him into a pit.	The first man Adam nails Jesus Christ to the cross by which the faithful are saved.
37:23–28	Joseph is stripped by his brothers.	The nakedness of Jesus Christ on the cross (Matt 27:35).
	Joseph is cast into a pit that has no water in it.	The thirst of Christ on the cross (John 19:28).
	The brothers sit down to eat bread.	The breaking, or killing, of the body.
	A caravan appears, carrying spicery and balm and myrrh.	The preparation of the body of Christ for burial (John 19:39–40).
	The brothers sell Joseph for twenty pieces of silver.	The life of Jesus valued in pieces of silver (Matt 27:9).
37:29–35	The firstborn Reuben rends his clothes.	The call to repentance of natural man.
	The sign of Joseph's death is his coat of many colors dipped in blood.	The robes of the faithful are washed, dipped, in the blood and made white (Rev 7:14).
	Jacob rends his clothes.	The Spirit testifies unto the Son.
37:36	Joseph is sold into Egypt.	We are bought with a price (1 Cor 6:19–20).

JOSEPH BEN JACOB

JUDAH AND TAMAR

	Material	Spiritual
38:1–2	Judah goes down from his brethren unto a certain place and takes a Canaanite wife.	The church age culminating in a wicked generation that will be judged.
38:3–5	Judah's Canaanite wife bears three sons, named Er, Onan, and Shelah.	The three millennia that connect the First and Second Advents.
38:6–7	Judah takes Tamar as a wife for Er, but God slays Er because of his wickedness.	The wickedness of the first millennium following the First Advent.
38:8–10	Judah tells Onan to raise up seed for Er, but Onan refuses. And the Lord slays Onan also.	The increasing apostasy that marks the second millennium following the First Advent.
38:11	Tamar is not allowed to conceive, but must wait until Shelah is grown.	The harvest of mankind must wait until the time of the maturity of the present age.
38:12–14	Tamar perceives that she is not being given unto Shelah, even though he has grown into adulthood.	The third born Shelah being supplanted by his father Judah represents the death and resurrection of the Body of Christ in the third millennium following the First Advent.
	Tamar puts off her widow's garments and sits in an open place as a harlot.	Tamar the widow and Tamar the whore reflect the two women of the book of Revelation (Rev 12:1, 18:7).
38:15–18	Judah gives unto Tamar his signet, bracelets, and staff as a pledge for a kid from the flock.	A threefold pledge representing the authority of the Father, the binding of the Son, and the guidance of the Spirit.
	And Tamar conceives the Messianic bloodline.	The movement from widow to harlot to mother reflects Adam followed by the First and Second Advents. This is also the three millennia connecting the conceptions of the Head and the Body, that is, the First and Second Advents.
38:19–23	Judah is unable to recompense Tamar with the promised kid from the flock.	The requirement of the kid from the flock represents the requirement under law of the blood sacrifice of Christ, while the kid being supplanted by the threefold pledge represents the Body being added by grace to the Head.
38:24–26	About three months later, Tamar is found to be pregnant and Judah condemns her to be burned.	Tamar the harlot is figuratively burned, representing the coming judgment by fire in the third millennium from the First Advent.
	Judah finally acknowledges that Tamar is more righteousness than he is.	Man is identified with justice and law, while woman is identified with mercy and grace.
38:27–30	Tamar, with twins, travails in childbirth.	The tribulation period.
	One son puts out his hand, and the midwife binds it with a scarlet thread. But the other son is born first.	The second man Jesus is the firstborn from the dead, and the faithful that follow Christ are likewise exalted in Christ.

HOUSE OF POTIPHAR

	Material	Spiritual
39:1	Joseph is brought down to Egypt, where he is bought by Potiphar.	The church age culminating in the Second Advent, but with an emphasis on the kingship of Christ, which is the suffering of Christ and likewise the suffering of the faithful in Christ.
39:2–6	And Joseph is prosperous because the Lord is with him.	The paradox of the prosperous slave is the paradox of Jesus Christ, who is fully God and fully man.
	Potiphar makes Joseph the overseer of his house and puts all that he has into his hand.	The ascendant Christ during the church age.
	The house of Potiphar is blessed for the sake of Joseph.	The children of God, who are the house of God, are blessed in the Son.

ESAU, JACOB, ISRAEL

39:7–10	Potiphar's wife seeks to lay with Joseph.	The whore of Babylon.
	Joseph refuses Potiphar's wife.	The Son rejects the faithless.
39:11–18	Potiphar's wife strips Joseph of his garment.	The death of the Body following the Head.
	Joseph is falsely condemned by his garment.	The Body of Christ, which is the garment of Christ, is falsely accused.
39:19	The wrath of Potiphar is kindled because of the wicked accusations of his wife.	The blasphemies of the whore of Babylon that will kindle the wrath of God in the end times.
39:20–23	Joseph is cast into prison, but all the prisoners are committed into his hand.	The death and resurrection of the Body of Christ culminating in the Second Advent.

BAKER AND BUTLER

	Material	Spiritual
40:1–2	The baker and the butler of Pharaoh offend their lord, the king of Egypt.	Bread and wine corresponding to the twofold offenses of the flesh and spirit.
	Pharaoh is wroth against the baker and butler.	Two tribulations corresponding to the crucifixion of the flesh of Christ followed by the crucifixion of the sinful nature, or sinful spirit, of the repentant in Christ.
40:3–4	Pharaoh puts the baker and butler into the prison where Joseph was bound.	Joseph represents the Son, while the baker and the butler represent the twofold natures of the Son, who is true man and true God.
40:5–8	The baker and the butler both dreamed a dream in one night.	The unity of the flesh and spirit, likewise the law and grace, that is affirmed by prophecy.
	The baker and butler are sad because there is no one to interpret their dreams.	The vexation of the baker and butler portends the rejection of Christ, likewise the Body of Christ, culminating in the Second Advent.
40:9–23	Joseph interprets the dreams of the baker and butler of Pharaoh.	The interpretation of dreams belongs to God the Father but is given unto God the Son, while the dream itself represents the presence and movement of God the Spirit.
	The heads of the baker and butler are lifted up on the third day on Pharaoh's birthday.	The birthday, or rebirthday, of the faithful in the third millennium from the First Advent.
	The butler does not remember Joseph.	The foretold delay represented by the final tribulation period.

INTERPRETER OF DREAMS

	Material	Spiritual
41:1–7	At the end of two full years, Pharaoh dreams a dream.	The millennial kingdom that follows two full millennia from the time of the First Advent.
	Seven good cows are devoured by seven bad cows, followed by seven good ears of corn being devoured by seven bad ears.	The cows being followed by the grain relates a looking backward from the Second Advent to the First Advent.
41:8	None of Pharaoh's magicians or wise men can interpret the dream.	The apostate cannot correctly perceive the signs of the times.
41:9–13	Pharaoh's butler remembers his sins and tells Pharaoh of the Hebrew Joseph that can correctly interpret dreams.	The remembrance of sins being linked to the butler's restoration, figuratively through Joseph, points to the sins of mankind being nailed to the cross.
41:14	Pharaoh hastily brings Joseph out of prison, shaves him, and changes his raiment.	The resurrection and rapture of the faithful.
41:15–16	Joseph stands before Pharaoh as the one and only person who can interpret his dreams, and the interpretation will certainly be an answer of peace from God.	Pharaoh is the dreamer of dreams, representing the Father. Joseph is the interpreter of dreams, representing the Son. And the dream itself represents the presence and movement of the Spirit.

JOSEPH BEN JACOB

41:17–24	Pharaoh recounts his two dreams to Joseph.	The second telling of Pharaoh's dreams, which is the first telling unto Joseph, is the First Advent following the formation of Adam, while the coming reality foretold by the two dreams is the coming Second Advent.
41:25	Joseph testifies that the two dreams are one.	The unity of law and grace.
41:26–32	Joseph interprets the two dreams of Pharaoh that are one dream.	The seven bad that follow the seven good is the tribulation period of the Second Advent of Christ, encompassing all of creation, that follows the ministry of the First Advent, underlying all creation.
41:33–37	Pharaoh is to identify a man who is discreet and wise and set that man over all the land.	The one man who is discreet and wise is Jesus Christ, the Son of God.
	The discreet and wise man is to collect the fifth of the land so the land will not perish.	The fifth that marks our salvation is the First Advent of Christ in the fifth millennium.
	HOUSE OF PHARAOH	
	Material	Spiritual
41:38–39	Pharaoh proclaims that there is none so discreet and wise as Joseph, in whom one can find the Spirit of God.	The one man Jesus Christ, who is the Head of the one Body of Christ.
41:40–44	Pharaoh sets Joseph over the land of Egypt.	The Father sets the Son over creation.
	Pharaoh puts his ring upon Joseph's hand, arrays him in vestures of fine linen, and puts a gold chain around his neck.	A threefold sign reflecting the triunity of God.
	Joseph is made to ride in the second chariot of Pharaoh, and there are cries made to bow the knee unto him.	The call unto repentance in the Son.
41:45–46	Pharaoh gives Joseph a new name.	The glorification of the Body of Christ.
	Pharaoh gives Joseph the daughter of a priest of Egypt as a wife.	The Second Advent identifies the priesthood of Christ with the kingship of Christ.
	Joseph was thirty years old when he stood before Pharaoh, king of Egypt.	Jesus would also be about thirty when he was lifted up on the cross, exalting the kingship under the law to the high priesthood of intercession that is by grace (Luke 3:23).
41:47–49	Joseph gathers corn as the sand of the sea during the seven plenteous years.	The assembly of the faithful throughout the first creation that is identified with the First Advent of Christ.
41:50–52	Two sons, Manasseh and Ephraim, are born unto Joseph.	The first and second men Adam and Jesus, reflecting the totality of creation, that is, the original creation and the new creation.
41:53–54	In all lands, the seven years of plenty end and the seven years of dearth begin.	The final tribulation at the end of time, encompassing all of creation.
41:55–57	The storehouses of Joseph are the only source of bread in all the countries of the land.	All peoples and nations must come unto Jesus Christ, for he is the one and only bread of life.

ISRAEL

יהוה

CHAPTER FIVE

Twelve Sons

The prime image in the account of the sons of Israel journeying to Egypt is Joseph revealing himself to his brothers as the ruler of all Egypt, effectively the ruler of the whole world. Jacob sending Joseph's brothers forth and Joseph's brothers finally being received by Joseph under Pharaoh prefigures the millennial reign of Christ at the Second Advent. Joseph's brothers represent the totality of humanity throughout the ages and culminating in the end times. Jacob sending his sons unto Joseph in order to live and not die reflects the Spirit directing humanity unto the Son and unto the salvation that exists only in the Son. The seven years of famine portend the final tribulation period (Dan 9:27). The binding of the second son Simeon during this period connects the first destruction in the second millennium to the second and final destruction in the end times (Gen 42:24). Joseph testifying that God had sent him ahead of his brothers into Egypt to cause a great deliverance reflects the relationship between the First and Second Advents (Gen 45:7). The silver money and cup, which connects but also separates Joseph and his brothers, foreshadows the value in silver placed upon the life of Christ, connecting but also separating the First and Second Advents (Gen 44:12, Matt 27:9). Joseph accusing his brothers of being enemies portends the judgment of the world (Gen 42:9), but Joseph finally accepting his brothers points to the salvation of the faithful (Gen 50:19–21). And Jacob going unto Joseph before he dies, or figuratively at the time of his death, represents the end of the age (Gen 45:28).

The twofold relationship emphasized in the account of Joseph revealing himself to his brothers is the unique brotherhood of Joseph and Benjamin. The second son Simeon is bound on the first journey in order to bring Benjamin unto Joseph (Gen 42:19–20, 42:24). And the brothers are only allowed into the presence of Joseph on the second journey because Benjamin is with them (Gen 43:3–5, 43:16). And Joseph finally reveals himself to his brothers only when Judah offers his own life in the place of Benjamin (Gen 44:33–45:3). The first and second sons Joseph and Benjamin reflect the first and second men Adam and Christ, likewise the First and Second Advents of Christ, and likewise the millennial kingdom of Christ and eternity in Christ. Further, the relationship between Egypt and Canaan, or Egypt and the surrounding nations, reflects the relationship between the kingdom of God and the kingdoms of the earth. And the relationship between the first and fourth born sons Reuben and Judah points to the relationship between Adam formed in the first millennium and Christ conceived in the fourth millennium. The relationship between Reuben and Judah marks Joseph originally being sold into slavery and also Joseph ultimately revealing himself (Gen 37:21, 37:26, 42:37, 43:8–9). And Joseph's brothers rejecting him followed by Joseph revealing himself unto them reflects the First Advent followed by the Second Advent.

The three journeys of the sons of Israel to Egypt reflect the Fall of Adam followed by the First and Second Advents of Christ. Joseph accusing his brothers on the first journey reflects the original condemnation of Adam and likewise all mankind in Adam. Joseph revealing himself to his brothers on the second journey reflects the incarnation of Christ at the First Advent. And Jacob coming unto Joseph on the third journey and bringing his entire household reflects the Holy Spirit bringing the faithful unto Christ at the Second Advent. This is the resurrection of the faithful in the Body of Christ by the power of the Spirit. Israel becoming a multitude in Egypt under Joseph, who ruled by the favor of Pharaoh, prefigures the millennial kingdom of Christ, which will be a literal kingdom on the earth. The triune Father, Son, and Spirit are reflected by the threefold Pharaoh, who possesses Egypt, Joseph, who rules under Pharaoh, and Joseph ben Jacob, or simply Jacob, who gathers all Israel unto himself. And the threefold successive Adam followed by the First and Second Advents of Christ is again reflected in Reuben offering his flesh, or fleshly offspring, as a guarantee for the life of Benjamin (Gen 42:37) followed by Judah offering his own personal sonship as a guarantee for Benjamin (Gen 43:8–9) followed by Judah abiding in the place of Benjamin and thereby revealing the identity of Joseph (Gen 44:33–45:3).

The First Journey

Genesis 42:1 Now when Jacob saw that there was corn in Egypt, Jacob said unto his sons, Why do ye look one upon another?

The twelve sons of Jacob reflect the totality of the millennia of creation proceeding from Adam, especially the multitude of faithful throughout all time, both before and after the cross. Jacob, as the progenitor of the twelve sons who would become the twelve tribes, is most closely identified with God the Holy Spirit. It is the Holy Spirit who marks the faithful and calls the faithful and directs the faithful. The intimate connection between Jacob and his sons recalls the relationship between Abraham, Isaac, and Jacob that is the relationship between the Father, the Son, and the Holy Spirit. But this Trinitarian relationship—Father, Son, and Spirit—is expressed in the present context by Pharaoh, Joseph, and Jacob. The Trinity being reflected in different ways in different contexts and at different times is a testimony to the allness embodied by God, not only in the original act of creation, but also with respect to the very fabric of creation—past, present, and future.

Jacob in Canaan is counterpoised to Pharaoh in Egypt. The journeys between the two extremes represent condemnation and preservation, likewise death and resurrection, and likewise desolation and restoration. Pharaoh represents God the Father, while Joseph represents God the Son. Jacob sending his sons unto Pharaoh represents the movement of God the Holy Spirit, the hand of providence, especially in the call of the faithful. The Father has life—represented here by corn, or grain—whereby the Holy Spirit directs the faithful unto the Father (John 5:26). The brothers cannot save themselves just as humanity is helpless facing the condemnation of the world. That the sons of Jacob are being directed unknowingly unto Joseph represents the ignorance of the world, not knowing the nature of God.

Jacob now seeing that there is corn in Egypt stands in contrast to Joseph having originally stored up corn in Egypt. Pharaoh dreamed, Joseph interpreted, and now Jacob perceives. Pharaoh originally dreaming the dream reflects the Father, who is the font of creation. Joseph interpreting the dream of Pharaoh reflects the Son, who reveals the Father. And Jacob now finally seeing the fulfillment of the dream represents the faithful being given understanding by the Holy Spirit, especially at the time of the resurrection and exaltation of the faithful in the Body of Christ in the end times. The emphasis on Jacob's sons looking upon one another, in contrast to looking upon Pharaoh, testifies to the way of flesh not seeing, or perceiving, the way of the Spirit.[1]

Genesis 42:2 And he said, Behold, I have heard that there is corn in Egypt: get you down thither, and buy for us from thence; that we may live, and not die.

Apart from Joseph having stored up corn in Egypt, Jacob and his sons would have died and therefore figuratively, or spiritually, they did indeed die. But Jacob's sons going unto Egypt to buy corn represents a reprieve, which signifies resurrection. This first of three journeys into Egypt specifically reflects the original condemnation and simultaneous preservation of the first man Adam. And the condemnation and preservation of Adam and Adam-kind is like a death and resurrection and, thereby, prophesies death and resurrection.

Genesis 42:3 And Joseph's ten brethren went down to buy corn in Egypt.

The emphasis on there being ten brothers sent to Egypt points to the law that is closely identified with the number 10. The famine afflicting the brothers represents the condemnation of the flesh under the law. The two brothers not

---

[1] The Messiah will only come to a world that is either wholly guilty or wholly innocent, *Sanhedrin* (Cohen, *Rabbinic Sages* 349). Both are simultaneously and without contradiction true: the former is the rejection of Jesus Christ at the First Advent, while the latter is the perfection of the faithful in Christ at the Second Advent.

counted among the ten are Joseph and Benjamin. And the two brothers not counted are identified with the seventh and eighth millennia, representing the promised new creation that comes by grace. In contrast, the ten brothers that are counted are identified with the first six millennia from Adam, specifically with the curse of the flesh proceeding from Adam that characterizes the first six millennia from Adam.

Genesis 42:4 But Benjamin, Joseph's brother, Jacob sent not with his brethren; for he said, Lest peradventure mischief befall him.

Jacob's youngest son, Benjamin, is identified with the eighth millennium, representing the coming reality of eternal life. Benjamin not being allowed to join his brothers on this first of three journeys recalls the first man Adam not being allowed to take of the tree of life and live forever (Gen 3:22). The connection between the youngest son Benjamin and the promise of life is further emphasized by Jacob protecting Benjamin's life from any mischief that might befall him. Jacob protecting the life of Benjamin represents the deposit of God the Spirit that guarantees the fullness of eternal life in God the Son, the Body of Christ, in oneness with God the Father.

Genesis 42:5 And the sons of Israel came to buy [corn] among those that came: for the famine was in the land of Canaan.

Many are called, but few are chosen (Matt 20:16).

Genesis 42:6 And Joseph [was] the governor over the land, [and] he [it was] that sold to all the people of the land: and Joseph's brethren came, and bowed down themselves before him [with] their faces to the earth.

Every knee will bow, and every tongue will confess to God (Rom 14:11). This means all people throughout all time, as represented in the present context by Joseph's brothers. The brothers of Joseph bowing their faces down to the earth represents an identification with the earth, or land, that is an identification with carnal nature, likewise with death. The way of all the earth is death (1 Kgs 2:2). For dust thou art, and unto dust shalt thou return (Gen 3:19).[2]

Genesis 42:7 And Joseph saw his brethren, and he knew them, but made himself strange unto them, and spake roughly unto them; and he said unto them, Whence come ye? And they said, From the land of Canaan to buy food.

---

[2] "The gesture of the brothers [bowing] is a deliberate recall of the dream [dreams] in [Gen 37:5–10; cf. 42:9a] . . . The narrator is playing off the knowledge of Joseph (and the readers) against the ignorance of the brothers" (Murphy, *New Jerome* 39; Gen 42:6–8). It is not happenstance that believers are called to be a people of the Book, for the transcendent perspective that is shared between the divine narrator and the faithful reader reflects the unity of the Body of Christ.

Joseph making himself strange unto his brothers and speaking roughly unto them is directly connected to their original betrayal of him. Joseph making himself strange unto his brothers reflects God separating himself from mankind because of our sin. And Joseph speaking roughly unto his brothers represents the condemnation of mankind under the law. This first of three journeys to Egypt reflects the original condemnation of Adam, likewise all mankind in Adam. And it is the time of Adam that marks the separation of mankind and God and the corresponding judgment of mankind under the law. But Joseph specifically represents God the Son whereby his brothers betraying him connects the second man Jesus Christ and the first man Adam. The relationship between the Passion of Christ and the Fall of Man is the reality of Adam and likewise all mankind in Adam having nailed Christ to the cross and specifically to the tree of knowledge.

Genesis 42:8 And Joseph knew his brethren, but they knew not him.

Joseph knows his brothers, but the brothers do not know Joseph. The identity of Joseph is not recognized by his brothers just as the nature of God is not recognized, or understood, by the world. The way of the flesh is death, forever opposed to the way of the Spirit, which is life.

Genesis 42:9–10 And Joseph remembered [H2142] the dreams which he dreamed of them, and said unto them, Ye [are] spies; to see the nakedness [H6172] of the land ye are come. 10 And they said unto him, Nay, my lord, but to buy food are thy servants come.

The word *remembered* [H2142] (Joseph remembered the dreams) is the same word used to describe God *remembering* [H2142] Noah in the ark (Gen 8:1). The word *nakedness* [H6172] (nakedness of the land) is the same word used to describe the *nakedness* [H6172] of Noah being covered by Shem and Japheth (Gen 9:23). The time of the Flood parallels the time of the First Advent of Christ, but the spiritual context of this first of three journeys to Egypt is the time of Adam. Nonetheless, the simultaneous condemnation and preservation of Adam and Adam-kind innately prefigures the death and resurrection of Christ. The first man Adam points to the second man Christ. Joseph remembering the dreams he had dreamed reflects God remembering, or fulfilling, his promises. The nakedness of the land during the time of Joseph recalls the original nakedness of Adam (Gen 3:21) and also prefigures the nakedness of Christ on the cross (Matt 27:35).

The sign of nakedness, specifically the covering of nakedness, represents the atonement of sin. The act of a spy seeing the nakedness of the land is here connected to the act of a servant buying food. The implied evil intent is the presumption of the wicked brothers that they can simply buy food from righteous Joseph. The corn of Egypt stored up by Joseph represents life, but life is a gift and, therefore, can only be received by grace and not by works. And the brothers not being able to buy food from Joseph will be affirmed when they

ESAU, JACOB, ISRAEL

find their money in the sacks of food received from Joseph (Gen 42:35). The brothers not literally spying the nakedness of the land is a further indication of a larger spiritual context—namely, the Fall of Man and the original nakedness, or lost innocence, of the garden of Eden (Gen 3:7). But this is also innately a looking forward from the curse of Adam to the time of the buying of life on the cross at the First Advent.

Genesis 42:11–12 We [are] all one man's sons; we [are] true [men], thy servants are no spies [H7270]. 12 And he said unto them, Nay, but to see the nakedness of the land ye are come.

The sons of Jacob are identified with the millennia of creation proceeding from Adam. And the emphasis on the brothers being the sons of one man points to the unity of creation. The brothers are true men, servants and not spies, despite their betrayal of Joseph. And this reflects the present fallen creation leading us inexorably to the new creation that is the law leading us to grace (Gal 3:24). The person of Jacob is identified with God the Holy Spirit, whereby the intimate identification of Jacob's sons with Jacob represents the multitude of the faithful being marked by the Holy Spirit.

The brothers have not come as spies, but Joseph nonetheless insists on identifying them as spies. The word *spies* [H7270] (thy servants are no spies) has a connotation "to go about maliciously, as a slanderer." It is the devil who is the slanderer, and thus the brothers are identified with the devil (John 8:44). The concurrent identification of the brothers with the millennia of creation from Adam, specifically with the six millennia from Adam, testifies to the devil continuing to be the god of the present world even unto the end times (2 Cor 4:4). That the devil now remains the god of this world, even after the cross, is evidenced by the continuing prevalence of evil, likewise the continuing death in the world and of the world.

Genesis 42:13 And they said, Thy servants [are] twelve brethren, the sons of one man in the land of Canaan; and, behold, the youngest [is] this day with our father, and one [is] not.

The account of Joseph coming to power in Egypt is most closely identified with the Second Advent, but the embedded accounts of the three journeys of Joseph's brothers into Egypt represent a recounting of the totality of creation from Adam to the First and Second Advents of Christ. The threefold successive formation of Adam followed by the First and Second Advents of Christ reflects the fundamental triunity of the Father, Son, and Holy Spirit. The image of God, which is triunity, is impressed upon, or embodied by, all creation, likewise the Scriptures that speak of creation and the promised new creation. And the triunity of God is therefore the only proper framework, or hermeneutic, for understanding the Bible, actually life in general, because all things testify to the universal triunity of God. Nonetheless, the recounting of the totality of creation within the account of Joseph points specifically to the Second Advent and the Body of Christ, which is the promised final embodiment of all creation.

The emphasis on the persons of Joseph and Benjamin points to the Second Advent in the end times since it is Joseph and Benjamin who are the sons of Jacob's old age (Gen 37:3, 44:20). It is their ten brothers identified with the Fall of Adam who make this first journey to Egypt, but this represents the time of Adam looking forward to the time of Christ and not simply the time of Adam in isolation. The persons of Joseph and Benjamin are connected by one mother just as the seventh and eighth millennia are connected by the one dominion of God the Holy Spirit. The emphasis on there being ten former, or original, sons separated from two final sons points to the law that governs the six millennia and connects the first Adam and the promised new Adam, that is, points from the body of Adam to the Body of Christ.

The youngest son Benjamin being with his father and not joining his brothers on this first of three journeys to Egypt reinforces the emphasis on the spiritual context being the time of Adam. But Joseph being identified as "one who is not" reflects the death of Christ at the time of the First Advent, even though this first journey of his brothers to Egypt is identified with the time of Adam and not with the time of the First Advent. The person of Joseph, the "one who is not," presiding over all three of the journeys of his brothers to Egypt, especially this first journey to Egypt, testifies to the preexistence of the Son, who is eternally begotten of the Father by the Spirit. The one man who presides over all three journeys is the one Son who reveals the threefold nature of the Godhead—Father, Son, and Spirit. The Lamb slain from the foundation of the world (Rev 13:8).[3]

SIMEON

Genesis 42:14 And Joseph said unto them, That [is it] that I spake unto you, saying, Ye [are] spies:

Joseph persistently identifying his brothers as enemies of the state represents the irrevocable condemnation of the natural body under the law. Joseph is accusing his brothers of being enemies ultimately because of their hidden treachery. Joseph's brothers figuratively, or spiritually, killed him, and of that they are truly guilty and utterly without excuse. Joseph's brothers casting him into a pit represents the death of Christ at the time of the First Advent (Gen 37:33), but this same rejection of Christ is finally understood to be the rejection of God by Adam, likewise Adam-kind (Gen 3:15). Christ is the perfect and complete image of the invisible God. Jesus Christ is God in the flesh, whereby

---

[3] "Orthodox doctrine confesses that God the Father is the eternal origin and source of the Spirit, just as He is the source of the Son. . . . For us it is enough to see that the difference between the two [Spirit and Son] lies in the distinction between the divine persons and actions of the Son and the Spirit in relation to the Father, and so as well to each other and to the world" (Hopko, *Orthodox Faith* 1:118). There has never been nor ever will be a time when the Trinity is either increased or decreased in number.

the rejection of Christ represents nothing less than the visible, tangible reality of rejecting God Almighty (Col 1:15).

Genesis 42:15 Hereby ye shall be proved: By the life of Pharaoh ye shall not go forth hence, except your youngest brother come hither.

The life of Pharaoh is here connected to the commandment of Joseph. This represents the Son speaking the commandment of the Father that is the undeniable, or relentless, promise of everlasting life unto the faithful in Christ (John 12:50). This first condemnation of the brothers in Egypt recalls the original condemnation of Adam. And this first going forth from Egypt with the corn of Pharaoh, spiritually the grain of life, recalls the preservation of Adam despite his being condemned. The person of Benjamin is identified with the eighth millennium, representing the promise of eternal life. And the connection between the life of Pharaoh and the coming of Benjamin is just this promise of eternal life. This is the life in the Father that is also in the Son (John 5:26). Joseph is most closely identified with the image of being rejected (by brothers), while Benjamin is most closely identified with the image of being accepted (by brothers). But both qualities of being rejected and being accepted reflect the one person of Christ, specifically the death and resurrection of Christ.[4]

According to the commandment of the firstborn Joseph, the coming of the second born Benjamin in the second journey to Egypt is connected to the first going forth from Egypt. The coming of Benjamin that must follow the first journey represents the coming of Christ that must follow the condemnation of the first man Adam. The first going forth from Egypt with the corn of Pharaoh, the grain of life, represents the preservation of Adam despite his being condemned. The connection between the first going forth from Egypt and the second journey into Egypt is the connection between the original preservation of Adam going forth from the garden of Eden and the coming of Christ unto the chosen people of God. The only reason why Adam can be preserved, or saved, is because of the promised coming of Christ. The preservation of Adam and the coming of Christ are the same call to repentance.

Joseph and Benjamin are both the sons of Jacob's old age (Gen 37:3, 44:20), but Benjamin is the living son while Joseph is (figuratively) the dead son (Gen 42:38). Joseph, when compared with Benjamin, is therefore most closely identified with the First Advent while Benjamin is most closely identified with the Second Advent. The firstborn Joseph precedes the second born Benjamin just as the First Advent precedes the Second Advent (Gen 30:22–24, 35:17–18). And Jacob's old age represents the last days connecting the First and Second Advents. The coming of Benjamin will ultimately be connected with the revelation of the true identity of Joseph, which again connects the two persons

---

[4] "From this formula of swearing [by the life of Pharaoh] a new question is raised; . . . nature dictates that this honour is to be given to God alone . . . ." (Calvin, *Commentaries* 2:341; Gen 42:15). Joseph ben Jacob ruling under Pharaoh points to nothing less than the triune reality of God.

of Joseph and Benjamin (Gen 45:12). The spiritual context of the coming of Benjamin in the second journey to Egypt is the First Advent. Accordingly, Joseph is most closely identified as the Son of man while Benjamin is most closely identified as the Son of God.

Genesis 42:16 Send one of you, and let him fetch your brother, and ye shall be kept in prison, that your words may be proved, whether [there be any] truth in you: or else by the life of Pharaoh surely ye [are] spies.

Joseph compared with Benjamin reflects the seventh millennium compared with the eighth millennium, or more specifically the millennial reign compared with eternity. Joseph compared with Benjamin is likewise the kingdom of God proclaimed in the First Advent compared with the Body of Christ to be revealed in the Second Advent. And the First and Second Advents parallel the first and second men Adam and Jesus. Adam compared with Jesus is like the law compared with grace, the birthright compared with the blessing, death compared with resurrection, and the kingship compared with the high priesthood. The necessity that Benjamin must be brought unto Joseph represents the essential oneness of Christ, who is true man and true God, fulfilling the law and revealing grace.

Joseph's ten brothers are identified with the totality of creation and specifically the six millennia of natural creation connecting the condemnation of Adam and the final judgment of Adam-kind. Joseph insisting that his brothers be kept in prison until Benjamin is brought unto him represents the present creation that precedes the new creation, likewise the death that precedes eternal life. The coming of Benjamin being identified with proving the veracity of the ten brothers, or simply proving the ten, represents the revelation of life that proves the law. That one brother alone will never actually be sent to bring Benjamin unto Joseph represents no man being found who can prove the law and reveal life (Isa 59:16). That one brother will ultimately be kept in prison in order to bring Benjamin unto Joseph (Gen 42:19) represents the one man Christ, the slain Lamb of God, finally being found worthy (Rev 5:12).

Genesis 42:17 And he put them all together into ward three days.

The three days in ward represents a period of waiting and searching to find the one man among the ten brothers who can be sent to bring Benjamin unto Joseph. That one man alone should represent all ten brothers signifies one man alone fulfilling the whole of the law. The three days in ward represents the three millennia connecting the First and Second Advents. The one man for whom we are waiting is the risen Christ, who will return at the time of the Second Advent. And the anticipated union of Joseph and Benjamin represents the unity of law and grace and likewise the unity of the First and Second Advents.

Genesis 42:18 And Joseph said unto them the third day, This do [H6213], and live [H2421]; [for] I fear God:

The fear of God being identified with the third day portends the final judgment of God in the end times corresponding to the third millennium from the time of the First Advent. The connection between *doing* [H6213] and *living* [H2421] represents the connection between repentance and redemption. However, the doing, or working, of repentance is not our work but rather the work of Christ on the cross fulfilling the totality of the law. The *doing* [H6213] that Joseph requires is the bringing of Benjamin unto him. And it is just this union of the first and second born Joseph and Benjamin that represents the union of the First and Second Advents of Christ, likewise the union of law and grace, and likewise the union of repentance and redemption. This is the unity of humanity and deity embodied by God the Son. And our repentance is therefore our turning unto Jesus Christ. And our redemption is our salvation in Christ, that is, the Body of Christ.

Genesis 42:19 If ye [be] true [men], let one of your brethren be bound in the house of your prison: go ye, carry corn for the famine of your houses:

The simultaneous condemnation and preservation of the ten brothers in this first of three journeys to Egypt recalls the preservation in condemnation of the first man Adam and that specifically under the law. The corn given to the brothers represents a preservation of their lives despite their condemnation as spies. The connection between the brothers being true men and the necessity that one man must be bound reflects the essential justification of the faithful by the suffering of the one man Jesus Christ.

Genesis 42:20 But bring your youngest brother unto me; so shall your words be verified, and ye shall not die. And they did so.

Rachel's two only sons, Joseph and Benjamin, must be united, or their ten brothers will die. This is the gift of eternal life that can only be received in the fulfillment of the law in grace. The bringing of Benjamin unto Joseph will verify the words of their ten brothers. This is the justification of the faithful by Jesus Christ and in Jesus Christ. The emphasis on all ten brothers obeying the commandment of Joseph does not reflect the salvation of the whole of humanity but rather points to the undeniable, or relentless, sovereignty of God. Only the faithful in Christ are saved by Christ.

Genesis 42:21 And they said one to another, We [are] verily guilty concerning our brother, in that we saw the anguish of his soul, when he besought us, and we would not hear; therefore is this distress come upon us.

Joseph reflects Christ, while his ten brothers reflect Adam, or Adam-kind, specifically the totality of mankind throughout the ages proceeding from Adam. And the brothers are correct in their understanding that their distress has come upon them because of their guilt concerning Joseph. Sin likewise entered the world through the first man, and death through sin (Rom 5:12). Adam and likewise all mankind in Adam nailed Christ to the cross, which is spiritually the tree of the knowledge of good and evil (Gen 2:17). The anguish of Joseph's soul prefigures the suffering of Jesus Christ for the sake of mankind, while the heartlessness of Joseph's ten brothers testifies to every imagination of the thoughts of the heart of man being evil continually (Gen 6:5). The emphasis on Joseph having beseeched his ten brothers testifies to the centrality of the call to repentance. But the unwillingness of Joseph's ten brothers to hearken unto him prefigures the rejection of Jesus Christ, particularly by those who are his own flesh and bone (John 1:10–11).

Genesis 42:22 And Reuben answered them, saying, Spake I not unto you, saying, Do not sin against the child; and ye would not hear? therefore, behold, also his blood is required.

The firstborn Reuben is most closely identified with the first millennium and specifically with the Fall of Adam. The emphasis on Reuben himself not wanting to sin against the child points to the serpent originally deceiving Eve and not Adam (1 Tim 2:14). The original apostasy proceeding from Eve to Adam reflects the spiritual origin of the corruption of creation. The nature of man is to the nature of woman as law is to grace, likewise as flesh is to spirit. Likewise, the nature of the serpent, who is the devil, is spiritual in comparison with the nature of humanity, which is carnal. Further, the emphasis on Joseph having been a child when he was originally betrayed points to the parallel between the life of Christ and the progression of the millennia of creation. The life of Jesus Christ is a recapitulation of the totality of creation and, thereby, is a sanctification of the totality of creation. The emphasis on the blood of Joseph being required points to there being no remission of sins without the shedding of blood (Heb 9:22). The blood of Joseph that his brothers (figuratively) shed represents the blood of Jesus Christ shed at the time of the First Advent. The rejection of Christ at the time of the First Advent is the visible image of the original rejection of the Lord God by Adam just as Jesus Christ himself is the visible image of the invisible God (Col 1:15).

Genesis 42:23 And they knew not that Joseph understood [them]; for he spake unto them by an interpreter.

Joseph speaking to his brothers through an interpreter reflects Jesus speaking to the faithful by, or according to, the Spirit (John 15:26). The ten brothers not realizing that Joseph understands them reflects the faithless not recognizing the truth of Christ that is the reality of God.

Genesis 42:24 And he turned himself about from them, and wept; and returned to them again, and communed with them, and took from them Simeon, and bound him before their eyes.

Joseph weeping over Simeon and his brothers reflects Jesus weeping over his friend Lazarus and, by extension, all his loved ones. And Jesus weeping over Lazarus is specifically Jesus weeping over the death of his loved ones (John 11:35). Simeon being bound in prison parallels Lazarus being wrapped in burial clothes (John 11:44). And the connection between Simeon being bound and the death of the natural body is affirmed in the connection between Simeon and Noah. The second born Simeon is identified with the second millennium and specifically with the condemnation of the world at the time of Noah. The necessity that Simeon be bound in order to bring Benjamin unto Joseph points to the essential suffering and death of Christ. The identification of Simeon with the Flood testifies to the relationship between the death and resurrection of the world at the time of Noah and the death and resurrection of Christ for the world at the time of the First Advent. The life of Christ is a recapitulation of the totality of creation and, thereby, is a sanctification of the totality of creation.

SILVER

Genesis 42:25 Then Joseph commanded to fill their sacks with corn, and to restore every man's money into his sack, and to give them provision for the way: and thus did he unto them.

This first of three journeys of the brothers to Egypt represents the original condemnation of Adam. The brothers are driven out of the promised land because of the famine of the land. Likewise, Adam and Adam-kind were driven out of the garden of Eden because of the sins, or sinful nature, of the flesh. Nonetheless, the brothers receiving the corn of Pharaoh represents the preservation of Adam despite the condemnation of the flesh. Simeon being bound represents both the death of Adam and the death of Jesus Christ in the place of Adam-kind. This first journey to Egypt is most closely identified with the first man Adam, but the first man Adam points to the second man Christ just as the first covenant, the Covenant of Law, points to the second covenant, the Covenant of Grace. Joseph commanding that the brothers' money be restored points to a grace that can be received only by the blood of Jesus Christ. The brothers trying to pay but not being allowed to pay represents the failure of the law to yield life in separation from Christ.

Genesis 42:26 And they laded their asses with the corn, and departed thence.

The corn of Pharaoh has saved the lives of the brothers, and thereby the corn of Pharaoh represents life itself and specifically a life that proceeds from Pharaoh. But the preservation of the brothers is transitory just as the preservation of natural man after the original sin is transitory (Gen 3:19). The brothers originally being driven from the promised land by a famine recalls Adam originally being driven from the garden of Eden because of the flesh, or sinful nature (Gen 3:22–24). But the brothers now returning to the land of

Canaan does not represent a returning to the garden of Eden or even a returning to the promised land. The land that has been promised is not a land wracked by famine and starvation, and thus in a real sense the promised land has been cut off from the brothers, even though they now return to the land that would otherwise signify the promised land. The garden of Eden has likewise been cut off from humanity in the world. That the land of Canaan has never truly been the realization of the promised land is not relevant, or vital. Everything in this life is a mere shadow of the promised life to come (1 Cor 13:12). The intentions of the Holy Spirit are always that which is vital, or life-giving, but the fulfillment of all promises must await the promised new earth and new heaven (2 Pet 3:13).

Genesis 42:27 And as one of them opened his sack to give his ass provender in the inn, he espied his money [H3701]; for, behold, it [was] in his sack's mouth.

The money of the brothers not being accepted reflects the grace of God coming only by grace and not by works. The word *money* [H3701] (money in the sack's mouth) means "silver, money," which prefigures the price of the life of Christ being valued in silver (Matt 27:9). The silver of the ten brothers would not be accepted by Joseph just as the silver of the chief priests and elders would not be accepted for Christ (Matt 27:5). And yet there is an equivalency between the money and the corn. The money being exchanged for the corn in the first place testifies to this equivalency. And the connection between the money and the corn is reinforced by the emphasis on the money being placed in the sacks of corn. Joseph accepting the money in the first place reflects the rejection of Christ preceding the redemption in Christ. This is not the will of God but simply the reality that there would be no need for our redemption by God if we had not first rejected God. It is not God that has condemned man, but rather man that has condemned himself. The brothers discovering their money when going to feed their animals reflects the truth that the gift of life we proclaim to others is not our own but rather proceeds solely from God.

Genesis 42:28 And he said unto his brethren, My money is restored; and, lo, [it is] even in my sack: and their heart failed [them], and they were afraid, saying one to another, What [is] this [that] God hath done unto us?

The natural man is terrified to find that money, representing the work of his hands, is worthless before God. And the brothers are absolutely correct that God has indeed done this. God doing all these things through Joseph reflects the Father accomplishing all things through the Son. The natural man ultimately realizes that the work of his hands is that of nailing Christ to the cross.

Genesis 42:29–30 And they came unto Jacob their father unto the land of Canaan, and told him all that befell unto them; saying, 30 The man, [who

is] the lord of the land, spake roughly to us, and took us for spies of the country.

Pharaoh in Egypt reflects God the Father, while Jacob in Canaan reflects God the Spirit. And Joseph mediating between his brothers and Pharaoh represents God the Son. The brothers are closely identified with Jacob and, thereby, reflect the faithful indwelt by the Holy Spirit. The three journeys between Canaan and Egypt that will finally bring Jacob and his entire household unto Pharaoh represent the totality of creation, specifically the formation of Adam followed by the First and Second Advents of Christ. The present journey being the first of three reflects the preservation of man after the original sin. Joseph speaking roughly to his brothers represents the condemnation of all mankind in Adam. The identity, or reality, of Joseph being unknown to his brothers represents Adam certainly but unknowingly nailing Jesus Christ to the tree of knowledge. And Joseph's brothers now returning unto their father, Jacob, represents the faithful returning unto the Spirit of life and truth, who raises up, or exalts, Christ and likewise the faithful in Christ (Rom 8:11).

Genesis 42:31–32 And we said unto him, We [are] true [men]; we are no spies: 32 We [be] twelve brethren, sons of our father; one [is] not, and the youngest [is] this day with our father in the land of Canaan.

The brothers are enemies who will be proved to be true men. The brothers represent the faithful in Christ, redeemed by God the Holy Spirit in God the Son, in the Body of Christ, according to the will of God the Father. The emphasis on Joseph, in contrast to Pharaoh, judging the brothers points to the Father committing all judgment unto the Son (John 5:22). But it will be Jacob representing the Holy Spirit who proves, or sanctifies, Joseph's brothers in the act of sending Benjamin unto Joseph (2 Thess 2:13, Gen 43:14). The brothers and half brothers being the sons of the one man Jacob reflects the essential identification of the faithful with the one Holy Spirit. And the brothers being unsympathetic characters is a testimony that salvation comes by grace alone and not by attempts at good works.

Genesis 42:33–34 And the man, the lord of the country, said unto us, Hereby shall I know that ye [are] true [men]; leave one of your brethren [here] with me, and take [food for] the famine of your households, and be gone: 34 And bring your youngest brother unto me: then shall I know that ye [are] no spies, but [that] ye [are] true [men: so] will I deliver you your brother, and ye shall traffick [H5503] in the land.

The word *traffick* [H5503] (traffick in the land) means "to go around, about, travel about in (as a merchant)." The three journeys to the land of Egypt, which will finally bring the house of Jacob under the authority of Joseph in Egypt, reflects the threefold creation of Adam followed by the First and Second Advents of Christ, which is the triune image of God impressed upon all creation. The brothers are specifically identified with the faithful, but the brothers are generally identified with the totality of humanity. And Joseph foretelling that his brothers will become traffickers in the land foreshadows the merchants of the earth connected with the end times and, thereby, with the second coming of Christ (Rev 18:3).

Genesis 42:35 And it came to pass as they emptied their sacks, that, behold, every man's bundle of money [was] in his sack: and when [both] they and their father saw the bundles of money, they were afraid.

Jacob being sore afraid represents a foreboding in the Spirit of God concerning the pain and suffering that will mark the final tribulation period. Jacob being afraid along with his sons reflects the empathy of the Spirit with humanity. The life of the Spirit is the breath of life that animates all humanity in the natural body. But the connection between Jacob being afraid and their money not being accepted is an affirmation that there can be no acceptance of the faithless. The money of each brother being returned represents no man being found righteous. And this should be understood to be the money of the brothers as representing Adam-kind, not the money of Jacob representing God the Spirit. The ambiguity between the brothers and their father arises from the fact that mortal life and eternal life both proceed from the one God the Spirit, who is the one Spirit of life.

Reuben and Judah

Genesis 42:36 And Jacob their father said unto them, Me have ye bereaved [of my children]: Joseph [is] not, and Simeon [is] not, and ye will take Benjamin [away]: all these things are against me.

Jacob connects the lives of Joseph, Simeon, and Benjamin, reflecting the omniscience of God and specifically God the Holy Spirit. And Jacob marks the relationship between Joseph, Simeon, and Benjamin with the sign of death. Joseph reflects God the Son. Simeon being bound in prison in order to bring Benjamin unto Joseph reflects the death of Christ for the sins of the world (Gen 42:24). And the necessity that Benjamin must be brought unto his brother Joseph reflects the essential unity of humanity and divinity in Christ, likewise the unity of the First and Second Advents of Christ, and likewise the unity of the millennial kingdom of Christ and eternity in Christ (Gen 43:5).

Genesis 42:37 And Reuben spake unto his father, saying, Slay my two sons, if I bring him not to thee: deliver him into my hand, and I will bring him to thee again.

The firstborn Reuben is identified with the first millennium, with fallen humanity in the first man Adam. And Reuben offering up his two sons to be killed reflects the connection between the sin of Adam and the condemnation of all flesh (Rom 5:12). It is from Adam and in Adam that all mankind, or all the sons of Adam, die. And Benjamin will not be delivered into the hand of Reuben just as fallen man cannot be the font of his own redemption (Gen 42:38). The symbolic deaths of Reuben's two sons, embodied by their being offered up, represent the two deaths of the faithless in separation from Christ. The two deaths are the twofold *destroying* [G622], or "putting out of the way entirely," of the *body* [G4983] and the *soul* [G5590] (Matt 10:28).[5] In contrast, the *spirit* [G4151] of man proceeds directly from the side of the Lord God, being identified with God the Spirit, and therefore can in no way be destroyed just as the freewill of man can in no way be denied (1 Thess 5:23). The second death is the lake of fire (Rev 20:14) that burns forever (Matt 25:41).[6]

Genesis 42:38 And he said, My son shall not go down with you; for his brother is dead, and he is left alone: if mischief befall him by the way in the which ye go, then shall ye bring down my gray hairs with sorrow to the grave.

Symbolically, Joseph is dead because of his brothers, which reflects the death of Jesus Christ in the place of Adam. Benjamin being preserved because Joseph is dead reflects the preservation of humanity, likewise creation as a whole, until and unto the promised new life in Christ. And Benjamin finally being allowed to go down to Egypt reflects his brother Joseph not being dead but being figuratively resurrected and likewise Benjamin being resurrected with Joseph (Gen 43:14). The coming of Benjamin unto Joseph represents the fulfillment of all things in Christ. Jacob asserting that he himself will die if Benjamin dies is a testimony that the failure, or death, of creation would be the death of the Creator himself. The promise of God cannot fail, but if the promise of God did fail, then God would cease being God. The promise of God is life just as God is life. And if life becomes death, then death becomes nothingness.[7]

Genesis 43:1–2 And the famine [was] sore in the land. 2 And it came to pass, when they had eaten up the corn which they had brought out of Egypt, their father said unto them, Go again, buy us a little food.

The reprieve from starvation and death granted in the first journey to Egypt has now expired. The preservation of the first man Adam, likewise natural

---

[5] G622 connotation "put out of the way entirely" per *Brown-Driver-Briggs*, but is also evident in *Strong's* etymology connecting G622 and G575.
[6] A form of leadership is here assumed by the firstborn Reuben for the final time (Sarna 297; Gen 42:37). The fall of the first man Adam.
[7] "The ways of Providence are often to us dark and perplexed, so that we are ready to imagine that good can never result from what appears to us to be directly contrary to our interest; and we are often tempted to think that those very providential dealings of God, which have for their object our present and eternal welfare, are rather proofs of his displeasure, or evidences of his vindictive judgment" (Clarke 1:242; Gen 42:38). The valley of the shadow of death, Ps 23:4.

mankind in Adam, is transitory as affirmed by the death of the second man Jesus Christ under the law. Jacob sending his sons unto Joseph in order to receive the corn of Pharaoh represents the Holy Spirit bringing the faithful unto the Son and likewise unto the Father.

Genesis 43:3–5 And Judah spake unto him, saying, The man did solemnly protest unto us, saying, Ye shall not see my face, except your brother [be] with you. 4 If thou wilt send our brother with us, we will go down and buy thee food: 5 But if thou wilt not send [him], we will not go down: for the man said unto us, Ye shall not see my face, except your brother [be] with you.

The fourth son Judah is identified with the fourth millennium, beginning with the Davidic kingdom and culminating in the birth of Jesus Christ as king of kings. And the firstborn Joseph is to the second born Benjamin as the kingship is to the perpetual priesthood. Joseph is to Benjamin as the millennial kingdom is to eternity as the First Advent is to the Second Advent as the first man Adam is to the second man Christ. Judah stating unequivocally that Benjamin must be brought unto Joseph reflects the birth, death, and resurrection of Christ as being one continuous series of events. And this represents a recapitulation of the totality of creation. This represents the birth, death, and resurrection of the faithful in Christ, who form the Body of Christ. The brothers of Joseph and Benjamin represent the faithful throughout all the ages, whereby their taking Benjamin unto Joseph, under the overall direction of Jacob, represents God the Holy Spirit leading the faithful from the law unto grace.

Genesis 43:6–7 And Israel [H3478] said, Wherefore dealt ye [so] ill with me, [as] to tell the man whether ye had yet a brother? 7 And they said, The man asked us straitly of our state, and of our kindred, saying, [Is] your father yet alive? have ye [another] brother? and we told him according to the tenor of these words: could we certainly know that he would say, Bring your brother down?

Joseph being exalted by Pharaoh represents God the Son being given all things by God the Father, while Jacob being the progenitor of the multitude of God's chosen people represents God the Spirit being the very life of the body of believers. Jacob ruing that Benjamin must be taken to Egypt reflects a deep foreboding in the Spirit concerning the rapidly approaching tribulation period. But the tribulation must precede the glorious reappearing just as death must precede resurrection just as law must precede grace just as the incarnation of Christ must precede the indwelling of the Holy Spirit. The name *Israel* [H3478] being used, in contrast to the name *Jacob* [H3290], represents just this transformation. The name *Israel* [H3478] being used in relationship to the second journey into Egypt reflects the guarantee of our redemption being manifested at the time of the First Advent of Christ.

Genesis 43:8 And Judah said unto Israel his father, Send the lad with me, and we will arise and go; that we may live, and not die, both we, and thou, [and] also our little ones.

The firstborn Reuben was the first son to ask to take Benjamin to Egypt, but the firstborn Reuben was rejected (Gen 42:37–38). The fourth born Judah is now the second son to ask to take Benjamin to Egypt, and the fourth born Judah will be accepted (Gen 43:13). Likewise, the firstborn Reuben was the first son to seek to deliver Joseph from his brothers (Gen 37:21–22) but it was the fourth son Judah who would succeed in delivering Joseph from his brothers (Gen 37:26). The first man Adam formed in the first millennium is supplanted by the second man Christ begotten in the fourth millennium. The original promise of Reuben to return Benjamin to their father is the promise of the death of Reuben's own sons, but Judah now promises life for everyone and especially for their little ones (Gen 42:37). This is the death that comes through Adam in contrast to the new life that is only in Christ.

Genesis 43:9 I will be surety for him; of my hand shalt thou require him: if I bring him not unto thee, and set him before thee, then let me bear the blame for ever:

The firstborn Reuben originally offered his sons, but the fourth born Judah now offers himself (Gen 42:37). This is the death that marks all Adam-kind in contrast to the eternal life that exists only in Christ. Reuben would have his own offspring bear the blame just as the offspring of Adam even now suffer because of the original sin. But Judah would bear the blame himself forever just as Jesus would bear all the sins of all the faithful from all the ages (Heb 9:25–28).

Genesis 43:10 For except we had lingered, surely now we had returned this second time.

The emphasis on the long time delay between the first and second journeys to Egypt points to the long time delay between the original formation of the first man Adam and the conception of the second man Christ and likewise the long time delay between the first coming of Christ and the second coming.

Genesis 43:11 And their father Israel said unto them, If [it must be] so now, do this; take of the best fruits in the land in your vessels, and carry down the man a present [H4503], a little [H4592] balm [H6875], and a little [H4592] honey [H1706], spices [H5219], and myrrh [H3910], nuts [H992], and almonds [H8247]:

The word *present* [H4503] (of the land) means "gift, tribute, offering" and has a connotation "offering made to God." This second of three journeys to Egypt is most closely identified with the First Advent of Jesus Christ. Joseph is identified with God the Son, while Jacob is identified with God the Holy Spirit.

And it is Jacob representing the Spirit who insists upon sending a present of the land unto Joseph, who represents the Son. The tribute that the Spirit gives the Son at the time of the First Advent is the dominion over death, likewise over all creation, in the resurrection from the heart of the earth, or dust of the land (Matt 12:40, Rom 8:11). The six gifts of Jacob represent the six millennia of creation proceeding from Adam. And the emphasis on the gifts of Jacob being "of the land" reinforces the identification of the gifts with creation, likewise with the physical body, and likewise with the resurrection.

The word *balm* [H6875] has a connotation "medicament (medicine)," whereby the first offering of *balm* [H6875] reflects sickness and death entering the world through the first man Adam in the first millennium. The word *almonds* [H8247] is derived from the root "to watch, wake" [H8245], whereby the sixth offering of *almonds* [H8247] reflects the watching and waiting for the glorious return of Jesus Christ that marks the sixth millennium. The word *little* [H4592] (little balm, little honey) connects the first and second offerings of *balm* [H6875] and *honey* [H1706] and, thereby, connects the condemnation of all mankind through the first man Adam in the first millennium and the condemnation of all the world by Noah, the second Adam, in the second millennium. The similarity of the fifth and sixth offerings of *nuts* [H992] and *almonds* [H8247] reflects the continuity of the church age, which connects the fifth and sixth millennia. And the similarity of the third and fourth offerings of *spices* [H5219] and *myrrh* [H3910] reflects the establishment of the chosen people and the formal law, which connects the third and fourth millennia.

Genesis 43:12 And take double [H4932] money in your hand; and the money that was brought again in the mouth of your sacks, carry [it] again in your hand; peradventure it [was] an oversight:

The *double* [H4932] (double money) sent by Jacob to Joseph reflects the *double* [H8147] (double portion) that belongs to the firstborn (Deut 21:17). And the close connection between the two words *double* [H4932] and *double* [H8147] is affirmed by their sharing a common root "to repeat, do again" [H8138]. The double portion that rightfully belongs to the second firstborn Joseph now at the time of this second of three journeys ultimately points to the double portion that belongs to Jesus Christ, who would become the firstborn from the dead at the time of the First Advent (Col 1:18). And the double portion of Christ is finally understood as the twofold lordship of Christ being both king of kings and our high priest forever (Heb 7:1, 7:15).

Genesis 43:13 Take [H3947] also your brother, and arise [H6965], go again [H7725] unto the man:

The word *take* [H3947] connotes "to be taken in marriage," reflecting the original covenantal relationship between creation and the Creator established at the time of the formation of Adam. The word *arise* [H6965] means "to arise, stand up, stand," reflecting the resurrection of Christ at the time of the First

Advent. And the word *go again* [H7725] means "to turn back, return," reflecting the glorious return of Christ at the time of the Second Advent. This second of three journeys to Egypt is specifically identified with the First Advent, but the life of Christ made visible at the First Advent represents a recapitulation of all creation just as the person, or coming, of Christ represents the revelation of the fullness of the Trinity. The First and Second Advents of Christ follow the original formation of Adam in the image of God just as the Son and Spirit proceed from the Father in the triunity of God.

Genesis 43:14 And God Almighty give you mercy [H7356] before the man, that he may send away your other brother, and Benjamin. If I be bereaved [H7921] [of my children], I am bereaved [H7921].

The word *mercy* [H7356] (before the man) connotes "brotherly feeling, of those born from the same womb," reflecting the yet hidden kinship between Joseph and his brothers and ultimately the kinship between Christ and the faithful in Christ. The word *bereaved* [H7921] (if I be) connotes "to make childless," whereby the loss of Joseph together with Benjamin is understood to represent the loss of all Jacob's children. The faithful in Christ are likewise lost without Christ. The person of Benjamin being set free during this second journey points to the glorification of the Body of Christ at the Second Advent being guaranteed at the First Advent.

The Second Journey

Genesis 43:15 And the men took that present, and they took double money in their hand, and Benjamin; and rose up, and went down to Egypt, and stood before Joseph.

The ten brothers bringing Benjamin unto Joseph represents the six millennia of creation being under the law of death but nevertheless connecting the first Adam and the promised new Adam. The six gifts, or presents, of the ten brothers are the same six millennia. The double money that rightfully belongs to Joseph is the double portion of the firstborn. And the double portion that belongs to Christ is the birthright and the blessing that is the kingship and the high priesthood. The necessity that Benjamin must be brought unto Joseph represents the unity of the First and Second Advents and likewise the unity of the millennial reign and eternity.

Genesis 43:16 And when Joseph saw Benjamin with them, he said to the ruler of his house, Bring [these] men home, and slay [H2873, H2874], and make ready; for [these] men shall dine with me at noon [H6672].

The word *noon* [H6672] (dine at noon) is closely related to the word *make oil* (press out oil) [H6671] and, thereby, points to the appointed time of anointing (Job 24:11). The ten brothers are admitted into the house of Joseph, not of themselves, but only through their identification with Benjamin and ultimately with Benjamin's brother Joseph. The faithful in Christ are likewise saved only by their identification with Christ. The emphasis on Joseph commanding the ruler of his house represents an emphasis on the authority and dominion of Joseph, which is ultimately the authority and dominion of Christ established at the First Advent by virtue of the cross. And the *slaying* [H2873, H2874] of an animal in order to feast points to the tribulation of the cross and also to the final tribulation period that will precede the promised millennial kingdom.

Genesis 43:17 And the man did as Joseph bade; and the man brought the men into Joseph's house.

The house of Joseph represents the Body of Christ that is the temple, or dwelling, actually indwelling, of God.

Genesis 43:18 And the men were afraid, because they were brought into Joseph's house; and they said, Because of the money that was returned in our sacks at the first time are we brought in; that he may seek occasion against us, and fall upon us, and take us for bondmen, and our asses.

The brothers' fear is justified because of their guilt. And the brothers have become acutely aware that all their attempts to hide their sin have been futile. The focus on the money having been returned at the time of the first journey to Egypt points to the original sin of the first man Adam. And the brothers' fear of becoming bondmen reflects the nature of sin being a form of slavery and actually the very worst form of slavery (Rom 6:16).

Genesis 43:19 And they came near to the steward of Joseph's house, and they communed with him at the door of the house,

The house of Joseph will be revealed to be the bosom of Joseph as a place of forgiveness and brotherhood (Gen 45:14–15, Luke 16:22) and, thereby, reflects the Body of Christ being the house, or dwelling, of God as the place of the indwelling Holy Spirit (1 Cor 6:19). Christ is the door, and if any man enters in by him, he will be saved (John 10:9).

Genesis 43:20–21 And said, O sir, we came indeed down at the first time to buy food: 21 And it came to pass, when we came to the inn, that we opened our sacks, and, behold, [every] man's money [was] in the mouth of his sack, our money in full weight: and we have brought it again in our hand.

The brothers, representing the totality of creation, confess that their money has not been accepted by the ruler over the land. The faithful are saved by grace alone and not by works (Eph 2:8–10).

Genesis 43:22 And other money have we brought down in our hands to buy food: we cannot tell who put our money in our sacks.

The nature of the natural man is ignorance, whereas the nature of the spiritual man is knowledge and wisdom.

Genesis 43:23 And he said, Peace [be] to you, fear not: your God, and the God of your father, hath given you treasure in your sacks: I had your money. And he brought Simeon out unto them.

Christ would be sold for money (Matt 27:9), and yet it is Christ who purchases many (Mark 10:45). Simeon is set free.

Genesis 43:24 And the man brought the men into Joseph's house, and gave [them] water, and they washed their feet; and he gave their asses provender.

Joseph is identified with Jesus Christ, while the brothers are identified with Adam. The brothers coming into the house of Joseph reflects the faithful being washed clean in the Body of Christ.

Genesis 43:25 And they made ready the present against Joseph came at noon: for they heard that they should eat bread there.

The symbol of bread represents the flesh, or physical body, of Christ, while eating bread represents the death of the body, specifically the natural body. The faithful must eat the flesh of Christ (John 6:51). The faithful in Christ must be united with Christ in death according to the law that governs flesh.[8]

Genesis 43:26 And when Joseph came home, they brought him the present which [was] in their hand into the house, and bowed themselves to him to the earth.

The sixfold gift, or present, given to Joseph represents the totality of the six millennia of creation proceeding from the first man Adam (Gen 43:11). The brothers all bowing themselves before Joseph prefigures every knee bowing before Jesus Christ (Rom 14:11).

Genesis 43:27–28 And he asked them of [their] welfare, and said, [Is] your father well, the old man of whom ye spake? [Is] he yet alive? 28 And

---

[8] "[T]he whole Torah [as summarized by Hillel:] . . . 'What is hateful to yourself, do not to your fellow-man' [*Shabbath*]. This is the Talmudic formulation of the Golden Rule . . . Hillel's maxim is worded in the negative, whereas the Gospels have it in a positive form ['whatsoever ye would that men should do to you, do ye even so to them,' Matt 7:12]" (Cohen, *Rabbinic Sages* 214). The negative form is subsumed by the positive just as law is subsumed by grace.

they answered, Thy servant our father [is] in good health, he [is] yet alive. And they bowed down their heads, and made obeisance.

The firstborn Joseph is identified with the Son, while Joseph's progenitor Jacob is identified with the Holy Spirit (Luke 1:35). The brothers represent fallen humanity sent by and brought by the Spirit unto the Son. The three journeys to Egypt reflect the time of Adam followed by the First and Second Advents, whereby the emphasis on Jacob being an old man throughout this entire period testifies to the eternal nature of the Spirit. The emphasis on Jacob being yet alive points to the time of the call of the Spirit. And the intense interest of Joseph in whether his father, Jacob, is yet alive represents the Son awaiting the time of the end appointed by the Father (Mark 13:32). The brothers being able to confirm the life and good health of their father is a testimony to the living and life-giving work of the Holy Spirit, calling a fallen world to the repentance in Christ.

Benjamin

Genesis 43:29 And he lifted up his eyes, and saw his brother Benjamin, his mother's son, and said, [Is] this your younger brother, of whom ye spake unto me? And he said, God be gracious unto thee, my son.

The two brothers Joseph and Benjamin are uniquely the beloved sons of their father, Jacob. The first and second born Joseph and Benjamin reflect the millennial kingdom of Christ followed by eternity in Christ, likewise the First Advent of Christ followed by the Second Advent, and likewise the formation of Adam followed by the conception of Christ. All creation relates the twofold natures of Christ, who is fully man and fully God. This is the kingship and high priesthood of Christ. And this is the Covenant of Law subsumed by the Covenant of Grace.

Genesis 43:30 And Joseph made haste; for his bowels did yearn upon his brother: and he sought [where] to weep; and he entered into [his] chamber, and wept there.

Jesus wept (John 11:35).

Genesis 43:31 And he washed his face, and went out, and refrained himself, and said, Set on bread.

The act of washing represents baptism, while the act of eating bread represents the death of the body. And the connection between washing and eating is ultimately the baptism of the cross (Matt 20:22). The baptism in water is to the baptism of the Holy Spirit as repentance is to redemption as law is to grace as flesh is to spirit as the natural body is to the spiritual, or glorified, resurrection body. The baptism in water is to the baptism of the Holy Spirit as the first destruction of the world (by water) is to the coming second destruction of the world (by fire).

Genesis 43:32 And they set on for him by himself, and for them by themselves, and for the Egyptians, which did eat with him, by themselves: because the Egyptians might not eat bread with the Hebrews; for that [is] an abomination unto the Egyptians.

The necessary separation between Joseph and his brothers reflects the necessary separation between a righteous God and sinful mankind. But the hidden kinship connecting Joseph and his brothers reflects the essential kinship connecting God and the faithful in the Body of Christ. The relationship between Joseph and his brothers being at first hidden but later revealed reflects the progressive nature of revelation. The revelation of God is progressive just as everything in creation is progressive. If one could somehow imagine revelation not happening in time, it would not be consistent with the inviolable sanctity of freewill. There is only one paradigm for all creation, and that paradigm is God himself, specifically the triune nature of God—bringing the faithful into the fullness of communion with him, through him, and in him.[9]

Genesis 43:33 And they sat before him, the firstborn according to his birthright, and the youngest according to his youth: and the men marvelled one at another.

The particular ordering of the brothers according to their birthrights reflects the providential ordering of all creation from the time of Adam. The amazement of the brothers reflects the amazement of all mankind at the progressive revelation of the triunity of God.

Genesis 43:34 And he took [and sent] messes unto them from before him: but Benjamin's mess was five times so much as any of theirs. And they drank [H8354], and were merry [H7937] with him.

The word *merry* [H7937] (brothers were merry) has a connotation "to be or become drunk," while the word *drank* [H8354] (brothers drank) has connotations "to drink blood (of slaughter)" and also "of drinking the cup of Yahweh's [Jehovah's] wrath." These undertones portend the final tribulation and likewise the final judgment. The concurrent emphasis on the portion of the second born Benjamin being five times that of his brothers points to the fifth millennium and specifically to the rejection of the second man Jesus Christ in the fifth millennium. But the judgment of Jesus Christ on the cross and the judgment of the world by the cross are one event. And the church age is rightly

---

[9] "Some people think they can imagine a creature which was free but had no possibility of going wrong; I cannot. If a thing is free to be good it is also free to be bad" (Lewis, *Mere Christianity* 52). Biblical Christianity is common sense.

viewed as a parenthetical period because the First and Second Advents are rightly viewed as a single continuous whole.

The Silver Cup

Genesis 44:1 And he commanded the steward of his house, saying, Fill the men's sacks [with] food, as much as they can carry, and put every man's money in his sack's mouth.

The brothers are sustained by Joseph a second time, but their money is also rejected a second time. This second journey to Egypt prefigures the time of the First Advent, while the brothers themselves are identified with the totality of creation proceeding from Adam. The preservation of the brothers this second time reflects the preservation of the world even after the crucifixion of the second man Christ. But the rejection of the brothers' money being reaffirmed testifies to the irrevocable nature of the condemnation of the natural body even after the cross. The silver offered by the brothers represents the value placed upon the life of Christ (Matt 27:9). And the first and second journeys being connected by the offering of silver points to the connection between the original curse of Adam because of the tree and the ultimate curse of Christ on the tree of the cross (Gen 3:17–19, Gal 3:13).[10]

Genesis 44:2 And put my cup, the silver [H3701] cup, in the sack's mouth of the youngest, and his corn money [H3701]. And he did according to the word that Joseph had spoken.

The silver cup of Joseph is a symbol of the power and authority of Joseph, representing the power and authority of Jesus Christ. And the dominion of Christ comes by virtue of the cross. The strange parallel between the *silver* [H3701] cup of Joseph and the *money* (silver) [H3701] of his brothers is the value placed upon the life of Christ that ironically becomes a ransom for many (Matt 27:9, Matt 20:28). The silver cup of Joseph being placed into the possession of his younger brother Benjamin points to the bond between the two brothers. The relationship between Joseph and Benjamin reflects the relationship between the First and Second Advents and likewise the relationship between the millennial reign and eternity.

Genesis 44:3–4 As soon as the morning was light, the men were sent away, they and their asses. 4 [And] when they were gone out of the city, [and] not [yet] far off, Joseph said unto his steward, Up, follow after the men; and when thou dost overtake them, say unto them, Wherefore have ye rewarded evil for good?

---

[10] The only possible expiation for profaning the name of God is death, *Joma* (Cohen, *Rabbinic Sages* 23). All Adam-kind has profaned the name of God.

The evil that the brothers have returned for good is directly connected to their taking the silver cup of Joseph and specifically with their attempting to return home with the cup. The silver cup of Joseph represents the dominion that comes by virtue of the cross. The faithful in Christ participate in the death and resurrection of Christ (Col 2:12), but it is Christ himself who actually holds the keys of hell and of death (Rev 1:18). The faithful are not saved by faith of itself but rather by grace through faith in Jesus Christ (Eph 2:8).

Genesis 44:5 [Is] not this [it] in which my lord drinketh [H8354], and whereby indeed he divineth [H5172]? ye have done evil in so doing.

The word *drinketh* [H8354] (from the silver cup) has connotations "to drink blood (of slaughter)" and also "of drinking the cup of Yahweh's [Jehovah's] wrath" and, thereby, connects the cup of the new covenant with the baptism of the cross (Matt 20:22, Luke 22:20). The word *divineth* [H5172] (by the silver cup) has a connotation "to observe the signs" and is translated *learn by experience* [H5172] in the description of Laban, who represents the devil, acknowledging the blessing of God that proceeds from the person of Jacob (Gen 30:27). The silver cup of Joseph is an emblem of the power and authority of Jesus Christ over death and the world, specifically the dominion that comes by virtue of the cross. And the connection between drinking from the silver cup and divining by the silver cup points to just this connection between the spilled blood of Christ for the world and the sovereignty of Christ over the world.

Genesis 44:6 And he overtook them, and he spake unto them these same words.

The sons of Israel believe that they can now return to the land of Canaan, but in fact they will not be allowed to return at the present time. And this false expectation of the sons of Israel prefigures the misplaced hope at the time of the First Advent that the Messiah would restore the kingdom to ethnic Israel (Acts 1:6). For Christ to have simply restored the kingdom to Israel would have been an affirmation of natural man under the law. But in truth it is the cross that fulfills and also affirms the law—testifying to the irrevocable condemnation of natural man (Gen 3:19). Christ would not come to destroy the law or the prophets but rather to fulfill them (Matt 5:17). It is appointed unto all men once to die, but after this the judgment of the world (Heb 9:27).

Genesis 44:7–8 And they said unto him, Wherefore saith my lord these words? God forbid [H2486] that thy servants should do according to this thing: 8 Behold, the money [H3701], which we found in our sacks' mouths, we brought again unto thee out of the land of Canaan: how then should we steal out of thy lord's house silver [H3701] or gold [H2091]?

The word *forbid* (God forbid) [H2486] (thy servants) is derived from the root "to pollute, defile, profane" [H2490] used to describe men *beginning* (profanely)

[H2490] to call upon the name of the Lord at the time of Adam (Gen 4:26). The brothers on this second journey again offer the silver of their first journey as a proof of their innocence. But the rejection of the silver of the first journey is identified with the irrevocable rejection of the first man Adam. The brothers insisting upon identifying themselves with the silver of the first journey represents their insisting upon identifying themselves with Adam, likewise with the sin of Adam, and likewise with the condemnation of Adam. But the connection between the first and second journeys to Egypt points to the connection between the Fall of Adam and the First Advent of Christ.

God in sacrificing himself in the place of the first man Adam, or Adam-kind, at the time of the First Advent truly does *forbid* (God forbid) [H2486] the faithful from doing the evil thing of rejecting God, or not being able to accept God, as signified by the brothers taking Joseph's silver cup. The brothers not realizing at first that they had taken the silver cup for themselves reflects the ignorance and spiritual immaturity of Adam not realizing the ramifications of his rebellion. Joseph having placed the silver cup in their sack represents the foreknowledge and sovereignty of God. The addition of the symbol of gold to the symbol of silver now at the time of this second journey to Egypt points to the exaltation of Jesus Christ on the cross. The gold of Joseph that is added to the silver of Joseph is the glorification in Jesus Christ, in the Body of Christ, that is guaranteed by the sacrifice of Christ.

Genesis 44:9 With whomsoever of thy servants [H5650] it be found, both let him die, and we also will be my lord's bondmen [H5650].

The one man who possesses the silver cup must die. All other men are *servants* [H5650] and finally *bondmen* [H5650]. The one man who must die is Jesus Christ and likewise the faithful in the one Body of Christ. All other men are judged under the law to be sinners and specifically to be bondmen to sin.

Genesis 44:10 And he said, Now also [let] it [be] according unto your words: he with whom it is found shall be my servant; and ye shall be blameless.

The first judgment, pronounced by the brothers, is that the one who possesses the cup must die and that the remaining brothers must become servants (Gen 44:9). The second and final judgment, pronounced by the steward of Joseph, spiritually Joseph himself, is that the one who possesses the cup must become a servant and that the remaining brothers will be blameless. And these two judgments exist side by side without any controversy, even though they are fundamentally different. The first judgment by the brothers represents that of natural man, while the second judgment by Joseph represents that of spiritual, or glorified, man. The possessor of the cup must die in the natural, but in the spiritual, in glory, the possessor of the cup is identified with Joseph. Benjamin and Joseph, who both in a sense possess the cup, reflect different aspects of the one man Jesus Christ. And the emphasis on the brothers being blameless points to the essential justification of the faithful in Christ, in the Body of Christ. The brothers themselves are servants to sin according to the first judgment in the natural, but the brothers are blameless according to the second judgment in the spiritual. The first judgment is that natural man is the servant of sin and death, but the second judgment is that spiritual man is blameless in Jesus Christ. The first judgment is that of the law, while the second judgment is that of grace. And though fundamentally different, the two judgments do not contradict one another.

Genesis 44:11–12 Then they speedily took down every man his sack to the ground, and opened every man his sack. 12 And he searched, [and] began at the eldest, and left at the youngest: and the cup was found in Benjamin's sack.

The brothers reflect the totality of creation proceeding from Adam. And the search beginning with the eldest and ending with the youngest reflects the progression of the millennia from the time of Adam. The sack of every brother being searched reflects the judgment of all peoples throughout all time under the same law. The silver cup of Joseph represents the power and authority of Christ that comes by virtue of the cross. And the silver cup of Joseph being found in the bag of Benjamin reflects the close relationship between the two brothers Joseph and Benjamin. The brotherhood of Joseph and Benjamin reflects the unity of the First and Second Advents and likewise the unity of the millennial reign and eternity. And Joseph put the silver cup into the bag of Benjamin in order to be united with Benjamin. This is the unity of the Head and the Body that is the brotherhood of Christ and the faithful in Christ.

Genesis 44:13 Then they rent their clothes, and laded every man his ass, and returned to the city.

The brothers originally stripped Joseph of his coat of many colors and cast him into a pit, representing the death of Jesus Christ at the time of the First Advent (Gen 37:23–24, 37:31–33). And now the brothers rent their own clothing in imitation of Joseph just as the Body of Christ must follow Christ in death and resurrection. This is the time of the second journey to Egypt— representing the time of the First Advent, according to which a person is either condemned by the cross or redeemed on the cross. The brothers now return unto Joseph in the city to face him as their judge, to face either condemnation by Joseph as strangers or justification in Joseph as his brothers.

JUDAH

Genesis 44:14 And Judah and his brethren came to Joseph's house; for he [was] yet there: and they fell before him on the ground.

TWELVE SONS

The three journeys to Egypt reflect the time of Adam followed by the First and Second Advents of Christ. The brothers spoke to Joseph in one voice at the time of the first journey (Gen 42:10–11). But now Judah alone speaks to Joseph at this time of the second journey (Gen 44:16). The brothers speaking in one voice at the time of the first journey represents the universal guilt of all humanity in Adam. The firstborn Reuben proclaiming their guilt at the time of the first journey also points to the first man Adam (Gen 42:22). But the emphasis on the one man Judah at the time of this second journey points specifically to the Messianic bloodline embodied by Judah and specifically at the time of the First Advent (Gen 49:10).

Genesis 44:15 And Joseph said unto them, What deed [is] this that ye have done? wot ye not that such a man as I can certainly divine [H5172]?

The word *divineth* [H5172] (by the silver cup) has a connotation "to observe the signs" and is translated *learn by experience* [H5172] in the description of Laban, representing the devil, acknowledging the blessing of God that proceeds from the person of Jacob (Gen 30:27). The silver cup from which Joseph drinks and by which Joseph divines represents the power and authority of Christ and specifically that which comes by virtue of the cross. The relationship between Jacob and Joseph, manifested in Jacob sending his sons unto Joseph, reflects the relationship between the Spirit and the Son. Joseph knowing the deeds of his brothers recalls the original sin of the brothers against Joseph. And Joseph knowing the deeds of his brothers ultimately reflects the omniscience of God. The brothers not knowing the identity of Joseph, or understanding the purposes of Joseph, reflects the ignorance of natural man. And Joseph judging his brothers finally prefigures Jesus Christ judging the world (John 5:22).

Genesis 44:16 And Judah said, What shall we say unto my lord? what shall we speak? or how shall we clear ourselves? God hath found out the iniquity of thy servants: behold, we [are] my lord's servants, both we, and [he] also with whom the cup is found.

Judah embodies the Messianic bloodline that is the promise of Jesus Christ, while Joseph is identified specifically with the kingship of Christ that is foremost the humanity of Christ. And the brothers represent the totality of humanity proceeding from Adam that is the totality of fallen mankind. Judah confessing the guilt of the brothers to Joseph points to the promise of Christ being fulfilled in the person of Christ. And Judah identifies their guilt not with their being the enemies of Joseph but rather with their being the servants of Joseph, which reflects the one true salvation of us sinners that comes through submission to the cross. And the guilt of the brothers is further connected with the symbol of the silver cup of Joseph.

The brothers taking the silver cup of Joseph is specifically identified with their original betrayal of Joseph. The only brother innocent of this betrayal is ironically the very one found with the silver cup, and thereby the one innocent brother completes the picture of the sinless Christ, sacrificing himself on the cross in the place of fallen mankind. The silver cup represents the power and authority of Christ that comes by virtue of the cross. The silver cup is found with Benjamin and, thereby, connects Joseph and Benjamin, but nevertheless the silver cup still belongs to Joseph. The brotherhood of Joseph and Benjamin reflects the unity of the First and Second Advents of Christ and likewise the unity of the millennial reign of Christ and eternity in Christ, which is ultimately the unity of Christ the Head and the Body of Christ.

Genesis 44:17 And he said, God forbid [H2486] that I should do so: [but] the man in whose hand the cup is found, he shall be my servant; and as for you, get you up in peace unto your father.

The word *forbid* (God forbid) [H2486] connects Joseph's prohibition—that no one other than the one man would be acceptable—with the brother's previous prohibition—that no man among them should return evil for good (Gen 44:7). And these two prohibitions together reflect the imperative that only God himself can fulfill the law that justifies the faithful. The natural and the spiritual are in agreement just as the law and grace are in agreement. The word *forbid* (God forbid) [H2486] is derived from the root "to pollute, defile, profane" [H2490] used to describe men *beginning* (profanely) [H2490] to call upon the name of the Lord at the time of Adam (Gen 4:26). And God in sacrificing himself in the place of Adam truly does forbid, or enables, the faithful, separated from the faithless, from doing the evil thing of rejecting God, as represented by the brothers taking the silver cup of Joseph for themselves. The identification of any man other than Jesus Christ with the cup of the new covenant would represent a profaning, or rejecting, of the one sinless man, who is nothing less than God in the flesh (Luke 22:20).

The brothers with one voice previously judged that the one man found with the silver cup must die and that the rest of them must be servants (Gen 44:9). In contrast, the one man Judah, speaking for the brothers, judges that they are all the servants of Joseph (Gen 44:16). The former is the judgment made before the cup is found, while the latter is the judgment made after the cup is found. The former represents the death of the one man Christ, while the latter represents the resurrection of the faithful in Christ. Joseph now reiterates the previous judgment that only the one man found with the silver cup will be his servant (Gen 44:10), which represents the service, or perpetual intercession, of the one man Jesus Christ in behalf of the faithful (Heb 7:24-25). The perspective of Judah is that of natural man, while the perspective of Joseph is that of spiritual man. The former represents the law that governs natural man, while the latter represents the grace that governs spiritual man. The law is our schoolmaster that leads us to grace (Gal 3:24).

Genesis 44:18 Then Judah came near unto him, and said, Oh my lord, let thy servant, I pray thee, speak a word in my lord's ears, and let not thine anger burn against thy servant: for thou [art] even as Pharaoh.

TWELVE SONS

The fourth son Judah embodies the Messianic bloodline, representing the promise of God that is foremost the promised Seed of woman realized in the fourth millennium (Gen 3:15). Jacob sending all his remaining sons unto his second firstborn Joseph reflects the Holy Spirit bringing the faithful throughout the ages unto the only begotten Son. And the progression of the Messianic bloodline through the ages represents the movement of the Spirit, whereby Judah is appropriately acting as the messenger of Jacob. Pharaoh represents the Father while Joseph represents the Son, whereby Judah correctly identifies Joseph with Pharaoh. The Son is one with the Father (John 10:30). The person of Joseph being identified with a burning anger finally portends the foretold tribulation period and the corresponding destruction by fire (2 Pet 3:7).

Genesis 44:19 My lord asked his servants, saying, Have ye a father, or a brother?

The intense interest of Joseph concerning Jacob and Benjamin reflects the desire of God to reveal the triune reality of himself to humanity and thereby redeem humanity in himself. Joseph represents God the Son, and Joseph is closely identified with Pharaoh, who represents God the Father. The brotherhood of Joseph and Benjamin, especially the pressing necessity that Benjamin be united with Joseph, represents the unity of the First and Second Advents and likewise the unity of the millennial reign and eternity. And Jacob sending his sons unto Joseph represents the movement of God the Spirit.[11]

Genesis 44:20 And we said unto my lord, We have a father, an old man, and a child of his old age, a little one; and his brother is dead, and he alone is left of his mother, and his father loveth him.

Jacob sending his sons unto his lost son Joseph represents the providential movement of the Holy Spirit. Joseph is presumed dead and figuratively has died, but Joseph will be found resurrected. The emphasis on Jacob being an old man points to the end of the church age. Joseph compared with Benjamin reflects the First Advent compared with the Second Advent and likewise the millennial reign compared with eternity. The emphasis on the beloved son Benjamin being the child of Jacob's old age points to the end of the current world that corresponds to the end of the church age. The emphasis on

---

[11] "There is no doctrine of the Trinity in the strict sense in the Apostolic Fathers [Clement of Rome, Ignatius of Antioch, Hermas, Polycarp, and Papias, among others], but the trinitarian formulas are apparent" (Rusch 3). A Trinitarian understanding, as evidenced by the Bible itself, has, at the very least, always been implicit, or tacit, even in Old Testament times, but it is simultaneously true that there is an ongoing discussion about the Trinity, even in the modern day, reflecting the progressive, or explicit, revelation of the Trinity that has been occurring throughout all history. The former tacit revelation testifies to the Trinity existing in eternity, transcending creation, while the latter progressive revelation affirms the Trinitarian redemption of the faithful occurring in creation, or in space and time, in accordance with freewill.

Benjamin having no mother recalls his mother's death giving birth to him and, thereby, portends the coming judgment (Gen 31:32, 35:18).

Genesis 44:21 And thou saidst unto thy servants, Bring him down unto me, that I may set mine eyes upon him.

Joseph, who rules with the power and authority of Pharaoh, requires that Benjamin be brought before his eyes. Jacob sends Benjamin unto Joseph so that they may all live and not die. And the brothers are compelled to bring Benjamin unto Joseph. The faithful are called by the Son according to the authority of the Father, and the faithful are brought unto the Son by the power of the Holy Spirit. Joseph can call his brothers by the authority of Pharaoh simply because he has the power, but Joseph can bring them and present them unto Pharaoh only because they are his brothers and spiritually one flesh, or one body, with him. The authority to call the brothers reflects the kingship, while the power to present the brothers reflects the priesthood. The call of the brothers represents the call to repentance, while the presentation of the brothers represents the sanctification of the faithful. The call to repentance in Christ compared with the sanctification by the Holy Spirit is the First Advent of Christ compared with the Second Advent. And the two are one just as the one man Jesus Christ is simultaneously the Son of man and the Son of God. The birthright and the blessing belong to the second firstborn who is Jesus Christ.

Genesis 44:22 And we said unto my lord, The lad cannot leave his father: for [if] he should leave his father, [his father] would die.

The hypothetical death of Jacob represents the hypothetical failure of the Holy Spirit to redeem the faithful in the Body of Christ. Jacob will die, reflecting the end of the final age corresponding to the end of the seventh millennium, but he will not die because of a separation from his beloved Benjamin and Joseph or, for that matter, from any of his sons. God the Spirit cannot fail. Nonetheless, a figurative, or spiritual, death of Jacob—signified by Jacob's temporary separation from Benjamin—is connected with this second journey into Egypt. And the figurative death of Jacob in this context represents the rejection of Jesus Christ, likewise the rejection of the Spirit of Christ, but specifically at the time of the First Advent, not in the Second Advent.

Genesis 44:23 And thou saidst unto thy servants, Except your youngest brother come down with you, ye shall see my face no more.

To see the face of Joseph is like seeing the face of Pharaoh. To see the Son is to see the Father (John 14:9). The promise of the Father is the indwelling Holy Spirit—sent by the Son in accordance with the will of the Father, calling the faithful in the Son unto the Father (John 14:16–20). The necessity that Benjamin must come unto his older brother, Joseph, represents the essential unity of the First and Second Advents of Christ, which is the absolutely necessary unity of the resurrection of Jesus Christ as the Head and the resurrection of the faithful as the Body of Christ (1 Cor 15:22–24). And the faithful even now wait and watch to see the face of the Son at the time of the resurrection and rapture (1 Cor 13:12).

Genesis 44:24 And it came to pass when we came up unto thy servant my father, we told him the words of my lord.

Jacob is the father of Joseph, together with all Joseph's brothers, and Jacob is also the servant of Joseph. God the Holy Spirit is sent by God the Son to nurture and raise up the faithful in the Body of Christ (John 16:7). Jacob hearing the judgment of Joseph from the mouths of Joseph's brothers reflects the Holy Spirit hearing the suffering of all humanity.

Genesis 44:25 And our father said, Go again, [and] buy us a little food.

The Spirit urges humanity to come unto the Son and receive eternal life.

Genesis 44:26 And we said, We cannot go down: if our youngest brother be with us, then will we go down: for we may not see the man's face, except our youngest brother [be] with us.

The world will not see the face of Jesus Christ until the appointed time of the Second Advent (Matt 23:39).

Genesis 44:27 And thy servant my father said unto us, Ye know that my wife bare me two [sons]:

The Holy Spirit points the faithful to the two sons of one mother in the last days. The first and second sons Joseph and Benjamin reflect the First and Second Advents of Christ, individually and sequentially embodying death and resurrection. This is likewise the Covenants of Law and Grace, likewise the birthright and blessing, and likewise the kingship and high priesthood. And this is finally the millennial reign followed by and connected with eternity.

Genesis 44:28 And the one went out from me, and I said, Surely he is torn in pieces; and I saw him not since:

The image of the second firstborn Joseph being torn in pieces by a wild animal points to the crucifixion of Jesus Christ (Ps 22:13). The emphasis on Jacob not having seen Joseph points to the formal separation, or distinction, between the work of the Spirit and that of the Son. The Holy Spirit is sent into the world to call the faithful, while the ascendant Christ prepares a place for the faithful (John 14:2–4, 14:16–18). And Christ himself actually is the place of faith unto which the faithful are called by the Spirit. This is the Body of Christ animated by the Holy Spirit.

Genesis 44:29 And if ye take this also from me, and mischief befall him, ye shall bring down my gray hairs with sorrow to the grave.

The movement of the Holy Spirit is evident in the progression from Adam to the promised new Adam, who is Jesus Christ, likewise the progression from the First Advent of Christ to the Second Advent, and likewise the progression from the millennial reign of Christ to eternity in Christ. The mischief that might befall Benjamin is connected with a hypothetical premature death of Jacob, but such a circumstance is denied by the providential will of God. The Spirit will not fail. Nonetheless, the speculation whirling around the possible premature death of Jacob portends a time of confusion and uncertainty, marking the tribulation of the crucifixion and likewise the final tribulation of the end times.

Genesis 44:30–31 Now therefore when I come to thy servant my father, and the lad [be] not with us; seeing that his life is bound up in the lad's life; 31 It shall come to pass, when he seeth that the lad [is] not [with us], that he will die: and thy servants shall bring down the gray hairs of thy servant our father with sorrow to the grave.

The life of Jacob is bound up in the life of Benjamin. The life of Jacob is bound up in the brotherhood of Joseph and Benjamin. The life of Jacob is bound up in the salvation of his offspring that comes by the brotherhood of Joseph and Benjamin. The promise of eternal life proceeds by the Holy Spirit in the Son from the Father (John 6:54).[12]

Genesis 44:32 For thy servant became surety for the lad unto my father, saying, If I bring him not unto thee, then I shall bear the blame to my father for ever.

The fourth son Judah embodies the Messianic bloodline (Gen 49:10). The person of Judah becoming the guarantee of the coming of Benjamin reflects the life of Jesus Christ becoming a ransom for many (Matt 20:28). The blood of Christ shed at the time of the First Advent is the guarantee of our redemption, the fullness of which will be revealed at the time of the Second Advent. The blame that Judah would bear forever reflects Christ becoming a curse on the cross for the sake of his faithful ones—past, present, and future (Gal 3:13).

Genesis 44:33 Now therefore, I pray thee, let thy servant abide instead of the lad a bondman to my lord; and let the lad go up with his brethren.

---

[12] "[E]very activity which pervades from God to creation and is named according to our manifold designs starts off from the Father, proceeds through the Son, and is completed by the Holy Spirit" (Rusch 155). The original creation, Adam-kind, proceeds from the Father by the Spirit through the Son, while the promised new creation, Christ-kind, is united by the Spirit in the Son with the Father.

Judah offering himself in the place of his brother reflects Christ offering himself in the place of the faithful. Joseph compared with Benjamin reflects the First Advent of Christ compared with the Second Advent and likewise the millennial kingdom of Christ compared with eternity in Christ. Judah bringing Benjamin unto Joseph reflects the bloodline that literally leads from Adam to Christ and spiritually leads Adam to Christ.[13]

Genesis 44:34 For how shall I go up to my father, and the lad [be] not with me? lest peradventure I see the evil that shall come on my father.

The personal evil that seeks to destroy the life of the Spirit, likewise the life that proceeds from the Spirit, is the great dragon, that old serpent, called the devil and also satan, which deceives the whole world (Rev 12:9).

Pharaoh, Joseph, Jacob

Genesis 45:1–2 Then Joseph could not refrain himself before all them that stood by him; and he cried, Cause every man to go out from me. And there stood no man with him, while Joseph made himself known unto his brethren. 2 And he wept aloud: and the Egyptians and the house of Pharaoh heard.

Joseph chooses to reveal himself now at the time of his brothers' second journey to Egypt. This second journey has a twofold structure in that the brothers attempt to leave but are forced to return (Gen 44:13). And the key distinction between these two parts of the second journey is the changing relationship between Joseph and his brothers. In the first part of the second journey, Joseph is lord and master over his brothers, but in the second part of the second journey, Joseph is also the blood relative of his brothers. The twofold structure marking this second journey is identified with the progressive revelation of the twofold natures of Jesus Christ that marks the First Advent. And the changing relationship between Joseph and his brothers reflects the changing relationship between Christ and his disciples. The disciples of Christ are servants who become friends by virtue of the cross (John 15:15). The natural precedes the spiritual just as the law precedes grace. Christ likewise reveals himself first as the Son of man and second as the Son of God.

---

[13] Judah sacrificing himself for [his younger half-brother] Benjamin is the specific point at which Judah supplants [his older brother] Reuben as the successor to the birthright of the firstborn (Coffman 523; Gen 44:32–34). The second man, or younger, Jesus Christ sacrifices himself to redeem his faithful ones and, in so doing, supplants the first man, or elder, Adam. The faithful in Christ come out of all the ages but are exalted only following Christ, wherein the faithful are themselves like a younger sibling. The further identification of the faithful with a half-brother reflects the faithful being adopted, while the further identification of Adam with a full brother reflects Adam being unbegotten and therein uniquely embodying the image of God.

Genesis 45:3 And Joseph said unto his brethren, I [am] Joseph; doth my father yet live? And his brethren could not answer him; for they were troubled at his presence.

The risen Christ would likewise stand in the midst of his disciples, and they would be terrified at his sight, supposing him to be a spirit (Luke 24:36–38). Joseph seeking an affirmation of the life of Jacob from the mouths of Joseph's brothers represents Christ seeking to relate the presence of the indwelling Holy Spirit unto his faithful ones. The mouth of a man testifies to the overflow of his heart (Luke 6:45). The mouth of a man represents the stirring of the breath of life that is the breath of God and specifically God the Holy Spirit (Gen 2:7). And the Holy Spirit must proceed from God if a man is to live and not die. Joseph questioning his brothers represents the movement of the Holy Spirit, while the desired response of the brothers represents the quickening of the Spirit. The one true God is the one and only font of life.[14]

Genesis 45:4–5 And Joseph said unto his brethren, Come near to me, I pray you. And they came near. And he said, I [am] Joseph your brother, whom ye sold into Egypt. 5 Now therefore be not grieved, nor angry with yourselves, that ye sold me hither: for God did send me before you to preserve life.

Christ would likewise teach his disciples that he must suffer many things, and be rejected of the elders and chief priests and scribes, and be slain, and be raised the third day (Luke 9:22). Joseph being sent into Egypt before his brothers in order to preserve life prefigures Jesus becoming the firstfruits from the dead (1 Cor 15:20). Joseph drawing his brothers near unto himself reflects Christ drawing his faithful ones in the Body of Christ (1 Cor 15:23).[15]

Genesis 45:6 For these two years [hath] the famine [been] in the land: and yet [there are] five years, in the which [there shall] neither [be] earing nor harvest.

The seven years of famine portend the final seven foretold through and by the prophet Daniel, namely, the final seven-year tribulation period (Dan 9:27). The focus here is the end of the second year and the beginning of the third year, and thus time is short for the house of Jacob to flee Canaan. The mid-tribulation point at three and one-half years will mark the beginning of the great tribulation (Matt 24:15–21). The house of Jacob is saved out of and through the

---

[14] "Their dismay [confronting their brother Joseph] is a shadow of what will happen when the Jews see Jesus for who He is again: '... whom they pierced....'" (Guzik 249; Gen 45:1–3). The time of the Second Advent will be like that of the First Advent, a remnant worshipping the Lord prefiguring a universal acknowledgment of the Lord.
[15] "This example teaches, that we must by all means comfort those, which are truly humbled and wounded for their sins" (Whittingham et al., *Geneva Bible* 22L n. b; Gen 45:5). The baptism of the law is followed by the baptism of grace.

tribulation represented by the famine—reflecting the resurrection and rapture of the faithful preceding the final tribulation and, simultaneously and without contradiction, the redemption through the tribulation of a remnant of new believers, or newly believing, in Christ.

Genesis 45:7 And God sent me before you to preserve you a posterity in the earth, and to save your lives by a great deliverance.

The great deliverance that follows, or proceeds from, the sending forth of Joseph prefigures the promised but yet future glorious reappearing that necessarily follows the death and resurrection of Jesus Christ. The emphasis on preserving posterity in the earth points to the re-creation of the earth that will accompany the rebirth and resurrection of the faithful (Rev 21:1).

Genesis 45:8 So now [it was] not you [that] sent me hither, but God: and he hath made me a father to Pharaoh, and lord of all his house, and a ruler throughout all the land of Egypt.

God making Joseph a father unto Pharaoh reflects the unity of the Father and the Son (John 10:30). This is all things being given into the hand of the Son (John 3:35). It is God and God alone that sent Joseph into the land of Egypt. The purpose of the brothers, apart from the will of God, would have been to kill Joseph and dispose of him forever. But no man would take the life of Christ; rather, Christ would lay it down and take it up again by his own power, or righteousness (John 10:18). Joseph being lord over the house of Pharaoh and ruling throughout the land of Pharaoh prefigures the millennial kingdom of Christ preceding and opening eternity in Christ (Rev 20:6).

Genesis 45:9 Haste ye, and go up to my father, and say unto him, Thus saith thy son Joseph, God hath made me lord of all Egypt: come down unto me, tarry not:

The enemies of the Lord have been made his footstool (Heb 10:13). This is the appointed time, and the Lord will not tarry (Heb 10:37).

Genesis 45:10 And thou shalt dwell in the land of Goshen, and thou shalt be near unto me, thou, and thy children, and thy children's children, and thy flocks, and thy herds, and all that thou hast:

The necessity that Jacob be near unto his son Joseph represents the essential twofold unity of the Spirit and the Son proceeding from the Father. And the final manifestation of the unity of the Son and the Spirit, in accordance with the promise of the Father, will be the one Body of Christ—a second, or new, reality, fundamentally twofold itself, Head and Body, to be fully established at the time of the Second Advent.[16]

Genesis 45:11 And there will I nourish thee; for yet [there are] five years of famine; lest thou, and thy household, and all that thou hast, come to poverty.

And the woman fled into the wilderness, where she hath a place prepared of God, that they should feed her there a thousand two hundred and threescore days (Rev 12:6).

Genesis 45:12 And, behold, your eyes see, and the eyes of my brother Benjamin, that [it is] my mouth that speaketh unto you.

The Spirit brings the faithful unto the Son, and the faithful testify concerning the identity of the Son. The testimony of the brothers marks the time of the coming of the second son Benjamin unto the first son Joseph that is the time of the Second Advent.

Genesis 45:13 And ye shall tell my father of all my glory in Egypt, and of all that ye have seen; and ye shall haste and bring down my father hither.

The nexus connecting Joseph and Jacob is the testimony of the brothers concerning Joseph. The visible revelation of the unity of the Son and the Spirit is the testimony of the Body of Christ.

Genesis 45:14–15 And he fell upon his brother Benjamin's neck, and wept; and Benjamin wept upon his neck. 15 Moreover he kissed all his brethren, and wept upon them: and after that his brethren talked with him.

The image of Joseph weeping upon his brothers reflects the baptism of repentance that is signified by water. The baptism in water precedes the baptism of the Spirit just as the law precedes grace just as the natural precedes the spiritual just as the First Advent precedes the Second Advent. This is the baptism of repentance that must precede the baptism of redemption, in accordance with the inviolable nature of the freewill of man. The tears of Joseph represent the tears of Jesus Christ, connecting the baptism in water and the baptism of the cross (Matt 20:22).

---

[16] "Glory to the Father, and to the Son, and to the Holy Spirit, the triune light of the Godhead, which is unity subsisting in trinity, divided, yet indivisible: for the Trinity is the one God Almighty, whose glory the heavens declare, and the earth His dominion . . . . [*Liturgy of James*]" (Roberts et al., *Ante-Nicene Fathers* 7:537). The one creation is the twofold earth and heaven proceeding from the triune God.

TWELVE SONS

Genesis 45:16 And the fame thereof was heard in Pharaoh's house, saying, Joseph's brethren are come: and it pleased Pharaoh well, and his servants.

Pharaoh being well pleased by Joseph bringing his brethren unto himself reflects the Father being well pleased in the Son drawing the faithful into himself (Matt 12:18–21). The servants of Pharaoh also being well pleased reflects the angels of God rejoicing over men turning from their myriad sins unto the one true God (Luke 15:10).

Genesis 45:17–18 And Pharaoh said unto Joseph, Say unto thy brethren, This do ye; lade your beasts, and go, get you unto the land of Canaan; 18 And take your father and your households, and come unto me: and I will give you the good of the land of Egypt, and ye shall eat the fat of the land.

Pharaoh represents God the Father, while Jacob represents God the Spirit. And it is in the bringing of Jacob unto Pharaoh that the blessing is received. This is the third and final journey to Egypt, reflecting the Second Advent. The brothers being blessed by Pharaoh through Jacob represents the promised new creation that comes by the indwelling Holy Spirit. The emphasis on the brothers themselves bringing Jacob unto Pharaoh represents an affirmation of the inviolable nature of freewill.

Genesis 45:19 Now thou art commanded, this do ye; take you wagons out of the land of Egypt for your little ones, and for your wives, and bring your father, and come.

Joseph's brothers must bring Jacob unto Pharaoh in order to live and not die during the famine of the land. The commandment of God is to come unto him and receive the seal of eternal life while yet enduring the famine of the natural body. Those who disobey the commandment of God are separating themselves from God and necessarily die in separation from God because God is the one and only font of life, that is, the fullness of eternal life.

Genesis 45:20 Also regard not your stuff; for the good of all the land of Egypt [is] yours.

The natural body, Adam-kind, is supplanted by the spiritual, or glorified, body, Christ-kind. The present earth and heaven will likewise be supplanted by the new earth and new heaven.

Genesis 45:21 And the children of Israel did so: and Joseph gave them wagons, according to the commandment of Pharaoh, and gave them provision for the way.

ESAU, JACOB, ISRAEL

The Lord himself gives us the strength and means to come unto him.

Genesis 45:22 To all of them he gave each man changes of raiment; but to Benjamin he gave three hundred [pieces] of silver, and five changes of raiment.

Joseph was stripped by his brothers, but now Joseph clothes all of them. And Joseph's power to cloth his brothers is actually derived from them having stripped him and cast him into a pit, representing the grave (Gen 37:23–24). Joseph giving changes of raiment to all his brothers represents the whole world being blessed by Jesus Christ. The special blessing of Benjamin by Joseph, which is marked by the sign of silver, reflects the unity of the First and Second Advents being based on the sacrifice of Christ, also marked by the sign of silver (Matt 27:9). The five changes of raiment point to the crucifixion of Christ in the fifth millennium from Adam. The three hundred pieces of silver point to the resurrection of Christ on the third day from the crucifixion, likewise to the resurrection of the Body of Christ in the third millennium from the crucifixion (Matt 12:38–40). The five changes of raiment (for the body) connect Adam and Jesus Christ according to the natural body, or Messianic bloodline, while the three hundred pieces of silver connect Christ the Head and the Body of Christ according to the value of life determined by the law and amplified by grace. And the changes of raiment, together with the pieces of silver, being given to the one brother Benjamin points to the summation and culmination of all things at the time of the Second Advent.

Genesis 45:23 And to his father he sent after this [manner]; ten asses laden with the good things of Egypt, and ten she asses laden with corn and bread and meat for his father by the way.

The emphasis on groups of ten beasts of burden bringing Jacob unto Joseph testifies to the central importance of the law bringing the chosen faithful unto grace (Gal 3:24). The number 10 is perhaps most notably identified with the law by the Ten Commandments (Deut 4:13).

Genesis 45:24 So he sent his brethren away, and they departed: and he said unto them, See that ye fall not out by the way.

Broad is the way to destruction, narrow is the way unto life (Matt 7:13–14).

Genesis 45:25–27 And they went up out of Egypt, and came into the land of Canaan unto Jacob their father, 26 And told him, saying, Joseph [is] yet alive, and he [is] governor over all the land of Egypt. And Jacob's heart fainted, for he believed them not. 27 And they told him all the words of Joseph, which he had said unto them: and when he saw the wagons which Joseph had sent to carry him, the spirit of Jacob their father revived:

TWELVE SONS

The call to believe that Joseph is alive represents the call to faith in the risen Lord. The intangible testimony of Joseph's brothers represents the subtlety of God the Spirit, while the tangible wagons of Joseph represent the visible gifts of the Spirit. The brothers testifying that Joseph lives and is lord over all Egypt reflects the Spirit, in accordance with the Father, testifying to the life that exists only in the Son (John 15:26). Jacob originally not believing portends a prevalent spirit of delusion existing in the end times, but Jacob ultimately believing testifies that God the Holy Spirit, the Spirit of truth, will save a remnant, even during the final tribulation (2 Thess 2:11–13).[17]

Genesis 45:28 And Israel said, [It is] enough; Joseph my son [is] yet alive: I will go and see him before I die.

The necessity that Jacob must see Joseph before he, Jacob, dies points to the fulfillment of all the promises of God in the offspring of Jacob. The death of Jacob prefigures the end of the final age that is the beginning of eternity.[18]

Ω Ω Ω

The three brothers Reuben, Judah and Joseph form the primary twofold relationships that usher Joseph into Egypt and finally the entire house of Jacob into Egypt. Reuben, Judah, and Joseph reflect Adam, Jesus Christ, and the Body of Christ, that is, Adam followed by the First and Second Advents of Christ. The firstborn son Reuben is identified with the first man Adam and also the first millennium during which Adam lived, while the fourth son Judah is identified with the Messianic bloodline and also the conception of Christ at the end of the fourth millennium. But Joseph as the preeminent son of Jacob is also identified with Jesus Christ. Reuben first casting Joseph into a pit reflects the spiritual reality of the rebellion of Adam, which is that Adam and likewise all mankind in Adam are culpable for the death of Christ (Gen 37:22). Judah is identified with Christ via the Messianic bloodline since Christ would emerge from the tribe of Judah (Gen 49:10), whereby Judah raising Joseph up out of the pit reflects the Holy Spirit—signified by the bloodline, or blood, or life in the blood, of Christ—raising Christ up from the dead (Gen 37:26–28).

The Messianic bloodline, representing the saving blood of Jesus Christ, would not be forever cut off at the time of the First Advent, but rather the

---

[17] "Every time in the Bible when a person is called upon to exercise faith, it's an intelligent faith. . . . The problem with most people is that they seem to stop with their hearts. The facts about Christ never get to their minds. We've been given a mind innovated by the Holy Spirit to know God, as well as a heart to love him . . . ." (McDowell, *Carpenter* 39). Mind and heart must work together just as flesh and spirit must work together just as law and grace must work together.

[18] "In Joseph's making himself known unto his brethren, he was a type of Christ, who manifests himself to his people alone . . . not unto the world . . . ." (Gill 1:228; Gen 45:28). The emphasis on blood kinship testifies to the personal nature of salvation, coming only through the blood of Jesus Christ.

bloodline of Christ would be continued in the Body of Christ and will culminate in the resurrection and rapture at the time of the Second Advent. The persons of Judah and Joseph are both identified with Jesus Christ—respectively, with the First and Second Advents of Christ—and thus the second firstborn Joseph eclipsing the fourth born Judah reflects the Second Advent of Christ fulfilling the First Advent. (It's completely normal for more than one personage to simultaneously reflect the Lord, and it's completely normal for roles to change in different narratives, also in different perspectives of the same narrative.) Joseph finally ruling in accordance with the will of Pharaoh and simultaneously for the benefit of the house of Jacob prefigures the millennial kingdom to be established at the time of the Second Advent (Gen 41:40, 50:21).

1	2
REUBEN	JUDAH
ADAM	CHRIST
JUDAH	JOSEPH
FIRST ADVENT	SECOND ADVENT

The comparison between Joseph and his ten half brothers parallels the comparison between Jesus Christ and Adam-kind, or humanity as a whole, while the unique full brotherhood of Joseph and Benjamin prefigures the relationship between the First and Second Advents, that is, between Christ and the Body of Christ. The authority of Joseph being established through his personal suffering prefigures the kingship of Christ at the time of the First Advent. The firstborn Joseph exalting the second born Benjamin reflects the First Advent being fulfilled in the Second Advent, that is, the resurrection of Christ as the Head being fulfilled in the resurrection of the Body of Christ (Gen 43:34, 45:22). And Joseph's younger brother being born in suffering as Benoni but then being raised up in love as Benjamin is an affirmation of the essential unity of the First and Second Advents of Christ (Gen 35:18). The silver cup of Joseph, which signifies the power and authority of Joseph, foreshadows the life of Christ being valued in silver, and therefore the silver cup of Joseph, which marks Benjamin as belonging to Joseph, again connects the First and Second Advents (Gen 44:2). And the suffering kingship of the First Advent compared with the sanctifying high priesthood of the Second Advent points to the millennial reign as compared with eternity.

1	2
JACOB'S SONS	JOSEPH
ADAM-KIND	JESUS CHRIST
THE SECOND FIRSTBORN JOSEPH	THE FINAL SECOND BORN BENJAMIN
A KINGSHIP ESTABLISHED THROUGH SUFFERING	A SECOND BORN EXALTED BY THE FIRSTBORN
FIRST ADVENT (KINGSHIP)	SECOND ADVENT (HIGH PRIESTHOOD)
MILLENNIAL KINGDOM	ETERNITY

The three journeys of Joseph's brothers into Egypt reflect the threefold successive formation of Adam followed by the First and Second Advents of

Christ. Joseph not being recognized by his ten half brothers at the time of the first journey represents the plan, or law, of God, likewise God himself, not being recognized, or understood, by the first man Adam. Joseph revealing himself to all his brothers at the time of the second journey represents Christ revealing himself, ultimately to all peoples, at the time of the First Advent (Gen 45:1). And Joseph nourishing Jacob on the third and final journey in order to make his house into a great nation and kingdom prefigures the Body of Christ being established in the millennial kingdom of Jesus Christ at the time of the Second Advent (Gen 45:7–11). And the judgment of the first man Adam followed by the revelation of God the Son followed by the exaltation of the faithful in the Body of Christ is finally recognized as the progressive revelation of God the Father, God the Son, and God the Holy Spirit.

The original identification of the brothers as subversives, which would result in the second born Simeon being bound, reflects the original condemnation of all mankind in Adam, which would culminate in the Flood of the second millennium (Gen 42:9, 42:24). The fourth son Judah being chosen, over the first son Reuben, to lead the second journey into Egypt points to the conception of Jesus Christ at the end of the fourth millennium (Gen 42:37–38, 43:8–11). The unique brotherhood of Joseph and Benjamin, sharing the same mother, reflects the unity of the First and Second Advents of Christ, bearing the one and same indwelling Spirit. The First Advent guarantees our redemption, but it is the Second Advent that is the actual manifestation of our redemption. Benjamin not being allowed to make the first journey reflects the utter condemnation of Adam in the natural body (Gen 42:4), while the absolute necessity that Benjamin must take the subsequent journeys reflects the essential connection between the First and Second Advents in the Body of Christ (Gen 43:3).

1	2	3
FIRST JOURNEY TO EGYPT	SECOND JOURNEY TO EGYPT	THIRD JOURNEY TO EGYPT
ADAM	FIRST ADVENT	SECOND ADVENT
BROTHERS	JOSEPH	HOUSE OF JACOB
CONDEMNED	REVEALED	ESTABLISHED
GOD THE FATHER	GOD THE SON	GOD THE HOLY SPIRIT

The three journeys into Egypt reflect the first man followed by the First and Second Advents that is ultimately understood to be the progressive revelation of the Father, Son, and Spirit. The fundamental Trinitarian pattern is reinforced by the threefold sequence of Reuben rejecting Joseph and casting him into a pit (Gen 37:21–22) followed by Judah raising Joseph up out of the pit and selling him into Gentile Egypt (Gen 37:26–28) followed by the brothers coming unto Joseph in Egypt in order to live and not die (Gen 42:1–2). The Trinitarian pattern is again reinforced by the threefold sequence of Jacob rejecting Reuben as a guarantee for the safety of Benjamin (Gen 42:37–38) followed by Jacob accepting Judah as a guarantee for Benjamin (Gen 43:8–11) followed by Joseph revealing himself to Jacob's house and exalting Benjamin (Gen 45:3). And the Trinitarian pattern is again reinforced by the threefold sequence of Joseph accusing his brothers and condemning Simeon (Gen 42:9, 42:24) followed by

Joseph uniting himself with Benjamin according to the sign of the silver cup (Gen 44:17) followed by Joseph identifying himself with Judah, saving the lives of his brothers and bringing them under his dominion (Gen 45:5).

1	2	3
REUBEN REJECTS JOSEPH (CAST INTO THE PIT)	JUDAH SAVES JOSEPH (SOLD TO GENTILES)	BROTHERS GO UNTO JOSEPH (TO LIVE & NOT DIE)
FALL OF ADAM	FIRST ADVENT OF CHRIST	SECOND ADVENT
REUBEN NOT ACCEPTED IN THE PLACE OF BENJAMIN	JUDAH IS ACCEPTED IN THE PLACE OF BENJAMIN	JOSEPH REVEALS HIMSELF TO THE HOUSE OF JACOB
FALL OF ADAM	FIRST ADVENT OF CHRIST	SECOND ADVENT
JOSEPH CONDEMNS HIS BROTHERS	JOSEPH UNITED WITH BENJAMIN	JOSEPH SAVES HIS BROTHERS
FALL OF ADAM	FIRST ADVENT OF CHRIST	SECOND ADVENT

Joseph being sent into Egypt ahead of his brothers in order to save them prefigures the death and resurrection of Christ being the way of redemption for the faithful in Christ (Gen 45:5). And Jacob sending Joseph's brothers unto him represents the Spirit directing the faithful unto Christ (Gen 42:1–2). Joseph compared with his brothers reflects Jesus Christ compared with all humanity, specifically the millennial reign of Christ compared with the six millennia of Adam-kind. In contrast, Joseph compared with his one brother Benjamin reflects the millennial kingdom compared with eternity. Nonetheless, the relationship between the first man Adam and second man Christ parallels the relationship between the First and Second Advents, also the relationship between the millennial reign of Christ and eternity in Christ. And showing the same basic twofold pattern, the beginning and end of the millennial reign will itself be marked by two tribulations (Rev 20:2, 20:7). And the fires that mark the beginning and end of the millennial reign are connected just as the original curse of Adam is connected with the final curse of all Adam-kind.

Further, the second son Simeon being bound on the first of the three journeys into Egypt recalls the destruction of the world in the second millennium (Gen 42:24). And Leah's second son, Simeon, being bound as a guarantee of the coming of Rachel's second son, Benjamin, connects the two second sons (Gen 42:19–20). The parallel between Simeon and Benjamin is the parallel between the first and second destructions, respectively, by water in the past and by fire in the future, which is the same parallel between the two fires, or sword (blood) followed by fire, bookending the millennial kingdom (2 Pet 3:3–13). The famine that drives the house of Jacob into Egypt recalls the original curse, or famine, of the ground, which is embodied by Adam and affirmed by the baptism in the floodwaters (Gen 3:17). And the famine of Jacob also portends the final curse, or tribulation, of all creation, which is prefigured by the sweat of Adam (unto death) and fulfilled by the baptism of fire (Gen 3:19). The famine of God that corresponds to the fire of God is the famine of the Word of God (Amos 8:11). Jacob's sons represent the totality of creation proceeding from the first man Adam, whereby the final journey of Jacob with his sons during a time of famine represents a recapitulation (sanctification) of all creation that is necessitated by the condemnation of all creation.

CHAPTER FIVE OUTLINE

Key Images

PRIME IMAGES

Material	Abstract	Spiritual
The sons of Jacob.	A progression of offspring.	The totality of history.
Seven years of famine.	An affliction of all creation.	Seven years of tribulation.
Jacob sends his sons unto Joseph in Egypt to buy corn.	A sending forth in order to live and not die.	God the Holy Spirit directs the faithful unto God the Son.
The sign of silver marking the bags of the brothers and causing their submission unto Joseph.	A law that binds the brothers unto Joseph.	The law of repentance that must precede the redemption by grace.
Joseph accuses his brothers.	A judgment that comes because they had rejected their brother.	The judgment of the world.
The binding of the second born son (of a freewoman) Simeon by the seventh born son (also of a freewoman) Joseph.	An affliction of the second born that connects the second born and the seventh born.	The first destruction marking the second millennium is linked to the second destruction heralding the seventh millennium.
Joseph as the ruler of all Egypt reveals himself to his brothers.	The innocent one who suffered becomes the ruler of the world.	The millennial reign of Christ.
Joseph accepts his brothers.	An unmerited forgiveness.	The salvation of the faithful.
Jacob goes unto Joseph so that he can die satisfied.	A completion of a life.	The end of the age.

TWOFOLD IMAGES

Material	Abstract	Spiritual
Rachel's first and second born sons, Joseph and Benjamin.	First and second sons. First longs for the second. Flesh and spirit.	Adam animated by the Spirit, Christ conceived of the Spirit.
The firstborn Reuben casting Joseph into a pit is followed by the fourth born Judah selling Joseph into slavery.	First son, fourth son. A sin causing a servitude. Flesh and spirit.	The curse of Adam in the first millennium followed by the humble condescension of Christ in the fourth millennium.
The land of Canaan, likewise all the nations, compared with the one nation of Egypt.	Weak and strong. Cursed and blessed. Flesh and spirit.	The nations surrounding the one city of God during the millennial reign (Rev 20:7–9).
The guarantee of the firstborn Reuben for the safety of Benjamin is rejected, but the guarantee of the fourth born Judah is accepted.	First son, fourth son. Former guarantee, latter. Rejected, accepted. Flesh and spirit.	Adam formed at the beginning of the first millennium compared with Jesus Christ being conceived at the end of the fourth.
The necessity that the second born Benjamin must be brought unto the firstborn Joseph.	First and second sons. First plus the second. Flesh and spirit.	Adam and Christ. First and Second Advents. Millennial reign and eternity.
Joseph as the ruler of Egypt not being recognized by his brothers is followed by Joseph revealing himself unto his brothers.	The possessor of power not being recognized is followed by a blood kinship being revealed. Flesh and spirit.	The First and Second Advents of Christ.

THREEFOLD IMAGES

Material	Abstract	Spiritual
The three journeys to Egypt.	Joseph accusing his brothers followed by Joseph revealing himself followed by Joseph receiving his whole family.	The Fall of Adam-kind followed by the First Advent of Christ followed by the Second Advent.

ESAU, JACOB, ISRAEL

(1) Reuben offers the lives of his own sons to Jacob as a guarantee for the life of Benjamin, (2) Judah offers his own life and honor, or sonship, to Jacob as a guarantee for the life of Benjamin, (3) Judah offers his own freedom, or life, to Joseph in order to free Benjamin and save the life of Jacob. Pharaoh, Joseph, and Joseph ben Jacob.	(1) The offering of one's own flesh, which signifies the law, is not acceptable, (2) a relationship according to the Sonship is the only acceptable offering, (3) the faithful are not redeemed of themselves, but only by their identification with the death and resurrection of the beloved Son. The one who possesses, the one who rules, and the one who calls his brothers unto himself.	(1) The primordial rejection of the natural man Adam, likewise all Adam-kind, (2) the acceptance of the spiritual man Jesus Christ, God the Son, at the time of the First Advent, (3) the acceptance of the faithful in Christ, in the Body of Christ, at the time of the Second Advent. Father, Son, and Holy Spirit.

Synopsis

	The First Journey	
	Material	Spiritual
42:1–5	Jacob sends his ten sons unknowingly unto Joseph to buy corn in Egypt.	The subtlety of the Spirit in calling the faithful throughout all the ages unto the one Son.
	Jacob sends his sons unto Joseph so that they may live and not die.	A figurative death and resurrection according to the way of law and grace.
	But Benjamin does not go on the first journey to Egypt with his brothers.	A sign of the death proceeding from Adam, since the eighth son embodies eternal life.
42:6	Joseph, being the governor over the land, sells corn to all the people of all the land.	The one font of life that exists in the one man Jesus Christ.
	And Joseph's brethren came and bowed down themselves before him.	Every knee will bow, and every tongue will confess to God (Rom 14:11).
42:7–8	Joseph made himself strange unto his brethren and spoke roughly unto them.	The separation between God and man at the time of the Fall of Adam.
	Joseph knew his brethren, but his brethren did not know him.	The way of the flesh does not comprehend the way of the Spirit.
42:9–10	Joseph remembers his dreams.	God remembers his promises.
	Joseph accuses his brothers of being spies in the land, but his brothers profess themselves to be his servants.	The brothers not being able to buy life-giving food represents a looking forward to Christ purchasing our lives on the cross.
42:11–13	The ten brothers identify themselves as the sons of one man.	The millennia of fallen creation.
	The brothers reject being called spies and seek to be recognized as servants.	The law that leads unto grace (Gal 3:24).
	The ten brothers identify themselves with Joseph and Benjamin.	The faithful can only be saved in Christ.
	Simeon	
	Material	Spiritual
42:14	Joseph again speaks the word that the brothers are spies.	The condemnation of the natural body under the law is irrevocable.
42:15–16	Joseph demands that the brothers be proved by the coming of Benjamin.	The faithful are saved only by the coming of Jesus Christ.
	One brother shall go and fetch Benjamin, while the other brothers remain in prison.	The one man Jesus Christ.

TWELVE SONS

		Material	Spiritual
		Otherwise, by the life of Pharaoh, the brothers will be judged as spies.	The life in the Father that is also in the Son (John 5:26).
42:17–20		The ten brothers are placed in ward three days.	The three millennia connecting the First and Second Advents.
		On the third day, Joseph proclaims that, in order to live, one brother must be bound so that the others may fetch Benjamin.	The essential death and resurrection of Christ and likewise the Body of Christ.
42:21–22		The brothers identify their distress with their not hearing the anguish of Joseph's soul.	Adam and likewise all Adam-kind nailed Christ to the tree of the knowledge of good and evil.
		Reuben professes that blood is required.	The blood of Christ shed for Adam-kind.
42:23		Joseph's brothers don't know that he can understand them, because he speaks to them by an interpreter.	The world, or figuratively flesh, does not perceive the movement of the Holy Spirit.
42:24		Joseph left his brothers and wept.	Jesus weeps over the world.
		And Joseph returned unto his brothers and bound Simeon before their eyes.	The condemnation of the natural body under the law is irrevocable.

SILVER

	Material	Spiritual
42:25–26	Joseph fills his brothers' sacks with corn and restores every man's money into his sack, and the brothers depart from thence.	The life of the Spirit that proceeds from the Father through the Son.
42:27–28	One of the brothers discovers that his money has been restored, and they are all afraid. And they ask what God has done unto them.	The faithful are saved by grace alone and not by good works.
42:29–34	And the brothers return unto Jacob, and they give an account of their journey to Egypt.	The faithful must be identified with the Spirit.
42:35	Jacob and his sons see that all their money is in their sacks, and they are afraid.	The empathetic foreboding of the Spirit with man, concerning the coming judgment.

REUBEN AND JUDAH

	Material	Spiritual
42:36–38	The firstborn Reuben offers the lives of his sons as a guarantee for the life of Benjamin.	The sons of the first man Adam die according to the way of Adam, the way of all the earth, of all flesh in and of the earth.
	But Jacob will not give Benjamin into the hand of his firstborn, Reuben.	The death of fallen Adam-kind cannot redeem the life of fallen Adam-kind.
43:1–9	The life of the fourth born Judah is accepted as a guarantee for the life of Benjamin.	The life of Jesus Christ, conceived of the Holy Spirit at the end of the fourth millennium, is acceptable.
43:10	Except the brothers had lingered, they could have already returned the second time.	The long delay between Adam and Jesus that prefigures the church age.
43:11–14	Jacob instructs his sons to take six gifts of the land unto the ruler of the land.	The Son receives dominion over the six millennia of creation that is all creation.
	And double money.	The double portion of the firstborn that Christ takes as the firstborn from the dead.
	And also Benjamin.	The multitude of faithful is added to Christ as eternity is added to the millennial kingdom.

THE SECOND JOURNEY

	Material	Spiritual
43:15	The brothers take their sixfold present, double money, and also Benjamin unto Joseph.	The six millennia of the law that connect the first Adam and the last Adam.
43:16–17	When he saw Benjamin, Joseph brought all his brothers into his house.	The faithful enter into the presence of God only by their identification with Christ.
43:18	Jacob's sons were afraid because they were brought into Joseph's house.	No one separated from the Spirit can stand before Christ and not be judged.

ESAU, JACOB, ISRAEL

43:19	The brothers commune with Joseph's steward at the door of Joseph's house.	Christ is the door (John 10:9).
43:20–22	The brothers profess that their money had been returned.	The faithful are saved by grace alone and not by works.
	The brothers confess that they do not know who returned their money.	The nature of natural man is ignorance, while the nature of spiritual man is knowledge.
43:23	Simeon is freed.	The faithful are redeemed.
43:24	Joseph's brothers are brought into his house, and their feet are washed.	The sins of the faithful are washed clean by the blood of Christ.
43:25–26	The brothers present their sixfold gift to Joseph, and they bow down before him.	Every person throughout all the millennia of creation will bow before Christ (Rom 14:11).
43:27–28	The brothers testify that their father Jacob is in good health and yet alive.	The living and life-giving work of the Spirit throughout all creation.

BENJAMIN

	Material	Spiritual
43:29	Joseph sees Benjamin and speaks the word that God would be gracious unto him.	The second is blessed according to the first, in testimony to grace following law.
43:30–31	Joseph weeps, washes his face, and has bread served.	The baptism of the cross.
43:32–33	Joseph must eat separately from his brothers.	A necessary but passing separation, veiling an essential kinship, in progressive revelation.
	The brothers are seated in the order of their births, and they marvel one at another.	The progressive revelation of the millennia of creation according to the image of God.
43:34	The allotment of food set before the second born Benjamin is five times as much as that set before his brothers.	The tribulation of the second man Christ in the fifth millennium is connected to the final tribulation of the end times.

THE SILVER CUP

	Material	Spiritual
44:1–2	Joseph outfits his brothers a second time with sacks of food.	The continuing preservation of the world even after the crucifixion of Christ.
	And Joseph again returns their money into their sacks.	The condemnation of the natural body is irrevocable.
	Moreover, Joseph puts his silver cup into the sack of Benjamin.	The power and authority of Christ that comes by virtue of the cross.
44:3–6	Joseph sends his brothers away, but he then sends his steward after them to confront them regarding the silver cup.	The kingdom of God would not be revealed at the time of the First Advent and not simply as an ethnic kingdom of Israel.
44:7–8	God forbid that thy servants should do such a thing.	The cross ensures the salvation of the faithful, calling the faithful as long as necessary.
44:9–10	The brothers proclaim that the one with the silver cup should be put to death and that the rest of them should become servants.	The one man who dies is Christ and likewise the faithful in the one Body of Christ, while the faithless are judged to be the slaves of sin.
	But Joseph's steward proclaims that the one with the silver cup should become a servant and that the rest of them would be blameless.	The judgment of grace that subsumes the judgment of the law, and in no way at all contradicts the judgment of the law.
44:11–13	The sacks of the brothers are searched in the order of the eldest to the youngest.	The millennia of creation proceeding from the first man Adam.
	And the silver cup of Joseph was found in the sack of Benjamin.	The brotherhood, or blood kinship, of Christ and the Body of Christ.
	And every man returned to the city.	All mankind will stand before Christ.

JUDAH

	Material	Spiritual
44:14	Judah and his brothers came to the house of Joseph and fell before him on the ground.	The emphasis on Judah in this second journey points to the First Advent.

44:15	Joseph asks his brothers what deed they have done and why they did not know that he could divine the thing.	The omniscience of the Son proceeding from the Holy Spirit compared with the ignorance of natural man in the way of flesh.
44:16–17	Judah confesses that God has found out their iniquity and that all of them are servants.	The servitude of submission unto God that marks true repentance.
	But Joseph replies that only the one with his silver cup will be his servant.	The Son and only the Son fulfills the law that justifies the faithful.
44:18–23	Judah approaches Joseph and recounts their first journey to Egypt.	The progression of the Messianic bloodline throughout the ages.
44:24–31	Judah proclaims that Jacob will die if anything were to happen to Benjamin.	The way of death that marks the tribulation of the cross and likewise the end times.
44:32–34	Judah explains that he himself is the surety for Benjamin.	The blood of Christ is the guarantee of the redemption of the faithful.
	And Judah offers himself in the place of Benjamin.	The bloodline that leads from Adam to the promised new Adam.

PHARAOH, JOSEPH, JACOB

	Material	Spiritual
45:1–2	Joseph makes himself known to his brothers.	Jesus reveals himself at the First Advent.
45:3	Joseph asks if his father Jacob yet lives.	The faithful testify according to the Spirit.
45:4–8	Joseph tells his brothers that God sent him before them in order to preserve life.	The faithful in Christ are joined unto Christ in death and resurrection.
45:9–15	Joseph sends his brothers to bring their father, Jacob, so that they can all be nourished during the famine.	The essential unity of the Son and the Spirit in the Body of Christ.
45:16–21	The coming of Joseph's brethren pleases Pharaoh and also his servants.	The Father is well pleased with the Son, who draws the faithful by the Spirit unto himself.
45:22	Joseph gives to Benjamin five changes of raiment and three hundred pieces of silver.	The millennia of Adam culminating in the Body of Christ.
45:23–24	The brothers return unto Jacob with ten asses and ten she asses, all laden with goods.	The law bringing the chosen faithful unto the grace that exists only in Christ.
45:25–27	Jacob does not at first believe that Joseph is alive, but finally Jacob does believe and his spirit revives.	The Spirit of truth will redeem a remnant of faithful in the end times despite a prevalent spirit of delusion.
45:28	And Jacob proclaims that it is enough for him to go unto Joseph and see him before he dies.	The fulfillment of all things in the unity of the Body of Christ.

CHAPTER SIX

Twelve Tribes

The prime images in the account of Israel going down to Egypt and dwelling in the land of Goshen are Joseph taking possession of the Egyptians and their belongings during a time of universal famine (Gen 47:23) and Jacob blessing his sons at the time of his death (Gen 49:28). The seventy souls of the house of Jacob represent the Table of Nations (Gen 46:26–27). Jacob bringing his household unto Joseph represents the Holy Spirit bringing the faithful unto the Son. Joseph ben Jacob taking possession of both man and land for Pharaoh prefigures Jesus Christ establishing the millennial kingdom on the earth at the time of the Second Advent. The sons of Jacob are identified with the progression of the millennia connecting Adam and Christ, whereby the blessings given by Jacob are identified with the movement of the Holy Spirit throughout the millennia of creation. The blessings given by Jacob to his sons represent the gifts of the Holy Spirit culminating in the fullness of the indwelling Holy Spirit. The famine that drives Israel into Egypt represents the original curse of the ground culminating in the final tribulation (Gen 3:17). The suffering of Joseph being the means of preserving and also prospering the house of Jacob reflects the connection between the First and Second Advents of Christ (Gen 50:20). The deaths of Jacob and Joseph point to the end of the time of the call to repentance in God the Son that comes by God the Spirit.

The twofold image emphasized in the account of Israel dwelling in Egypt under Pharaoh is the relationship between the Egyptians and the Israelites. The offspring of Jacob are removed to the land of Goshen and, thereby, are separated from the larger Egyptian population. The offspring of Jacob are detestable to the Egyptians because they are shepherds (Gen 46:34). The house of Jacob embodies the dominion of the Spirit and, thereby, represents the community of faithful, while the larger Egyptian population represents the world as a whole. Joseph taking possession of the Egyptians reflects Christ having authority and dominion over the whole world, whereas Joseph nourishing his brothers in Goshen reflects the special relationship between Christ and the faithful in Christ. The emphasis on Joseph taking possession of both the property and the people of Egypt points to the essential connection between the body and the spirit, likewise between physical and spiritual reality (Gen 47:23). The faithful in Christ are not looking for some disembodied resurrection of the human spirit in isolation but for a resurrection of creation as a whole and of the individual as a whole, including the physical body (Rev 21:1). Further, the two blessings of Ephraim and Manasseh are the double inheritance given to Joseph and signifying the dual kingship and priesthood of Jesus Christ (Gen 48:5). The firstborn Manasseh being supplanted by the second born Ephraim reflects the relationship between the first man Adam and the second man Jesus Christ, likewise the relationship between the First Advent of Christ and the Second Advent, and likewise the relationship between the millennial kingdom of Christ and eternity in Christ.

The threefold Pharaoh, Joseph, and Jacob reflect the Father, Son, and Spirit and likewise the formation of Adam followed by the First and Second Advents of Christ. Jacob blessing Pharaoh followed by Jacob blessing Joseph followed by Jacob blessing his twelve sons reflects the blessing of life and creation proceeding from God the Father to God the Son and finally to the faithful by the power of God the Holy Spirit (Gen 47:10, 48:15, 49:28). Joseph in the place of Pharaoh taking possession of the silver of Egypt followed by the livestock of Egypt followed by the people and their land reflects the same threefold progression of the Father, Son, and Spirit that marks all creation (Gen 47:14, 47:16, 47:23). And Joseph coming to Egypt followed by his brothers followed by Jacob again reflects the one and same threefold progression of creation. Concurrently, the representation of the Father, Son, and Spirit that overarches the account of Joseph ben Jacob is the threefold Abraham, Isaac, and Jacob. The deaths of Abraham followed by Isaac followed by Jacob reflect the ending of three successive ages, or eras. The first is the age of Adam, ending with the death and resurrection of Christ. The second is the age of the church, ending with the resurrection of the faithful, that is, the death and resurrection of the Body of Christ. And the third is the foretold millennial reign of Christ, ending with the promised new earth and new heaven, that is, the death and resurrection of all creation and the corresponding opening of eternity.

The Third Journey

Genesis 46:1 And Israel [H3478] took his journey with all that he had, and came to Beer-sheba [H884], and offered sacrifices unto the God of his father Isaac.

The word *Beersheba* [H884] means "well of seven (as a place of swearing by seven)," which reflects the seven millennia of creation embodying the promise of God that is the promise of eternal life. The wilderness of *Beersheba* [H884] is identified with the second and final flight of Hagar (Gen 21:14), while the ownership of *Beersheba* [H884] is identified with the second and final treaty between Abraham and Abimelech (Gen 21:30). The actual dwelling place at *Beersheba* [H884] is identified with the Second Advent. And the present third and final journey of the brothers into Egypt is also identified with the Second

ESAU, JACOB, ISRAEL

Advent. The dwelling place at *Beersheba* [H884] is closely connected with the second coming of Christ but also looks past the seven millennia of creation into eternity just as the second coming heralds the opening of eternity.

The emphasis on Jacob offering sacrifices to the God of Isaac, specifically at the present time of this third journey to Egypt, points to the unity of the First and Second Advents of Christ. The threefold Abraham, Isaac, and Jacob reflect the triune Father, Son, and Spirit and likewise the formation of Adam followed by the First and Second Advents of Christ. The person of Jacob is most closely identified with God the Spirit, specifically with the Second Advent, while the person of Isaac is most closely identified with God the Son, with the First Advent. And the shifting emphasis from the name *Jacob* [H3290] to the name *Israel* [H3478] reflects the shifting emphasis from birthright to blessing that is the blessing of the multitude of faithful that will form the Body of Christ.

Genesis 46:2 And God spake unto Israel in the visions of the night, and said, Jacob, Jacob. And he said, Here [am] I.

The nighttime of Jacob connected with this third and final journey portends the tribulation period that will precede the Second Advent of Christ.

Genesis 46:3 And he said, I [am] God, the God of thy father: fear not to go down into Egypt; for I will there make of thee a great nation:

The fear connected with this third and final journey portends the tribulation period that must precede the Second Advent.

Genesis 46:4 I will go down with thee into Egypt; and I will also surely bring thee up [again]: and Joseph shall put his hand upon thine eyes.

Joseph is identified with the Son, while Jacob is identified with the Spirit. And the Son sending the Holy Spirit is the defining characteristic of the age of the church (John 16:7–16). Joseph closing the eyes of Jacob in death prefigures not the end of the time of the Spirit but rather the end of the parenthetical church age of the Spirit. And the descent into Egypt with God followed by the promised return to the land of Canaan with God points to the resurrection of all the dead and the corresponding rebirth of all creation.

Genesis 46:5 And Jacob rose up from Beer-sheba: and the sons of Israel carried Jacob their father, and their little ones, and their wives, in the wagons which Pharaoh had sent to carry him.

The faithful marked by the sign of the indwelling Holy Spirit come unto the Son in accordance with the will of the Father.

Genesis 46:6 And they took their cattle, and their goods, which they had gotten in the land of Canaan, and came into Egypt, Jacob, and all his seed with him:

To the goods of Canaan are added the goods of Egypt. The gifts of the Holy Spirit in the natural body will be magnified in the spiritual, or glorified, body.[1]

Genesis 46:7 His sons, and his sons' sons with him, his daughters, and his sons' daughters, and all his seed brought he with him into Egypt.

The totality of the seed of Jacob represents the faithful throughout all the ages, anointed by the Spirit of God and forming the one Body of Christ.

Genesis 46:8–15 And these [are] the names of the children of Israel, which came into Egypt, Jacob and his sons: Reuben, Jacob's firstborn. 9 And the sons of Reuben; Hanoch, and Phallu, and Hezron, and Carmi. 10 And the sons of Simeon; Jemuel, and Jamin, and Ohad, and Jachin, and Zohar, and Shaul the son of a Canaanitish woman. 11 And the sons of Levi; Gershon, Kohath, and Merari. 12 And the sons of Judah; Er, and Onan, and Shelah, and Pharez, and Zerah: but Er and Onan died in the land of Canaan. And the sons of Pharez were Hezron and Hamul. 13 And the sons of Issachar; Tola, and Phuvah, and Job, and Shimron. 14 And the sons of Zebulun; Sered, and Elon, and Jahleel. 15 These [be] the sons of Leah, which she bare unto Jacob in Padan-aram, with his daughter Dinah: all the souls of his sons and his daughters [were] thirty and three.

Only thirty-two living offspring of Jacob, not thirty-three, are here recorded. There is possibly an unborn child in the womb, who is counted though yet unnamed, but in any case the unnamed soul can be connected with the yet unrevealed Messiah coming through the line of Judah and Pharez (Matt 1:3). The counting of the Messiah before the time of the First Advent reflects the preexistence of the Messiah. God the Son is without beginning or end, eternally begotten of God the Father through God the Holy Spirit (Luke 1:35). The counting of the Messiah as part of the camp of Jacob is an affirmation that God is with Jacob and his offspring. The counting of the Messiah now, expressly at the time of the third and final journey into Egypt, points to the glorious reappearing of Jesus Christ at the time of the Second Advent. The listing of Leah's six sons reflects the progression of the six millennia connecting the original creation of Adam with the conception of Jesus Christ, the promised new Adam, that will be finally fulfilled in the birthing of the Body of Christ.

---

[1] The traditional Rabbinic use of the term *Ruach Hakodesh*, "the Holy Spirit," is sometimes equivalent to *Shechinah*, literally "dwelling"—*Lamentations Rabbah*; but more often it is used to denote the enduing of a person with special gifts—*Genesis Rabbah* (Cohen, *Rabbinic Sages* 45). An obscure view of the third person of the Trinity, God the Holy Spirit, who indwells the believer and thereby gifts the believer.

Genesis 46:16–18 And the sons of Gad; Ziphion, and Haggi, Shuni, and Ezbon, Eri, and Arodi, and Areli. 17 And the sons of Asher; Jimnah, and Ishuah, and Isui, and Beriah, and Serah their sister: and the sons of Beriah; Heber, and Malchiel. 18 These [are] the sons of Zilpah, whom Laban gave to Leah his daughter, and these she bare unto Jacob, [even] sixteen souls.

The offspring of the sons of Leah's handmaid, Zilpah, being listed here following the offspring of Leah's own six sons points to the period connecting the sixth and seventh millennia from Adam. The bondage identified with Zilpah portends a bondage of the end times, specifically the final tribulation period. And the emphasis on Laban having given Zilpah to Leah points to the coming of the evil one at this time. The bondage of the coming tribulation is the bondage to the coming anti-christ (Rev 13:17).[2]

Genesis 46:19–22 The sons of Rachel Jacob's wife; Joseph, and Benjamin. 20 And unto Joseph in the land of Egypt were born Manasseh and Ephraim, which Asenath the daughter of Poti-pherah priest of On bare unto him. 21 And the sons of Benjamin [were] Belah, and Becher, and Ashbel, Gera, and Naaman, Ehi, and Rosh, Muppim, and Huppim, and Ard. 22 These [are] the sons of Rachel, which were born to Jacob: all the souls [were] fourteen.

The listing of the offspring of the two sons of the younger sister Rachel reflects the seventh and eighth millennia from the formation of Adam, which corresponds to the third and fourth millennia from the first coming of Christ. The power and authority of the second firstborn Joseph over all the land prefigures the millennial reign of Jesus Christ. The second born Benjamin being added to the firstborn Joseph reflects Christ being added to Adam, likewise the Second Advent being added to the First Advent, and finally eternity being added to the millennial reign.

Genesis 46:23–25 And the sons of Dan; Hushim. 24 And the sons of Naphtali; Jahzeel, and Guni, and Jezer, and Shillem. 25 These [are] the sons of Bilhah, which Laban gave unto Rachel his daughter, and she bare these unto Jacob: all the souls [were] seven.

The persons of Joseph and Benjamin are identified with the millennial kingdom followed by eternity, which corresponds to the seventh and eighth millennia from Adam. The offspring of the sons of Rachel's handmaid, Bilhah,

---

[2] Zilpah's son Gad is the seventh son listed, has seven sons himself, and the numerical value corresponding to his name is also seven (Sarna 315; Gen 46:16). Zilpah's other son, Asher, also has seven offspring, including his daughter and also his grandsons, and the Bible testifies to this number, which might otherwise seem contrived, in stating that the total offspring of Zilpah should be reckoned as sixteen souls.

being listed here following the offspring of Rachel's own two sons, Joseph and Benjamin, points past eternity, or rather throughout eternity. This cannot be the end of time, because time will never end; rather, this signifies the eternal condemnation of the evil one and his angels. The bracketing of the offspring of Joseph and Benjamin by the offspring of Zilpah's and Bilhah's sons reflects a special continuity between the millennial reign and eternity. The emphasis on Laban having given Bilhah to Rachel points to the eternal bondage, or condemnation, of the evil one (Rev 20:7–10). This is not the end of time but rather the end of death and hell that defines eternity as following the millennial kingdom (Rev 20:14). The bondage identified with this final listing of the offspring of Bilhah portends the final eternal bondage of the lake of fire.

Genesis 46:26–27 All the souls that came with Jacob into Egypt, which came out of his loins, besides Jacob's sons' wives, all the souls [were] threescore and six; 27 And the sons of Joseph, which were born him in Egypt, [were] two souls: all the souls of the house of Jacob, which came into Egypt, [were] threescore and ten [H7657].

One unnamed soul here mysteriously shifts to the house of Joseph.[3] And the shift is spiritually from the house of Judah to the house of Joseph since Judah and Joseph are the two dominant sons. The comparison between the threescore and six (sixty-six) souls of Jacob and the combined threescore and ten (seventy) souls of Jacob plus Joseph indicates four souls corresponding to the house of Joseph, but Joseph and his two sons represent only three souls in the natural. The shift from Judah to Joseph at this time of the third and final journey to Egypt represents the Messianic bloodline (Judah) leading the world into the millennial kingdom (Joseph). The progression of the Messianic bloodline is identified with the movement of the Holy Spirit just as the incarnation of the Son would come by the overshadowing of the Holy Spirit (Luke 1:35). And the Messianic bloodline (Judah) continues during the church age in the formation of the Body of Christ, culminating in the millennial kingdom (Joseph).[4]

---

[3] "The statement that there were but seventy souls, while Stephen [Acts 7:14] adds five more, is made, I doubt not, by an error of the transcribers" (Calvin, *Commentaries* 2:391; Gen 46:8). Calvin casually admitting that he prefers human speculation over the inspired Word of God shows that the historical-critical worldview is nothing new.

[4] Though noting that the counting of 70 souls may include Jacob himself, Sarna asserts that the number is probably typological, himself recognizing only the listed offspring of Jacob and only 66 of those souls by subtracting Er and Onan, who died in Canaan, and by also subtracting Manasseh and Ephraim, who were born in Egypt (Sarna 317; Gen 46:26–27). Judah could possibly have carried the remains of Er and Onan into Egypt in order to establish a new buryingplace, while Manasseh and Ephraim can be counted just as their father Joseph is counted. And the unnamed soul, which is identified with the progression of the Messianic bloodline, can indeed be connected to Jacob since the life of Jacob is closely identified with the movement of the Holy Spirit. Also, the emphasis on the word *soul* implies a counting that transcends the merely corporeal.

The seventy souls proceeding from the loins of Jacob reflect the seventy nations of the world proceeding from God (Gen 10:1–32). The house of Jacob, which is the nation of Israel, is a microcosm of all the nations. The community of families and peoples and nations is the dominion of God and will endure throughout the millennial kingdom (Rev 20:7–8). The word *seventy* (threescore and ten) [H7657] (seventy souls) and also the word *seventh* [H7637] (seventh day of rest) are closely related to the word *swear* [H7650], meaning to "to seven oneself, or bind oneself by seven things" (Gen 2:2). The oath, or promise, of God is the indwelling Holy Spirit, the fullness of which will be revealed to the whole world at the time of the Second Advent in the seventh millennium. Our promised new creation in the Body of Christ, which represents the fullness of communion with God, can only come by the power of the indwelling Spirit.[5]

Goshen

Genesis 46:28 And he sent Judah before him unto Joseph, to direct his face unto Goshen; and they came into the land of Goshen.

Jacob sending Judah before him unto Joseph in order to direct his house to the safe haven of Goshen represents the Messianic bloodline leading the faithful in Christ from repentance to redemption. And this is specifically the fullness of redemption and new creation that will be established by, or through, the millennial reign of Christ. Jacob sending Judah unto Joseph and finally unto the safe haven of Goshen represents the movement of God the Holy Spirit.[6]

Genesis 46:29 And Joseph made ready his chariot [H4818], and went up to meet Israel his father, to Goshen, and presented himself unto him; and he fell on his neck, and wept [H1058] on his neck a good while.

The word *chariot* [H4818] (of Joseph) has a connotation "war chariot," which foreshadows the glorious return of Jesus Christ, judging and making war in all righteousness (Rev 19:11). The chariot of Joseph represents the seat of power given to him by Pharaoh (Gen 41:43). And the power and authority of Joseph points to the power and authority of Christ and specifically that manifested at the time of the Second Advent. Jacob is identified with God the Spirit, while Joseph is identified with God the Son. The previous account of Jacob coming unto Joseph represents the Holy Spirit leading the faithful unto the Son during

---

[5] "Like many [all?] great works of God, Israel had a slow beginning. . . . It took this family 215 years to grow from 1 to 70. In another 430 years, they grew to 2,000,000" (Guzik 254; Gen 46:5–27). The culmination of the Body of Christ in the end times. The perspective of man is the slowness of beginning, whereas the perspective of God is the exponential fulfillment of all things.

[6] Joseph being the savior of the Egyptians, Gen 40:1–41:57, mirroring his also being the savior of his family, 46:28–47:12, marks the dual center of a counterpoint, concentric structure spanning 37:2–50:26 (Waltke 581–82). The promised redemption in the Body of Christ is the meaning of all creation and thus the manifest focus of all creation.

the church age (Gen 45:28). The present account of Joseph coming to Jacob represents the glorious return of Christ. The Spirit was sent by Christ at the time of the First Advent to prepare the faithful for the glorious return at the time of the Second Advent (John 16:7). And the time of the Second Advent, establishing the millennial kingdom, marks the end of the age of the Spirit calling the faithful in the Son unto the Father.

Joseph *wept* [H1058] at the time of the first journey to Egypt, specifically in separation from his brothers, representing the exile of Adam from the garden of Eden (Gen 42:24). This is the suffering of God because of the suffering of all humanity in Adam. Joseph *wept* [H1058] with his brothers at the time of the second journey, representing God being with us at the time of the First Advent (Gen 45:15). This is the suffering of the cross for the sake of and in the place of all humanity. And Joseph now *weeps* [H1058] with Jacob at the time of this third and final journey, representing the unity of the Son and the Spirit in the Body of Christ. This is the suffering of the final tribulation period and likewise the coming final judgment of the world. Further, Jacob originally *weeping* [H1058] over the figurative (spiritual) death of Joseph marks his (their) original betrayal and, thereby, reflects the mourning of the Spirit over the original rebellion of Adam (Adam-kind) (Gen 37:35). Joseph finally *weeping* [H1058] over the death of Jacob points to the end of the age, which is marked by the final judgment of the damned that have rejected the saving grace of the Spirit (Gen 50:1).

Genesis 46:30 And Israel said unto Joseph, Now let me die, since I have seen thy face, because thou [art] yet alive.

Jacob is identified with the Spirit, while Joseph is identified with the Son. Jacob finally seeing the face of Joseph prefigures the glorious return of Jesus Christ in the end times. The imminent death of Jacob does not represent the death of God the Holy Spirit but rather the end of the age of grace that comes by God the Holy Spirit.

Genesis 46:31 And Joseph said unto his brethren, and unto his father's house, I will go up, and shew Pharaoh, and say unto him, My brethren, and my father's house, which [were] in the land of Canaan, are come unto me;

Pharaoh reflects God the Father, Joseph reflects God the Son, and Jacob reflects God the Holy Spirit. The Spirit leads the faithful unto the Son, who presents the faithful unto the Father (1 Cor 15:24).

Genesis 46:32 And the men [are] shepherds, for their trade hath been to feed cattle; and they have brought their flocks, and their herds, and all that they have.

Jesus Christ is the good shepherd, and the faithful become shepherds in imitation of Christ (John 10:14). When Christ appears, we will be like him, for we will see him as he is (1 John 3:2).[7]

Genesis 46:33–34 And it shall come to pass, when Pharaoh shall call you, and shall say, What [is] your occupation? 34 That ye shall say, Thy servants' trade hath been about cattle from our youth even until now, both we, [and] also our fathers: that ye may dwell in the land of Goshen; for every shepherd [is] an abomination unto the Egyptians.

The Egyptians compared with the Israelites represent separate and distinct peoples under the one administration of Pharaoh. The Israelites being an abomination to the Egyptians represents the faithful being an abomination to the unfaithful. And it is the faithless of their own freewill that insist upon being separated from the faithful. The brothers identifying themselves as shepherds is directly connected to their being allowed to settle in Goshen, which represents the best of the land and therefore spiritually the promised land (Gen 47:6). And it is absolutely essential that the brothers explicitly identify themselves as shepherds before Pharaoh. This is the identification of the faithful with the Son before the Father. And the only thing that can make us acceptable to the Father is just this identification with the Son in the Body of Christ that comes by the perfecting power, or new life, of the Holy Spirit.

Genesis 47:1 Then Joseph came and told Pharaoh, and said, My father and my brethren, and their flocks, and their herds, and all that they have, are come out of the land of Canaan; and, behold, they [are] in the land of Goshen.

Joseph presents his brothers, together with their father, unto Pharaoh. Joseph reflects God the Son, while Pharaoh reflects God the Father. The brothers reflect the faithful, while their father reflects God the Holy Spirit. Jacob being presented with Joseph's brothers reflects the indwelling Holy Spirit by which the faithful in the Son may enter into the fullness of the presence of the Father. The chosen are saved by grace through faith, namely, by the grace of the Holy Spirit through the faith in the Son that proceeds from the Father.

Genesis 47:2 And he took some of his brethren, [even] five [H2568] men, and presented them unto Pharaoh.

---

[7] "... 'For this is why the Word became man, ... so that man, by entering into communion with the Word and thus receiving divine sonship, might become a son of God' [Irenaeus, *Adversus haereses*]. 'For the Son of God became man so that we might become God' [Athanasius, *De incarnatione Verbi Dei*]" (Rom. Catholic Church, *Catechism* 128–29). Yes, a return to, or fulfillment of, the promise established in the garden of Eden, but not simply a return to the garden itself, or some state of naiveté.

All of Joseph's brothers, their totality, are presented unto Pharaoh, but they are represented in the present context by only five brothers. The five representing all the brothers points to the death and resurrection of Christ in the fifth millennium, by which all the faithful throughout all time are redeemed. Joseph presenting the five unto Pharaoh at the time of this third and final journey to Egypt connects the death and resurrection of Christ in the fifth millennium (fifth from Adam) to the death and resurrection of the Body of Christ in the third millennium (third from Jesus, seventh from Adam). And the emphasis on the number *five* [H2568] is reinforced throughout the account of the second and third journeys to Egypt, which affirms the connection between the First and Second Advents being the relationship between Christ and the Body of Christ. Joseph gives five portions to Benjamin (Gen 43:34); Joseph promises to preserve posterity during the five remaining years of famine (Gen 45:6–7, 45:11); Joseph gives five changes of raiment to Benjamin (Gen 45:22); and now Joseph finally presents five brothers unto Pharaoh (Gen 47:2).

Genesis 47:3 And Pharaoh said unto his brethren, What [is] your occupation? And they said unto Pharaoh, Thy servants [are] shepherds, both we, [and] also our fathers.

The occupation of man is handed down, actually inherited, from our first father Adam and ultimately from our Father in heaven, God the Father, who is spiritually the true progenitor of all mankind. The preordained occupation of Adam-kind is to keep the garden of God (Gen 2:15). And the image of keeping the sheep of Israel can be compared to keeping the garden of God because the garden, or domain, of God is finally understood to be the body, or assembly, of the faithful. The garden of God is to the sheep of God as the garden of Eden is to the kingdom of God as the Covenant of Law is to the Covenant of Grace as the body of Adam is to the Body of Christ.

Genesis 47:4 They said moreover unto Pharaoh, For to sojourn in the land are we come; for thy servants have no pasture for their flocks; for the famine [is] sore in the land of Canaan: now therefore, we pray thee, let thy servants dwell in the land of Goshen.

The wasteland of Canaan ravaged by famine is the present world marked by death, while Goshen representing the best of the land is the promised new creation. And this promised new reality, which will embody the fullness of communion with the Lord God, will be revealed first in the millennial reign and finally in eternity. The house of Israel sojourning in Goshen because of a passing famine during the life of Joseph implies that their sojourn will also be transitory. And the millennial kingdom corresponding to the time of the Second Advent will likewise be transitory. The first man Adam is to the second man Christ as the First Advent of Christ is to the Second Advent as the millennial kingdom of Christ is to eternity in Christ.

Genesis 47:5–6 And Pharaoh spake unto Joseph, saying, Thy father and thy brethren are come unto thee: 6 The land of Egypt [is] before thee; in the best of the land make thy father and brethren to dwell; in the land of Goshen let them dwell: and if thou knowest [any] men of activity among them, then make them rulers over my cattle.

Joseph's brothers being elevated to positions of authority with Joseph prefigures the faithful living and reigning with Jesus Christ during the millennial kingdom (Rev 20:4).

Genesis 47:7 And Joseph brought in Jacob his father, and set him before Pharaoh: and Jacob blessed Pharaoh.

The threefold Pharaoh, Joseph, and Jacob reflect the Father, Son, and Spirit. Joseph bringing Jacob unto Pharaoh represents the Son presenting the faithful unto the Father by the power of the indwelling Holy Spirit. Pharaoh being supreme in the land and yet being blessed by the lowly Jacob reflects the supreme joy of the Father over the salvation of his children.

Genesis 47:8 And Pharaoh said unto Jacob, How old [art] thou?

The emphasis on the old age of Jacob points to the progressive revelation of the Spirit throughout the millennia of Adam and Adamic creation.

Genesis 47:9 And Jacob said unto Pharaoh, The days of the years of my pilgrimage [H4033] [are] an hundred and thirty years: few and evil have the days of the years of my life been, and have not attained unto the days of the years of the life of my fathers in the days of their pilgrimage [H4033].

The word *pilgrimage* [H4033] (of Jacob) means "sojourning place, dwelling place, sojourning" and is elsewhere translated *stranger* [H4033] (Gen 17:8). The pilgrimage of Jacob reflects the movement of the Holy Spirit, indwelling the believer in the present mortal life and finally leading the believer into eternal life. The pilgrimage of Jacob being evil reflects the suffering of the Holy Spirit with all humanity throughout the history of the present creation. The pilgrimage of Jacob being short compared with that of his fathers reflects the transience of the mortal life of Adam-kind, likewise the present creation as a whole, that will finally be embodied by the rapid culmination of all things in the end times.[8]

---

[8] "Jacob's life was very emphatically and literally a pilgrimage . . . Canaan . . . Padan-aram . . . Canaan again . . . Succoth . . . Shechem . . . Hebron . . . Egypt . . . he had spent 130 years of his life in this way . . . ." (Gill 1:233; Gen 47:9). The pilgrimage of Jacob is the pilgrimage of Abraham, Isaac, and Jacob.

TWELVE TRIBES

Genesis 47:10   And Jacob blessed Pharaoh, and went out from before Pharaoh.

The image of Jacob going out from the presence of Pharaoh foreshadows the end of the millennial kingdom. The first heaven and the first earth will not pass away until the end of the millennial kingdom (Rev 21:1). And in the successive dawning of eternity, the holy city will descend from God out of heaven, representing not merely a new heaven and a new earth but a new heaven and a new earth united together in one creation (Rev 21:2). The new heaven and the new earth will be one creation just as the faithful are one in the Body of Christ in accordance with the indwelling Holy Spirit (John 17:21).

Genesis 47:11   And Joseph placed his father and his brethren, and gave them a possession [H272] in the land of Egypt, in the best of the land, in the land of Rameses, as Pharaoh had commanded.

The word *possession* [H272] (of the best of the land) has a connotation "possession by right of inheritance," reflecting the promised inheritance of the children of God, which is the fullness of communion with God in the resurrection of the body and the corresponding restoration of all creation. The close connection between Jacob and the destiny of Joseph's brothers reflects the centrality of the indwelling Holy Spirit. Pharaoh commanding Joseph to give the house of Jacob a possession in the land represents the resurrection of the faithful in God the Son, in the Body of Christ, by the power, or new life, of God the Spirit according to the will of God the Father.

Genesis 47:12   And Joseph nourished [H3557] his father, and his brethren, and all his father's household, with bread, according to [their] families.

Joseph *nourishing* [H3557] the household of Jacob is God *nourishing* [H3557] the household of Jacob (Gen 45:11). This is the unity of the Father and the Son that is the same unity of the faithful that comes by the indwelling Holy Spirit. The bread that nourishes the faithful is ultimately the flesh of Christ and finally the blood of Christ (John 6:53).

Two Tithes

Genesis 47:13   And [there was] no bread in all the land; for the famine [was] very sore, so that the land of Egypt and [all] the land of Canaan fainted [H3856] by reason of the famine.

The word *fainted* [H3856] (by reason of the famine) has a connotation "madman" (Prov 26:18). The famine of bread at the time of Joseph portends a famine in separation from Christ, a famine of the words of God, specifically at the time of the end (Amos 8:11). The faintness of the end times that is like a madness is the great delusion that will consume the unfaithful (2 Thess 2:11).

Genesis 47:14 And Joseph gathered up all the money [H3701] that was found in the land of Egypt, and in the land of Canaan, for the corn [H7668] which they bought: and Joseph brought the money [H3701] into Pharaoh's house.

Joseph now begins the process of taking for Pharaoh complete possession of the people and the land, and Joseph begins this process by gathering all the *money* (silver) [H3701] of the land. Joseph reflects the Son, while Pharaoh reflects the Father. And Jacob prospering in the land during this period reflects the movement of the Holy Spirit. The seven years of famine at the time of Joseph prefigures the final seven years of tribulation that will herald the Second Advent of Christ. And the dominion established at the time of the final tribulation period is connected to the dominion established at the time of the tribulation of the cross. Likewise, the ascendancy of Joseph is connected to the suffering of Joseph. Joseph first accepting all the *money* (silver) [H3701] of the land in exchange for corn, signifying life, reflects the value in silver placed upon the life of Jesus Christ at the time of the First Advent (Matt 27:9). The two tribulations are connected just as the two advents are connected.

The tribulation of the cross at the time of the First Advent and the final tribulation at the time of the Second Advent both represent the pouring out of the wrath of God (Rom 3:25). The word *corn* (grain) [H7668] (silver for corn) is closely related to the word "breaking, crushing" [H7667], variously translated as *destruction* [H7667] (Prov 16:18) and *affliction* [H7667] (Amos 6:6). The grain (bread) of affliction received in exchange for silver is the affliction of the cross—namely, the affliction of Christ himself at the First Advent, likewise the affliction of the faithful in Christ culminating in the Second Advent. And the image of crushing corn, or grain, equally recalls the original curse of Adam to eat bread in the sweat of his face (Gen 3:19). The rebellion of Adam is the rejection of Jesus. The triune formation of Adam followed by the First and Second Advents of Christ reflects the triune Father, Son, and Holy Spirit.

Genesis 47:15–17 And when money [H3701] failed in the land of Egypt, and in the land of Canaan, all the Egyptians came unto Joseph, and said, Give us bread [H3899]: for why should we die in thy presence? for the money [H3701] faileth. 16 And Joseph said, Give your cattle [H4735]; and I will give you for your cattle [H4735], if money [H3701] fail. 17 And they brought their cattle [H4735] unto Joseph: and Joseph gave them bread [H3899] [in exchange] for horses, and for the flocks, and for the cattle [H4735] of the herds, and for the asses: and he fed them with bread for all their cattle [H4735] for that year.

The death of the Egyptians is connected with the failure of money, and the Egyptians therefore do figuratively die when the money fails. The word *cattle* (livestock) [H4735] (cattle for bread) is elsewhere translated *possession* [H4735] and is derived from the root "to get, acquire (property)" [H7069] (Gen 26:14). The symbol of cattle, or livestock, is a living possession representing the possession of life itself. The word *bread* [H3899] (cattle for bread) is closely related to the word "to fight, do battle" [H3898], elsewhere translated *maketh war* [H3898] (Jer 21:2). The bread exchanged for livestock is the death of the natural body and that expressly by the sword. This is ultimately the death of Christ on the cross as king of kings proclaimed by a soldier's spear of war piercing his side (John 19:34), and this is finally the rising tide of wars and rumors of wars in the last days beginning at the time of the cross (Matt 24:6). But death is supplanted by resurrection just as the natural body is supplanted by the spiritual, or glorified, resurrection body.[9]

Joseph exchanging grain for silver followed by Joseph exchanging bread for livestock reflects the first and second millennia from Jesus Christ, which correspond to the fifth and sixth millennia from Adam (Gen 47:14, 47:17). The fifth millennium from Adam marked by the rejection of Christ is followed by the sixth millennium marked by the apostasy of the visible church, which reflects the original rebellion of Adam followed by the visible rejection of Christ at the First Advent. The failure of *money* (silver) [H3701] representing the death of the Egyptians is specifically the death of the cross representing the condemnation of the natural body under the law. And the progression from silver representing life to livestock embodying life parallels the progression from grain to bread. But this is finally understood to be the progression from the promise of Adam to the reality of Jesus and likewise the progression from the guarantee of the cross to the reality of the resurrection.

Genesis 47:18–20 When that year was ended, they came unto him the second year, and said unto him, We will not hide [it] from my lord, how that our money [H3701] is spent; my lord also hath our herds [H4735] of cattle; there is not ought left in the sight of my lord, but our bodies, and our lands: 19 Wherefore shall we die before thine eyes, both we and our land? buy us and our land for bread [H3899], and we and our land will be servants unto Pharaoh: and give [us] seed [H2233], that we may live, and not die, that the land be not desolate. 20 And Joseph bought all the land of Egypt for Pharaoh; for the Egyptians sold every man his field, because the famine prevailed over them: so the land became Pharaoh's.

The people of the land finally yield their bodies and their land in order to live and not die. And Joseph completes his acquisition of all things on behalf of Pharaoh. The implied unity of body and land points to the essential re-creation

---

[9] "Just as a word has a variety of connotations, so also it may have more than one denotation. . . . This variety of denotation, complicated by additional tones of connotation [connotations and associations], makes language confusing and difficult to use. . . . [But] the poet will often take advantage of the fact that the word has more than one meaning by using it to mean more than one thing at the same time" (Perrine 587). The whole of the Bible is poetic, reflecting the God of the Bible being all things.

of physical creation as a whole being concomitant with the resurrection of individual believers. Joseph first exchanged *corn* (grain) [H7668] for silver (Gen 47:14), followed second by *bread* [H3899] for livestock (Gen 47:17). And Joseph finally exchanges *bread* [H3899] and *seed* [H2233] for the bodies and land of the people. To possess seed is to possess an endless harvest, whereby the symbol of seed represents eternal life. This third and final purchase of Joseph points to the Second Advent of Christ in the third millennium from the First Advent that is the seventh, or Sabbath, millennium from Adam. The word *seed* [H2233] has a connotation "offspring (children)," which reflects the multitude of faithful throughout the ages entering into the one Body of Christ.

The threefold *corn* (grain) [H7668] and *bread* [H3899] and *seed* [H2233] of Joseph reflects the three millennia connecting the First and Second Advents, likewise the threefold successive formation of Adam followed by the First and Second Advents of Christ, and finally the triunity of the Father, Son, and Spirit. The bread of Joseph is the bread of affliction, while the similarity between corn and seed is the connection between creation and new creation. The seven years of famine, which testify to the dominion of Joseph and culminate in the formation of national Israel, prefigure the final seven years of tribulation, which will testify to the dominion of Jesus Christ and culminate in the millennial kingdom. The new Adam will be formed in the image of God just as the original Adam was formed in the image of God, whereby the dominion of the new Adam and likewise the establishment of the dominion of the new Adam must embody the triunity of God. The new Adam is foremost Christ and finally the Body of Christ taken from the side of Christ. The original Adam was very good (Gen 1:31), but the new Adam must be perfect (Gen 17:1).[10]

Genesis 47:21 And as for the people, he removed them to cities from [one] end of the borders of Egypt even to the [other] end thereof.

The cities of Pharaoh under Joseph represent the nations living in peace during the millennial reign of Jesus Christ (Rev 20:7–8). The household of Jacob being established separately in Goshen represents the beloved city of God (Gen 47:27, Rev 20:9).

Genesis 47:22 Only the land of the priests [H3548] bought he not; for the priests [H3548] had a portion [assigned them] of Pharaoh, and did eat their portion which Pharaoh gave them: wherefore they sold not their lands.

The *priests* (kohen) [H3548] of Pharaoh are protected from the ravages of the famine and are united with Joseph through the marriage with Asenath, the

---

[10] Joseph's enslavement by the Egyptians, Gen 39:1–23, corresponds to Joseph's purchasing of the Egyptians, 47:13–31, in a counterpoint, concentric structure spanning 37:2–50:26 (Waltke 581–82). The death and resurrection of Christ is the death and resurrection of creation as a whole.

daughter of Potipherah, priest of On (Gen 41:45). And the union of Joseph with the priests of Pharaoh reflects the union of kingship and priesthood in the Body of Christ. The priests of Pharaoh being protected during the seven years of famine prefigures the 144,000 being sealed with the seal of the living God at the time of the final tribulation period (Rev 7:2–4). And the 144,000 will finally stand with the Lamb on Mount Zion (Rev 14:1) and will follow the Lamb wherever he goes (Rev 14:4). The 144,000 of the twelve tribes will all be kings and priests just as all the faithful will be kings and priests. The reign of Joseph under Pharaoh prefigures the Second Advent. The First Advent is fulfilled in the Second Advent. And the First Advent is to the Second Advent as the kingship is to the high priesthood.[11]

Genesis 47:23 Then Joseph said unto the people, Behold, I have bought you this day and your land for Pharaoh: lo, [here is] seed [H2233] for you, and ye shall sow the land.

The word *seed* [H2233] (of Joseph) has a connotation "offspring (children)." The people belonging to Pharaoh being given seed to sow in the land recalls the primal vocation of Adam, likewise Adam-kind, in being called to dress and keep the garden of Eden (Gen 2:15). The directive to sow the land also reflects the commandment to be fruitful and multiply and to subdue the earth (Gen 1:28). The kingdom of God recalls the garden of Eden, but the kingdom of God is not simply a return to the garden of Eden. If the movement from the garden to the kingdom represented a circular path, then man would inevitably fall from grace again and again throughout all eternity. And Jesus Christ would need to be crucified again and again throughout all eternity, which is not possible (Heb 6:4–6). The kingdom is not the body of Adam but rather the Body of Christ, representing the fullness of communion with God.[12]

Genesis 47:24 And it shall come to pass in the increase, that ye shall give the fifth [part] unto Pharaoh, and four parts shall be your own, for seed of

---

[11] "[W]hatever the religion of Egypt was, it *was established by law* and supported by the state. . . . This is the earliest [explicit] account we have of an *established religion supported by the state*" (Clarke 1:259; Gen 47:22). The land of Egypt reflects the larger world in which we live, the good and the bad, and thereby Egypt can and does prefigure the promised millennial reign of Christ and, simultaneously, the false system of anti-christ that will precede the return of Christ.

[12] Man was originally created in a state of holiness, but man was destined to be fully divinized—Maximus the Confessor, *Ambigua* (Rom. Catholic Church, *Catechism* 112). The garden of Eden at no time yielded the fullness of communion within the Trinity, that is, by God the Holy Spirit in God the Son with God the Father. For if the presence of the Lord God walking in the garden had represented the fullness of relationship, or communion, with God, and, therein, the fullness of the knowledge of the Lord, then fallen mankind, Adam-kind, like the fallen angels, could not have been afforded, as a second chance, the freewill choice of being redeemed.

the field, and for your food, and for them of your households, and for food for your little ones.

The fifth part given to Pharaoh recalls the sacrifice of Christ in the fifth millennium from Adam. A fifth part represents two tenths, or two tithes. And the double tithe expected in the last days (beginning with the First Advent) is the tithe of the Body of Christ added to the tithe of Christ himself. The tithe is a requirement of the law and, thereby, signifies the whole of the law (Jas 2:10)— especially since the tithe is identified with the firstborn representing the first man Adam, who embodies all of fallen mankind condemned under the law (Num 3:12, 18:24). The double tithe is the final tribulation of the Second Advent added to the tribulation of the cross of the First Advent. The Lord did not come to destroy the law but to fulfill the law (Matt 5:17).

Further, the tithe originally promised by Jacob at Bethel is connected to the peace and safety of his house (Gen 28:20–22) but is ultimately the taking of Joseph from him and finally the adding of Benjamin to Joseph (Gen 42:38). For it is Joseph being taken and Benjamin being added to Joseph that finally ensures the peace and safety of Jacob's house (Gen 45:5). The first and second sons Joseph and Benjamin reflect the First and Second Advents and likewise the millennial reign and eternity. The tribulation of the Body of Christ has no meaning separated from the tribulation of Christ, but nonetheless the tribulation of the Body must be added to that of the Head because the Body and the Head are one. And the fire that concludes the millennial kingdom must be added to the fire that announces the millennial kingdom (Rev 18:8, 20:7–10). The natural body and likewise the present creation remain condemned under the law even after the tribulations of Christ and the Body of Christ. In subsuming the original creation, the promised new creation must wholly supplant the old.

Genesis 47:25 And they said, Thou hast saved our lives: let us find grace [H2580] in the sight of my lord, and we will be Pharaoh's servants.

The *grace* [H2580] that the Egyptians find in the eyes of Joseph is the same *grace* [H2580] that Noah found in the eyes of the Lord (Gen 6:8). The grace that will be manifested in the Second Advent is the same grace established in the First Advent just as the foretold second destruction (by fire) will be the fulfillment of the first destruction (by water) (2 Pet 3:5–7). There is a persistent connection between the Flood and the First Advent. The Egyptians become the possessions of Pharaoh because they find grace in the eyes of Joseph, and as a result their lives and their land are saved. This is the eternal life of the Father that the faithful receive by grace through faith in the Son according to the anointing of the Spirit. The death and resurrection of the world by the wooden ark prefigures the death and resurrection of the world by the wooden cross.

TWELVE TRIBES

Genesis 47:26 And Joseph made it a law over the land of Egypt unto this day, [that] Pharaoh should have the fifth [part]; except the land of the priests only, [which] became not Pharaoh's.

The double tithe required by the law of Joseph represents the double judgment of the law, which is the death of the natural body together with the death of the present natural creation. This is also the twofold *destroying* [G622], or "putting out of the way entirely," of soul and body (Matt 10:28).[13] This is the second death following the first (Rev 20:6). The priests being protected under the auspices of Pharaoh and therefore not paying this tithe prefigures the 144,000 being sealed by the living God and thereby passing through the final tribulation period without dying a natural death (Rev 7:2–3). But the 144,000 are the firstfruits and, therefore, are themselves identified with a yet larger harvest of the faithful (Rev 14:4). The 144,000 of the twelve tribes will all be kings and priests just as all the faithful will be kings and priests. And the completed harvest will be added to the firstfruits just as grace is added to law.

Genesis 47:27 And Israel dwelt in the land of Egypt, in the country of Goshen; and they had possessions therein, and grew, and multiplied exceedingly.

Jacob directing his sons unto their brother Joseph reflects the Holy Spirit guiding the faithful unto the Son. The prospering and multiplying of the house of Jacob in the kingdom of Egypt, which is the land of Joseph, prefigures the multitude of faithful that will inherit the promised fullness of the indwelling Holy Spirit in the kingdom of God, which is the Body of Christ. The seven years of famine driving the house of Jacob into the kingdom of Egypt foreshadows the seven years of tribulation that will herald the millennial kingdom. Joseph ruling Egypt under Pharaoh prefigures the Son judging the world according to the will of the Father.

Genesis 47:28 And Jacob lived in the land of Egypt seventeen years: so the whole age of Jacob was an hundred forty and seven years.

Joseph called Jacob into Egypt after two years of famine, when there was yet five years of famine remaining (Gen 45:6). Jacob living in the land of Egypt in total seventeen years implies that he lived in the land twelve years after the famine had ended. The twelve years of Jacob following the seven years of famine reflects the millennial reign of Christ following the tribulation period. The twelve years of Jacob reflect the twelve sons of Jacob and finally the twelve thrones set up over the nation of Israel during the reign of Christ (Matt 19:28). The connection between the twelve sons of Jacob and the one thousand years of Christ is the same connection between the twelve sons and the seven

---

[13] G622 connotation "put out of the way entirely" per *Brown-Driver-Briggs*, but is also evident in *Strong's* etymology connecting G622 and G575.

thousand years of Adam. The millennial kingdom of Christ is the promised seventh, or Sabbath, millennium from Adam, and therefore the seventh millennium, which is the fulfillment of the seven millennia, represents the totality of the seven millennia. The twelve sons of Jacob are identified with the progression of the millennia connecting Adam and the promised new Adam and, therefore, are also identified with the seventh, or Sabbath, millennium.[14]

The twelve years of Jacob following the seven years of famine prefigure the one thousand years of Christ, but the twelve years of Jacob also look past the millennial kingdom just as the millennial reign itself heralds the opening of eternity. Jacob living in a relative paradise for the twelve years following the seven years of famine parallels the exaltation of his twelve sons at the same time. The prosperity of the twelve tribes following the seven years of famine prefigures the millennial reign of Christ, but the exaltation of the twelve finally points to the promised new creation and new Jerusalem, which will be marked by the names of the twelve tribes of Israel and also by the names of the twelve apostles of the Lamb (Rev 21:12–14). The twelve apostles do not replace the twelve tribes but are added to them just as the Body is added to the Head just as eternity will be added to the millennial reign. The Covenant of Grace likewise completes and subsumes the Covenant of Law. The spiritual, or glorified, resurrection body likewise completes and subsumes the natural body, for the spiritual body is a true physical body.[15]

Genesis 47:29–30 And the time drew nigh that Israel must die: and he called his son Joseph, and said unto him, If now I have found grace [H2580] in thy sight, put, I pray thee, thy hand under my thigh, and deal kindly and truly with me; bury me not, I pray thee, in Egypt: 30 But I will lie with my fathers, and thou shalt carry me out of Egypt, and bury me in their buryingplace. And he said, I will do as thou hast said.

Joseph putting his hand under the thigh of Jacob and swearing to not bury him in Egypt recalls the eldest servant of Abraham putting his hand under the thigh of Abraham and swearing to bring only a near-kin bride unto his son Isaac (Gen 24:2–4). In the former account, Isaac represents the Son, the eldest servant represents the Spirit, and Abraham represents the Father. The bride of Isaac was called following his figurative death and resurrection in Moriah (Gen

---

[14] "Abimi b. Abuhu taught: Seven thousand years will be the days of Messiah, as it reads [Isa 62:5]: 'And as a bridegroom is glad over the bride, so will be glad over thee thy God,' which is seven days, and each day of the Lord is a thousand years" (Rodkinson, *Talmud: Sanhedrin* 8[16]:312). To the bridegroom of blood belongs the whole of the seven thousand years of creation, Exod 4:26.

[15] Jacob's 17 years with Joseph in Egypt recalls Joseph's 17 years with Jacob in Canaan, Gen 37:2, just as Abraham's 75 years with Isaac in Canaan recalls Abraham's 75 years with Terah outside Canaan, 12:4, 21:5, 25:7 (Sarna 324; Gen 47:28). The Son with the Father, or begotten of the Father, becomes the Father with the Son, or revealed in the Son. Isaac ben Abraham points to Joseph ben Jacob just as the First Advent points to the Second Advent just as the first man Adam points to the second man Christ.

22:2) just as the bride of the (slain) Lamb would be called following the crucifixion of Christ (Exod 4:24–26). The necessity that Abraham's eldest servant must himself bring the bride unto Isaac reflects the Holy Spirit indwelling and guiding the faithful unto the Son (Gen 24:6). In the present local context corresponding to the millennial kingdom of Christ, Joseph represents the Son, Jacob represents the Spirit, and Pharaoh generally represents the Father, though in this case Pharaoh is supplanted by Abraham (as the Father), which represents a looking past the millennial reign into eternity. The necessity that Jacob must be buried with Abraham and not with Pharaoh reflects the imperative that the Holy Spirit must bring the faithful into what is the fullness of communion with the Father.[16]

The approaching death of Jacob, who represents God the Holy Spirit, signifies, not the death of the Spirit, but rather the end of the age of the Spirit, that is, the end of the age of calling the faithful unto repentance in God the Son. The *grace* [H2580] that Jacob now finds in Joseph is the same *grace* [H2580] that the Egyptians found in Joseph (Gen 47:25). The *grace* [H2580] that Jacob finds in Joseph is the saving grace and redemption of the Holy Spirit that can only be received by grace through faith in Jesus Christ. The threefold Pharaoh, Joseph, and Jacob reflect the Father, Son, and Spirit, specifically in relation to the time culminating in the millennial kingdom. In contrast, Abraham, Isaac, and Jacob represent a universal image of the Father, Son, and Spirit—as indicated by God referring to himself as the God of Abraham, Isaac, and Jacob but never according to any other highly localized title, such as the God of Pharaoh, Joseph, and Jacob (Exod 3:6). And the universality of Abraham, Isaac, and Jacob can be attributed to the universality of Abraham, who uniquely symbolizes the father of all the faithful (Rom 4:16). And it's appropriate that the universal image represented by Abraham, Isaac, and Jacob, which applies throughout all the Scriptures and likewise throughout all time, is now evoked in the context of the eternity that will proceed from the millennial reign.[17]

Genesis 47:31   And he said, Swear [H7650] unto me. And he sware [H7650] unto him. And Israel bowed himself upon the bed's head.

The word *swear* [H7650] (Joseph swears unto Jacob) literally means "to seven oneself, or bind oneself by seven things," which reflects the fulfillment of the original seven days of creation and likewise the fulfillment of the present seven millennia of creation. Joseph swearing unto Jacob represents the fulfillment of

---

[16] "He [Jacob] would be buried in *Canaan* . . . because it was a type of heaven, that better country, which he was in expectation of" (Wesley 1:182; Gen 47:29). Not simply a type of heaven, but of a new creation, a new earth and a new heaven, representing a unified whole, of Christ and in Christ.

[17] Other Trinitarian titles are "the God of Shadrach, Meshach, and Abednego," Dan 3:29, and "the God of Abraham, and the God of Nahor, the God of their father [Terah]," Gen 31:53. But these titles of deity are not emphasized beyond their local context and, not coincidentally, neither are they applied by God to himself, rather by the people of the world to God, Exod 3:6.

the promise of the Spirit in the Son, in the Body of Christ. The coming death of Jacob signifies the end of the age of God the Holy Spirit calling the faithful unto repentance in Christ. The death of Jacob points to the end of the millennial kingdom of Christ, corresponding to the end of the seventh, or Sabbath, millennium, which in turn marks the opening of eternity in Christ, signified by the eighth millennium. It is not until the end of the Sabbath millennium that death and hell will be cast into the lake of fire (Rev 20:14). The foretold eighth day represents the first day of the new week that is the promised new and eternal creation (Rev 21:1).

Ephraim and Manasseh

Genesis 48:1–2 And it came to pass after these things, that [one] told Joseph, Behold, thy father [is] sick [H2470]: and he took with him his two sons, Manasseh [H4519] and Ephraim [H669]. 2 And [one] told Jacob, and said, Behold, thy son Joseph cometh unto thee: and Israel strengthened [H2388] himself, and sat upon the bed.

The word *sick* [H2470] (Israel is sick) has a connotation "to be grieved" (Amos 6:6), while the word *strengthened* [H2388] (Israel strengthened himself) has a connotation "to prevail" (Gen 47:20). The Spirit is grieved by the faithless rejecting the Son, but the Spirit nonetheless prevails in establishing the faithful in the Son. Joseph bringing his first and second born sons unto Jacob at this critical time reflects the redemption of the faithful being established in the unity of the First and Second Advents of Christ. The name *Manasseh* [H4519] (the firstborn) is connected with God making Joseph forget all his toil and also all his father's house, which reflects the preservation of Adam in the land, with Christ ultimately assuming the curse of Adam (Gen 41:51). The name *Ephraim* [H669] (the second born) is connected with God causing Joseph to be fruitful in the land of his affliction, which reflects the harvest of the church age and finally the exaltation of the multitude of faithful in the Body of Christ (Gen 41:52).

Genesis 48:3–5 And Jacob said unto Joseph, God Almighty appeared unto me at Luz in the land of Canaan, and blessed me, 4 And said unto me, Behold, I will make thee fruitful, and multiply thee, and I will make of thee a multitude of people; and will give this land to thy seed after thee [for] an everlasting possession. 5 And now thy two sons, Ephraim and Manasseh, which were born unto thee in the land of Egypt before I came unto thee into Egypt, [are] mine; as Reuben and Simeon, they shall be mine.

The blessing of Jacob to become a multitude is here identified with the first and second sons of Joseph being begotten in Egypt. The dominion of Joseph under Pharaoh reflects the First Advent of Christ being fulfilled in the Second Advent. And the sons of Joseph under Pharaoh becoming the sons of Jacob reflects the reality of sons being begotten after the same kind as their father, in this case after Jacob and not Pharaoh. The faithful in Christ are always marked by a conforming unto the image of Christ (John 13:35, 1 John 3:2). But the emphasis on Ephraim and Manasseh having been born unto Joseph before Jacob had arrived in Egypt points specifically to the church age connecting the First and Second Advents. And Joseph's first and seconds sons, Manasseh and Ephraim, being like Jacob's first and second sons, Reuben and Simeon, finally represents the sons of Joseph supplanting the sons of Jacob. And this is an image of rebirth in the Body of Christ by the power of the Spirit culminating in the Second Advent and unifying the First and Second Advents.

Genesis 48:6 And thy issue, which thou begettest after them, shall be thine, [and] shall be called after the name of their brethren in their inheritance.

The offspring of Joseph begotten after the coming of Jacob are identified with Joseph and not Jacob and, thereby, reflect the offspring corresponding to the millennial kingdom of Jesus Christ. The future offspring of Joseph will nevertheless receive their inheritance through the offspring of Jacob, which is an affirmation of the promise of the indwelling Spirit continuing throughout the millennial kingdom. The second firstborn Joseph not actually having any recorded offspring following Manasseh and Ephraim points the faithful to the fulfillment of all things in the end times. A tribe not being formally named after the preeminent son Joseph reflects the singular position of Christ, who is sovereign over all the tribes of Jacob and not confined to any one tribe (Num 2:1–34), while a tribe under the explicit name of Joseph being identified with the end times in the book of Revelation points to the promised brotherhood of Christ and the faithful in Christ (Rev 7:5–8). The Lord is simultaneously and without contradiction fully God and fully man.

Genesis 48:7 And as for me, when I came from Padan, Rachel died by me in the land of Canaan in the way, when yet [there was] but a little way to come unto Ephrath: and I buried her there in the way of Ephrath; the same [is] Beth-lehem.

Jacob recalling the death of his wife Rachel connects her death with his own death. The deaths of Jacob and Rachel both point to the end of the millennial kingdom that is the end of the Second Advent. Joseph is identified with the seventh millennium, while Benjamin is identified with the eighth millennium. And the death of Jacob's second wife, Rachel, giving birth to their second son, Benjamin, points to the end of the millennial kingdom of Christ, specifically to the apostasy marking the end of the millennial kingdom (Rev 20:7–8). The death of Rachel is identified with childbirth and likewise with children. And through her burial near Bethlehem, the death of Rachel is further identified with the slaughter of the innocents—which has always been the final harbinger of the evil one, not only at the time of the First Advent, but always throughout all time (Jer 31:15). The pillar set upon Rachel's grave represents the resurrection unto damnation that will mark the end of the millennial kingdom of Christ (Gen 35:20, John 5:29, Rev 20:11–15).

Genesis 48:8–11 And Israel beheld [H7200] Joseph's sons, and said, Who [are] these? 9 And Joseph said unto his father, They [are] my sons, whom God hath given me in this [place]. And he said, Bring them, I pray thee, unto me, and I will bless them. 10 Now the eyes of Israel were dim for age, [so that] he could not see [H7200]. And he brought them near unto him; and he kissed them, and embraced them. 11 And Israel said unto Joseph, I had not thought to see [H7200] thy face: and, lo, God hath shewed [H7200] me also thy seed.

The image of Jacob *beholding* [H7200] Joseph's sons without actually being able to *see* [H7200] reflects a walk that is by faith in contrast to sight. Jacob reflects the Holy Spirit, while Joseph reflects the Son. Jacob needing Joseph to identify his offspring and bring them unto him represents the essential identification of the faithful with Jesus Christ that comes by the Spirit. The blessing of the Spirit is finally the indwelling of the Spirit, and the faithful receive the indwelling of the Holy Spirit in the Body of Christ and only in the Body of Christ, which is why the fullness of the Spirit could come only after the time of the First Advent (John 16:7). Jacob identifying his seeing Joseph with his seeing the offspring of Joseph again reflects the essential identification of the faithful with Christ. Jacob seeing Joseph represents the coming of Jesus Christ, while Jacob seeing the offspring of Joseph represents the anointing of the faithful in Christ. The sons of Joseph being born unto Joseph in Egypt at the time of his ruling over Egypt under Pharaoh points to the exaltation of the children of God, generally during the church age and specifically as culminating in the time of the Second Advent of Christ.[18]

Genesis 48:12 And Joseph brought them out from between his knees [H1290], and he bowed himself with his face to the earth.

Joseph bringing his sons out from between his *knees* [H1290] recalls Bilhah bearing children upon the *knees* [H1290] of Joseph's mother Rachel (Gen 30:3). This is the figurative birthing of Joseph's sons in the presence of Jacob. And this image is naturally identified with Rachel's handmaid, Bilhah, and not with Leah's handmaid, Zilpah. Joseph being identified with the spiritual birthing of his sons in the presence of Jacob represents the faithful being born again in the Body of Christ by the power, or new life, of the Holy Spirit. The powerful and mighty Joseph ruling with the authority of his king and master, Pharaoh, and yet simultaneously bowing himself before his humble father, Jacob, reflects the

---

[18] "And he [Joseph] brought Manasseh and Ephraim, desiring that Manasseh should be blessed, because he was the elder.... But Jacob saw in spirit the type of the people to arise afterwards [*Epistle of Barnabas*]" (Roberts et al., *Ante-Nicene Fathers* 1:145). Yes, the peoples of Manasseh and Ephraim, but also the peoples of Adam and Christ.

fundamental unity of the will of God the Father, God the Son, and God the Spirit in the Trinity (Gen 41:40).

Genesis 48:13–14 And Joseph took them both, Ephraim in his right hand toward Israel's left hand, and Manasseh in his left hand toward Israel's right hand, and brought [them] near unto him. 14 And Israel stretched out his right hand, and laid [it] upon Ephraim's head, who [was] the younger, and his left hand upon Manasseh's head, guiding his hands wittingly; for Manasseh [was] the firstborn.

According to the human perspective, Joseph and Jacob are at odds with each other, but the fact is that both Joseph and Jacob place their right hands upon the second born Ephraim and, thereby, together affirm the blessing of Ephraim in the place of the firstborn. Joseph taking his second born, Ephraim, in his right hand (the "wrong" hand) spiritually anticipates Jacob also taking Ephraim in his right hand. And thus, though seemingly opposed according to the way of flesh, Joseph and Jacob both point to the essential ascendancy of the second born son. The Son and the Spirit both testify to the one will of the Father that is the one will of the Godhead. And the unexpected and seemingly impossible nature of Jacob guiding his hands wittingly despite being dim-eyed reflects the providential movement of the Spirit, working all things together for good in the redemption of the faithful unto the Father in the Son (Rom 8:28).[19]

Genesis 48:15–16 And he blessed Joseph, and said, God [H430], before whom my fathers Abraham and Isaac did walk, the God [H430] which fed me all my life long unto this day, 16 The Angel [H4397] which redeemed me from all evil, bless the lads; and let my name be named on them, and the name of my fathers Abraham and Isaac; and let them grow into a multitude in the midst of the earth.

The threefold Abraham, Isaac, and Jacob reflect the triune Father, Son, and Spirit. Jacob is the one who blesses his offspring, and Jacob is also the blessing itself, his name marking, or resting upon, his offspring. Jacob is God the Holy Spirit, who is our sanctifier. The contrast between the Angel of God and the name of God echoes the relationship between the persons of Isaac and Abraham and, thereby, expands upon the representations of the Son and the Father. The *Angel* [H4397], or "messenger," that redeems is the Son, the Word made flesh, who is our redeemer (John 1:14). The *God* (Elohim) [H430] that feeds, or gives life, is God the Father, who is our creator, or spiritually our true progenitor, our namesake. Further, the blessing of Joseph's offspring is distinct compared with the detailed blessings that will be identified with Joseph and his

---

[19] "It is observable how God from the beginning has preferred the younger to the elder, as *Abel* before *Cain*; *Shem* before *Japheth*; *Isaac* before *Ishmael*; *Jacob* before *Esau*; *Judah* and *Joseph* before *Reuben*; *Ephraim* before *Manasseh*; *Moses* before *Aaron*; and *David* before his *brethren*" (Clarke 1:263; Gen 48:14). The pattern is clear and cannot be ignored.

brothers (Gen 49:1–28). The blessings of the Lord God are distinct but intimately related, reflecting the unity of the Trinity.[20]

Jacob identifies his own name, together with the names of his fathers Isaac and Abraham, with the blessing of Ephraim and Manasseh. And this blessing of Joseph's sons, who are adopted by Jacob, is connected with their becoming a multitude in the earth. The one and only blessing of the faithful in the Body of Christ is the fullness of the indwelling Holy Spirit (Jacob) that is the fullness of the promised communion with the Father (Abraham) in the Son (Isaac). All other blessings flow from this one blessing. Further, Jacob's adopted sons, Ephraim and Manasseh, are marked by their being born in Egypt during Joseph's rule under Pharaoh but before Jacob's arrival and most significantly before Jacob's death, which foreshadows the end of the millennial kingdom. Ephraim and Manasseh specifically prefigure the multiplication of the faithful in a literal millennial kingdom on the earth, which will be established during the millennial Sabbath.[21]

Genesis 48:17–18 And when Joseph saw that his father laid his right hand upon the head of Ephraim, it displeased [H3415] him: and he held up his father's hand, to remove it from Ephraim's head unto Manasseh's head. 18 And Joseph said unto his father, Not so, my father: for this [is] the firstborn; put thy right hand upon his head.

The word *displeased* [H3415] (it displeased Joseph) means "to quiver or tremble (in terror and distress)." The distress of Joseph over his firstborn Manasseh being displaced is the distress of Jesus over the condemnation of the first man Adam, likewise the distress of Jesus over the condemnation of all natural mankind in the first man Adam. The condemnation of natural man is administered under the law. In the context of Jacob coming unto Joseph in Egypt, figuratively the present world, this is specifically the judgment of the tribulation period that will precede the millennial reign.[22]

---

[20] "Christ the angel of the covenant is he that redeems us from *all evil*" (Wesley 1:184; Gen 48:16). The title *Angel*, "messenger," is to the title *Word*, "the essential, personal Expression of God," (Gen 48:16, John 1:1) as the name *Immanuel*, "with us is God," is to the name *Jesus*, "YHWH is salvation" (Isa 7:14, John 1:17).

[21] ". . . Sarah adopted Ishmael, and Leah her handmaid's son[s], and Pharaoh's daughter Moses. Jacob, too, adopted his grandsons, the children of Joseph. . . . That act, then, by which God, when we were not born of Him, but created and formed, begot us by His word and grace, is called adoption. So John says, 'He gave them power to become the sons of God' [John 1:12] [Augustine, *Reply to Faustus the Manichæan*]" (Schaff, *Nicene and Post-Nicene Fathers: First Series* 4:160). We are adopted, not left orphaned, just as the Lord himself is begotten, not merely created.

[22] "It has been observed that Joseph spoke here as he was moved by *natural* affection, and that Jacob acted as he was influenced by the *Holy Spirit*" (Clarke 1:264; Gen 48:18). Joseph ben Jacob forms a dichotomous image of Jesus Christ, God the Son, who is fully man and fully God.

Genesis 48:19 And his father refused, and said, I know [it], my son, I know [it]: he also shall become a people, and he also shall be great: but truly his younger brother shall be greater than he, and his seed shall become a multitude of nations.

The firstborn Manasseh represents a people who come first, and the people who come first (in time) are the Israelites, the one nation of Israel. But greater (in number) than Manasseh will be the second born Ephraim, representing a multitude of peoples that will come second, namely, the peoples and nations of the world redeemed in Christ through the one nation of Israel. The second supplanting the first reflects the Body of Christ supplanting the body of Adam. The second born and the firstborn are related by blood just as the second covenant, the Covenant of Grace, subsumes the first covenant, the Covenant of Law, by virtue of the shed blood of Jesus Christ. The second born son supplanting the firstborn is the incarnation of the second man Jesus Christ transcending and subsuming the formation of the first man Adam, likewise the Second Advent of Christ subsuming the First Advent, and likewise eternity in Christ subsuming the millennial reign of Christ.[23]

Genesis 48:20 And he blessed them that day, saying, In thee shall Israel bless, saying, God make thee as Ephraim and as Manasseh: and he set Ephraim before Manasseh.

The blessing pronounced by the one nation of Israel is finally the blessing of all the nations, in accord with the original covenant made with father Abraham (Gen 12:3, 18:18). The twofold blessing of God, to be as the two sons Ephraim and Manasseh, is in truth one blessing. The blessing of God is the blessing of the firstborn in the second born, that is, the blessing of the first man Adam in the second man Jesus Christ.[24]

Genesis 48:21 And Israel said unto Joseph, Behold, I die: but God shall be with you, and bring you again unto the land of your fathers.

The death of Jacob foreshadows the end of the age of the Holy Spirit, which is the end of the call unto repentance in Jesus Christ. And this age will not be wholly fulfilled until death and hell are cast into the lake of fire at the end of the

---

[23] "... *Jacob* gave him [Joseph] to understand that he knew what he did, and that he [Jacob] did it neither by mistake nor in a humour, nor from a partial affection to one [child] more than the other, but from a spirit of prophecy" (Wesley 1:184; Gen 48:16). The testimony of Jesus Christ is the spirit of prophecy, namely, the spirit of truth that is the person of the Holy Spirit.

[24] "For though Manasseh was first-born, how could it be that Ephraim should take the birthright? . . . Lo! John [the Baptist] as a herald declares that he [Jesus] is later, though he was elder-born; for he said, 'Behold a man cometh after me, and yet He was before me' [John 1:30] [Ephraim the Syrian, *Nisibene Hymns*]" (Schaff and Wace, *Nicene and Post-Nicene Fathers: Second Series* 13:200). The Lord himself is the paradigm of creation.

millennial kingdom of Christ (Rev 20:14). It is clear that the sin nature will not be completely eradicated during the millennial reign of Christ, because people will continue to die during this period (Isa 65:20) and also because the nations will rebel at the end of the millennial reign (Rev 20:7–9). God's promise to bring Joseph again unto the land of his fathers, after the time of Jacob's death, points to the foretold new creation being established at the end of the millennial kingdom (Rev 21:1–4).

Genesis 48:22 Moreover I have given to thee one portion above thy brethren, which I took out of the hand of the Amorite with my sword and with my bow.

The bifurcation of the one tribe of Joseph into the two tribes of Ephraim and Manasseh is the double portion given to Joseph.[25] The double portion reflects the First Advent followed by the Second Advent, likewise the original creation followed by the promised new creation. The emphasis on Jacob having taken the portion of Joseph by force points to the promised dominion of Christ at the Second Advent coming by the victory of the cross at the First Advent. And the hand of the Amorite reflects the evil one, from whom Christ takes the dominion (2 Cor 4:4). The double portion of Jesus Christ is the birthright and the blessing and likewise the kingship and the high priesthood. The double portion of the kingship and the priesthood is affirmed by the tithe given to the king (1 Sam 8:15–17) paralleling the tithe given to the Levites (Num 18:24). And this is finally the tithe of the Second Advent added to the tithe of the First Advent, namely, the final tribulation of the Body of Christ being added to the tribulation of Christ himself on the cross.

Twelve Prophecies

Genesis 49:1 And Jacob called unto his sons, and said, Gather yourselves together, that I may tell you [that] which shall befall you in the last [H319] days [H3117].

The last days will culminate with the final judgment of the world, but the judgment of the world began with Christ assuming the condemnation of the faithful on the cross (Isa 2:2–4).[26] The *eschaton*,[27] "the final event in the divine

---

[25] "The *one portion above your* [Joseph's] *brothers* speaks of Joseph being father of two tribes, while each of his brothers only fathered one" (Guzik 259; Gen 48:21–22). The spiritual blessing represented by and given to physical offspring reflects the essential unity of blessing and birthright.

[26] "[*Eschatology*:] The branch of theology that deals with the four last things (death, judgment, heaven, and hell) and the final destiny of the soul and of humankind; . . ." (*Shorter Oxford English Dictionary on Historical Principles*, 5th ed., s.v. "eschatology"). The individual is connected with humanity as a whole. The First Advent of Christ is the beginning of the Second Advent, culminating in the Body of Christ.

[27] A related form is *eschatos* [G2078], meaning "extreme, last in time or in place."

plan,"[28] properly began at the time of the First Advent of Christ (1 John 2:18).[29] And the church age connecting the First and Second Advents therefore points to the fulfillment of all creation. The telling of the things that will befall Jacob's sons in the last days looks beyond their individual fates to this larger meaning. And the character of the blessings of Jacob testifies to this reality of looking beyond the individual sons (Gen 49:10). Nevertheless, Jacob's blessings do still comprehend his literal sons. It is actually a universal attribute of true prophecy to have layered significances, referring simultaneously to both individual circumstances and the larger world. This being the intrinsic nature of prophecy is consistent with man being a microcosm of creation as a whole. The individual and creation as a whole are both formed in the image of God because God, who is self-existent, is all that is and therefore the only practicable mold with which creation can be formed and conformed.[30]

Yet the prophetic names of Jacob's twelve sons, representing birthrights or birth prophecies and given by their respective mothers, are distinct from the much later prophetic blessings given by Jacob at the time of his death (Gen 29:31–30:24, 36:18). The birthrights are identified most closely with the kingship, while the subsequent blessings are identified most closely with the high priesthood. The former points to the First Advent, while the latter points to the Second Advent. The former connects the condemnation of Adam with the crucifixion of Christ, while the latter connects the victory of the cross with the glorious reappearing of Christ. The birthrights being spoken by Jacob's wives recalls the promised Seed of woman, who would be conceived of God the Holy Spirit. In contrast, the blessings being spoken by father Jacob himself looks forward to the promised union with God the Father, which is our promised new creation. At the time of birth, man originally proceeds from the womb of woman, which is spiritually from the side (rib) of Adam (Gen 2:21–24, 3:20), but at the time of rebirth, a man finally proceeds from the side of Christ (John 19:34, 1 John 5:8, John 3:5).[31]

Genesis 49:2 Gather yourselves together, and hear [H8085], ye sons of Jacob; and hearken [H8085] unto Israel your father.

---

[28] *Shorter Oxford English Dictionary on Historical Principles*, 5th ed., s.v. "eschaton."
[29] The phrase *in days to come* (last [H319] days [H3117]) is a technical formulation in Biblical prophetic literature for the "end-time" or "eschaton," representing the fulfillment of God's plan for humanity (Sarna 332; Gen 49:1). The three millennia, or prophetic days, of God connecting the First and Second Advents.
[30] Created man, seemingly in every detail, is viewed as a microcosm of creation, *Aboth d'Rabbi Nathan* (Cohen, *Rabbinic Sages* 70). Prophecy is fractal.
[31] The myriad attempts to refute Messianic prophecies, such as those prophecies uttered by Jacob on his deathbed, are based entirely upon a rejection of the supernatural reality of God and not in any way upon the actual historical or literary facts (Coffman 561–62; Gen 49:1). The Spirit moves simultaneously in the natural and in the supernatural just as the Son is fully man and fully God.

The word *hearken* (hear) [H8085] has a connotation "to obey." The brothers are identified with the progression of the millennia connecting Adam and the promised new Adam. And the brothers hearing and obeying their father reflects the providential movement of the Spirit throughout the ages. The sons of Jacob being called upon to hearken unto Israel their father represents the essential movement from the way of the flesh to the way of the Spirit. The sons of Jacob must hearken unto Israel just as Jacob himself must become Israel.

Genesis 49:3–4 Reuben, thou [art] my firstborn, my might, and the beginning of my strength, the excellency of dignity, and the excellency of power: 4 Unstable as water [H4325], thou shalt not excel; because thou wentest up to thy father's bed; then defiledst [H2490] thou [it]: he went up to my couch.

The firstborn Reuben reflects the first man Adam. And Reuben will not excel just as Adam will not be accepted. The word *defiledst* [H2490] (the firstborn defiled his father's bed) is the same word describing men *beginning* (profanely) [H2490] to call upon the name of the Lord during the time of Adam (Gen 4:26). And the comparison of the firstborn Reuben to *water* [H4325] (unstable as water) reflects the connection between the rejection of the first man Adam and the first destruction of Adam-kind that came by water. This is also the rejection of Adamic natural man in the death and resurrection of repentance that is signified by the baptism in water. The image of adultery, particularly in the defilement of a father's bed, reflects the rejection of the Lord God inherent in the embrace of idolatry, finally understood to be the primordial sin of pride, or vain self-worship, shared by serpent and man alike (Gen 3:4–5). The rejection of the firstborn represents the rejection of the natural body that is condemned under the law. The adultery of the firstborn, who defiles his father's bed, portends the final apostasy in the end times. The first rebellion of Adam and the final rebellion of Adam-kind represent the same apostasy.[32]

Genesis 49:5–7 Simeon and Levi [are] brethren; instruments of cruelty [are in] their habitations. 6 O my soul, come not thou into their secret; unto their assembly, mine honour, be not thou united: for in their anger they slew a man, and in their selfwill they digged down a wall. 7 Cursed [be] their anger, for [it was] fierce; and their wrath, for it was cruel: I will divide them in Jacob, and scatter them in Israel.

---

[32] "[H]e [Reuben] was deprived of this pre-eminence, belonging to the birthright [of the firstborn], which included, according to Jewish writers, a double portion of the inheritance, the priesthood, and the kingdom, and which were distributed amongst his brothers,—the first being conferred on Joseph, the second on Levi, and the third on Judah" (Jamieson et al. 1:265; Gen 49:3). The kingship, the priesthood, and the blessing of the double portion being identified with three different brothers, or tribes, relates no simple separation of the three but a simultaneous separation and brotherhood—namely, the triune reality of the kingship of Judah and the priesthood of Levi being nurtured by, or proceeding from, the double portion of Joseph.

The brotherhood of cruelty that marks Simeon and Levi hearkens back to their destroying Shechem (Gen 34:30). Simeon and Levi requiring the men of Shechem to be circumcised and then killing them points to the connection between circumcision and the judgment of the law. The sign of the law is the circumcision of natural man, while the judgment of the law is the death of the natural man (Gen 34:15, 34:25). That the men of Shechem were in fact deserving of judgment and death because of Dinah is a testimony to the righteousness of the law (Gen 34:31). Further, the image of being scattered in Israel foretells of the Levites not receiving an inheritance in the land (Deut 14:27). The ministry of the Levites serving in the temple connects the Levites to animal sacrifice and, thereby, to the death of the natural body required by the law. The cruelty and anger and wrath of Simeon and Levi—slaying a man, representing all flesh—reflect the nature of the law, which is of itself without mercy. The destruction of Shechem portends the final tribulation period in the end times. In contrast, Jacob refusing to be united with their wrath represents God refusing to let the law be the final word.[33]

The brotherhood of Simeon and Levi ultimately reflects the connection between the second and third millennia from the first man Adam, which is the relationship between the judgment of the floodwaters in the second millennium and the law established by Moses in the third millennium. The first covenant, the Covenant of Law, precedes the second covenant, the Covenant of Grace, just as the first destruction (by water) precedes the second destruction (by fire). The First Advent of Christ precedes the Second Advent just as the millennial kingdom of Christ precedes eternity in Christ. Likewise, the natural man precedes the spiritual man. And the brotherhood of Simeon and Levi, which connects the second and third millennia, finally points to the brotherhood of Issachar and Zebulun, which connects the fifth and sixth millennia leading up to the end times (Gen 30:17–20, 49:13–15). The final word of the Father is the grace that comes by faith in the Son, which will be fully manifested by the power of the Holy Spirit at the time of the Second Advent. This is the grace that subsumes law. This is the spiritual, or glorified, resurrection body that is a true physical body.[34]

Genesis 49:8–12 Judah, thou [art he] whom thy brethren shall praise: thy hand [shall be] in the neck of thine enemies; thy father's children shall bow down before thee. 9 Judah [is] a lion's whelp: from the prey, my son,

---

[33] "[C]ertainly a prophecy, 'I will divide them in Jacob, and scatter them in Israel'; . . . as for the tribe of Simeon, that had not a distinct part by itself in the land of Canaan, but had their inheritance out of the portion, and within the inheritance of the tribe of Judah, [Josh 19:1–9]: . . . And as for the tribe of Levi, it is well known that it had no inheritance in the land of Canaan, [Deut 18:1] . . . ." (Gill 1:242; Gen 49:7). The scattering of Jacob in the nation of Israel is the law being subsumed by grace in the Body of Christ.

[34] "We ought always in the expressions of our zeal carefully to distinguish between the sinner and the sin, so as not to love or bless the sin for the sake of the person, nor to hate or curse the person for the sake of the sin" (Wesley 1:187; Gen 49:7). Persons and prophecies are also distinguished just as the literal and spiritual are distinguished.

thou art gone up: he stooped down, he couched as a lion, and as an old lion; who shall rouse him up? 10 The sceptre shall not depart from Judah, nor a lawgiver from between his feet, until Shiloh come; and unto him [shall] the gathering of the people [be]. 11 Binding his foal unto the vine, and his ass's colt unto the choice vine; he washed his garments in wine, and his clothes in the blood of grapes: 12 His eyes [shall be] red with wine, and his teeth white with milk.

The hand of Judah being on the neck of his enemies points to the enemies of Jesus Christ being made his footstool (Heb 10:12–14, 1 Cor 15:25–26). The parallel between hand and foot, between higher and lower things, in the exaltation of Christ, in the ascending and descending of Christ, is ultimately the twofold natures of Christ, being true God and true man. The children of Judah's father bowing down before Judah prefigures the time when every knee will bow to the Lord and every tongue will confess to God (Rom 14:11). Judah as the lion hunting prey portends the coming judgment of the world. The identification of Judah with holding the scepter (David) and also with giving laws (Moses and Aaron) reflects the unity of the kingship and the high priesthood in the one man Jesus Christ.[35] The coming of Shiloh and the gathering of the people and the binding to the vine points to the resurrection of the faithful in Jesus Christ, in the Body of Christ.[36] And the ironic washing of Judah's garments in wine prefigures the holy saints finally coming out of the seemingly unholy great tribulation of the world after washing their robes white in the blood of the Lamb (Rev 7:14).[37]

---

[35] "From David until the Herods, a prince of Judah was head over Israel (even Daniel in captivity). The promise was that Israel would keep this *scepter* until *Shiloh* [Messiah] *comes*. Even under their foreign masters . . . Israel had a limited right to self-rule, until in 7 [AD]. Under Herod and the Romans, their right to capital punishment was taken way. . . . At the time, the rabbis considered it a disaster of unfulfilled Scripture. Seemingly, the last vestige of the scepter had passed from Judah, and they did not see the Messiah. . . . Certainly, [however,] Jesus was alive then. Perhaps this was the very year He was 12 years old and discussing God's Word in the temple with the scholars of His day" (Guzik 264; Gen 49:8–12). Ironically, the Jews would still condemn Jesus and have him put to death, despite having lost the right to wield capital punishment.

[36] "Almost all commentators, both Jewish and Christian, agree in regarding this ['until Shiloh come'] as a Messianic prophecy. But they differ very much as to whether the reference is direct or indirect. Many . . . interpret the clause, 'until peace come,' . . . But the most prevalent opinion is . . . *Shiloh* means 'the man of rest,' the 'pacificator,' the 'peace-bringer' . . . ." (Jamieson et al. 1:267; Gen 49:8–10). The two interpretations are not mutually exclusive, and actually one would expect simultaneous supernatural and natural fulfillments.

[37] "The prerogatives of the birth-right which *Reuben* had forfeited, the *excellency of dignity and power*, were thus conferred upon *Judah*" (Wesley 1:187; Gen 49:7). In bypassing Simeon and Levi, Judah becomes a type of a new, or second, firstborn with respect to the law as well as the scepter.

TWELVE TRIBES

Genesis 49:13 Zebulun shall dwell at the haven of the sea; and he [shall be] for an haven of ships; and his border [shall be] unto Zidon.

Though he is the sixth son, Zebulun is identified with the fifth millennium because he is listed fifth (Gen 30:17–20). The safe haven of the sea embodied by Zebulun points to the Gentile nations that would receive the Gospel and characterize the church age connecting the First and Second Advents. The interchange of the ordering of Issachar and Zebulun highlights the unity of the fifth and sixth millennia and is counterpoised to the monolithic brotherhood of Simeon and Levi that marks the unity of the second and third millennia (Gen 49:5). The parallel between these two pairs of millennia points to the death and resurrection of the whole world in its entirety. The symbolic rotation of the fifth and sixth millennia additionally reflects a special parallel between the times of the First and Second Advents. The reconstitution of the nation of Israel and the Roman Empire are perhaps the two most notable examples of this parallel between the time of Christ and the time of the Body of Christ. And the unique relationship between the fifth and sixth millennia reflects the essential kinship between Christ and the faithful in Christ.

Genesis 49:14–15 Issachar [is] a strong ass couching down between two burdens: 15 And he saw that rest [was] good, and the land that [it was] pleasant; and bowed his shoulder to bear, and became a servant unto tribute.

Though he is the fifth son, Issachar is identified with the sixth millennium because he is listed sixth (Gen 30:17–20).[38] Issachar can see the pleasant land and the rest thereof, and so he bows his shoulder under the burden to come, which is specifically the final tribulation period heralding the glorious return of Christ. The rotation of Issachar from the fifth to the sixth position points to the essential unity of the tribulations of the Body of Christ in the end times and Christ himself on the cross. This is also the unity of Gentiles and Jews in the one Body of Christ.[39]

Genesis 49:16–21 Dan shall judge his people, as one of the tribes of Israel. 17 Dan shall be a serpent by the way, an adder in the path, that

---

[38] Additionally, Zebulun is listed ahead of Issachar, contrary to birth order, in the Blessing of Moses, Deut 33:18, while the Song of Deborah depicts Zebulun both before and after Issachar, Judg 5:14–15, 5:18 (Sarna 337–38; Gen 49:13). Redundancy and variation triangulate signification.

[39] "Being consumed by divine love . . . his [Issachar's] mind was captivated not by the old alone, but by both the heritages [himself resting between the two heritages or realities] . . . [H]e beheld afar off 'the rest' which is in heaven, and,—since this 'land' consists of such beautiful works,—how much more truly the heavenly [country] must also [consist] of such; . . . [Athanasius, *Festal Letters*]" (Schaff and Wace, *Nicene and Post-Nicene Fathers: Second Series* 4:540). The unification of creation, earth and heaven, that comes only by the death and resurrection in Christ.

biteth the horse heels, so that his rider shall fall backward. 18 I have waited for thy salvation, O LORD. 19 Gad, a troop shall overcome him: but he shall overcome at the last. 20 Out of Asher his bread [shall be] fat, and he shall yield royal dainties. 21 Naphtali [is] a hind let loose: he giveth goodly words.

Now at the time of blessing, Jacob's offspring by bondwomen are listed between the sixth and seventh sons of Jacob by freewomen, and thereby the offspring by bondwomen collectively point to the time of the Second Advent, which will herald the blessing of the seventh, or Sabbath, millennium. In the original proclamations of the births and birthrights, Jacob's offspring by bondwomen are listed between the fourth and fifth sons of Jacob by freewomen, which points to the First Advent and the time of the birth of Christ (Gen 30:3–13). The birthright is to the blessing as the First Advent of Christ is to the Second Advent as the kingship is to the high priesthood as the Covenant of Law is to the Covenant of Grace. This is the law that condemns Adam compared with the grace that is received only through faith in Jesus Christ. The birthright is to the blessing as the natural body is to the spiritual, or glorified, body as the death of Christ is to the resurrection of the Body of Christ.

The cursing and blessing of Jacob's four sons of bondwomen point to the juncture connecting the sixth and seventh millennia. The judgment embodied by Dan as a serpent prefigures the judgment of the world in the last days, which is signified by the serpent bruising the Heel, specifically as culminating in the time of the final tribulation period (Gen 3:15).[40] The final judgment of the world will be the wicked given over to their father the devil, but what is commonly called the final tribulation period will be only the beginning, or formal beginning, of this final judgment.[41] The judgment of the world will not be completed until the devil, with his children, is consigned to the lake fire at the end of the millennial kingdom (Rev 20:9–15). Yet Gad overcoming in the end prefigures a remnant being saved during the tribulation period and passing through the tribulation. And the fatness and royal dainties of Asher point to the table of God that is prepared for the faithful. And Naphtali being let loose and

---

[40] "But that no one may err by supposing that this is said of the Saviour, let him attend carefully to the matter. . . . For as Christ springs [like an old lion] from the tribe of Judah [Gen 49:9], so Antichrist is to spring [like a lion's whelp] from the tribe of Dan [Deut 33:22] [Hippolytus, *On Christ and Antichrist*]" (Roberts et al., *Ante-Nicene Fathers* 5:207). Christ and anti-christ are often confused, as is somewhat the case in the present example, because anti-christ presents himself as Christ, 2 Thess 2:4, and also because Christ became a curse on the cross, Gal 3:13. This dynamic is particularly evident in Moses using a brazen (brasen) serpent on a pole to represent the cross, Num 21:9, and that same serpent becoming an object of idolatry, 2 Kgs 18:4.

[41] The ordering of the blessings of Jacob's sons shows a chiastic structure, which is obviously deliberate since it deviates from all other Biblical orderings of the tribes: Leah, Bilhah, Zilpah, Zilpah, Bilhah, Rachel (Sarna 331; Gen 49:1–33). Zilpah's sons being inserted between Bilhah's sons forms a pivot within a pivot, calling attention to the mid-tribulation point, Dan 9:27, 12:11.

giving goodly words is the faithful praising God after having been set free of the bondage of sin and death.[42]

Genesis 49:22–26 Joseph [is] a fruitful bough, [even] a fruitful bough by a well; [whose] branches run over the wall: 23 The archers have sorely grieved him, and shot [at him], and hated him: 24 But his bow abode in strength, and the arms of his hands were made strong by the hands of the mighty [God] of Jacob; (from thence [is] the shepherd, the stone of Israel:) 25 [Even] by the God of thy father, who shall help thee; and by the Almighty, who shall bless thee with blessings of heaven above, blessings of the deep that lieth under, blessings of the breasts, and of the womb: 26 The blessings of thy father have prevailed above the blessings of my progenitors unto the utmost bound of the everlasting hills: they shall be on the head of Joseph, and on the crown of the head of him that was separate [H5139] from his brethren.

The second firstborn son Joseph is here listed as the seventh son of a freewoman and, thereby, is identified with the seventh, or Sabbath, millennium, corresponding to the millennial kingdom of Christ. The promised fruitfulness of Joseph is the multiplication of the faithful in the kingdom of God, in the Body of Christ. Joseph being hated and attacked portends Christ and likewise the faithful in Christ being hated and attacked. Joseph having been sorely grieved reflects the suffering of Jesus Christ, but the hands of Joseph being made strong by the very hands of God Almighty prefigures the glorification of the faithful in Christ, in the Body of Christ. Joseph receiving all the blessings of heaven and earth, representing the spiritual and physical domains, points to the resurrection of the body and the corresponding restoration, or re-creation, of all creation, earth and heaven. The blessings of Joseph being everlasting testifies to the promised new creation being eternal.

The crown on the head of Joseph, closely identified with the blessings of God, is the crown of the high priest. The scepter of Judah is identified with the conception of Christ, while the crown of Joseph is identified with the glorification of Christ (Gen 49:10). The scepter of Judah is to the crown of Joseph as the birthright is to the blessing as the kingship is to the high priesthood as the first coming is to the second coming. The birthright is to the blessing as the law is to grace as the natural body is to the spiritual, or glorified, body as the suffering of Jesus Christ is to the glorification of the faithful in Christ. The king and the high priest both wearing crowns (Exod 29:6) finally points to the dual offices of Christ, being both king of kings and high priest (Heb 7:17). The crown of Joseph reflects both the kingship and the high

---

[42] "And he (Naphtali) is adopted as a figure of things pertaining to us, as the Gospel shows: 'The land of Zabulun, and the land of Nephthalim, by the way of the sea, beyond Jordan,' etc.; and, 'To them that sat in darkness light has arisen' [Matt 4:15–16]. And what other light was this but the calling of the Gentiles, . . . [Hippolytus, *On Genesis*]" (Roberts et al., *Ante-Nicene Fathers* 5:167). The haven of the sea that is the way to freedom in the land.

priesthood just as grace subsumes law. The spiritual, or glorified, resurrection body is a true physical body.[43]

Genesis 49:27 Benjamin shall ravin [as] a wolf: in the morning he shall devour [H398] the prey, and at night he shall divide [H2505] the spoil.

Benjamin is listed as the eighth son of a freewoman and, thereby, is identified with the eighth millennium, which represents the opening of eternity. The word *devour* [H398] (devour the prey) has a connotation "to devour by fire," which foreshadows death and hell being cast into the lake of fire at the conclusion of the seventh, or Sabbath, millennium (Rev 20:7–15). The word *divide* [H2505] (divide the spoil) means "to divide, share," which reflects God Almighty sharing his glory with all his faithful ones. And God sharing with the faithful in Christ should be recognized as the unmerited giving of the promised inheritance of the fullness of the indwelling Holy Spirit. And then finally the wolf will dwell with the lamb (Isa 11:6).[44]

Genesis 49:28 All these [are] the twelve tribes of Israel: and this [is it] that their father spake unto them, and blessed them; every one according to his blessing he blessed them.

Twelve sons mark the seven millennia of creation[45] just as twelve months mark the year (Esth 3:7) just as twelve hours mark the day (John 11:9).[46]

THE DEATH OF JACOB

Genesis 49:29 And he charged them, and said unto them, I am to be gathered unto my people: bury me with my fathers in the cave that [is] in the field of Ephron the Hittite,

---

[43] The word *separate* (Nazarite) [H5139] is used here for the first time in the Scriptures.
[44] ". . . Jacob, when he turned his attention to Benjamin . . . foresaw that Paul would arise out of the tribe of Benjamin, a voracious wolf, devouring his prey in the morning: . . . as a persecutor of the churches; but in the evening he would give them nourishment, . . . as the teacher of the Gentiles [Tertullian, *Against Marcion*]" (Roberts et al., *Ante-Nicene Fathers* 3:430). And the Holy Spirit inspiring Jacob would have also been looking beyond the tribulation wrought by Saul to the final tribulation period foretold through and by the prophet Daniel.
[45] "Moses would teach us by these words [referring to Jacob's sons as tribes], that his predictions [inspired by the Holy Spirit] did not apply only to the sons of Jacob, but extended to their whole race" (Calvin, *Commentaries* 2:470; Gen 49:28). Not only the Israelites, but ultimately the whole race of humanity.
[46] Twelve is a recurring number in both Jewish and non-Jewish cultures, which is not surprising given the twelve months of the year and the twelve constellations of the zodiac (*Jewish Encyclopedia*, s.v. "tribes, the twelve"). Pagans and also humanists attempt to identify themselves with nature—the earth, moon, stars, and so forth—but in reality it is God who has placed the signs in heaven and in earth.

The necessity that Jacob must be buried with his fathers is a testimony to the unique relationship between Abraham, Isaac, and Jacob. And the covenant of blood kinship shared by Abraham, Isaac, and Jacob represents nothing less than the unity of God the Father, God the Son, and God the Holy Spirit. The implied equality between Jacob being buried with his fathers and Jacob being gathered unto his people reflects the essential joining of the death of the faithful to the death and resurrection of Jesus Christ. This is the faithful entering into the presence of the Father in the Body of Christ by the power of the Spirit. This is Adam formed in the image of God followed by the First Advent of Christ followed by the Second Advent.[47]

Genesis 49:30 In the cave that [is] in the field of Machpelah, which [is] before Mamre, in the land of Canaan, which Abraham bought with the field of Ephron the Hittite for a possession of a buryingplace.

The emphasis on father Abraham being the rightful owner of the buryingplace of his people points to the righteousness of the Lord God being the guarantee for the promised resurrection of the dead. Further, the act of being buried should be contrasted with the act of being immolated. The act of being buried reflects a faithful expectation of being resurrected unto eternal life, while the act of burning a body reflects ostensibly an expectation of being annihilated but ironically prophesies an eternal lake of fire since a body, or the ash thereof, cannot be fully consumed by fire.

Genesis 49:31 There they buried Abraham and Sarah his wife; there they buried Isaac and Rebekah his wife; and there I buried Leah.

Abraham, Isaac, and Jacob reflect the Father, Son, and Holy Spirit. The three successive generations represented by Abraham, Isaac, and Jacob reflect the progressive revelation of the Father, Son, and Spirit embodied by the formation of Adam followed by the First and Second Advents of Christ. And the wives of the patriarchs represent the faithful, the bride of the Lamb, called to repentance throughout the progressive revelation of creation. Sarah represents all humanity being called to repentance following the Fall of Adam, or Adam-kind. Rebekah reflects the call to repentance corresponding to the time of the First Advent of Jesus Christ. And the wives of Jacob finally represent the call to repentance as connected with the time of the Second Advent of Christ.

---

[47] "The same charge he [Jacob] had given to Joseph he here renews, and lays it upon his sons . . . 'I am to be gathered unto my people'; the people of God, the spirits of just men made perfect, the souls of all the saints . . . called his people, because he and they were of the same mystical body the church, belonged to the same general assembly, and church of the firstborn; the company of God's elect, who were in the same covenant of grace, and partakers of the same blessings and promises of grace . . . ." (Gill 1:247–48; Gen 49:29). One God, one salvation, one Body of Christ.

Genesis 49:32 The purchase of the field and of the cave that [is] therein [was] from the children of Heth.

The buryingplace of Abraham is purchased from the children of Heth, who represent the people of the world and likewise the god of this world, the devil (2 Cor 4:4). The buryingplace of Abraham is identified with the resurrection. The price that is required for a buryingplace is symbolically the death of the body, which is ultimately the death and resurrection of Christ and finally the death and resurrection of the Body of Christ. This is the lost dominion of Adam that is redeemed by the blood of Jesus Christ.

Genesis 49:33 And when Jacob had made an end of commanding his sons, he gathered up his feet into the bed, and yielded up the ghost, and was gathered unto his people.

The end of the age of the Holy Spirit. The end of the age of the call unto repentance in Christ. The final judgment of the faithless, separated from God.

Genesis 50:1 And Joseph fell upon his father's face, and wept [H1058] upon him, and kissed [H5401] him.

Jacob originally *wept* [H1058] over the symbolic death of his son Joseph (disappearing into Egypt), but now Joseph *weeps* [H1058] over the literal death of Jacob (also in Egypt) (Gen 37:35). The deaths of Jacob and Joseph ben Jacob both point to the end of the present age. Jacob is identified with the Spirit, while Joseph is identified with the Son. And the Son and the Spirit are uniquely connected with each other because it is the Spirit and the Son together that proceed from the Father. The progressive revelation of God is the revelation of creation followed by the revelation of redemption followed by the revelation of sanctification, which is finally recognized as the progressive revelation of God the Father, God the Son, and God the Spirit in the formation of Adam followed by the First and Second Advents of Christ.

The procession of God the Son and God the Holy Spirit from God the Father converge at the end of the age, reflecting the singular will of God to save all the faithful in Christ. The righteousness of God is a burning fire, whereby no sinner can enter into the fullness of the presence of God and live (Exod 33:20). And this is why God cannot simply reveal the fullness of himself to the faithful, but rather the faithful must be brought unto God the Father in God the Son, in the Body of Christ, by the power, or new life, of God the Holy Spirit. The word *kissed* [H5401] (Joseph kissed Jacob) connotes "to fasten together, arrange in order," which reflects the fastened together, or unified, will of God to fasten together, or unify, the faithful in Christ by the power of the Spirit.[48]

---

[48] Jacob mourning Joseph, Gen 37:12–36, corresponds to Joseph mourning Jacob, 49:33–50:14, in a counterpoint, concentric structure spanning 37:2–50:26 (Waltke 581–82). Joseph ben Jacob.

Genesis 50:2 And Joseph commanded his servants the physicians [H7495] to embalm [H2590] his father: and the physicians [H7495] embalmed [H2590] Israel.

The word *physicians* [H7495] (physicians embalmed Israel) means "to heal," which prefigures the healing of the nations at the end of the present age of the present heaven and earth (Rev 21:1, 22:2). The word *embalm* [H2590] (embalmed Israel) means "to spice, make spicy, embalm" and has a connotation "to make spicy or ripen (putting forth green figs)," which points to a concurrent ripening, or maturing, of the promises of God at the end of the present age (Song 2:13).

Genesis 50:3 And forty days were fulfilled for him; for so are fulfilled the days of those which are embalmed [H2590]: and the Egyptians mourned [H1058] for him threescore and ten days.

The forty days of *embalming* [H2590] represent an appointed time of maturity, reflecting the first coming of Jesus Christ, as marking the end of the fourth millennium and forming the basis for the promised new creation. The seventy (threescore and ten) days of *mourning* (weeping) [H1058] reflect the seven millennia of creation ending with the faithless being cast into the lake of fire (Rev 20:7–15). And the forty days are presumably the first forty days of the seventy days, which reinforces the identification of the forty days with the first four millennia connecting Adam and Jesus.[49]

Genesis 50:4–6 And when the days of his mourning [H1068] were past, Joseph spake unto the house of Pharaoh, saying, If now I have found grace in your eyes, speak, I pray you, in the ears of Pharaoh, saying, 5 My father made me swear [H7650], saying, Lo, I die: in my grave which I have digged for me in the land of Canaan, there shalt thou bury me. Now therefore let me go up, I pray thee, and bury my father, and I will come again. 6 And Pharaoh said, Go up, and bury thy father, according as he made thee swear [H7650].

Joseph reflects the Son, while Pharaoh reflects the Father. Jacob reflects the Spirit, while the house of Pharaoh reflects the children of God. The death of Jacob is the occasion that causes the house of Pharaoh to identify with the suffering of Joseph, which reflects the movement of the Holy Spirit to redeem sinners being finally fulfilled, or completed. The days of *mourning* [H1068], or "weeping," is a weeping of Joseph together with, or shared with, the house of Pharaoh. And the grace that Joseph symbolically finds in human eyes is just this shared weeping of the eyes that identifies the house of Pharaoh with the

---

[49] There is no reason to think that the mourning process would have been delayed 40 days, until after the embalming was completed (Coffman 576; Gen 50:1–3). The silence of the sacred text implies no delay spiritually, even if the literal reality was otherwise, particularly since the total 110, 40+70, has no Biblical precedent.

suffering of Joseph. And the suffering of Joseph is ultimately the suffering of the cross. The grace that Joseph finds in the eyes of the house of Pharaoh is the promised new creation that comes only by grace through faith in Jesus Christ. Pharaoh's house seeing the suffering of Joseph is contrasted with Pharaoh himself simply hearing their petition, which reflects the incarnate nature of the Son compared with the purely spiritual nature of the Father and the Spirit. The Son is the one who would suffer on the cross, shedding human tears and feeling human pain, not the Father and not the Spirit.

Pharaoh, Joseph, and Jacob reflect the Father, Son, and Spirit, while the house of Pharaoh reflects the faithful moved by the Spirit, saved in the Son, and belonging to the Father. Joseph swearing unto Jacob, at least figuratively, in the presence of the house of Pharaoh represents the Son testifying to the truth of the Spirit and pointing the faithful to the Spirit. The Son directs us unto the Holy Spirit, while the Holy Spirit brings us unto the Son. The word *swear* [H7650] (Joseph swears unto Israel) literally means "to seven oneself, or bind oneself by seven things," reflecting the fulfillment of the original seven days of creation and likewise the fulfillment of the present seven millennia of creation. The fulfillment of the sevenfold creation is the new heaven and the new earth that is our promised new creation in Jesus Christ. Joseph does not petition Pharaoh through the house of Pharaoh, because the Son himself needs no intercessor. Joseph petitions Pharaoh in concert with the house of Pharaoh, representing the unity of the Body of Christ. The faithful in the Son enter into the presence of the Father by the power of the Holy Spirit, purifying and changing the hearts of sinners.

Genesis 50:7–9 And Joseph went up to bury his father: and with him went up all the servants of Pharaoh, the elders of his house, and all the elders of the land of Egypt, 8 And all the house of Joseph, and his brethren, and his father's house: only their little ones, and their flocks, and their herds, they left in the land of Goshen. 9 And there went up with him both chariots and horsemen: and it was a very great company.

The great company of Egyptians and Israelites represents the redeemed of the earth together with the host of heaven, both heralding the promised new creation that is the union of earth and heaven in the one kingdom of God. The promised land is not simply Canaan but rather the lands of Egypt and Canaan together, representing the whole of the earth and by extension the whole of creation. And the whole of creation is earth and heaven together, representing the totality of the physical and the spiritual domains of creation. The relationship between Egypt and Canaan—representing, respectively, earth and heaven—is reflected in Pharaoh having fed all of Egypt and Canaan during the famine but only purchasing, symbolically redeeming, the Egyptians and their land (Gen 47:13–15, 47:20–21).

Genesis 50:10–11 And they came to the threshingfloor of Atad [H329], which [is] beyond Jordan, and there they mourned with a great and very

sore lamentation: and he made a mourning for his father seven days. 11 And when the inhabitants of the land, the Canaanites, saw the mourning in the floor of Atad [H329], they said, This [is] a grievous mourning to the Egyptians: wherefore the name of it was called Abel-mizraim, which [is] beyond Jordan.

The Canaanites observe the grievous mourning of the Egyptians for seven days, but the Canaanites do not join the Egyptians in their mourning. The separateness of the Egyptians and Canaanites represents the separateness of the faithful and the faithless, likewise the separateness of the spiritual and physical domains, and likewise the separateness of heaven and earth. (The Canaanites are distinct from the land of Canaan, since it is the Israelites, not the Canaanites, that are rightfully identified with the promised land.) The emphasis on separateness is reinforced by the connection of the mourning of the Egyptians with the floor of Atad, in that a threshing floor is a place of separating wheat and chaff (Luke 3:17). The name *Atad* [H329] (threshing floor of Atad) means "bramble, buckthorn," which evokes an image of threshing and separating thorns, portending the resurrection unto damnation at the end of the millennial kingdom of Christ (John 5:29, Rev 20:5). And the Canaanites not joining the Egyptians during the entire seven days of mourning represents the wicked rejecting the Lord God throughout the whole of the seven millennia of the present heaven and earth.

Genesis 50:12 And his sons did unto him according as he commanded them:

The emphasis on the sons obeying their father points to the promised new creation that will embody the fullness of the indwelling Holy Spirit. In their betrayal of Joseph and their lying to Jacob, the sons were previously the epitome of disobedience (Gen 37:31–32). But the sons now being completely obedient to Jacob, specifically at the time of his death, reflects the reality of the promised new creation supplanting the present creation in the death and resurrection of the body and only in the death and resurrection of the body.

Genesis 50:13–14 For his sons carried him into the land of Canaan, and buried him in the cave of the field of Machpelah, which Abraham bought with the field for a possession of a buryingplace of Ephron the Hittite, before Mamre. 14 And Joseph returned into Egypt, he, and his brethren, and all that went up with him to bury his father, after he had buried his father.

Joseph leaving Egypt and then returning to Egypt, throughout in a dramatic public procession, reflects the new creation supplanting the present creation. The company leaves as twelve sons but returns as twelve tribes. The remnant of faithful will likewise inherit all creation. And the basis for the faithful, the children of Abraham, assuming possession of all creation is the righteousness of

God, not man, as affirmed by the emphasis on father Abraham, representing God the Father, being the legal owner of the land of the buryingplace.

Genesis 50:15–17 And when Joseph's brethren saw that their father was dead, they said, Joseph will peradventure hate us, and will certainly requite us all the evil which we did unto him. 16 And they sent a messenger unto Joseph, saying, Thy father did command before he died, saying, 17 So shall ye say unto Joseph, Forgive, I pray thee now, the trespass of thy brethren, and their sin; for they did unto thee evil: and now, we pray thee, forgive the trespass of the servants of the God of thy father. And Joseph wept when they spake unto him.

Jacob is identified with the Spirit, while Joseph is identified with the Son. Joseph's brothers seeking to be accepted according to the commandment of Jacob represents the faithful entering into the Body of Christ by the power of the Holy Spirit. The brothers being wicked sinners is a testimony that salvation comes by grace through faith and not by works. The feeling that the brothers might be lying about the posthumous instructions of Jacob only adds to the sense that they are of themselves undeserving in all ways. And whether or not Jacob's sons are lying, Jacob certainly did expect Joseph to protect and prosper his household in accordance with the promises of God, which again points to the righteousness of God, not man, being the basis for our salvation.[50]

Genesis 50:18 And his brethren also went and fell down before his face; and they said, Behold, we [be] thy servants.

We are not our own, for we have been bought with a price (1 Cor 6:19–20).

Genesis 50:19 And Joseph said unto them, Fear not: for [am] I in the place of God?

Joseph represents God the Son, and therefore Joseph actually does symbolically stand in the place of God. The implication that Joseph does not stand in the place of God reflects the essential condescension of God the Son, presenting the faithful in him by the power of God the Holy Spirit unto God the Father (1 Cor 15:24). Accordingly, Christ would ironically proclaim his essential condescension by asking, "Why callest thou me good? none is good, save one, that is, God," and Christ would speak thus specifically in the context of being asked how one can receive eternal life (Luke 18:18–19).[51]

---

[50] "Thus in humbling ourselves to Christ [to God the Son] by faith and repentance [by God the Holy Spirit], we may plead that it is the command of his father and our father [God the Father] we should do so" (Wesley 1:193; Gen 50:16). The petition of Joseph's brothers to him for forgiveness in the name of their father, Jacob, is our one and same petition for grace in the triunity of God—with the Father, in the Son, by the Spirit.
[51] "[T]he assumed superhuman character of the Messiah [as understood by some rabbis] appeared to be in conflict with the tradition that spoke of his death, and therefore the

TWELVE TRIBES

Genesis 50:20–21 But as for you, ye thought evil against me; [but] God meant it unto good, to bring to pass, as [it is] this day, to save much people alive. 21 Now therefore fear ye not: I will nourish you, and your little ones. And he comforted them, and spake kindly unto them.

God works all things together for the good of his children (Rom 8:28). The will of God is undeniable, or relentless, despite our sins. The world killed Christ, but Christ saves the world. The hatred and rejection of God by mankind is manifested in death, but the love of God for his faithful ones is established in the resurrection unto eternal life.

The Death of Joseph

Genesis 50:22 And Joseph dwelt in Egypt, he, and his father's house: and Joseph lived an hundred and ten years.

The deaths of Abraham, Isaac, and Jacob reflect the end of three successive dispensations. And closely following the account of the death of Jacob is the account of the death of Joseph, which reflects the close relationship between Joseph and Jacob. The deaths of Jacob and Joseph both point to the end of the millennial kingdom. The convergence of the lives of Jacob and Joseph points to the fulfillment of all things in the one God at the end of the present age, corresponding to the end of the present heaven and earth (Rev 21:1). The death of Isaac is closely connected to Jacob's return to Canaan with great wealth and with a large family, all of which he had taken from evil Laban (Gen 35:27–29). The return of Jacob with a multitude prefigures the glorious return of Christ. And the death of Isaac then points to the end of the church age, connecting the First and Second Advents. The death of Abraham is closely connected with the birth of Jacob unto Isaac, which reflects the Son sending the Spirit at the time of the First Advent (Gen 25:11). And the death of father Abraham then points to the end of the dispensation of father Adam, or fallen man, corresponding to the victory over the serpent at the time of the First Advent (1 Cor 15:55–57).

Genesis 50:23 And Joseph saw Ephraim's children of the third [generation]: the children also of Machir the son of Manasseh were brought up upon Joseph's knees.

The dominion of Joseph being counted as three generations reflects the dominion of Christ being identified with the three days of Jonah (Matt 12:38–

---

figure of a Messiah who would come from the tribe of Joseph, or Ephraim, instead of from Judah, and who would willingly undergo suffering for his nation and fall as victim in the Gog and Magog war [representing a final battle with evil], was created [perceived] .... The Messiah from the tribe of Ephraim falls in the battle with Gog and Magog, whereas the Messiah from the house of David kills the superhuman hostile leader ... with the breath of his mouth; then he [the Messiah] is universally recognized as king ...." (*Jewish Encyclopedia*, s.v. "eschatology"). Death and resurrection.

40). And the three days of Jonah ultimately point to the triunity of God. The three generations of Joseph's reign are simultaneously over the house of Jacob and under Pharaoh, which reflects the Son ruling by the power of the Holy Spirit and according to the will of the Father. The representation of the Father, Son, and Spirit by three successive generations reflects the progressive revelation of the Father, Son, and Spirit throughout the Scriptures and likewise throughout the millennia of creation. The three generations of Joseph further recall the three generations corresponding to Abraham, Isaac, and Jacob and, thereby, the progressive revelation of the triune God of the threefold Abraham, Isaac, and Jacob, for it is not incidental that the Lord names himself the God of Abraham, the God of Isaac, and the God of Jacob (Exod 3:6).

Genesis 50:24 And Joseph said unto his brethren, I die: and God will surely visit you, and bring you out of this land unto the land which he sware to Abraham, to Isaac, and to Jacob.

The land is promised to Abraham, Isaac, and Jacob by the God of Abraham, Isaac, and Jacob. The promised return to the promised land points to the restoration of the land and the corresponding resurrection of the body. This is the Father receiving his children and all creation through faith in the Son by the power of the indwelling Spirit. Father, Son, and Holy Spirit. Creator, Redeemer, and Sanctifier. Joseph's brothers are identified with the progression of the millennia connecting Adam and the promised new Adam, whereby the emphasis on Joseph instructing his brothers about the promised bodily deliverance points to the fulfillment of the totality of creation in the promised divine deliverance at the end of the present age. The connection between the death of Joseph and the certainty of divine visitation points to the death and resurrection of Jesus Christ being the certain guarantee of our redemption. The connection between the literal death of Joseph while ruling over Egypt and the figurative, or spiritual, death of Joseph when he was originally sold into Egypt is the connection between the death and resurrection of the Body of Christ and the death and resurrection of Christ as the Head (Gen 37:33).[52]

Genesis 50:25 And Joseph took an oath of the children of Israel, saying, God will surely visit you, and ye shall carry up my bones from hence.

Abraham, Isaac, and Jacob reflect the immanent reality of the formation of Adam followed by the First and Second Advents of Christ and, simultaneously, the transcendent reality of God the Father, God the Son, and God the Holy Spirit. Joseph ben Jacob governing under Pharaoh prefigures the millennial kingdom, or Sabbath millennium, of Christ, corresponding to the Second

---

[52] "As the Father is called Creator and the Son is called Redeemer, so on account of his work the Holy Spirit must be called Sanctifier, the One who makes holy" (Luther, *Large Catechism* 59). The titles *Creator*, *Redeemer*, and *Sanctifier* reflect, respectively, the same relational roles as God the Father, God the Son, and God the Holy Spirit.

Advent of Christ. The deaths of Jacob and Joseph then prefigure the end of the present heaven and earth. Nevertheless, the deaths of the twelve patriarchs and the subsequent enslavement of the twelve tribes signal the beginning of a new threefold cycle of revelation (Exod 1:6–14). And this next cycle, as with all cycles, reflects the progressive revelation of the same triune reality of God that is impressed upon all creation. The coming enslavement of the Jews in Egypt juxtaposed to their becoming a great multitude reflects the preservation of the present world after the original exile of Adam-kind from the garden of Eden. Further, Joseph connects his death with the promised future deliverance of the Israelites by God, and thereby Joseph links himself with Moses, who would carry Joseph's bones out of the land of Egypt into the promised land (Exod 13:19). And the identification of the death of Joseph with the deliverance by Moses points to the next threefold cycle of revelation being centered upon the life and times of Moses.

Genesis 50:26 So Joseph died, [being] an hundred and ten years old: and they embalmed him, and he was put in a coffin [H727] in Egypt.

The word *coffin* [H727] (containing the body of Joseph) is the same word denoting the *ark* [H727] (containing the tables of stone), which connects the person of Joseph not only to the prophet Moses but also to the law carried by Moses (Deut 10:2). The identification of Joseph, specifically Joseph's dead body, with the law given by Moses points to the condemnation of Jesus Christ for the sake of Adam-kind being the essential fulfillment of the law (Matt 5:17). The (mortal) natural body is to the (immortal) spiritual, or glorified, resurrection body as the Covenant of Law is to the Covenant of Grace. And the progressive cycle of revelation continues forward with Moses carrying the bones of Joseph up out of Egypt, foreshadowing the First Advent of Christ (Exod 13:19, Josh 24:32). Lord God have mercy.[53]

Ω Ω Ω

The three patriarchs Abraham, Isaac, and Jacob reflect the triune God the Father, God the Son, and God the Holy Spirit and likewise the formation of the first man Adam followed by the First and Second Advents of Christ. Abraham is the father of all the faithful, recalling the first man Adam formed in the very image of God (Rom 4:16). Father Abraham sacrificing his one and only (legitimate) son, Isaac, in Moriah reflects the Father giving his only begotten Son, Jesus Christ, for the world (Gen 22:2, John 3:16). Isaac, the second patriarch, afterward sending forth Jacob, his second born son, to establish his

---

[53] "In striking contrast to the honors accorded Jacob [after his death], no ritual or mourning is recorded [for Joseph]. The atmosphere, heavy with the anticipation of enslavement, is filled with foreboding" (Sarna 351; Gen 50:26). The white throne judgment that marks the end of the millennial reign of Christ and forms the nexus between the millennial reign and eternity, Rev 20:11.

household and his offspring prefigures the second man Jesus Christ, after his ascension, sending forth the Holy Spirit to call the faithful in Christ (Gen 28:1–2, John 14:26). And Jacob finally returning unto the promised land and meeting the company of his brother, Esau, en route represents the resurrection and rapture of the faithful in the Body of Christ (Gen 32:6). But the destruction of Shechem in retribution for the rape of Dinah, which also marks the return of Jacob unto the promised land, portends the concomitant judgment of the world during the tribulation period (Gen 34:25).

Jacob returning with his entire household unto Bethel represents the glorious return of Jesus Christ unto the earth in order to establish the house of God in the earth (Gen 28:19–22, 35:1–3). The physical death of Isaac in his old age echoes the destruction of Shechem and portends the end of the present world, but the death of Isaac, following long after his figurative sacrifice in Moriah, is also closely identified with the return of Jacob to Bethel, which points to the end of the church age that will finally be the opening of eternity (Gen 22:2, 35:29). The previous account of the death of Abraham, immediately preceding the ascendency of Jacob over his brother Esau, reflects the end of the dispensation of Adam, that is, the dominion of the serpent ending with the victory of Christ over death at the First Advent (Gen 25:11). The death of Jacob coming only after seeing the son of his old age, Joseph, ruling Egypt, figuratively the whole world, under Pharaoh represents the end of the time of the call unto repentance in Christ, corresponding to the end of the present creation as embodied by the millennial kingdom (Gen 45:28).[54]

1	2	3
ABRAHAM	ISAAC	JACOB
GOD THE FATHER	GOD THE SON	GOD THE HOLY SPIRIT
ABRAHAM CALLED AS THE FATHER OF THE FAITHFUL	ISAAC SACRIFICED AS AN ONLY SON IN MORIAH	JACOB ESTABLISHES THE HOUSE OF ISRAEL
CREATION OF ADAM	FIRST ADVENT OF CHRIST	SECOND ADVENT OF CHRIST
THE DEATH OF ABRAHAM	THE DEATH OF ISAAC	THE DEATH OF JACOB
THE END OF THE DISPENSATION OF ADAM	THE END OF THE CHURCH AGE	THE END OF THE PRESENT WORLD

The journey of Jacob from the land of Canaan to the east country of Padanaram to establish his household and all his future offspring reflects the church age connecting the First and Second Advents of Christ and culminating in the millennial kingdom of Christ (Gen 28:1–2). The subsequent journey of the entire house of Jacob to Goshen in Egypt because of the seven years of famine over the land foreshadows the final seven years of tribulation over the whole earth that will herald the millennial kingdom of all the faithful in Christ (Gen 42:1–2). The account of the destruction of Shechem followed by the return of Jacob unto Bethel, likewise Jacob's entire exile followed by his return, reinforces the image of tribulation heralding exaltation that is ultimately

---

[54] "Now, today, this moment, is our chance to choose the right side. God is holding back to give us that chance. It will not last for ever. We must take it or leave it" (Lewis, *Mere Christianity* 66). To say otherwise is to say that this life has no meaning.

repentance preceding redemption (Gen 34:25, 35:1). And Jacob returning to the land of Canaan followed by Joseph ben Jacob going into the safe haven of Goshen is itself a tribulation followed by exaltation. And the two fires, or sword (blood) followed by fire, that delimit the millennial kingdom of Christ testify to this same twofold reality.

The fire that marks both the beginning and the end of the millennial kingdom of Christ, which is the seventh, or Sabbath, millennium, is the one and same fire (Rev 20:1–15), whereby the seven good years of plenty being followed by seven bad years of famine represents the totality of the seven millennia of creation being consumed by the seven evil years of the final tribulation period (Gen 41:28–29). The two fires, or sword (blood) followed by fire, delimiting the Sabbath millennium parallel the two creations, the present creation followed by the promised new creation, also the two destructions of the world, water followed by fire, also the first and second men, Adam followed by Christ, and also the First and Second Advents, Jesus Christ followed by the Body of Christ. This is the natural body under law followed by the spiritual, or glorified, resurrection body under grace, the baptism in water followed by the baptism of fire, repentance followed by redemption, and finally the millennial kingdom of Christ followed by eternity in Christ.

The three separate journeys of the house of Jacob into Egypt represent a recapitulation of the history of the world, which is demarcated by the formation of Adam followed by the First and Second Advents of Christ (Gen 42:2, 43:15, 46:5). And the fundamentally threefold history of creation is finally understood to be a proclamation of the triunity of God, existing eternally as God the Father, God the Son, and God the Holy Spirit. The famine in all the land is the rejection of Adam, while Joseph revealing himself in Egypt is the incarnation of Christ. Joseph setting the house of Jacob apart in the land of Goshen is then the salvation of the faithful in the Body of Christ. The ascendancy of Joseph ben Jacob echoes the ascendancy of Jacob and, thereby, reinforces the prophecy of the Second Advent of Christ, which will be the Body of Christ, while the inherent unity of Joseph and Jacob, or Joseph ben Jacob, is itself a prophecy of the unity of the Son and the Spirit in the Body of Christ. The life and death and resurrection of Christ Jesus, reflected by Joseph ben Jacob, relate spiritually the recapitulation of man and literally the sanctification of the faithful in Christ. The creation and destruction and rebirth of the world through Christ relate the sanctification of all creation, which is also necessarily in Christ.[55]

---

[55] "The rabbis taught: . . . But as the Messiah b. David will have seen that the Messiah b. Joseph who preceded him was killed, he will say before the Lord: Lord of the Universe, I will ask nothing of Thee but life . . . This was prophesied already for thee by thy father David [Ps 21:4]: 'Life hath he asked of thee, thou gavest it to him' " (Rodkinson, *Talmud: Succah* 7:80). Messiah ben Joseph and Messiah ben David are the one and same Christ as related by Joseph ben Jacob.

ESAU, JACOB, ISRAEL

1	2	3
First Journey to Egypt (Unto Pharaoh)	Second Journey to Egypt (Unto Joseph)	Third Journey to Egypt (Unto a Separate Land)
God the Father	God the Son	God the Holy Spirit
The Whole Land Ravaged by Famine	Joseph Reveals Himself to His Brothers	Jacob Established by Joseph under Pharaoh
Rejection of Adam	First Advent of Christ	Second Advent of Christ

The seventy souls of the house of Jacob that enter into Egypt represent the nations and specifically the faithful called out of all nations (Gen 46:27). Joseph ben Jacob taking the money and livestock of Egypt, together with the people and their land, prefigures God the Son taking complete and absolute possession of the entire world and all creation in the end times (Gen 47:14, 47:16, 47:19–21). The distinction between Joseph purchasing the Egyptians as slaves but nourishing his own blood relatives as freemen represents the division between the children of the world and the children of God, particularly that which will continue throughout the millennial reign of Christ (Gen 47:21, 50:21). This is the distinction between the city of God and the nations surrounding the city of God, which will mark the millennial kingdom (Rev 20:7–9). This is the end of death and hell that must await the end of the thousand-year reign of Christ (Rev 20:14). Finally, Pharaoh's priesthood, compared with the peoples of Egypt and Israel, represents a distinct third group that is closely identified, not only with Pharaoh, but also with Joseph by his marriage relationship to Pharaoh's priesthood (Gen 41:50).

The enslavement of the Egyptians under the law of the land represents an affirmation of the condemnation of Adam-kind because of sin and the corresponding condemnation of the natural body together with the present creation. The offspring of Jacob to be born in Egypt prefigure the offspring of the Spirit that will be born during the Sabbath millennium, but the house of Jacob must remain, on account of Egyptian prejudices, separated from the whole of Egypt, signifying the wholeness, or perfection, of creation. And the priests of Pharaoh, who eat from the table of Pharaoh and remain completely unfettered, represent the angels of God (Gen 47:22) and simultaneously the faithful in Christ, who will become, at least in some ways, like the angels in the promised glorified body (Matt 22:30). Further, the threefold distinction between the Egyptians, Israelites, and Pharaoh's priests is paralleled by the threefold distinction between Egypt, Goshen, and Canaan. And the distinction between Egyptians, Israelites, and Pharaoh's priests is ultimately the threefold progressive revelation of Adam followed by Christ followed by the Body of Christ. The land of Egypt being purchased represents the present creation under the law. The land of Goshen being given freely to the blood relatives of Joseph represents Christ redeeming his faithful ones freely according to grace. And the land of Canaan, which is formally the promised land, represents the promised new creation, that is, the new earth and the new heaven and the new body and the new song (Rev 21:1–4).

TWELVE TRIBES

1	2	3
EGYPTIANS ENSLAVED UNDER LAW	ISRAELITES NOURISHED BY JOSEPH	PRIESTS JOINED UNTO JOSEPH BY MARRIAGE
FALL OF MAN	FIRST ADVENT	SECOND ADVENT
EGYPT UNDER THE LAW OF PHARAOH	GOSHEN GIVEN AS A GIFT	CANAAN SIGNIFYING THE NEW CREATION
ADAM	CHRIST THE HEAD	THE BODY OF CHRIST

In the account of Jacob and Joseph reunited in Egypt, Jacob first blesses Pharaoh in the presence of Joseph (Gen 47:10). Jacob then blesses Joseph and his two sons, Manasseh and Ephraim (Gen 48:15). And Jacob last of all blesses all twelve of his sons, Joseph together with all of Israel (Gen 49:28). The threefold Pharaoh, Joseph, and Jacob reflect the triune God the Father, God the Son, and God the Holy Spirit and likewise Adam formed in the image of God followed by the First and Second Advents of Christ. The first blessing of Jacob being given to Pharaoh in the presence of Joseph is closely linked with Jacob proclaiming his personal suffering and is terminated by Jacob purposefully going out from Pharaoh (Gen 47:9–10). The suffering of Jacob reflects the birth pangs afflicting all creation formed in the image of God. And Jacob going out from Pharaoh reflects the Holy Spirit proceeding from the Father in the conception of the world in the image of the Son (Gen 1:1–2). The second blessing of Jacob being given to Joseph and his sons is connected to Jacob switching the blessings of Manasseh and Ephraim (Gen 48:17–19). The second born Ephraim supplanting the firstborn Manasseh reflects the second man Christ supplanting the first man Adam, specifically at the time of the First Advent. The third blessing of Jacob being given to his whole household, all of Israel, as signified by his twelve sons, represents the movement of the Holy Spirit throughout the totality of creation, which will culminate in the promised new creation at the time of the Second Advent.

1	2	3
PHARAOH	JOSEPH	JACOB
GOD THE FATHER	GOD THE SON	GOD THE HOLY SPIRIT
JACOB BLESSES PHARAOH IN THE PRESENCE OF JOSEPH	JACOB BLESSES JOSEPH & HIS TWO SONS	JACOB BLESSES JOSEPH TOGETHER WITH ALL ISRAEL
FORMATION OF ADAM	FIRST ADVENT OF CHRIST	SECOND ADVENT OF CHRIST

The sons of Jacob reflect the millennia connecting the original creation and the promised new creation. The prophetic blessing of the twelve sons proclaimed by their father at the time of his death is contrasted with the prophetic naming of his sons proclaimed by their mothers at the times of their births (Gen 29:31–30:24, 35:18, 49:3–27). The prophetic naming of the sons is identified with the birthright of Christ, while the prophetic blessing of the sons is identified with the blessing in Christ. The prophetic naming precedes the prophetic blessing just as the natural body precedes the spiritual, or glorified, resurrection body just as the Covenant of Law precedes the Covenant of Grace just as the birthright precedes the blessing. Death precedes resurrection just as the kingship precedes the high priesthood just as Christ Jesus precedes the Body of Christ. The first man Adam precedes the second man Christ just as the First Advent of Christ precedes the Second Advent just as the millennial kingdom of Christ precedes the opening of eternity in Christ.

1	2
FIRST MAN ADAM	SECOND MAN JESUS
(DEATH)	(LIFE)
NATURAL BODY	SPIRITUAL, OR GLORIFIED, BODY
FIRST ADVENT	SECOND ADVENT
(KINGSHIP)	(HIGH PRIESTHOOD)
COVENANT OF LAW	COVENANT OF GRACE
MILLENNIAL KINGDOM	ETERNITY
(HEAD)	(BODY)
BIRTHRIGHT OF THE FIRSTBORN	BLESSING OF THE FIRSTBORN

The firstborn Leah is identified with the Covenant of Law, while the second born Rachel is identified with the Covenant of Grace. The sons of Leah are identified with the present creation, represented by the six millennia leading up to the Second Advent of Christ. The sons of Rachel are identified with the promised new creation to be announced in the seventh millennium, corresponding to the Sabbath millennium and finally established in the eighth millennium, representing eternity. The progression of revelation points inexorably to the fulfillment of all things in the last days, or last three millennial days, which connect the First and Second Advents. The births of Jacob's sons by bondwomen are interjected after the birth of Jacob's fourth son by Leah, which reflects the intercession of Christ in the history of creation at the time of the First Advent, specifically at the beginning of the fifth millennium and specifically as a suffering bondservant (Gen 30:1–13). In contrast, Jacob blesses his sons by bondwomen after he blesses his sixth son by Leah, which points to the glorious return of Christ to establish the millennial kingdom in the seventh millennium (Gen 49:16–21).

1	2
LEAH	RACHEL
COVENANT OF LAW	COVENANT OF GRACE
LEAH'S SONS	RACHEL'S SONS
PRESENT CREATION	PROMISED NEW CREATION
(SIX MILLENNIA FROM ADAM)	(SEVENTH & EIGHTH MILLENNIA)
BONDWOMEN'S SONS INTERJECTED	BONDWOMEN'S SONS BLESSED
FIRST ADVENT	SECOND ADVENT

The life of Jacob reflects the movement of the Holy Spirit calling the faithful unto the life that is only in the Son. Jacob establishing for himself a household and descendants and also taking possession of a great material wealth reflects the establishment of the faithful in the world but not of the world (Gen 31:16). This is the spiritual, or glorified, body that is a true body. And Jacob expressly taking his house out of the house of Laban represents Jesus seizing the faithful out of the hand of the devil and out of a fallen creation. The tithe, or tenth, that Jacob promises the Lord at the beginning of his journey eastward would be fulfilled in the sacrifice of Joseph, his eleventh son (tenth excluding Levi), being sold by his brothers into slavery (Gen 28:20–22). The tithe of the Spirit is the sacrifice of the Son under the law. The journey of Jacob into Egypt to establish the nation of Israel under Joseph and with the blessing of Pharaoh reflects the Spirit ushering the faithful into the millennial kingdom of Christ according to the will of the Father (Gen 46:26–27). The double portion that Joseph receives from the hand of Jacob is a double inheritance among the twelve tribes of Israel as embodied by Joseph's two sons, Ephraim and Manasseh. And in the blessing of the second firstborn Joseph, Ephraim and Manasseh are necessarily adopted by Jacob in order to have their place among the twelve tribes. Therein the double portion that Jacob gives Joseph is also received by Jacob from Joseph. The double portion given by the Spirit is also received by the Spirit indwelling the faithful in the one Body of Christ.[56]

The close identification of Jacob and Joseph ben Jacob reflects the Body of Christ being animated by the power of the Holy Spirit. The single tithe that Jacob pledges to God is embodied by Joseph and represents the death of Jesus, but the double portion that Joseph receives is the resurrection of the Body of Christ being added to the resurrection of Christ. The Body is added to the Head as grace is added to law as blessing is added to birthright as the priesthood is added to the kingship. Christ Jesus fulfilled the law so that the faithful could be redeemed by grace in him. The Head must precede the Body just as law must precede grace just as the natural body must precede the spiritual, or glorified, resurrection body. The kingship must precede the high priesthood just as the dominion of Christ over death must precede the intercession of Christ in the resurrection of the dead. The birthright must precede the blessing just as our freewill created in the image of God must precede our choosing God and becoming one with God. The linking of the accounts of the deaths of Jacob and Joseph again identifies Joseph as Joseph ben Jacob (Gen 49:33, 50:26). The death of Jacob represents the end of the call of the faithful by the Holy Spirit to repentance in Christ at the time of the Second Advent, while the death of Joseph represents the corresponding end of the present creation that is the end of the millennial kingdom of Christ. And the seventh, or Sabbath, millennium, corresponding to the millennial reign of Christ, represents the opening of eternity in Christ.[57]

---

[56] "By adopting Joseph's two sons, Ephraim and Manasseh, and giving each of them a portion of the inheritance, Jacob virtually gave Joseph Reuben's extra portion of the land [entitled to the firstborn]. And Judah became the tribal leader in Reuben's place [Gen 49:8–10]" (*Amplified Bible* 64 n. a; Gen 49:3). The two sons Judah and Joseph supplanting the first son Reuben represents the First and Second Advents of Christ succeeding the creation of Adam.

[57] "Whereas other peoples of antiquity placed their Golden Age in the dim and remote past, the Jews relegated it to the future. The prophets of Israel repeatedly allude to 'the latter days,' . . . centered around the person of a *Mashiach* [Messiah], 'an anointed one,' . . ." (Cohen, *Rabbinic Sages* 346). The kingdom of God is not of this world, John 18:36.

ESAU, JACOB, ISRAEL

CHAPTER SIX OUTLINE

Key Images

PRIME IMAGES		
Material	Abstract	Spiritual
The promise of God that Israel will become a great nation in the land of Egypt.	A multitude established through a great suffering and finally out of bondage.	The faithful to be redeemed in the Body of Christ out of the earth but in the earth.
The seventy souls of the house of Jacob that enter into Egypt.	The Table of Nations as related by the souls of Jacob.	The whole of the world, all of which belongs to the Lord.
Joseph taking possession of the Egyptians and their property.	An absolute dominion of and over flesh and earth.	The millennial kingdom of Christ established on the earth.
Jacob blessing his sons at the time of his death.	Jacob's offspring embody the progression of the millennia from Adam to the new Adam.	The gifts of the Spirit through the ages culminating in the fullness of the indwelling Spirit.
The deaths of Jacob and Joseph.	The beginning of national Israel.	The end of the present age.
TWOFOLD IMAGES		
Material	Abstract	Spiritual
Egyptians and Israelites.	Indigenous versus aliens. Of the land, not of the land. Flesh and spirit.	The whole world contrasted with the community of faithful that are separate from the world.
Joseph takes possession of the Egyptians, but he nourishes his brethren.	Slavery versus freedom. Master versus benefactor. Flesh and spirit.	The rightful dominion of Christ by law in contrast to the faithful in Christ redeemed by grace.
The two blessings of Joseph's sons, Manasseh and Ephraim, given by Jacob.	A people (firstborn), a multitude (second born). Flesh and spirit.	The one man Adam supplanted by the Body of Christ.
The brotherhood of Manasseh and Ephraim.	First supplanted by the second. Flesh and spirit.	Adam and Christ. First and Second Advents. Millennial reign and eternity.
THREEFOLD IMAGES		
Material	Abstract	Spiritual
Joseph coming to Egypt followed by his brothers followed by all the house of Israel.	One man exiled followed by his brethren being saved followed by the formation of a great nation blessed by God.	Adam followed by the First and Second Advents of Christ.
Jacob blessing Pharaoh followed by Jacob blessing the house of Joseph followed by Jacob blessing all his sons.	From the possessor of all things to the ruler over all things to those who are nourished in all things.	The blessing of life proceeding from the Father through the Son unto the faithful by the power of the indwelling Holy Spirit.
Joseph takes unto Pharaoh the silver of Egypt followed by the livestock followed by the people with their land.	An inanimate, or lifeless, wealth followed by a sign of blood followed by living souls together with their dominion.	The death in Adam followed by the sacrifice of Christ followed by the redemption of the faithful in Christ in the end times.
The death of Abraham followed by the death of Isaac followed by the death of Jacob.	The end of three successive generations, or prophetic eras.	The end of the three progressive dispensations: Adam followed by the church age followed by the millennial kingdom.

TWELVE TRIBES

Synopsis

THE THIRD JOURNEY

	Material	Spiritual
46:1–3	God speaks to Jacob in night visions and tells him to not be afraid.	The tribulation period that must precede the establishment of the millennial kingdom.
	God directs Jacob to go into the land of Egypt in order to become a great nation.	A literal millennial kingdom on the earth.
46:4	God will go down with Israel into Egypt, and God will surely bring them up again.	The death and resurrection of the faithful that is united with that of Christ.
	Joseph will close the eyes of his father.	The end of the age of the church.
46:5–7	The sons of Israel carry all Jacob's house unto Pharaoh in the wagons Pharaoh provided.	The faithful are presented unto the Father in the Son by the power of the Holy Spirit.
46:8–25	The souls of Israel begotten through the elder sister Leah are recorded.	The six millennia of creation leading Adam-kind unto the promised new Adam.
	The souls of Israel begotten through Leah's handmaid, Zilpah, are recorded.	The bondage of the tribulation connecting the sixth and seventh millennia.
	The souls of Israel begotten through the younger sister Rachel are recorded.	The seventh and eighth millennia, demarcating the millennial kingdom and eternity.
	The souls of Israel begotten through Rachel's handmaid, Bilhah, are recorded.	The eternal bondage, or judgment, that is represented by the lake of fire.
46:26–27	And all the souls of the house of Jacob that came into Egypt were seventy.	The Table of Nations will endure throughout the millennial kingdom (Gen 10:1–32).

GOSHEN

	Material	Spiritual
46:28	Jacob sends Judah ahead unto Joseph to direct his face unto the land of Goshen.	The Spirit ushering the Messianic bloodline unto the millennial kingdom.
46:29	Joseph makes ready his chariot to go up and meet his father, Jacob.	The second coming of the Son, in power and glory, at the end of the age of the Spirit.
	And Joseph weeps on the neck of Jacob a good while.	The unity of the Son and Spirit in the Body, weeping over the judgment of all flesh.
46:30	Jacob proclaims that he can now die, because he has seen the face of his son Joseph.	Jesus Christ is the fulfillment of all things.
46:31–34	Joseph warns his brothers that, to dwell in Goshen (the best of the land), they must testify to Pharaoh that they are shepherds.	The faithful must be identified with the Son, the good shepherd, in order to enter into the blessing of the Father.
47:1–6	Joseph takes five of his brothers, representing Israel, and presents them unto Pharaoh.	Joseph's brothers, their totality, are identified with the cross of the fifth millennium.
47:7	Joseph brings Jacob unto Pharaoh, and then Jacob blesses Pharaoh.	The joy of the Father over the blessing of the faithful in the Son.
47:8–10	Jacob testifies that the days of his life have been few and evil.	The suffering of the Holy Spirit with humanity throughout the present creation.
47:11–12	Joseph gives Israel a possession in the best of the land, as Pharaoh had commanded.	The will of the Father to raise up the faithful in the Son by the power of the Holy Spirit.
	And Joseph nourishes them with bread.	The body of Christ and finally the blood.

TWO TITHES

	Material	Spiritual
47:13	And there was no bread in all the land.	A famine of the words of God (Amos 8:11).
47:14	In exchange for corn, Joseph gathers unto the house of Pharaoh all the money in the lands of Egypt and Canaan.	The value in silver to be placed upon the life of Jesus Christ in the fifth millennium from Adam (Matt 20:28, 27:9).

ESAU, JACOB, ISRAEL

47:15–17	Joseph gathers up all the livestock.	The end of livestock, or life, that follows the end of silver money is the apostasy of the sixth millennium that follows that of the fifth.
47:18–20	Joseph takes possession of the people and their lands.	God takes possession of all things in the seventh millennium.
47:21	Joseph removes the people of the land of Egypt into cities.	The nations of men surrounding the city of God during the millennial reign (Rev 20:7–9).
47:22	And only the land of Pharaoh's priests did Joseph not purchase, because the priests had a portion of Pharaoh assigned to them.	The 144,000 sealed at the time of the final tribulation period (Rev 7:2–4).
47:23	Joseph gives seed to the people of the land for them to sow in the land.	The original calling of Adam-kind to keep the garden of God will be fulfilled.
47:24–26	The fifth part must be given to Pharaoh.	The tithe of the Body of Christ added to the tithe of Christ.
47:27	And Israel dwelled in Goshen, and they had possessions and multiplied exceedingly.	The multiplication of the children of God at the time of the millennial kingdom.
47:28–31	Joseph swears that Jacob's body will be carried out of the land of Egypt and buried with his fathers in the promised land.	The end of the age of the Spirit, heralding the fullness of triunity, corresponding to the end of the millennial kingdom and the beginning of the promised new creation.
EPHRAIM AND MANASSEH		
	Material	Spiritual
48:1–2	Jacob is sick.	The Spirit is grieved.
48:3–6	As Reuben and Simeon, now Ephraim and Manasseh belong to Jacob.	The rebirth in the Body of Christ established in the unity of the First and Second Advents.
	Joseph's future children will be counted with their brothers in their inheritance.	The offspring that will be begotten during the millennial kingdom of Christ.
48:7	Jacob recounts the death of Rachel.	The coming end of the millennial kingdom.
48:8–20	Jacob blesses the second born Ephraim ahead of the firstborn Manasseh.	The city of God that becomes a blessing to the nations of the world.
48:21–22	Jacob testifies that God will be with Joseph, also to Joseph's double portion.	The Second Advent added to the First Advent of Jesus Christ.
TWELVE PROPHECIES		
	Material	Spiritual
49:1–2	Jacob gathers his sons to tell them what will befall them in the last days.	The culmination of creation in the church age that connects the First and Second Advents.
49:3–27	Reuben.	The rejection of Adam-kind.
	Simeon and Levi.	The judgment of flesh that comes by Noah and Moses.
	Judah.	The call of the faithful in Christ.
	Zebulun and Issachar.	The Gentiles are added to the Jews.
	Dan, Gad, Asher, and Naphtali.	The tribulation delimiting the millennial kingdom of Christ.
	Joseph and Benjamin.	The Sabbath millennium heralding eternity.
49:28	This is the blessing of the twelve tribes of Israel, everyone according to his blessing.	Twelve tribes mark the millennia of creation just as twelve months mark the year just as twelve hours mark the day.
THE DEATH OF JACOB		
	Material	Spiritual
49:29–32	Jacob charges his sons to bury him with his fathers in the land of Canaan.	The faithful can only be redeemed unto the Father in the Son by the power of the Spirit.
	Jacob recounts that Abraham had purchased their buryingplace as a possession.	The righteousness of God himself is the basis for our salvation.

TWELVE TRIBES

49:33	When Jacob had finished commanding his sons, he yielded up the ghost.		The end of the age of the call unto repentance in Jesus Christ.
50:1	And Joseph fell upon his father's face and wept upon him and kissed him.		The unity of the Son and the Spirit that is the unity of the Body of Christ.
50:2–3	Forty days are fulfilled for Jacob's embalming.		The four days, or millennia, connecting Adam and Jesus Christ.
	And the Egyptians mourn for seventy days.		The seven days, or millennia, connecting the first Adam and the promised new Adam.
50:4–6	Joseph seeks grace in the eyes of Pharaoh's house, and Pharaoh hears Joseph's petition to bury his father, Jacob, as he had sworn.		The faithful are established in the Body of Christ by the power of the Holy Spirit and according to the will of the Father.
50:7–12	Joseph, along with his family and with a great company of Egyptians, goes up to bury Jacob.		The promised union of heaven and earth in the new creation.
	The Canaanites see but do not join in the grievous mourning of the Egyptians.		The essential separation of the faithless from the faithful.
	And his sons did unto Jacob everything as he had commanded them.		The fullness of the indwelling Holy Spirit that will define the promised new creation.
50:13–14	And Joseph and his brethren returned unto the land of Egypt.		A remnant will inherit all creation.
50:15–18	Joseph's brothers tell him that Jacob had commanded that they should be forgiven.		The redemption of the faithful is unmerited, coming by grace through faith in Jesus Christ.
	Joseph's brothers profess themselves to be the servants of Joseph.		We are not our own, for we have been bought with a price (1 Cor 6:19–20).
50:19–21	Joseph tells his brothers to not be afraid, asking them if he is in the place of God.		The essential condescension of God the Son, presenting the faithful by God the Spirit unto God the Father.
	Joseph promises to nourish his brothers and their little ones.		The will of God is undeniable, or relentless, despite our sins.

THE DEATH OF JOSEPH

	Material		Spiritual
50:22–23	Joseph lived an hundred and ten years and saw his offspring of the third generation.		The sign of Jonah, signifying the progressive revelation of the triunity of God.
50:24–25	Joseph tells his brothers that he is dying and that God will surely bring them into the land promised to Abraham, Isaac, and Jacob.		The death and resurrection of Christ is the guarantee for the resurrection of the faithful and the restoration of creation.
50:26	Joseph dies and is embalmed and placed into a coffin (ark) in Egypt.		The opening of the age of the nation of Israel, the next cycle of progressive revelation.

AFTERWORD

The most basic symmetry patterns characterizing the Biblical text and likewise reality as a whole are the *prime*, *twofold*, and *threefold* pattern types. The next level of complexity is characterized by the *serial*, *chiastic*, and *staircase* pattern types, which are temporal analogues of the prime, twofold, and threefold types. And the third and final level of complexity is characterized by the *historical*, *individual*, and *generational* pattern types, which are nonuniform analogues of the serial, chiastic, and staircase types. The dividing line between the three sets, or layers, of three pattern types is creation itself and specifically time, or space-time. And it is the dimensionality of creation formed in the image of God that indicates a minimum set of nine unique and irreducible pattern types. This is in contrast to relegating the more complex pattern types (serial, chiastic, staircase; historical, individual, generational) as mere derivatives of the three basic pattern types (prime, twofold, threefold). The connection, specifically the parallel, between the three sets of three pattern types is not simply derivative but derivative and relational, or rather progressive and Trinitarian. The three sets, or layers, of pattern types parallel the three persons of the Father, Son, and Holy Spirit just as the three types composing each set also parallel the Father, Son, and Holy Spirit.

The irreducible pattern types prime, twofold, and threefold—representing the most basic types—are fundamentally archetypal, or image-based, and therefore are fundamentally disconnected from time. Examples are one God, two brothers, and three sons. And the quality of being outside time is most closely identified with God the Father, from whom all creation, including time itself, proceeds like an offspring. The irreducible pattern types serial, chiastic, and staircase—representing the second level of complexity—are characterized by a rigid conformity to diurnal and corresponding millennial intervals of time. And the quality of being strictly organized in relation to time is most closely identified with God the Son, who was conceived at an appointed time and will return again at an appointed time. The irreducible pattern types historical, individual, and generational—representing the highest level of complexity—are characterized by a deviation from rigidly organized time and, thereby, convey a reality that spans all space and time, representing all creation, earth and heaven. And the quality of being everywhere always is most closely identified with God the Holy Spirit, who not only spans all creation always but also connects creation in God the Son unto God the Father.

AFTERWORD

The three pattern types prime, twofold, and threefold can also individually be identified with the Father, Son, and Holy Spirit. This is (1) the oneness of the Father, from whom the Son and the Spirit proceed, (2) the twofold natures of the Son, who is fully man and fully God, and (3) the threefold agency of the Holy Spirit, presenting the faithful in the Son unto the Father.[1] The three pattern types serial, chiastic, and staircase can also be identified with the Father, Son, and Holy Spirit. This is (1) the sevenfold, or six-plus-one, creation that proceeds from the Father, (2) the whole of creation pointing to the promised conception of Jesus Christ in the fourth millennium, and (3) the Spirit moving inexorably unto the fulfillment of all things in the last days. The three pattern types historical, individual, and generational can also be identified with the Father, Son, and Holy Spirit. This is (1) creation throughout time as a whole, reflecting the abstract transcendence of the Father, (2) individual living souls being identified with the one man Jesus Christ, and (3) the universality of the Holy Spirit, enveloping all creation at all times. The three sets, or layers, of pattern types, likewise the three types composing each set, are connected to God the Father, God the Son, and God the Spirit, and such interwoven relationships are both inevitable and essential because all reality is formed in the image of the Father, Son, and Spirit. The nature of individual man is triune just as the nature of creation as a whole is triune because the triune God, being the one self-existent one, is the only practicable basis, or paradigm, for the reality of creation. The Trinity is reality.[2]

FATHER	SON	SPIRIT	
PRIME	TWOFOLD	THREEFOLD	FATHER
SERIAL	CHIASTIC	STAIRCASE	SON
HISTORICAL	INDIVIDUAL	GENERATIONAL	SPIRIT

The three irreducible sets of three pattern types are naturally organized in a 3x3 symmetry matrix table, such that the fundamentally Trinitarian properties of the basis set are more transparent. The columns and rows mark the boundaries of the system and also the internal coordinates of the system. The symmetry matrix being delimited by the Father, Son, and Spirit reflects creation being enveloped and also permeated by the Trinity. Creation is viewed as expanding

---

[1] "Therefore, since the Father, the Son and the Holy Spirit are one God, and certainly God is holy, and God is a spirit, the Trinity can be called also the Holy Spirit. But yet that Holy Spirit, who is not the Trinity, but is understood as in the Trinity, is spoken of in His proper name of the Holy Spirit relatively, since He is referred both to the Father and to the Son . . . . [Augustine, *On the Trinity*]" (Schaff, *Nicene and Post-Nicene Fathers: First Series* 3:93). God the Holy Spirit, as the third person of the Trinity, is most closely identified with the triunity of God.

[2] "[T]he idea of the triadic [Father, Son, Spirit] manifestation [existence] of the Godhead was present from the earliest period [including that represented by the New Testament writings] as part of Christian piety and thinking. . . . The triadic pattern supplies the raw data from which the more developed [explicit] descriptions of the Christian doctrine of God will come" (Rusch 2). Not only the doctrine of God but ultimately all doctrines are connected to the triune reality of God.

AFTERWORD

from nothing in the midst of the Trinity and according to the will and nature of the Trinity. This is not only man in isolation but also creation as a whole being formed in the very image of God. Simple position within the matrix is designated by the two coordinates <row, column>, but operative position must comprehend a less obvious third coordinate representing the unidirectional, or vectorial, progression in time from the original creation to the promised new creation. And this unidirectional time component corresponds to the progressive revelation of creation moving from the Father to the Son to the Spirit. Time, or space-time, representing the totality of creation, can also be identified with the basic demarcation of reality because time is the most basic aspect of both progressive revelation and also freewill, both of which necessarily existing in time. The progression of revelation and the exercise of freewill are actually not independent of each other, because it is in our choosing of God that God reveals himself to us.

The movement of progressive revelation in the symmetry matrix is from left to right and from top to bottom. The trend is periodic and toward complexity and completeness, representing our promised new creation. The movement toward completeness is specifically the progressive revelation of the Holy Spirit, which is the providence of God unfolding in creation as a whole and simultaneously in the life of the individual. Creation as a whole (including mankind) and the individual living soul are in fact the only two things that reflect the fullness of the image of God. The individual, who is physical and spiritual and animated by the Spirit, is triune (body, soul, spirit). And likewise creation as a whole, which is earth and heaven and sustained by the Spirit, is also triune (natural, spiritual, divine). A rock of itself is not triune. Neither is a plant triune. Not even an animal is triune. Only an individual person is animated by the Holy Spirit (Gen 2:7) as creation as a whole is held together by the Holy Spirit (Col 1:15–17). Nonetheless, creation as a whole includes mankind and is not alive separated from mankind, with creation ultimately being viewed as a mere extension of the physical body. The progressive revelation of individual man and the progressive revelation of creation as a whole cannot be viewed as independent of one another, and thus the directionality within the symmetry matrix should be counted as only one additional coordinate, or dimension, the third of three coordinates <row, column, direction>.

The trend, or movement, from left to right in the symmetry matrix is most closely identified with the progressive revelation of the promised new man, which is the progressive revelation of God unto man. The progressive revelation of man begins with the oneness of the Father and is followed by the twofold natures of the Son and finally the threefold movement of the Holy Spirit in presenting the faithful in the Son unto the Father. The movement from top to bottom is most closely identified with the progressive revelation of the promised new creation, which is the revelation of creation itself in becoming a unified whole. The progressive revelation of creation begins with the original creation and is followed by the present fallen creation and finally the promised new creation. The progressive revelation of the promised new creation, paralleling that of the promised new man, is ultimately one revelation—namely,

AFTERWORD

the one and same triune image of God, which is our promised inheritance from God and in God. The three symmetry matrix dimensions <row, column, direction> also reflect the oneness of God that is the three persons of God the Father, God the Son, and God the Holy Spirit, who themselves are ultimately the most fundamental three relational dimensions of reality. The <row, column> first and second dimensions—which represent a single type, or likeness, both being position coordinates—reflect the Father and Son relationship, God the Son being the likeness of God the Father. The more subtle third dimension of direction, or time—which represents the stream, or movement, of progressive revelation—reflects the normally difficult to perceive and understand movement of God the Holy Spirit.

→ Progressive Revelation of Man →			↓ Progressive Revelation of Creation ↓
Prime	Twofold	Threefold	
Serial	Chiastic	Staircase	
Historical	Individual	Generational	

The three pattern types prime, twofold, and threefold—representing the most fundamental and abstract types—are most closely identified with the original creation before the Fall of Man and likewise with Adam originally formed in the image of God. And this is foremost an identification with God the Father. The original creation was fleeting, necessarily doomed upon inception in accord with the foreknowledge of God, and thereby the original creation that existed before sin entered the world embodies an ironic and abstract sense of (figuratively) having never actually existed. And this is reinforced by the implication that some predilection for sin must have existed in Adam before the actual manifestation of sin and death. Adam was formed in the image of God but not in equality with God, and though he was created very good, Adam could not have been perfect in the same sense that God is perfect, because God is peerless (Gen 1:31). Nonetheless, the original creation is identified with the perfect and sinless will of God. For the original creation existed before sin and death entered into the world. This is specifically an identification with God the Father as our creator, or spiritually procreator. And therefore the original creation before death, reflecting God the Father as our creator, is connected to the abstract nature of the Father, transcending time, existing outside of time. God is eternal, timeless, and without change, and therefore the will of God for the welfare of his children is still evident, fundamentally undeniable, or relentless, despite even the (temporal) death that entered through sin.

The three temporally uniform pattern types serial, chiastic, and staircase are most closely identified with the present creation, which is a fallen, or crucified, creation, under the curse of God and forsaken by God. And this is ultimately an identification with God the Son. The present creation has been appointed an exact time just as every individual has been appointed an exact time. This is not predetermination, but the reality that man necessarily exists in space and time.

AFTERWORD

The First Advent of the Son was appointed an exact time connecting the fourth and fifth millennia just as the Second Advent of the Son has been appointed an exact time corresponding to the seventh, or Sabbath, millennium. The present creation is a fallen creation, moaning for redemption, and is therefore identified with the incarnation of God the Son, specifically as our redeemer. And the present fallen creation, like God the Son, our redeemer, is identified with a nature of being rigidly tied to time and likewise to flesh and the law of flesh. This is the same law governing the flesh violated by Adam but obeyed and fulfilled by Christ and in Christ. This is the personal and individual nature of the Son, existing in space and time, face to face with humanity. And the present time of the law is the corresponding call to repentance, in accordance with the inviolable sanctity of individual freewill.

The three temporally nonuniform pattern types historical, individual, and generational are most closely identified with the promised new creation that is yet to be fully revealed. And this is finally an identification with God the Holy Spirit. The promised new creation is not simply being translated to heaven, and neither is it a restoration of the garden of Eden. It is a new heaven and a new earth, not divided or separated, but rather the perfect union of earth and heaven, reflecting the perfect union of law and grace that is the will of God, likewise the perfect union of flesh and spirit in Jesus Christ and also in the Body of Christ (Rev 21:1–5). The spiritual, or glorified, resurrection body, our promised new creation, is a true body of flesh and blood, but it will also transcend the limits of the present natural body, which are the limits of space and time. This being the case is made clear in the account of the resurrected Christ (John 20:19–20), in whose likeness we shall be conformed in the promised new creation (Rom 8:29–30). But the nature of simultaneously being in space and time and also transcending space and time identifies the new creation most closely with God the Spirit, who is always everywhere. It is the fullness of the indwelling Spirit that animates and sanctifies the resurrection body, and this is the essential connection between the promised new creation and God the Holy Spirit.[3]

1	2	3
GOD THE FATHER	GOD THE SON	GOD THE HOLY SPIRIT
ORIGINAL CREATION	FALLEN CREATION	NEW CREATION
PRIME, TWOFOLD, THREEFOLD	SERIAL, CHIASTIC, STAIRCASE	HISTORICAL, INDIVIDUAL, GENERATIONAL

The progression within the symmetry matrix is demarcated not only by the persons of the Trinity but also by the distinct characteristics of the persons of the Trinity. Biblical Trinitarianism is not only oneness but also relational distinctiveness. And this simultaneous unity and distinctiveness is reflected by

---

[3] "Christianity appeared . . . as a movement with a message of salvation . . . God was bringing 'the restoration of all things' (Acts 3:21)—the new age promised by the prophets—when wrong would be righted and humanity reconciled to God" (Norris 1). The promise is a new age, not simply a return to the old age.

AFTERWORD

the progressive revelation of man—namely, Adam followed by the First Advent of Christ followed by the Second Advent—and also by the progressive revelation of creation—namely, the original creation followed by the present fallen creation followed by the promised but yet future new creation. Focusing on the progression from left to right, the three pattern types (1) prime, (2) twofold, and (3) threefold express a timeless, abstract quality characteristic of the original creation and, thereby, reflect the reality of the Father, Son, and Holy Spirit as being eternal and unchanging, respectively, in (1) oneness, (2) duality, and (3) triunity. This is the oneness of the Father, which is the will, or freewill, of the Father. This is the twofold natures of the Son, which forms the paradigm of all creation and also the very nexus between God and man. And this is the threefold movement of the Spirit, which is the breath of life, animating and unifying all creation. God the Son is not simply begotten through the Spirit and of the Father but eternally begotten.

Continuing to focus on the left to right within the symmetry matrix, the three pattern types (1) serial, (2) chiastic, and (3) staircase express a rigid conformity to time characteristic of the present fallen creation and, thereby, reflect the sequential revelation, in the appointed seasons, of the Father, Son, and Holy Spirit, respectively, as (1) creator, (2) redeemer, and (3) sanctifier. The whole of creation proceeds from the Father like an offspring, whereby the faithful are called the children of God, the children of the Father. The Son is our redeemer, being the one person of the Trinity nailed to the cross. And the Holy Spirit is our sanctifier, indwelling our new creation in the Body of Christ. The three pattern types (1) historical, (2) individual, and (3) generational express a quality of being everywhere always, which is characteristic of the promised new creation and, thereby, reflect the Father, Son, and Holy Spirit as, respectively, (1) transcendent, (2) personal, and (3) universal. God the Father, whom we cannot see, is abstract and transcendent, existing outside of time and space (John 14:9). God the Son, with whom we have a human relationship, is personal, existing inside time and space. And God the Spirit, being everywhere always, is universal, existing simultaneously throughout all time and space and also outside time and space.[4]

---

[4] "For it was the Son alone in the Trinity who assumed the form of a servant, a form which in His case was fitted into the unity of His person, or, in other words, that the one person, Jesus Christ, should be the Son of God and the Son of man; and so that we should be kept from preaching a quaternity instead of the Trinity, which God forbid that we should do [Augustine, *Tractates on the Gospel of John*]" (Schaff, *Nicene and Post-Nicene Fathers: First Series* 7:381). It is more complete to say that the incarnation is the eternal Sonship made visible.

→ Progressive Revelation of Man →					
Adam	First Advent	Second Advent			
Father	Son	Spirit			
Prime (Freewill)	Twofold (Nexus)	Threefold (Unity)	Father	Original Creation	↓ Progressive Revelation of Creation ↓
Serial (Creator)	Chiastic (Redeemer)	Staircase (Sanctifier)	Son	Fallen Creation	
Historical (Transcendent)	Individual (Personal)	Generational (Universal)	Spirit	New Creation	

The temporally uniform pattern types serial, chiastic, and staircase are expected to be those types that most directly encode the unfolding of the present fallen creation. A prophecy is a foretelling of what is to come, foremost what is to come in the present reality of the present fallen creation. Therefore, the domain of prophecy—as it is normally conceived in the context of the present fallen creation—corresponds to the symmetry types most closely identified with the present fallen creation. Further, since the analysis of patterns requires the existence of patterns, necessarily established in the past, the domain of prophecy is generally restricted to the last days, connecting the First Advent of Christ and the Second Advent (Dan 12:4).[5]

As to the relevancy of Bible prophecy, it should be understood that the study of the Bible is the study of prophecy, for the organizing principle of the Bible is prophecy, specifically the overarching prophecy of the redemption of the faithful in Christ. All prophecies ultimately point to the First and Second Advents, and every aspect of the Bible should be understood prophetically. And it is no coincidence that the pattern types identified with fallen creation are exactly those which are rigidly demarcated by time, for prophecy is inherently entangled with the timing and ordering of events. Further, the faithful love the Lord and desire to be with the Lord. Therefore, the focus of the faithful living in the present church age could be nothing other than the prophesied resurrection and rapture, or catching up, to be with the Lord (1 Thess 4:15–17). In contrast, the natural focus of the faithless, the people of the world, the present fallen world, is their own destiny following the rapture but separated from the rapture, namely, the tribulation period and the battle of Armageddon. And it is exactly these horrific images of destruction, actually judgment, that are even now titillating an enthralled world.

The remnant of faithful, now preparing for the Lord's return, have a natural interest in the timing of the resurrection and rapture, not simply from a practical viewpoint, but ultimately in relationship to, as a matter of conformity to, the Biblical worldview. Given the increasingly universal apostasy of the people of the world, particularly within the church, the Lord returning imminently compared with his returning in the unfathomably distant future implies contradicting perspectives of God and, therefore, mutually exclusive

---

[5] "A poem, in fact, can only be re-read, not read, since some of its structures can only be perceived retrospectively" (Eagleton 89). The Word of God is poetic in the sense that it is always operating on all levels of reality.

AFTERWORD

fundamental realities. There is a common misconception, actually a guile of the flesh, that the Lord has stated that no one can ever know anything about the timing of the resurrection and rapture. The power of this deception lies in its close similarity to the truth, its mingling of fact and fiction. It recalls the original deception of Eve in the garden of Eden (Gen 2:16–17, 3:4–5). While it is true that no one can know the exact day or hour of the resurrection and rapture (Matt 24:36), the faithful in Christ are actually commanded to know the season thereof (1 Thess 5:4). And this in no way contradicts the doctrine of the imminency of the return of Christ.

First, God is sovereign. And thus God can certainly choose to return at any time. But God has already, from the very beginning of creation, sovereignly appointed the times of his coming (Isa 46:10). And it is the love of God to foretell all things to his faithful for the sake of his faithful (Mark 13:23). Second, the often-cited image of the Lord coming like a thief in the night applies primarily to the faithless and not to the faithful (1 Thess 5:4). The Lord comes to give freely unto the faithful, not to rob the faithful. But the blessing of the Lord, from which the faithless unknowingly benefit, will be secreted away with the faithful at the time of the resurrection and rapture. And being secreted away is appropriate since the faithless deny the very existence of the blessing of the Lord. Third, there is a parallel between the death of the individual and the destruction of the world. And the coming of the Lord has been truly imminent for the individual throughout all the ages. The individual is a microcosm of creation in that both the individual and creation as a whole reflect the triunity of God. The individual and creation as a whole therefore both have infinite value to God. And thus in the eyes of the Lord the death of the individual is like the destruction of the entire world or universe. Fourth, it has been foretold that knowledge would increase in the last days. And our knowledge that the resurrection and rapture has not yet happened is, not coincidentally, a knowledge that is intrinsic to the last days. This knowledge, which not even the faithful in Christ could have (by its very nature) held previously (in the natural), represents an ever-decreasing window in which the resurrection and rapture of the faithful can happen, especially given the convergence of signs being increasingly manifested in the modern day (Dan 12:4).

→ PROGRESSIVE REVELATION OF MAN →		
(THE REDEMPTION OF THE FAITHFUL)		
ADAM	FIRST ADVENT	SECOND ADVENT
FATHER	SON	HOLY SPIRIT
SERIAL	CHIASTIC	STAIRCASE
(CREATOR)	(REDEEMER)	(SANCTIFIER)

The symmetry types serial, chiastic, and staircase, demarcating the present fallen creation, point to the seventh, or Sabbath, millennium from Adam as the time corresponding to the second coming and the millennial reign of Christ. The overarching symmetry of creation is sevenfold, whereby the faithful now expect the Lord to keep the seventh-millennium Sabbath (closing the present creation as a whole) just as we remember the Lord keeping the first seventh-day

AFTERWORD

Sabbath (closing the original act of creation) (Exod 20:8–11). Nevertheless, as in the original act of creation, a general darkness necessarily precedes the light of creation (Gen 1:2–3). This is every day beginning with the evening, according to the words "the evening and the morning were the first day," and so forth (Gen 1:5). And the present modern day is the darkness, or beginning of the darkness, that even now heralds the light of the millennial kingdom. Further, the second coming of Christ is identified with the seventh millennium. But the second coming, viewed as being heralded by the resurrection and rapture and the concomitant tribulation period, will be foremost the nexus between the sixth and seventh millennia ending the church age. Likewise, the conception and birth of Christ as king at the time of the First Advent marked the end of the fourth millennium (Matt 2:2) while the death and resurrection of Christ as the king of kings marked the beginning of the fifth millennium (Matt 27:37). The First Advent is the incarnation and exaltation of Christ, while the Second Advent is the incarnation and exaltation, or glorification, of the Body of Christ.

Focusing on the present fallen creation, the fifth millennium parallels the second millennium when viewed from the perspective of the serial pattern symmetry. The fifth millennium is marked by the death and resurrection of Christ at the time of the First Advent, while the second millennium is marked by the death and resurrection of the world at the time of the Flood. Further, the death and resurrection of Christ is connected to the sending of the Holy Spirit in the establishment of the church age while the death and resurrection of the world is connected to the descending of God to judge the tower of Babel in the establishment of the nations. The sign that marks the second and fifth days and millennia in the serial pattern is the sign of water, specifically water baptism as related to the repentance of sins. The parallel between the baptism of Christ on the cross and the baptism of the world by the floodwaters identifies the death and resurrection of Christ with the death and resurrection of the whole world and all creation. And the establishment of the nations after the time of the Flood prefigures the establishment of the different churches, or assemblies, after the time of the First Advent. The serial pattern type is most closely identified with God the Father, specifically God the Father as our creator, or spiritual progenitor. The death and resurrection of all creation in the person of God the Son is the promised new creation that proceeds from God the Father.

The fifth millennium parallels the third millennium when viewed from the perspective of the chiastic pattern symmetry. The third millennium is marked by the call of faithful Abraham out of the world and the corresponding establishment of the nation of Israel under the law of Moses. In comparison, the fifth millennium is marked by the faithful submission of Christ to the cross in accordance with the law and the corresponding establishment, or founding of, the Body of Christ. The sign that marks the third and fifth days and millennia in the chiastic pattern is the sign of life, specifically the life of the body that comes by the law. The life that comes by the law of Moses is the promise of mortal life, to live long in the land (Deut 11:8–9), while the life that comes by Christ in fulfillment of the law on the cross is the promise of eternal life, the guarantee of our salvation in the Body of Christ (2 Cor 5:4–5, 5:14–15). The

AFTERWORD

Covenant of Law precedes the Covenant of Grace just as the natural body precedes the spiritual, or glorified, resurrection body just as repentance precedes redemption just as the baptism in water precedes the baptism of the Holy Spirit. The chiastic pattern type is most closely identified with God the Son, specifically God the Son as our redeemer. It is the Son, the second person of the Trinity, who is identified with our redemption under the law, because it is the Son who was nailed to the cross.

The fifth millennium parallels the third and seventh millennia when viewed from the perspective of the staircase pattern symmetry. The seventh millennium is the Sabbath millennium, representing the culmination of the present creation and corresponding to the promised millennial kingdom of Christ. The sign that marks the third, fifth, and seventh days and millennia in the staircase pattern is again the sign of life but specifically the fulfillment of the promise of life that comes through the Messianic bloodline. The establishment of Israel under the law of Moses in the third millennium represents the fulfillment of the promise to preserve Adam, or mankind, in the world despite the fall in Adam. The death and resurrection of Christ in the fifth millennium is the climactic fulfillment of the whole of the law, representing the absolute guarantee of eternal life for the faithful in Christ. And the promised establishment of the Body of Christ in the seventh millennium is the fulfillment of the Covenant of Law in the Covenant of Grace that is represented by the resurrection. The movement from the third millennium to the fifth to the seventh is the progression from the fulfillment of the law in Adam to the fulfillment of the law in Jesus Christ to the fulfillment of the law in the Body of Christ. The staircase pattern type is most closely identified with God the Holy Spirit, specifically God the Holy Spirit as our sanctifier. The progressive revelation of eternal life in Christ, which is our promised sanctification and exaltation in the Body of Christ, is the movement, or quickening, of the Holy Spirit in our midst and in our persons.

The sixth millennium parallels the third millennium when viewed from the perspective of the serial pattern symmetry. The sixth millennium is marked by the schism of the visible church culminating in the greatest schism, or division, of all—namely, the resurrection and rapture of the faithful in Christ out of a world that has rejected Christ. The sign that marks the third and sixth days and millennia in the serial pattern is again the sign of life but specifically the life of creation and new creation. The creation, or new life, of God identified with the third millennium is the establishment of the children of Abraham through whom Jesus Christ would come. The creation, or new life, of God identified with the sixth millennium is the establishment of the children of God in the Body of Christ. The serial pattern type is most closely identified with God the Father as our creator, or spiritually our progenitor. God the Father is the true father of all the faithful (Matt 23:9). The sign of creation, the life of the Creator, the Father, connecting the third and sixth millennia is the regeneration that comes only by grace through faith in Jesus Christ, the only begotten who eternally proceeds from God the Father (Eph 2:8).

The sixth millennium parallels the second millennium when viewed from the perspective of the chiastic pattern symmetry. The sign that marks the second

AFTERWORD

and sixth days and millennia in the chiastic pattern is the sign of division, specifically the division of the faithful and the faithless that comes by the judgment of all flesh under the law. The division of the second millennium is the separation of the one perfect man Noah (Gen 6:9), while the division of the sixth millennium is the separation of the one Body of Christ (Deut 18:13). The former is the baptism in water, or literally floodwaters, while the latter is the baptism of fire, or spiritually the Holy Spirit. But only the faithless are judged under the law and not the faithful, for anyone who is judged under the law, separated from Christ, will be condemned (John 3:18). The chiastic pattern type is most closely identified with God the Son as our redeemer. The redemption of the faithful comes by water and by fire (Luke 3:16). This is the duality of the Son, who is true man and true God. This is law and grace together fulfilled perfectly in the one Son. The presence of the Lord is a burning fire that destroys the faithless but purifies the faithful (Heb 12:23–29).

The sixth millennium parallels the second and fourth millennia when viewed from the perspective of the staircase pattern symmetry. The fourth millennium is marked by the establishment of the Davidic kingdom culminating in the incarnation of Jesus Christ (Luke 1:32–33, Matt 2:2). The sign that marks the second, fourth, and sixth days and millennia in the staircase pattern is again the sign of division but specifically the division that comes by the exaltation and dominion of the faithful. The division of the second millennium is the exaltation of Noah on the floodwaters. The division of the fourth millennium is the exaltation of the kingdom of David, that is, the conception of Christ as king of kings. And the division of the sixth millennium is the exaltation of the faithful in the Body of Christ. The staircase pattern type is most closely identified with God the Spirit as our sanctifier. The progression of the one Messianic bloodline through the ages from Adam to Jesus Christ to the Body of Christ represents the movement of the Holy Spirit. The ministry of the Holy Spirit is the setting apart of the faithful in the Son for the Father. The sign, or mark, of the Holy Spirit that separates the faithful from the faithless is faith itself and very specifically the one faith in the one man Jesus Christ.

The seventh millennium parallels the fourth millennium when viewed from the perspective of the serial pattern symmetry. The sign that marks the fourth and seventh days and millennia in the serial pattern is the sign of kingship, specifically the kingship identified with the kingdom of God, which is ultimately the light of God, the light of creation and redemption. The kingship that marks the fourth millennium is the Davidic kingship culminating in the conception of Jesus Christ as king of kings. The kingship that marks the seventh, or Sabbath, millennium is the long awaited millennial kingdom of Christ. The serial pattern type is most closely identified with God the Father as our creator, or spiritually our progenitor. The kingdom of God is our promised new creation in the Body of Christ that proceeds from the Father as the light of God. The millennial kingdom corresponds to the Sabbath millennium because our promised new creation in the Body of Christ is foremost our peace and rest in Christ and our reliance upon Christ. This is the ultimate meaning of the seventh-day Sabbath

AFTERWORD

that the faithful are commanded to keep according to the will and light of the Father, as proclaimed by the law and the prophets (Exod 20:8, Isa 56:1–7).

The seventh millennium parallels the first millennium when viewed from the perspective of the chiastic pattern symmetry. The first millennium is marked not solely by the Fall of Man but also by the concurrent preservation of man despite sin. The preservation of Adam and likewise Adam-kind is expressly the preservation of the natural body in the present fallen state. The sign that marks the first and seventh days and millennia in the chiastic pattern is the sign of peace. The peace of the first millennium is the peace of God represented by the preservation of Adam and the innate promise of life embodied by Adam. The peace of the seventh millennium is the peace of the new creation that is our promised peace in God in the Body of Christ. And the present time of preservation is the time of repentance that necessarily precedes the time of redemption. The chiastic pattern type is most closely identified with God the Son as our redeemer. The relationship between the first and seventh millennia is the relationship between Adam and the promised new Adam that is our promised redemption in the Body of Christ.

The seventh millennium parallels the third and fifth millennia when viewed from the perspective of the staircase pattern symmetry. The sign that marks the third, fifth, and seventh days and millennia in the staircase pattern is again the sign of life represented by the fulfillment of the promise of life but specifically that in eternity. In the staircase pattern type a unique relationship is evident between the fifth and seventh millennia that is not evident in either the serial or chiastic pattern types. The fifth and seventh millennia are both identified with the 3-position in the repeating 1-2-3 staircase pattern, which demarcates the last days connecting the First and Second Advents of Christ. The connection between the fifth and seventh millennia is the connection between Christ as the Head and the faithful as the Body of Christ. And the establishment of the church that connects the fifth and seventh millennia parallels the establishment of Israel that connects the third and fifth millennia. The staircase pattern type is most closely identified with God the Holy Spirit as our sanctifier. And the sign of life points to our promised sanctification in Christ by the power of the Holy Spirit. The Spirit specifically is identified with the church age, which connects the fifth and seventh millennia, because the call of the faithful unto Christ during the church age represents the pinnacle of the earthly ministry of the Spirit. And it is for this purpose that Christ sent forth the Holy Spirit upon his ascension unto the Father (John 16:7). The ministry of the Son precedes the ministry of the Spirit just as the Head precedes the Body just as repentance precedes redemption.[6]

---

[6] "[T]he Holy Spirit is the first to awaken faith in us and to communicate to us the new life, which is to 'know the Father and the one whom he has sent, Jesus Christ' [John 17:3]. But the Spirit is the last of the persons of the Holy Trinity to be revealed" (Rom. Catholic Church, *Catechism* 196). The Alpha is the Omega.

AFTERWORD

	→ THREE DAYS OF CHRIST →			
FIFTH MILLENNIUM (FRIDAY)	SIXTH MILLENNIUM (SATURDAY)	SEVENTH MILLENNIUM (SUNDAY)		
BAPTISM OF THE WORLD (WATER)	RESURRECTION & RAPTURE (LIFE)	KINGDOM OF GOD (LIGHT)	SERIAL (CREATION)	↓ THREE DAYS OF CREATION ↓
LAW FULFILLED BY CHRIST (LIFE)	RESURRECTION & RAPTURE (DIVISION)	MILLENNIAL SABBATH (PEACE)	CHIASTIC (REDEMPTION)	
QUICKENING OF THE SPIRIT (BLOOD)	RESURRECTION & RAPTURE (DOMINION)	THE BODY OF CHRIST (LIFE)	STAIRCASE (SANCTIFICATION)	

    The pattern types identified with fallen creation—serial, chiastic, and staircase—are the domain of prophecy as it is normally conceived, but the pattern types identified with the original creation—prime, twofold, and threefold—and those identified with the promised new creation—historical, individual, and generational—also relate what are essential aspects of the complete prophetic image. And the complete prophetic image—that is, all levels of prophecy viewed as a unified whole—should finally be recognized as the progressive revelation of the absolute fullness of the triune image of God (Rev 19:10). The fundamental parallel between the physical and the spiritual, which persists even in our fallen creation, testifies to the unity of the original creation and accordingly to the (prerequisite) wholeness and oneness of the Creator. And the very fabric of all creation—past, present, and future—weaving increasingly complex patterns from archetypal elements is itself a prophecy of the fullness of God permeating and encompassing all reality in the promised new creation. The progressive unfolding of the revelation of Christ, in contrast to the simple proclamation of Jesus, reflects the essence of the Messianic bloodline—which is our salvation coming by the flow of blood (in time and space), in accordance with freewill and representing the movement of the Spirit. The bloodline of Christ is a flow of blood connecting Adam to Jesus to the Body of Christ. The bloodline of the Son is a lifeblood relating a life that is always living and, therefore, necessarily spans all creation—past, present, and future—in contrast to a life that is simply acquired or possessed at some specific moment in time.

    The original creation before sin entered the world and the yet future new creation are difficult to comprehend for the same reason. Our experience is limited to our fallen creation. And this problem includes our very perception of creation being confused just as all creation has been corrupted. The symmetry patterns corresponding to the present fallen creation are by no means trivial, but the patterns corresponding to the original creation and the yet future creation are inherently foreign, in addition to being fundamentally disconnected from time and space. The symmetry patterns serial, chiastic, and staircase are rigidly uniform in space and time, which reflects Christ being conceived in the flesh at an appointed time and place in the very midst of creation. Jesus Christ is corporeal and relatable, and these qualities of Christ are expressed in the individual lives of the faithful and likewise in the assembly of the faithful, the

AFTERWORD

nature of which is characterized by experiencing the personhood of Christ in time and space. True Christianity, which is Biblical and therefore Trinitarian, is antithetical to the idea that God is disembodied from physical creation and personal relationship. The abstract symmetry patterns prime, twofold, and threefold testify to this same reality, but with an emphasis on the unmovable and unchanging will of the Father. The nonlocalized symmetry patterns historical, individual, and generational also testify to this same reality, but with an emphasis on the Spirit enveloping and permeating all time and space and all spiritual and physical creation in the Body of Christ.

The progressive nature of revelation—connecting the original creation to the present creation to the promised new creation—relates the Son and the Spirit proceeding from the Father in the creation, redemption, and sanctification of the faithful unto the Father in the Son, the Body of Christ, by the power of the indwelling Spirit. The elemental pattern types prime, twofold, and threefold are static and abstract, representing the timeless will of God, which is immutable and transcends creation. But the will of God is the nature of God and the reality of creation formed in the image of God. The progressive revelation of God is a projection, or unfolding, of creation from God, while the redemption of all creation is a subsuming, or folding, of creation unto God. The pattern types prime, twofold, and threefold are simultaneously concrete and abstract just as the Trinity is simultaneously immanent and transcendent just as creation is simultaneously simple and complex. The pattern types prime, twofold, and threefold project into the present fallen creation, as evidenced by the serial, chiastic, and staircase types being founded upon the prime, twofold, and threefold types. And the historical, individual, and generational pattern types being analogues of the serial, chiastic, and staircase types relates a promised new creation that will not only supplant but also subsume the original creation.

The observed unfolding of complexity in creation, founded upon the Messianic bloodline, is the progressive revelation of God, the image of God, unto man, but there is also an implied simplicity of creation, or concurrent folding of creation, which corresponds to the redemption of all the faithful in the Body of Christ. The unfolding and folding of creation represents all things being created through and in Christ. For example, the Flood of Noah points to the Passion of Christ in the progressive revelation of creation, but the correspondence between the death and resurrection of the world, marked by the wooden ark, and the death and resurrection of the world in Christ, marked by the wooden cross, implies an overlapping of the two watersheds. The parallel between the Flood and the Passion represents a folding of the sevenfold creation into a threefold creation, death, and resurrection of the whole world and all creation. The formation of Adam followed by the First and Second Advents of Christ forms the basic framework for the unfolding of the sevenfold creation, but it additionally implies a concurrent folding of the sevenfold creation of Adam-kind into a threefold creation of, or through, Christ. And the threefold creation through Christ is finally the one Body of Christ.

The folding of the sevenfold body of creation, or body of Adam, into the threefold creation of Jesus Christ and finally into the one Body of Christ is

AFTERWORD

simultaneously the judgment, or displacement, of the threefold serpent, devil, and satan by the triune Father, Son, and Spirit. The unfolding and folding of progressive revelation is not a repeating cycle. Progressive revelation is a coming into the fullness of form in accordance with the inviolable sanctity of freewill. The kingdom of God is not simply a return to the garden of Eden and likewise to the serpent of the garden of Eden. The nature of progressive revelation is the spirit of prophecy. Progressive revelation looks forward and not backward. The garden was not the kingdom; the garden was a prophecy of, or path to, the kingdom. The perfect image of God is freewill in the second man Jesus Christ, not slavery to sin in the first man Adam. The fullness of the Body of Christ will not be the annihilation of self—that is, not the annihilation of freewill—but the realization of perfect freedom in the spiritual, or glorified, resurrection body. The promised resurrection body is spiritual and supernatural in the sense of transcending natural limits, but it is necessarily also a true physical body, as required by the nature of freewill operating in time and space. The present natural body is governed by the flesh and the law of the flesh, whereas the promised spiritual body will be governed by the indwelling Holy Spirit and the grace of the Spirit. Nonetheless, the natural body and the spiritual body are both true physical bodies. The prophecy of the Body of Christ is the promise of the fullness of a personal and palpable communion with the Lord God.

The unfolding and folding of creation in the progressive revelation of God unto man—relating the will of God, likewise the nature of God—is innately prophetic just as the will of God is inherently undeniable, or relentless. And the will and nature of God is the Body of Christ, not the body of Adam. The perfect image of God is not Adam, but Jesus Christ and likewise the Body of Christ. Adam is the very good image (Gen 1:31), whereas Christ is the perfect image (Col 1:15). The oneness of reality, which is the folding of the totality of creation into the one Body of Christ, parallels the oneness of prophecy, which relates the one Body of Christ and likewise the one nature of God. The prophecy of the Body of Christ is in actuality the singular promise of God in that all prophecies and promises are ultimately relating what are different aspects or perspectives of the one Body of Christ. And the fundamental parallel between creation as a whole, formed in the triune image of God, and individual man, likewise formed in the triune image of God, implies the folding of the totality of creation into just such a singularity, or oneness, as represented by the Body of Christ. The one inheritance of all the faithful in Jesus Christ is the Holy Spirit, the fullness of which will be received in the one Body of Christ at the appointed time of the Second Advent of Christ. And what could ever be added to the fullness of the indwelling Holy Spirit to make such an inheritance yet greater? The unfolding of creation is God the Holy Spirit proceeding from God the Father in the conception of God the Son (Father, Spirit, Son), while the folding of creation is God the Holy Spirit presenting the faithful in God the Son, the Body of Christ, unto God the Father (Father, Son, Spirit).

EPILOGUE

The seven churches of the book of Revelation, 2:1–3:22, diagrammed by millennia and corresponding Biblical personages. The King James Bible standard English text is quoted, with editorial clarifications delimited in brackets.[1]

FIRST MILLENNIUM	
THE CHURCH OF EPHESUS:	THE FALL OF ADAM:
... These things saith he that holdeth the seven stars in his right hand, who walketh in the midst of the seven golden candlesticks; ... (Rev 2:1).	The seven stars and seven candlesticks reflect the six plus one days of creation. The stars and candlesticks represent all things, heaven and earth, being created through the Son (John 1:3).
I know thy works, and thy labour ... and how thou ... hast not fainted (2:2–3).	In the sweat of thy face shalt thou eat bread (Gen 3:19).
Nevertheless ... thou hast left thy first love (2:4).	The sons of God begin to take the daughters of men (Gen 6:2).
Remember therefore from whence thou art fallen, and repent, and do the first works; or else I will come unto thee quickly, and will remove thy candlestick out of his place, except thou repent (2:5).	Remember the garden of Eden and the Fall of Man, and return to the obedience unto God—which is according to the righteousness of the law—or the time of Adam (foremost antediluvian man) will be swept away in judgment.
But this thou hast, that thou hatest the deeds of the Nicolaitanes, which I also hate (2:6).	The time before and the time after the Flood of the second millennium are both marked by the sons of God going in unto the daughters of men. Likewise, the Nicolaitanes mark the first and third churches, paralleling the first and third millennia (Gen 6:4).

---

[1] The inspired ordering of the seven churches in the book of Revelation is sometimes compared to the progression of the church age, but such a comparison is not mutually exclusive with the comparison to the history of creation as a whole. Nonetheless, the comparison to the church age does require a strong reliance upon extra-Biblical history and therefore is less certain.

EPILOGUE

. . . To him that overcometh will I give to eat of the tree of life, which is in the midst of the paradise of God (2:7).	The tree of life, which marked the garden of Eden, will be transplanted into the promised kingdom of God (Gen 3:22–24).

SECOND MILLENNIUM

THE CHURCH IN SMYRNA:	THE FLOOD OF NOAH:
. . . These things saith the first and the last, which was dead, and is alive; . . . (Rev 2:8).	Yes, the death and resurrection of Jesus Christ (as linked to the wooden cross), but also the death and resurrection of the whole world in Christ (as linked to the wooden ark) (1 Pet 3:18–22).
I know thy works, and tribulation, and poverty, (but thou art rich) and [I know] the blasphemy of them which say they are Jews, and are not, but [are] the synagogue of Satan (2:9).	The synagogue of satan recalls the dominion of the serpent that was renounced in the Flood. And the blasphemy of the chosen people recalls antediluvian Adam-kind beginning to call upon (profanely) the name of the Lord (Gen 4:26).
[T]he devil shall cast [some] of you into prison, that ye may be tried; . . . (2:10).	Those imprisoned at the time of the Flood, unto whom Christ would preach (1 Pet 3:19).
. . . He that overcometh shall not be hurt of the second death (2:11).	Righteous Noah, together with his family, passing alive through the floodwaters.

THIRD MILLENNIUM

THE CHURCH IN PERGAMOS:	THE CALL OF ABRAHAM:
. . . These things saith he which hath the sharp sword with two edges; . . . (Rev 2:12).	The establishment of the children of Abraham as the nation of Israel is the beginning of the time of the sword (Deut 20:17).
I know thy works, and where thou dwellest . . . and thou holdest fast my name, and hast not denied my faith . . . . (2:13).	Faithful Abraham represents the father, or first, of all the faithful (Rom 4:16).
[T]hou hast there them that hold the doctrine of Balaam, who taught Balac to cast a stumblingblock before the children of Israel, to eat things sacrificed unto idols, and to commit fornication (2:14).	The nation of Israel is commanded by the Lord God to take possession of the promised land of Canaan, but they are opposed by the soothsayer Balaam, even though Balaam knows very well the plan of the God (Josh 13:22).
So hast thou also them that hold the doctrine of the Nicolaitanes, which thing I hate. Repent; or else I will come unto thee quickly, and will fight against them with the sword of my mouth (2:15–16).	The time before and the time after the Flood of the second millennium are both marked by the sons of God going in unto the daughters of men. Likewise, the Nicolaitanes mark the first and third churches, paralleling the first and third millennia (Gen 6:4).

EPILOGUE

... To him that overcometh will I give to eat of the hidden manna, and will give him a white stone, and in the stone a new name written, which no man knoweth saving he that receiveth [it] (2:17).	The hidden manna recalls the manna from heaven given to the children of faithful Abraham when they were called out of slavery in Egypt (John 6:32), while the promised new name of righteousness recalls Jacob being renamed Israel (Gen 32:28).

FOURTH MILLENNIUM

THE CHURCH IN THYATIRA:	THE DAVIDIC KINGSHIP:
... These things saith the Son of God, who hath his eyes like unto a flame of fire, and his feet [are] like fine brass; ... (Rev 2:18).	The Son of God is conceived of the Holy Spirit, the breath of fire, as the king of the Jews at the end of the fourth millennium, representing the culmination of the fourth millennium.
I know thy works, and charity, and service, and faith, and thy patience, and thy works; and the last [to be] more than the first (2:19).	The last Adam will be greater than the first Adam, and likewise the latter works will be greater than the former works (1 Cor 15:45).
Notwithstanding I have a few things against thee, because thou sufferest that woman Jezebel, which calleth herself a prophetess .... (2:20–21).	That whore and witch Jezebel, who slew the very prophets of God during the time of the kings of Israel (2 Kgs 9:22).
Behold, I will cast her into a bed, and them that commit adultery with her into great tribulation, except they repent of their deeds. ... (2:22–23).	The adulteries of the kings of the promised land, especially the (counterfeit) kings of Israel (Samaria), portend the final tribulation period, which will precede the millennial kingdom of Christ.
But unto you I say ... as many as have not this doctrine, and which have not known the depths of Satan, as they speak; I will put upon you none other burden (2:24).	The satanic doctrine of Jezebel, which preceded the First Advent, prefigures the (unforgiveable) mark of the beast, which will precede the Second Advent (Rev 20:4).
But that which ye have [already] hold fast till I come. And he that overcometh, and keepeth my works unto the end, to him will I give power over the nations: ... (2:25–26).	A prophetic warning that the time following the First Advent will be a time of waiting and watching that will last until the faithful in Christ finally reign with him at the time of the Second Advent (Rev 20:6).
And he shall rule them with a rod of iron; as the vessels of a potter shall they be broken to shivers: even as I received of my Father (2:27).	The rod of iron identified with the millennial reign was first established as an inheritance at the time of the conception of Christ (Ps 2:7–9, Rev 12:5).
And I will give him the morning star (2:28).	Jesus Christ is the one true morning star (Rev 22:16), whereby his birth in Bethlehem would be marked by the sign of his star (Matt 2:2).

EPILOGUE

He that hath an ear, let him hear what the Spirit saith unto the churches (2:29).	The Word of the Holy Spirit is foremost the holy conception of the Son (Luke 1:35).

FIFTH MILLENNIUM

THE CHURCH IN SARDIS:	THE FIRST ADVENT OF CHRIST:
. . . These things saith he that hath the seven Spirits of God, and the seven stars; I know thy works, that thou hast a name that thou livest, and art dead (Rev 3:1).	There is no life in separation from the death and resurrection of Jesus Christ, for Christ alone holds the sevenfold reality, which is creation and likewise new creation.
Be watchful, and strengthen the things which remain, that are ready to die: for I have not found thy works perfect before God (3:2).	The corrupted natural body is that which is ready to die. The perfect work of the cross does not pardon the natural body, but rather transforms it through death and resurrection.
Remember therefore how thou hast received and heard, and hold fast, and repent. If therefore thou shalt not watch, I will come on thee as a thief, and thou shalt not know what hour I will come upon thee (3:3).	That which has been received is the revelation of the immanent dominion of Jesus Christ as true man and true God. And accordingly his return for his own has always been imminent, even from the time of the fifth millennium.
Thou hast a few names even in Sardis which have not defiled their garments; and they shall walk with me in white: for they are worthy (3:4).	The relatively small number of Jews in Israel that believed in Jesus Christ, before the Gospel was sent unto the Gentile nations.
He that overcometh, the same shall be clothed in white raiment; and I will not blot out his name out of the book of life, but I will confess his name before my Father, and before his angels (3:5).	The faithful Jews and Gentiles to be redeemed during the church age.
He that hath an ear, let him hear what the Spirit saith unto the churches (3:6).	The Word of the Spirit is the call of the faithful unto repentance in the Son.

SIXTH MILLENNIUM

THE CHURCH IN PHILADELPHIA:	SCHISM AND RAPTURE:
. . . These things saith he that is holy, he that is true, he that hath the key of David, he that openeth, and no man shutteth; and shutteth, and no man openeth; . . . (Rev 3:7).	The key held by Jesus Christ, which opens and shuts, is the death of the cross, which separates the faithful and the faithless, the faithful unto eternal life and the faithless unto eternal damnation (John 5:29).
I know thy works: behold, I have set before thee an open door, and no man can shut it: for thou hast a little strength, and hast kept my word, and hast not denied my name (3:8).	The open door that Christ sets before the faithful is the resurrection and rapture, through which the faithful enter by grace through faith in Christ, not by their own strength.

Behold, I will make them of the synagogue of Satan, which say they are Jews, and are not, but do lie; behold, I will make them to come and worship before thy feet, and to know that I have loved thee (3:9).	The synagogue, or assembly, of satan is the coming together not only of Jews but Jews and Gentiles, presenting themselves as the chosen people of the Lord God. This is the anti-christ system that will mark the end times.
Because thou hast kept the word of my patience, I also will keep thee from the hour of temptation, which shall come upon all the world, to try them that dwell upon the earth (3:10).	A remnant of faithful will be raptured before the final period of tribulation.
Behold, I come quickly: hold that fast which thou hast, that no man take thy crown (3:11).	The faithful in Jesus Christ will be resurrected and raptured suddenly and unexpectedly, in the twinkling of an eye (1 Cor 15:52).
Him that overcometh will I make a pillar in the temple of my God, and he shall go no more out: and I will write upon him the name of my God, and the name of the city of my God, [which is] new Jerusalem, which cometh down out of heaven from my God: and [I will write upon him] my new name (3:12).	The promised temple of God and new Jerusalem is the Body of Christ and the kingdom of God, which will be fulfilled at the end of the millennial reign of Christ, when the promised new creation, the new heaven and new earth, is revealed (Rev 21:1).
He that hath an ear, let him hear what the Spirit saith unto the churches (3:13).	The Word of the Spirit is finally the promised eternal life in the Body of Christ.

Seventh Millennium

The Church of the Laodiceans:	The Second Advent:
... These things saith the Amen, the faithful and true witness, the beginning of the creation of God; ... (Rev 3:14).	The millennial reign of Christ, corresponding to the Sabbath millennium, is not yet the new heaven and new earth, but it is the beginning of the promised new creation.
I know thy works, that thou art neither cold nor hot: I would thou wert cold or hot. So then because thou art lukewarm, and neither cold nor hot, I will spue thee out of my mouth (3:15–16).	The Body of Christ is divers, in accordance with the innumerable gifts and ministries of the Holy Spirit, but anything that exists of itself, not in accordance with the loving purposes of God, must be vomited out as something disgusting.
Because thou sayest, I am rich, and increased with goods, and have need of nothing; and knowest not that thou art wretched, and miserable, and poor, and blind, and naked: ... (3:17).	The sin of pride is the original sin of angels and men alike (Gen 3:5, Isa 14:13). And since like begets like, the sin of pride is the offspring of all sin as well as the mother of all sin.

EPILOGUE

I counsel thee to buy of me gold tried in the fire, that thou mayest be rich; and white raiment, that thou mayest be clothed, and [that] the shame of thy nakedness do not appear; and anoint thine eyes with eyesalve, that thou mayest see (3:18).	The purchasing of all things from God is the Son purchasing our salvation for us on the cross (Eph 2:8). The gold and riches of God is the grace of the Father. The white raiment of God is the sinless life of the Son. The eyesalve of God is the anointing of the Holy Spirit.
As many as I love, I rebuke and chasten: be zealous therefore, and repent (3:19).	All things work together for good to them that love God, to them who are the called ones according to his purpose (Rom 8:28).
Behold, I stand at the door, and knock: if any man hear my voice, and open the door, I will come in to him, and will sup with him, and he with me (3:20).	Blessed are they which are called unto the marriage supper of the Lamb (Rev 19:9).
To him that overcometh will I grant to sit with me in my throne, even as I also overcame, and am set down with my Father in his throne (3:21).	Our promised communion with the Father in the Body of Christ according to the power of the Spirit, which is the kingdom and throne of God established in fulfillment of all things.
He that hath an ear, let him hear what the Spirit saith unto the churches (3:22).	The fullness of the indwelling Holy Spirit that is the perfected inward hearing of faith (Gal 3:2).

EIGHTH MILLENNIUM

THE ONE TRUE CHURCH:	ETERNITY:
I Jesus have sent mine angel to testify unto you these things in the churches. I am the root and the offspring of David, [and] the bright and morning star (22:16).	The culmination of all seven churches, likewise the culmination of all seven of the millennia of twofold creation—originally through Christ and finally in Christ, by Christ on the cross.

SELECTED BIBLIOGRAPHY

Source materials are divided into subsections to highlight differences in genres and traditions as well as to facilitate referencing and to organize further reading. Not listed are original sources cited only via secondary sources, since in such cases the chief interest is in the secondary sources themselves, including their intrinsic filtering of the original sources. All such original sources are documented in the footnotes at least generally, along with complete citations for the secondary sources. Also not listed are a small number of general-purpose reference works.

SACRED TEXT

The Amplified Bible: Containing the Amplified Old Testament and the Amplified New Testament. Expanded edition. Grand Rapids: Zondervan, 1987.

The Holy Bible: Authorized King James Version. Pew Bible. Nashville: Holman Bible Publishers, 2014. Advocated by Bible Protector Ministries, Australia, as representing a pure presentation of the standard English text, first typeset circa 1900 and mass-produced by Bible and missionary societies in the twentieth century, ISBN 978-1-5864-0942-5.

The Holy Bible: The Catholic Bible, Douay-Rheims Version; Translated from the Latin Vulgate and Diligently Compared with the Hebrew, Greek and Other Editions; With Notes by Bishop [Richard] *Challoner and the Encyclical Letter "On the Study of the Holy Scriptures" by Pope Leo XIII, also a Presentation of the Essence of the Encyclical Letter "On Biblical Studies" by Pope Pius XII, and a Preface by Rev. William H. McClellan, S. J.; Also an Appendix Containing an Historical and Chronological Index, a Table of References and Maps.* New York: Benziger, 1941.

The Holy Bible: New International Version; Containing the Old Testament and the New Testament. Grand Rapids: Zondervan, 1984.

The New American Bible: Translated from the Original Languages with Critical Use of All the Ancient Sources; And the Revised New Testament Authorized by the Board of Trustees of the Confraternity of Christian Doctrine and Approved by the Administrative Committee/Board of the National Conference of Catholic Bishops and the U. S. Catholic Conference. Nashville: Catholic Bible Press, 1987.

Tanakh: A New Translation of the Holy Scriptures according to the Traditional Hebrew Text. First special-format edition. Philadelphia: Jewish Publication Society, 1985.

BIBLIOGRAPHY

WORD STUDIES

Brown, Francis, S. R. Driver, and Charles A. Briggs. *The Brown-Driver-Briggs Hebrew and English Lexicon: With an Appendix Containing the Biblical Aramaic; Coded with the Numbering System from Strong's Exhaustive Concordance of the Bible; Based on the Lexicon of William Gesenius, as Translated by Edward Robinson, and Edited with Constant Reference to the Thesaurus of Gesenius as Completed by E. Rödiger, and with Authorized Use of the German Editions of Gesenius' Handwörterbuch über das Alte Testament.* Peabody: Hendrickson, 2007. Reprinted from the 1906 edition published by Houghton, Mifflin & Company. Strong's numbering added by Hendrickson.

Green, Jay P., Sr., ed. *The Interlinear Bible, Hebrew-Greek-English: With Strong's Concordance Numbers above Each Word.* Grand Rapids: Hendrickson, 1986. The Masoretic Text was type set in 1866 by the British and Foreign Bible Society. The Textus Receptus was type set in 1976 by Stephen Austin and Sons for the Trinitarian Bible Society and was based upon Scrivener's 1894–1902 *The New Testament in the Original Greek according to the Text Followed in the Authorized Version*.

Strong, James. *The Exhaustive Concordance of the Bible: Showing Every Word of the Text of the Common English Version of the Canonical Books, and Every Occurrence of Each Word in Regular Order; Together with a Key-Word Comparison of Selected Words and Phrases in the King James Version with Five Leading Contemporary Translations; Also Brief Dictionaries of the Hebrew and Greek Words of the Original, with References to the English Words.* Thirty-eighth printing. Nashville: Abingdon, 1980. Copyrighted 1890. Key-word comparison updated by Abingdon.

Thayer, Joseph H. *Thayer's Greek-English Lexicon of the New Testament: Coded with Strong's Concordance Numbers.* Peabody: Hendrickson, 2007. Reprinted from the 1896 fourth edition published by T&T Clark. Strong's numbering added by Hendrickson.

TALMUDIC WRITINGS

Cohen, Abraham. *Everyman's Talmud: The Major Teachings of the Rabbinic Sages.* New York: Schocken, 1995. Reprinted from the 1949 edition published by E. P. Dutton.

Rapaport, Samuel., ed. *A Treasury of the Midrash.* New York: KTAV, 1968. First published in 1907 as *Tales and Maxims from the Midrash*.

BIBLIOGRAPHY

Rodkinson, Michael Levi, Isaac Mayer Wise, and Godfrey Taubenhaus, eds. *New Edition of the Babylonian Talmud: Original Text, Edited, Corrected, Formulated, and Translated into English.* Bound in 10 vols. Boston: New Talmud, 1896–1903. Internal tract/volume, not bound volume, divisions are used in footnote citations.

PATRISTIC WRITINGS

Augustine of Hippo. *The City of God.* 1993 Modern Library edition. Translated by Marcus Dods. New York: Modern Library, 1994. Augustine lived 354–430.

Augustine of Hippo. *Confessions.* Oxford World's Classics. Translated by Henry Chadwick. New York: Oxford UP, 1998.

Norris, Richard A., Jr., ed. *The Christological Controversy.* Sources of Early Christian Thought. Series editor: William G. Rusch. Philadelphia: Fortress, 1982.

Roberts, Alexander, James Donaldson, A. Cleveland Coxe, and Allan Menzies, eds. *Ante-Nicene Fathers: The Writings of the Fathers down to AD 325.* Revised and chronologically arranged, with brief prefaces and occasional notes. 10 vols. Peabody: Hendrickson, 1995. Reprint edition of the American edition published 1885–1897 by Christian Literature Publishing.

Rusch, William G., ed. *The Trinitarian Controversy.* Sources of Early Christian Thought. Series editor: William G. Rusch. Philadelphia: Fortress, 1980.

Schaff, Philip, ed. *Nicene and Post-Nicene Fathers: A Select Library of the Christian Church; First Series.* 14 vols. Peabody: Hendrickson, 1995. Reprint edition of the American edition published 1886–1889 by Christian Literature Publishing.

Schaff, Philip, and Henry Wace, eds. *Nicene and Post-Nicene Fathers: A Select Library of the Christian Church; Second Series.* 14 vols. Peabody: Hendrickson, 1995. Reprint edition of the American editions published 1890–1898 by Christian Literature Publishing (vols. 1–8, 10–13) and 1899–1900 by Charles Scribner's Sons (vols. 9 and 14). Pagination of vols. 9 and 12 both subdivided.

BIBLICAL COMMENTARIES

Alter, Robert. *Genesis: Translation and Commentary.* New York: W. W. Norton, 1996.

BIBLIOGRAPHY

Calvin, John. *Commentaries on the First Book of Moses, Called Genesis.* Translated by John King. 2 vols. Edinburgh: Calvin Translation Society, 1847–1850.

Clarke, Adam. *The Holy Bible Containing the Old and New Testaments: The Text Carefully Printed from the Most Correct Copies of the Present Authorized Translation, including the Marginal Readings and Parallel Texts; With a Commentary and Critical Notes Designed as a Help to a Better Understanding of the Sacred Writings.* A new edition, with the author's final corrections. 6 vols. New York: Abingdon-Cokesbury, [n.d.]. The first edition of Clarke's commentary was published in 1826.

Coffman, James Burton. *Commentary on Genesis: The First Book of Moses.* James Burton Coffman Commentaries. Abilene: ACU Press, 1985.

Gill, John. *Gill's Commentary.* 6 vols. Grand Rapids: Baker, 1980. Reprinted from the 1852–1854 edition published by William Hill.

Guzik, David. *Verse-by-Verse Commentary on the Book of Genesis.* Enduring Word Commentary Series. Simi Valley: Enduring Word, 1998.

Henry, Matthew. *Matthew Henry's Commentary on the Whole Bible: Wherein Each Chapter Is Summed Up in Its Contents; the Sacred Text Inserted at Large in Distinct Paragraphs; Each Paragraph Reduced to Its Proper Heads; the Sense Given, and Largely Illustrated with Practical Remarks and Observations.* Carefully revised and corrected. 6 vols. New York: Fleming H. Revell, [n.d.]. The first volume of Henry's original commentary was published in 1708.

Jamieson, Robert, A. R. Fausset, and David Brown. *A Commentary, Critical, Experimental and Practical, on the Old and New Testaments.* 6 vols. Grand Rapids: Eerdmans, 1945. The first edition appeared 1864–1870.

Murphy, Roland E. Commentary on Genesis 25:19–50:26 in *The New Jerome Biblical Commentary*, 28–43. Edited by Raymond E. Brown, Joseph A. Fitzmyer, and Roland E. Murphy. Englewood Cliffs: Prentice-Hall, 1990. Previously published as *The Jerome Biblical Commentary.*

Sarna, Nahum M. *Genesis: The Traditional Hebrew Text with New JPS Translation/Commentary.* The JPS Torah Commentary. Philadelphia: Jewish Publication Society, 1989.

BIBLIOGRAPHY

Scofield, C. I. *The Scofield Reference Bible: The Holy Bible; Containing the Old and New Testaments; Authorized Version; With a New System of Connected Topical References to All the Greater Themes of Scripture, with Annotations, Revised Marginal Renderings, Summaries, Definitions, Chronology, and Index, to Which Are Added, Helps at Hard Places, Explanations of Seeming Discrepancies, and a New System of Paragraphs.* New and improved edition. New York: Oxford UP, 1945. Reprinted from the 1917 edition.

Waltke, Bruce K., with Cathi J. Fredricks. *Genesis: A Commentary.* Grand Rapids: Zondervan, 2001.

Wesley, John. *Explanatory Notes upon the Old Testament.* 3 vols. Salem, Ohio: Schmul, 1975. Reprinted from the 1765–1766 edition. Script updated when quoted.

Whittingham, William, Miles Coverdale, Christopher Goodman, Anthony Gilby, Thomas Sampson, William Cole, John Knox, William Kethe, Rowland Hall, John Pullain, John Bodley, John Baron, and William Williams. Marginal annotations in *The Geneva Bible: A Facsimile of the 1560 Edition.* Facsimile introduction by Lloyd E. Berry. Madison: University of Wisconsin Press, 1969. Attribution uncertain, including the influence of John Calvin. Pagination by leafs, not pages; script updated when quoted.

MODERN CHRISTIAN THOUGHT

Lewis, C. S. *Mere Christianity.* A revised and enlarged edition, with a new introduction, of the three books *The Case for Christianity*, *Christian Behavior*, and *Beyond Personality.* New York: Macmillan, 1984. The revised edition was first published in 1952.

Lewis, C. S. *The Screwtape Letters, with Screwtape Proposes a Toast.* Revised edition. New York: Macmillan, 1982. Lewis's preface dated 1960.

McDowell, Josh. *More Than a Carpenter.* Living Books edition. Wheaton: Tyndale House, 1988.

CATECHISMS, ENCYCLOPEDIAS, DICTIONARIES

Aquinas, Thomas. *Summa theologica.* First complete American edition. Translated by Fathers of the English Dominican Province. 3 vols. New York: Benziger, 1947–1948. *Summa theologica* was originally written ca. 1265–1273.

Elwell, Walter A., ed. *Evangelical Dictionary of Theology.* Second edition. Grand Rapids: Baker Academic, 2001.

BIBLIOGRAPHY

Herbermann, Charles G., Edward A. Pace, Condé B. Pallen, Thomas J. Shahan, and John J. Wynne, eds. *The Catholic Encyclopedia: An International Work of Reference on the Constitution, Doctrine, Discipline, and History of the Catholic Church*. 15 vols. New York: Robert Appleton, 1907–1912.

Hopko, Thomas. *The Orthodox Faith*. Second edition. 4 vols. New York: Department of Religious Education, OCA, 1976–1981.

Luther, Martin. *The Large Catechism of Martin Luther*. Translated by Robert H. Fischer. Philadelphia: Fortress, 1959. Luther's *Large Catechism* was formulated in 1529.

McFarland, Ian A., David A. S. Fergusson, Karen Kilby, and Iain R. Torrance, eds. *The Cambridge Dictionary of Christian Theology*. Cambridge: Cambridge UP, 2011.

Roman Catholic Church. *Catechism of the Catholic Church: With Modifications from the Editio typica*. Second edition. New York: Doubleday, 1997.

Singer, Isidore, ed., assisted by American and foreign boards of consulting editors. *The Jewish Encyclopedia: A Descriptive Record of the History, Religion, Literature, and Customs of the Jewish People from the Earliest Times to the Present Day*. 12 vols. New York: Funk & Wagnalls, 1916.

Unger, Merrill F. *The New Unger's Bible Dictionary*. Revised and updated edition. Edited by R. K. Harrison, Howard F. Vos, and Cyril J. Barber. Chicago: Moody Press, 1988. Original work copyrighted 1957.

HERMENEUTICS

Alter, Robert, and Frank Kermode, eds. *The Literary Guide to the Bible*. Cambridge, Mass.: Belknap Press of Harvard UP, 1987.

Blaising, Craig A., and Darrell L. Bock, *Progressive Dispensationalism*. Grand Rapids: BridgePoint, 2000.

Eagleton, Terry. *Literary Theory: An Introduction*. Second edition. Minneapolis: University of Minnesota Press, 1996.

Perrine, Laurence. *Literature: Structure, Sound, and Sense*. Second edition. New York: Harcourt Brace Jovanovich, 1974.

Ramm, Bernard. *Protestant Biblical Interpretation: A Textbook of Hermeneutics*. Third revised edition. Grand Rapids: Baker, 2004. Copyrighted 1970.

BIBLIOGRAPHY

Ryrie, Charles C., *Dispensationalism*. Revised and expanded edition. Chicago: Moody Press, 1995. Original work copyrighted 1966.

HISTORICAL WORKS

Aland, Kurt, and Barbara Aland. *The Text of the New Testament: An Introduction to the Critical Editions and to the Theory and Practice of Modern Textual Criticism*. Second edition, revised and enlarged. Translated by Erroll F. Rhodes. Grand Rapids: Eerdmans, 1995.

Armstrong, Karen. *The Bible: A Biography*. Books That Changed the World. First American edition. New York: Atlantic Monthly Press, 2007.

De Hamel, Christopher. *The Book: A History of the Bible*. London: Phaidon, 2001.

Ehrman, Bart D. *Misquoting Jesus: The Story behind Who Changed the Bible and Why*. First Edition. New York: HarperSanFrancisco, 2005.

Fuller, David Otis, ed. *Which Bible?* Third edition, revised and enlarged. Grand Rapids: Grand Rapids International, 1972.

Jones, Timothy P. *Misquoting Truth: A Guide to the Fallacies of Bart Ehrman's Misquoting Jesus*. Downers Grove: IVP, 2007.

Josephus, Flavius. *The Works of Josephus: With a Life Written by Himself; Translated from the Original Greek; Including Explanatory Notes and Observations*. Translated by William Whiston. 4 vols. Boston: C.T. Brainard, [n.d.]. Flavius Josephus [Joseph ben Matityahu] lived AD ca. 37–ca. 100.

Law, David R. *The Historical-Critical Method: A Guide for the Perplexed*. London: T&T Clark, 2012.

Maier, Gerhard. *The End of the Historical-Critical Method*. Translated by Edwin W. Leverenz and Rudolph F. Norden. St. Louis: Concordia, 1977.

Meinardus, Otto F. A. *Two Thousand Years of Coptic Christianity*. Cairo: American University in Cairo Press, 1999.

Metzger, Bruce M. *The Canon of the New Testament: Its Origin, Development, and Significance*. Oxford: Clarendon, 1987.

Metzger, Bruce M. *An Introduction to the Apocrypha*. New York: Oxford UP, 1957.

McDonald, Lee Martin. *The Biblical Canon: Its Origin, Transmission, and Authority*. Updated and revised third edition. Peabody: Hendrickson, 2007.

BIBLIOGRAPHY

Nicolson, Adam. *God's Secretaries: The Making of the King James Bible*. New York: HarperCollins, 2003.

Ussher, James. *The Annals of the World*. Revised and updated by Larry and Marion Pierce. Green Forest: Master, 2003. The first English edition was published in 1658.

Demonology

Martin, Malachi. *Hostage to the Devil: The Possession and Exorcism of Five Living Americans*. [San Francisco]: HarperSanFrancisco, 1992.

Spanos, Nicholas P. *Multiple Identities and False Memories: A Sociocognitive Perspective*. Washington, DC: American Psychological Association, 1996.

REX FROST was born in the late 1960s and was raised in the Midwestern United States. The religious backdrop of the author's youth was Separate Baptist and Southern Baptist, though he is now a nondenominational Bible Christian. The author holds bachelor's degrees in chemistry and chemical engineering and a doctor's degree in physical chemistry, and he has worked in the field of microprocessor fabrication research and development. The author's earliest publications are technical, comprising epitaxy modeling, atmospheric photochemistry, and molecular spectroscopy journal articles, as well as various semiconductor lithography patents.

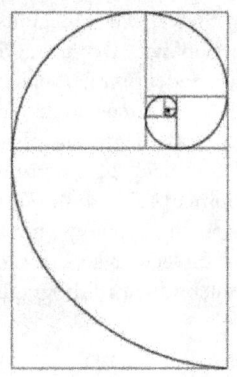

www.ingramcontent.com/pod-product-compliance
Lightning Source LLC
Chambersburg PA
CBHW022000100426
42738CB00042B/955